# Psychology

## FIFTH EDITION

### Robert S. Woodworth
COLUMBIA UNIVERSITY

### Donald G. Marquis
UNIVERSITY OF MICHIGAN

HENRY HOLT AND COMPANY · NEW YORK

# Preface to the Fifth Edition

Without changing the general character of the book, the authors of this fifth edition have subjected it to a rather thorough revision. They have introduced new material when feasible, eliminated some old material that the beginning student will not seriously miss, simplified many passages with avoidance of superfluous technical terms and synonyms, and clarified the organization both of the separate chapters and of the book as a whole. The first part, on differential psychology, has been pruned of topics more logically belonging in the larger part devoted to general psychology, which begins with chapters on interaction with the environment and on development, along with a chapter on the nervous system, and proceeds to motives and emotions, observation and the senses, and finally learning, memory and thinking. The book will probably be found to become more difficult as it proceeds. An elementary treatment of learning is introduced fairly early, in the chapter on development. The chapter on imagination has disappeared but its essential content will be found in the chapter on thinking and in other chapters. The final chapter of the fourth edition, on personal applications, has also disappeared but much of its content is now incorporated into the chapter on choice, conflict and frustration.

A new feature is the analytical summary at the close of each chapter. All the important psychological terms used in the text are defined in these summaries, and significant general principles are stated.

The references have been assembled chapter by chapter at the end of the book and provided with a separate index of names.

We are happy to recognize the important assistance received from several friends and colleagues. Professor Mary Rose Sheehan has given the proof her expert scrutiny and criticism. Mrs. Enrica Tunnell has made herself responsible for the completeness and accuracy of the references and indices. Lt. Commander Dean Farnsworth has provided the much-improved color chart. Professor G. Milton Smith, in preparing a Work Book to accompany our text, has read the proof and made valuable suggestions.

The new edition throughout, it should be stated, is the joint work of both authors.

New York and Ann Arbor               R.S.W. and D.G.M.
   February 26, 1947

# Contents

v

ORIGIN AND DEVELOPMENT OF MOTIVES: Unlearned motives necessary for life; Effects of learning. CLASSIFICATION OF MOTIVES: Organic needs; Emergency motives; Objective motives and interests; Purposes. STRENGTH OF MOTIVES: Measurement of animal drives; Suggestions for human application. MOTIVATION OF WORK: Pacemaking, competition and self-competition; Morale, military and civilian.

FEELING: Wundt's three dimensions; Feeling distinguished from motor and sensory activities; Sources of pleasure and displeasure; Sympathy and empathy; Esthetic enjoyment. EMOTION: The great variety of emotions. EMOTIONAL EXPRESSION: Expressive movements; Learning to control them; Facial expression, gesture and voice. ORGANIC STATES IN EMOTION: The autonomic nerves; Breathing and blood pressure; The "lie detector"; Stomach changes in anger; The organic state a useful preparation in emergencies. THEORY OF THE EMOTIONS: The famous James-Lange theory and recent counterevidence; Cortex and interbrain.

THE WILL: Choosing, intending, overcoming obstacles. CONFLICTING MOTIVES: Choice, compromise, vacillation; Decision. FRUSTRATION: Sources of emotional frustration; Behavior in emotional frustration, defense "mechanisms." ADJUSTMENT AND MALADJUSTMENT: Severe maladjustments; Ways of helping maladjusted individuals: psychotherapy, psychoanalysis, nondirective counseling.

ATTENTION: Degrees of consciousness; Catching and holding attention; Interest; Sustained attention. PERCEPTION: Observing objects a necessity in dealing with the environment; Signs and meanings. FIGURAL FACTORS IN PERCEPTION: Figure and ground; Gestalt principles; Hidden figures, camouflage. ACCURACY AND INACCURACY OF OBSERVATION: The span of apprehension; Constant and variable errors; Weber's law; Illusions of various

# The Aim and Method of Psychology

What's in a name? Words have a way of changing their meaning, and the names of our older sciences do not indicate clearly the nature of those sciences as they have developed in the course of the centuries. Mathematics, literally understood, includes all the sciences and all branches of learning. Physics is literally the science of growth or of nature in general. Chemistry was originally the art of extracting medicinal juices from plants. Psychology, also one of the older sciences, means literally the science of the "breath of life," and for many centuries it was defined as the science (or philosophy) of the soul. But neither that literal meaning nor that old definition gives a true picture of psychology today. At the beginning of the present century, when the psychologists of that day were making strenuous efforts to establish a science in the modern sense, one of their leaders was asked to formulate a definition of psychology. His reply, often quoted since then, was that psychology is "what psychologists are interested in," and that the only way to discover the nature of this science is to observe the work of psychologists and notice what they are trying to accomplish (1).[1]

[1] Italicized numbers in parentheses refer to the References on pages 639–658.

During World War II, even more than during the first one, psychologists had an opportunity to make a contribution toward meeting the national emergency. Their existing knowledge and methods could be applied to various military problems, and their war work was quite varied. One large problem, already worked at in industries before the war, was that of "fitting the man to the job and the job to the man." The problem has several angles. The man is tested and interviewed so as to discover his abilities and interests; and the job is analyzed, or rather many jobs are analyzed, to determine what abilities and interests are called for in each job. But the problem involves more than selecting the right man for the right job. The man must be trained for his new job of airplane pilot or radio-code operator, and psychologists developed efficient methods of training. Then too, the job itself often makes excessive demands on the operator's powers of seeing or hearing or on his skill of hand, and can be improved by careful study from the psychological point of view.

The psychologists were not concerned wholly with the abilities of a man; his emotional stamina and fitness for the severe stresses of warfare were also considered. The morale of a company, division or other group, and ways of building up morale and combatting disruptive propaganda and rumors—these were the problems committed to some of the psychologists. The rehabilitation of injured or emotionally maladjusted men, and the counseling of the veterans on their plans for education and civilian occupation, were another type of psychological work (11).

These various applications of psychology to the specific problems of war are of course different from peacetime applications, but in war and peace alike psychology has to do with the human factor. There is a human factor in industry, in government, in the building of a world organization for promoting peace and prosperity. The machines of industry and the machinery of government accomplish nothing without the will and skill of human operators. If we follow the psychologists into their peacetime laboratories where they are occupied with funda-

mental research rather than practical applications, we still find
them working on problems of human behavior. A science of
human behavior—now in the making, though less far advanced
than some other sciences—will eventually provide a sound basis
for good management of human affairs both public and private.

**Psychology studies the activities of the individual.** The science of human behavior is actually a group of sciences. On one
side we find physiology investigating the organs and cells that
do the work of the organism, and on the other side we see the
social sciences studying nations and groups of mankind. There
is room for a middle science that shall focus its attention on the
*individual*. That middle science is psychology. Psychology studies the individual's activities throughout his span of life, from
his small beginnings before birth up through infancy, childhood
and adolescence to maturity, and still further on through the
declining years. During this life history he remains the same
individual, and his behavior shows continuity along with many
changes. Psychology compares child and adult, the normal and
the abnormal, the human and the animal. It is interested in the
differences between one individual and another, and still more
interested, if possible, in the general laws of activity holding
good even of very different individuals—laws, for example, of
growth, learning, thinking and emotion. Psychology can be
defined as the *science of the activities of the individual.*

The word "activity" is used here in a very broad sense. It includes not only motor activities like walking and speaking, but
also cognitive (knowledge-getting) activities like seeing, hearing, remembering and thinking, and emotional activities like
laughing and crying, and feeling happy or sad. These last may
seem passive, yet they are activities, for they depend on the
life of the organism. Any manifestation of life can be called an
activity. No matter how passive an individual may seem to himself in watching a game or listening to music, he is really carrying on an activity. The only way to be completely inactive is to
be dead.

**Human activity as viewed by different sciences.** Largely,
though not exclusively, psychology is concerned with what we

ordinarily call "mental" activities such as learning, remembering, thinking, planning, observing, wishing, loving and hating. They are sometimes grouped under the main heads of knowing, feeling and doing. But any mental activity is at the same time a bodily activity. The brain is active in any such performance, and usually the muscles and the sense organs play a part. To discover how the various organs operate is the province of physiology. Physiology picks the organism to pieces, literally or figuratively, and tries to see what each organ contributes to the life of the whole. It asks what goes on in the eye during seeing and in the speech organs during talking. It asks how the muscles work the fingers in grasping an object; and how that enormously complicated organ, the brain, integrates the activities of the individual and enables him to deal effectively with the environment.

If, then, we wish to understand human behavior, does not physiology furnish all we want, so far as any knowledge is available? If the individual's activity can be analyzed into the activities of his organs, why should we study the individual as a whole? The answer is that physiology furnishes only part of what we need to know. The individual is a real unit. It is the individual that loves and hates, succeeds or fails. He has tasks to perform, problems to solve. He deals more or less effectively and happily with other persons and with things. There is a vast network of interaction between the individual, taken as a whole, and the world about him, and this interaction calls for scientific investigation. Psychology studies the individual's activities in relation to the environment.

The human individual, much of the time, is interacting with other individuals and taking part in group activity. The group can be taken as a unit and its activities described, as is done by sociology; or the individual can be taken as a unit and his behavior described in its relations with the other individuals; or, again, the activity of the individual can be analyzed physiologically. A football game, for example, could be reported as a struggle between two teams without any mention of the individual players. Team A, having the ball, first tries a certain mass formation which advances the ball a yard, and next tries a certain open play which loses ground. Team A then forms for a kick, but Team B breaks through and captures the ball. And so on. The game could also be described as consisting of the actions of the individual players; to be complete, the description would have to tell what each player heard, saw and felt, what he attempted to do, what obstacles he encountered and how he came out of each play. It would make a very involved story. Theoretically the same game could be described in physiological terms, for certainly the muscles, lungs, heart and brain of every player are active throughout the game. The physiological description, if at all complete, would fill the Sunday newspaper and contain much valuable information, but would be disappointing to any reader who wanted to follow the game.

So we can have physiological, psychological and sociological pictures of human activity, each picture true and valuable. They are like maps of the same country drawn to different scales. One map shows much more detail, another gives a better idea of the general shape of the country. Human life can be charted in its broad social relations or in its internal organic details. Psychology, however, uses a medium scale such as brings out the activities and relations of the individual.

## SCIENTIFIC METHOD IN PSYCHOLOGY

During its long history down to the middle of the nineteenth century, psychology was cultivated by able thinkers who did not realize their need of carefully observed facts. They relied on general impressions derived from past experience. They felt, as many persons do today, that having observed people all their lives they must know psychology pretty well, or at least must know all the necessary facts. When they came to discuss psychology with each other, however, they were often in disagreement and saw no way of settling the disputed questions. It became clear that psychology, like other sciences, must gather more facts in order to make any substantial progress (6, 7).

There was an anecdotal period when the need for concrete facts was recognized but no systematic investigations were undertaken. Anecdotes in some cases are true reports of actual behavior, but in other cases the facts were not accurately observed in the first place and have since been partly forgotten or even distorted in memory. Scientists find it necessary to sharpen their powers of observation by the use of instruments and by setting up definite questions of fact to be answered by observation; and they find it necessary also to record their observations on the spot and not trust to memory.

Anecdotes and general impressions derived from past experience are likely to give a one-sided view of the facts on any controversial question. Someone tells you he knows from his own experience that bad luck comes on the 13th of the month, for he has taken pains to notice and feels sure of his facts. But has he duly taken note of the *negative instances*, when good luck came on the 13th and bad luck on some other day, or did only the positive instances make any deep impression? If anyone thought it worth while to make a scientific study of the matter, he would keep a diary and note down each day his good and bad luck—taking care to use the same standards of good and bad luck throughout the investigation—and finally sum up the results over a long period of time. In this way the memory error, the error of one-sided selection of cases, and the error of too few cases would all be avoided.

**The experimental method.**   Finally psychologists decided they must follow the lead of physics, chemistry and physiology and transform psychology into an experimental science. Whenever a process or activity is to be studied, experiment is the ideal means of getting the facts.

An experiment is sometimes described as a "question put to nature." A successful experiment is one that gets a clear answer from nature. The experimenter approaches nature with a question, and his skill lies in so putting the question as to obtain an answer. What is implied by the word "nature"? We speak of the "uniformity of nature," meaning that under the same conditions the same thing will happen, the same result be obtained. A psychological experiment carries the implication that human behavior belongs in the system of nature, so that, given the same conditions, the same behavior will occur.

To put a question to nature is to arrange the conditions in a certain known way and then observe what happens. Sometimes, in a preliminary survey, the question asked is very general and amounts simply to this: Under these known conditions, what happens? Often apparatus is used either to produce the desired conditions or to assist in observation.

Let us take an example. Knowing that an aviator or balloonist trying for an altitude record is likely to lose his good sense and finally to lose consciousness at extreme heights, an experimenter makes a preliminary survey of what happens under these conditions. He might make an ascent with an aviator, and devote himself to obtaining records of breathing, heart rate, blood pressure, sight, hearing, muscular strength, and performance in psychological tests at different altitudes. (A difficulty with this simple plan of experiment is that the experimenter himself is probably not immune to the effects of altitude, so that he would lose his efficiency as an observer; but there are ways around this difficulty as we shall see.)

The preliminary survey may raise specific questions on which it is important to be perfectly sure of the facts. For example, at what altitude do the first symptoms appear? A new experiment is conducted with attention and equipment concentrated on this one point. It is found that breathing is noticeably hastened at about 12,000 feet and that muscular weakness and headache begin to appear at about 14,000. Many specific questions must be answered before the whole story is known, and some important questions may be very difficult to answer. What form of psychological test, for example, can be used to show that the pilot is beginning to lose his good judgment, so that he may be warned in time? Such a question is likely to require many experiments before it is settled.

*Analyzing the conditions.* Much more penetrating questions than those so far suggested are tackled by the experimental method. We said that when all the conditions are the same the result will be the same. But some conditions may be unimportant. The day of the month, whether the 13th or some other, is a condition that certainly makes no difference. Given the same weather conditions, the same condition of the plane and the same handling of the plane, it will fly the same on any day of the month. But in respect to some conditions we cannot judge in advance whether they will or will not make any difference.

Going up in the air changes several conditions at once, and we wish to dissect this complex and find which conditions count in producing altitude effects.

1. The mere fact that one is in the air may cause fear and nervousness. We can rule this out as relatively unimportant because essentially the same altitude effects occur on very high mountains when there is no danger of falling.

2. The motion of the plane can cause something akin to seasickness. But the air is smoother at high altitudes and even when the plane is steady altitude effects will occur.

3. We might think of the cold of high altitudes, but we know that the same cold at low altitudes has no such effects.

4. The atmospheric pressure decreases as one ascends. At 12,000 feet it is reduced to $\frac{2}{3}$, at 18,000 feet to $\frac{1}{2}$, and at 28,000 to about $\frac{1}{3}$ of the pressure at sea level. This condition is found to be unimportant (unless at extremely high altitudes) by experiments in which a man is placed in a steel chamber, the air pumped out to $\frac{1}{3}$ or less of normal atmospheric pressure, but the man supplied with a tank of pure oxygen to breathe.

5. The last experiment suggests that the amount of available oxygen may be the important variable. The oxygen is 21 per cent of what air there is at any altitude, but in the rare air of high altitudes the amount of oxygen in a lungful is scanty. It is proportional to the atmospheric pressure, being accordingly $\frac{2}{3}$ of the normal amount at 12,000 feet, $\frac{1}{2}$ at 18,000, $\frac{1}{3}$ at 28,000. Place a man in a chamber in which the composition of the air can be controlled. Without changing the total atmospheric pressure in the chamber, imitate an ascent so far as oxygen is concerned by gradually replacing the oxygen by

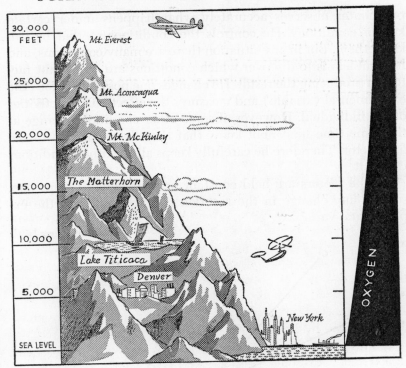

FIG. 1.—Dearth of oxygen at high altitudes.

nitrogen; and you get the same symptoms as in an actual ascent, height for height. The important condition, the "cause" of altitude effects, is shown to be the shortage of oxygen.

6. There are other factors of some importance residing in the individual himself. Some individuals succumb at much lower altitudes than others, or at much smaller reductions of the oxygen in a chamber. The individual's "condition," in the athletic use of the word, makes a difference. If he lives for days or weeks on a mountain at 12,000–18,000 feet, he becomes acclimated, loses his mountain sickness and can work fairly well, though perhaps not so well as in more usual human habitations (up to 6,000 feet) (5, 8).

These experiments on the effect of altitude are introduced here simply to illustrate the nature of an experiment. The experimenter observes accurately what happens under certain known conditions. He controls the conditions so that he can know them. But in any situation there are many conditions, and his problem is to discover which conditions are significant factors in producing the result. He changes one possible factor (the experimental variable) and measures the effect on the activities of the individual. However, if some other conditions change at the same time he cannot know that the effect was due to the first factor. Therefore he carefully keeps all the other conditions constant.

All the factors are held constant or kept equal, except one, so that any change in the reaction can be pinned to the experimental variable.

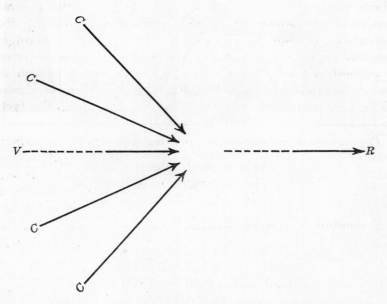

Fig. 2.—Scheme of an experiment. R is the particular phase of the individual's activity under study, the subject's "reaction." The converging arrows are the influences or conditions which may affect the reaction. Those marked C are held constant throughout the experiment, whereas the one marked V, called the experimental variable, is made to change, and the resulting effect in R is observed. What effect does V have upon R? —That is the question to be answered by the experiment.

Instead of saying that an experiment is designed to answer a question, scientists often say it is designed to test a *hypothesis*. A hypothesis is a possible answer to a question and the experiment aims to discover whether this answer is correct. With regard to altitude effects, one hypothesis was that the low atmospheric pressure at high altitudes was the cause. If so, a man will show the effects in a steel chamber in the laboratory, even though he has oxygen to breathe, provided only the pressure is reduced sufficiently. But when these conditions were produced, the effects did not occur. The answer was "No" and the hypothesis was disproved. Another hypothesis was then suggested: the effects are due to lack of oxygen at high altitudes. If so, the effects will come on in the chamber when the oxygen is sufficiently reduced, even though the total atmospheric pressure remains normal. When these conditions were produced, the effects did occur, pretty well confirming the hypothesis, though not absolutely proving it, for there might possibly be some other cause not yet thought of, some other hypothesis not yet put to the test of experiment. A hypothesis cannot be absolutely proved to be correct, but it may be shown to be very probable because it is consistent with all the facts so far known.

*Psychological experiments.*   We may designate the experimenter by the letter *E,* and the subject (individual) whose activity is observed by the letter *O,* standing for "organism" or "one observed." Some reaction or phase of *O*'s activity is observed or measured. *E* is to discover what *O* does under certain conditions, how he behaves, what his reaction is, how he is affected by the experimental variable. If *O* is a human individual, he usually receives certain *instructions* from *E;* he is assigned a certain *task* to perform. He is not usually told the ultimate purpose of the experiment, but he knows what he has to do. The experiment is *E*'s, not *O*'s. *E*'s immediate job is in many cases to discover how successfully *O* performs his task under the conditions of the experiment.

The conditions to be controlled in a psychological experiment are partly environmental and partly lie in *O* himself. To control the external situation is a matter of laboratory technique; for example, a dark room may be needed and a piece of apparatus for exposing a picture exactly $\frac{1}{10}$ of a second. But how shall $E$ control the conditions that lie within $O$? Of course, if $O$ is ill on a certain day, he is excused from the experiment. His emotional condition cannot be wholly controlled, since he may be excited or worried about the task he has to perform; but with experience as a laboratory subject his emotional condition becomes stabilized. To a surprisingly great extent $O$'s attitude is controlled by $E$'s instructions. $O$ accepts the assigned task and sets himself to do it as well as possible. His effort, obviously an important factor, remains fairly constant at a high level. However, certain difficulties may arise.

1. If the task becomes monotonous, $O$ may lose interest and slacken his effort, so giving a false result.

2. If the external conditions become unfavorable, $O$ may be stimulated to greater effort. Here we see an important psychological fact, but one which conceals the natural effect of the external condition. If $O$ is a candidate for admission to an aviation school and is subjected to tests under low oxygen, his effort often increases with the "altitude" and conceals the effect of shortage of oxygen—up to a certain point.

3. If $O$ knows, or thinks he knows, the purpose of the experiment, he may take a partisan attitude. In experiments on the effect of moderate doses of alcohol on mental efficiency, $O$ may be convinced in advance that alcohol is a depressant, and this belief may lower his effort in the alcoholic condition. If on the contrary he believes that alcohol is a stimulant, hopes so at any rate, he may put in greater effort when he has received the dose. $E$ endeavors to forestall such changes in $O$'s attitude by giving a control dose part of the time—some drink free from alcohol but indistinguishable in taste—so that $O$ does not know whether or not he has received any alcohol. Such experiments, incidentally, give no evidence of any real stimulating effect of alcohol on mental processes.

Because the conditions lying within $O$ cannot be wholly controlled, and because different individuals behave differently in the same situation, it is often necessary to plan a psychological experiment on a grand scale, with repeated trials on large groups of subjects, and to use the average results as the basis of any conclusions that are drawn (2, 4).

The developmental method. One important job of psychology is that of tracing the mental and behavioral development of the individual from birth, or better from before birth, up to maturity. There are many difficult questions here regarding the influences of heredity and environment, the conditions favorable to normal development, and the factors that produce such abnormalities as delinquency and insanity. Tests and laboratory methods can be used for measuring the stage of development reached at different ages and for determining growth curves. But to conduct a decisive experiment on development, one would need to have control over the conditions in which the child is reared, and even to subject certain children to conditions presumed to be unfavorable, so as to make sure whether they are really unfavorable in any important degree. Such experiments might yield extremely valuable information. But the psychologist is not going to take it on himself to subject a child to unfavorable conditions. He will not, for example, stunt the child's physical development by an inadequate diet so as to determine whether mental growth suffers. He will perform such experiments on animals, or he will find undernourished children in the community and try to discover whether the malnutrition has had any demonstrable effect on their mentality. At the best, his results will not be so decisive as those of a complete experiment.

Much can be learned, without such an experiment, by simply observing and recording behavior up through childhood. We say "simply" observing and recording; but the task is far from simple if dependable results are to be obtained. The child behaves *so much* that an observer cannot record more than small samples. Moreover, the records of a child's behavior, though interesting, may not prove or disprove anything, unless the observer has had definite questions in mind, definite hypotheses to be checked by observation. When we know that some important development is about to occur, as that the child will soon begin to talk, or that he is soon to have a baby brother or sister to whose presence in the family he must adjust himself, we can formulate specific questions to be answered from observations of his behavior. The whole job of tracing child development is large and many-sided, but fortunately it is being seriously undertaken by many scientific observers (9).

**The case history method.** In the true developmental method the observer is on the spot and watches the process as it occurs. But often the psychologist has before him a genius, a criminal, a "problem child," or a remarkably fine personality, and the question is how this individual came to be what he is. The psychologist is forced to adopt a substitute for the true developmental method by reconstructing the individual's developmental history as well as can be done from the memory of the individual and his associates and from whatever records have been preserved. This *case history method* has obvious disadvantages, much like those of the anecdotal method. It depends largely on fallible memory of incidents that were not scientifically observed in the first place. But it seems to be the only way to make a start toward answering some very important questions.

The case history method, up to the present time, has been employed mostly with individuals whose behavior is undesirable in some respect. When a person has broken down mentally, the psychiatrist with the assistance of a social worker obtains information on this person's heredity and family environment, noting such conditions as are believed to be important. The patient's own story is taken down and an attempt is made to get back to earlier emotional conflicts which may have a bearing on his present trouble. When a child presents a serious behavior problem—such as stealing, overaggressiveness, destructive "meanness," or shyness and dependence—he may be taken to a child guidance clinic, where a staff of experts considers his history from several points of view, medical, psychological and social. These experts approach the child in a friendly spirit, and make him see they are not trying to "get something on him," but wish to help him by first understanding him. They need cooperation from him and from his parents, and their inquiries must be conducted with tact as well as skill. They work on the assumption that the child's misconduct has causes which should be discovered, causes lying in his environment and in his own limitations.

The guidance clinic does more than reconstruct the history of the case to date. In cooperation with the home and the school, it tries an experiment on the child, by way of treatment. Any treatment of such a case is experimental in some degree, since there is no certainty of success. The case history and present state of the child suggest some cause of the misconduct; and the treatment tests this hypothesis by altering certain conditions of the child's life. The hypothesis may be that the child is spoiled or overprotected or denied affection at home, or that his school placement is above or below his mental age, or that his silly behavior, enuresis, fussy eating habits or temper tantrums are just his way of bidding for attention. Treatment in line with any such hypothesis evidently calls for cooperation from parents or teachers. If the treatment succeeds, the hypothesis works and is verified to that extent; if the treatment fails, some other hypothesis must be given a trial (3).

Case histories of outstandingly fine or successful persons are decidedly lacking so far. The behavior clinics are conducted for the benefit of those who have got into trouble; and the adult, unless he has got into trouble of some sort, is sensitive about being probed. If we could tell in advance that a given newborn baby was going to become great or fine, we could study his development as it proceeded. A biography, written long afterward, is almost sure to be meager and unpsychological in its account of the subject's early development. Now that many children, including some of great promise, are being studied, we may hope in time to possess some authentic developmental biographies of normal and superior people.

**Objective and introspective data.** A *datum* (plural, *data*) is an observed fact used in testing a hypothesis or reaching any conclusion. What kinds of data are available in psychology?

Shall we ask O to observe his own activities, or shall *we* observe them? We can observe his behavior objectively; he can give us inside information of his thoughts, feelings and intentions and of what he sees, hears and knows. [When he observes his own activities, he is said to introspect, and the data he furnishes are introspective data. They are also called subjective data, because they are furnished by the subject from self-observation.]

Introspection, as understood in psychology, is not brooding over one's troubles or worrying about one's personality. It is not even attempting to explain one's actions. It is distinctly a form of observation. One kind of introspection is illustrated by observations of the "after-image." If you look fixedly for 20 seconds at a black square and then look at a gray wall, you will see a white square on the wall. The square moves when you move your eyes, and so must be a subjective phenomenon, occurring in you, not on the wall. Everyone, after a little practice, can observe his own after-images but no one can observe those of another person, just as no one can observe another person's toothache. In experiments on the senses, with human subjects, the customary procedure is to present a suitable stimulus and ask O to report what he sees or hears or smells. Introspection in such experiments is the same as any ordinary observation, except that O understands that his senses are being tested and does not try to beat the game by utilizing extraneous sources of information. If his eyes are being tested he does not sneak up close to the test chart beforehand so as to know the letters he is supposed to read from a distance. He simply reports the impression he gets from the given stimulus.

Sometimes the introspection is a little more complex. In an experiment on reading, the letter group

## PYSCHOLOGY

is shown for a fraction of a second, and O reads "psychology" but reports experiencing some strain and dissatisfaction and noticing a messy appearance of the first part of the word. We see from this report that the misspelling made some impression on *O* though not enough to enable him to read the actual sequence of letters. Still more complex is the introspection of the thought process in solving a puzzle. As soon as the solution is reached, *O* reviews the process and reports what he can remember of it. He recalls the steps he went through and so gives a more complete picture of the process than the experimenter can get from observing his behavior.

Some psychologists would exclude introspective data altogether, believing them untrustworthy. Undoubtedly the more complex kinds of introspection make rather heavy demands on the subject. But results show that you can trust introspection if you do not expect it to go into minute detail. Who can doubt, for example, that a well-practiced act goes on almost automatically, or that inner, silent speech is commonly present in the process of thinking? Yet we have only introspection to vouch for these statements. In conversation we accept a person's introspection if he says, "I didn't hear what you said," or "I agree with you," or "That proposition leaves me cold," or "I feel strongly on the matter." We could not dispense with introspection in everyday life and there is no reason for excluding it from psychology. It is true that a person needs some training before he can be trusted to give very accurate introspection. He is apt to explain his conduct rather than simply to report what he can observe of his thoughts, feelings and actions.

To say, as used to be said, that psychology is *purely* an introspective science, making no use of objective data, is absurd in face of the facts. We have animal psychology where the data are wholly objective. The animal performs, the psychologist does the observing. The same is true of child psychology, at least for early childhood. In studying anger in children, we describe their angry behavior and endeavor to determine the conditions which elicit this behavior. Older children and adults are capable of introspection but even here the bulk of experimental work is of the objective type. Nearly all psychological tests are objective. The subject is given a task to perform and the psychologist measures the speed or the accuracy and excellence of the performance. In laboratory experiments, as well as in tests, most of the data obtained are objective; the performer is one person, the observer another.

In studying memory, you assign a lesson to be learned under certain conditions, and note how quickly and perfectly O learns the lesson; then you give him another, equally difficult lesson to learn under altered conditions and observe whether he does better or worse than before. Thus you discover which conditions are more favorable for learning and draw some conclusion as to the nature of the learning process. In the whole experiment you may not have called for any introspections—or you may have secured some introspective data in addition to the objective data.

Objective psychological data usually record what O did under certain conditions. They record his overt, external behavior. Another type of objective observation seeks to discover what goes on inside the organism during anger, joy, work or any specified kind of behavior. It employs apparatus to record O's breathing, heart beat, stomach movements, flow of saliva, electric currents in the brain, involuntary eye movements, muscular tension in the legs, etc. The purpose is to see how different organs take part in the behavior of the whole organism. We wish to know not only *that* O learns, perceives, thinks, loves and hates, but also *how* he does these things. Physiology affords one line of attack on this question, introspection another. But the usual line of attack is neither physiological nor introspective. It is, rather, an objective study of behavior and performance under different conditions, so chosen as to test some hypothesis. This is the line of attack just suggested for the study of memory, and illustrated earlier by the experiments on altitude effects.

At one time it was customary to distinguish psychology sharply from the natural sciences and to say that it dealt with an inner world of experience, altogether separate from the external world. But this distinction has been shown to have no logical basis. Introspective data and objective data are fundamentally the same—both depend on observations by people. The principal difference lies in the fact that introspective data are private—there can be only one observer, while objective data are public—several persons may observe the same fact and we can check the agreement of the observers. The field of psychology is not separate from the fields of the natural and social sciences. It is part of the same big field. The individual's behavior belongs squarely in the world of natural phenomena and his conscious experience is bound up closely with his external behavior, both being parts of the same activity (10).

**The terms used in psychology.** The terminology of psychology is often a source of unnecessary difficulty. Since we are to be studying activities, our terms should properly be verbs and adverbs. We shall need one noun, *individual* or *organism*, as the subject of all the verbs. When we dip into physiology we need the names of bodily organs, and when we speak of external objects we need their names. But the reader will encounter a host of other nouns, names of activities and ways of acting, such as intelligence, personality, memory, imagination, thought, will, sensation, emotion, attention, perception, consciousness, behavior. Most of these nouns are properly verbs with "individual" understood as their subject.

Instead of "memory" we should properly say "remembering" or "*O* remembers"; instead of "sensation" we should say "seeing," "hearing," etc.; and instead of "emotion" we should say that someone feels eager or angry or afraid. But, like other sciences, psychology finds it convenient to transform its verbs into nouns. Then what happens? We forget that our nouns are merely substitutes for verbs, and start hunting for the *things* denoted by the nouns—for substances, forces, faculties—but no such things exist; there is only the individual engaged in these different activities.

Intelligence, consciousness and the unconscious belong with such terms as skill and speed. They are properly adverbs, the facts being that the individual acts intelligently, consciously or unconsciously, skillfully, speedily. A safe rule, on encountering any abstract psychological noun, is to change it into the corresponding verb or adverb. Much difficulty and unnecessary controversy can thus be avoided.

**Plan of the book.** The various topics in psychology could be taken up in many different orders almost equally well. This is not because the various processes are separate and independent of each other but, just the contrary, because they are all so interdependent that whichever you take up first you will have some reason to wish you already knew the others. We might begin with the senses which are used in almost everything we do, or for the same reason we might begin with the nervous system. We might begin with learning and memory since our thoughts and actions at any time depend on what we have previously learned. As this book is arranged—it could be rearranged without causing serious difficulty—the first general question considered is "How do people differ?" They differ in their abilities and personal characteristics, and the causes of these differences are sought in heredity and environment. After that, the processes common to all individuals are considered: their reactions to the environment, their development, their motives and emotions, and their powers of observing, learning and thinking. Many cross references are made from one chapter to another in the hope that the student will bind all the chapters together into a comprehensive view of the individual's activities.

## SUMMARY

1. Psychology is the scientific study of the activities of the individual in relation to his environment.
   a. *Physiology* also studies human activities, but in more detailed terms of the separate organs of the body.
   b. *Sociology* studies human activities in terms of the groups and institutions of society.
2. The *scientific method* in psychology involves the collecting and recording of accurate and unbiased observations in sufficient number to provide reliable answers to theoretical and practical questions.
   a. In the *experimental method* one of the many conditions in a situation is changed (experimental variable) and the effect on some activity of the individual (reaction) is meas-

ured. All other conditions are controlled and the result can then be attributed to the influence of the experimental variable.

b. The *developmental method* observes and records selected samples of the activities of individuals during their growth.

c. The *case history method*, usually employed in the study of patients with mental or behavioral disturbances, attempts to reconstruct the individual's developmental history and to determine the conditions influencing his behavior.

d. *Introspective data* are observations by an individual of his own activities. *Objective data* are observations which can be made by more than one observer. Introspective data are private, while objective data are public. Psychology makes use of both types of data.

e. *Psychological terms* refer to activities of the individual, and should therefore be verbs and adverbs. Nouns such as "memory" and "intelligence" are convenient substitutes for longer phrases.

# CHAPTER TWO

# *Individual Differences in Ability*

The problem before us in this first part of the book, devoted to individual differences, has often been suggested to a democratically minded psychologist—as most psychologists are—by an attentive reading of that charter of democracy, the Declaration of Independence adopted by the American Continental Congress, July 4, 1776:

We hold these truths to be self-evident, that all men are created equal, that they are endowed by their Creator with certain unalienable Rights, that among these are Life, Liberty and the pursuit of Happiness.

It is the first of these "self-evident truths" that gives psychologists cause to stop and think. Can the signers of the Declaration have really meant that all men are equal, when they had among their own number so many individuals of strikingly different personalities, and when certainly Benjamin Franklin and Thomas Jefferson were obviously more able than many of the rest? From the context it is probable that what was meant by equality of mankind is implied in the second "truth," that all men have *equal rights* to life, liberty and the pursuit of happiness. Probably these eminent men did not really mean that

all men are equal in ability and personality or even that they
are all created equal in the sense that they are equal by nature
and heredity and differ only by education and opportunity.
Whatever they may have meant, there is no doubt that the fact
of individual differences creates a problem for democracy.

It is worth noting that one of the old communist slogans implied that men were different rather than all equal: "From each
according to his abilities, to each according to his needs." One
thing is certain: a successful government must be based on the
facts of human nature; it cannot be based on a misreading of
the facts. If individuals differ, this fact must be taken into account in our planning for a better world.

The fact that adult individuals differ in ability and personality is so obvious that the reader may be impatient to get on
to the question of why they differ, regarding that as the only important question. However, it is not worth while to attempt an
explanation of the facts until we know the facts. Take adults as
we find them, or take children as we find them, and ask in what
ways they differ, how much they differ, and whether these differences are important or not in the life of man. The facts of
individual differences go far beyond the mere statement that
people differ. The differences turn out to show law and regu-
larity, and their laws are interesting and significant (2).

That important question of the causes of individual differences will be in the back of our minds as we consider ability
and personality, and will come to the front in the later chapter
on heredity and environment.


## MEASURING ABILITY

Achievement and capacity. [The word *ability* is somewhat
ambiguous, having two meanings which, though closely related,
need to be carefully distinguished. It may mean *actual ability*
or it may mean *potential ability*.] A visitor in Paris was amazed
at the "wonderful ability of the little French children. They
speak French so well, so much better than our children at
home!" Now of course, from lack of training, children in other

countries do not have the actual ability to speak French, but every normal child the world over has the potential ability to speak French or any other language. A child who has the actual ability to speak French *can do it* now, while a child who has the potential ability to speak French *can learn to do it*.

To avoid this ambiguity we will use the word *achievement* to mean actual ability, and the word *capacity* to mean potential ability.

Anyone's capacity exceeds his achievement, since he is not trained to his limit in every line, and probably not in any line. He is capable of learning more kinds of things than he has actually learned, and he is capable of improving his achievement in almost everything that he already can do.

But capacity itself is not unlimited. No human being, probably, has the capacity to run a mile in three minutes, for many fine runners have subjected themselves to the most intensive training for the mile run, and no one has approached any such record. A child's capacity, for the time being, is limited by his immature stage of development. With further development his capacity for both muscular and mental performances will increase. Yet his ultimate, mature capacity also is limited, and it seems certain that the limit is different for different individuals.

**Determining achievement and capacity.**  When we say that an individual has attained a certain achievement, i.e., that he can do a certain thing, our best evidence is that we have seen him do it. The direct evidence of achievement is actual performance. The direct evidence for lack of achievement is that the person tries to do a thing but does not succeed.

Evidence for capacity, i.e., for undeveloped, untrained capacity, is necessarily indirect. If we are asked whether a certain normal child has the capacity to speak French we can safely answer "Yes," because all normal children in a French-speaking environment do learn to speak French. But capacity is a matter of degree, and if we are asked *how much* capacity this child has for speaking French we need to be cautious, since individuals who have had the best opportunities and training differ greatly in their mastery of the French language. Their capacities for speaking French evidently differ in degree. In any line of activity—athletic, musical, literary, political—individuals who have had equally intensive training and experience come out with unequal achievements, from which we infer that they must have started with unequal capacities.

**Achievement tests.** (We can measure achievement by actual performance, provided we can measure the performance and provided the subject (the person tested) does his best. In attempting to measure performance accurately, psychologists have devised standard tasks to be performed under standard conditions. Such a task performed under such conditions is called a *test* (8).[1])

For example, a test for truck-driving consists of several items: backing the truck around a curve, driving up and down hill, parking, and so on. In order to make a fair comparison of the candidates for the job it is necessary to have the conditions the same for all of them. The curves must be the same, the hills must be the same, the trucks must be of the same size and power. The scoring or marking of the individual's performance must be the same for all.

Educational achievement tests show how much knowledge and skill an individual has obtained (and retained) in a school subject such as arithmetic, history or geology. Achievement is sometimes best measured in the field, the practical situation. Other performances, such as speed of reaction or accuracy of sense perception, can best be measured in the laboratory with the aid of very precise apparatus. Many psychological tests demand only pencil and paper as apparatus, along with a clock or stop-watch, and resemble ordinary school examinations except that the questions have been prepared with unusual care and that the credit to be given for each possible answer is worked out in advance.

(A preliminary tryout is an essential part of the process of constructing a test.) Many test items must be tried and some of them eliminated because they do not distinguish very well between superior and inferior performers. Ambiguities must be

[1] See References, p. 639.

taken out, and the time allowed for each test and the amount of explanation given to the subjects must be determined, so that in the actual use of the test all of these matters shall be the same for all the subjects tested.

In "speed tests" very simple tasks are given and the point is to see how rapidly the subject performs them. Such a task would be the crossing out of every a and d in the preceding paragraph. Individuals differ in their speed of performance, and it is interesting to note that this test in a standardized form is a good index of clerical ability of office workers. The test can also be used to measure the impairment of performance resulting from fatigue, emotion, or oxygen lack.

In "accuracy tests," such as throwing darts at a target or estimating the speed of a passing automobile, the amount of error is measured.

In "difficulty tests," no emphasis is placed on speed. The test items are of graded difficulty, some being so easy that scarcely any individual who is to be tested will miss them, and some so difficult that scarcely anyone will pass them. The aim is to discover how difficult a task (of a certain kind) each individual can perform correctly. For example, the subject is asked to tell the opposite of each word in the following list:

| | |
|---|---|
| good | soothing |
| early | stubborn |
| north | helpless |
| beautiful | lonesome |
| gentle | resentful |
| vague | remarkable |
| doubtful | sticky |

**Aptitude tests.**    If a person's capacity could be measured or at least estimated before he begins a course of training, much wasted effort could be spared. Many young men aspire to be airplane pilots but some of them crack up or wash out during training. The more accurately their capacity for this performance is known in advance of actual training, the better for all concerned. Some students do not have sufficient capacity to complete college work; if they could be spotted before college entrance and advised to follow another line, much time, money and effort would be saved.

It is unfortunately true that capacity cannot be directly observed and measured. The best we can do is to devise tests and methods for estimating *aptitude, which is predicted achievement*. An aptitude test, in itself, is nothing more than an achievement test, but it is used not simply as a measure of present performance in the special task, but as an index of future performance in other and broader tasks. The psychologist has to discover by experiment and follow-up how accurately future achievement can be predicted from present performance in the aptitude tests.

One way of estimating aptitude for a given line of work is to take a group of individuals who are ignorant of that work at present, and give them a certain amount of training. Some of them will make more rapid progress than others. For example, in the first hour of practice in learning radio code signals (p. 549) some students learn two or three times as much as others. It is found that those who make a good start usually continue to do well in the later stages of learning while those who make a poor start usually remain relatively poor performers. But because there are many exceptions to this rule, prediction from the initial success or failure is not perfect by any means. Some students who really have good aptitude for this work are frightened or self-conscious at the beginning and fail to do themselves justice. Some very intelligent students know just how to learn efficiently and make excellent initial scores even though their aptitude for this special line of work is nothing remarkable. For these reasons psychologists will agree that measuring aptitude, or predicting future achievement, is much more difficult than measuring present achievement.

Raw scores and meaningful scores. An individual who takes a test achieves a certain score, which is his raw score. In athletic contests, the raw score is the number of seconds it takes a given individual to run 100 yards, or the number of feet and inches he clears in the pole vault, or some such number. A raw score tells very little without certain background information.

A raw score becomes meaningful by being compared in some way with other scores. In general there are two ways of making such a comparison.

1. In some situations the individual's score is compared with certain absolute standards or requirements. A code operator must be able to receive radio signals as fast as a certain standard before he is accepted for regular service. An airplane pilot must reach a certain standard of basic skill and knowledge before being allowed to fly solo. But rigid standards, however desirable, are often difficult to maintain. When competent code operators are scarce and in great demand, the requirement must be lowered a bit; it could be raised again only if the supply of good candidates should increase. Indirectly, then, a candidate who passes or fails to meet the "absolute" requirements is being compared with other candidates.

2. More commonly the individual's score is compared directly with the scores of other individuals in the same performance. A representative sample of the population or of some section of the population such as twelve-year-old children, college students or candidates for a certain job, is tested. The average is computed, and the individual's score is compared with the average and with the whole run of the scores. So the individual's relative standing is found and his raw score is made meaningful. We must consider these matters more fully.

**The distribution of scores.** The best over-all picture of individual differences is given by a *distribution curve,* such as the one showing the scores of college students in an addition test (Fig. 3). Similar distributions have been obtained many times with various tests and various groups of subjects, either children or adults. The minor ups and downs differ from one curve to another and have no general significance, but the following general laws of individual differences have been confirmed again and again.

1. There is a fairly definite *range* within which all the scores of a certain class of subjects in a certain test will fall. In Figure 3 the range extends from a minimum of 2 examples to a maximum of 24. Of course these limits are not absolutely fixed; they

would differ somewhat, though not very much, with different samples of college students and with different samples of addition examples.

2. Medium scores are the most common. The curve reaches its peak near the middle of the range. That is, individuals of moderate ability (achievement) are the most numerous.

3. The farther you go from the peak, in either direction, the fewer scores you find. The curve tends to flatten out or tail off toward both ends, as can be seen better in the intelligence distributions given later in this chapter. The whole curve tends to have a symmetrical shape much like that of a bell. A symmetrical, bell-like distribution is called a *normal distribution*.

4. There is no gap anywhere (provided a large enough sample of individuals has been tested), no sharp break separating the superior individuals from the medium or the medium from the inferior. Instead, there is a continuous gradation from one extreme to the other.

Measuring a distribution. If you wish to describe a particular distribution such as the one in Figure 3, you have to tell where it centers and how widely it spreads out; you need some measure of the *center* of the distribution and some measure of its *scatter*. By inspection of a distribution curve you can tell where the peak score falls and what is the whole range of the scores.

An accurate measure of the center of the distribution is afforded by the *average*. To measure the scatter we can see how far each individual deviates up or down from the average, and having all the individual deviations we can find the average deviation (or the *standard deviation* which is more useful in mathematical treatment of the scores).

Another way of blocking out the distribution is by the use of *centiles*, as briefly explained in the legend of Figure 3. The 50-centile point or *median* is a good measure of the center of a distribution, and the distance along the base line from the 25-centile to the 75-centile gives a good measure of scatter.

Measuring the individual's position in the distribution. With the distribution curve before you, you can see where any in-

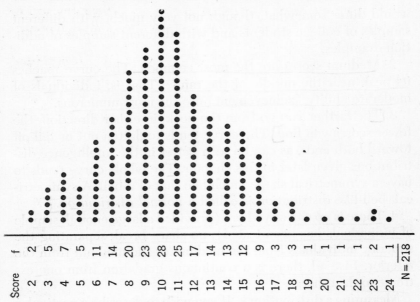

FIG. 3.—Distribution of scores in a test for speed of addition. Three minutes were allowed for adding columns of 2-place numbers like this example:

$$
\begin{array}{r}
18 \\
56 \\
43 \\
88 \\
37 \\
22 \\
65 \\
\hline
329
\end{array}
$$

The test sheet provided 24 such examples, and the score was the number right. The subjects were 218 college students. (Data from Thurstone, 17.)

To construct the chart you lay off the possible scores in order along the base line, and record each individual's score by a dot or tally mark at the proper point, making the vertical spacing uniform so that the height of each column of dots will picture the "frequency" (f) of the particular score. To bring out the "curve" you may connect the tops of the columns.

With the distribution pictured before us, what can we say about it? We can say that the peak score is 10 examples. But let any two students who got 10 right get just one more, and the peak goes up to 11, just as if everybody scored one more. The peak is only a rough, undependable measure of the center of the distribution, and for a similar reason the range is only a rough measure of the scatter. Much more dependable are the average and the standard deviation.

dividual's score falls, whether near the peak, near the top or
near the bottom. To describe the individual's standing more accurately you may proceed in either of two ways.

1. *Standard Scores.* The individual's plus or minus deviation
from the average, divided by the standard deviation, gives an
exact statement of his position in the distribution, for the plus
or minus sign shows whether he stands above or below the
average, and the size of the standard score shows how much he
deviates in relation to the scatter of the group as a whole. To

---

Here the *average* score (obtained by getting the sum of the 218 individual scores and dividing by 218) is 10.6 examples. Each individual's
*deviation* is reckoned up or down from the average. The *standard deviation* (obtained by squaring each of the 218 individual deviations, getting
the sum of these squares, dividing by 218, and finally extracting the
square root) is 4.0 examples.

The 10-centile point (a point such that 10 percent of the individuals fall
below it and the rest above it) is obviously about 6 examples; more exactly
computed it is 5.8 examples. Similarly the 25-centile point is 8.0 examples,
the 50-centile (or *median*) point is 10.3 examples, the 75-centile point is
13.0 examples, and the 90-centile point is 15.5 examples. Other centile
points can be added but these particular five block out the distribution
in a useful way, because the distances along the base line between the
successive points are approximately equal.

An individual's relative standing can be expressed either as a centile
score or as a standard score. In the present distribution there are 14 individuals who made a score of 13 examples, just about on the 75-centile
line. Their deviation from the average, $13.0 - 10.6 = 2.4$ examples, divided by the standard deviation of 4.0, gives them a standard score
of $+ 0.6$.

In a perfectly "normal" distribution each centile corresponds exactly
to a certain standard score, as for example:

The 10-centile score is the same as a standard score of $- 1.28$
" 25-centile " " " " " " " " " $- .67$
" 50-centile " " " " " " " " " $0$
" 75-centile " " " " " " " " " $+ .67$
" 90-centile " " " " " " " " " $+ 1.28$

In a "skew" (lopsided) distribution or whenever there are any irregularities, these correspondences are only approximate.

The brief statements here and in the main text are intended simply to
convey a general idea of the quantitative study of individual differences,
which is a very interesting study to those who go into it more adequately
(*6, 9, 11, 13*).

get rid of decimals and negative signs the standard score is often changed to a more convenient form, as in Fig. 8 (p. 57).

2. *Centile Scores.* With the distribution blocked out into centiles as minutely as may be desired, each individual can be assigned a centile score, showing what percent of the group he surpassed in the test, whether 10 percent, or 25, or 68, or 90, or what. This system is very convenient for indicating an individual's relative standing in the group, though it is open to some misinterpretation in comparing one individual with another, because the centiles are close together in the middle of the distribution where the scores pile up, while they lie farther apart near the ends of the distribution. So the difference of 10 centile points between the 45-centile and the 55-centile individuals amounts to very little, while the difference between the 85-centile and the 95-centile individual may be quite large.

## INTELLIGENCE

There are many kinds of achievement and many different aptitudes. Some persons who are good at drawing are not very good in making a speech, and some who learn history easily find mathematics quite difficult. This matter of different kinds of ability will be taken up in the next chapter. At present we will consider the type of tests that are best known and most used by the psychologist: intelligence tests.

*Intelligence* is a noun with the meaning of a verb or adverb. Intelligence is not a thing of which you have more or less but it is a way of acting. A person shows intelligence when he handles a situation intelligently; he is stupid when he attacks a problem stupidly.

As a word, *intelligence* is closely related to *intellect*, which is a comprehensive term for observing, understanding, thinking, remembering and all ways of knowing and of getting knowledge. Intellectual activity yields knowledge. Intelligent activity does this and something more. It is *useful,* helpful in solving a problem and reaching a goal. Counting, for example, is an intellectual activity and yields knowledge, but whether this knowledge is useful or not depends on the matter in hand. Counting the chairs in your room and the guests you expect is an intelligent way of finding out whether you have enough chairs, but counting the letters on a page would scarcely be an intelligent start toward learning a lesson printed on the page. Intelligence means *intellect put to use.* It is the use of intellectual abilities for handling a situation or accomplishing any task.

Intelligence depends upon knowledge, but it is using knowledge rather than merely having it. Sometimes we say of a person that he knows a lot and yet is rather stupid because he makes so little use of what he knows. He knows how to count, add, subtract, multiply and divide, but it does not occur to him to make use of these arithmetical operations when they are just what he needs to solve a practical problem. He has the tools but he does not use them. One person may have a good set of carpenter's tools but be stupid in the way he tries to use them, while another, with only a few simple tools, makes out very well. The second person is the better mechanic, the more intelligent in mechanical matters. Just so, numbers are tools, and one who has learned arithmetic has these tools in his intellectual tool chest; the question is whether he uses them when they are needed. In the same way words are tools. It is not intelligent merely to jabber words. It is intelligent to use words in explaining to another person exactly what you wish him to do. There are many other intellectual tools, and intelligence consists in putting those tools to use in solving problems and handling the situations of life.

**Feeblemindedness.** Long before any attempt was made to measure intelligence, it was obvious that some individuals in any large community were mentally deficient. They were too stupid to manage their own lives. Those showing the greatest deficiency are called idiots, those somewhat less deficient are the imbeciles. The least defective group, the morons, far outnumber the idiots and imbeciles.

Idiots do not even avoid the common dangers of life, but will put their hands into fire, walk heedlessly into deep water, or remain in front of a moving automobile. They cannot learn to wash and dress themselves, and the most deficient among them do not learn to feed themselves or care for their bodily needs. They do not talk beyond a few monosyllables.

Imbeciles do learn to avoid the common dangers of life. They talk a little but cannot learn to read. Nor can they learn to do much useful work; the least intelligent of them are incapable of any work, those somewhat higher in the scale learn to perform a few useful acts under supervision, and those near the upper limit of the imbecile class learn to dress, wash and feed themselves, but cannot be left to perform any but the simplest and briefest tasks without constant supervision.

Morons can be taught to do simple routine work without close supervision. In an institution they make the beds and run errands, and some "high-grade morons" become skillful in taking care of animals, in tending babies, doing carpenter work, or operating a lathe or sewing machine. Progressive institutions for the feebleminded are having considerable success in sending out well-trained high-grade morons for employment in the community; but even these need general supervision by someone who understands their limitations and has their welfare at heart. Without such assistance the morons are likely to spend their money foolishly and to make poor use of their leisure time; the girls are easily led into prostitution and the boys into thievery. In general morons do not handle a novel situation or complicated problem with much success.

In a simple, friendly, easy-going community the presence of a few feebleminded children or adults creates no serious problem, as it does when the community becomes complex and industrialized. Then the community finds it necessary to make special provision for the education and supervision of the feebleminded. Laws are passed attempting to define feeblemindedness and to prescribe what shall be done for the feebleminded child or adult.

In law, a feebleminded child is one who is unable to master the ordinary school subjects with anything like the usual speed and thoroughness. Special provision has to be made for his education.

A feebleminded adult is defined legally as one who because of his mental deficiency is unable to support himself and keep out of trouble in the community. The community has to provide "care, supervision, and control" for the protection of the feebleminded individual himself and for the protection of other people as well. Some individuals who are unable to master the school subjects do manage to take care of themselves as adults, performing some useful work for pay and keeping out of serious mischief. Such adults are not legally feebleminded in spite of their meager mental ability.

When scientific interest was first attracted to the feebleminded early in the nineteenth century, some hope was entertained that they could be brought up to normal intelligence by suitable education. This hope has never been realized, but the moron at least can be taught much that will help him in life, provided his limitations are recognized. Many idiots and imbeciles would have been normal individuals except for damage to the brain by birth injury, encephalitis, cerebrospinal meningitis, etc. Morons, in the majority of cases, have not suffered from brain injury but are simply very dull individuals not markedly different from the low-normal group except that they do not get on in the community. There is a continuous gradation from the moron through a large borderline group into the great mass of the normal population.

Estimates of the number of the feebleminded in the population, run from half of one percent to one or even two percent. No exact percent can be determined simply because there is no sharp line between the feebleminded and the low-normal, and because the individual's normality or subnormality depends in part on the environment with which he has to cope (1, 18).

**Genius and exceptional intelligence.**   At the other extreme of ability from the feebleminded are those persons whose achievement in intellectual lines is outstanding. Though they are famous for their accomplishments in some special field such as literature, music, science, or government, they probably would have made very high scores in a general intelligence test. They seem always to have been very bright children. When we find that Ralph Waldo Emerson, at the age of ten years, composed a long poem, of which these two lines are a sample:

> Six score and twenty thousand 'gan the fray,
> Six score alone survived that dreadful day,

we must admit that the performance was remarkable for his years. Similar indications of exceptional brightness are found in the childhood records of all great men and women whenever these records are at all complete. Other qualities besides intelligence stand out in the records and certainly contributed to the later achievements of these individuals—such qualities as persistence of effort, confidence in their own powers, force of character, ambition or the desire to excel, and often a passionate love for their chosen work (*10, 14,* Vol. 2).

## INTELLIGENCE TESTS

Intelligence tests are measures of aptitude; i.e., they attempt to predict the intellectual achievement of individuals, especially of children and adolescents.

**The Binet tests of intelligence.** About the year 1900 the school authorities of the city of Paris, disturbed by the large number of children who were backward in their school work, wished to find out whether this backwardness was due to inattention and mischievousness, as the teachers were apt to assume, or to insufficient mental capacity. These children were not feebleminded in the full sense of the word, yet they were not succeeding well in school. Now if a child is not feebleminded, he must be normal in intelligence—so the older theory ran—and if he is normal he can master ordinary school work. The alternative possibility, that mental capacity may shade off by imperceptible degrees from high to average and from average to low, was not so familiar in 1900 as it is today.

Alfred Binet, one of the leading psychologists of that time, undertook to find the answers to these important questions. He saw that some method must be found to *measure* intelligence.

After experimenting with different methods that were suggested he came to the conclusion that no single task would be
equally fair to all individuals. He invented a new type of test
which gives the child a variety of tasks to perform and plenty
of chances to show what he is able to do. The Binet-Simon
measuring scale, prepared by Binet and a collaborator, was an
assembly of many different tasks or "test items" (3).

Tests of graded difficulty, ranging from easy to hard, were
obviously needed; and here Binet had the brilliant idea of utilizing the undoubted fact that children increase in ability as
they grow older. His easiest tests were just within the reach of
three-year-olds, those next in order were just beyond the reach
of the average three-year-old but within the power of the four-
year-olds, and so on up the scale. Since no one can tell by inspection the exact difficulty of any task, Binet tried out his test
items on children of different ages and modified them if necessary till each item was fitted to some particular age level. Years
of experimentation and several revisions were needed before
the Binet tests were shaped into a fairly accurate measuring
instrument. Binet himself died in 1911, before the job was fully
accomplished. But his tests, quickly found useful by the psychologists of various countries, have been adapted, revised
again and again, and extended in scope down to the first-year
level and up to the level of superior adults.

In the recent Stanford revision (15) the investigators first
collected thousands of possible test items and tried out the
most promising on 1500 subjects ranging in age from the preschool to the adult level. Any item that proved uninteresting to
the children or adults for whom it was intended had to be rejected, since the interest and cooperation of the subject are required for accurate measurement of his ability. Any item that
meant different things to different subjects, and any item that
could not be scored objectively as passed or failed, had to be
rejected, and exact rules for scoring every item had to be formulated. In this manner the test items were weeded out and
400 kept for a second trial. The selected items were tried on
3000 subjects ranging from 2 to 18 years of age, all white Amer-

icans, native-born though of different ancestral groups. So as to represent the country at large, the subjects were obtained in 11 states, from Vermont and Virginia to California. Urban and rural districts and the various occupational groups (professional, business, clerical, agricultural, skilled and unskilled labor) were sampled in such proportions as fairly to represent the white population of the country. From the results of this second tryout, two equivalent batteries of 129 items each were selected, each battery being so arranged and standardized as to give a person the same score as the other. Several other intelligence tests of the Binet type have been prepared, some intended specially for the younger children and some for adult subjects.

In order to get some idea of what the intelligence tests are really measuring we need to scrutinize the test items and consider what sort of mental operations they demand from the subject. Some notion of the varied material employed by Binet and his successors is afforded by the sample items below, taken from several sources. Usually six items are used at each age level.

4-month level: sitting with back supported for 30 seconds.

6-month level: reaching for a small bright object dangled before the child within his reach.

12-month level: imitating the examiner who shakes a rattle or rings a small bell.

2-year level: removing the paper wrapping from a piece of candy before putting the candy in the mouth.

2½-year level: naming 4 out of 5 familiar objects presented in the form of toys.

3-year level: stringing beads, at least 4 beads to be strung within a time limit of 2 minutes.

6-year level: finding omissions in pictures of faces, from which the nose, or one eye, etc., is left out. Four such pictures are shown and 3 correct responses are required to pass the test.

9-year level: telling how wood and coal are alike and also how they are different. Both likeness and difference must be given for each of 4 such pairs named by the examiner.

12-year level: correct interpretation of a picture showing an incident.

14-year level: explaining the physical absurdity involved in a certain picture.

Adult, 4 levels: free definitions of 20, 23, 26 and 30 words from a graded list of 45 words.

The question may be raised, "Why such arbitrary scoring rules—4 out of 5 correct answers required in one test, 4 out of 4 in another, 20 out of 45 words to be defined?" The answer is that the scoring rules are really not arbitrary; they have been carefully adjusted to correspond to the actual success of average children at the different ages.

Special training, as well as tact, is necessary for the psychological examiner. Unless he can enlist the subject's interest and still give the test in the standard manner without helping the subject over the difficult places, his measurements may be absurdly inaccurate. The Binet test system is one of the psychologist's instruments of precision, and the novice must learn the requisite technique from the expert.

In order to broaden our acquaintance with test materials we may glance at other types of intelligence tests which differ somewhat from those of Binet.

Performance tests, as compared with the Binet type, make little use of oral question and answer, and much use of concrete materials. Some persons do much better when dealing with concrete objects than when answering questions. A person who does well in either the oral or the performance tests has a good chance of finding a niche in the workaday world and making a good social adjustment. The *form board* is an example of a performance test. Blocks of different shapes are to be fitted into corresponding holes in a board; the time is taken and the errors are counted. An error is an attempt to insert a block into a hole of different shape. For the average adult this is too simple a task to serve as a test of his intelligence, but the young child finds it difficult, and the adult of low intelligence goes at it in the same haphazard way as the young child, trying to force the square block into the round hole. He does not clearly grasp the principle of matching blocks and holes according to their shape.

A *man-drawing test* is useful from ages four to ten (7). The child is given pencil and paper and simply told, "Make a man, the best man you can make." His drawing is scored not for beauty but for completeness and coherence. The child's ad-

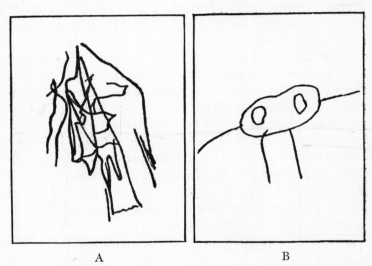

A                                                B

Fig. 4.—Children's drawings of a man. (From Goodenough, 7.)

A. Score 0, M.A. (mental age), less than 3 years.

B. Score 4 points, for head, legs, arms, eyes; M.A., 4 years.

C. Score 8 points, for head, legs, trunk, trunk longer than wide, eyes, pupils of eyes, mouth, forehead; M.A., 5 years.

D. Score 14 points, for head, legs, arms, trunk, trunk longer than wide, arms and legs attached to trunk, eyes, nose, mouth, ears, hands, legs in fair proportion to trunk, some clothing, firm and well-controlled lines; M.A., 6 years, 6 months.

E. Score 26 points, including most of those mentioned above, and in addition: shoulders, neck, neck continuous with head, hair, clothing non-transparent, fingers, thumbs, arms and legs shown in two dimensions, heels, head in fair proportion, eyebrow; M.A., 9 years, 6 months.

F. Score 44 points, including most of those mentioned above, and in addition: lips, nostrils, elbow, knee, projecting chin, profile, eye detail (4 points), ears in correct position and proportion, arms attached at right point, hair non-transparent and well shown, good proportion of head, arms, legs and feet, good lines and motor control (3 points), costume complete without incongruities (5 points): M.A., 13 years or over.

*psychology psch psychiatry*

vance with age consists partly in including more details in his picture, partly in placing the details in better relation to each other (attaching the arms to the trunk rather than to the head), and partly in representing the man as he could be seen at one time (not putting two eyes in a profile face, nor showing the legs through the trousers).

C    D

E    F

$$MA = \frac{IQ}{CA.}$$

$$\frac{CA}{IQ}$$

Still another performance test presents a maze through which the shortest path must be traced with a pencil. Success here depends on looking ahead and avoiding blind, impulsive moves. Many other concrete tasks are used in intelligence testing.

FIG. 5.—A pencil maze. With the pencil or with your finger trace the most direct path from the entrance to the exit. No back tracing allowed. A series of mazes can be provided, some easier than this one, others more difficult. The question is how difficult a maze the subject can do perfectly on the first trial. Or several trials can be given on the same maze, and the number of trials necessary before the subject reaches a perfect performance can be taken as his score.

Group tests, as they are called because given to many individuals at the same time, are usually paper-and-pencil tests of the short-answer form now familiar to many students. On the whole they may be less adequate than the individual tests in which an experienced examiner can make sure that there is optimal adjustment to the testing situation. Both forms may well be included in a complete mental examination. Group testing got its impetus from the psychologists in the American Army in 1917–1918. Their job was to examine thousands of recruits in short order and to discover which men were too dull to learn the duties of a soldier and which ones were bright enough to learn the duties of an officer or non-commissioned officer (20). They devised the *Army Alpha*, a group test consisting of several parts. The test booklet contained a page of arithmetical problems increasing in difficulty from the top to the bottom of the page; a page of information items; and a page of synonyms and antonyms to be distinguished, as for example:

ascend—rise                    same or opposite?
nadir—acme                     same or opposite?

These three sub-tests depend strongly, though not entirely, upon the subject's stock of *knowledge*. Among the other sub-tests were three that depended mostly on *alertness* and mental flexibility. One of these gave oral directions, as for example:

"Look at the row of letters. When I say 'Go,' cross out the last letter in the row, circle the letter F, and underline the two letters next after K. Go!" (10 seconds allowed.)

A  B  C  D  E  F  G  H  I  J  K  L  M  N  O  P

Another required the continuation of number series, such as:

1      3      2      6      3      . . .        . . .
49     36     25     16     9      . . .        . . .

Another one, in the multiple choice form, presented "analogies" to be completed as:

left—right :: up—(front, rear, down, town)
knife—blade :: arrow—(spear, head, bow, shoot)

There was also an *Army Beta,* intended to be fair to the illiterate subject and to the immigrant who knew no English. Instructions were given by pantomime and blackboard illustration. Beta included among other sub-tests: pictures to be completed by drawing the missing part; mazes; and "XO" series to be continued, as in the two lines below:

OXOXO......
OXXXOOXXOOOXOXXX..............

**The nature of intelligence as indicated by the tests.**   Intelligence tests use a variety of material because they are designed to take a broad sample of the individual's mental performances. They call for activities that appeal to his spontaneous interests. If we look over the test items, asking what the subject must do in order to pass them and how he may fail them, we may glean some information regarding the nature of the "intelligence" that is being tested.

1. We notice that many test items require the use of knowledge gained in the subject's *past experience.* This is obviously true when he is asked to define a word and whenever he has to understand the meaning of words. It is no less obvious with the man-drawing test and with any picture test. It is not quite so obvious with the maze test, since the subject may never have encountered anything just like a maze. Yet even here he may be guided by past experience; he may have learned the advantage of being foresightful rather than hasty and impulsive. Probably some use could be made of past experience in performing any task that could possibly be devised. Intelligent behavior depends on making use of what the individual has previously learned.

2. Very few test items, however, call merely for a recitation of something previously learned. Most of them place the subject in a more or less *novel situation.* He is well acquainted with baseballs and oranges but has never before been asked to explain how they are alike and how they are different. He has done many examples in arithmetic, but each new example sets

a new problem, especially when different kinds of examples are intermingled in the test. The mingling of different tasks has the effect of making each test item a fresh problem.

3. So far, we should judge that intelligence consists in meeting new situations by applying knowledge acquired in past experience. Such a definition is all right as far as it goes, but it does not penetrate deeply into the process of meeting new situations. How are novel situations handled successfully? Some light is thrown on this question by the ways in which subjects *fail* to solve the test items. There are several ways of failing.

a. Failure to see the problem, failure to aim at the target at all. A young child, confronted with the form board, may simply play with the blocks and make no effort to place them in the holes.

b. Failure to see the problem precisely, failure to aim at the bull's-eye. In an opposites test (p. 26) a subject may be contented with vague, general responses, not considering the exact meaning of the given words or trying to find their exact opposites.

c. Failure to take account of the *whole* problem. The subject may impulsively react to a part of the problem without considering whether his reaction meets all the requirements. In tracing a maze he may enter a promising path without first looking ahead far enough to make sure it is not a blind alley. In describing a picture he may simply enumerate one object after another without noticing the meaning of the picture as a whole.

d. Failure to check or prove his first answer, lack of self-criticism. In continuing a number series (p. 43) the subject may put in two numbers and leave the matter there without going back to make sure that all the numbers fit together. Somewhat similar is the "sentence completion test," which requires one word to be inserted in each blank space. For example:

Near the ........ of the mountain, where there are ..........
trees, you get a ........ view of the broad plains to the north and
........ and of many still ........ mountains to the south and
west.

Subjects will sometimes hastily fill in one blank after another with words that make some kind of sense, without reading over the completed sentence to make sure the whole thing hangs together.

All in all, it appears from the problems used in the tests, and from the ways in which subjects succeed or fail in the tests, that intelligent behavior consists in seeing a problem clearly and completely, in making use of past experience to solve the problem, and in not accepting a solution without checking back to make sure that the problem is really solved (12).

## MENTAL AGE AND INTELLIGENCE QUOTIENT

The raw score obtained from an intelligence test is simply the number of test items the subject is able to pass. As with other tests, so here, the raw score is practically meaningless and must be converted into some form that will show *how the subject compares with other individuals*. Binet introduced the very convenient measure known as *mental age* (MA).

**Mental Age.** Age norms are established by testing large samples of children at each age. The average score of a sample of eight-year children is the eight-year norm. The norms increase year by year up to about 15 years of age, and thus provide a scale of mental ages. An individual's raw score can now be converted into a mental age. Any child or adult has a mental age of 8 years if his score just equals the 8-year norm. If his score falls exactly half-way between the 8-year and 9-year norms his mental age is 8½ years.

Mental age is a measure of the individual's level of intelligence at a given time. To say that a child or adult has reached the mental age of 8, that is, the mental level of the average 8-year-old, conveys a definite meaning. It means, for one thing, that he is just about qualified, intellectually, to begin the work of the third grade in school and that he is by no means capable of handling the work of the fourth or fifth grade. In industry a mental age of 8 means that the individual is not qualified for any kind of clerical work but that, given adequate physical maturity, he can do satisfactory work in simple packing jobs or in certain other jobs that make no great demands on intellectual ability.

**Intelligence Quotient.**    Mental age does not tell all we want to know about a child's intelligence. If this child with an MA of 8 years is only 5 years old we should call him a bright child, but if he is 12 years old we should regard him as quite dull. Along with his mental age we want to know his brightness relative to other children of his own *chronological age* (life age counted from birth, abbreviated CA) A convenient way of calculating brightness is to divide mental age by chronological age, so obtaining the *intelligence quotient,* the IQ.

$$IQ = \frac{MA}{CA}$$

With MA 8 years and CA 12 years, a child's IQ is $\frac{8}{12}$ or .67; another child with the same MA but a CA of only 5 years has the much higher IQ of $\frac{8}{5}$ or 1.60. The exactly average child of any age has an IQ of 1.00, because his MA is just up to the norm for his own age.

Usually the decimal point is omitted and the exactly average child is said to have an IQ of 100. A child with an IQ of over 100 is above the exact average for his age, and one with an IQ under 100 is below the exact average. Individuals with an IQ only a few points above or below 100 are practically average.

The two measures, MA and IQ, have different uses depending on what you want to know about the individual. Consider the two children, 5 and 12 years old, each having an MA of 8 years. At the moment, both are at the same level, both have equal present intelligence (so far as indicated by the tests). But the younger child is exceptionally intelligent for his age, while the older one is far behind his age. So we call the younger of these two children much brighter, as indicated by the two IQs. Mental age, then, is a measure of the level of intellectual achievement, while IQ is an index of brightness, or achievement relative to others of the same age. It is also a prediction of potential intellectual achievement.

As a child grows up, his intelligence increases; he gains in mental age. His IQ need not increase. In fact the *average* IQ remains at 100 through the years of childhood and youth. This is clear from the way MA and IQ are defined and computed.

**Constancy of the IQ.** Though the average of all IQs remains constant at 100, this does not necessarily mean that the individual's IQ must remain constant. John might go up and James go down without disturbing the average. But in general, and within certain limits, individual IQs tend to remain the same.

Some fluctuation of the individual's IQ is to be expected. He feels better and works better on some days than on others; and some test items suit him better than others even at the same difficulty level. The examiner may be a bit too strict or too lenient on a certain day in scoring some of the subject's definitions, for example, in the vocabulary test. It is really remarkable that intelligence testing is as accurate as it is, but we have to expect the IQ to shift up or down a few points even when the subject is retested before any genuine change in intelligence has time to occur. When children have been tested *within one week* on the two equivalent batteries of the revised Stanford-Binet, the high IQs went up or down about 6 points, the middle ones about 5 points, the low ones about 2.5 points, and some individuals of course changed quite a little more than these average amounts. Greater fluctuation is found in bright than in dull children, and in younger than older children (*15*).

With an allowance of 5–10 points for chance fluctuations, we cannot take seriously most of the shifts of an individual's IQ which are obtained on retesting after *much longer intervals*. Here, for example, is the record of a little girl, tested five times over a period of six years.

| | Chronological Age | | Mental Age | | IQ |
|---|---|---|---|---|---|
| First test | 6 years | 8 months | 5 years | 6 months | 83 |
| Second test | 7 | 1 | 5 | 4 | 75 |
| Third test | 8 | 2 | 6 | 10 | 84 |
| Fourth test | 8 | 7 | 7 | 0 | 82 |
| Fifth test | 12 | 10 | 9 | 10 | 77 |

She varies from 80 only a few points up or down. Here is another girl with higher IQ and more variation:

| | Chronological Age | | Mental Age | | IQ |
|---|---|---|---|---|---|
| First test | 8 years | 0 months | 9 years | 9 months | 122 |
| Second test | 9 | 1 | 11 | 5 | 126 |
| Third test | 10 | 0 | 11 | 4 | 113 |
| Fourth test | 10 | 11 | 11 | 7 | 106 |
| Fifth test | 12 | 0 | 13 | 6 | 113 |

Individual records could easily be selected to give the impression of either constancy or inconstancy. Retests of hundreds of children over long periods of time show, on the average, a shift of 5 or 10 points up or down, with a few changes as large as 20 or 25 points. On the whole, the individual child's IQ remains fairly though not absolutely constant, and the bright child becomes the intelligent adult. Thus the IQ obtained in childhood has considerable predictive value. If a child at the age of 6 has an MA of 8, and an IQ therefore of 133, we can predict that probably though not certainly his MA at the age of 10 will be about 13 years and that later he will be able to do superior college work. Prediction is not as good, however, from tests made in the preschool years as from tests made after the age of about 6.

The constancy of the IQ has sometimes been used as an argument to prove that the individual's intelligence is completely determined by heredity and wholly unaffected by education and other environmental influences. The flaw in this argument is the fact that under ordinary conditions the child's environment remains fairly constant. If he has a good home, it ordinarily remains good. If he has the advantages of a good school and neighborhood in his early years, he usually has similar advantages later on in childhood. Logically, then, his constant IQ might be explained either by his constant environment or by his heredity, or by a combination of both.

Children relieved of the handicap of partial blindness or deafness sometimes show a definite and permanent rise in IQ. They are receiving much more stimulation from the environment, and have much greater opportunities to practice intellectual tasks. Other pronounced environmental changes have been tried out experimentally, in order to find out how much can be accomplished by improved environment. Some of the results will be discussed in a later chapter (p. 178).

**Adult intelligence.** How intelligent is the average adult? This seems like a simple question but there are two difficulties, one in devising adequate tests for adults, and the other in obtaining a fair sample of the adult population.

With adults specializing in many different directions one difficulty is to construct tests fair to all alike and still hard enough for the superior individual. Test items demanding high intel-

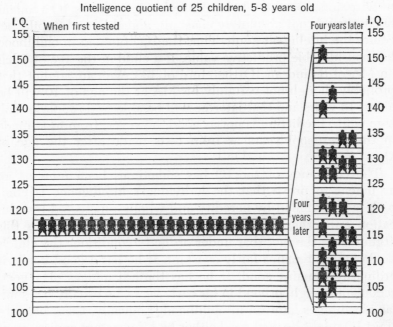

Intelligence quotient of 25 children, 5-8 years old

FIG. 6.—Changes in IQ of 25 children whose IQ was 115 on first test. During four years in these stimulating schools, the IQ of some of these children went up, while the IQ of others went down. The changes were not large in comparison with the whole IQ range of 0–200. The average change was a gain of 5 points. (Data from the psychological records of the Horace Mann and Lincoln Schools of Teachers College, Columbia University.)

ligence could easily be drawn from law, medicine, engineering
and other such fields, but would evidently not be fair to all.
What the psychologists have done is to devise items similar to
those used in testing children, but more difficult. These adult
items are occasionally passed by a bright boy or girl of twelve,
but the superior adult is more consistently successful.

The sampling difficulty is troublesome. So long as practically
all children attend school, representative samples of the various
age groups can be drawn from the schools, and accurate age
norms determined. But as soon as a considerable proportion
of adolescents have left school, those still in school are not an
adequate sample of their age groups. How shall we get hold of
a fair sample of men or women of 21, for instance, so as to test
them and determine the 21-year norm? During the war of
1917–18 many thousands of drafted recruits, 20–30 years of age,
were given the Army Alpha and Beta tests—a very large sample,
this, but not entirely representative because of numerous ex-
emptions from the draft. The average score made by the recruits was equal to that of 13-year-old children, indicating that
intelligence did not develop very much beyond that age. A
shocking conclusion, so it seemed—grown men with the mental
age of the 13-year-old child!

In standardizing the revised Stanford-Binet tests (p. 37)
great pains were taken to obtain fair samples of the age groups
up through 18 years, and also to raise the "ceiling" of the tests
so that even the brightest 18-year-old could show his full ability.
The average score increased slowly beyond age 13 but scarcely
at all after 15. According to this finding adult intelligence is
reached at the age of 15, though doubtless with much variation, some individuals maturing more slowly than others. Other
samples have shown a slight increase up to 16 or even 18 years
of age (5, 16).

The growth of intelligence in adolescence can be followed by
another method which avoids the sampling difficulty: test the
same individuals repeatedly, year after year, with due allowance for the improvement to be expected from practice in taking the tests. Some studies of this sort have found no advance

beyond age 14; other studies have shown a slight improvement up to 18 or even 20 years of age. (See the later discussion of the whole question of mental development, p. 297.)

On the whole the evidence indicates that mental growth, like physical growth, tapers off in adolescence and reaches its adult level at the age of 15–18 years. There is no reason to be shocked at such a conclusion. If the adult level of intelligence could be raised, that would be fine. But suppose you had it in your power to hasten or retard the process of mental development. Would you see any advantage in prolonging the process so that the adult level would not be reached till the age of 30 or 40? Is it not better for everyone to reach his full mental power during adolescence, so as to be equipped for taking on his adult responsibilities? Reaching the adult level means that he has attained his full powers of learning, acquiring new ideas and attacking new problems. The alert adult goes on learning for many years. His increasing knowledge of the world in general, as well as of his own affairs, enables him to deal more successfully with the environment, even though his capacity and power are not increasing. In handling new problems he is probably no brighter at 40 than he was at 20, but the problems he has to handle are no longer strictly new because of his background of experience.

**Computing an IQ for adults.**    The IQ of a child tells something about his rate of mental development. He has reached a certain level of achievement (his MA) and it has taken him a certain number of years (his CA) to reach this level. In the case of an adult, however, the IQ cannot have this clear meaning. His test score or MA gives us his level of achievement, but his CA does not tell how many years of growth he required to reach this level. Probably he reached his adult level during the teens, and we can assume that he reached it at the age of 15 years, and use this figure for his CA in computing an IQ for him. This is a customary procedure in computing the so-called IQ of adults. What we really wish to know about an adult is his standing in comparison with other adults, i.e., his position in the distribution of adult intelligence (19).

## THE DISTRIBUTION OF INTELLIGENCE
### IN THE POPULATION

The point of intelligence testing lies in the comparison of one individual with another or, better, in the comparison of any individual with the run of the population. The individual's IQ should be compared with IQs in general. We need to know the range of IQs with the number or percent of people falling in each part of the range.

The point at issue can be brought out by asking how much a child's IQ tells about his standing in the population. If his IQ is 100 he is exactly average; if above 100, above the exact average. So much we already know. But if we are interested in a particular child we insist on knowing more. If his IQ is 110 we want to know whether that is so far above the average that he is a remarkably bright individual, or whether it is not at all exceptional.

We get a partial answer to this question when we know the *range* of IQs which, as already stated, extends from nearly zero to nearly 200. Since 110 falls near the middle of the range we conclude that this individual cannot be very far above the average. But we want a more exact statement.

The distribution of IQs will tell how frequently each value of IQ is found in the population. A fair sample of the population must be tested and their IQs computed. The range of IQs is divided into equal steps, 100 to 105, 105 to 110, 110 to 115, etc., and the number or percent falling within each step is counted. So a distribution table is obtained and a distribution curve constructed (p. 30). We have to depend mostly on results obtained from children since they have been more adequately sampled than adults. The IQ distribution obtained from a large and representative sample of children (Fig. 7) probably holds good for adults as well. Like other distribution curves it shows more people near the average than anywhere else (p. 28), with a gradual tapering off toward either extreme. IQs of 120 are less common than those of 110, those of 130 are still less common, and so on up the scale. Below 100 it is the same in reverse

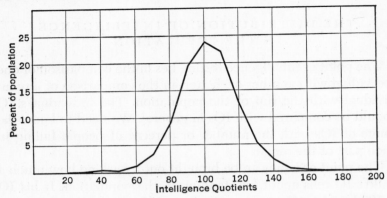

FIG. 7.—Distribution of IQs in a sample of about 2900 children, ages 2–18 combined. This sample was carefully selected, as explained on page 37, to represent as fairly as possible the native white children of the United States. The height of the curve above any point of the base line shows the percent of the child population having an IQ within 5 IQ points of 40 or 60 or 100, etc. (Data from Terman & Merrill, 15.)

order. And there is no gap anywhere—no sharp break between the superior and the average, between the average and the dull, or even between the dull and the feebleminded. These are not distinct classes of people; they are degrees in a continuous scale of brightness and dullness.

These same facts, somewhat differently stated, are presented in a table showing the percent of individuals falling within each part of the range of IQ values.

DISTRIBUTION OF IQ VALUES

| IQ | Percent of the Population | |
|---|---|---|
| over 140 | 1 | genius |
| 130–139 | 2 } | very superior |
| 120–129 | 8 } | very superior |
| 110–119 | 16 | superior |
| 100–109 | 23 } | average |
| 90–99 | 23 } | average |
| 80–89 | 16 | dull average |
| 70–79 | 8 | borderline |
| 60–69 | 2 } | mentally deficient |
| below 60 | 1 } | mentally deficient |

If we now come back to our question, how exceptional an IQ of 110 is in the population, this distribution table gives us an answer. We see that an IQ of 140 stands for quite a high degree of brightness, such as is surpassed by only 1 percent of people. An IQ of 130 is surpassed by $1 + 2 = 3$ percent, an IQ of 110 by $1 + 2 + 8 + 16 = 27$ percent. Similarly, at the other end of the scale, an IQ of 60 stands for a degree of *dullness* which is exceeded by only 1 percent, while an IQ of 70 is exceeded in dullness by 3 percent.

This table can be recast to show what percent of IQs are *surpassed by* an IQ of 140, or 130, etc. The following table is the result.

| An IQ of | 140 | surpasses | 99 | percent of all IQs |
|---|---|---|---|---|
| "    "    " | 130 | " | 97 | "    "    "    " |
| "    "    " | 120 | " | 89 | "    "    "    " |
| "    "    " | 110 | " | 73 | "    "    "    " |
| "    "    " | 100 | " | 50 | "    "    "    " |
| "    "    " | 90 | " | 27 | "    "    "    " |
| "    "    " | 80 | " | 11 | "    "    "    " |
| "    "    " | 70 | " | 3 | "    "    "    " |
| "    "    " | 60 | " | 1 | "    "    "    " |

**Centile intelligence scores and standard intelligence scores.** The facts given in this last table can also be stated by saying that 140 is the 99-centile IQ, that 110 is the 73-centile IQ, that 90 is the 27-centile IQ, etc. Centile values can be worked out in greater detail. The 50-centile IQ is of course 100, and the 25-centile and 75-centile IQs are found to be 89 and 111, respectively, so that half of the population falls between these narrow limits.

Standard scores can be derived from these same data. The average IQ is 100, and the standard deviation is 16 IQ points, as determined for this revised Stanford-Binet test. Accordingly, an IQ of 116 is equivalent to a standard score of +1, an IQ of 132 to +2, an IQ of 140 to +2.5; and similarly an IQ of 84 is equivalent to a standard score of −1, an IQ of 68 to −2, an IQ of 60 to −2,5, etc. In fact any IQ can be regarded as a standard score stated in these terms: that the average is called 100 and the standard deviation is 16 IQ points. So regarded, an adult's IQ is more directly meaningful than when regarded as a ratio of MA to CA (p. 52).

When we say that an individual with an IQ of 110 surpasses 73 percent of the population in intelligence, we need to have two serious qualifications in mind. First, an individual's IQ varies a few points up and down in repeated tests, so that the most we can say is that he surpasses *about* 73 percent of the population. And second, it makes a difference what kind of intelligence test is used—whether a Binet, a paper-pencil test, or a performance test—for an individual who gets a 73-centile rating in one intelligence test may earn only a 60-centile rating in another, or may go up instead of down. It seems there are several kinds of intelligence; certainly there are many kinds of ability; and a person who ranks high or low in one ability does not often rank equally high or low in all other abilities. Here we touch on the problem of the next chapter.

**Results from the new Army Intelligence Tests.**    With the experience of World War I and of the succeeding years to go on, psychologists during World War II improved their group tests for adults. The principal tests for literate men consisted of (1) verbal items calling for a grasp of the precise meanings of words; (2) arithmetical items calling for computation and problem solution; and (3) spatial items. The items ranged in difficulty from very easy to very hard. These tests were first standardized on a sample of about 3000 men and then given to 10,000,000 recruits, certainly the largest sample of the adult population ever tested. Though so large, the sample was not perfectly representative of the population because some of the lowest grade were excluded from the draft while some of the highest grade (Regular Army officers, doctors and other professionals) were not required to take the test. Some of the men tested did not do themselves full justice because of inadequate schooling. For these and similar reasons the actual distribution of test scores did not conform exactly to the "normal" distribution which probably would hold in ideal conditions.

The better-educated men got the higher scores, on the whole. But some men achieved grade-one scores who had not even completed grammar school, and some college graduates made only mediocre scores. More important is the converse fact that a great many young men whose high intelligence scores showed them to be capable of college and professional education had not gone beyond the secondary school.

The tests demonstrated their value in many ways. In general they indicated very well, though not infallibly, how capable a man was of learning the manifold duties of a modern soldier.

So far, results have not been published to show how these young adults compared with children of different ages. Many other questions, scientific and practical, will probably be helped toward an answer by more complete results when they are known.

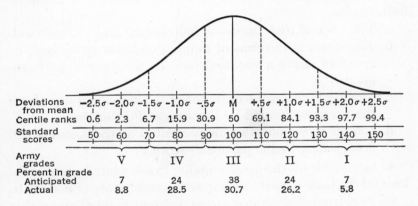

| Deviations from mean | −2.5σ | −2.0σ | −1.5σ | −1.0σ | −.5σ | M | +.5σ | +1.0σ | +1.5σ | +2.0σ | +2.5σ |
|---|---|---|---|---|---|---|---|---|---|---|---|
| Centile ranks | 0.6 | 2.3 | 6.7 | 15.9 | 30.9 | 50 | 69.1 | 84.1 | 93.3 | 97.7 | 99.4 |
| Standard scores | 50 | 60 | 70 | 80 | 90 | 100 | 110 | 120 | 130 | 140 | 150 |

| Army grades | V | IV | III | II | I |
|---|---|---|---|---|---|
| Percent in grade Anticipated | 7 | 24 | 38 | 24 | 7 |
| Actual | 8.8 | 28.5 | 30.7 | 26.2 | 5.8 |

Fig. 8.—A normal distribution of intelligence test scores, compared with the results of Army testing. Here the average is denoted by M, and the standard deviation by σ. The "standard scores" are derived from the deviations by calling the average 100 units and the standard deviation 20 units. These standard scores look like IQs but they are not IQs because they were not obtained by dividing MA by CA, and because the standard deviation is taken as 20 points instead of 16. They would be more comparable to IQs if 16 were substituted for 20, so that they would run from 60 to 140 by 8-point steps instead of from 50 to 150 by 10-point steps. Comparing the actual with the anticipated percent in each Grade we see that the actual distribution was flatter in the middle than the theoretical or normal distribution shown by the curve. (From Bingham, 4.)

## SUMMARY

1. *Individual differences* are found in all psychological characteristics: physical abilities, mental abilities, knowledge, habits, personality and character traits.

2. *Ability* has three distinct meanings:
   a. *Achievement* is actual ability, and can be measured directly by the use of tests.
   b. *Capacity* is potential ability, and can be inferred indirectly from the unequal achievements of individuals who have had equally intensive training and experience.
   c. *Aptitude* is predictable achievement, and can be measured by specially devised tests.

3. *Test scores* are interpreted by relation to a standard criterion, or by relation to the distribution of scores in a group of individuals.
   a. The *normal distribution* is bell-shaped and symmetrical.
   b. *Raw score* is in terms of number of items completed, or speed of doing a specified task, or accuracy of performance.
   c. *Standard score* is the deviation of the individual score from the average, divided by the *standard deviation.*
   d. *Centile score* indicates the percent of all the scores which is surpassed by the particular score.

4. *Intelligence* is the general ability to solve intellectual problems on the basis of past learning and present grasp of essentials.
   a. *Feebleminded* persons are so deficient in intelligence that they cannot manage their own lives without supervision. Three grades of feebleminded are distinguished: moron, imbecile and idiot.
   b. *Geniuses* are exceptionally intelligent persons who, with favorable opportunities, reach outstanding intellectual achievement.

5. *Intelligence tests* are standardized, objective measures of intellectual aptitude.

4/2

a. *Binet test* is an individual examination made up of items graded in difficulty and arranged in groups corresponding to the average level of children of each age.

b. *Performance tests* make much use of concrete non-verbal materials.

c. *Group tests* are collections of short-answer items which can be administered to many persons simultaneously.

6. *Intelligence test scores* of children can be expressed by relation to age norms, as well as in standard scores or centile scores.

a. *Mental age* is the score attained by a child who passes all the test items which are normally passed by average children of the specified age.

b. *Intelligence quotient* is the mental age divided by the chronological age. It is an index of the relative brightness of the child and remains approximately constant throughout his life.

7. *Growth of intelligence* is continuous throughout childhood. Mental age increases steadily to age 13 or 15, more slowly to age 16 or even 18, when no further increase occurs.

8. The *distribution of intelligence* in the population conforms to the normal curve, and the brightness of any individual can be determined by his relative position in this distribution.

# CHAPTER THREE

# *The Correlation of Abilities*

I n the last chapter we discussed the measurement of intelligence without raising the question of different kinds of ability. But we would like to know whether ability is generalized or specialized, and whether the intelligence tests give an adequate measure of a person's all-round intellectual ability. When a person is described as a "very able individual," or another as having "little ability," there is an underlying assumption that individuals differ in their general, all-round ability. Quite a different assumption is implied when a politician is said to possess great oratorical ability but little ability in administration, or when an athlete is said to have greater ability in running than in pole vaulting, or when a young woman is said to have a gift for salesmanship or for millinery. With all these special abilities, the question is whether there is any such thing as general ability. This is one of the questions to be investigated in a scientific study of individual differences. It is part of the broader question how different abilities are related to each other and to success in different lines of activity.

Idiots savants. This term, meaning "talented idiots," is applied to certain feebleminded individuals, not usually low enough in intelligence to be properly classed as idiots, who show remarkably high ability in some special line. Different ones have shown different abilities. Some have shown great musical ability, at least so far as concerns memory for music and performance on some musical instrument. "Blind Tom," fifty years ago, used to give public concerts, playing difficult pieces very well indeed (one of the present authors heard him play), pieces which he had learned by hearing them played, and he would demonstrate his ability to reproduce new pieces, even very difficult and intricate ones, after a single hearing. Blind Tom was reputed to be feebleminded. After he finished each piece, he joined heartily in the applause of the audience.

Other idiots savants have shown ability in drawing or in mechanical construction—the making of model ships in one case—each individual having his own specialty. Perhaps the commonest specialty—though it must be understood that all these cases are extremely rare—has to do with numbers in some way. One feebleminded boy could promptly tell the day of the week for any date you chose to mention within the preceding five years, and another could even do this correctly for any date within the past thousand years. These were not pure feats of memory but depended partly on computing and allowing for leap years. These individuals are very proud of their special abilities and spend a large share of their time perfecting their knowledge and technique (22).[1]

Arithmetical prodigies. Far from the feebleminded level, and yet only moderate in intelligence as compared with their remarkable achievements with numbers, are a small group of persons celebrated for their ability in mental calculation. A few of them have been carefully studied by psychologists. They have excellent memory for numbers. Most educated adults can repeat from 7 to 10 one-place numbers after one hearing, while several of these arithmetical prodigies have been able to repeat from 20 to 25. They also have unusual memory for numbers heard days or weeks before. Their ability to multiply large numbers in their heads, find the squares of numbers, square roots and cube roots is so unusual as to arouse wonder in an

[1] See References, p. 639.

audience. People have been so mystified as to suppose the performer must have supernatural powers, or at least that his "unconscious mind" must be doing the rapid calculations. In reality these performances are the very opposite of unconscious, for the "lightning calculator" is giving the keenest possible attention to what he is doing, and the more intelligent of them are able to explain how they go to work. Their rapid performance depends on two main factors: first, great familiarity with many numbers and number relations; and second, the use of short-cut methods which they have picked up or invented.

From childhood on, these calculators have taken a great interest in numbers. One child, as soon as he was able to talk and had learned a few number words, amused himself by counting things, and he kept up this habit of counting everything till he was about 12 years old, when his interest switched from mere counting to calculation. He began to extend his knowledge of the multiplication table much beyond the usual $10 \times 10$ limit, and in a few years knew all the products up to $100 \times 100$ and even farther. Knowing by heart the answer to any example such as $54 \times 87$, it was no more difficult for him to find the product of four-place numbers than for most people to find that of two-place numbers.

With sufficient time and interest, you could become perfectly familiar with all the numbers up to 1000 and with many beyond that. These calculators have had the interest, have taken the time—for they are continually thinking of numbers—and have become as well acquainted with these larger numbers as most of us are with numbers like 12 and 25. To them 576 and 676 being the squares of 24 and 26 stand out as familiar friends, while 776 is the date of the Declaration of Independence minus 1000. You can find something rememberable about almost any number because of its relations to other numbers; and if you were proud of your skill with numbers and could win applause and amazement by your seemingly miraculous feats of calculation, you might be tempted to devote a good share of your time to the study of numbers. The short-cut methods of the lightning calculator include such everyday devices as dividing by 2 instead of multiplying by 5, and other less familiar devices making use of factors and squares in various ways to fit specific types of problems.

Most of the noted arithmetical prodigies have not progressed beyond arithmetic to higher mathematics, though there have been a few who became eminent mathematicians.

**Reading disability.** Just as some persons may possess one ability that is outstandingly superior to the general run of their abilities, other persons may have a particular lack of ability in one special line. Perhaps you know a college professor who, in spite of his obvious general intelligence, couldn't fix a doorbell or replace a burned-out fuse if he had to. Or a fellow student who does well in all his courses so long as he avoids mathematics which he knows he would fail.

Recently attention has been given to a rather large number of school children who have great difficulty in learning to read in spite of their normal abilities in other lines (8). It is not uncommon to find an eighth-grader with an IQ of 115 who is not able to read any better than the average third-grade child. He has been able to get along in school by puzzling out key words in his books, by careful attention to the teacher's oral presentations and by satisfactory work in arithmetic. He seems to have a specific disability in reading. Special training, particularly if it is available early, can do much to improve his reading, but he may always be slow. There are many adults who find reading so difficult and unpleasant that they never undertake to read anything except signs and newspaper headlines.

## THE METHOD OF CORRELATION

The striking instances just given of individuals with very unequal achievements in different lines lead us directly to ask whether equality or inequality of abilities is the general human characteristic. We are interested not only in separate abilities but in the relationship between different abilities. This is the problem of correlation. The problem may be stated in several ways:

1. Do the individuals who stand high, medium, low in one ability have the same standing when they are measured in another ability?

2. How accurately can you predict from an individual's standing in one ability (say in a certain test) what his standing will be in another ability?

3. How much do different abilities have in common?

The first and second questions obviously amount to the same thing.. For if each individual's standing in two abilities should be the same, and if we knew this to be the case, we could test him in one ability and predict exactly how he would stand in the other. If his standing in two abilities were only roughly the same, we could make a rough but not accurate prediction from one to the other. But if there were no correspondence at all, we could make no prediction from the standing in one test to the standing in another.

The third of the above questions is not so obviously the same as the other two and we will delay considering it till later on in the chapter.

**Positive, negative and zero correlation.**   Let us go over this matter in a little more detail. Suppose the same 20 individuals have taken two tests. We wish to know how closely their standings in one test correspond with their standings in the other. Is No. 1 in the first test No. 1 in the second also, is No. 2 in the first No. 2 in the second, and so on down the line till No. 20 in the first is No. 20 in the second? If so, there is perfect correspondence or agreement between the scores in the two tests, and we say, then, that there is a "perfect positive correlation" between the two sets of scores—or between the two tests.

Conceivably there might be perfect negative correlation between two abilities. There might be a law of compensation such that any individual who was poor in the first ability would certainly be good in the second one. If compensation between two tests were perfect, the individuals scoring highest in the one would score lowest in the other, and the order of individuals in one test would be just the reverse of their order in the other test.

Again, the two tests might show a zero correlation. The top man in one test might be found anywhere along the range in the other test, and so with the bottom man and with every other man. There would be no relation between the two abilities—no correspondence, no compensation, but pure chance like a shuffled deck of cards.

Actually, we never find perfect negative correlation, nor anything like it, between the scores in two tests. Compensation is conspicuous by its absence. We never find perfect positive correlation, either, though we sometimes get approximations to

Fig. 9.—Correlation of height and weight. Arrange the individuals first in order of height and then in order of weight, and see how much or little the positions change. The correlation of these particular individuals, by the rank-difference formula (p. 66), is +.60.

it. We often find zero or near-zero correlation. Most often, there is *more or less* correspondence, more or less of positive correlation.

We obviously need some *measure* of correlation which will tell us *how much* agreement there is between the scores on two tests. Perfect positive correlation is represented by the number +1, perfect negative correlation by −1, and mere chance relationship by 0. Then we can see that a correlation of +.8 means rather close correspondence, that a correlation of +.3 is low but positive, and that a correlation of −.3 is low and negative. Correlations of +.4 to +.7 can be called moderate.

We appeal to the mathematical statisticians for some method of computing the correlation, and we find that such methods have been developed for use not only in psychology but also in biology, economics and many other fields. Some of the methods have been devised by psychologists, for psychology has plenty of use for such statistical techniques.

**How to measure correlation.** There are several formulas, all based on the same general principle. For perfect positive correlation, each individual must have the same standing in both tests—the same, that is, in relation to the group as a whole. When the group is small, the simplest method is to rank the individuals in order from best to worst, in each test. Each individual then has two rank numbers, indicating his standing in the two tests. If every individual's two rank numbers are the same, the correlation is perfect; if they differ a good deal the correlation is low. Find the difference between an individual's two rank numbers and denote this difference by the letter *D*. Square *D*. Do the same for each individual. Find the sum of these squares and use the following formula:

$$\text{Rho} = 1 - \frac{6\,\text{Sum}\,D^2}{n(n^2 - 1)}$$

Here *n* is the number of individuals. "Rho" is a measure of correlation, known as the *rank-difference* measure. One can easily see that rho = 1 for perfect correlation, for then each and every

$D$ is zero. (It also works out mathematically that rho $= -1$ for perfect negative correlation, and that rho $= 0$ for a purely chance relationship between the two sets of scores.)

As an example of this method of computing correlation, take the scores of 10 individuals who have taken an addition test and a division test, and rank the scores in order, as is done below.

COMPUTATION OF RHO BY RANK-DIFFERENCES

| Individual | Addition | | Division | | $D$ | $D^2$ |
|---|---|---|---|---|---|---|
| | Raw Score | Rank Number | Raw Score | Rank Number | | |
| A | 18 | 1 | 9 | 2 | 1 | 1 |
| B | 14 | 2 | 11 | 1 | 1 | 1 |
| C | 12 | 3 | 8 | 3 | 0 | 0 |
| D | 11 | 4 | 4 | 8 | 4 | 16 |
| E | 10 | 5.5 | 5 | 6.5 | 1 | 1 |
| F | 10 | 5.5 | 7 | 4 | 1.5 | 2.25 |
| G | 8 | 7 | 3 | 9 | 2 | 4 |
| H | 7 | 8 | 6 | 5 | 3 | 9 |
| I | 6 | 9 | 5 | 6.5 | 2.5 | 6.25 |
| J | 4 | 10 | 2 | 10 | 0 | 0 |

$n = 10$

$n^2 - 1 = 99$

Sum $D^2 = 40.50$

6 Sum $D^2 = 243$

$$\text{Rho} = 1 - \frac{6 \text{ Sum } D^2}{n(n^2 - 1)}$$

$$= 1 - \frac{243}{10 \times 99}$$

$$= 1 - .25$$

$$= +.75$$

An important technical point comes out in the rank numbers for addition. Individuals $E$ and $F$ are tied for 5th place, and we might think the thing to do was to give them both a rank number of 5 and proceed to rank $G$ 6, $H$ 7 and so on. Then we should have no rank number 10 and our formula would be spoiled. It is fully as logical to say that $E$ and $F$ are tied for

6th place as well as for 5th and therefore to give both a rank of 5.5. In the same way, if three individuals were tied, say, for places 7, 8 and 9, we should rank all of them 8.

Computing correlations is a special technique for which excellent guides can be found in books on the application of statistical methods in psychology (*4, 6, 7, 11*). What we want here is not technical mastery of statistics but some understanding of the relation between different abilities.

**Some sample correlations.** Even though you have no occasion to compute correlations, you run across correlations of .50 or of .80 in general reading and need a realistic sense of the closeness of correspondence indicated by such numbers. Some idea of the concrete meaning of the correlations can be gained from the following table of values actually obtained. We see that stature and arm spread are correlated to the extent of +.82; here we should expect a close relation, and +.82 is pretty high correlation as things go, though it is by no means perfect. Stature and weight are less closely correlated ($r =$ +.59) as we might expect since a person may change his weight considerably without altering his height. Correlations higher than .85 are seldom obtained except from the use of almost identical tests. Zero values and small positive and negative values are the usual thing where the abilities are obviously quite different in kind, such as hand grip, adding, and color vision. A true, significant negative correlation between any two abilities is practically unknown. The general result is perfectly clear: abilities are positively rather than negatively interrelated, though the relationship is usually moderate rather than close.

### A FEW CORRELATIONS
#### (from various sources)
Anthropometric and strength tests

| | |
|---|---:|
| Stature and arm spread, men | .82 |
| Stature and weight, men | .59 |
| Stature and grip, men | .43 |
| Grip, right hand vs. left hand, men | .74 |

Grip and tapping, men .25
Grip and 100-yard dash, women .16
Scholastic tests
Word meaning and paragraph meaning .80
Arithmetic: computation and reasoning .70
Punctuation and spelling .60
Vocabulary and spelling .50
Reading and general information .40
High school grades
Algebra and geometry .65
English and French .50
English and art .15
College grades (West Point)
Two English courses .77
English and history .68
English and physics .48
English and mathematics .49
English and drawing .25
Mathematics and physics .78
Mathematics and history .44
Mathematics and drawing .48

## GENERAL ABILITY OR SPECIAL ABILITIES?

Alongside of the experimental and developmental methods of investigation, described in the first chapter, the correlational method deserves a place. It is much used today in the hope of discovering the relations between different abilities. From the correlation of +.70 between computation and arithmetical reasoning we see that the two abilities have much in common and yet are by no means the same ability, since this correlation is some distance from 1.00. From the low correlation of +.25 between English and drawing we infer that these two abilities have a little in common but only a little. In general, correlation indicates how far two abilities are the same and how far they are different.

Correlations afford a line of attack on the question mentioned at the beginning of the chapter, whether ability is generalized or specialized. Is there such a thing as *general ability?*

Let a group of individuals be put through many varied tests of their abilities. If certain individuals always stood at the top, certain others always at the bottom, and others always in the same intermediate position, with no one shifting around very much, these results would indicate the existence of just one general ability. Some individuals would simply be more able than others. But we never get that result. The correlations are never close to +1.00, except where two tests are obviously tests of the same ability, like two tests in adding, or two tests in giving opposites. When the tests call for different kinds of work, adding and multiplying, defining words and giving their opposites, memory for numbers or for the sense of a paragraph, the correlations run from 0 up to about +.70 and average about +.30. Such are the basic facts to be considered in analyzing human intellectual ability.

**Two outmoded theories.**   These facts are sufficient to disprove two theories of ability that have been suggested in the past. One theory was that every task calls for a separate specific ability, and that individuals differ in any task simply because they possess this specific ability in different degrees. If abilities were as separate as all that, any two tests should give a zero correlation instead of the positive correlation usually found. The other extreme theory held that all ability was a unit, some individuals simply having more, others less, of this general, all-round ability. In that case the correlation between any two tests should be up near +1.00, which is not at all what we find. The facts compel us to seek for some intermediate theory.

**General ability plus many very specific abilities.**   One possibility is to assume both a general ability and a lot of specific abilities. The positive correlations would then be due wholly to the general ability, since the specific ability is assumed to be different for each different task. The individual's performance in any test would depend on two factors, the amount of general ability he possesses and his specific ability to deal with certain materials in a certain way (for example, to deal with numbers by adding them). Some tests, we may assume, depend more on general ability, others more on specific abilities. Two tests which depend mostly on general ability will show a high correlation, while two tests depending mostly on different specific abilities can have only a low correlation. This theory calls for a graded series of correlations such as we actually obtain. But there is one serious difficulty, now to be presented.

**Group factors—abilities of intermediate scope.** The just-noticed theory assumed only very narrow specific abilities in addition to one general, all-round ability. The correlations obtained between various tests, however, reveal the existence of abilities that are not broad enough in scope to be called general ability and yet are not narrowly limited to very specific tasks. Clusters of tests are found, the correlations being high between the tests in a cluster, but much lower between tests in one and in another cluster.

For example, tests of college students for speed of addition, subtraction, multiplication and division were found to correlate around +.60 with each other; and tests of opposites, synonyms, reading and vocabulary correlated with each other about +.55; but the correlation between any of these verbal tests with any of the arithmetic tests was only about +.20 (19). In another study the subjects were boys ten years old, and the correlations were higher, as is usually the case with young subjects. In a group of verbal tests the correlations were about +.63, and in a group of spatial perception tests about +.66, while between verbal and spatial they were about +.43 (2). We see evidence here of three rather broad abilities which have come out of other studies as well and which have been called verbal, numerical and spatial abilities. Other data indicate the existence of additional group factors such as word fluency, perceptual ability, and reasoning. In areas outside of the strictly intellectual tasks research has pointed to an artistic ability, a mechanical ability and a musical ability, and there are probably still others which are too broad to be called specific and yet not broad enough to be identified with general ability.

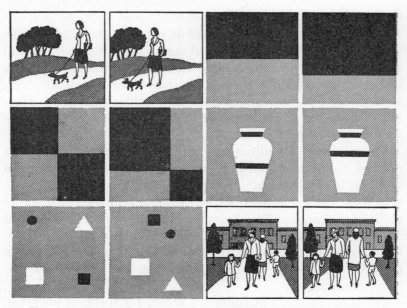

Fig. 10.—A test of esthetic judgment. Which drawing in each
pair is the more artistic?

Let us examine verbal, numerical and spatial abilities more
closely.

*Verbal ability* is not very well named. At least it is not exactly
what one might suppose. The tests for this ability are not such
as would be used in a speech clinic or in a school or college
course in "better speech." They are not tests for clear pronuncia-
tion, grammatical correctness, fluency in conversation, or speed
of reading. The ability tested is not simply "verbal." Rather, it
is the ability to deal with ideas by use of words. Since words
stand for things, events, qualities and relations, a vocabulary
test is not merely a test of word knowledge but is rather an
index of the subject's knowledge of things, etc. An opposites
test calls for getting the exact meaning of words. A sentence
completion test calls for putting in words to complete the meaning of the sentence. These are typical verbal tests.

Verbal ability is broad in scope because language is a tool for
conveying many kinds of meaning. But not every kind is readily

conveyed in words. Imagine geography with no maps, or mathematics with no diagrams and other symbols! Verbal tests cannot do justice to all varieties of human ability.

*Numerical ability* includes knowledge of numbers and their relations, and facility in the fundamental arithmetical operations. Problems in arithmetic often call also for arithmetical reasoning which seems to be a different ability. Numerical ability itself is rather narrow in scope, though very important for some purposes. Tests for this ability include straight adding, multiplying, etc., and also tests in number relations such as the "number series completion test" illustrated below:

Fill in the blank spaces so as to make the numbers in each horizontal line follow a given rule, the rule being different for each line.

| | | | | | | |
|---|---|---|---|---|---|---|
| 2 | 4 | 6 | 8 | 10 | 12 | 14 |
| 10 | 9 | 8 | 7 | 6 | 5 | 4 |
| 1 | 2 | 4 | 8 | 16 | 32 | 64 |
| 3 | 5 | 10 | 12 | 24 | 26 | 52 |
| 100 | 90 | 81 | 73 | 66 | 60 | 55 |
| 1 | 4 | 9 | 16 | 25 | 36 | 49 |

*Spatial ability* is the ability to grasp and use spatial facts and relations. It probably includes such outdoor skills as finding one's way, keeping one's bearings and remembering locations. It is often tested by use of drawings representing shapes and sizes and three-dimensional objects (Fig. 11). Such questions as the following would depend on spatial ability (and on verbal ability, too, because the problems are set in words).

At what time between half-past-five and half-past-six are the hour and minute hands exactly opposite?

If I go southeast one mile and then southwest one mile, in what direction am I from my starting point?

What point on a rolling hoop is moving forward most rapidly at any moment?

**Is there a general ability, too?** The facts of correlation of abilities therefore make it necessary to recognize very specific abilities and somewhat broader abilities. Whether it is necessary also to assume the existence of general ability is not cer-

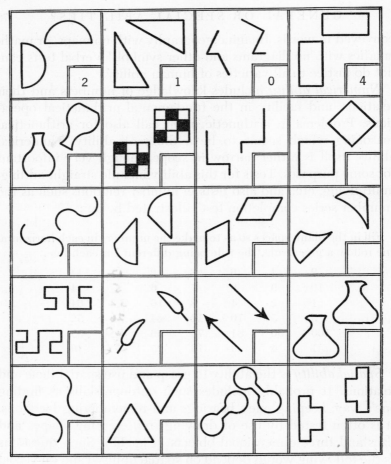

FIG. 11.—Matching forms. Directions:

Imagine the upper figure in each box to be a flat block, and the lower figure a hole into which the block is to be fitted. In how many ways will it fit? Write the answer in the small square.

The semicircle in the first box can be slid around flat and inserted. Then it can be picked up and turned over (like a penny, heads up to tails up) and inserted again. The answer is 2.

The triangle cannot be fitted by sliding but must be turned over. Answer: 1.

The jagged line in the third box will not fit in any position.

The rectangle can be fitted in two positions (end for end) without turning over, and then turned over and fitted twice more.

With a time limit of 5 minutes, the average score of correct items was about 9, for college students.

74

tain. The experts in this line of work have developed very elaborate mathematical methods for treating their data, but are not yet in agreement on this important question (*17*). The notion of general ability is rather attractive. It might amount (a) to *quick learning and good retention* of what has been learned. For suppose that one person is superior in learning and retention: he will accumulate a large stock of knowledge and skill ready for use in tackling any new problem he encounters, and the new learning required by the new problem will also be easy for him. One who learns and retains little is not much helped by his past experience and will make the same mistakes repeatedly. General ability, if there is such a thing, might also consist (b) in quick and accurate *grasping of relationships*, for the intellectual mastery of a problem depends on seeing the essential relations involved. These two views of general ability, put forward respectively by Thorndike (*18*) and Spearman (*13*), may amount to the same thing; for the intellectually useful facts that we learn consist largely of relationships.

The correlation between the special or group abilities is quite high in young children. This is strong evidence for a general ability—perhaps a general capacity. The correlations decrease in older children. For example, the correlation between verbal ability and number ability in third-grade children was found to be .83; in adults it was .26 (*9*). Similar results have been found with other tests and different age groups (*5*), indicating a progressive specialization and differentiation of abilities with age.

The differences in achievement of adults are not due wholly to their different capacities; in part they are due to differences in training and effort. One person specializes in one line, another in another, and thus achievement becomes specialized. Achievement is doubtless more specialized than capacity.

## PREDICTION OF VOCATIONAL SUCCESS

Up to this point in the chapter we have been interested in the relation of abilities to each other. But tests are chiefly used for the practical purpose of predicting how well individuals will succeed in a particular line of work. When tests are used in this way they are termed *aptitude tests*. They are measures of present achievement, to be sure, but they are also predictors of future achievement to be reached after further training or experience.

**Requirements of an aptitude test.** For a test to have any value it must be carefully constructed and standardized. It must, moreover, be tried out in advance to find out how useful it is in predicting success in a given field. Great care must be taken to make the tests as dependable as possible. A dependable test has two characteristics which psychologists call reliability and validity.

*Reliability* is present when a test gives a consistent measure of each individual's standing in the test itself. To find out how reliable a test is, you give it to a large group of persons at two different times. If each person gets just about the same score both times, the test is reliable, but if the scores shift around a good deal from one time to the other, the test is unreliable because it does not enable you to tell who stands better and who stands worse in the ability you are trying to measure. The correlation between test and retest is called self-correlation. Self-correlation should be as high as .90 for a very reliable test, though many usable tests do not quite come up to this standard.

*Validity.* A reliable test will give you a good measure of the ability you are directly testing, but if this ability is not closely related to the performance you wish to predict, your test will not be valid as a basis for prediction. The dynamometer test for strength of grip is very reliable but it is of little use in predicting how rapidly a person can run 100 yards, as can be seen from the low correlation of .16 between these two abilities (p. 69).

Validity is present when a test furnishes a good indication of the performance you wish to predict. If you can tell from the test scores just about how well different individuals will succeed in a given line of work, your test is a valid one for this purpose. Let a psychologist prepare a test (or battery of tests) for predicting success and failure in a certain occupation, let him give his test to a large number of persons who are entering this occupation, and then follow them up and see how well each person succeeds. If the test is valid, his predictions based on the test scores will check with the actual success or failure in the occupation. Success in the occupation is a *criterion* against which the test must check, and the test must show a good correlation with the criterion in order to have validity. Since the correlation between two abilities is never as high as the self-correlation of a good test, validity will not be as high as reliability. A validity correlation of .75 permits reasonably good prediction of individual performance, and tests of lower validity are useful for certain practical problems involving the average performance of large groups of persons, rather than a single individual.

**Prediction of school success.** A practical question with regard to intelligence tests is whether the individual differences they reveal count for very much in the daily activities of the child or adult. If they do, good use can be made of these tests in educational and vocational guidance. A boy can be encouraged to go to college if his IQ is high enough to make success reasonably sure, provided of course he will do the work. Or a boy may be advised not to attempt college because his IQ is not high enough. The counselor must use good judgment, not depending on the results of an intelligence test alone, but taking into account other factors such as character, personality, environmental conditions and vocational opportunities.

On the whole, there is very good correlation between the child's IQ and his school success. The correlation is especially close when each child, no matter how bright, is afforded an opportunity to advance at his own rate. As the higher grades of the elementary school are reached, the children of low IQ lag behind. Probably an IQ of 90 is needed to master the regular work of the eighth grade, an IQ of 100 to finish the junior high school and an IQ of 110 to do satisfactory work in the senior high school, though these numbers are only rough indications. Many colleges try to limit their freshmen to individuals of superior ability, succeeding to such an extent that intelligence tests of freshmen show them to represent a high selection from the general population.

<u>But the correspondence between intelligence test scores and academic achievement is less close in the secondary school than in the elementary school, and still less close in college</u>. The correlation between IQ and school marks goes down from about .75 in the lower grades to .60–.65 in the secondary school, and to .50, more or less, in college (3). The reason is in part that the college group is highly selected; those of low IQ who would certainly fail in college have been weeded out, and the achievement of those who are admitted depends largely on their interest. Some students of high intelligence prefer to concentrate on something else than the college courses, while some students simply take it easy. Motivation as well as ability has to be considered.

*An example of the prediction of college grades from intelligence test scores.* A sample of 100 students admitted to college, varying considerably in their intelligence test scores, was followed up to see how well their course marks could have been predicted from the test. The results are shown in the correlation chart, or "scatter diagram," given in Fig. 12. Each dot represents one of the 100 students. The farther to the right his dot is located, the better he did in the intelligence test; the farther up, the better his average college grade. The chart as a whole shows some tendency for the dots that are farther to the right to be farther up also, indicating some degree of positive correlation. But the correlation is far from high, because the scatter is so wide. How much could we predict from the test scores? Let us see whether they have any validity as indicators of the college marks.

The scatter diagram gives an all-over view of the relationship between two measures—here the test scores and the college marks—but it requires analysis before the correlation can be estimated in any useful way. One method of analysis starts with contrasting groups. Divide the group of 100 into quarters on the basis of the test scores, and compare the college marks

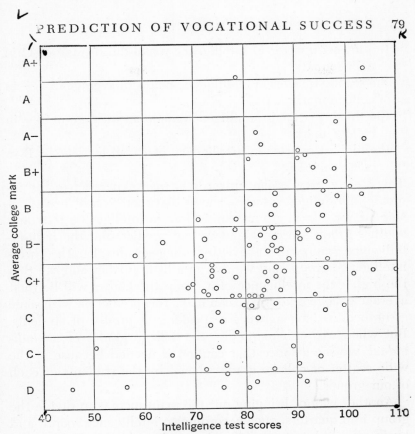

Fig. 12.—A scatter diagram showing the correlation between intelligence test scores and college grades of 100 students. If the correlation were +1.00, all the dots would lie in a diagonal line extending from the left-hand lower to the right-hand upper corner. If the correlation were zero, the dots would show no trend. As it is, with a correlation of +.40, the dots do show a diagonal trend in spite of much scattering. (These intelligence test scores are not IQs.) (Data from Sommerville, 12.)

of the lowest and highest of these quarters. You will find that the lowest quarter in intelligence averaged C in college grades, while the highest quarter in intelligence obtained an average of B. In a broad way, then, those who stood well in the intelligence test also stood well in college grades.

The two intervening quarters may also be taken into consideration. When that is done we find that:

the lowest quarter in intelligence made an average of C in
   college marks
the second quarter in intelligence made an average of C+ in
   college marks
the third quarter in intelligence made an average of B— in
   college marks
the highest quarter in intelligence made an average of B in
   college marks.

This steady progression upwards in marks, parallel to the increase in intelligence scores, shows that there is a real relationship. If we take a group scoring low in intelligence tests and
another group scoring high, we can predict that the high-in-
telligence group will make better college grades than the lower-
intelligence group, and we can go a little further and say that
the higher the intelligence of a group the higher will be their
average college grades. We can make this prediction with some
assurance, so long as we are speaking of *groups* of students.
But when we wish to predict the college grades of an *individual,* we see at once that caution is needed because of the
wide scatter of college grades shown by the students of each
of our groups.

Another way of bringing out the main facts is to divide the
group into quarters, once according to intelligence scores, and
again according to college grades, and see how well the quarters correspond. We obtain the table on page 81 which shows
for the 25 students making the low intelligence scores that 1
made the highest quarter in college grades, and 6 the next-
highest quarter, while 7 and 11 fell in the two lower quarters.
In the same way each of the quarters shows considerable scatter; but about half of all the students are in the same quarter
in both measures.

All the information contained in the diagram and table can
be condensed into a single number, which is the measure of
correlation between the intelligence test scores and the college
grades. Computed by the rank-difference method or by other
methods the correlation is about +.40. Other groups of college
students have given somewhat higher correlations, about +.50

or .55. That is by no means a high correlation, though high enough to prove that intelligence is a real factor in determining a student's mark in college. At the same time it is low enough to prove that other factors are operating. Thus the two students in the scatter diagram who made the highest scores in intelligence and still got only C+ in college would certainly have done better except for interfering factors such as lack of time or interest, or perhaps poor health. Intelligence is only one of several factors which influence college achievement.

STUDENT GROUP DIVIDED INTO QUARTERS, HORIZONTALLY BY IN-
TELLIGENCE TEST SCORES, VERTICALLY BY COLLEGE GRADES

| College Grades | | | | |
|---|---|---|---|---|
| High | 1 | 6 | 5 | 13 |
| | 6 | 3 | 11 | 5 |
| | 7 | 10 | 5 | 3 |
| Low | 11 | 6 | 4 | 4 |
| | Low | | | High |

Intelligence Test

**Prediction of success in pilot training.** At the beginning of the last war it was necessary to undertake the rapid training of hundreds of thousands of young men for flying duty. Of those who entered training, approximately one-third failed to complete the course and earn their wings. Since planes and instructors were limited in number, it was desirable to select the students who would have the greatest likelihood of surviving the training. Psychologists were therefore directed to devise aptitude tests to be given to all applicants.

A variety of tests were tried out in the Army Air Force and the test scores were correlated with success and failure in pilot training. No single test was found to have a high enough validity to warrant its use alone. Intelligence tests, for example, had only a low correlation with success, perhaps because the applicants were mostly college students who all had sufficient intelligence for pilot training. Abilities other than intelligence were apparently responsible for the different degrees of success. Accordingly, 18 tests of various sorts were combined to form a *battery* for prediction. The validity of any single test was not high, but when the scores of all the tests were combined, the validity was adequate. Twelve tests of the paper-and-pencil variety gave a combined validity of .51 and the same was true for six apparatus tests of motor coordination (see Fig. 13). Combined, the 18 tests had a validity of .60. Figure 14 shows how well this battery was able to predict success in pilot training (14).

**Selection of employees.** Many business and industrial organizations make use of aptitude tests in the selection of employees most likely to be satisfactory. Their selection procedures, just as those in the Air Force, will be valuable to the degree that the tests are reliable and valid predictors of the job requirements. One kind of work is quite different from another kind of work and an aptitude test that gives good prediction in one company may be useless in another (1, 20).

The first step in setting up a program of aptitude testing is an analysis of each job to find out its requirements and to discover the actual differences between good and poor workers on the job. On the basis of this analysis a variety of different tests are selected or constructed. This step involves judgment and a certain amount of guessing. Then the battery is administered to a group of successful workers and to a group of less success-

FIG. 13.—Complex coordination test employed by Army Air Force.

The candidate sits in front of three double rows of lights in each of which one red light is illuminated. By manipulating a stick with his hand and a rudder with his feet, he causes the position of a green light in each of the three rows to match the red light. When all three pairs are simultaneously matched, a new pattern of three red lights automatically appears. The candidate's performance is measured by the number of settings he completes in a certain period of time. Photograph courtesy of A. W. Melton (15).

This test was developed in 1934 by Colonel Neely C. Mashburn at the AAF School of Aviation Medicine, and was found to have the highest validity of any single test in predicting pilot success during World War II. Other tests of visual-motor coordination which were included in the total battery were a two-hand coordination test requiring the use of both hands simultaneously in manipulating two lathe-type handles, a test of discrimination reaction time, a finger dexterity test in which the candidate lifts small pegs, turns them over and returns them to their holes, and a multidimensional pursuit test requiring attention to three instrument meters.

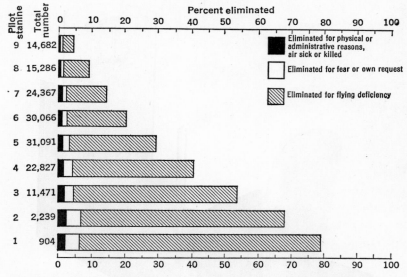

FIG. 14.—Prediction of failures in pilot training with a battery of aptitude tests. This figure is based on results from 153,000 cases in 15 consecutive pilot classes. Each bar shows the percentage of students with a particular aptitude score who failed to complete the training. Adapted from (14).

ful workers. Only those tests which show different scores for the two groups are kept.

Now the battery of aptitude tests is ready for tryout on new applicants, and the subsequent work record of each person is carefully followed. Production rates, supervisor's ratings, absenteeism and other measures are recorded to form a criterion of each worker's success. The validity of the battery is measured by correlation with the criterion. Further improvement is usually possible by continued checking of the tests.

Vocational guidance.   Some of the same techniques and procedures used in selecting employees are useful in vocational guidance. The two tasks are much alike, but differ in emphasis. In selecting employees, the emphasis is on finding the best man available for the job; in vocational guidance the emphasis is on finding the best job available for the man (10, 16, 21).

The problem of choosing the most suitable line of training and work is of paramount importance to all students. And it is far from being a simple, easy problem. The U. S. census lists about 25,000 different occupations, and many of these, like the learned professions, include a large variety of particular occupations. The student does not have at hand the necessary information to make a wise choice. Probably the logical first step would be to go to a vocational counselor and have an appraisal of his ability and special aptitudes. These facts might quickly rule out a large number of occupations, some as demanding too much ability, some as demanding too little. Evaluation of his personality characteristics, his values, and his pattern of interests (see next chapter) would help to narrow further the range of possibilities. But there would still remain a large number of alternatives. The vocational counselor seldom takes the responsibility of making a definite final recommendation. The individual must eventually choose for himself.

## SUMMARY

1. Some individuals possess strikingly greater ability of one sort than of other sorts.

   a. *Idiots savants* are rare feebleminded persons who show remarkably high ability in one special line.

   b. *Arithmetical prodigies* are normal in general ability but outstanding in rapid mental calculation.

   c. *Reading disability* occurs frequently in children whose IQ is normal or above.

2. Correlation is a measure of the degree of correspondence between the standings on two tests of a group of individuals. Perfect correspondence is represented by a correlation of +1.00; perfect but reversed correspondence by —1.00; and chance relationship by 0.

3. The degree of correlation between two tests indicates the degree of identity or overlap in the abilities measured.

   a. The fact that most correlations are low indicates that there must be many *specific abilities*.

   b. The fact that most correlations are positive indicates that there must be a *general ability* which enters into each test performance to some degree.

c. The fact that a group of tests will correlate high with each other but low with any other test indicates that there must be *group factors*—abilities of intermediate scope. Examples include:

   (1) *Verbal ability,* the ability to deal with ideas and meanings by use of words.

   (2) *Number ability,* the ability to calculate and to deal with numerical relations.

   (3) *Spatial ability,* the ability to grasp and use spatial facts and relations.

d. Correlations between special abilities are greater in children than in adults. This increasing differentiation of ability may be the result of differences in training and acquired interests.

4. Prediction of vocational success can be based in part on the use of *aptitude tests* which are measures of present ability designed to predict future achievement with training.

a. Dependable aptitude tests must be well constructed and standardized. Their usefulness depends on their

   (1) *Reliability*—consistency of measurement, as determined by correlation between test and retest; and

   (2) *Validity*—correlation of test with the criterion (the measure of eventual success or failure).

b. Prediction of school success on the basis of intelligence test scores is better in the lower grades than in college, with correlations ranging from .50 to .75.

c. Prediction of success in pilot training has utilized a battery of 18 different tests, the validity of which is much higher than of any single test.

d. Aptitude tests for the selection of employees must be tried out and validated in each job situation where prediction is desired.

e. Vocational guidance makes use of aptitude tests to narrow the range of possible vocational choices from which the individual makes his selection.

# CHAPTER FOUR

# *Personality*

Still keeping to our general theme of individual differences, we turn now from differences in ability to those less measurable but often very striking characteristics of the individual which fall under the head of character and personality. *Character* refers mostly to conduct that can be called right or wrong, that meets or fails to meet the accepted social standards. *Personality* refers to behavior which, though not necessarily right or wrong, is pleasing or offensive to other people, favorable or unfavorable to the individual's standing with his fellows. The distinction is not always sharp and for our purposes may be disregarded.

If your friend, in applying for a position, has named you as one of his references, you will be asked by the appointing officer to tell what you know of the candidate's ability and experience, and also what you know of his personality. In replying you state, so far as you conscientiously can, that the candidate has a pleasing yet forceful personality, that he is energetic and persistent but cheerful and even-tempered, self-reliant without being selfish, and that he cooperates well with other members of a group. There are literally thousands of adjectives that can be used to characterize a personality, and certainly these qualities are of immense importance in work, in the home and in all forms of social life.

A moment's thought shows that these adjectives are properly adverbs. They tell how the individual behaves. One person behaves in a pleasing way, another in an irritating way; one acts energetically, another languidly. Personality words are not names of different activities, but names of qualities of behavior. Any little act may "reveal the personality" by showing the individual's characteristic style of action. Personality can be broadly defined as the *total quality of an individual's behavior*, as it is revealed in his habits of thought and expression, his attitudes and interests, his manner of acting, and his personal philosophy of life.

Personality is potentially the most interesting part of psychology. If a psychologist is asked to "Tell us something about your subject" he will probably ask his audience to be more specific. "What topic would you like to have me discuss?" "Oh, tell us about personality," is usually the answer. "Well, what would you like to hear about personality—in case I know it myself?" The two most likely questions are: (1) how to judge personality, and (2) how to develop and improve personality. "Tell us how to size up a new acquaintance, so as to know whether he is going to wear well. And tell us how to develop personality ourselves." This second question broadens out when one is responsible for other people. A parent, teacher, priest, psychiatrist or psychological counselor wants to know how to improve the personality of other people.

When addressing students, the psychologist is not going to hand out a set of mechanical rules for judging or improving personality. His job with students is to lead them to some basic knowledge. Just as the electrical engineer bases his practical control on scientific knowledge of electricity, so the psychological engineer must proceed from a knowledge of cause and effect.

The present chapter gives a scientific approach to the problem of judging personality, and the following chapter looks into the question of causes or sources which must be known by anyone who seeks to improve personality.

## DESCRIBING PERSONALITY

It is not easy by any means to give an adequate picture, description or characterization of an individual's personality. It is not easy to obtain an intelligible description from those who know him. You may be interested to learn about a certain person so as to judge whether he will make a good friend or a desirable addition to your group. Someone who knows him tells you, "Well, he's this sort of a man," and goes on to relate an incident or example of the individual's behavior, leaving you to draw your own conclusions. Instead of dramatizing in this way, your informant may be more analytical and apply a number of descriptive adjectives to the person. Either the dramatic picture or the analytical description is likely to leave you with a false or inadequate impression of the unknown man. An adjective by itself is abstract and you may go wrong in giving it concrete meaning. An incident shows how the person behaved in a concrete situation, but you wish to know how he would behave in other situations.

Personality traits.    In the scientific description of personality, the psychologist tries to identify the most significant traits which the individual displays. A personality trait is some particular quality of behavior such as cheerfulness or self-reliance, which characterizes the individual in a wide range of his activities and is fairly consistent over a period of time. The total personality would be the sum of these traits, except that it is more than a mere sum of separate qualities. It has some unity. For example, a certain person is not merely cheerful and self-reliant; he is cheerfully self-reliant. Another person is peevishly dependent, and still another may be cheerfully dependent. Each individual has his own style or quality which is only roughly characterized by naming his traits (1, 24).[1]

[1] See References, p. 639.

Many traits are recognizable only in social or interpersonal situations. Perhaps you are told that the person in question is very congenial. That is something worth knowing, but it is not enough. Because A and B are congenial it does not necessarily follow that A and C will be so. Congeniality is a relation between two (or more) people and depends on the *interaction of personalities.* If we make a study of happy and unhappy marriages, hoping to discover what personality traits make for the one or the other, we find all kinds of people happily married and all kinds unhappily. We find some very amiable people unhappy and some unamiable ones perfectly contented. The aggressive and the yielding, the touchy and the thick-skinned, the stable and the unstable, all may be either happy or unhappy in wedded life. It depends on the interplay of personalities and to some extent on external circumstances (35).

From such facts as these some students of the subject draw the conclusion that personality is not an individual matter. They say it is a relation between individuals. They deny that the individual has any personality apart from his associates, and ridicule any attempt to describe an individual's separate personality. Such a conclusion, however, goes far beyond the facts and is quite inconsistent with certain facts. Though all kinds of people are happily married, it does not follow that you could mate two individuals at random and assure them of wedded bliss. Individuals differ, and therefore pairs of individuals differ. If the individuals were all alike and neutral in respect to personality, then pairs of individuals also would be all alike, which is obviously contrary to the facts.

Nor should we accept the assertion that personality reveals itself only in social life. An irritable man quarrels with his tools, a persistent man sticks to a lonely task. A man may "let himself go" when alone more than in company. He may like to give vent to a buoyant *joie de vivre* by singing at the top of his lungs, but does so only when safely out of hearing.

But what can we mean by saying that person now dozing in an easy chair is a vivacious person, or irritable, or persistent, or that he "possesses" any other trait? We mean about the same as when we say that he possesses a certain ability, unused at the moment. Our evidence in both cases is that we have "seen him do it." We assume with good reason that he still retains, carries around with him, the ability or the trait that he has demonstrated in active behavior. Personality is a relatively permanent characteristic of the individual.

**Distribution of personality traits.** Of the enormous number of trait names in common use, many come in pairs of opposites, as cheerful—gloomy, masterful—submissive, kind—cruel. Because opposites are so convenient we easily slip into the error of classifying people as either cheerful or gloomy, as if these were two sharply separated classes. The distribution curve (p. 30) stands as a warning. People do not fall into contrasting types. They scatter all the way from one extreme to the other, with the greatest number falling in the middle of the range. So we find whenever we are able to measure people in any respect. It may not be possible to measure cheerfulness but certainly people are more or less cheerful rather than either cheerful or gloomy. The best way to utilize the everyday vocabulary of trait names is to place a pair of opposites at the ends of a line and regard this line as a dimension of personality, with individuals located at different parts of the line.

These dimensions, or traits, are analogous to the verbal, numerical and spatial abilities which are dimensions of ability. The question is whether any outstanding dimensions can be identified in the field of personality. By using pairs of opposites we could find names for hundreds of possible dimensions, but they would not be wholly different. The many traits overlap and can be reduced to a smaller number. The correlation method provides a check. Arrange a good sample of the population along the cheerful-gloomy dimension, and arrange the same individuals along the kind-cruel dimension. If the order of individuals is nearly the same in the two arrangements, i.e., if the correlation between the two arrangements is high, the two dimensions are largely the same. If the correlation is zero they are separate and independent dimensions, like latitude and longitude in geography. Several systematic studies of the interrelation of traits have recently been carried out, and the table below presents a list of the most clearly established *primary traits* (6). The method of correlation, applied to the results of rating, questionnaire, and test researches, enables us to systematize the multitude of personality traits into a smaller number of primary traits. A primary trait includes several specific traits which are correlated with each other and therefore have much in common. The twelve primary traits are relatively independent, having very low correlations with each other.

| Primary traits | Opposites |
|---|---|
| 1. Easygoing, genial, warm, generous | Inflexible, cold, timid, hostile, shy. |
| 2. Intelligent, independent, reliable | Foolish, unreflective, frivolous |
| 3. Emotionally stable, realistic, steadfast | Neurotic, evasive, emotionally changeable |
| 4. Dominant, ascendant, self-assertive | Submissive, self-effacing |
| 5. Placid, cheerful, sociable, talkative | Sorrowful, depressed, seclusive, agitated |
| 6. Sensitive, tenderhearted, sympathetic | Hard-boiled, poised, frank, unemotional |
| 7. Trained and cultured mind, esthetic | Boorish, uncultured |
| 8. Conscientious, responsible, painstaking | Emotionally dependent, impulsive, irresponsible |
| 9. Adventurous, carefree, kind | Inhibited, reserved, cautious, withdrawn |
| 10. Vigorous, energetic, persistent, quick | Languid, slack, daydreaming |
| 11. Emotionally hypersensitive, high-strung, excitable | Phlegmatic, tolerant |
| 12. Friendly, trustful | Suspicious, hostile |

**The introversion-extroversion cluster of traits.** Some writers have proposed more comprehensive personality traits than any of the twelve listed on page 92. For many years no traits attracted so much attention as this pair originally proposed by Jung (17). Extroversion, according to Jung's definition, consists primarily in interest directed toward the external world (including the world of people) and in finding the values of life in the external world; while introversion consists in finding interest and value primarily in one's own thoughts, feelings and ideals. The two interests are present in every normal person, and everyone shifts from one to the other. But some individuals, it may be, are *usually* interested in the immediate environment and deserve the name of extroverts, whereas individuals of the opposite tendency may be called introverts.

How would these tendencies manifest themselves? Jung and others worked out many ways in which introverts and extroverts could be distinguished. The extrovert would live in the present and value his possessions and social success, while the introvert would dream or plan for the future and value his own standards and sentiments. The extrovert would be interested in the visible, tangible world, while the introvert was interested in the underlying, invisible forces and laws of nature. The extrovert would be practical, the introvert intuitive and imaginative. The extrovert would like action and would make decisions quickly and easily, while the introvert would prefer thought and planning and hesitate in reaching a final decision.

So far, the differences could be classed under *intellectual* introversion-extroversion. But questions like the following deal specifically with social life:

Do you like to talk before a group of people?
Do you always try to make others agree with you?
Do you make friends easily?
Are you at home among strangers?
Do you like to take the lead in a social gathering?
Do you worry over what people think of you?
Are you somewhat suspicious of other people's motives?
Do you suffer from a feeling of inferiority?
Are you easily embarrassed?
Are your feelings easily hurt?

The "Yes" answer to the first five of these questions is supposed to be characteristic of the extrovert; to the last five, of the introvert. These questions refer to what might be called *social* introversion-extroversion.

The last five of these questions are also concerned with emotional stability and integration (*12*). Introversion combines and confuses three dimensions: liking for thought as against action, liking for solitude as against society, and proneness to find trouble in life. Introversion-extroversion is thus a very broad and comprehensive way of describing personality, and includes many characteristics which later research (p. 92) have shown to be separate and independent traits.

However much we may like the extroversion-introversion distinction, we should not allow ourselves to fall into the habit of classifying everybody as either an extrovert or an introvert. Whenever any large sample of people has been examined by use of appropriate methods, they have been found to fall mostly along in the middle between the two extremes. A "mixed type," the ambivert, has been recognized and most individuals belong to this mixed type (*15*). In any dimension of personality, the peak of the distribution lies near the middle between the extremes (p. 29).

One obstacle in the way of any penetrating analysis of personality is our inveterate tendency to tell how we like a person instead of seeking to discover what it is about him that we like or dislike. We say he is pleasing, interesting, useful or in some similar terms state his *value to us.* Often we give our impression of his moral value, by calling him good or bad. None of these value judgments really describe the individual. We need to ask *in what way* he is pleasing, interesting, good or bad. We need to lay our own feelings aside and see him as objectively as possible. Even if he is offensive to everyone else and not merely to ourselves, so that he must be "really" offensive, calling him offensive does not get us far toward a description of his personal characteristics nor help us much if we undertake to improve his personality. As soon as we try to be more specific we find ourselves forced away from valuation toward a study of cause and effect. Offensiveness is only an effect; we must discover the characteristics of the individual that make him offensive.

## JUDGING PERSONALITY

To the student who desires to develop his power of judging character and personality the psychologist can offer no easy short-cut system of rules and signs. He has no faith at all in astrology, for it seems to him that the distant stars can have about as much influence on your behavior and fortunes as your actions have on the star. Coming down to earth, you may find the psychologist not quite so skeptical regarding the anatomical signs stressed by some self-styled character analysts, like the shape of the chin or size of the nose; for the bodily structure and the behavior of the individual both belong to the same organism. But the psychologist would expect only very low correlations between anatomical and behavioral traits, and the correlations he finds are actually too low for any practical use (26). From a person's forehead, nose or chin you can learn practically nothing regarding his character. When the character analyst is successful, it is by observing the subject's behavior and not his mere anatomy (16). You can learn something from the subject's facial *expression,* or from his speaking voice, or from a two-minute silent film of the subject in action (9). You can learn something from his written themes or essays, and the expert can even make some fair deductions from his handwriting. Some people reveal their personal traits more freely than others, some traits are more open than others to inspection, and of two judges, both afforded the same opportunities for observing an individual, one will obtain a much truer and fuller impression than the other.

To be a good judge of character, you obviously need experience. You must know the particular person to be judged and other persons to compare him with, and you need experience in checking first impressions against later acquaintance, and in viewing people objectively, not as friends or enemies.

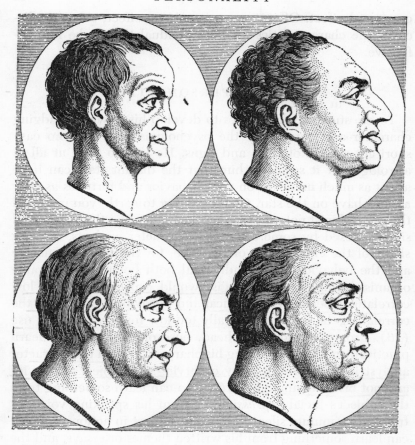

Fig. 15.—Physiognomy. Many such faces were studied by Lavater (1741–1801) and by others from time to time, in the hope of finding connections between the facial anatomy and character and personality. The first face in this selection was supposed to indicate a lack of vigor, the second some crudity and love of ease, the third very fine qualities, and the fourth sensuality. Such correlations have never stood up when subjected to statistical tests.

but as persons in their own right, with their own problems and their own resources and handicaps.]

**Interviewing.** [It has been said that to know a personality you must live with the individual for three months, preferably seeing him in a variety of situations.] A vocational or psychological adviser has to get along with somewhat less than this. An hour's interview must often suffice. A good interviewer quickly establishes *rapport,* by winning the subject's confidence, putting him at his ease as far as possible, overcoming the subject's tendency to be on the defensive or to assume a pose, and in short securing the subject's cooperation in the effort to understand his problems, assets and liabilities. The good interviewer has a genuine interest in people and still maintains the objective attitude. Since he interviews many individuals, his real task is that of comparing one with another. He must place them to some extent in the same situation, following a standardized plan, and at the same time he must be flexible and responsive to the person interviewed. From the information given by the subject and from his behavior, the interviewer is able to form some judgment regarding his personal characteristics. The good interviewer avoids premature judgment. Knowing that first impressions are often misleading he maintains the attitude of suspended judgment till the subject has a good chance to reveal himself. Even the best interviewer makes some mistakes, if only because the same visible behavior does not always spring from the same cause. The subject who will not look you straight in the face may have a shifty character, or may be very docile and submissive, or may simply prefer some less interesting object to fix his eyes on while thinking out the answer to your question. Good interviewing is a fine art (5). See also the methods used in *non-directive counseling,* mentioned on page 397.

The case study.   A person becomes a "case" because of some breakdown or misconduct, usually, and the study is aimed at his rehabilitation. The methods have already been indicated under the head of "case history" in the first chapter of this book. His parents or other early associates and especially the subject himself are interviewed for the purpose of reconstructing his personal history during the most formative years. His academic and occupational history are scrutinized. He comes under the eye of several specialists who observe him from their respective points of view and bring their findings together in staff meeting.

His abilities are tested. His desires, hopes and plans, his goals and the means he tends to adopt for securing his goals, are part of the picture. The whole inquiry is directed toward a recommendation as to how the subject may best be put on his feet, and as far as possible he himself has a share in formulating this recommendation and accepts it as the most hopeful plan of action. Subsequent check on the success of the recommended "disposition of the case" is an essential part of the whole procedure.

Though so incisive a case study is seldom possible except where the subject has got into trouble and is in desperate need of help, the college student would probably derive some benefit from being the subject of a somewhat similar study, and the student of personality would learn something from conducting such a study. It might be feasible for two students to collaborate, each serving as subject to the other, as in a laboratory experiment. The two should be reasonably congenial but not emotionally attached to each other—for the study must be objective. Without attempting to reach the deep undercurrents of personal life, the study could bring out the background, interests, attitudes, goals and traits and work up to a comparison of the two personalities.

The individual student may even find it instructive to take himself as a "case," and examine his interests, hopes and prospects, viewed in the light of his life history, with emphasis on formative influences in family, neighborhood and school, and the satisfactions and frustrations of his life so far. Intimate personal autobiographies of young adults sometimes make very illuminating sources for the study of personality (24, 33).

## PERSONALITY TESTS AND MEASUREMENTS

In describing an individual we compare him directly or indirectly with others. If we do not think specifically of any other individuals at the moment, we compare him with the general run of people. Experience with various people has given us a rough idea of the average person and of the scatter along any dimension. It is the same in judging personality as in judging ability or even bodily size. When we exclaim, "Isn't he a big fellow!" we need not be thinking of anyone else except the individual now before us, but we are evidently comparing him implicitly with the average and range of people with whom we are familiar. If we should be transported to Brobdingnag, where all the inhabitants are giants, our scale of bigness would be altered and our "big fellow" would appear comparatively small. In the same way a companion whom we think exceedingly grumpy may later seem a very mild case by comparison with certain other individuals. A science of personality attempts to locate individuals on various dimensions of personality, and to measure personality traits as accurately as possible. The numerous methods used are classified under the head of rating scales, questionnaires, situation tests and projective tests.

**Rating scales.**   Instead of saying that a person is "very persistent," "moderately so," or "lacking in persistence," we must attempt to be more precise and quantitative. There are many situations where an adviser or supervisor will make good use of accurate estimates if they can be obtained. Teachers are rated as to teaching ability, students as to promise of academic and other success, army officers in respect to general value to the service. Promotions and other important decisions are sometimes based, in part at least, on such estimates.

An estimate can be expressed as a percent, the most cheerful person imaginable being called 100 percent cheerful, the average person 50 percent, the low extreme 0 percent. Ratings of most personality traits cannot, however, be accurately made on scales with more than 5 or 10 steps. For example, a scale running from 0 to 5 can be used, 0 and 5 being used for extreme cases, 1 and 4 for markedly high or low individuals, 2 for just below average and 3 for just above average in the designated trait. The "graphic rating scale" is convenient. A certain dimension or trait is represented by a line and the individual's estimated place in this dimension is denoted by a check mark somewhere along this line. For example, rate some acquaintances in the six traits shown in Fig. 16. Or take two acquaintances, denoted by X and Y, and rate them both on the same chart.

The average individual in any trait belongs at the middle of the line. Raters are likely to commit the "generosity error" by placing their acquaintances on the more desirable side of the average. Some raters are more generous than others, but there are statistical means for correcting this error, provided the same rater rates a large number of individuals, so that his distribution can be compared with the normal distribution (11).

Another error is known as the "halo effect." If an individual creates a favorable impression by his excellence in one trait, you are apt to rate him near the top in every trait without discrimination. If he has created a bad impression at one time, you find it difficult to shake off that impression when rating him in various traits.

The main advantages of using such scales are that intermediate degrees of a trait can be better expressed than in words, and that the judgments of two or more raters can be pooled and averaged. Any single rater is likely to be one-sided or prejudiced, but the prejudices of different raters will often be in different directions and neutralize each other, leaving a fairly unbiased average rating. Apart from prejudice, the different raters have seen the subject in different situations and obtained different impressions which need to be combined into the final rating in any trait.

In order not to present too optimistic a view of the value of pooled ratings, two qualifications should be mentioned. First, different raters may have the same bias, and their combined ratings will retain this bias. High school teachers rating a student have seen him mostly in the classroom and cannot easily escape the halo effect of the student's classroom performance. They may agree in rating a student low in the scale of ambition, while others seeing him in another situation would come away with quite a different impression.

The second qualification is that it does no good to pool ratings unless the single judgments are better than a mere guess. If three judges assign ratings to an entirely unknown individual,

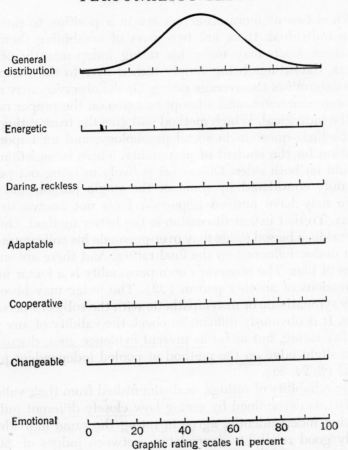

FIG. 16.—A graphic rating scale. In rating a person for energy, place him at the left of the line if he has no energy at all, and at the very right if he shows an enormous amount of energy; if he seems just about average place him near the middle. The distribution curve at the top is intended as a warning against the tendency to place everybody at one extreme or the other and against the tendency to place everybody indiscriminately in the middle. With a large number of individuals rated in any trait, the marks should scatter about as in the distribution curve.

X, merely pooling the ratings will not yield any approximation to a true judgment. But if each judge has even a slightly true impression, their combined judgment tends to be truer still (27, 36).

When two or more observers are in a position to rate the same individual, there are two ways of combining their impressions. Each may make his rating independently of the others, the ratings being simply turned over to the computer who determines the average rating. Or the observers may meet and compare notes, and attempt to agree on the proper rating for the individual. Which method will give the truer ratings?— a nice little question in social psychology, and an important question for the student of personality. There is something to be said on both sides. Discussion is likely to bring out points not duly considered by some of the single judges, and one judge may have noticed important facts not known to the others. To that extent discussion is the better method. On the other side, a biased judge may over-persuade his colleagues and have undue influence on the final rating. And there are subtle forms of bias. The observer's own personality is a factor in his impressions of another person (32). The judge may be especially sympathetic or unsympathetic with the subject's personal traits. It is obviously difficult to check the validity of any personality rating, but as far as present evidence goes, discussion has a slight edge on the method of pooled independent judgments (8, 24, 36).

The reliability of ratings, as distinguished from their validity (p. 76), is determined by seeing how closely different judges, working independently, agree in rating the same individuals. Fairly good reliability (correlation between judges of .80 or .90) has been obtained when the rating scale is carefully prepared and when the judges are well-trained and have sufficient acquaintance with the persons judged.

Self-ratings are found on the whole to run higher, in desirable traits, than ratings by other people, but there are exceptions and the tendency toward self-aggrandizement is largely offset by a tendency to rate oneself as "about average."

Questionnaires. In general a questionnaire is a list of questions to be answered in writing or by checking "Yes" or "No." It may be intended to obtain information on any matter. There is a special psychological type of questionnaire designed to lead an individual to reveal where he stands along a given dimension of personality. Suppose the dimension extends between the extremes, "finding trouble everywhere in life" and "finding no trouble at all in life." The appropriate questionnaire lists a large number of troubles.

### LIST OF POSSIBLE TROUBLES

Poor general health
Physical inferiority
Poor appetite
Insomnia
Disagreeable dreams
Mysterious aches and pains
Spells of dizziness
Nervousness
Persistent tired feeling
Persistent headache
Persistent worry
Persistent irritability
Loneliness
Ennui
Lack of true friends

Shyness
Lack of self-confidence
Mind-wandering
Foolish fears
Remorse
Being criticized
Being humiliated
Being misunderstood
Bad luck
Unfair treatment
Constant failure
The insecurity of life
The futility of life
The wickedness of people
No pleasure in life

The subject is asked to indicate which of these are genuine troubles in his own life. The list usually consists of direct questions and may go into much greater detail.

The troubles included in the list are supposed to depend on the individual rather than mainly on accidents of his environment. A high trouble score suggests that the individual may need some expert advice in adjusting himself to his environment. These trouble scores vary enormously. A list containing about 200 trouble questions (37) was given to a large freshman class and the scores ranged from near zero to over 100, with the average about 35. Not all who report many troubles are "neurotic" in any proper sense, and not all patients whom the psychiatrist finds to be psychoneurotic get a high trouble score in the questionnaire, though most of them do (20). Probably a neurosis consists not so much in being aware of many troubles as in "caving in" under their weight.

A trouble questionnaire has a rather high reliability in the sense that subjects do not change their scores much on a re-test. They may change the answers to a few questions but still they check about the same total number of troubles. The question of validity is more difficult. Validity depends on the use to be made of the scores. If the purpose is to discover individuals of "neurotic tendency" who are likely to have a nervous break-down or to become seriously maladjusted, the best check is to give the questionnaire to a large number of individuals, say freshmen, and to follow them through their college course and determine whether those with large trouble scores do develop personal difficulties from which those with small scores are free. On this basis the questionnaire is found to have some validity but not very much, since some students with large scores come through all right, while some with small scores allow their personal affairs to become terribly tangled (*13*). Improved questionnaires have been found to have some value in sifting out individuals in the Air Force for more intensive psychiatric examination (*31*).

If our object is to select the best candidates for a certain job where emotional stability is an asset, we must remember that the subject can easily misrepresent himself in filling out a questionnaire. If he wants the job, say a government position, he can be coached in advance to make a low trouble score; so that a Civil Service Commission cannot legitimately use such a questionnaire. If he does not want the job, as in case of some drafted recruits to the army in time of war, he can be coached to give a very large trouble score in the hope of being assigned to a noncombatant service. Of course the malingerer is running the risk of being detected in a subsequent individual examination.

We have used the trouble questionnaire as an illustration of a much-used method in personality studies. Questionnaires have been prepared for several other traits, such as ascendance, sociability, and introversion-extroversion.

The nature and range of a person's *interests* can be determined by means of a questionnaire containing many items covering a large variety of likes and dislikes. One widely used test of this sort has 168 questions which are scored to indicate the strength of the subject's interest in each of the following areas: mechanical, computational, scientific, persuasive, artistic, literary, musical, social service and clerical (*19*). Information on an individual's interests is important for a psychologist who is attempting to guide him toward the particular educational and vocational pursuit in which he will be most successful and best satisfied. Another interest questionnaire is scored to indicate how closely an individual's miscellaneous interests correspond to the interests actually reported by successful adults in each of 36 different occupations and professions (*34*). It may seem strange that psychologists go to the trouble of administering and scoring these long questionnaires when they could simply ask the individual what vocation most interests him. The test, however, has several clear-cut advantages over the simpler direct question. In the first place it permits a comparison with other persons. It yields a measure of the relative strength of interests. Often, too, a person does not really know his own vocational interests; he may be quite convinced that he wants to be a doctor like his father, while his test responses indicate that his general interests are very unlike those of physicians and much more like those of engineers. On seeing these results he may realize that his vocational choice was really determined by his father and that he would like to try engineering. Many persons cannot know their own vocational preferences because they have never had an opportunity to sample or even observe such lines of work as law, accounting, social case work, or advertising copy writing.

The questionnaire device is much used also for measuring attitudes on such matters as religion, economic conservatism or radicalism, and nationalism versus internationalism. A list of questions might include the following:

Is the hope of permanent peace an idle dream?
Is an occasional war needed to maintain the vigor of a people?

Is it the duty of the peace-loving citizen to refuse to participate in any war?

Some of the questions are intentionally made much stronger than others. If possible an additional refinement is introduced by scaling the questions, i.e., by selecting such questions as are spaced out by equal intervals from one extreme to the other of the dimension in question. The attitude questionnaires can be used for comparing different groups, or for comparing the same group at different times, as before and after being subjected to certain propaganda (7).

**Situation tests of personality.**   It is easy to test an individual's *knowledge* of the rules of good conduct or good manners or tact, but sometimes one who knows the rules does not obey them. We desire tests that will sample his actual behavior. The tests must be camouflaged somewhat, for you cannot very well tell the subject, "This is a test to discover how cheerful a disposition you have" or "This is a test to measure your willingness to cooperate." You might not get a fair sample of his behavior. In an ability test you discover what the subject *can* do, but in a personality test you wish to discover what he *will* do in life situations. Obviously it is going to be difficult for the psychologist to devise true tests of character and personality.

Many attempts are being made and some are fairly successful, especially with children. The camouflage employed is well illustrated by some tests for honesty (*14*).

A spelling test, conducted in the schoolroom, contained rightly and wrongly spelled words with instructions to check each misspelled word with a pencil mark. Next day the papers were handed back with a key by which the child was asked to score his own paper. To cheat he had only to change his wrong check marks, so that cheating was easy. But meanwhile a copy of the child's original check marks had been made by the experimenter, who thus detected all the cheating.

Similar to the honesty tests are tests of "overstatement." For example, in a vocabulary test the subject is asked to check the words he knows. Some fictitious words are included in the list, and checking of these is evidence of overstatement. A check list of "books I have read" can be similarly loaded with a few fictitious titles.

Some results of these tests will be discussed later in the chapter (p. 112).

Persistence, it would seem, must be an easy trait to test objectively. Give the subject a task without time limit and note how long he sticks to it. Here, too, some concealment is necessary, for if a group of subjects understand that persistence is the only point at issue, they may "gang up on" the experimenter and wear him out, beat him at his own game. Tasks found useful in persistence tests include the building of as many words as possible from the letters of a given word; standing on the toes as long as one can and will; etc. Any single task brings in other factors besides pure persistence, but a battery of tests may measure persistence rather well. The persistence score shows almost zero correlation with intelligence, but an appreciable positive correlation with academic achievement (30).

Objective tests have been devised for several other traits: aggressiveness, recklessness, suggestibility (23).

Situation tests were extensively used during the last war in a program for the selection of men for special secret duty in the Office of Strategic Services (2). In groups of 18, the candidates lived together with a staff of psychiatrists and psychologists for three and a half days on an estate just outside Washington, D. C. They were observed and rated as they were put through a series of situation tests as well as interviews, aptitude tests and questionnaires. The situations were designed to reveal the degree of such traits as practical effectiveness, initiative, leadership, emotional stability, cooperation, etc. Each man, for example, was observed while he tried to construct a five-foot cube out of poles and blocks, a sort of giant Tinker Toy, with the "help" of two assigned assistants who proceeded to delay and obstruct the task and harass the candidate in every way possible. Then a group of six candidates was instructed to figure out a way and get a 100-pound boulder across a brook which they were told to consider a roaring torrent too wide to jump. The available equipment was several boards, all of which were too short, a few pieces of rope, a pulley, and a barrel with both ends knocked out. Each candidate was rated by staff members on traits such as leadership, cooperation, ingenuity and so forth.

Another method by which a large variety of real-life situations could be simulated was the improvisation test. Two men would be given different and opposing roles to play. They were then directed to perform before the class and to behave as they normally would under the circumstances outlined. For example, A was told only that he had recently arrived in a certain city and had been proposed for membership in its most exclusive club by his friend B, who was on the membership committee. He was to call on B to check on a rumor that the committee had acted on his application. B was told that on hearing that the other committee members would vote against his friend, he had dropped in a blackball himself, but that when the votes were counted, there was only one blackball, so that he alone was responsible for his friend's rejection. A and B were seated at a table together, each informed of his own part but ignorant of the part the other was to play. Sometimes those who played the B part lied their way out; sometimes they evaded; sometimes they blurted out the truth. In each case the staff got a revealing glimpse of a man's personality in action and were enabled to rate him on significant traits which might not be apparent in less stressful situations like the interview.

**Projective tests of personality.** If we present an individual with a task which permits him to give free rein to his imagination, we can analyse his production to obtain indications of his characteristic modes of response, his emotional trends, and his ways of thinking. He tends to reveal or project his personality in free, unrestricted activity.

Several types of projective test situations have been devised. We might simply ask the subject to daydream and tell us his imaginings, but it will be better to give him some kind of a start. A story is begun for him and he is asked to complete it. A list of words is presented one at a time and he is asked to respond to each by saying the first word that comes to mind (p. 220). A hazy picture is shown and he is asked

Fig. 17.—Thematic apperception (*not* one of the standard series).
Write a short story suggested by the picture.

to weave a story around the picture. A cloud picture or an ink-blot is shown him and he is asked to tell what he sees.

If the psychologist is to obtain more than a very impressionistic view of the subject's personality from the response to such tests, the responses of many persons must be compared, and some system of scoring must be worked out. Such standardization has been attempted by Rorschach and his followers. A collection of ten blots is used, some being plain black on white, and some in colors. They are blots in which most people will "see something." This standard set of blots is shown to the subject, one blot at a time, and he tells what he sees. He may see one thing after another in the same blot. His responses are scored so as to answer such questions as these:

How often does he see human figures, how often animals, plants, landscapes, etc.?
Does he see the figure as a whole or fasten on details?
Is his impression governed by the form of the blot or by the colors?
How often does he see objects, especially human beings, in motion?
How good are the figures that he sees?
How original or unusual are his imaginings?

From these various scores taken together the Rorschach tester draws many surprising deductions. Seeing the blots as wholes indicates abstract and synthetic ability, while response to details indicates a preference for the concrete. Response to colors denotes impulsiveness, while seeing human forms in motion indicates a preference for inner thought. Seeing mostly animals denotes a stereotyped limitation of thought. Seeing good, clean-cut forms indicates good control When all the indications are combined, the examiner may judge that a certain individual is "outwardly calm but with dammed-up emotion,

FIG. 18.—An inkblot (*not* one of the Rorschach series).

undergoing conflict but keeping himself well in hand, his productivity not up to his capacity." It seems too good to be true. Can these findings be valid? The best check on validity is to size up the subject's personality entirely from the Rorschach results and then to compare the finding with what is known of the individual from other sources. In some clinical cases this check has come out in favor of the method, but it would be premature to express a judgment, either favorable or unfavorable, on all the claims of the Rorschach testers. In the hands of an experienced clinical psychologist the Rorschach results check favorably with other methods and further stand-ardization will probably render the test more objective (*4, 18*).

## SELF-CONSISTENCY AND TRAIT GENERALITY

When we call a person a cheerful individual, we mean more than that he acts cheerfully in pleasant circumstances. We might allow him to lapse into gloom when everything was gloomy, but would insist on his being cheerful most of the time. Any such adjective applied to an individual implies that he behaves in a certain way with some uniformity. But since the environment affecting him is anything but uniform, how can we expect uniformity in his reactions?

As a matter of fact, almost no individual shows any special trait with perfect uniformity. No one gives all extrovert answers, or all introvert, in filling out a questionnaire. And when the same individual is observed day after day in a series of situations, as in a boys' camp, his behavior is found to veer sometimes toward the extrovert pole and sometimes toward the introvert. Behavior seems to depend on the situation fully as much as on the individual (25).

Two kinds of uniformity. We should distinguish (1) self-consistency from (2) trait generality. The meaning of self-consistency is easily understood. An individual is self-consistent if he always acts the same way in the same situation, even though in different situations he acts in surprisingly different ways. He is always even-tempered, let us say, except on one particular subject which never fails to get him angry. Well, he is perfectly consistent with himself. Another person shows a lack of self-consistency by behaving differently at different times though the circumstances are the same.

Trait generality implies that a certain trait manifests itself in varied situations. If even temper were a perfectly general trait, the individual possessing this trait would show it under all conditions.

The distinction is clear in case of scholarship. If scholarship were a perfectly general trait, the student who gets A in one course would get the same in all courses (provided the markings were accurate), and every other student would always get a certain mark. Such not being the case, we see that this trait lacks complete generality. But if a certain student always gets high marks in the languages but low marks in the sciences, he is perfectly consistent with himself. He is dependable, his future marks are predictable, once you know his pattern of scholarship.

The traits listed in the Table on page 92 were chosen largely on the basis of their consistency and generality in most individuals. Other traits such as prompt—tardy, polite—rude, which vary greatly from situation to situation and from time to time are not as useful in the study of the stable personality.

**Self-consistency and trait generality in respect to honesty.** This distinction should be borne in mind in considering the results of an extensive study of school children, aged 8 to 15 years, in which use was made of the honesty tests already described (*14*). Each test in the battery yielded a "cheating score," ranging from zero when a child did no cheating up to a maximum when he took every chance to cheat. If the children's scores in two tests should correlate +1.00, that would mean that the child who did most cheating in one test did so in the other, and that every child similarly maintained the same position in the group from test to test. Now consider the actual results.

1. In the same test or practically identical tests, the correlation was high, but it became lower as the situations became more different. For example, there were several schoolroom

tests in which cheating meant copying answers from a key; the correlation among these tests was +.70. There were several other tests in the gymnasium where cheating consisted in over-stating one's performance; and the correlation among these tests was +.46. But the cross correlation between cheating in these two very different situations was only +.20. Cribbing in one test indicated that a child would probably crib in another test but afforded very little ground for predicting that he would overstate his gymnastic performance.

2. Of the individual children, some were much more uniform in their behavior than others. Some were always honest but scarcely anyone was always dishonest. The most honest children were highly favored individuals, with high intelligence, good homes and neighborhoods, and good emotional adjustment. The most dishonest children were not especially low in intelligence but were not favored by home and neighborhood conditions.

3. One schoolroom class sometimes stood out as much more honest than other classes in the same town and neighborhood, as if each class, perhaps largely through the teacher's influence, had developed its own code with regard to cheating.

What conclusions can be drawn from this investigation? Since each child responded similarly to similar situations, there was considerable self-consistency. But since the correlation was low between different situations, the trait of honesty showed only a small degree of generality. Instead of speaking of dishonesty as a single trait we must specify the type of dishonesty and the type of situation, at least when speaking of school children. Cribbing in the schoolroom is one trait and cheating in a gymnastic contest is another trait only slightly related to the first. There may be a common factor present in all honest conduct, but it is cut across by other factors.

The fact that a minority of children were honest in all the tests suggests still another conclusion. Those children gave evidence of a general trait of honesty, while the children who cheated a great deal, not being consistent about it, gave no evidence for a general trait of dishonesty. Probably there is no such thing as a general "need for dishonesty." There are numerous temptations or incentives to cheat, lie or steal, and some incentives are stronger with one individual, some with another, but there is probably no natural propensity to be always dishonest. But a general ideal of honesty is held up before most children and those who adopt this ideal will tend to be honest under the most varied conditions. Some individuals—many of them in the aggregate—can be rightly described as thoroughly honest, but perhaps no one deserves the name of a thoroughly dishonest individual.

## PERSONALITY INTEGRATION

When measures or ratings have been obtained on several traits of the same individual, they may be combined in a diagram known as the personality profile, which shows to the eye in what respects the individual stands high, low or average in comparison with the general run of people. His standing in each trait is indicated by a point suitably located above or below a middle line which represents the average of the population. The fact that this middle line is straight and horizontal does not mean that the average person is uniform in all re-

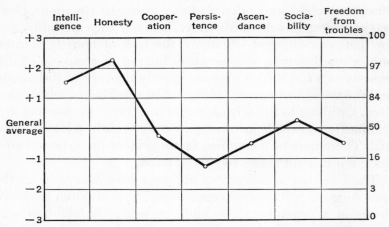

Fig. 19.—A personality profile. The scale at the left indicates standard scores, that at the right centile scores (p. 31).

spects, but simply that the group average in every trait is taken as the standard or base from which to measure the individual. If an individual should stand slightly above the average in every trait, his profile would be a horizontal line slightly above the middle line. The hypothetical individual whose profile is shown stands much higher in some traits than in others. The profile conveys an impression of the individual's high or low standing in general and of the evenness or unevenness of his personality. We cannot pretend that it pictures the "total personality," for it fails to show how the several traits *work together* in the individual's behavior.

**Interaction between personality traits.** A trait can be thought of as a behavior tendency. Sociability is a tendency to behave sociably, to seek company and to participate eagerly in group activities. Ascendance is a tendency to be masterful in any situation, whether involving other people or not. A person strong in both these traits would accordingly be a social leader, provided his other traits and abilities made him acceptable to the group. For another example, suppose a person to be strong in self-seeking but weak in energy. He would work when his own interests were directly involved, but in cooperative enterprises he would be a laggard. The individual's several traits, conceived as tendencies or forces, interact and are combined in his behavior (1, 24).

One trait cannot be changed without changing the significance of the others. For example try to imagine the individual whose profile is shown in Figure 19 with a high degree of ascendance. The entire picture now changes. His below-average rating in cooperation, which previously seemed only natural in a generally colorless, not-very-social person, now becomes a positive menace—he must be a tyrant and bully. Or picture to yourself an individual with the following traits,

energetic, assured, talkative, cold, ironical, inquisitive, persuasive,

and also this one,

energetic, assured, talkative, warm, ironical, inquisitive, persuasive.

In spite of a difference in only one trait, the total personalities are likely to seem very different (3).

The traits which we can analyze out of a total personality are not separate things or even separate tendencies. The laziness and selfishness of a certain individual are not two separate tendencies but are analyzed out of behavior which is limited to getting everything possible for the self with the least expenditure of effort. The traits pictured in a profile may seem unrelated and even incongruous, but if we observe how they express themselves in the individual we can usually see that they work together in harmony so that the individual has an integrated personality. After we have picked a personality to pieces, tested and rated him in various dimensions in comparison with other people, we need to go back to our individual and envisage him as a living, unique person (1).

**Lack of integration in personality.** Though the individual is an integral whole, he may lack something of perfect integration. All of us are inconsistent in the sense that we pass back and forth between different states in which our behavior is quite different. In one state we are energetic, in another state sluggish; in one state we are responsive to the environment, in another state very much withdrawn; in one state we are wide awake, in another state fast asleep. We behave differently when hungry and when well fed, when in a hurry and when at our ease. Human personality is a many-sided affair, and different sides become prominent in different states and activities. Our desires pull us in different directions, our interests are not easily integrated into a single all-inclusive purpose in life. Some individuals are relatively well integrated, while others appear distracted and unstable.

Children develop their habits, traits, and attitudes by responding to the specific influences and situations of their daily life, and there is usually a noticeable lack of harmony among them. For example, a child may love and hate his mother in quick succession; he may lie and disapprove of lying at the same time. Only gradually in the process of growing up do the various aspects of his personality become modified so that the parts are integrated with each other. Some adults do not achieve this harmonious integration and they are sometimes referred to as "immature" in their personality (21). In certain mental disorders, too, there is a disintegration of the personality pattern. In schizophrenia, for example, it is characteristic to find that the emotional feelings of the patient are not in harmony with his beliefs.

**Multiple personality.** Disintegration appears with dramatic vividness in those rare cases (22) that go under the name of double personality. The individual passes from one state to another, showing a very different personality in the two states, and forgetting in the primary or more lasting state everything he has done in the secondary state. In the secondary state he generally remembers the primary state but speaks of it as belonging to another person. The primary state is somewhat abnormal or limited, as if the individual were not his complete self, while the secondary state is a sort of complement to the primary, though very incomplete in itself. An individual who in the primary state is excessively quiet and submissive may be excessively mischievous in the secondary state. He seems to live in fractions and never as a whole.

In the celebrated Doris case (29) a little girl at the age of three years was thrown to the floor by a drunken father angry at finding her asleep in his place in the marital bed. From that moment she became an extremely quiet, industrious and conscientious child, except for intervals when she was wild and mischievous. The sober Doris had no memory of the pranks of the mischievous Doris, though the latter knew all about the former and spoke of her with scorn. The still more celebrated Beauchamp case (28) was that of a young woman whose difficult early life caused her to adopt an extremely religious, conscientious and self-effacing attitude, but who had brief, unaccountable episodes of mischievous conduct. In the psychotherapist's hands her mischievous side took shape in a secondary childish state, and a third personality emerged with normally aggressive and self-seeking tendencies. The primary, self-effacing state had no memory of what happened during either the self-seeking or the childishly mischievous state. The case thus developed under treatment into one of triple rather than double personality. The psychotherapist attempted to assemble these three fractions into a complete person, and apparently succeeded after years of effort. His chief method was to put the subject into the passive, suggestible state known as hypnosis, in which she could remember all three of her alternating states, and then to suggest that she would awake from hypnosis with all her memories retained. In the case of an ex-soldier whose split personality resulted from war strain, the separate memories were brought together by recall of certain events which served as bridges between the two states (10). Whether the essential achievement in these cases is the integration of the subject's memories, or the integration of goals and tendencies, is still open to question.

## SUMMARY

1. *Personality* is the total quality of an individual's behavior, as it is revealed in his characteristic habits of thought and expression, his attitudes and interests, his manner of acting, and his own philosophy of life.

2. Descriptions of personality are usually given in terms of traits.

a. A *personality trait* is some particular quality of behavior which characterizes the individual in a wide range of his activities, and which is fairly consistent over a period of time.

b. Although many traits are revealed most clearly in the interplay of personalities in a social situation, they also characterize the individual at other times as well.

c. Traits are usually named by a pair of opposite adjectives referring to the two extremes, but individuals are found distributed normally over the entire range of the trait.

d. Certain traits correlate highly with others and together may be considered a *trait cluster*.

e. The most comprehensive kind of personality classification, such as introversion-extroversion, attempts to include many significant traits in one single dimension.

3. *Judgment of personality* will be better if the judge observes the most revealing aspects of the individual, and if he has thorough experience in interpreting those aspects.

a. *Interviewing* offers a method of judging a person in a relatively short, somewhat standardized conversational situation.

b. *Case study* is a comprehensive analysis of a person based on all available types of information about him, including his life history.

4. *Measurements of personality* are designed to locate individuals accurately in comparison with other individuals in various dimensions of personality.

a. *Rating scales* provide a method for indicating intermediate degrees of a trait, and permit averaging the judgments of two or more raters.

b. *Questionnaires* are used to secure measures of traits such as trouble finding, ascendance, sociability, and extroversion-introversion, and of interests and attitudes. The reliability of questionnaires is adequate if they are carefully constructed, but their validity must be determined for each particular purpose for which they are used.

c. *Situation tests* are sample life situations in which certain traits can be observed which are hard to measure by any type of paper-and-pencil test.

d. *Projective tests* present ambiguous stimuli evoking imaginative responses which can be scored to reveal basic personality traits and patterns.

5. Personality traits are manifest in an individual's behavior with more or less *uniformity*.

a. *Self-consistency* is uniformity in manner of reaction to a situation at different times.

b. *Trait generality* is uniformity in manner of reacting to a wide range of varying situations.

6. Personality traits are not separate and independent characteristics; they are closely interrelated and interdependent.

   a. An *integrated personality* is one in which the several traits, interests and desires are combined in an effective harmonious unity. This unity is more characteristic of mature adults than of children.

   b. Lack of integration of personality is clearly seen in certain mental disorders, and in extreme form in cases of *multiple personality*.

# CHAPTER FIVE

# Physiological and Social Factors in Personality

In order to approach an answer to the problem of control and improvement of personality—whether the personality to be improved is one's own, that of one's children, or that of people in general—it is necessary to have some knowledge of cause and effect in this field. It is necessary to look into the factors that produce individual differences in personality, and to see what experiment and practical experience have revealed as to ways of changing personality. Though each individual is in a sense unique, each is not "a law unto himself." The same causal laws operate in all people, even in the most eccentric and abnormal. If there were no general laws of personality, the task of the psychological adviser would be hopeless. He must apply to one individual what he has learned from the study of other individuals and what he knows of the organism and its relations with the environment.

Physiological psychology and social psychology meet in the study of personality. Their meeting sometimes has the appearance of a battle, with one side shouting for the biological factors, the other for the social factors. Some will tell us that personality depends on "the glands," others that it depends on social influences. We will listen to both sides, beginning with the physiological.

The individual's *physique* is certainly a factor in his personality. The mere size of a person affects his attitude toward other people and their attitude toward him, though the big fellow is not always inclined to be dominant nor the little one to be submissive. Muscular development and "looks" also have their effect.

Individuals also differ in constitution—the proportions of the body—and these differences are possibly associated with personality characteristics. It is common observation that a round-shaped person is more apt to be jovial, comfort-loving, and sociable; a thin person more apt to be restrained, tense and introverted. The contrast is clearly expressed in the Shakespearean characters Falstaff and Hamlet. Research is now being carried out to investigate more fully the relation between constitution and personality.

Another biological factor may be spoken of as the *chemique* of the individual. It corresponds to what the ancients called *temperament*. They attempted to connect the "four temperaments" with four important "humors" of the body. The sanguine individual, they said, had a surplus of blood, the choleric a surplus of bile, the phlegmatic a surplus of phlegm, and the melancholic a surplus of spleen. Sometimes a fifth temperament, the nervous, was admitted, resulting from a surplus of the "nerve fluid."

Though this particular physiological theory is out of date, the possibility remains that chemical substances have much to do with the quality of one's behavior. Some of these chemical substances are introduced from outside in food and drink or through infections. There are also chemical substances manufactured in the body which have marked effects on growth and behavior.

The chemical factors in personality are dependent on the circulation. No less than the nervous system though in a very different way, the circulation is an integrator of the organism.

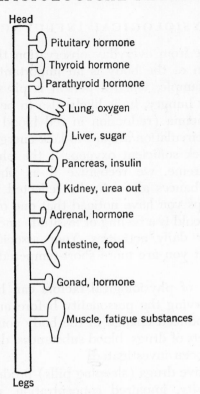

FIG. 20.—Organs contributing substances to the blood stream.

The circulation is like a railroad in carrying substances; the nervous system is like the telegraph and telephone in carrying messages; but neither of them operates much like any man-made system. The transportation of substances proceeds in this way: each organ delivers its output of substances into the blood; driven by the heart, the blood circulates through all the organs, and each organ helps itself to substances as they stream past. The circulation is surprisingly rapid; it may take only fifteen seconds for a substance delivered into the blood stream by one organ to be transported throughout the entire system to reach all the organs and affect the activity of the muscles or of the brain.

## PHYSIOLOGICAL INFLUENCES

It is apparent from everyday observation that the physiological condition of the body is an important factor in personality. For example, when a person is physically tired, or when he is very hungry, he is likely also to be more irritable. Persons with anemia (reduction in red blood corpuscles) or deficient blood circulation are apt to lack energy and initiative because they lack sufficient oxygen. If the physiological disturbance is extreme, we recognize it as illness, but more moderate disturbances also may be reflected in the person's behavior. Perhaps you have noticed that one of the first signs of an oncoming cold is a feeling of lassitude and a reduction of interest in your daily activities. Your associates may have noticed also that you are more short-tempered and generally disagreeable.

The influence of physiological factors can be most clearly studied by observing the personality before and after an experimentally produced change in the body condition. By this method the effects of drugs, blood substances, diet, and disease processes have been investigated.

**Drugs.** Sedative drugs (sleeping pills) produce a reduction in general activity, impaired concentration, muscular incoordination, drowsiness and eventually sleep. These effects are the result of paralysis or depression of certain portions of the brain. Alcohol is sometimes considered to have an opposite or stimulating effect, but closer study has shown that it also acts by depression of brain function. The talkativeness, sociability and perhaps pugnaciousness of the person who is "stimulated" by alcohol result from the depression of brain processes which normally control and moderate such behavior (8). Similarly there is often a stage of apparent stimulation during the period when a sedative drug is gradually taking effect.

Other drugs have certain specific effects depending on the part of the brain which is affected. Morphine, for example, induces a pleasurable dreamy elation, and marijuana upsets time perception so that short intervals seem long. Caffeine and

benzedrine increase alertness and efficiency slightly and reduce fatigue temporarily (32).

**Blood sugar.** The sugar content of the blood must be maintained above a certain level for the normal functioning of the
brain and other organs. When the blood sugar falls below this
critical level, mental function is impaired and alterations in
personality result. Most outstanding are changes in mood, increased irritability and vague feelings of apprehension. Lack
of oxygen, as mentioned in the first chapter (p. 7), leads to
similar temporary alterations in personality (32).

**Diet.** Relief workers have noticed that persons suffering
from prolonged malnutrition in regions devastated by war or
famine are psychologically affected. A carefully controlled experiment was carried out in this country during the last war
on 32 young men who voluntarily submitted to partial starva-
tion for a period of six months, losing about 25% of their
weight (11). Although there was no loss of intellectual abilities,
there were marked alterations in personality characteristics.
The men were continually preoccupied with thoughts and
dreams of food; their usual interests in sex, athletics, movies,
etc., were reduced. They were generally depressed, irritable,
and unsocial; they lost their sense of humor. These changes
gradually disappeared during the subsequent period of rehabilitation. Equally marked changes in personality have been
noted in patients whose food intake was not reduced in total
amount but was deficient in vitamin B.

**Disease.** During the acute stages of any illness there is likely
to be marked change in personality. Some of the change is the
direct result of the temporary impairment of brain function by
fever temperature and disease poisons, but illness can also
produce indirect effects such as an attitude of dependency and
lack of self-sufficiency which may persist beyond the period of
illness. The psychological after-effects of severe illness, particularly in growing children, deserve careful attention as a factor in understanding adult personality.

Encephalitis is an example of a disease which produces
marked effects on personality as a result of damage to the brain.

It occurs in children as well as adults and frequently gives rise to symptoms which persist years after the primary illness. The changes in conduct include exaggerated emotionality and irritability with overactivity and impulsive behavior, often resulting in antisocial or delinquent acts. Sometimes this behavior is associated with mental deterioration and retarded development, particularly in young children, but intelligence is usually not greatly affected in older persons (3, 4).

The following case study illustrates the type of personality change which can occur with encephalitis:

Angelo was committed to the State Home for Boys at the age of 12.5 years following his third arrest for stealing. He was born in the United States of respectable Italian parents, the seventh in a family of thirteen children. His parents and siblings are law-abiding and his home is comfortable. He was an ordinarily amenable youngster, showing no peculiarities of conduct as far as has been noted, up to the age of eight years when he suffered from encephalitis. Immediately following this illness he was extremely nervous and awkward.

A few months later he was operated on for appendicitis. During this long illness he was naturally much petted and humored, and when he began to show extreme irritability, obtrusiveness and restlessness his parents and others said he had been "spoiled." But discipline which had sufficed for his brothers and sisters failed to influence him. As soon as he was able to get about he began stealing "anything he could lay his hands on." He would run out of a moving picture show after a very few minutes of a vain attempt to sit still. Periods in a detention home and admonitions of parents, physicians and courts alike wrought no change. In school he was a failure, being still in the second grade at twelve years of age.

On his admission to the State Home for Boys the psychologist found his intelligence test scores to indicate borderline level, but deferred diagnosis because of the marked personality disturbance present. His attention was very mobile and it was considered probable that increased stability might enable him to attain higher scores. He was rated by the examiner as irritable, talkative and obtrusive. Medical and neurological examination led to a diagnosis of post-encephalitic instability.

Although a program of school and work activities with constant supervision was arranged for Angelo, his eight-month stay was a stormy period. For a time he appeared to be constantly inciting discord. He played tricks on his associates, fought, stole, lied, etc. Every officer who dealt with him agreed in declaring him to be a thorn in the flesh. Yet withal, he was a likeable chap, for he was always buoyant, never depressed, and his confidence in himself was amazing. Although he made a little progress in his school work, no significant improvement in his conduct was observed during his eight months stay in the institution (36).

## THE ENDOCRINE GLANDS

An endocrine gland, or gland of "internal secretion," is one that delivers its product to the blood. It produces one or more *hormones*, substances having the power to raise or lower the activity level of the body or of certain organs. For example, the pancreas produces two secretions. One, the well-known pancreatic juice, is not an internal secretion because it passes from the gland not into the blood but into the intestine, where it acts on the food and plays an important part in digestion. The pancreas, however, discharges into the blood a substance called *insulin.* This hormone, being carried by the blood to the muscles, enables them to use sugar as a fuel, i.e., to burn or oxidize sugar. If the pancreas fails to produce insulin, the organism lapses into the condition of diabetes in which the sugar, not being oxidized, accumulates in the blood till removed by the kidneys. Variations in the output of insulin cause variations in the individual's level of blood sugar, with the effects on the personality and behavior just described under that head (p. 125).

In general, the endocrine glands are small organs and not at all important in appearance, but physiology and clinical medicine have found these little chemical factories to be of vital importance (14). The physiologists work on animals by two main methods: by removing a gland and noting the effects of the loss on the animal's growth, health and behavior; and by replacing the gland or supplying the hormone by the mouth or by injection. The clinicians take note of diseases resulting

from overactivity and underactivity of the glands and treat
them by glandular extracts, following the leads discovered in
animal experiments. Chemists are playing their part by isolat-
ing from the glands the chemical substances which actually do
the work. Some of these hormones can now be produced
synthetically in the chemical laboratory; others are extracted
from animal glands obtained at slaughter.

The thyroid gland.    This lies at the base of the neck in front
of the windpipe and normally weighs less than an ounce. Its
enlargement into a goiter may or may not indicate anything
seriously wrong in its functioning. When this gland is destroyed
by disease, the individual loses his former vim and alertness
and sinks into a sluggish condition known as *myxedema.* The
skin is puffy. The muscles and brain are inert. The individual
is slow, stupid, forgetful and unable to concentrate or to think
and act effectively. If the gland is defective from birth or is
lost in childhood, growth is stunted and intelligence does not
develop. In the worst cases, called *cretins,* the individual remains a dwarf, misshapen and imbecile, though placid in disposition.

One of the dramatic discoveries of endocrinology was the
cure for myxedema. It was found that simply feeding sheep's

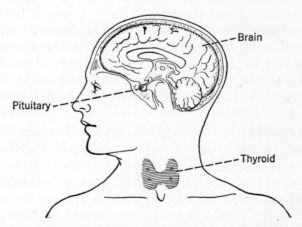

Fig. 21.—Locations of the pituitary and thyroid glands. For
another view of the pituitary, see page 248.

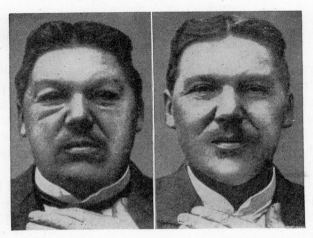

Fig. 22.—A case of myxedema, before and after treatment with thyroid extract. (From Joll, in Best & Taylor, *The Living Body*, 1944, published by Henry Holt & Co.)

thyroid quickly restored the normal state, as if by magic. An extract of the gland can be taken with the same results. The cure does not, to be sure, develop new thyroid glands in the patient, but so long as he continues to receive adequate doses of the thyroid substance his condition remains normal. Even the poor little cretins can be helped if the use of thyroid substance is begun early enough. Their IQ can be brought far above the level of the untreated cretin although it cannot be pushed above the normal level.

The thyroid hormone, called *thyroxin,* has been chemically analyzed and found to have a composition indicated by the formula $C_{15}H_{11}O_4NI_4$. The carbon, hydrogen, oxygen and nitrogen in this formula are the commonest chemical elements in the body, while the iodin is almost peculiar to thyroxin. The iodin taken into the body in food and drinking water, in very small amounts, is concentrated by the thyroid gland into this chemical compound. In regions where the iodin has almost all been leached from the ground and carried down to the sea —as in Switzerland and the Great Lakes region of North America—the task of the thyroid gland is made doubly hard by the scarcity of iodin taken in. Thyroid deficiency is common in these regions but can be forestalled by iodizing the table salt.

The primary work of thyroxin is to speed up the metabolism or chemical activity of the body, especially the process of oxidation. When this hormone is deficient in amount, metabolism sinks to a low level; less oxygen is consumed and less carbon dioxide given off. When the thyroid produces an excess of the hormone, the rate of metabolism is raised above the normal level.

When the thyroid is greatly overactive the individual is restless, tense, irritable, worried, unstable. If he is still in the growing period, his growth is rapid, especially in length, and he becomes, physically, just the opposite of the cretin dwarf. It does not appear, however, that his mental growth is accelerated or his intelligence raised.

Besides the extreme cases of thyroid excess or deficiency, there are probably many cases deviating moderately up or down from the norm. As far as known, there is little correlation between such deviations and intelligence, but there is some evidence that children's school achievement may drop below their intelligence level because of the apathy induced by moderate thyroid deficiency and indicated by a low metabolism (37). Personality differences in the dimension of overactivity and underactivity are sometimes due to the thyroid, but can also result from other causes. A diagnosis of thyroid abnormality cannot be made from personality traits alone.

**The adrenal glands.** These little glands were named from their location close to the kidneys, though they are quite distinct from the kidneys in function. Each adrenal consists of an outer part called the cortex (bark) and an inner part called the medulla (pith or marrow). The two parts differ in structure and function, and each is an endocrine gland in its own right. The hormone produced by the medulla is *adrenin;* that produced by the cortex is *cortin.*

*Adrenin* is a powerful hormone, very small quantities in the blood being sufficient to produce the following effects:

Strong, rapid heart beat

High blood pressure, forcing blood predominantly through the muscles and the brain, rather than through the skin or viscera

Suspended activity of stomach and intestines

Wide opening of the air passages in the lungs

Release of stored sugar from the liver

Delay of muscular fatigue

Free perspiration

Dilation of the pupil of the eye

These effects are also produced by activity of the sympathetic division of the autonomic nervous system (p. 360). The sympathetic nerves produce these results quickly and for short periods of time, while adrenin, discharged from the gland into the blood, gives the same results more slowly but for longer periods. Thus the adrenal medulla is an adjunct of the sympathetic nerves.

Is there any coherence among the varied effects listed above? Cannon has shown that all these changes occur in an animal in an emotional situation and that they serve to mobilize the animal's resources to meet a sudden emergency (6).

Cortin is involved in the bodily utilization of sodium, potassium and sugar, and has marked influence on muscular and sexual functions. It tones up the organism in some way that is not yet perfectly clear. It is necessary for life. Complete destruction of the adrenal cortex in man, usually by tuberculosis, results in a fatal disease named, after its discoverer (1855), Addison's disease. The symptoms are: progressive weakness and lassitude, loss of sex interest, low metabolism, and low resistance to any infectious disease. The skin darkens; the patient cannot endure heat or cold; he suffers from insomnia. His behavior is marked by poor judgment, irritability and lack of cooperation. These symptoms are removed by administration of cortin.

Overactivity of the adrenal cortex seems to be one cause of an excess of masculine characteristics in either man or woman. In a woman it causes loss of the rounded feminine contours, deepening of the voice and growth of a beard.

The gonads.   The primary sex organs, female ovary and male testis, besides producing the reproductive cells (ovum and spermatozoon, p. 164), also secrete hormones that have important effects on growth and behavior. There are several of these hormones and some of them are present in both male and female. A balance of male hormones steers development in the direction of masculinity, a balance of female hormones steers it toward femininity. At puberty these sex hormones promote the development of the genital organs and of such sex characteristics as the mammary glands of women and the beard and deep voice of men. Lacking the gonads, the individual of either sex develops into rather a neutral specimen without strong sex characteristics.

The internal reproductive processes in the female, including the menstrual or ovulation cycle, pregnancy and lactation, are controlled very largely by hormones. Even the urge to give maternal care to the infant seems to depend on hormones, although the efficiency of maternal behavior depends on the brain (2, 19).

The sex hormones, though present in childhood, increase during adolescence and are certainly necessary for the development of sex interest. As to personality traits, some individuals appear to be oversexed and others undersexed. Such differences may be due to the hormones, though real evidence on this point is scanty. Some individuals who lack the normal amount of spontaneous sex interest are criticized by their associates and react by engaging in sex activities, usually of some peculiar sort. Other individuals with normal hormones are driven into atypical sex attitudes by peculiarities of their social environment and by other interests which compete or combine with the sex interest.

The pituitary gland.   This is called the "master gland" because of the control its hormones exert on the other endocrine glands. The pituitary is a small body attached to the under side of the brain. It can be seen in Figure 21, page 128. Part of it, the posterior lobe, produces hormones which regulate bodily processes such as blood pressure and water metabolism.

The anterior lobe supplies hormones that stimulate the thyroid, the gonads, the adrenal cortex and perhaps other glands; without the pituitary hormones these glands do not develop or function normally.

The anterior pituitary also has great influence on bodily growth. If this gland is overactive in childhood, the bones and muscles grow rapidly and the individual may become a veritable giant, seven to nine feet tall. The gland, after this period of overactivity, is likely to become exhausted with the result that the giant loses muscular strength and dies young. If this same gland, after being just normally active during the growth period, becomes overactive during adult life, the individual, without growing any taller, develops large hands, feet, nose, lower jaw, etc.—a condition known as acromegaly (meaning "big extremities"). Underactivity of the anterior pituitary during the growth period is known to produce dwarfs of a symmetrical type, "midgets," who are quite different from cretins, being often rather attractive in appearance and normal in intelligence. While they are still young their growth can be increased by pituitary extracts.

**Endocrine balance.**   The relation of the pituitary to behavior and personality is very difficult to discover, partly because this gland works so largely by stimulating other glands. Endocrinologists are convinced that moderate overactivity of the pituitary makes the individual muscular, aggressive, self-controlled and calculating, while underactivity of this gland produces muscular weakness, sluggishness, easy discouragement and a tendency to give up and cry. These states of the organism may be produced, however, not by excess or deficiency in the pituitary hormones alone but by a lack of proper *balance* of all the hormones. Diagnosis of a particular endocrine disturbance is scarcely possible from the individual's behavior alone. For the same reason it would be useless for anyone to attempt to analyze his own personality in endocrine terms and then to try to improve it by glandular treatment.

Another complicating factor is the subject's reaction to the comments of his associates on his condition. Thyroid deficiency tends to sluggishness, but if the subject is constantly criticized for his sluggishness he may develop an irritable behavior quite different from what one would expect from the thyroid deficiency alone. Lack of gonadal hormones naturally leads to lack of sex interest, but the subject's reaction, as already stated, may lead him into some atypical form of sex behavior. Some endocrine imbalance may make an adolescent drowsy and unable to concentrate, while his appetite is enormous and he lays on great quantities of fat. Much comment is sure to arise and his reaction may be to withdraw from society, or to be sullen and resentful against authority, or to acquire the habit of stealing to satisfy an appetite for sweets (23).

The endocrine balance of most people is probably about normal. Although extreme overactivity or underactivity of one of the glands results in unmistakable alterations in behavior and personality, such cases are relatively rare. It is not known whether the small variations in personality which occur among normal individuals are related to small variations in hormone function. Some writers have tended to overemphasize the importance of the hormones as determiners of individual differences in personality. Within the normal range of glandular function personality differences are probably due to other causes. Some of these other causes are biological and some social. The best we can say is that the endocrines are among the basic biological factors in personality (15).

## SOCIAL FACTORS

That fundamental principle of psychology, to see the individual in his environment, is nowhere more important than in tracing the development of a personality. Like ability, personality is developed by the individual's activity, and activity depends on stimuli received from the environment as well as on the individual himself. There is no reason for laying all our emphasis on the *social* environment. A tropical climate may foster an easy-going disposition, while a temperate climate, with marked seasonal changes, may foster a more energetic

temperament. Such possibilities have not received the scientific
study that they deserve, but much attention is being directed to
the influence of the social environment upon personality.

The words *code* and *role* suggest two important influences
of the social environment. The individual acquires a code of
conduct. He adopts the code of his group or at least builds up
his personal code in living with the group; and he finds or
makes a role for himself in the group.

The group code.   Any social group seeks to enforce certain
rules of conduct on its members. The group code covers manners as well as morals. It comprises the mores and folkways and
differs greatly from family to family, from gang to gang, and
from region to region. The child picks up many of these rules
easily and cheerfully, and where he resists he is subjected to
criticism, ridicule, punishment or ostracism, until he conforms.
He usually ends by adopting the group standards of behavior.

Besides its rules of morals and manners, any group has more
subtle nuances of behavior which come closer to personality
traits. Just as one picks up the dialect of a place, with its
drawl or twang or "Oxford accent," so one takes on the local
*style* of behavior. This kind of social influence is well brought
out by studies of isolated communities. One small mountain
community, back in the forests of the Blue Ridge, without even
a wagon road from outside, had lived and inbred for a hundred
years with scarcely a thought for the progress of national
events. There was little traffic in or out, and those who went
out and tried town life sometimes came back with relief because they could live with less effort in the mountains, and
could get up when they pleased and dress as they pleased.
The tone of the community was easy-going, unambitious,
fatalistic, and such was the tone of the individuals. It seems a
clear case of the individual's taking up personality traits from
the environment. But we must not overdraw the picture. Even
in this community the individuals differed. There was a steady,
industrious man, there was a relatively enterprising man, there
was a boy ambitious to succeed in the world, there was at least
one young woman who repudiated the local fatalism in respect

to every woman's predestined large family of children. Here we see the individual more or less successfully *resisting* the social environment, and we learn that personality is not forced on the individual. It is his reaction to the environment and depends on his individual organism as well as on the environment (*31*).

There are "black sheep" in every group, deviates from the standard behavior of the group. Those who deviate too much are suppressed, but some latitude for deviation is probably always allowed, though some groups are much stricter than others in enforcing conformity. Because codes differ greatly from group to group, an individual who is a misfit in one might be quite at home in another. Some groups are openly and blatantly competitive, so much so that an individual who surpasses others in wealth or prowess is expected to boast openly of his superiority. Other groups, if competitive at all, are much more subtle about it; an individual can win social approval and praise, but he does so by service and modesty. Our own culture is highly complex in this regard. We enjoy competition, for example in games, but it runs to teamwork and rivalry between sub-groups, and boasting of personal success or sulking under personal defeat is decidedly bad form. Being a misfit in one's group tends to create a personality difficulty, sometimes of the rebellious sort, sometimes of the shrinking and neurotic sort. A person may become a misfit on moving from one community to another where the style of life is very different, as happens sometimes to immigrants. Or a person may be a misfit because his natural inclinations conflict with the group standards. Personality difficulties are thus sometimes the result of a disharmony between the individual and the group. Undoubtedly some personality difficulties have nothing in particular to do with the group but result simply from internal conditions such as thyroid deficiency. The causes of the neuroses and insanities are not thoroughly worked out but we should have our eyes open for both physiological and social factors.

**Acquiring the group code in childhood.** Any group game

affords a concrete instance of a code which must be obeyed if the game is to run smoothly. A study of Swiss boys (28) traced the gradual development of their grasp of the rules of the game of marbles. The experimenter had boys play the game before him and quizzed them on the rules. The very youngest children need no rules, as each child plays entirely by himself. Somewhat older boys follow some rules in a lax way, but have no great need of them because they are not definitely competing. Each boy is simply trying to make his marble hit the marbles in the "square" and both players can win the same game. Only later does the real competitive game appear, with its numerous rules, the purpose of which is apparently to put a premium on skill and to magnify the social aspect of the game.

When first learned by the younger boys, the rules are regarded as sacred and authoritative. Each little boy is likely to say that his father invented the game and established its rules. The older boys are fully aware that the rules exist simply to insure a good game and could be changed by common consent of the players, provided the game would be improved. Probably few adults understand the true nature of their own group code as well as boys of twelve or thirteen see around their game of marbles.

The Swiss investigator inquired into children's ideas regarding lying; he asked them what lying is, why it is bad, and which of two suggested lies would be worse. The six-year-olds defined lying as "saying naughty words" and explained that lying was bad because it was punished. They thought it not very bad to tell a lie to a child, "because the child will believe you." A child who falsely reported to his mother that the teacher had given him a good mark in school did not lie, for his mother believed him and gave him a cookie; but a boy who told the assembled family of seeing a dog as big as a cow told a very bad lie because no one believed him.

The children of eight to ten years have completely changed their ideas. To them a lie is a statement that deceives someone. It is worse to lie to a child than to a grown-up because the child will believe you. Lies are bad "because if everyone lied no one would know where he was." Thus, with the older children, lying no less than the rules of a game is evaluated according to its social effects.

The logic of the younger child, who thinks a lie is bad because it is punished, may seem perverted, but it is perfectly good from the child's standpoint. He has to discover the code by trying out various acts and seeing which are acceptable to his elders. When he thus discovers a rule of conduct, it is sanctioned by adult authority before he discovers its social utility. Exactly how he advances from the authoritarian to the utilitarian conception of rules, we do not know.

**Social roles.** However rigid a group code may be it always allows for a variety of individual roles. Each person has his own particular role to play. To some extent the available roles are determined by group organization. There must be a provider, there must perhaps be a leader, and it is nice to have an entertainer. If all individuals were potentially alike, the roles might be distributed at random, and then each individual in filling his assigned role would develop the potentialities appropriate to that role. According to his role he would develop different traits of personality. The provider would become provident, the leader would become masterful, the entertainer would become entertaining. Personality, from an ultra-social point of view, is the individual's response to the role imposed on him by the group. To a student of individual differences it would seem more likely that each individual gravitates toward a role that suits his own characteristics, and that he finds his role or makes it rather than having it thrust upon him by arbitrary group action. Once in a role he certainly develops according to the requirements and opportunities of that role. The personality of an adult would then depend partly on the roles he has filled and partly on his inherent characteristics, the social and the individual factors working together at every stage of his development.

**The role of the child in the home.** Because of his inherent characteristics as a child, the individual's first social role is to be weak and dependent but also to grow and become more and

more independent. His role is anything but static and he comes
to feel, himself, that the main thing for a child to do is to grow
up. His role is also to be loved and admired. But the exact
nature of a given child's role depends very much on the parents
—not entirely, for each child early shows characteristics that
have to be reckoned with by the rest of the family. Some parents do not give the child half a chance to grow up. Children
come to the behavior clinics suffering from personality difficulties which are the result of injudicious handling by their parents. In one family the parents are so solicitous to protect the
child from every danger and hardship that they prevent his
learning to do anything for himself, while in another family the
child is held in such rigid subjection that he, too, remains overdependent. The spoiled child and the cowed child in their
different ways show personality traits due to the roles imposed
on them at home. The favorite child, too, and the unwanted
child are given roles in the home which have an effect on personality (22, 29).

With two children in the family the home environment is not
the same for both. Even if the parents treat them the same,
each one has a different child for companion. The older of two
brothers has a younger brother as part of his environment,
while the younger has an older brother—quite a different thing.
Some psychologists, especially Alfred Adler, have laid great
stress on the child's family position or *birth order*. The only
child, never supplanted, never having to share, might well become overdependent and at the same time tyrannical. The
oldest child, after playing the role of the only child for a few
formative years, is deposed; we might expect him to become a
jealous person, striving to keep what he has, believing in authority and privilege. The second child is always trying to catch
up and might become an especially eager person and a rebel
against the established order. The youngest child, as the per-
petual baby, might permanently cling to the role of everybody's pet who always looks to others for help. Except in large
families, it would seem, every child is cast for an unfortunate
role (1).

Investigators in the behavior clinics have attempted to verify these suggestions regarding birth order but with little success. On the whole, no position in the family comes out worse than any other. The same kinds of personality difficulty are found in children of every position, and with about equal frequency. The only child is not as a matter of record unduly represented among the problem children referred to behavior clinics, and he presents no peculiar type of behavior difficulties but shows the same variety of problems as other children. Among university students the "trouble score" (p. 103) is not larger on the average for only children than for others, nor does it show any consistent relation to the birth order (17). The clinical psychologist regards the child's birth order as a fact worth knowing because it suggests what his difficulties *may be,* but it is no sure indicator of what his difficulties actually are. Too much depends on the atmosphere of the home, and too much depends on the inherent characteristics of the individual child.

Adler, to do him justice, fully recognized the importance of other factors in the home besides birth order. Much depends on the mother's skill in initiating the child into group life and helping him to develop a social disposition, an understanding of other people and a willingness to give and take and to become a participating member of the group, a social being. Even if he adopts this desirable general role, each child specializes his own role according to his early experiences. The spoiled child expects always to be the center of attention, while the rejected child adopts the attitude of keeping at a safe distance. So every child, according to Adler, develops in his first few years a "style of life" which remains fundamentally unchanged for the rest of his life.

Freud and his followers, the psychoanalysts, have contributed to our understanding of the child's role and code the concept of *identification.* The child imitates his elders, not passively but intentionally and eagerly. He wants to be like his father, or she wants to be like her mother—sometimes the other way around. The father has the prestige of bigness and strength, he shows affection for the boy and usually has the advantage of being held up by the mother as a fine person. On the other side the father may be stern at times, he may be delegated to do the severe punishing, and so he comes to represent the disagreeable factor of *authority* which the child tends to resist. The child's attitude toward his father thus contains contradictory elements, but the contradiction is resolved by identifying himself with the father.

By identifying with the authority the child becomes an authority himself, responsible for his own conduct (and also authorized, as he assumes, to pass judgment on the conduct of other people). The code that was originally imposed on him becomes his own personal code of right and wrong. So the child develops his *conscience,* which is more than a matter-of-fact collection of rules, however, since this whole process of identification has a strong element of loyalty, first to the parents and the family, later extended to wider social groups with which the individual comes to identify himself (9).

Freud and Adler agree in tracing the individual's fundamental role in life back to the family situation in the very early years. They are one-sided in discounting the social influences affecting the child and youth from outside the home. They regard the effect of these later influences as being superficial and not reaching to the heart of the personality, which they believe to become fixed in early childhood. Their evidence, drawn from the study of adult neurotic individuals, is inconclusive because these individuals seem to be those who have not grown up in personality. Most people, we may believe, are more flexible, more responsive as children to influences from the school and playground, and as young adults to the larger social group. Development is of course a continuous process, with no sharp break between babyhood and adulthood, and yet the child's attitudes and style of life may be profoundly modified as he participates in the varied activities of community life.

**The child's role in the gang.**   The study of play groups is a valuable lead in social psychology and in tracing the development of the individual's personality. In spite of the importance of the home environment in fixing the individual's traits, the child often takes more interest in his playmates and may find his role and adopt his code in the play group more than in the home situation. Among his fellows he escapes from the role of a dependent and has scope for his love of adventure. Whether adventure shall mean lawlessness depends largely on the facilities and standards of the neighborhood. Boys' gangs often have a leader and an inner circle, besides regular members and hangers-on. The activities of the gang provide a framework in which the individual boy finds his place. One boy may be the "brains" of the gang, one the dare-devil, and one the funny boy. One may serve as the "goat" or the cat's-paw. The more desirable roles are won by competition. In a fighting gang the leader has to prove himself the best fighter. Personal traits such as generosity count heavily in winning the important roles. The roles are not handed out at random but are determined in large measure by the existing traits of each boy. Therefore we cannot say that the role makes the boy, though we must agree that the boy who has found a congenial role develops his personality according to his role (30, 34).

Many boys' gangs are lawless and include boys with court records who must be classed as juvenile *delinquents* and potential criminals. How about the intelligence of the delinquents? Since the invention of intelligence tests much attention has been paid to this matter. The first studies indicated that a majority of delinquents and criminals were feebleminded, but with the improvement of the tests the results have taken on a different color. It now appears that only a small fraction are feebleminded. Some are average and a few well above average, but an IQ of 80–90 is more typical. As a whole, juvenile delinquents are below the average, and are better in performance and mechanical aptitude tests than in the more verbal tests such as the Binet. Such boys feel themselves misfits in school and are easily led into habitual truancy, a start toward delinquency. When the school, perhaps by the introduction of shop work, provides an opportunity for these boys to enjoy a measure of school success and achievement, a delinquent career is much less likely (5, 25, 33).

We should know much more than we do of the changes in personality that occur in *adolescence*. We know from studies already made that play groups in early adolescence show a rather sudden shift of interest to dancing and other forms of companionship between the sexes—a shift that occurs about two years earlier in girls than in boys, in conformity with the earlier puberty of girls, and that seems therefore to depend on physiological factors. At this period there is a rapid loss of interest in marbles, stilts, kites and other favored games of childhood, and a loss of enthusiasm for some spectacular roles in life, like those of the cowboy and circus performer, which greatly appeal to children (10, 21). The "storm and stress" traditionally supposed to characterize the period of adolescence is by no means always present even in our own culture, and seems to be quite absent from certain other, freer cultures (24). But the "growing-up" of childhood is accentuated in adolescence by an active search for individual roles in the world's work and social life (35).

**Adult roles.** A boy who has been a leader in his school naturally expects to play the same role in college, but may come up against strong competition from those who have been leaders in other schools. A similar necessity may confront the young adult when he becomes a member of an adult social or occupational group. Even those who have never aspired to be leaders may not like to be bossed. In any large organization the managerial function is important, but the workmen are apt to be very critical of the management, as the GI was of the "brass." For many individuals it is not easy to accept a subordinate role. This organizational difficulty, not yet fully mastered by any means, is met to some extent by delegating responsibility and initiative to the subordinate. More use should be made of the psychology of individual differences in various abilities and in personal traits and interests.

## IMPROVING PERSONALITY

This is a big subject and there is little of a scientific nature to say on such questions as how to develop good qualities like

sympathy and frankness, or how to eradicate excessive tense-
ness and touchiness. It is dangerous to hand out general rules
and maxims, for the persons who take them most to heart may
be the very ones who would profit by just the opposite advice.
For example, frankness is certainly a desirable trait, and a
calmly voiced objection to some irritating behavior of your
friend is much better than letting your irritation go unrevealed
till it reaches the bursting point and explodes in a serious quarrel. But the person who takes this rule to heart and continually
nags his friend builds up irritation in the friend or drives him
away altogether. "Grin and bear it" would be a better rule for
some persons and some situations than "Be frank."

An individual's personality has usually crystallized into a
pretty stable pattern by the time he becomes aware that some
changes in it would be desirable. Nevertheless considerable
improvement can often be achieved by one who is willing to
expend the necessary effort and who can face his own characteristics frankly and clearly. The easiest modification is in the
sphere of social manners, for which a good book on "etiquette"
is a useful guide. By observing his successful associates, too, a
person can learn the kinds of behavior which his group considers appropriate. When carried to extremes, or when done too
blatantly, this effort is apt to be labelled "social climbing."
More fundamental traits like self-confidence and ascendance
are not so easily acquired.

Ascendance and submission are a pair of traits, neither of
which should be developed to excess. The person who always
wants to dominate and is never willing to follow a leader makes
an undesirable companion; so does the person who will never
take the lead nor stand up for his rights. How do these opposite
traits develop? Judging from a study of college girls, the most
dominant ones have had a large degree of independence as
children and have sought satisfaction in achievement rather
than in being good or in being admired (7). We cannot be sure
that the family situation was entirely responsible, for some
children, more than others, insist on independence and active
achievement.

**An experiment in training for ascendance.** Nursery children were the subjects in this experiment, and they are probably the best subjects for experiments in changing personality traits, being less self-conscious and wary than older persons would be. The shyest, least ascendant children in a class of four-year-olds were given certain training after which their ascendance score rose considerably. The experiment included a fore-test, a training period, and an after-test. In the fore-test, each child was placed with another child to play in a sand box while the experimenter watched from behind a screen and noted down the child's attempts to secure play materials by verbal or forcible means, his efforts to lead and direct the other child, his success in these efforts and his compliance with the demands of the other child. The children who made very low ascendance scores in the fore-test were then trained by the experimenter till they had complete mastery of certain play materials— blocks for building certain designs, a jigsaw puzzle, a picture book with its story—and then each trained child was placed with another child to build the block design, to work the puzzle, or to tell the story in the picture book. The trained child had the advantage of the untrained child, and proceeded to use his advantage, usually by assuming the role of teacher. After quite a bit of such experience, the trained child was given an after-test identical with the fore-test, and his ascendance score was much higher in general than before. Control tests showed that the gain was not the result of the few weeks' increase in age (*16, 26*).

In a similar experiment, children who showed little self-confidence in solving a problem were brought to a higher level of independent work by starting them with easy problems and promoting them to progressively difficult ones, always with encouragement but no actual assistance (*18*). Much the same experiment was tried some time ago on soldiers temporarily incapacitated by wounds so that at first they could not raise the arm. Their progress was hastened by use of a little instrument which showed exactly how high the arm was being raised. At first their achievement was slight, but the instrument made it visible and gave them a mark to reach and surpass the next day. Many experiments in the psychological laboratory have shown that visible achievement promotes self-confidence and is an incentive to further efforts.

**Treatment of personality difficulties.**   Which is worse, to lack self-confidence or to have no confidence in anybody else? The worst of all is to have no confidence in either self or others, and such is the state of some badly disturbed individuals. The first step toward a "cure" is, often at least, to get the subject to have confidence in some competent adviser. The mental hygienist, when working with a maladjusted child, tries first to win confidence by seeing the difficulty from the child's own point of view, and then to secure the child's cooperation in some hopeful plan for improvement. The child, as well as the adviser, must be hopeful. Often the cooperation of the parents and a more confident attitude on their part toward the child are essential for successful treatment.

When the child's difficulty brings him into serious conflict with society, as in cases of stealing or incorrigibility, a change of home environment may be necessary. Antagonisms may have grown up between the child and other members of the family which cannot be overcome, and the child would slip back into his old role if replaced in his old surroundings. A foster home is found for him after careful study of that home as well as of the child to make sure that the two will fit together. Follow-up of several hundred boys and girls placed out in this way revealed improvement in the great majority of cases (about 90 percent), except where the child's personality showed from the beginning distinctly abnormal trends. Stealing, lying and running away ceased, though not all at once, and timidity, irritability and distrust disappeared in a favorable home atmosphere. Precocious sex interest was allayed. Yet the children, after all, remained the same children. The overactive one remained overactive, though less disturbingly so, and the easygoing one retained that characteristic through all the change of behavior. In short, the biological, temperamental factors in the child's constitution continued to operate in the changed environment (12).

The individuals who are most dominating and aggressive in their overt behavior are not always the most self-confident at heart; they may be "compensating" for an inner sense of distrust and insecurity. They may be drawing too sharp a line between the self and the environment and so failing to participate wholeheartedly in group activities (13).

We shall return to problems of this general sort in chapter 12.

## INTERPLAY OF INTERNAL AND EXTERNAL FACTORS IN THE PERSONALITY

We have the endocrines and other biological factors in personality, and we have the environmental factors such as the group code, the family situation and the role of the individual in the group. Shall we wave aside the biological factors in favor of the social, or the reverse? What we must do is to recognize the importance of both kinds of factors, and to insist that personality is not a sum of these factors, but rather a product of their interaction. The individual is not molded like putty; he is aroused to activity by the environment and is developed by his own activity. At any moment his behavior depends on stimuli received from the environment and on his own personal characteristics, physiological and psychological. That is, it depends on both internal and external factors.

Two individuals playing practically the same role will play it differently because of their different internal constitutions. They may accomplish almost the same results, but do so in different ways according to their personal characteristics. Two leaders, for example, may both be effective and yet very different in their ways of leading. One may be forceful and the other gentle. Two unlike individuals placed in similar roles will develop differently because their own tendencies cause them to act differently. But it is also true that two similar individuals placed in very different roles will develop differently, because of the different activities demanded. As these statements hold good even of young children, we may conclude that the internal and external factors interact from the beginning and probably to the end of life.

There is another point to consider. The individual passes back and forth from group to group, between the gang and the home circle, or between the classroom and the football team, playing very different roles in different groups. If personality depended wholly on the role, multiple roles would mean multiple personality. Yet most of us who play two or more roles are not disintegrated. The typical case of multiple personality arises from the *refusal* of the subject to play the multiple roles that normally fall to the same individual. He tries to confine himself to the role of the serious and self-effacing person, without ever being normally aggressive or normally playful; and the roles which he refuses to play get played in special states into which he lapses against his will. By contrast the normal individual passes freely from one role to another and maintains his own unity and continuity throughout. This unity and continuity are certainly not provided by the environment but depend on the fact that the organism is itself a unit.

**The continuity of personality illustrated by a case history.** That the individual preserves a good measure of sameness as he grows up and comes into different environments is well brought out in the numerous case histories that have been published of neurotic and delinquent persons, "problem children" and the like. One would expect to find the same continuity in the biographies of the great, but these biographies are apt to be rather meager on the formative years. Much of psychological interest can be found in the life of the American humorist, Samuel Langhorne Clemens, better known as Mark Twain (*20, 27*).

Mark Twain grew up in the semifrontier town of Hannibal, Missouri, on the Mississippi River. His father, a lawyer of high character and aspirations, was a poor money-getter, and the family was always close to poverty. His mother came of a family of optimistic people, full of projects for getting ahead, and was herself a woman of great vitality, courageous and outspoken, with a peculiar, interesting drawl in her speech and the art of saying a humorous thing "with the perfect air of not knowing it to be humorous." Mark Twain resembled his mother in all these respects. She once replied to a neighbor who asked if she put any credence in the boy's astonishing tales of his adventures, "Oh yes, I know his average. I discount him 90 percent. The rest is pure gold." Sam, or Mark, was the sixth in order of seven children. He was cared for largely by Negro slaves, was very fond of the stories they told, and retained a strong affection for the Negro. Sympathy for the "under dog" was always one of his strong characteristics. He was the leader of a gang of boys who roamed the woods, swam in the River and explored it in "borrowed" boats. He was full of adventurous projects and practical jokes, and it was said of him that he always had a ready audience for whatever he had to say in his drawling way. One of his gang was the original of "Huckleberry Finn," the neglected son of the town drunkard, whose company was forbidden to the children of respectable families. Mark did not like school and when he was eleven, his father having died, his mother permitted him to work in a local printing office, where he soon learned to be an expert typesetter. Leaving home at the age of seventeen, he plied his trade in several large cities, and then suddenly, during a steamboat trip, determined to become a River pilot —the great ambition of his boyhood. He "learned the River" and piloted large steamboats between St. Louis and New Orleans for several years, until the outbreak of the Civil War put a stop to the river traffic. Soon afterwards we find him in Nevada, then in the height of the silver boom. He dabbled in mining, optimistically, for a few months, but soon became a reporter on the leading newspaper of the region. (He had written a few sketches from time to time during his youth and early manhood.) A few years later he began to travel as a newspaper correspondent, and he ventured with much trepidation to try his hand as a lecturer. He had already, on one or two occasions, met with much success as an after-dinner speaker; and when he stood before his audience and just talked to them in his characteristic way, he carried all before him. He embodied some of his travel letters in his first book, *Innocents Abroad*. The success of this book led him to settle down, more or less, to the life of an author and man of means. He had found a wife after his own heart and was much devoted to his children. His wife became his censor and kept his writing within the bounds of respectability, from which he was

*Courtesy, Cyril Clemens, Mark Twain Soc.*

Fig. 23.—Mark Twain as a young man.

prone to stray. Besides the creditable array of books and sketches which he published, there were many which were censored and left unfinished. He was always willing to take a chance on what seemed like a promising invention, and sank a fortune in a type-setting machine. He became partner in a publishing house which after rather a brilliant career went bankrupt, and then, at the age of nearly sixty, set about paying off his indebtedness by going back to the lecture platform. He suffered many disappointments and sorrows from time to time and felt them deeply but always came back to high spirits.

There is an undercurrent of serious purpose in Mark Twain's writing—to strip off cant and prejudice and see things as they really are. He was extremely critical of much that was current in religion and public life, and used to rant about the "damned human race" which was to his way of thinking inferior to the animals except in the one point of intelligence. But his readers and hearers always suspected a joke, and would burst into laughter at his most serious statements. He had made his role and was held to it. Apparently he found his role even as a boy in his gang. Certainly his behavior shows continuity in spite of the varied environments in which he lived and the varied oc-cupations in which he engaged. One should mention also certain

*Underwood-Stratton*

Fig. 24.—Mark Twain in later life.

personality traits which had much to do with his career and which were certainly biological or constitutional: his resilience and high spirits, his great endurance (he would play billiards all night without feeling tired) and his inventiveness and disposition to take a chance.

Mark Twain's marked ability and striking personality reveal quite clearly the interaction of biological and social factors. The direction in which he developed was obviously determined by the social role that he filled, but his role was not handed out to him by society, for he showed unusual initiative in making a role for himself. He made his role by finding what an individual of his biological constitution could do that would have social value and acceptance.

Such a life history brings us squarely in front of a problem around which we have been skirting for a long time—the problem of the influence of heredity on personality, on intelligence, and on behavior generally. We have been willing to recognize the importance of the "biological factor," but we have not assumed by any means that this factor is identical with heredity.

## SUMMARY

1. Personality development is clearly influenced by both biological and social factors.
   a. The *physique* of the individual—his size, strength, looks, and constitution—affects his attitude toward others and their attitude toward him.
   b. The *chemique* of the individual refers to the chemical substances which circulate in the blood and affect the brain and other organs of the body.

2. The physiological condition of the body influences the behavior and personality by its effect on the functioning of the brain.
   a. *Sedative drugs* depress brain activity, and result in reduced activity, impaired efficiency and drowsiness. Alcohol depresses certain control functions and results in an apparent stimulating effect.
   b. *Low blood sugar* results in mood changes, irritability and apprehensive feelings.
   c. *Reduced diet,* and especially lack of vitamin B, produces lethargy, irritability and depression.
   d. *Disease* may affect personality directly by brain damage, or indirectly by inducing attitudes of dependency.

3. *Endocrine glands* deliver chemical substances, *hormones,* to the blood stream.
   a. The *thyroid* gland produces *thyroxin,* which maintains the rate of bodily metabolism. Lack of thyroxin in early development results in *cretinism;* in older persons, in *myxedema.*
   b. The *adrenal* gland manufactures two hormones. *Adrenin* produces a variety of internal bodily effects during emotional states. Deficiency in *cortin* results in weakness, loss of sex interest, and lowered metabolism. Overproduction of cortin results in exaggerated masculinity.
   c. The *gonads* secrete hormones which determine the development of secondary masculine or feminine characteristics, and the degree of sex interest.

d. The *pituitary* gland regulates the rate of growth; overactivity resulting in giants, underactivity in midgets.

e. The amount of secretion of the various glands is regulated by hormones from the pituitary, and a balance of all the hormones is necessary for normal functioning.

f. Although extreme overactivity and underactivity of a gland result in clear-cut personality changes, it is not definitely known whether normal personality differences are related to small variations in hormone output.

4. *The group code* is the set of conduct rules, manners, morals and folkways which are common to the group.

a. The group tends to enforce conformity to its code, with more or less latitude for individual deviation.

b. Social misfits are individuals who do not conform to the group code, and they are likely to have personality difficulties.

c. Children learn the group code gradually and progressively. Rules which are at first sanctioned by authority are later supported by social utility.

5. *Social roles* of various kinds are available in every group, and the individual tends to develop the personality which is appropriate to the role which he adopts.

a. The child's role in the family is determined largely by the parents. If the parents are over-solicitous and protective, the child may develop a dependent personality. If the parents are lacking in affection and harsh in punishment, the child may develop a defensive, negativistic personality.

b. The child's role in the gang may support or conflict with his role in the family.

c. Adult roles vary most with occupation and with social class.

6. *Improvement of personality* is a difficult task for which there are no cut and dried rules.

a. Experimental studies have shown that ascendance in children can be fostered by teaching them mastery of games and skills which their group values.

b. The treatment of personality difficulties is best undertaken by a thoroughly trained mental hygienist. Sometimes the person can work out his difficulty with such professional help; sometimes a change in environment is helpful.

7. The development of the individual is influenced by both physiological and social factors. The personality is not a sum of these factors, but rather a product of their interaction.

# CHAPTER SIX

# *Heredity and Environment as Causes of Individual Differences*

U p to this point in our study of individual differences in ability and personality we have been building up a knowledge of the facts without much attention to causes, and it is time now to round out the subject by looking into this question of causes. Why do people differ, what makes them different? If anyone should ask for *the* cause of individual differences, it would be impossible to answer his question, because there is not just one cause. Many causes or factors combine to make people differ. Physiological and social factors were noticed in the last chapter. We saw how people differ in personality because one is getting plenty of hormone from his thyroid gland while another is getting very little; and we saw how people develop different traits by filling different roles in the social group. But we can push the question farther back by asking what caused the glands to differ, and by asking what made two persons undertake their different social roles.

The numerous special factors that cause people to differ can be traced back to heredity and environment. The thyroid gland depends on the environment for a supply of iodin, and if very little iodin is available the individual will almost surely suffer from lack of the thyroid hormone. But that is not the whole story, for even in the same environment individuals differ, some having less active thyroid glands than others. People differ "naturally," i.e., by heredity, in this respect and in many other physiological characteristics. So a physiological cause of personality differences may itself be the result of both heredity and environment. Social factors, too, can be traced back to heredity and environment. Individuals differ in many cases because one has had better opportunities than another—an environmental factor—but even when given the same opportunities one person makes better use of them than another because he is better equipped by heredity to take advantage of what the environment has to offer.

Heredity covers all the factors that were present in the individual when he began life (not at birth but at the time of conception, about nine months before birth), while environment covers all the outside factors that have acted on him since that time. Between them, it would seem, heredity and environment must cover everything that can have any effect on the individual's life and development. But these factors combine and interact in so intricate a way that it is often impossible to distinguish the effects of heredity and environment.

## INTERACTION OF HEREDITY AND ENVIRONMENT

[Heredity consists of tendencies to develop in certain ways: to grow into a human being instead of some other kind of animal or plant, to become a blond or brunet person, tall or short, lively or quiet, etc. These hereditary tendencies are not left behind in infancy but are carried along through life] But they would come to naught unless provided with opportunity and stimulation from the environment. The hereditary tendency to form muscles would have no result if the environment supplied no food; and the muscles would not become strong if the environment afforded no opportunity for exercise. The muscles of an adult, then, are the result of heredity and environment combined; and the same is true of every part of his anatomy and of all his behavior.

The heredity of a plant is contained in the seed, while the environmental factors are soil, moisture, sunlight, weeds, etc. If you plant a cabbage seed and a tomato seed side by side, you get a cabbage plant from one and a tomato plant from the other, in spite of giving them the same environment. No amount of care will change one into the other. But cultivation can make the difference between a poor and a fine specimen of the same kind.

**Comparative importance of heredity and environment.** Sometimes you will hear people excitedly debating the question, "Which is more important, heredity or environment?" No wonder they become excited, for in this bald form the question is unanswerable and really absurd. It is like asking whether it is more important for an automobile to have an engine or some gas. If you want to raise cabbages, which is more important, to have some cabbage seed or to have a place to plant them? Without a proper environment the seed would not germinate and develop, and without seed there would be nothing to develop.

If you are thinking of a *single individual,* it makes no sense to ask whether heredity or environment is more important in his development and behavior. Each of them is absolutely essential.

Usually, however, when anyone asks whether heredity or environment is more important, his question really refers to *differences between individuals* or between groups. What he wants to know is whether people differ because their heredity is different or because they have had different environments. This question makes sense. One automobile might behave better than another because it had the better engine or because it was burning better gas. Two persons, like two cabbage plants, might be exactly the same in heredity and still develop differently because reared in different environments; and two persons reared in the same environment might develop differently, like seeds of different kinds, because of their different heredity. Yes, this form of the question makes sense, but it has no simple and easy answer.

**The individual as a product of heredity and environment.** The relation of heredity and environment is not like addition but more like multiplication. The individual does not = heredity + environment, but does equal heredity × environment. He is a product of the two factors, not a sum of certain parts due to heredity and other parts due to environment. We may represent heredity by the base of a rectangle, environment by the altitude, and the individual by the area of the rectangle, the product of base and altitude.

In considering any single individual, we cannot say that he is more the result of his heredity or of his environment, any more than the area of a rectangle depends more on the base or more on the altitude. If either should drop out there would be no area left. Both are absolutely essential.

But when we are comparing two or more individuals, represented by different rectangles, we see that they may differ in the heredity factor alone, in the environment factor alone, or in both factors. In Fig. 26 individuals A and B have equally good (or poor) environments but differ because of their un-

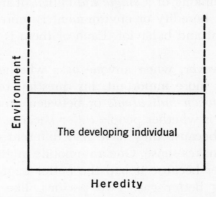

The developing individual

**Heredity**

FIG. 25.—The individual a product of heredity and environment. Increase the environmental stimulation (height of the rectangle) and you increase the area, but the hereditary factor (width) remains as important as ever.

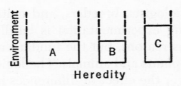

Fɪɢ. 26.—Individuals may differ because of differing heredity or because of differing environment. Thus A and B receive the same amount of
environmental stimulation, but differ (in area) because of their different
heredity; whereas B and C, though having the same heredity, differ because they receive different amounts of environmental stimulation. The
*size of the difference* between two individuals always depends on both
factors. Take A and B and double the environmental factor (height): you
double the amount of their difference (8). Let A be an elephant and B a
mouse. If food is scarce their weights differ by a certain number of pounds,
but if food becomes plentiful the elephant will gain more pounds than the
mouse and the absolute (not relative) difference in weight will be larger
than before.

For the same reason we should expect a naturally bright child and a
dull one to differ somewhat in knowledge even if brought up in a very
meager environment, but if the environment became richer and more stimulating the bright child would pick up more new knowledge than the dull
one, so that their stocks of knowledge would differ more than before. In
general, improving the environment for all alike should increase the
amount of individual differences.

equal heredity, while B and C have the same heredity but differ because of unequal environment.

Further study of the rectangles suggests that the following
statement would probably hold good: Improving the environment for all alike would not tend to make individuals equal.
It would not even diminish individual differences but would
increase them. For example, some children are naturally more
musical than others, but in an unmusical environment none of
them can develop much musical ability, while in a musical
environment the gifted ones may go far, leaving the unmusical
ones away in the rear. It would be the same with intelligence
or any special ability. It takes a rich, stimulating environment
to bring out the full extent of differences in heredity.

Two fundamental experiments on heredity and environment.
Modern knowledge of the effects of heredity and environment
on plants and animals is very extensive, thanks to numerous

experiments by biologists, breeders, and cultivators. In man's case thoroughgoing experimentation is hardly possible, for a number of obvious reasons, but the fundamental laws seem to be the same as in plants and animals. The logic of investigation is clear. To discover the effect of differences in heredity, make heredity your experimental variable, holding environment constant (p. 10). That is, take individuals of different heredity and expose them to identical environments; any difference that results must be due to heredity. Similarly, to investigate the influence of environment, take individuals of identical heredity and expose them to different environments. These two types of experiments have been tried many times and in various ways on plants and animals.

_Hybrids prove the importance of heredity in producing individual differences._ If a male of one species is mated with a female of a different (though necessarily similar) species, the offspring is known as a hybrid. With the male a donkey and the female a horse (mare), the offspring has the same prenatal environment as a normal horse and should therefore be born a horse, if only environment counts. But the offspring turns out to be a mule, differing considerably from a horse at birth and becoming more and more of a mule as he grows up. From this often-repeated experiment we learn:

1) that the difference between a horse and a mule is due to heredity, i.e., to the fact that the mule's father was a donkey and not a horse;

2) that creatures of different heredity are not made alike by developing in the same environment;

3) that hereditary differences come out more and more as development proceeds.

In a less striking way the same facts can be observed in human children whose parents differ, for the child does not (on the whole) "take after" his mother more than after his father, though his prenatal environment is so exclusively maternal. The environment does not "mold" him so as to eliminate his hereditary characteristics.

_Monsters prove the importance of environment in producing_

*individual differences.* If we give up the idea that the environment shapes the growing individual like a piece of putty so that development is a "molding" process, shall we swing to the opposite extreme and think of development as simply a process of "unfolding" the natural inherited characteristics of the individual? That this cannot be the true solution of our problem is proved by a second type of experiment in which an individual of normal heredity is subjected to an abnormal environment during the early stages of his development. Such experiments are difficult to carry out in the case of unborn mammals, but birds' eggs can be subjected to abnormal temperatures during incubation, and fish or frog eggs, which develop in water, can be heated or chilled or exposed to the action of chemicals, electricity, X-rays, etc. The result is often a "monster," an individual differing grossly from the norm of the species. In one experiment fish embryos, just at the developmental stage when the eyes are formed, were placed in the icebox for a few hours, with the result that the eyes were imperfectly formed, some individuals developing only a single eye. The difference between the one-eyed fish which developed in the cold and the two-eyed fish which develop under normal conditions was clearly due to the difference in environment (32).

## THE ACTION OF THE ENVIRONMENT

The environment influences the development of the individual in many different ways. The growth processes are necessarily dependent upon adequate supplies of oxygen, water and food and upon favorable environmental temperatures. The habits and skills of the person depend upon environmental situations permitting practice. The individual's knowledge depends on the teaching he has received, and his social attitudes depend on the social situations in which he has participated.

The effective environment. [Many things that are present in the environment have little effect on a given individual because they do not stimulate him to react or do anything.] He has no interest in them, he cannot use them. A field of luscious green grass would be a barren environment to a hungry dog, as a field full of rabbits would be to a cow. The environment is effective so far as it appeals to some need or interest of the individual and stimulates him to react in some way. What shall be effective depends on the individual, on his heredity, his previous experience, his chronological age and his mental age. A room full of adults absorbed in discussing politics is not a stimulating intellectual environment to a young child. You cannot tell whether a child has a good home environment simply by examining the home and family, with the child left out. You have to see the child in the home and notice his reactions. Two children in the same home do not necessarily have the same effective environment, and the more the children differ from each other the greater difference there is in their environments. This important point will come out more clearly later in the chapter.

**How environment can iron out individual differences.** According to our previous reasoning (p. 159) individuals of differing heredity are, not made alike by exposure to the same environment. In order to make them equal in ability we should have to *compensate* for the greater capacity of the one by giving the other more stimulation, more intensive training. In many schools certain ground is assigned to be covered in a certain grade. Some of the children master this material easily, others only with difficulty. The teacher labors with the laggards to bring them up to grade and is thankful that the bright ones need no special attention. At the end of the year most of the children have about equal mastery of the assigned material. Individual differences have been ironed out to a certain extent by applying unequal social pressure. In schools that encourage each child to advance at his own pace, individual differences have a clear field and come out strongly. Free, unlimited opportunity favors individual differences, while restricted opportunity tends toward regimentation of ability. In many other ways the social group sets up standards of conduct —quite moderate standards—and enforces conformity with the standards by using pressure where it is needed. Unequal environmental pressure compensates in some measure for inequalities in heredity.

Regimentation operates on personality traits as well as on abilities. George, let us say, is inclined to be overactive and boisterous, and his parents try to calm him down. His brother John is almost too quiet and they try to wake him up. So the two boys are brought somewhere near a uniform standard of motor activity, at least in the home. Outside, their natural tendencies may still show themselves. In a group of playmates, Mary is ridiculed for excessive timidity while Ruth is criticized for taking foolish risks, and so the group brings its members toward a common standard of visible behavior, though the natural tendencies may still persist and create different personal problems for different individuals.

**Summary on effects of environment.** While the environment does not force the individual into a mold as if he were passive in the process of development, it does provide opportunity and stimulation. Anything in the environment to which the individual does not react is not part of his effective environment. What shall be effective depends on the needs, tendencies and capacities of the individual. So the same objective environment will have different effects on differently constituted individuals. Individual differences are due to environment when individuals having the same heredity are subjected to different environments. But individuals of differing heredity are not made alike by exposure to the same environment. They can be made alike (in some respects) by unequal environmental pressures compensating for their unequal heredities. For the most part, individual differences are the result of heredity and environment combined.

## HEREDITY

We should not be contented with vague, abstract ideas about heredity. What we have said so far about it is rather abstract, even though perfectly logical. In the same environment, we said, individuals of differing heredity will develop differently and come out with unequal abilities and various personalities. Yes, but do individuals actually differ in heredity? What is heredity as a concrete biological fact? To obtain the answers to such questions we appeal to the biological science of *genetics*, a science which has made remarkable advances during the present century (*9, 13, 26, 33*).

**Heredity in the cells of the body.** Each individual plant or animal begins life as a single cell. The human individual begins as a tiny egg, the fertilized ovum, about $\frac{1}{200}$ of an inch in diameter. This single cell has been formed by the union of an ovum from the mother's ovary with a spermatozoon from the father. In the protected environment of the mother's womb the fertilized ovum grows and divides into 2 cells, these into 4, these into 8, 16, 32, and so on up into the millions and billions. Though all descended from the fertilized ovum, these cells develop differently, some becoming muscle cells, some gland cells, some nerve cells, and so on.

Each cell contains a small *nucleus* which differs chemically and physiologically from the rest of the cell body. While the rest of the cell body does the work of contracting in the case of the muscle cell, secreting in the case of the gland cell, or conducting in the case of the nerve cell, the nucleus takes the lead in growth and cell division and in maintaining the life and vigor of the cell. The nucleus of the fertilized ovum grows and divides into two nuclei, one for each of the two cells formed by division of the fertilized ovum; and the same thing happens in every cell division. The result is that every cell in the body contains a nucleus descended from the nucleus of the fertilized ovum. Concretely, an individual's heredity consists of his billions of cell nuclei, all descended from the nucleus of the fertilized ovum, which was formed by the union of two nuclei, one from each parent.

We already have three important points on heredity: (1) the child's heredity is derived from both his parents; (2) it is fixed and determined at the moment of fertilization or conception —no additional heredity can get into him later, even from the mother who carries him and provides his nourishment for the next nine months; (3) his heredity pervades his entire organism, being present in every one of his cells.

**The chromosomes.**   The nucleus contains little rod-like bodies called chromosomes, some of them longer and some shorter, some straight and some curved, but always the same number of them in all the cells of the same individual and in all the individuals of the same species. Every human cell contains 48 chromosomes; in some animals and plants the number is much smaller or even much larger than this. In cell division, each chromosome splits into two duplicates, one going to each of the two resulting cells, so that every cell of the human body contains 48 chromosomes, descended from those of the fertilized ovum.

Instead of speaking of 48 human chromosomes, it is better to speak of 24 pairs; the fact that they come in pairs is very important. The nucleus of the fertilized ovum, then, contains

Fig. 27.—Two sets of human chromosomes, male in the upper line, female in the lower. The 24 pairs are here arranged in order of size. (Their arrangement in the nucleus of a cell is much less regular.) For convenience they may be lettered: two A's, two B's, etc., but the last pair is designated X and Y, Y being the little one. Every male person has the XY pair, every female a double X. (Evans & Swesy, *11*.)

The mother's ovum before fertilization and the father's spermatozoon have only 24 chromosomes each, one of each pair; so their combination, the fertilized ovum, gets the full 48, two of each pair.

Since the female carries only the X and never the Y chromosome, every one of the many ova she produces contains the X. The male carries the XY pair, and half of his millions of spermatozoa contain X and half Y. The sex of a child, then, depends on whether an X or a Y spermatozoon gets to the ovum first and unites with it. The chances are about even, though it appears that the Y spermatozoa do somewhat better, since there are about 120 male to 100 female fertilized ova. The mortality is higher among the males; at the time of birth there are only 105 boys to 100 girls, a few years later the numbers are equal, and in old age there are more women than men surviving. Maybe Y is livelier than X but less tenacious of life. At any rate the hereditary difference between the sexes is the difference between X and Y.

24 pairs of chromosomes. Tracing these back we discover a remarkable fact. One chromosome of each pair came from the spermatozoon, while the other was present in the ovum before fertilization. The child gets one chromosome of each pair from his father and the other from his mother.

**The genes, elementary factors in heredity.** A child's father may have blue eyes and a slender build, while the mother is stocky and brown-eyed; and the child may be slender and brown-eyed, inheriting one trait from the father and another from the mother. The elementary genetic factors, or genes, were first discovered by comparison of parents and children when the parents were different in certain respects. (The "parents" and "children" in most of this research work are animals or plants rather than human beings.) Later it was found possible to localize certain genes in certain chromosomes, and even in certain parts of a chromosome. Examined under the high powers of the microscope a chromosome is somewhat like a string of beads, and essentially it is a string of genes arranged in a definite order. The human genes probably number a thousand or more, distributed unequally among the 48 chromosomes. The genes, like the chromosomes, come in pairs, one gene of each pair from the father and the other from the mother.

**Alternative genes.** For the most part the genes of a given pair are alike and give rise to the resemblances rather than the differences between parents and child; the resemblances greatly outnumber the differences. But in certain pairs the genes may differ, one tending to produce brown eyes, for example, while the other tends to produce blue eyes. If a child has a pair of the brown-eye genes, one from each parent, he will have brown eyes; if each parent has given him a blue-eye gene, he will have blue eyes; but if he got a brown-eye gene from one parent and a blue-eye gene from the other, his eyes will be more or less brown, for the brown-eye gene is dominant over the blue-eye gene.

**Mixed populations.** In an isolated mountain valley, let us suppose, there is a pure-bred population of brown-eyed people. They all have brown eyes, as all their ancestors have had for

many generations. Every individual in that valley has a pair
of brown-eye genes. In another valley there is a similar isolated
group, all with blue eyes, every individual possessing a pair of
blue-eye genes. Now let inter-marriage occur between the two
stocks. Let a dozen couples, a brown-eyed and a blue-eyed
person in each couple (first generation), colonize a third valley
and start a new population there. Every one of their children
(second generation) has a blue-brown gene pair and therefore
eyes that are more or less brown. When these children marry
among themselves, a curious thing happens: about a quarter of
their children (third generation) have blue eyes. The reason
is clear when we consider that a child in this generation has
a 50–50 chance of getting a blue-eye gene from his father,
and a 50–50 chance of getting a blue-eye gene from his mother,
so that his chance of getting two blue-eye genes and being
blue-eyed are 1 in 4. Now let the people of this third valley
marry among themselves freely generation after generation,
and we shall find brown eyes always more numerous but blue
eyes continually appearing in some of the children. Nations are
mixed populations with respect to many traits such as eye
color, hair color, size, body build, vigor and mental capacity.
Alternative genes for these traits are present in the population,
the gene pairs differ from individual to individual, and consequently the individuals differ in these traits.

**Trying to infer a child's heredity from a study of his parents.**
The word "heredity" is somewhat misleading since it makes us
think of the parents instead of the child's own assortment of
genes. If both parents are brown-eyed we are apt to assume
that "by heredity" the child should have brown eyes, while he
may have got a blue-eye gene from each parent and so be
blue-eyed, strictly by heredity. The child gets all his genes
from his parents but his assortment differs from that of either
parent, from that of any of his brothers or sisters, and even
from that of any other individual anywhere, for the number
of possible combinations of genes is practically infinite. The
child's heredity is his own unique combination of genes.

You wish, for example, to predict how tall the child of certain parents will be. This trait of stature depends in part on such environmental factors as nutrition, disease and injury, and allowance must be made for these factors. Stature depends on the genes, too, but not on a single pair of genes. It takes several pairs to make the difference between a very short person and a very tall one. Most individuals carry some genes for tallness along with some for shortness, so that the children of a given couple get different assortments of the stature genes. On the whole, the taller the parents the more tallness genes they pass on to their children, and the taller their children will *average*, but prediction for a single child is never sure but only a matter of probabilities.

Many other important human traits, including vigor and intelligence, depend on several gene pairs, and on environmental factors as well, so that prediction from parents to children is subject to the same difficulties as in the case of stature.

**Are acquired characteristics passed on by heredity?** An older theory of evolution assumed that changes produced in the individual by his environment and by his own activities could be passed on to his children and accumulate in successive generations. In spite of many attempts to find evidence favoring this theory, none has been found and the theory has been abandoned by biologists. With our modern knowledge of the mechanism of heredity it seems almost impossible that acquired characteristics could be inherited. If a man and his wife both develop horny hands by manual labor, how can that change in the skin have any effect on the genes in their gonads? As a matter of fact it has no effect on the skin of their children. If you learn to speak a language, can you pass this knowledge on to your child by way of the genes? There is no sign of any such result. You can pass on your knowledge and skill and your good or bad habits to your child by teaching him and setting him a good or bad example, but not by way of heredity. Even diseases such as tuberculosis or syphilis, which are often seen to run in families, are not transmitted by way of the genes. The child catches the disease by exposure to infection in the home environment.

## DIFFERENCES IN INTELLIGENCE AND
## PERSONALITY

The question whether individual differences in intelligence are due to heredity or to environment has been much debated in recent years (42). A similar question regarding the causes of personality differences is equally important but not so much studied, largely because of the difficulty of measuring personality. These are fascinating scientific problems and also have obvious practical bearings. If superiority and inferiority are due mostly to heredity, the best hope for the future of mankind lies in improving the human stock as far as possible and certainly not allowing it to degenerate. But if differences are due mostly to environment, society should continue to concentrate its efforts on providing for the population better nutrition and hygiene, better education, and better working conditions, recreational facilities and environmental opportunities of all kinds. Those who are called "environmentalists" lay stress on improving the environment. They believe their view is the most hopeful one. The extreme environmentalists go so far as to assert that heredity counts for very little in human affairs. Any healthy baby, they say, could be given superior personality and ability by suitable training and influences. This would indeed be a hopeful view to take if they could point out the influences and methods of training required to produce the desired results. But if they were actually given the job of developing any baby into a great artist or scientist or statesman, they would soon admit that their knowledge of environmental factors was much too scanty for undertaking any such task.

To the hereditarian the view just stated smacks strongly of wishful thinking. Impressed by the facts of biological heredity he argues that the importance of the genes must not be overlooked. The extreme hereditarians doubt whether any kind of training or influence can raise the child's IQ appreciably or change his fundamental personality.

There are really two questions before us: (1) whether suitable environmental factors can raise the IQ or improve the personality, and (2) whether the differences that we actually find present among individuals are due to heredity or to environment, or to both.

Even if we are willing to grant that differences are due to both, the question remains whether heredity or environment is more important. The answer cannot be had by simply observing people as we find them in the community, because the hereditary and environmental factors are so jumbled together. Some sort of experiment is needed.

The logic of investigation is the same as in the biological experiments described earlier in the chapter (pp. 159–161). To bring out differences due to heredity, we must take children who differ in heredity and bring them up in the same environment; and to bring out the effects of environment, we must take individuals of the same heredity and subject them to different environments. Clean-cut experiments such as are made on plants and animals are scarcely to be expected. We have to be satisfied with approximations to a true experimental setup.

It is easy to find children who presumably differ in heredity, but how shall we provide them with the same environment? Some approximation to uniform environment is found in an orphanage or even in an ordinary family.

Some approximation to the other type of experiment, with individuals of the same heredity exposed to different environments, is found in the case of identical twins, especially when separated and brought up in different families, and in the case of individuals who are taken from their own parents and brought up in foster homes.

The orphanage.   Children who certainly differ in heredity, since they are from many different parents, are brought up together in the same home. We might expect the children who are reared in the same orphanage to be very uniform in intelligence. As a matter of fact, when tested, they differ in IQ almost as much as the children of an average community. The orphanage does not make them all alike in intelligence, or in personality either. This result would seem to dispose of the view of the extreme environmentalist who believes that all individuals are equal in native capacity and that differences in ability are due entirely to environment. He can raise a reasonable objection to the experimental set-up, however. He can say that the same orphanage is not necessarily the same *effective* environment for all the children in it, for the children are not all treated exactly alike (*39*).

The family.   Children of the same parents—*siblings,* as they are called to include brothers and sisters—have sometimes been supposed to have the same heredity, but we have already seen that they differ in their genes, though they are more alike in this respect than children of different families. A family of children, then, consists of siblings of somewhat unlike heredity, brought up in the same home. Will they all be equal in intelligence?

No one would expect to find siblings always exactly the same in intelligence, any more than in other ways, but careful investigation is necessary to find out how much they differ from each other and from their parents. In one investigation over fifty families were tested, each consisting of the parents and at least four children. The IQs are shown in Fig. 28. Several facts can be made out from the figure:

1. It is easy to see that in almost every family the children differ considerably from each other and from their parents.

2. On the whole the more intelligent parents have the more intelligent children. The correlation between a parent and his or her child is +.58.

3. Careful study of the figure will reveal that the children of the most intelligent parents tend to fall below their parents, while the reverse is true of the children of the least intelligent parents. When the two parents average over 110 IQ, only 35 percent of their children surpass them; but when the two parents average less than 90 IQ, 80 percent of their children surpass them.

All these results conform to what would be expected from heredity. Several gene-pairs are concerned in making the difference between the lowest and the highest grade of intelligence. The question is not whether an individual has *the* intelligence-

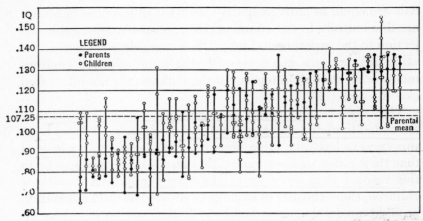

Fᵢɢ. 28.—The IQs of parents and children. (Data from Outhit, 23). Each line shows the distribution of IQs in a single family including both parents and at least four children. Besides the facts brought out in the text, there is one more that can be seen in the Figure: the IQs of the father and mother are usually rather close together. The correlation between father's and Mother's IQ in this sample is + .74. This is an example of "homogamy," of like marrying like. An effect of homogamy is to make the children of the same family more alike, and the children of different families more different, than they would otherwise be. There is some homogamy also in personality traits, though not as much as in intelligence (3).

gene or not, but *how many* of the intelligence-genes he has. One child may get more than another child of the same parents. The more of them the parents carry, the better the child's chance of getting a good supply. And whenever an individual has a very large number of these genes, his child or parent or sibling is likely to have a smaller number; or, if a certain individual has a very small number, the chances are that his child, parent or sibling has more.

So far, we should be inclined to draw the conclusion that siblings differ because of their differing genes, since the genes would explain the facts while the environment seems to be the same for the children in the same home. But is the same home the same effective environment for all the children there? No. The parents do not treat them all alike. One child has older brothers and sisters while another has younger ones—which sometimes makes quite a difference to the child. And outside of the home circle, one child is likely to have different friends, to visit different homes, to have different teachers.

Besides, it can fairly be said that each individual selects his own effective environment to a very large extent. Siblings differing in heredity will show different preferences in choosing toys, games, companions, reading matter, radio programs. The one of friendly disposition will find friends, while the quarrelsome one makes enemies, and thus they create very different personal environments for themselves. One learns to read easily, enjoys reading and so gets acquainted with the environment as it is presented in books; while another has difficulty in learning to read and much prefers to do things with his hands or to get acquainted with the things and people in the neighborhood.

With regard to families, then—to sum up what has been said —siblings differ among themselves in heredity, though less than unrelated children differ. They also differ in home environment—effective home environment—though this, too, is on the whole more alike for them than for unrelated children. With the effects of heredity and environment interacting as they do, the fact that siblings differ in intelligence does not by itself prove much for either the environmentalist or the hereditarian.

**Twins, identical and fraternal.** Though siblings do not generally have the same heredity, some twins are an exception. It sometimes happens that two individuals are derived from the same fertilized ovum; the embryo splits at a very early stage of development and gives rise to two individuals. Since all the cells derived from a given fertilized ovum have exactly the same genes, these two individuals have identical heredity. At birth they usually resemble each other so closely as to be barely distinguishable, and their physical resemblance becomes more striking as they grow up. These are the one-egg or *identical* twins (21).

The majority of twin pairs, called *fraternal* or two-egg twins, are twins simply because two separate ova were fertilized, each by a different spermatozoon, at practically the same time. They

Wide World Photos

Fig. 29.—Two pairs of identical twins.

have no more in common, so far as heredity is concerned, than other siblings. Fraternal twins are boy-girl pairs as often as of the same sex, while identicals are necessarily of the same sex, female or male according as the fertilized ovum was XX or XY.

Identical twins, when tested, prove to be much more alike in intelligence than fraternal twins or than other siblings. The following table gives the net result of many investigations, the two individuals compared being of the same sex in each case.

AVERAGE DIFFERENCE IN IQ POINTS

| Between Identical Twins | Between Fraternal Twins | Between Brothers or Sisters | Between Unrelated Individuals |
|---|---|---|---|
| 5 | 9 | 11 | 15 |

We see that the identicals differ no more from each other than the *same individual* commonly differs from himself in repeated tests (p. 48). There is nothing in the averages to show that identical twins differ *at all* in intelligence, though they certainly do in exceptional cases, as when one twin has suffered some brain injury. The results in the table conform very well to what would be expected from heredity, except for the fact that fraternals are a little more alike than other siblings. Since fraternals have no more genes in common than other siblings, their closer resemblance must be an effect of environment. They do have more environment in common than most siblings, being exposed simultaneously to the same home and school influences (and usually being tested at the same age as is usually not the case with the sibling pairs). We must also recognize that the environment is more alike for identicals than for fraternal twins, because two children who are themselves alike will be treated alike and will tend to select the same environment. Identicals are together more than fraternals and are more likely to have the same chums and to like the same games and the same school subjects (38). So the environmentalist can argue that the facts conform perfectly to his theory: the environment differs least for identicals, next for fraternals, then for siblings, and most for children from different families; and the IQ differences correspond. The data so far considered do not enable us to throw out either of the rival theories.

**Identical twins reared apart.**   If we were planning an experiment on the psychological effects of environment, we could not do better than to have identical twins separated in infancy and brought up in different homes. We would keep track of these twins and examine and test them at suitable intervals. We would make their environments very different in the particular environmental factors we wished to try out. If we were interested in the factor of schooling we would carry one twin of each pair along through high school and college while the other one was given only the first three grades. If we wished to study the effect on personality development of being reared as an only child, we would place one twin in an otherwise childless home, the other one in a family with several other children.

No such carefully planned experiment has been carried out, but there are probably many pairs of identical twins who have been separated in early childhood and brought up in different environments. By the strenuous efforts of investigators more than twenty such pairs have been discovered and their abilities sampled by tests during adolescence or adult life (22). In several instances the twins grew up in ignorance of each other's existence and only discovered each other because their close resemblance had attracted someone's attention.

In some instances one twin had a much more friendly home than the other, or one twin had travelled a great deal while the other had always lived in the same town. In a few cases one of the twins received much more schooling than the other. One girl went through college and became a school teacher, while her twin grew up largely in the backwoods and had only two years of regular schooling though she later obtained a good business and clerical job in a large city. Her IQ at the age of 35 years was 92, while that of her college-educated twin was 116. This difference of 24 points in IQ is the largest yet found between identical twins. In five other cases that have been tested, one twin received much more schooling than the other. On the average of the six cases, the better-educated twin had an IQ 13 points higher than the other one. It appears, then, that a fairly large difference in education can produce a fairly large difference in tested intelligence.

But how much will identical twins differ in IQ when they have been brought up in different homes but without much difference in amount of schooling? The difference found runs from 1 to 15 points, with an average of 5 points. They differ no more than identicals reared together or than the same individual commonly differs from himself on retest. This is strong evidence against the extreme environmentalist view. If the differences which we find among the children of a community were due to their differing home environments, children of the same heredity placed in different homes should differ on the average by as much as 15 points (see the Table on p. 174) instead of 5 points.

The evidence from separated identicals cannot be regarded as conclusive, because of the small number of such pairs so far discovered and tested. Yet it tends to disprove the extreme views of both the environmentalists and the hereditarians. The evidence is worth restating. The extreme environmental hypothesis is that the children of a community differ in IQ because of their differing environments, largely home environments, and that if the children of the community were all identical in heredity they would still differ just as they do now because of the differing home environments. This hypothesis is tested by taking pairs of identical heredity and rearing them in different homes. The separated pairs should be found later to differ by an average of 15 points in IQ, but they actually differ by an average of only 5 points. We can therefore rule out the extreme environmental explanation of individual differences in intelligence.

The extreme hereditarian view would be that each individual's IQ is fixed by his heredity and cannot be raised by education or any other environmental influence. It could be lowered, of course, by such an environmental cause as brain injury during birth—everyone would have to grant that—but it could not be lowered by lack of education or by a dull, unstimulating environment such as that of the backwoods or the ordinary orphanage. In opposition to this view we have the case of the girl brought up in the backwoods with little schooling who obtained an IQ of only 92 while her twin got 116. Since the two had the same heredity, the backwoods girl was capable of reaching the same IQ as her sister. In the case of another identical pair of girls, one was reared on a farm and had only eight grades of school, while the other lived in a small city and went through high school; the farm girl's IQ came out at 89 and the city girl's at 106. Though only a few such cases have been found there are enough of them to make it practically certain that a large difference in education can make a considerable difference in the IQ. Although there is some question whether our present intelligence tests are broad enough to give the backwoods girl and the farm girl a fair chance, we can safely conclude that education and environmental opportunity can stimulate intellectual activity, steer it into useful channels, and so practically raise the level of intelligence not of a few individuals only but of the whole population. Improving the environment would raise the general level of intelligence in the population, but it would not make the individuals all alike. Instead of doing so it would tend to make them more unlike, because the differences in heredity would have more chance to express themselves fully, as we saw before in discussing our "rectangles" (p. 159).

As regards the effect of environment on personality, the studies of separated identicals have not succeeded in proving anything very definite. The general impression of investigators who got to know the separated pairs is that their social attitudes are sometimes quite different while their temperaments seem not to have been affected by their different social environments. The college-educated school teacher had a polished manner, was careful of her personal appearance and took pains to make a favorable impression; while her twin from the backwoods and later in a business job was "all business, without social charm or concern about how she impressed others." Another pair (6) were temperamentally very active, talkative, impulsive, irritable, fond of outdoor sports, and these traits remained the same for both up to the age of 18 at least. One twin had been reared in a more sociable family and was herself much more sociable at the age of 12, though her twin seemed to be catching up with her in this respect by the age of 18. Both of these girls lacked perseverance as children, but one had much more training than the other in perseverance and responsibility, and this difference in their training showed results by the age of 18.

**Improving personality and intelligence by improving the environment.** One sure way, it would seem, to keep heredity constant is to expose the same individual first to an unfavorable environment and then to one that is more favorable. If we could transfer a group of children from a dull to a more stimulating environment, their IQs should be raised. The question would be how much we could accomplish in this way. There is a difficulty due to the fact that a young child does not always show all of his inherent personality traits, nor all of his assets in the way of intelligence. The abilities which depend on the use of language are very important factors in the intelligence of older children and adults. Before the child learns to talk we cannot test these abilities, and for that reason intelligence tests of a very young child are of little value in predicting how intelligent he will become during school age and later. Though the same individual certainly carries the same genes throughout life, it does not follow that all these genes come into play in the early years. Consequently this line of investigation is not quite so simple as it seems at first sight.

Yet we have some good evidence that improving the environment will improve a child's personality or intelligence. In the previous chapter (pp. 143–147) we saw how certain training helped children to overcome their shyness and timidity, their distrust of other people, and their tendencies to lie and steal. Such social traits were much affected by the social environments, although the more physiological and temperamental traits remained about as they were. Glandular treatment is sometimes useful in improving the temperamental traits.

In a neglected neighborhood in Chicago the boys had a very bad record for lawless behavior. Giving them the use of a playground and meeting place eliminated most of the lawlessness (28). Improving the schools in a mountain region of Tennessee was followed by a rise in the average IQ of the children in that region (37).

**Foster children.**   The orphans and other dependent children who come into the hands of child-placing agencies are in the main from relatively inferior homes and are placed in relatively superior homes. The agencies are careful to place children only where they will be well treated. The agencies are careful, too, not to place for adoption any child who is apparently feebleminded or abnormal. A couple wishing to adopt a child are naturally concerned to know whether they should look into the child's heredity or whether they can depend on themselves, and on the good home and education which they will provide, to produce an intelligent child of good character and personality.

Follow-up studies of foster children show that they turn out quite well, better than their own parents on the whole. For example, if a child's own father or mother was alcoholic, the child himself after being brought up in a good foster home seldom shows any tendency towards alcoholism (24).

As to intelligence, the average IQ of several samples of foster children (in Chicago, 12; California, 4; Minnesota, 18) has proved to be about 105 or 110 when these children were tested after being adopted as babies and living several years in good foster homes. Their own parents were not tested but from what is known of them their average IQ would probably be about 100. If the parents averaged 100 we should expect the children to average 100 also, and their extra 5–10 points can reasonably be laid to the good influence of their foster homes and parents. In a sample of foster children in Toronto all the own mothers (though not the fathers) were tested and found to have an average IQ of 84. The children after several years in their foster homes had an average IQ of 98. Here we should expect the children to surpass their mothers since the mothers stood so low (as explained on p. 172), but we should expect them to average about 92 instead of 98, so that there is a margin of 6 points to credit to the influence of the foster home.

In the Chicago study of foster children, and also in an Iowa study (29, 30), quite a number of children whose own mothers were almost or quite feebleminded were tested after several years in foster homes, and many of these children were found to have average intelligence or better. Shall we say that a good environment has enabled these children to develop good intelligence "in spite of poor heredity"? There is a temptation to say this, but it is illogical, for certainly no one can develop beyond what his heredity makes possible. If a child develops an IQ of 110, he certainly had the native capacity to do so. We cannot say that a child does well in spite of poor heredity, but we can say that he does well in spite of poor or inferior parentage. We have already noticed two main reasons why a child's own individual heredity—his genes—cannot be judged with certainty from a knowledge of his parents. The first reason is that the child's stock of genes is a new combination, differing from that of either of his parents. The second reason is that the parents themselves may have suffered from some environmental handicap and so have fallen short of their hereditary possibilities. The mother, in a few cases, might have suffered a brain injury, which is one cause of feeblemindedness. More often the mother grew up in an unfavorable environment and failed to measure up to her genes.

But if we cannot surely judge a child's heredity from his parentage, how can we judge it? There is only one sure way—Give him a chance! Make sure, as far as possible, that he has the advantages of a good home, neighborhood and school. Be on the watch for any signs of unusual intelligence or special ability, and keep on giving him a chance! When this is done, children of "inferior" parents will often develop quite desirable personality traits and good intelligence. So much at least has been proved by the environmentalists. This does not prove the unimportance of heredity in making individuals differ, but it does prove the importance of environment.

## GROUP DIFFERENCES

Human beings exist not simply as individuals but also as groups of individuals: families, religious and occupational groups, races, and nations. Do groups differ one from another as we have found individuals to differ? In considering this question we must take account not only of group averages but also of the distribution of individuals within each group. As a general rule, individuals differ more widely than groups. Our figure on page 172 shows clearly that different families differ in IQ; the average is definitely higher in some families than in others. But notice also the distribution of individuals in each family and the overlap of different families. Some members of the lower-averaging family do as well as some members of the higher-averaging family. What is true of families is true of other groups: one group may surpass another group on the average, but the overlap is often large and important.

**Urban and rural intelligence.**  While city children average 100 in IQ, or a little higher, country children have usually

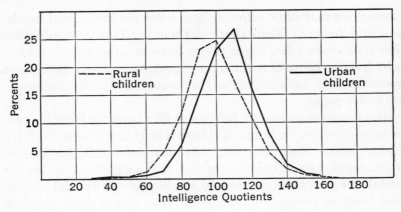

FIG. 30.—IQ distributions of urban and of rural children. (Terman and Merrill, 35.)

given an average of 90–95, with of course a large amount of overlapping. The difference, such as it is, may be due in part to heredity, since able young people often migrate to the city to enter the more intellectual occupations, and their children have a good chance of getting better than average genes. On the side of environment, city children are apt to get better schooling which would give them some advantage in taking the intelligence tests. When children of the same heredity, i.e., separated identical twins, are reared in the city and the country, the city child usually shows a higher IQ, especially if his education has been more extensive. But where the country schools are kept up to a high standard, country children may average just as high as city children. This is the result obtained in Scotland on testing all the children born on four specified days in 1926. They were tested when 9–11 years old, and the average IQ of these 874 children was 100, with the city and country children almost exactly equal (19).

City people are apt to assume that the city, quite apart from its superior schools, is a more stimulating intellectual environment than the country; but this has never been shown to be true. The majority of the men included in Who's Who in America were born in cities and towns, and yet about 23 percent of them were born on farms, and sometimes the rural environment was distinctly stimulating, especially to boys with a scientific bent (36). The country child's mind may be as active as the city child's, though occupied with different things; and the intelligence tests, prepared as they are by city psychologists, may unintentionally favor the city child. Notice the following test item, a disarranged sentence to be put in order:

*for the started an we country early at hour*

It makes better sense to the city child than to the country child. A few test items that are foreign to the child's environment may throw his IQ down by as much as 5 or 10 points. It is very difficult, if not impossible, to prepare a test that shall be equally fair to persons from different environments (16). Even the differences found between occupational groups may be *partly* spurious, because the tests may unintentionally favor the professional people in comparison with those engaged in mechanical and outdoor work.

**Occupational differences in intelligence.** Because of the different demands of different occupations, we should expect to find occupational differences in intelligence, and we do find on the average that professional men score the highest in intelligence tests, bookkeepers and stenographers rather high, mechanics moderately high, and unskilled laborers lowest (Fig. 31). What we should not expect, and what is really very surprising, is the wide range of intelligence found in every occupation, with the extensive overlapping of the different occupations. The spread of intelligence scores is enormous in each occupation. A small percent of the professional men get low scores, and a small percent of the laboring men get high scores. A "small percent" of a large group like the laborers means of course a large number of individuals (2, 14).

Now here is a challenging fact: children grade off more or less according to the occupations of their fathers. The children of professional men and executives score highest in an intelligence test, the children of unskilled laborers lowest. This gradation of the children has been found to exist in many localities

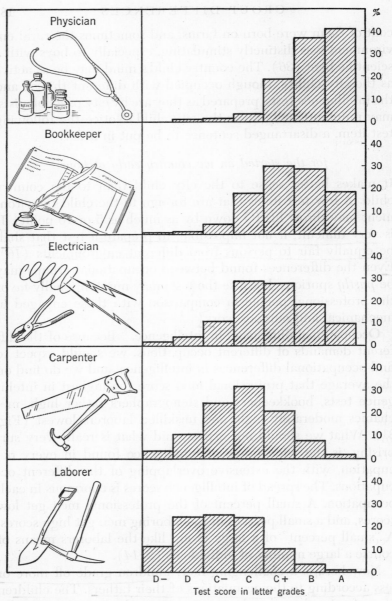

FIG. 31.—Intelligence in different occupations, according to the Army tests of 1917–18. Two facts stand out clearly: the higher scores in the more intellectual occupations, and the large overlapping of all the occupations. (Data from Yerkes, *43*.)

and in different countries. A good sample of the results is shown
in the following table.

IQ AVERAGES OF CHILDREN WHOSE FATHERS ARE IN VARIOUS
OCCUPATIONAL GROUPS

| Occupation of Father | Average IQ of Child |
|---|---|
| Professional | 116 |
| Semiprofessional and managerial | 111 |
| Clerical, skilled trades and retail business | 107 |
| Semiskilled, minor clerical, and minor business | 104 |
| Slightly skilled | 99 |
| Day laborers | 96 |

These are the averages obtained by Terman and Merrill (see p. 37)
in their large sample of the white U.S. population. Similar occupational differences have been found in our colored children and also in
Japan and in several European countries.

Though the table shows true differences between the occupational groups, the figures are misleading unless we bear
in mind that they are simply averages, and that the children in
each group scatter widely. Bright children and dull children are
found in every occupational group. The distributions of the
children overlap even more widely than those of the fathers
shown in Fig. 31. The total number of bright children coming from the less intellectual occupations is very large, even
though the more intellectual occupations supply more than
their quota of bright children and especially of the very brightest (7, 34).

Now why should the children from certain occupations have
a higher IQ on the average than the children from certain other
occupations? Is it because of heredity, the more intelligent
parents passing on a better supply of intelligence genes to their
children? Or is it because the more intelligent parents provide
a more stimulating intellectual environment for their children?
The mere fact that the children resemble their parents intellectually proves nothing for either heredity or environment,
since the parents who pass on good heredity usually provide

good environment as well. Something can be learned here from foster children adopted by parents belonging to different occupations. On the whole foster children adopted by professional people show a slightly higher average IQ than those adopted by skilled workmen. But there is less difference between the adopted children than between the own children from different occupational groups. The results obtained in the California study of foster children (see p. 180) are shown in the following table, and the results from the Minnesota study were about the same.

AVERAGE IQ OF FATHERS AND OF OWN AND ADOPTED CHILDREN

| Occupation of Fathers | IQ of Fathers | IQ of Own Children | IQ of Adopted Children |
|---|---|---|---|
| Professional | 123 | 119 | 109 |
| Semiprofessional, etc. | 119 | 119 | 109 |
| Lower Business | 110 | 116 | 108 |
| Skilled Labor | 101 | 106 | 105 |

The adopted children and the own children were not from the same homes, but they were from homes matched for father's occupation and for general goodness of the home (5).

The table shows that the fathers differ more from group to group than their own children and much more than their adopted children. From the highest to the lowest group the fathers differ by 22 points (on the average), the own children by 13 points, the foster children by only 4 points. The foster children differ slightly because of environment alone, the own children differ more because of heredity and environment combined. According to these and other similar results, both heredity and environment are factors tending to produce occupational differences in the intelligence of children, heredity being at least as potent a factor as environment. But even in the case of the own children, the occupational differences are rather small compared with the whole range of individual IQs extending from below 50 to over 150. A large share of the bright children of the nation come from the large middle occupational groups.

**Race differences.** The belief that races and nations are unequal in ability and general excellence is almost universal throughout the world, each race or nation being firmly convinced of its own superiority! These irrational beliefs cause friction between nations and between different races making up the population of each nation. If science could knock the props from under these old prejudices, it would be all to the good. However, we cannot command science to prove race equality, any more than race inequality. Science has to find the facts. The scientist, to be of any value to society, must avoid wishful thinking and report the truth as far as he has discovered it, without pretending to know more than he actually does know.

Race superiority should mean better heredity, better genes in one race than in another. Popular beliefs are not very clear on this point. When people speak of racial superiority they often mean what could better be called "cultural superiority," i.e., superiority in art, literature, science, industry, government, religion, manners and customs and standard of living. Friction between groups arises from cultural prejudice as well as from race prejudice. The assumption that "our own" culture is superior in all respects is as irrational as race prejudice. Anthropological study of various cultures leads to a broad and tolerant view of mankind in general.

Cultural superiority might of course be due to racial superiority. The race with the best genes would develop the best civilization, other things being equal. But other things have never been equal. The Eskimo and the Mexican Indians could not be expected to develop the same culture. Climate and other environmental factors differ for different races, and the contacts of one group with another have been very important, since culture spreads from group to group. Superior civilization is no proof of superior genes, because no nation has created its own civilization "out of whole cloth." The greatest nations have been the greatest borrowers. The ancient Greeks borrowed the alphabet from the Phoenicians and the rudiments of their art from the Egyptians. So, though we rank the Greeks extremely high in culture, we are not sure that they possessed superior genes.

With the argument from culture levels shown to be unreliable, we turn to the intelligence tests and ask whether they can be used to demonstrate racial equality or inequality. We immediately see two difficulties: the difficulty of devising tests that will be equally fair to races that have different cultures, and the difficulty of securing fair and equivalent samples of different races to test. When Indian or Negro school children in various parts of the United States have been tested, their average IQ has usually appeared to be rather low, not over 90. But we know that the tests are not completely fair to them since their schooling has not been as good as that of white children and since their cultural backgrounds have been different. How much allowance to make for these factors we cannot tell. Some samples of Indian or Negro children have shown an average IQ of 100, the same as white children. This is true of the Osage Indians in Oklahoma, a prosperous, English-speaking tribe (25). It is good to know this, but we are not sure that the Osage are a fair sample of the Indian population; they may be a superior stock. The children of the Hopi Indians in Arizona score above the white average in the man-drawing and other performance tests, while other tribes have given an average as low as 85 (10, 15). The tests may not be equally fair to all tribes, or the different tribes may differ somewhat in their genes, as families are known to differ.

Negro children do better in the intelligence tests where their schooling is good than where it is very meager. It is possible that all the difference usually found between Negroes and whites is due to schooling and other environmental factors. That is possible but as yet far from being proved. One encouraging fact is that a number of Negro children have been found in the public schools of Chicago, New York and Washington with IQs in the top levels (140 to 200), and with excellent school and college records. Some of these gifted children are mulattoes and some fullblooded Negroes. The existence of such individuals proves that the necessary genes for superior intellectual ability are present in the Negro population, but, for all we know yet, these genes may be less abundant, i.e., even scarcer, among the Negroes than among the whites (*17, 40, 41*).

Conditions in Hawaii are well worth studying. There we have an exceedingly mixed population composed of native Hawaiians, white Americans and Europeans, Chinese, Koreans, Japanese, Filipinos, Portuguese and others. All these races have intermarried and there is almost a complete absence of racial discrimination. Children of all races attend the same schools and speak English. It is a favorable situation for testing children of different races and there is no obvious environmental factor that should cause one race to come out ahead of any other—at least if the whites are left out of account. Yet the Chinese, Korean and Japanese children do considerably better on the average than the others in both verbal and performance tests. All the groups did considerably better in 1938 than in 1924, probably because of better schooling, etc., but the more backward groups did not gain on the more advanced ones (*31*).

It is sometimes said by those working for better race relations that psychologists have now proved all races equal in intelligence. Psychologists themselves make no such strong claim. They are too well aware of the difficulties already mentioned, of the actual differences in achievement revealed by the tests, and of the uncertain allowances that should be made for environmental factors. Besides, there are many races and tribes that have not yet been tested. But psychologists can properly make certain significant statements. They have established two important facts:

1. If races do differ in native intelligence, they differ much less than was formerly supposed.

2. Even if the average intelligence should differ from race to race, the distributions overlap greatly. Many Indians and Negroes surpass the white man's average. Many Hawaiians and Filipinos surpass the Chinese average. Individual differences are much greater than race differences.

**Sex differences.** Research shows that sex differences in ability and personality, like race differences, are much smaller than was formerly assumed to be the case. Even in the old days, when women were commonly supposed to be incapable of great intellectual achievement, exceptions must have been allowed, for all through the centuries there have been women who demonstrated superior ability in literature. In management and administration, too, eminent ability was shown by some of those women who came into positions of power, such as Queen Elizabeth of England or Catherine the Great of Russia. In a less public way many women have shown themselves to be good managers in business as well as in the home.

While the literary achievements of women, especially in poetry and fiction, have been notable for a long time, few women before the present century did much in the way of scientific investigation. At present there are not very many, but a fair number of women scientists, some of whom have won wide recognition for their discoveries. There are fewer eminent women scientists than novelists, and it may be that women have more of a natural bent for literature than for science.

In general intelligence as measured by our standard tests there seems to be no difference between the sexes. The average IQ for girls, as for boys, is 100, and the range is the same for both sexes. This does not mean that no sex differences come out in the intelligence tests. The boys do better in some parts of the test, the girls in other parts, while in most items there is no difference. The girls do better in comparing pictures of people's faces for beauty or for age, while the boys do better in space tests. It would be easy for the psychologist to construct tests that would give the advantage to either sex, since girls commonly excel in language and boys in anything of a mechanical nature. When a variety of tasks is included, as in the Binet tests, no sex difference appears in the total score (20).

In the elementary schools girls on the whole are more attentive and faithful in their work and they get better marks than the boys. This difference largely disappears in achievement tests (see p. 25), though even in them the girls surpass in reading while the boys are likely to surpass in arithmetic. In the secondary schools girls continue to surpass in the language tests while boys are ahead in geometry and the sciences. In college entrance tests, again, the girls do better in the linguistic part and the boys in the mathematical part. These differences, though small, are consistent from year to year and from place to place.

In industry and business, certain jobs fall to the women and others to the men. In clerical work, women are quicker, more accurate and more contented than men, while the reverse is true in mechanical work (1, 27). Are these differences due simply to custom and social causes? It is hard to be sure, but we find the same differences in tests for clerical aptitude and for mechanical understanding even in girls and boys who are below the working age. So, in tests calling for the quick, accurate reading of names or numbers, only 20–25 percent of boys do as well as the average girl; while in tests based on pictures of pulleys, gears, boats, trains and airplanes, only 2–4 percent of girls do as well as the average boy. In this last test a large part of the sex difference is probably due to the different interests and play habits of boys and girls. But why should the girls surpass in the clerical type of activities?

Girls and women surpass their male contemporaries in many kinds of linguistic tests such as reading, word knowledge, opposites, sentence completion, color naming, and the clerical tests just mentioned. Girl babies begin to talk a month earlier than boys, they pick up words more quickly and they use longer sentences in the early years of childhood. They hesitate and stutter less than boys. And in school they outdo the boys in language work. Can all this language superiority be explained by some difference in the environment or training of boys and girls? No one has yet suggested any reasonable environmental explanation.

Boys and girls are steered in different directions by their parents and by older boys and girls, and it might be that all the sex differences in abilities and interests are the result of this environmental factor and not to any difference in the male and female genes. Of the 24 pairs of chromosomes, we remember, 23 pairs are the same for both sexes, and only the 24th pair differs, being XX for the female and XY for the male. All the hundreds of genes in the 23 chromosomes, then, while differing from individual to individual, would not differ from sex to sex, and only the comparatively few genes carried by the X and Y chromosomes could make the sexes differ. These few sex genes produce the fundamental biological characteristics of the male and female. All the other sex differences might be due to environment, but more probably to the interaction of heredity and environment. Let us see how this interaction works out.

Early in development, long before birth, the genes determine the development of the structure of the sex glands as either male or female. The hormones which are later produced by the male and female gonads differ and cause the boy and girl to develop differently. Differences in bodily size and shape, in hairiness, amount of subcutaneous fat, and depth of the adult voice are due to the sex hormones.

Very important are two differences which are less obvious, being physiological rather than anatomical. One is the difference in muscular strength and energy, and the other is the difference in rate of growing up or maturing. The male surpasses not so much in physical endurance as in intensity of muscular action. He runs faster and punches harder. His muscles use fuel and oxygen more rapidly, and his red blood corpuscles, which carry oxygen from the lungs to the muscles, are 10 percent more abundant than those of women. His output of physical energy is naturally greater. So, as a boy, he is less contented than his sister in sitting quietly and playing with dolls. He wants to run around and use his muscles. This physiological difference leads boys and girls to select different effective environments and to develop different interests.

Girls mature more rapidly than boys. They reach adult size and sex maturity a couple of years earlier than boys. Their interests in the early teens are more mature than those of boys of the same age. Their greater interest in persons may be connected with this more rapid maturing, or with the maternal

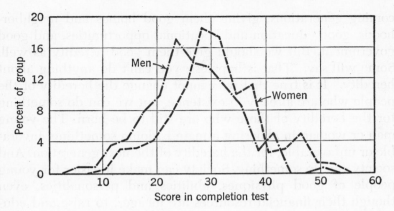

Fɪɢ. 32.—Overlapping distribution of male and female students in a sentence completion test. The average score of the men was 26 points, and of the women 30 points; and 70% of the women surpassed the average man. This is a large difference in comparison with most of those found in testing the sexes.

function toward which, biologically, they are heading. If we grant to the girls a greater interest in people, as well as a greater willingness to sit still and use their small rather than their large muscles, we can see how they might devote themselves to talking and reading more than boys do and develop their language functions more fully.

It is important to remember that sex differences in interests and abilities are merely *average* differences and that the male and female distributions overlap. Even in stature, though men average two or three inches taller, many individual women are taller than the male average and many men shorter than the female average. The same overlap is found in muscular strength. In mental abilities the sex difference is small in comparison with the variation within each sex.

**Final word on heredity and environment.** From all the evidence it is fairly certain that both heredity and environment are potent factors in causing human beings to differ in ability and personality. As to which is the more potent factor, the evidence is not so clear and perhaps the question is not very important. By all means let us improve the environment for the coming generations, giving them good homes and neighborhoods, good education and vocational opportunities, and good government. But we should give them good heredity as well. Some will say, "That is hopeless; you can't do anything about heredity." It is true that we cannot change the heredity of the people who are already in existence, but we can do something for the heredity of those who are still to be born. The young man or woman in choosing a mate is doing something, favorable or unfavorable, for the heredity of the next generation. And society can do something. Society can make it easier for young people of good physiques, abilities and personalities, even though their financial resources are meager, to raise and educate children. These children, on the whole, will have good heredity and good home environment as well. The children of intelligent and well-adjusted parents have the best start in life, and the number of such children should be increased—certainly not allowed to decrease. The next generation has a just claim on the present generation to provide it with the best parents possible.

After all, we would not desire to have all people alike, like peas in a pod. Their differing personalities make life interesting, and their differing abilities enable them to do the manifold work of the world. Democracy does not require that all the people should be alike. It demands that every one should have his chance, and that the welfare of all should be the concern of all.

## SUMMARY

1. The various special physiological and social factors influencing individual differences can be traced back to hereditary and environmental causes.

2. Both heredity and environment are essential for development. Any characteristic of the individual is the *product* of heredity and environment.

   a. *Differences* between individuals, however, can be attributed to differences in one cause, if there is no difference in the other.

b. Experimental study of the influence of heredity must hold environment constant; experimental study of the influence of environment must hold heredity constant.
 (1) Hybrids prove the importance of heredity in individual differences.
 (2) Monsters prove the importance of environment in individual differences.

3. The *effective environment* can be determined only by observing what the individual reacts to.
 a. An environment with free, unlimited opportunity favors individual differences.
 b. Unequal environmental influences can compensate for individual differences, tending to bring everyone to a uniform standard.

4. The hereditary factors are carried in the *nucleus* of every cell of the body. Each nucleus contains 24 pairs of *chromosomes*, derived from the nucleus of the fertilized ovum. The elementary units are the genes.
 a. The reproductive cells (ova and sperm) contain only 24 chromosomes. The fertilized ovum thus contains 24 chromosomes from the mother and 24 from the father.
 b. For any trait, such as eye color, there are *alternative genes*. The gene pairs differ from individual to individual, and consequently the individuals differ in the trait.
 c. A parent may possess and transmit to his child genes for traits which he himself does not display. Prediction from parents' characteristics to children's characteristics is therefore never completely accurate.
 d. Characteristics developed in an individual by his environment and by his own activities are not transmitted by heredity to his children.

5. The question of the relative importance of heredity and environment is important for practical social programs for improving personality and intelligence.
 a. Studies of orphanage children, parent-child relationships, and twin-similarities are equivocal; the results can be in-

terpreted in terms of hereditary influences or environmental influences.

b. Identical twins have identical heredity; any difference between them must necessarily be due to environmental factors. Such twins, on the average, do not differ in intelligence any more than individuals differ from themselves when retested. Identical twins brought up with extremely different educational opportunities differ 13 IQ points on the average.

c. When children are transferred to an improved environment, their social traits and their IQs are improved. Children adopted into superior foster homes have IQs 5 to 10 points higher than their own parents.

6. *Group differences* are usually expressed as a comparison of the averages of the groups; it is important to note the overlap of the distributions of the individuals in the groups.

a. The slight superiority in intelligence of city children over country children disappears where the country schools are of high quality. It is also probable that certain test items are not as fair to country children.

b. Average intelligence of adults varies according to occupational groups. Children also differ according to the occupations of the fathers, and studies of foster children show that this difference results from both heredity and environment.

c. The widespread popular belief in the superiority of one race over others is based more on prejudice than on scientific fact.

d. No differences in general intelligence exist between men and women, but women do relatively better in certain tests involving language, while men excel slightly in mechanical and mathematical tests.

# CHAPTER SEVEN

# Interaction with the Environment

At this stage in our study of psychology we may well pause and take our bearings, for we have reached a turning point. So far our whole emphasis has been on ways in which people differ and on the causes that make them differ, but now we shall consider ways in which people are alike. What we have studied in the previous chapters, except the first, is called *differential psychology,* while now we shall be studying *general psychology.*

We have already taken note in passing of some ways in which people are alike. The distribution curve does not divide them into separate classes. Individuals differ in degree rather than in kind. Some are more intelligent than others but they all have some intelligence. They all have the verbal, numerical, spatial and other abilities in some degree, they all make some use of past experience in handling a novel situation, they all have some ability to grasp relationships. Even in personality traits they do not show the absolute differences which are often assumed. No one is entirely good or entirely bad. Everyone, when tested, reveals some introversion and some extroversion. Everyone is affected by the physiological and social factors in personality. And the interaction of heredity and environment is an important general law. There are many principles of psychology which apply to the activities of all individuals.

From now on, individual differences will not be forgotten, for they are present in all forms of human activity, but the emphasis will be laid on the general laws of learning, thinking, desiring and other important processes.

**The fundamental questions of general psychology.** Since, according to the definition of psychology (p. 3), we are interested in the activities of the individual, let us consider what we want to know about them. What do psychologists in their investigations try to discover about these activities? In the simplest possible words the psychologist and the student of psychology are seeking answers to three questions:

What does the individual do?

Why does he do it?

How does he do it?

What does he do?—i.e., what activities does he engage in and what results does he accomplish? Why does he do it?—i.e., what causes lead him to engage in certain activities and to strive for certain results? How does he do it?—i.e., what processes does he go through in reaching a certain result?

For a very simple example, take the following conversation.

"What are you doing this morning?"

"I'm going down town."

"Why are you going?"

"I want to buy a hat."

"How are you going?"

"I think I'll walk down through the Park."

Not much psychology here, perhaps, but it gives a sort of diagram of the problems of psychology. Goal, motive, route to the goal are, in other words, the three problems. Goal is the result aimed at, motive is what makes the individual try for that goal, and route is the way he takes, the method he follows, in reaching the goal. Logically, it might seem, we should say "Motive, route, goal," or "Why, How, What," since this is the time order in the individual. But in observing another person we can usually see what he is doing before we can discover why he does it or exactly how he does it. His motives and mental processes are not visible. Even the individual himself may know better what he wants than why he wants it or how he will obtain it, for he is not fully aware of his own motives and mental processes. He tries to please and interest a certain girl without realizing that he is in love, and without being conscious of the little tricks he is using. We can gladly allow him to remain naive, but as psychologists we bring these motives and processes out into the open as far as possible.

The Why question, for the most part, is reserved for later consideration in the chapter on Motives. The What and How questions are considered throughout the remainder of the book, but here they are taken up in a very general way, though with some specific examples.

## WHAT THE INDIVIDUAL DOES—DEALING WITH THE ENVIRONMENT

A catalogue of hundreds and thousands of varied activities would be one answer to the question, What. More psychological would be a list of mental activities such as learning, observing, thinking—a list like the table of contents for the remainder of this book. But there is one broad, general answer that covers most of the subject even if not quite all of it: The individual deals with his environment. By "dealing" we mean active give-and-take relations such as the customer has with the grocer in buying and paying for some of his goods. The individual interacts with his environment—that is another way of saying the same thing. Of course it is only the "effective environment" (p. 161) with which he deals or interacts. But in the effective environment are numerous things of many kinds, and many physical forces and conditions such as gravitation, heat and cold, light and darkness, space and time. He deals with all of these, and he is in constant interaction with the social environment.

The words, "dealing with the environment," may seem to cover only the external activities and not the inner life of thought and feeling. Still, when you are absorbed in thought and almost unconscious of your present surroundings, are you not usually remembering what has happened or planning what you wish to do in reality? When you feel strongly, are you not usually pleased or displeased with some person or object in the real world? When the novelist is inventing his imaginary story and characters, he draws on his experience of real persons and happenings. This must be true even of an insane person who loses contact with the real world and lives a life of fantasy. Our point is not that the individual is always perfectly realistic; the point is, rather, that he has this fundamental attitude of always dealing with something, and that usually he is dealing directly or indirectly with something in the environment.

Since the individual's active relations with the environment are so important, that fact has been included in our definition of psychology as the science of the activities of the individual in relation to the environment (p. 4). Now let us examine this relation more closely and ask what the individual does to and with the environment.

**The individual resists the environment.**   For a perfect general answer to the question of what the individual does, we might have said, "He lives, with all that word implies." He stays alive, he survives, if he is to do anything at all. In order to survive he resists the environment in many ways, for there are many ways in which the environment is hostile or unfavorable to life. Sometimes it is too hot or too cold, but the warm-blooded animal resists these extremes and maintains his own body temperature at almost a constant level. Sometimes he is cut or bruised by the environment, but he has natural means of preventing much loss of blood and repairing the injured tissues. He has natural means, too, for resisting many kinds of disease germs. More in the line of behavior are his ways of resisting gravitation and keeping his balance while standing or walking, and his ways of counteracting the force of the wind and other forces that tend to push him around.

The social environment as well as the physical exerts pres-

Fig. 33.—Resisting the environment.

sure on the individual, making demands, requiring this and for-
bidding that, commanding or coaxing him, and he makes considerable resistance to these social pressures, as anyone knows
who has observed little children or even adolescents.

Often the individual runs away from something in the environment, avoiding it rather than exactly resisting it; but
avoidance and resistance are simply two ways of combatting
the unfavorable things in the environment.

**The individual uses the environment.**   Most of us would not
agree with those unfortunate persons who regard the environment as predominantly hostile and dangerous and who spend
their lives in the effort to resist or escape from it. The environment has many positive values. The organism takes in food and
oxygen and so provides itself with energy for its activities.

*Ewing Galloway*

Fɪɢ. 34.—Participation.

Many things from the environment the organism appropriates and uses—so many that it would be hardly possible to enumerate them, especially when the organism in question is a human being. In general, the individual needs and gets *stimulation* from the environment to wake him up and keep him active; without any stimulation he would lapse into a dormant state, surviving perhaps but not much more. And the individual needs what we may call *outlet* or *opportunity* for his activities. He needs something to act upon, as a squirrel needs trees to climb. A talking organism needs something to talk about (stimulation) and somebody to talk to (outlet).

**The individual participates in what is going on in the environment.** The negative reactions of resisting and the positive reactions of using the environment, even taken together, do not tell the whole story of interaction. An expert diver stands erect on the diving platform, resisting the force of gravity till the proper moment arrives, when he bends forward, springs and lets gravity carry him down into the water. Which makes the dive, the man's muscles or the pull of the earth? Both really play a part. The diver is participating in a process of nature.

He manages the process by taking part in it. A child in a swing does the same, and so he does when he throws a ball. Anyone who uses a tool or operates any machine takes part in a natural process which extends out beyond the limits of his body. So the individual's activity dovetails with what goes on in the environment. When we think of the social environment, such examples as conversation, games, choral singing and teamwork of any kind readily convince us that the individual participates in group activities and that social life consists very largely in such participation.

Getting to *know the environment* is one important kind of interaction. For the individual to know the environment it must act on him and he must be active, too. He must be awake, he must use his senses, and he must understand what he sees or hears. Often his activity in getting acquainted with the environment is very obvious as he goes around exploring, handling objects to find out more about them, and asking other people for information.

**Adjustment.**   If we wish a single statement to cover all that the individual does to or with the environment, perhaps the following will serve the purpose: The individual adjusts his relations with the environment. By "adjust" we mean "change for the better (as far as possible)." Sometimes the individual changes himself in relation to the environment, as when he goes from one place to another, or as when he builds up an immunity to an infectious disease. Sometimes he changes the environment in relation to himself, as when he pulls an object toward him or pushes it away, or as when he sterilizes his room to destroy the infectious germs. Whether he changes himself or changes the environment, in either case he changes the relation between himself and the environment.

Sometimes we should say that the individual adjusts himself to the environment, and at other times that he adjusts the environment to himself. In the one case he is more yielding, in the other more masterful. If there is a troublesome rock in his driveway, he adjusts himself by always dodging the rock, or he adjusts the driveway by removing the rock. If two friends have different ideas as to what they should do, the more yielding one may change his plans to suit the other's wishes, and the more masterful one may bully or persuade the other into adopting his plan. Both are engaged in a process of adjustment, and we can use the word broadly to cover both the yielding and the masterful sort of adjustment.

**A formula for interaction.** The fundamental fact that the individual deals with the environment can be represented by the formula,

$$W—O—W_2$$

with $W$ standing for the world or environment, and $O$ standing for the organism or individual. The formula means that $W$ acts on $O$ and $O$ back on $W$. This interaction goes on continually, back and forth, so that the formula might be extended into an indefinite series of $O$s and $W$s.

### STIMULUS AND RESPONSE, THE "HOW" OF INTERACTION

The $W—O—W$ formula gives a broad, general answer to the question, What the individual does, and immediately raises the question, How he does it. How does the individual interact with the environment? How does it act on him—the $W—O$ question—and how does he act on it—the $O—W$ question. Let us consider this second part-question first, asking how the individual acts on the environment and "does things to it," i.e., produces changes in it.

**The effectors.** We see someone doing a simple act such as moving a chair. At first we are contented to say, *He* moves it. Analyzing this $O—W$ process a little, we say he moves it with his *hands*. But the hands, as we learn from physiology, are inactive except when moved by their *muscles*. The muscles are inactive unless stimulated by their nerves, and these *motor nerves* are inactive unless stimulated by the *nerve centers*, especially the *brain*. In ordinary life we do not see the individual's brain, nerves and muscles, but it is safe to assume he

receptors
effectors

has them. He himself may be totally unaware of such details, as he moves the chair, for his attention is directed to that thing in the environment and to the change he is accomplishing by his act.

The muscles are called effectors because they produce effects, changing the individual's relations with the environment. The only other effectors possessed by the human organism are certain glands, such as the salivary glands which moisten food in the mouth. (Food in the mouth or even in the stomach or intestine is still in the environment, and the digestive juices poured out by the glands change the food before it is actually absorbed into the body.) The light-producing organ of the firefly and the electric-shock-producing organ of certain fishes are effectors.

The receptors. Now for the W-O question. How does the environment act on the individual so as to change his behavior? How does it reveal itself to him so that he knows what is going on? It acts primarily on his sense organs. Light from an object strikes his eyes and he sees the object; or sound from the object strikes his ears and he hears the object. Pressure and heat act on his skin, odors and tastes on his nose and mouth. In a word, forces from the environment act on his sense organs or *receptors* (as they are called because they receive stimulation from the environment). But the process does not end in the receptors. When they are thrown into activity by forces from the environment, they stimulate their sensory nerves, and these nerves in turn stimulate the brain. Through the brain the receptors are connected with the motor nerves and so with the effectors. Quite a chain of internal processes occurs in O's simple act of seeing a chair and changing its position.

Stimuli. Any force acting on a receptor and making it active is called a *stimulus*. This word originally meant a goad or sharp stick used as an "accelerator" in driving an animal. In psychology we speak of a stimulus to a receptor, as when light stimulates the eye or sound the ear, or we speak of a stimulus to the organism as a whole, since by way of the receptor, the sensory nerve and the brain, the light or sound may arouse the whole organism to activity. Within the organism one part often stimulates another to activity. The sensory nerves stimulate the brain, the brain stimulates the motor nerves and they stimulate the muscles.

Responses. Any activity aroused by a stimulus is a response to that stimulus. A stimulus is what arouses a response, and a response is what is aroused by a stimulus. The two terms belong together. The response, it should be noticed, is an activity of the organism and not a mere passive motion. The goad does not push the ox forward but stimulates him to walk faster. If a heavy wave bowls me over on the beach, no stimulus-response relationship is involved, but if I react in any way, as by jumping or maintaining my footing, the wave is a stimulus and my act is a response. The two words, *react* and *respond,* mean the same.

Sometimes only muscular acts are called responses, but this limitation is unnecessary. Any kind of activity aroused by a stimulus can properly be called a response. I hear a noise—this *hearing* is an activity aroused by the noise, a sensory response to the noise. I recognize the noise as the whistle of a steamboat and am reminded of last summer's vacation by the sea—this *remembering* is a second activity aroused by the noise, an indirect response to the noise. From the memory of last summer I may go on quickly to planning for next summer and so to the muscular response of reaching for a timetable. All these activities are responses, less and less direct ones, to the original noise. Or we can say that each act in the series is a response to the just preceding act. The main point is that one activity arouses another and that an external stimulus often starts such a series going.

Weak or monotonous stimuli, while producing some activity in the receptors, often have very little effect on behavior. You do not notice them or do anything with them. When a stimulus does have an effect on behavior, that effect may be a starting up of activity, a changing of activity, or even a stopping of activity. If you are sound asleep, the alarm clock stimulus will arouse you to activity. If you are already active, a stimulus may cause you to modify the present activity or to shift to another activity. Sometimes a sudden stimulus will make you stop what you are doing and simply wait for what is coming next. This stopping of activity is called *inhibition.* Even when a stimulus makes you shift suddenly from one activity to another, the activity which you drop is inhibited, and as this occurs frequently, inhibition is obviously an important type of response to a stimulus.

For a simple example, suppose you are walking smoothly along and see a slippery spot in the path. Your response is to modify your gait and walk more carefully. Next you see a friend ahead of you and shift from walking to running. Then the sound of an explosion inhibits all this activity; it makes you stop in your tracks (or, perhaps, if you have been exposed to bombing, it makes you throw yourself flat on the ground). Whenever a stimulus causes you to change your activity in any of these ways, the act which you were just about to perform is checked or inhibited. In any response, as a physiologist would say, both excitation and inhibition are involved.

**The stimulus-response formula.** To represent this fundamental biological fact, that activity depends on stimulation, a simple formula is often used:

$$S—R, \quad \text{or} \quad S{\rightarrow}R$$

with S standing for the stimulus and R for the response, so that the formula reads, "A stimulus arouses a response," or, "A response is aroused by a stimulus." Sometimes the word "elicit" is used instead of "arouse" and there are other words that carry the same meaning, namely, that activity of the individual is called forth by stimuli from the environment. The formula suggests such questions as these: "What response will a person make to such and such a stimulus?" and "What stimulus is necessary to get him to make a certain response?" As a guide to psychological research, the S—R formula leads to experiments in which certain changes are made in the stimulus to see what changes in the response will result. For example, let the physical intensity of a sound be raised gradually from very weak to very strong. What is the effect on the sensory response? Of course you know the answer: the sensation of sound grows louder. A great variety of similar questions can be asked and usually the answers are not known till the proper experiments are made. Other questions start with a known response and ask for the stimulus. Anger is a known response, but what are the stimuli that arouse anger, and what stimuli will inhibit anger that is already present? A large share of psychological problems can be tied to the S—R formula.

**Factors in the individual which influence his response.**  The S—R formula means that the response depends on the stimulus, but must not be taken to mean that it depends *wholly* on the stimulus and that no other factors have any influence on the response. We know that different individuals will respond differently to the same stimulus, and that the same individual will not always give the same response. An adult will respond differently from the way he responded as a child. If we wish to predict what response will be made to a given stimulus, we have to take account of the individual as well as of the stimulus. We have to take account of O as well as of S. Therefore a more adequate formula is:

$$( S—O—R )$$

This reads that the stimulus acts on the individual and gets him to respond, and that the response depends on him as well as on the stimulus. Focusing our attention on what the individual does at a particular moment, we ask what factors determine his action. When he receives a stimulus, his response depends partly on stimulus factors, S-factors, such as the strength of the stimulus; but it depends also on O-factors. The various O-factors can be classified under the three heads of structure, state, and activity in progress.

*Structure, permanent characteristics.*  By the individual's structure we mean his bodily structure, his anatomy, and we say that all his permanent characteristics are embodied in his structure. The genes are bits of structure, small but important. Arms and legs, muscles and glands, sense organs, nerves and brain—all parts of the bodily structure—have developed through the interaction of the genes with the environment. Structure thus includes both the hereditary factors and all permanent effects of the individual's past environment. Whatever he has learned, all his knowledge, habits and skills, are carried along in his structure. For suppose he learned to swim last summer and does not swim at all during the winter. Still he will be able to swim again next summer without having to learn over again. He retains this ability through the winter. Where does he retain it? Presumably in his brain structure which was modified in some way by his practice in swimming. Similarly, all his abilities and personality traits are carried along in his structure. It is true, however, that we cannot inspect much of the individual's internal structure and that we have to judge his permanent characteristics from his behavior. Practically, then, we mean permanent characteristics when we say structure, and they may be only *relatively* permanent, provided he is carrying them along out of the past into the present moment when he makes his response to a stimulus. The study of such permanent characteristics provides the basis for prediction of future activity.

*Temporary state*. At a given moment the individual, no matter how vivacious in general, may be in a drowsy state and make only a drowsy response to a question or other stimulus. Drowsiness is just one example of the many temporary states which have their different effects on the individual's responses. His response to food will be very different when he is in a state of hunger and when he is in the state that follows a full meal. His response to a couch will be very different when he is fatigued and when well rested. Intoxication and fever are other examples, and so are the emotional states of excitement or depression, of worry or jollity. Any such state of the organism is a strong factor in behavior, so that in trying to predict what response $O$ will make to a given $S$ you have to take account of $O$'s state at the moment.

*Activity in progress.* At a given moment $O$ is usually engaged in activity directed toward some goal. He is doing something, and his response to a stimulus that comes at that moment will depend on what he is doing. If the stimulus has no connection with what he is doing he will disregard it as far as possible; if it threatens to block his progress he will resist or avoid it; if it promises to help him along he will make a positive response.

We have noticed four general factors which work together in producing a response: the permanent characteristics of the individual, his internal state, his goal or activity in progress, and the stimulus reaching him at the moment. The response depends on all four, sometimes more clearly on one and sometimes on another. What response will a young woman make to the advances of a young man? It depends on the young woman, on her temperament and character, on her habits and past experiences. It depends on her physiological and emotional state at the time. It depends on what she is doing at the time. And it depends on the young man and his "appeal." Evidently it is impossible to give a general answer to the question, which of the four factors is most potent and compelling. Sometimes one dominates, sometimes another. Very strong stimuli such as a stab of pain usually make a person drop what he is doing and attend to them. Under anesthesia, however, he makes no response to the knife, his dormant state being the dominant factor. In the heat of battle a wound may pass unnoticed because the intense activity in progress is dominant. And some individuals are characteristically tougher than others.

## PRINCIPLES OF EFFICIENT DEALING WITH THE ENVIRONMENT

Our answer to the question "What does the individual do?" was incorporated in the formula, $W—O—W$, meaning that he deals with the environment; and our answer to the question "How does he do this?" in the formula, $S—O—R$, meaning that he responds to stimuli in accordance with his structure, state, and activity in progress. Since the stimuli typically come from the environment and the responses act on the environment, the two formulas can be combined into one,

$$W—S—O—R—W$$

which can be easily read and understood. It might seem that this combined formula provided the answer to our questions, What and How. So it does in bare outline, but a great deal of filling-in is still necessary. The outline does not answer the question of how the response is made to fit the environment as well as it usually does. The mere fact that O responds to stimuli from the environment and so produces effects in the environment does not prove that the effects are good. When you think of the multitude of stimuli that reach O's receptors at any moment and of the great variety of movements that he might make in response, you wonder how his behavior can be as well organized and well adjusted to the environment as it is.

Two main factors in dealing efficiently with the environment are *selectivity* and *set*. Both belong under the general head of activity in progress. Selectivity refers to the fact that the activity of any moment is *focused* on certain stimuli and certain responses instead of being spread over all the stimuli present and all the possible responses. Set refers to the fact that the organism is usually *prepared* at any moment for the stimuli it is going to receive and for the response it is going to make. The words, "focalization" instead of "selectivity," and "preparation" instead of "set," would serve equally well to suggest the two principles.

**Selective reception.**  The radio has made us familiar with selectivity. It can be tuned to any one of the many radio frequencies that are "on the air." The organism selects stimuli in a different way. Looking and listening are the best examples. Looking at an object brings the light from that object to the center of the retina where reception is best. The whole "field of view" at any moment is quite wide, but only the center of the field is clear and distinct. Listening is a visible performance in animals that have movable ears, and man also turns his head so as to get the best reception for a particular sound.

Another kind of selective reception consists in "focusing attention" on a certain sound without turning the head, or on a certain object without turning the eyes. In the midst of a babel of sounds, like the buzz of general conversation, you are able to "hear out" one particular sound or voice that interests you. It is not so easy to attend to an object without looking at it, but it can be done, though reception is of course not so good as when the eyes as well as the attention are focused upon the object. In the same way you can bring out clearly the sensations from your neck, your back, your feet by attending to one part at a time. When you notice one, the others recede into the background, and you cannot keep them all distinct at once.

**Selective response.**   Of the many acts that the individual is capable of performing, he does perform only one, or only one main one, at the same moment. Some movements are antagonistic to each other—bending and straightening the elbow, or approaching and avoiding an object—and only one of such a pair is attempted at the same time. If the organism did attempt to make two contrary movements at the same time, there would be no efficient dealing with the environment. Often two stimuli are present calling for contrary responses, but the response is selective. Suppose two interesting objects make their appearance at the same instant, one off to the right and the other to the left. If you tried to look at both at the same time, you would be staring between them and not getting a clear view of either one. What the eyes do in such a case is to look *either* to the right *or* to the left, and this either-or type of response is quite characteristic of the organism, especially in relatively simple matters.

Together with the principle of selectivity two other principles should be mentioned in order to avoid a one-sided view of behavior. These are the principles of shifting and combination.

**Shifting of response.**   From the principle of selectivity alone we should expect the eyes to turn toward one of the two interesting objects (in our last example) and to remain there. What they do is to shift to the second object after a good look at the first. Then they may shift back to the first object or to other objects until they have examined everything of interest that is in sight. This type of behavior, as well as selectivity, is characteristic of the organism and we shall meet it again in studying the topics of learning, observation and thinking.

**Combination.**   When the organism is receiving many stimuli, we might expect that each stimulus would arouse its own separate response. Or, because of selectivity, we might expect that only one stimulus would have any effect at a given time; and we might expect the response to be confined to just one muscle at a time. What happens is very different. In any ordinary field of view there are thousands of elementary stimuli, thousands of bits of light, shade and color; but you do not see these points separately, nor do you simply see a vast, variegated mass. You see objects, some large and some small, most of them certainly much larger than a single point of light. You see a face, for example, and it is easier to see the face as a whole than to fix your attention on the nose alone or on a single freckle. Seeing the face is evidently a response to a large combination of stimuli organized into a unit, but at the same time it is a selective response since the face is only a part of the whole field of view.

A movement of the eyes or of the hand or foot is performed by a combination of several muscles working together as a team. At the same time it is selective since only certain muscles take part, not all the muscles indiscriminately. It is a well-coordinated unit and accomplishes some definite result. Even such a big, powerful movement as the lifting of a heavy weight by the combined action of arms, legs and trunk is a unit, a single response. So is a horse's gallop; it is a unit in execution, and when you watch the horse's movement you see the movement as a whole and not as a series of different positions.

We see, then, that the organism responds to a combination of stimuli rather than to a single stimulus, and that a response brings into play a combination of muscles rather than a single muscle.

**Preparatory set.**   Just as activity is unified and made efficient by being focused or concentrated upon one thing at a time, so it is unified and made efficient over a period of time by de-

Pictures Incorporated

FIG. 35.—A snapshot of horses in active motion catches them in positions that appear strange because we usually see the motion as a whole and not the momentary positions through which the motion passes. Notice also the great complexity of the running movement which is nevertheless a single, unitary response.

voting part of the time to preparation for the crucial moment when something important is to be done. If we think of very important matters such as an examination, a dramatic performance, or a battle, we realize at once the necessity of preparation. But perhaps we have not noticed how deep-seated this preparing tendency is in the organism and how necessary it is even in very simple forms of behavior. Very often what we regard as a single act is composed of two parts, a preparatory response and an end response. A cough or sneeze is a relatively simple act, certainly, but it consists of two parts, inspiration followed by expiration. The end response which does the work is the forcible expulsion of a large quantity of air, and the preparatory response is the drawing in of this large quantity of air. The same two parts can be found in the acts of singing, shouting and even ordinary speaking. In striking a blow it is necessary first to "haul off" in preparation. In hammering it is necessary to raise the arm in preparation for the effective down stroke.

*Pictures Incorporated*

Fig. 36.—Preparatory set.

Preparatory set is the organism's preparation for the act that is soon to be performed. The runner on the mark, waiting for the starting signal, gives a vivid picture of preparedness. Notice his posture, how it is adjusted for the quickest possible getaway. He is all set to spring forward. If he were not ready he would make a slow start. But he must not allow himself to become so eager as to make a false start before the pistol shot. He must listen for the pistol, be prepared for the stimulus as well as for the response. His set is sensory as well as motor. It is a highly selective set, preparing for one particular response to one particular stimulus. Other incidental sounds are disregarded, and other responses ordinarily made to the sound of a pistol, such as turning to look for the source of the sound, are inhibited.

*Reaction time.* If the runner's starting time were measured, instead of the time he takes to run 100 yards, it would be well under a second, according to the results of a well-known laboratory experiment in which O has simply to press a telegraph key as soon as he receives a certain stimulus. He knows in advance what the stimulus will be and what response he has to make. A couple of seconds before the stimulus a "ready" signal is given, and at this signal he gets set, listens for the sound or looks for the light, and holds his finger poised on the key. When

FIG. 37.—Reaction time. When *E* (the experimenter) on the right presses his key, the neon lamp shines into *O*'s eyes and he responds by pressing his own key as promptly as possible. The clock on *E*'s side measures the reaction time to the hundredth of a second.

the stimulus arrives, his finger movement follows in $\frac{1}{5}$ of a second or less, provided he has had a little practice and is fully ready at the moment. This stimulus-response interval is the reaction time.

In this short interval quite a series of internal processes occur: stimulation of the sense organ, conduction along the sensory nerve to the brain, brain response, conduction along the motor nerve to the muscle, stimulation of the muscle, and moving of the hand by the muscle. Some individuals make this reaction in $\frac{1}{10}$ of a second, which seems to be about the human limit. (This is not a satisfactory or valid test for all-round quickness; one may have a short reaction time without being especially quick in other performances, or be slow in this test without being slow in more complex performances.) A curious fact, due to the photochemical processes in the reception of light by the eye, is that the reaction time to a light is longer than to a sound or to a touch on the skin, being about .18 sec. for light as against .14 sec. for sound or touch. There are many other interesting facts about reaction time, but those related to

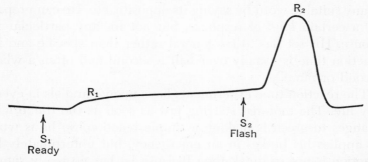

FIG. 38.—Preparatory set in the reaction time experiment. Here $R_1$ is the muscular tension in O's arm as he prepares to receive the stimulus, $S_2$, and make the response movement, $R_2$. See page 522.

the principle of *set* are listed in the paragraphs below (*6, 10*).

1. The "ready" signal is important. If none is given, *O* cannot tell just when to be ready and his reaction is slow. To get the quickest and most uniform reactions you have to allow about two seconds between the "ready" signal and the stimulus. Less than a second is definitely not time enough for him to get ready. More than five seconds is too much; his readiness fades out; his set loses some of its maximum efficiency.

2. What has been considered so far is the "simple reaction"; it is about the simplest task that can be given a subject and about the quickest response he can make (except for certain reflexes, p. 243). Other tasks make greater demands on him. In the "choice reaction" he is required to make different responses to different stimuli. For example, he must raise his right hand whenever a red light is shown, his left hand whenever a green is shown. Since he cannot tell which light is going to come next he cannot focus his preparation on either hand exclusively, for fear of making a false reaction. His readiness to respond cannot be pushed to so high a pitch as in the simple reaction. Consequently the choice reaction takes longer than the simple reaction, about $1/10$ of a second longer.

3. The "associative reaction" is still slower. Here *O* is to name any color that is shown, or to respond to any number that is shown by saying the next larger number, or to respond

to any suitable word by saying its opposite, etc. He can prepare for a certain *kind* of response, but not for any particular response. His set has to be general rather than specific and his reaction time is usually over half a second and often a whole second or more.

The reaction time experiments have many parallels in everyday life. The motorist starting just as soon as the traffic light changes to green is making a simple reaction. So he is when he applies his brakes in an emergency, but unfortunately his reaction is not so quick then because he has no ready signal. The boxer, dodging to right or left according to the blow aimed at him by his opponent—like the tennis player in a similar situation—is making choice reactions, and this kind is common in steering, handling tools and managing machinery. Associative reactions occur in calling a person's name on sight, in answering a question, in reading, adding and many kinds of mental work.

**The set to start and the set to continue.** The runner on the mark and the laboratory subject in a reaction time experiment are set to *commence* an act when the proper moment arrives. Whenever you know what is about to happen, you get ready to respond.

Usually, however, the goal of an activity is not reached in a single leap. It has to be reached by a series of steps. The activity continues and there is a *continuing control* which steers toward the goal. Besides the postures preparatory to starting there are postures for continuing an activity efficiently. While running you lean forward, and while running around a corner you lean inward (Fig. 39). Then there is the posture for carrying a load on the back, or under one arm, etc., and there is the posture of searching for an object on the ground or for spotting an airplane in the sky. Each such posture shows readiness for a certain continued activity. Since the postural muscles are controlled by the brain, the visible posture proves that the invisible brain is set for carrying on a certain activity.

Any set is selective, favoring certain responses and preventing others. Looking for a lost object is a set which favors the

*Ewing Galloway*

Fig. 39.—Continuing set.

seeing of that object. Listening to a person is a set which favors hearing what that person says. While listening intently you may easily fail to see something that is right before your eyes, and while looking eagerly for a lost object you may not notice what your companion is saying. That is to say, readiness for one act is at the same time unreadiness for other acts. If a motorist approaching an intersection is all intent on the possibility of a car from the right he may overlook a car coming from the left. A less sharply focused set is safer in such a situation.

**Mental sets.**   Some kinds of work we call "mental work" or "brain work," and a set for doing any certain kind of mental work is called a mental set. Just as tasks such as trying to see or hear distinctly are predominantly sensory, and as tasks calling for muscular strength or skilled movement are predominantly motor, so there are many tasks which are predominantly mental—for example, trying to remember anything, planning a trip, digging out the meaning of a difficult sentence, thinking out any problem. And just as we have sensory sets in looking and listening, and motor sets in running and skating, so we have a mental set for remembering or for planning or for solving a problem. (These distinctions are only relative and not absolute, for sensory and motor activities certainly involve brain activity, and mental tasks may always involve some activity of the sense organs and muscles.) What evidence have we for the reality of these mental sets? The evidence comes partly from introspection—a person can usually tell you what he is trying to do—and partly from experiments which show how *efficiently* a person can perform a mental task when he is well set for that task.

In what psychologists call a "word association test" disconnected words, the stimulus words, are pronounced or shown to the subject and he responds to each stimulus word by saying another word. In the "free" association test the only requirement is that he shall say the first other word suggested by the stimulus word. You can see what this test is like by responding freely to each word in the following list.

| | |
|---|---|
| rapid | difficult |
| wealthy | wicked |
| numerous | feeble |
| distant | quiet |
| ancient | costly |

Since any word is used in various connections and has various associations, different persons will make different responses to the same word, and the same person is likely to make different responses at different times, if the test is repeated. The reaction time may be taken to see how quickly the subject does this kind of work, and there are other uses for the test in studying personality.

In a "controlled association test" the task is more specific. The subject is told to respond to each stimulus word by saying a word that stands in a certain relation to it. For example, he has to give the opposite of each word. It might seem that this task would take more time than free association and that other words besides opposites would suggest themselves from the subject's vast stock of associations. You can try this out with the previous list of stimulus words.

Provided the stimulus words really have familiar opposites, the usual result is that this task is done very quickly and efficiently and with little interference from irrelevant associations. This particular list of words has been selected so as to be suitable also for two other tasks, that of giving synonyms, and that of naming an object to fit each of the given adjectives (for example, "rough—road").

Such experiments bring out the fact that the response is determined partly by the stimulus and partly by the subject's set at the moment. The set favors certain responses and prevents others from occurring. Set promotes quickness, accuracy and efficiency. Its practical value can be illustrated in arithmetical work. When you are adding a column of numbers, the set for adding holds you to sums and keeps you from following other suggestions. A pair of numbers might from your previous training suggest their sum, difference, product, or quotient, but if you set yourself to add you get the sums, while if you set yourself to subtract you get the differences, and so on.

| 12 | 10 | 6 | 9 | 20 | 8 | 30 |
|----|----|---|---|----|---|----|
| 6  | 5  | 2 | 3 | 4  | 2 | 3  |

In arithmetic and other branches of mathematics there are many rules or standard procedures for solving certain classes of problems, and once you have a problem classified you get set for following through the standard procedure. If you have many problems of the same class to solve, the set becomes very efficient and carries you smoothly through the regular procedure. In handling less standardized problems your set may be too routinized, too cut-and-dried, and so make you blind to more original solutions which you could find if your set were more flexible.

A set may be intentional or unintentional. Sometimes you tell yourself what you are going to do, or someone else tells you what to do and you accept his suggestion. In other cases something in the situation leads you to adopt a certain set without being clearly aware of it. You are more apt to know your goal than the exact way you are taking to reach the goal, and you may become set for a regular way of acting without knowing it (5, 8).

Each group of letters when rearranged will make a five-letter word. If the reader will work straight down the list, recording his solutions, the results may be of interest, as explained later.

| | | |
|---|---|---|
| 1. | y m e p t | *empty* |
| 2. | e u j d g | *judge* |
| 3. | p r g o u | *group* |
| 4. | y a d i s | *daisy* |
| 5. | n r d o w | *drown* |
| 6. | l a c m e | *camel* |
| 7. | n i w d e | *widen* |
| 8. | y a p r t | *party* |
| 9. | m t s o r | *storm* |
| 10. | t a h b i | *habit* |
| 11. | r i c g a | *cigar* |
| 12. | y a p n s | *pansy* |
| 13. | n a b c o | *bacon* |
| 14. | e n k i f | *knife* |
| 15. | t l p a n | *plant* |
| 16. | t h c e a | *cheat* |
| 17. | w h t r o | *throw* |
| 18. | d l c o u | *cloud* |
| 19. | t i n g h | *thing* |
| 20. | n r a g o | *groan* |
| 21. | n a r t i | *train* |
| 22. | g a r n y | *angry* |
| 23. | m h t o u | *mouth* |
| 24. | s o h r e | *shore* |
| 25. | e w t i r | *write* |

**Situation set.** We have been speaking of set as a preparation for doing something, for reaching some goal. Evidently O cannot act effectively unless he knows the environment with which he is dealing. He has to be set for the situation as well as for the goal. By "situation" we mean the present environment, including the place, the things and people in it, and what is going on.

Situation set is a grasp of the situation. For the baby in his crib the present situation is a small affair, not extending far in space or time. As he grows older his horizon will widen. He will know, for example, that these people in the car with him are his family on a journey to the seashore for a vacation. If he should ever become a Senator of the United States and be addressing the Senate on the subject of a peace treaty or a plan for international organization, the "present situation" for him then would be worldwide in space and historical in time perspective.

The words just used, "grasp of the situation," have an intellectual sound, but the situation set in simple cases is not very intellectual. You look out of the window in the morning and see that the weather is cold, wet and windy, and so you become set for dealing with that kind of an environment. When a singer has just finished a beautiful solo, your reaction will be different according as you have a concert set or a church set; in church you are not likely to burst into applause, and you do not expect the singer to bow to the congregation. Being set for the occasion you are ready for the kind of events that happen and for your customary behavior on such an occasion. If something happens contrary to your set you have a shock of surprise.

In regard to situation set, it is important to notice (1) that it is built up by observing the situation; (2) that it persists after you have completed your observations, so long as you remain in the same situation, though it may be lost if you become absorbed in your own thoughts and forget where you are; and (3) that it is objective. This last statement means that what you retain after observing a situation is not a memory of the stimuli received, but rather a memory of the objective facts discovered by use of these stimuli. For a good example of this objectivity, explore a room while keeping your eyes closed. By feeling your way around and touching this thing and that you get a series of touch stimuli but you do not remember these touches. Rather, you observe and remember a table near the door, a couch across the room, and other objects in their approximate location. So you build up a framework of the objective situation and can go to the different objects as you wish, though of course your orientation is not so good as if your eyes were open. You get to know the objects by use of stimuli but your interest is usually focused on the objects and not on the stimuli.

Goal set, too, is objective since it aims at reaching a certain place, or obtaining a certain object, or producing some change in the environment. And goal set is bound up with situation set, since the goal has its place in the situation.

Because of the importance of the combined situation-and-goal set for dealing efficiently with the environment, our formula should include some symbol for the set. Let a small $w$ appended to $O$ mean that the individual is so set, and our formula takes this final form:

$$W—S—O_w—R—W$$

It reads as follows: While the individual is set for reaching a certain goal in a certain situation he receives stimuli and makes responses which have an objective meaning because of his objective set, the stimuli revealing the objective situation and the responses being aimed at an objective result. His behavior is adjusted to the environment.

In spite of its great importance in behavior, the situation-and-goal set, being sometimes imperfect, may lead to very strange and ineffective actions. It is imperfect when $O$ has not sufficiently observed and understood the situation. Because of some bias of his own he has not faced the facts squarely but is set for a situation which is partially imaginary, and his actions guided by such a set are unrealistic. Or he fails to keep pace with a changing situation; his set is too rigid and his actions are out of date when performed. Something more about such maladjustments will be brought out in Chapter 12.

## EVERYDAY EXAMPLES OF THESE PRINCIPLES

**The process of reading.** Evidently reading is a stimulus-response process of a complicated sort. The stimulus is the light reflected from the printed page into the reader's eyes.

The motor response includes speech movements in oral reading, and eye movements along the lines of print even in silent reading. The complete response includes also the understanding and enjoyment (or otherwise) of what is read.

Since understanding is the main response, let us ask what factors are concerned in getting the meaning of a word or sentence. Suppose the reader comes to the word "watch" and responds by thinking of a timepiece. His understanding of this word goes back to his previous experience in learning this word and learning to read; this factor belongs under the head of "structure." Another factor is his "temporary state" of awakeness, for if he were very drowsy he might read the word without getting any meaning. And his "activity in progress"—the reading of a certain story—is a powerful selective factor, since the word "watch" has several meanings, and the meaning he gets depends on the context, *i.e.*, on his "set" for the story situation.

The process of reading affords some good examples of combination and of shifting. It was formerly supposed that the eyes moved steadily along a line of print, bringing each letter in turn into clear vision, and that the reader rapidly spelled out the words. But if you watch a reader's eyes (as you can conveniently by aid of a mirror laid flat on the table beside the reading matter) you will find that the eyes are moving not steadily but by a series of little jumps. They shift from point to point. In a newspaper line a good reader's eyes will make about 3–6 stops or fixations. During the rapid jumps he gets no clear view, but during each fixation he has a clear view of a couple of words. He glimpses the first word or two in the line, shifts a couple of words forward and takes a look there, shifts again and takes another look, and so on to near the end of the line from which his eyes make a long jump backward to near the beginning of the next line. This behavior of the reader's eyes is examined most accurately by aid of photography. Evidently the eyes are responding to combinations of letters rather than to single letters (10).

The reaction time method proves that a short, familiar word

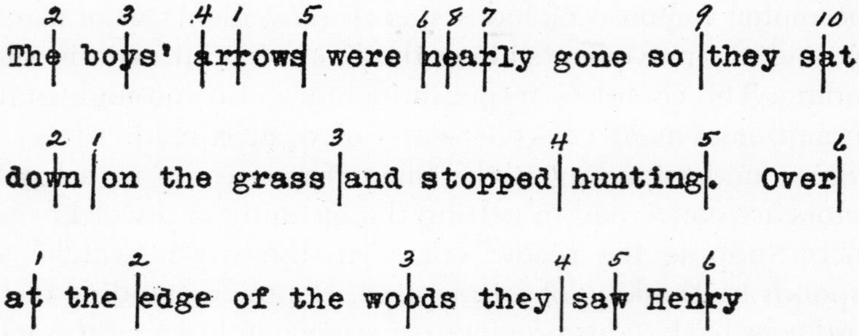

$$\overset{2}{\text{Th}}\overset{3}{\text{e}}\ \overset{.4}{\text{bo}}\overset{1}{\text{y}}\overset{5}{\text{s}}'\ \overset{}{\text{arrows}}\ \overset{6}{\text{were}}\ \overset{8}{\text{nea}}\overset{7}{\text{rly}}\ \text{gone}\ \text{so}\ \overset{9}{\big|\text{they}}\ \text{s}\overset{10}{\text{at}}$$

The boys' arrows were nearly gone so they sat

down on the grass and stopped hunting. Over

at the edge of the woods they saw Henry

FIG. 40.—Fixation points in reading. While a boy was reading these three lines, his eye movements were photographed. From the photographic record it was possible to locate the successive points on which he focused his eyes. The first line evidently gave him a little trouble; he had to go back from the first fixation point so as to see the first words clearly; and the word "nearly" seemed to offer some difficulty. The second and third lines were comparatively easy for this reader. (From Buswell, 2.)

can be read as a whole. Single letters are read as quickly as possible, and the reaction time is about $\frac{4}{10}$ of a second. Short words, too, are read in $\frac{4}{10}$ of a second. Since it takes no more time to read a short word than a single letter, the word is certainly not read by spelling it out. It is seen and read as a whole. Even a long word, if familiar, is read as a whole. A child can learn to read words before he knows his letters.

The speed of silent reading is much too great to allow time for spelling out the letters, or even for pronouncing the separate words. Easy reading goes at the rate of 2.5 words per second in a slow adult reader, and as fast as 10 words per second in a rapid reader. Difficult material is read more slowly because more time has to be allowed for comprehension.

[What are the limiting factors in speed of reading and why does one person read so much more slowly than another? Speed of comprehension is probably the most important factor.] Difficult material holds you back, while easily grasped material lets you move ahead rapidly. Comprehension depends on the reader's mental quickness and on his knowledge of the subject. But is the slow reader necessarily slow in comprehending and forever doomed to remain a slow reader? Not at all. He may not realize that his reading is slow, or he may even prefer to read slowly so as to savor each phrase to the full. Still he is missing something if he has not developed the skill to read rapidly. Some reading matter that is not worth a lot of time may be read rapidly for pure enjoyment or for culling out a few ideas. It is one thing to finish an exciting story in an hour or two, and quite another thing to let it keep you up all night.

No single prescription can be given to all slow readers who wish to increase their speed. Some have one bad reading habit, some another. Some have never abandoned the child's habit of whispering the words or at least moving the lips. This oral activity holds them back, for silent reading can go much faster than oral reading. Some adults keep up the beginner's habit of examining each word minutely, while others have the opposite fault of skimming too hastily over the words, misreading some words and having to go back. Some adults have a surprisingly meager vocabulary and do not know many words they meet in adult reading matter. Some have never mastered the neat little eye movements of rapid reading and may be helped by special exercises for regularizing these movements and cutting out superfluous fixations. Usually the main thing is to convince the slow reader that he has something to learn, something worth while to which he should give some attention with the confident expectation of making a considerable gain. When all is done, some persons will continue to read more rapidly than others (2, 3, 9).

**Doing two things at once.** In emphasizing the principle of selectivity, some pages back (p. 212), we almost made the assertion that the individual performs only one act at a time. We did not quite say that, but we did say that he performs only one "main act" at a time. As a matter of fact, the individual is usually doing at least two things at a time, one being the act of breathing. He has no trouble in breathing and walking at the same time, or even in thinking while both breathing and walking. But breathing and walking are _automatic_, that is, they can go on while attention is being given to something else. Other physiological processes such as digestion and the heart beat are automatic, and so are many acts that have been thoroughly learned. The expert typist can copy ordinary material while thinking of something else, and the pianist can play a familiar piece while listening to a conversation. However, when the typist is trying for high speed, and when the pianist is playing with much expression, they give close attention to what they are doing. Many kinds of routine work can be done moderately well while the thoughts are on something else. Of course the question might be raised as to which is the "main act" in such cases, but it is fair to say that to the individual at a particular moment the "main act" is the one to which he is giving his attention. In this sense, can the individual perform two main acts at the same time?

Julius Caesar, it was reported, used to dictate several letters "at the same time," each letter to a different copyist. He would give the first copyist the opening sentence of the first letter, shift to the second copyist and start him on the second letter, and so on, coming back to the first copyist in time to keep him busy, and never becoming confused himself. An intellectual feat, certainly! But not a feat requiring absolutely simultaneous attention to different matters or absolutely simultaneous performance of two main acts.

If you try to carry on two intellectual tasks at the same time, you find yourself *shifting* back and forth between them. You can add a column of numbers while reciting a familiar poem; you start the poem and let it run on automatically for a line or two while you add a few numbers, switch back to the poem and then back to the adding. Individuals differ greatly in their ability to do this sort of thing, but most people work much more efficiently when they do one thing at a time.

Besides this shifting procedure, another way of carrying on two tasks simultaneously is sometimes possible. Two acts can sometimes be *combined* into a single integrated performance. The beginner at the piano prefers to play with the right hand alone, because striking the bass note with his left hand interferes with his playing the main tune with his right hand. After some practice he easily combines both hands and really plays the music, much to his satisfaction. Other examples of combination are seen in driving a car, piloting an airplane, and numerous skilled performances.

**Resisting distractions.** Usually when you are trying to do one thing there are other things competing for your attention. But if you are sufficiently interested and absorbed in what you are doing you put extra energy into it and overcome the distraction.

There have been many experiments on the effects of noise and other distractions. In one experiment (4) a large class of college sophomores was first given a paper-and-pencil intelligence test, and then divided into two "matched groups," so that for each student in the one group there was a student in the other group who made the same score in this preliminary test. Each group contained 90 students. Some weeks later these matched groups took another similar intelligence test, but this time one group (the "experimental group") worked under distracting conditions, while the other group (the "control group") worked under normal quiet conditions. For distracting stimuli there were bells, buzzers, organ pipes, whistles and other noise makers, intermittent music, a spotlight flashing around the walls of the room, and people moving roughly about, talking and carrying strange apparatus. The conditions were outrageous, except that the whole thing was an experiment. The average scores came out as follows:

|  | Score in points |
|---|---|
| Control group, working in quiet | 137.6 |
| Experimental group, working under distraction | 133.9 |
| Loss through distraction | 3.7 |

The effect of distraction was very slight on the average, and none of the students broke down in the 19 minutes of intense work under severe distraction, though a few reported considerable strain.

In another experiment (1) matched groups were not used, but the same subjects worked sometimes in normal conditions and sometimes under distraction. Here, too, the effect of distraction was slight, and it could be warped one way or the other by suggestion. If the subjects were led to believe that the sound of music would disturb their arithmetical work, they lost a little; but if they were led to believe that the music would help them work, they gained a little; without any suggestion they neither gained nor lost. Some students say that soft radio music helps them to study; this supposed help may be a matter of suggestion, or perhaps of habit. In some kinds of factory work—which however is quite different from the student's job—music has been found to increase output (7).

So much intellectual work is done nowadays in noisy surroundings that the question is very important whether such conditions make any steady drain on the organism. Further investigation is necessary before this question can be answered. A great deal depends on the individual's emotional reaction. If he is irritated to the point of thinking, "Such conditions are an outrage," his work and perhaps his health will suffer. Internal distractions such as fear, anger and boredom have much more effect than the ordinary run of external distractions.

*Key to Anagrams,* page 222: 1. empty. 2. judge. 3. group. 4. daisy. 5. drown. 6. camel. 7. widen. 8. party. 9. storm. 10. habit. 11. cigar. 12. pansy. 13. bacon. 14. knife. 15. plant. 16. cheat, teach. 17. throw, worth. 18. cloud, could. 19. night, thing. 20. argon, organ, orang, groan. 21. train. 22. rangy, angry. 23. mouth. 24. horse, shore. 25. write.

The point of the experiment is that the letters have always to be rearranged in a certain order in the first 15 examples, but not in the last 10. If the subject becomes unconsciously set for this order he misses the most obvious words in examples 16–20, and experiences difficulty with 21–25 which must be rearranged differently.

## SUMMARY

1. *General psychology* seeks to discover and formulate the laws and principles that apply to the behavior of all persons. *Differential psychology* is concerned with the ways in which people differ.

2. The activities of the individual are ways in which he deals with the environment.

   a. The individual *resists and avoids* certain environmental forces in ways that insure his survival and continued activity.

   b. The individual *uses* the environment, appropriating food, etc., and finding stimulation and outlet for activity.

   c. The individual *participates* in what goes on in the environment.

   d. *Adjustment* to the environment involves changes in the environment or changes in the individual in his relation to it.

   e. The formula $W-O-W$ represents the continuous interaction of the environment and the individual.

3. The interaction of the individual and the environment takes place through the medium of stimuli and responses.

   a. *Effectors* are the individual's organs of response—his muscles and certain glands.

   b. *Receptors* are the individual's sense organs—the mechanisms for receiving stimulation from the environment.

   c. *Stimuli* are forces (external or internal) acting on a receptor and affecting the individual's activities.

   d. *Responses* are changes in the individual's activity aroused by stimuli. When the response is a stopping of activity it is called *inhibition*.

   e. The formula $S-R$ expresses the principle that the forces of the environment act as stimuli to arouse responses.

4. Responses to stimulation depend in part on the nature of the stimulus and in part on factors in the individual. This principle is expressed in the formula $S-O-R$.

   a. Responses depend on the *structure* of the individual—his permanent abilities and characteristics which have developed through the interaction of heredity and past learning.

   b. Responses depend on the *temporary state* of the individual.

    c. Responses depend on the *activity in progress* at the time of stimulation.

    d. The two previous formulas can now be combined to give $W—S—O—R—W$.

5. The interaction between environment and individual is made adjustive and efficient by the operation of factors of *selectivity* and of *preparatory set*.

    a. *Selective reception* involves adjusting the sense organs and directing the attention to only some out of many stimuli present at the moment.

    b. *Selective response* is necessary when the stimulus situation tends to arouse two antagonistic responses.

    c. Even when the situation remains the same the individual characteristically *shifts* the focus of his activity from one stimulus to another and from one response to another.

    d. Response is not typically to single isolated stimuli but to a *combination of stimuli* which are organized into a unit. Combination of muscles is also the rule for response.

    e. Most activity, if it is to be unified and efficient, requires preparation. *Preparatory set* is sensory as well as motor; it is selective for a particular stimulus and a particular response. *Reaction time* is the shortest interval in which an individual can respond to a stimulus. The better the preparatory set, the shorter the reaction time.

    f. Set may be preparatory for a single act, or it may be a *continuing control* directing ⁓ series of steps toward a goal.

    g. *Mental set* is preparation for a mental task. It promotes speed and accuracy by eliminating other responses which are not relevant to the task.

    h. *Situation set* is preparation to take account of the present environment in any activity. Situation sets are built on observation, are continuing, and are objective.

    i. The formula $W—S—O_w—R—W$ indicates that the interaction of the individual with his environment depends on his set.

# CHAPTER EIGHT

# *The Nervous System*

T he preceding chapter made clear that the environment acts on the individual by stimulating his receptors, and that the individual reacts to the environment by responses of various kinds. We learned that behavior also depends on the individual—his structure, his temporary state, and his activities in progress. In this chapter we turn to the study of what happens inside the body—what happens between stimulus and response.

The nervous system is the mechanism by which the individual's behavior is controlled and regulated. When he sees, learns, thinks or desires, he is using his nervous system, as well as his receptors and muscles. There is much detailed knowledge of the structure and function of the nervous system. For a century and more many physiologists, anatomists and clinicians have studied it, hoping to throw light on behavior. Much of this knowledge is remote from our ordinary range of ideas. In psychology we are primarily concerned with those factors influencing behavior which can be manipulated and modified, and there is little that the student can do in the way of manipulating his nervous system directly. But a few basic facts are helpful in getting below the surface of human behavior (*10*).

We approach the physiologist for information bearing on such questions as these: how the organism, for all its multiplicity of parts, is able to act as a whole; how, being a unit, it can still act in so many different ways; how it responds to stimuli; how it selects and combines—for we saw that selectivity and combination were very characteristic of both the reception of stimuli and the execution of movements; how it maintains a set toward a goal through a series of acts; and how it builds up and holds a "situation set." Looking ahead to later chapters we should hope that physiology would throw some light on learning and retention and on the sensory processes. Even if we do not get complete answers to all our questions, we shall see them from a new point of view (6).

## HOW THE NERVES OPERATE

Going back to first principles we see that individuals are alike in the general problem they have to solve, the problem of dealing effectively with the environment. Such dealing is dependent on the receptors and effectors, the receptors receiving stimuli from the environment, the effectors (muscles, particularly) producing changes in the environment. The receptor cells are very numerous (millions of them in the eyes alone), and the muscles are composed of very numerous muscle fibers. All this contact with the environment would be of no use to the organism unless there were some connection from the receptors to the effectors. The muscles must react to stimuli received by the receptors, and in an emergency the reaction must be quick. Rapid communication from the receptors to the effectors is provided by the *nerves,* which conduct so rapidly (about 75 yards per second) that they consume only a small fraction of a second in a simple reaction (p. 216).

How the organism is enabled to act as a unit. A general view of the nervous system (Fig. 41) shows nerves ramifying to every part of the body; they really divide into much finer and more numerous branches than the figure shows. They supply every muscle and every receptor. But a second glance shows

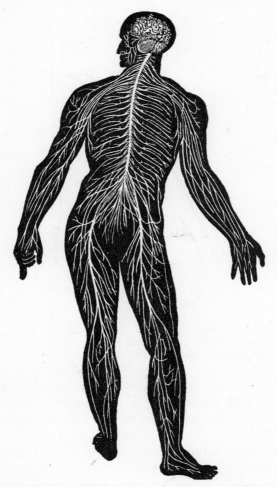

FIG. 41.—Geneal view of the nervous system, showing
brain, spinal cord and nerves (Martin, 9).

that these parts are not connected directly with each other but
only with a central mass consisting of the brain in the head and
the spinal cord extending down the back. All the nerves lead
to or from this general nerve center. The sensory nerves, supplying the receptors, conduct into the center; the motor nerves,
supplying the effectors, conduct out from the center. The

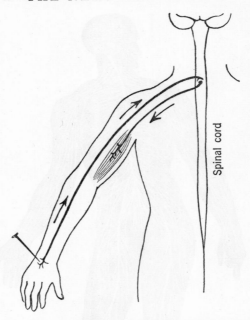

Fig. 42.—Nerve connection from the back of the hand, which is receiving a stimulus, to the arm muscle which executes the response. The nerve pathway leads into the spinal cord and out again.

sensory nerves report to the center, while the motor nerves take orders from the center and in turn arouse activity in the muscles. Thus the organism is centralized and capable of unified action.

**How variety of action is possible.** It is just as important for the organism to do different things under different conditions as for it to act as a unit. If the nerve center were simply a big reservoir receiving stimulation from the sensory nerves and pouring it out into the motor nerves, every act would be a general spasm. Microscopically examined, the nerve center proves to be anything but a mere reservoir. It has a very intricate structure. Even a single nerve consists of many minute fibers. The largest nerve in the body, the optic nerve conducting from the eye to the brain, contains as many as 400,000 fibers. Nerve fibers are extremely slender, but some of them

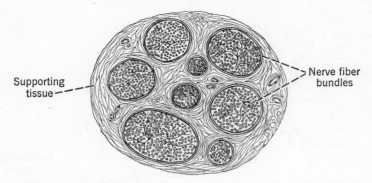

Fig. 43.—Cross section of a small nerve. It consists of several bundles bound together by supporting tissue. Each bundle contains many nerve fibers, showing in cross section as little circles.

are a yard long, each being long enough to reach from some receptor to the nerve center, or from the center to some muscle. These fibers are conducting units like the insulated wires in a telephone cable. Each sensory nerve fiber runs from a receptor to some definite part of the nerve center and each motor nerve fiber runs from some part of the nerve center to a particular muscle. The conduction along any sensory or motor nerve is not diffuse in the least but entirely localized and specific. The structure of the nervous system is somewhat like that of a city telephone system. The nerves are like telephone cables in being bundles of insulated conductors, each conductor leading to a separate point outside of the center but all converging to a common center where connections are made. But the connections made in the nerve center are very different from those in a telephone central. One incoming call is switched to a selection of the outgoing lines and many incoming calls may be switched to the same outgoing line. Thus the organism acts as a whole even while acting in a thousand different ways.

If the nerve supplying a muscle is broken or cut in an accident, the muscle is helpless. Receiving no stimuli from its nerve it remains inactive and paralyzed. Similarly if one optic nerve is cut the person is blind in that eye. No stimuli can reach

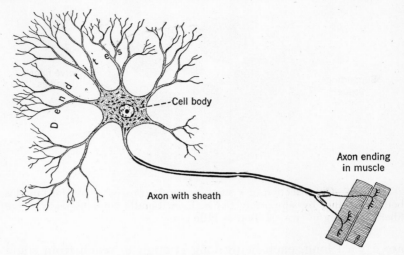

FIG. 44.—A motor neuron from the spinal cord, highly magnified. It has many dendrites, and a single axon that extends out to a muscle and there divides and makes close contact with a few muscles fibers. The axon is relatively much longer than shown in the figure.

the brain, no messages, because with the nerve cut there is no means of communication from the eye to the brain.

Nerve cells. If we wish to know how the nervous system operates, there is little to learn from the mere gross appearance of the brain, cord and nerves, just as we could learn little of the operation of a telephone system by inspecting the cables strung along the street and the building housing the central exchange. We need to examine the internal structure of the system, the microscopic structure in the case of the nervous system.

A *neuron* is a nerve cell including its branches. The whole nervous system is made up of neurons along with supporting tissue and the necessary blood vessels. Most nerve cells have two kinds of branches, a single *axon* and many *dendrites*. The dendrites are short tree-like branches, while the axon may be several feet long (Fig. 44).

Each nerve fiber contains an axon surrounded by an insulating sheath. The axons of the motor nerves are branches of

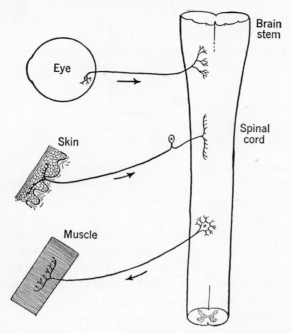

Fig. 45.—Sensory and motor axons and their nerve cells. The arrows
show the directions in which the several axons conduct.

nerve cells situated in the brain or cord. Each of these motor
axons extends from some part of the brain or cord out to a
muscle (or gland). Being stimulated in the nerve center it
passes the stimulation along to its muscle (Fig. 45).

The axons of the sensory nerves are branches of nerve cells
lying outside of the nerve center. Thus the axons of the optic
nerve come from cells in the retina, the light-sensitive part of
the eye (p. 441), and extend into the brain. The axons for the
sense of smell are branches of cells in the nose. The axons of
the other sensory nerves are branches of nerve cells which lie
in little bunches close to the brain or cord, and which are exceptional in having no dendrites. Each of these axons divides
and extends outward to a receptor in the skin or elsewhere and
inward into the cord or brain, so providing a path of connection
from that receptor to the nerve center.

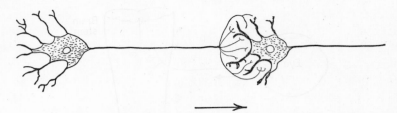

FIG. 46.—The synapse between the two neurons lies above the arrow. The arrow shows the direction of conduction across the synapse.

**The synapse.** Variety of response is made possible by the peculiar mode of connection between neurons. Long before birth the neurons begin life as separate, round cells. A little latter they take on the character of neurons by sending out an axon and dendrites. Though they establish close contact with each other by these branches, they never grow together, but each neuron always remains a separate cell. This form of connection, by contact only, is called synaptic connection and the contact between one neuron and another is called a synapse.

For simplicity let us first consider just two neurons and their synaptic connection. The axon of one neuron terminates in fine branches which interlace with the dendrites of the other neuron or attach themselves to its cell body. The contact between the two neurons is close enough to enable one to stimulate the other. Communication across a synapse is always in one direction, from the axon of the first neuron to the dendrites or cell body of the other. The axon is a conductor and stimulator, the dendrite a receiver (Fig. 46).

One misconception that might be created by our simplified diagram should be corrected at once. The neurons are not linked up in single chains. Each axon terminates so as to establish synapses with several other neurons; it can deliver stimuli to any or all of them. Each neuron also receives stimuli from the axons of several neurons. We see the principle of combination coming in here in two forms: combination of stimuli upon a single neuron, and combination of elementary responses by an axon branching and stimulating several neurons. We will say more of these two forms of combination later.

The principle of selectivity also comes in, for the axons do not run at random and form synapses with any chance neuron. The sensory axon from a certain bit of skin runs to a certain part of the spinal cord and connects with a certain group of neurons; and the motor axon from a certain part of the cord runs to a group of muscle fibers in a certain muscle and stimulates those particular fibers. The neuron connections are extremely intricate but highly organized.

**The nerve impulse.** When a sensory nerve fiber is stimulated, say in the skin, it swiftly transmits a message to the cord or brain. When a motor neuron is stimulated in the brain or cord it swiftly transmits a message to a group of muscle fibers and makes them contract. What are these "messages"? What does the nerve conduct or transmit? We call it the nerve impulse, and as far as known it is an electrochemical wave in the nerve fiber, which is very weak and consumes very little energy, but still is capable of arousing a muscle or a nerve center to action.

**The all-or-none law in nerve and muscle.** The meaning of "all or none" is illustrated by reference to a charge of dynamite. If the charge explodes at all it explodes completely. You cannot graduate the force of the explosion by varying the force of the spark with which you set it off. The charge can differ in amount, but whatever amount is present explodes as a unit. The all-or-none law holds good of the single muscle fiber and of the single nerve fiber. At any instant a muscle fiber contains a certain charge of available energy and any stimulus which arouses the muscle fiber to discharge uses up all this energy. In a fraction of a second the muscle fiber recovers, and has a new charge ready. Similarly a single nerve fiber discharges all of its available energy when it discharges at all. A stimulus may be too weak to arouse the fiber, but if it is strong enough to arouse any response it arouses the full response of which the fiber is capable at that particular moment (*1*).

**Varying strength of response.** A stronger stimulus to the organism usually brings a stronger response. A stronger light gives a brighter sensation of light, and a stronger effort gives a stronger muscular contraction. This gradation of response seems at first thought to be inconsistent with the all-or-none law.

There are two ways, in spite of the all-or-none law, in which a stronger stimulus can produce a stronger response. First, a stronger stimulus arouses a larger number of nerve fibers or muscle fibers. Even a pin point on the skin presses the endings of several sensory nerve fibers, and the more strongly it presses, the more nerve fibers will be stimulated.

In the second place, a stronger stimulus, though it cannot increase the strength of a single impulse, can arouse more impulses per second. The nerve fiber is so quick that a single wave of action is finished in a small fraction of a second. A continued stimulus applied to a nerve fiber arouses a series of impulses, and the stronger the stimulus the quicker the succession of impulses. In a single nerve fiber there may be as few as 5 impulses per second or as many as 200, depending on the strength of the stimulus. Muscle fibers, too, discharge a smaller or larger number of times per second according to the strength of the stimulus received.

Putting these two factors together we see that the strength of a response depends upon the total number of nerve impulses occurring per second, this number depending partly on the number of impulses in each fiber and partly on the number of active fibers. So we get graded sensations and graded muscular action.

## THE STIMULUS-RESPONSE MECHANISM

When the axon of one neuron stimulates another neuron to activity, or when a motor axon stimulates a group of muscle fibers, we have stimulus and response in their most rudimentary form. One cell stimulates another. Such rudimentary responses make up the internal detail of behavior. Now take the organism as a whole: a stimulus is applied to a receptor and a muscle or group of muscles responds. What is the nature of these larger stimulus-response units?

**Reflex action.** In the simple reaction (which is not a reflex) the subject is told to be ready and then a stimulus applied to his ear starts nerve impulses running to the brain; because of the way the brain is "set" the incoming impulses quickly give rise to outgoing impulses running down the spinal cord and out to the muscles which move the hand; and the total reaction time is about .15 second (p. 216). This reaction is fairly quick, but the reflex wink of the eyelids in response to a touch on the eyes is even quicker, taking about .05 second. Still quicker is the knee jerk obtained by striking the tendon just below the bent knee while the lower leg is hanging freely. The reflex time here is about .03 second. Not every reflex is especially quick, however, and some are slower than the simple reaction. The pupillary reflex, the narrowing of the pupil in response to a bright light suddenly shining into the eyes, takes a second or two.

The organism has many other reflexes, such as withdrawal of the hand from a burn, coughing, sneezing, and many internal reactions such as the movements of the stomach and intestines, and the widening and narrowing of the arteries which cause the skin to flush or pale. These are muscular responses, and there are also glandular reflexes such as the flow of saliva in response to a tasting substance in the mouth, and the flow of tears when a cinder gets into the eye.

A reflex is a direct muscular or glandular response to a sensory stimulus, an involuntary and unlearned response. Unlike the simple reaction, it does not depend upon the subject's being prepared or "set." The reflex does not need a "Ready" signal.

**The reflex arc.** The reflex depends on certain definite connections laid down in the growth of the nerve centers between the incoming sensory fibers and the outgoing motor fibers. The path from a sense organ through the nerve center to a muscle is called a reflex arc and some of these paths have been worked out in detail by physiologists.

A minimum diagram of the reflex arc shows the sensory axon leading from a receptor to the nerve center and there

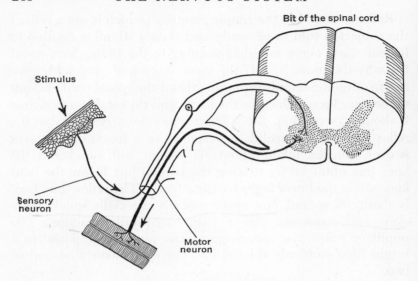

FIG. 47.—A two-neuron reflex arc.

forming a synaptic connection with the motor neuron whose axon extends out to the muscles (Fig. 47). This combination of a sensory and a motor neuron makes up a two-neuron reflex arc. Most reflex arcs have at least three neurons and some have more than that.

These simple diagrams are instructive in showing some of the less complicated interconnections in the nerve centers and so giving us some idea of what to expect in the brain. They are misleading if taken too literally; they need to be supplemented by a few fundamental statements regarding nerve center activity.

1. *Multiple nerve paths.* Each single fiber in the diagrams stands for a whole company of fibers working abreast.

2. *Converging paths.* The single reflex arc does not ordinarily act in isolation from the rest of the nervous system. Every nerve center receives axons from several other parts of the nervous system and is thus subjected to a combination of influences rather than to one single stimulus. The breathing center for

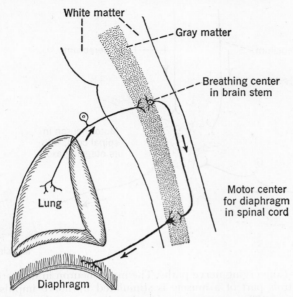

White matter

Gray matter

Breathing center
in brain stem

Motor center
for diaphragm
in spinal cord

Lung

Diaphragm

FIG. 48.—A three-neuron arc concerned in breathing. During expiration the sensory nerves of the lung are stimulated and arouse the breathing center in the brain stem. This in turn arouses the motor center for the diaphragm (in the spinal cord) and so brings on the movement of inspiration.

example receives not only sensory nerve impulses from the lungs but also impulses from many other sensory nerves as well, so that breathing is easily modified by a painful stimulus, by a loud noise, or by a dash of cold water on the skin. The breathing center also receives nerve fibers from higher up in the brain, as we can infer from the fact that the breath can be hastened or slowed voluntarily. The rate and depth of breathing are affected also by the amount of carbon dioxide in the blood circulating through the breathing center itself. So the three-neuron arc shown in Figure 48 is very far from a complete picture of the mechanism of breathing.

3. *Branching paths.* An adequate picture must show not only converging axons, but also branching axons by which any single neuron exerts an influence on several others. The nerve impulses coming from one part are distributed to many parts. The

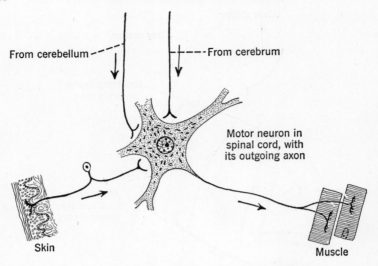

FIG. 49.—Converging nerve paths. The motor neuron in the cord which directly controls part of a muscle is stimulated by nerve impulses from several sources. (The motor neuron in this diagram is drawn disproportionately large.)

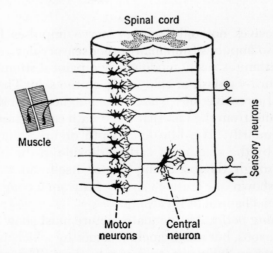

FIG. 50.—Branching of neurons. The result is the passing on of stimulation to many muscle fibers (of which only two are shown).

numerous muscle fibers in a single muscle are made to act together, and several muscles can be aroused at the same time in a coordinated movement (Fig. 50).

4. *Continued activity.* The reflex arc diagram may suggest a nerve center resting quietly until a stimulus arrives—whereas the typical condition of the nervous system as a whole is one of continued activity, activity in progress. The activity going on in the brain and cord is modified by the incoming nerve impulses. We should think of the system as constantly active and constantly receiving stimuli which modify its activity.

## THE BRAIN

There are many parts of the brain with many names, but the large divisions are these: the *brain stem* continuing the cord upward on an enlarged scale, and terminating in the *interbrain;* and two large outgrowths from the brain stem, the *cerebrum* and *cerebellum.* The brain stem and spinal cord, taken together, are the axis of the whole nervous system.

All the nerves of the arms and legs and most of the nerves of the trunk connect with the spinal cord, which contains the "lower centers" for these parts of the body. The nerves of the heart, lungs and stomach and the nerves of the head and face connect with the brain stem which contains the lower centers for these parts. The "higher centers" in the cerebrum and cerebellum are connected directly with these lower centers, and only by way of the lower centers do the higher centers have any connection with the muscles and sense organs, or with the environment. The lower centers coordinate the muscles into relatively simple teams; the higher centers coordinate the lower centers and so secure more elaborate teamwork from the muscles.

The cerebellum is located at the back of the head and is almost covered by the cerebrum. Large bundles of nerve fibers lead from the brain stem to the cerebellum, which receives sensory messages from the muscles of the body and coordinates messages going to motor neurons in such a way as to result in

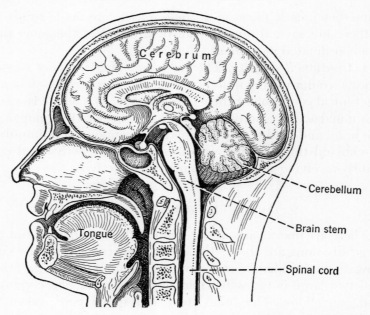

FIG. 51.—Location of the cord, brain stem, cerebrum and cerebellum.

the smooth working together of the muscles involved in any complicated movement.

The cerebrum in man is much larger than all the rest of the nervous system put together; it fills most of the skull. Its right and left halves are called hemispheres. The right hemisphere is connected for the most part with the left side of the body and the left hemisphere with the right side of the body. Of what service to the organism this crossed relation may be, no one has yet discovered.

The surface of the cerebrum as seen in Figure 52 shows the well-known *convolutions* or *gyri* separated by *fissures* which extend down a little into the substance of the cerebrum but do not really divide it into separate parts. Even the major divisions of the cerebrum, called *lobes,* are not separate organs for they are continuous underneath. The *frontal lobe* inside the forehead extends back as far as the *central fissure,* behind which lies the *parietal lobe;* behind that is the *occipital lobe,* lying at

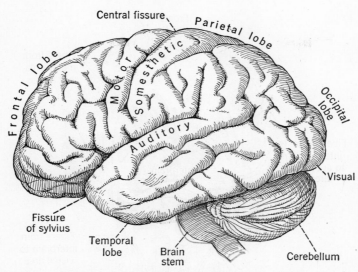

FIG. 52.—Side view of the left hemisphere of the cerebrum, showing the lobes and the motor and sensory areas. The olfactory area lies in a secluded position shown in Figure 54.

the rear of the brain. On the side of each hemisphere is the conspicuous *fissure of Sylvius* which separates the *temporal lobe* below from the frontal lobe above.

The *motor area* lies in the frontal lobe just forward of the central fissure; the *somesthetic area,* which is the area for the cutaneous and muscle senses, lies just behind the central fissure in the parietal lobe. The *auditory area* lies in the upper margin of the temporal lobe. The *visual area* lies at the rear of the brain in the occipital lobe. The justification for so naming these particular areas will be explained presently.

**Internal structure of the brain.** The external views of the brain give practically no idea at all of its mode of operation. It looks merely like a big mass and might be an overgrown gland of some sort. A section through the brain, either horizontal or transverse (Figs. 53 and 54), gives a very different impression. Even to the naked eye it shows a difference between white and gray matter. A large share of the gray matter lies on the surface and is called the *cortex* (bark) of the cere-

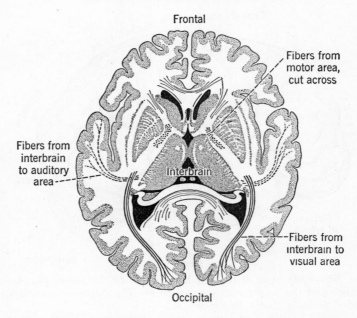

FIG. 53.—Horizontal section through the brain. White matter is shown in white, gray matter in gray, and fluid spaces in black.

brum. The cortex extends around the bottom of the fissures. There are also large interior masses of gray matter.

Viewed through the microscope, after suitable stains have been applied to the tissue, the white matter is seen to consist of nerve fibers passing in various directions. The gray matter is found to consist of nerve cells with their dendrites and of axons entering and terminating. The lower centers are masses of gray matter lying inside the spinal cord and brain stem, while the higher centers are largely in the cortex. About 50 percent of the brain and cord is white matter and 50 percent gray. The white matter consists of nerve fibers connecting all parts of the gray matter, just as the external nerves consist of fibers linking the lower centers with the muscles and sense organs.

When highly magnified any mass of gray matter shows a very intricate internal structure of nerve cells, dendrites and axons. Some idea of this intricate structure can be obtained

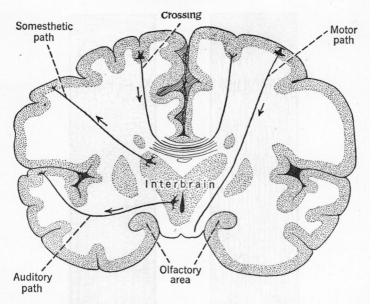

Somesthetic path

Crossing

Motor path

Interbrain

Auditory path

Olfactory area

Fig. 54.—Transverse section through the brain. (The scale is larger than that of the previous figure.) Single fibers, each of which stands for many thousands, indicate some of the principal pathways: from the motor area down toward the lower centers, from the interbrain to the auditory and somesthetic areas of the cortex, and from one hemisphere to the other.

from Figure 55. This particular bit of the cortex comes from the motor area and contains some giant pyramid cells, one of which is shown in Figure 56. Most of the cortex appears to be less well developed than the motor area. In fact all parts of the cortex differ in the fine detail of their inner structure.

The total number of nerve cells in the cerebral cortex is estimated to be about 14,000,000,000. Many of these are small and apparently undeveloped as if they constituted a reserve stock not yet used in the individual's cerebral activities.

With regard to individual differences, the question most likely to arise concerns the relation of brain size to intelligence. Some individuals of outstanding ability have been found, on postmortem examination, to have had very large brains, and some idiots very small brains. But the relationship is

F<small>IG</small>. 55.—A small bit of the human cerebral cortex magnified to show
something of its internal structure. One view shows the nerve cells
and dendrites with a few axons, while the other, being differently stained,
brings out the axons and their branches. Imagine one view superposed on
the other and you have some impression of the intricate interweaving of
axons and dendrites in the cortex. Convergence of paths is carried to a
maximum here (Ramon y Cajal).

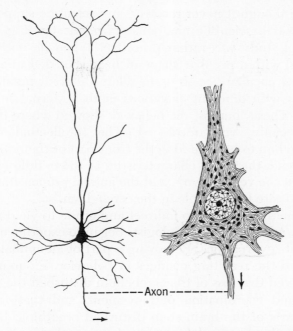

Fig. 56.—A giant pyramid neuron from the motor area. The second view shows its cell body still further magnified. The axon goes into the motor path shown in Figures 54 and 57.

far from close. Brain size (as judged from head measurements of living individuals) and intelligence (as tested) give a correlation of only +.10 or +.15, indicating that individual differences in intelligence are accounted for only to a very small extent by differences in the mere gross size of the brain. Other factors such as the fineness of internal brain structure and the chemistry of brain tissue are probably more important.

## MOTOR AND SENSORY AREAS OF THE CORTEX

The question whether different parts of the brain differ in function has an interesting history. It has been a live scientific question ever since about 1800 when Gall propounded his famous theory of phrenology, a theory which had a vast popular vogue though it never received any scientific support. Gall himself was a scientific anatomist of good standing, but his method of study was rather primitive. When he noticed any individual with a peculiar shape of head, he tried to ascertain his mental peculiarities so as to relate different mental characteristics with different elevations in the external surface of the skull. These "bumps," he believed, showed where the brain was especially well developed. The intellectual faculties seemed to him to be located in the front part of the brain inside the forehead, the moral characteristics in the middle (as "veneration" at the very crown), and the animal propensities in the rear, sex desire for example in the cerebellum.

Gall's methods were too indirect and crude to yield any real evidence. A little later physiologists began to experiment by the method of "extirpation." Removing a part of an animal's brain, they noted the resulting changes in behavior. Flourens about 1825 showed that loss of the cerebellum disturbed the animal's posture and coordination of movement, and that injury to certain parts of the brain stem disturbed breathing, heart action and other internal functions. Loss of the cerebrum destroyed initiative, memory and understanding, but as far as he could determine the cerebrum functioned as a unit. In direct opposition to phrenology he set up the doctrine that the cerebrum acts as a whole. Flourens' view was accepted doctrine till about 1860, when evidence began to accumulate showing that it made a difference what part of the cerebrum was injured. The human evidence comes from cases of brain tumors, gunshot wounds and other injuries to parts of the brain. Definite losses of function have been noted during life and at autopsy localized brain injuries have been found. By the end of the nineteenth century there was general agreement on the location of the chief sensory areas and the motor area; and with further advance in technique and increase in case material these areas have been definitely established.

The methods used in studying brain localization are:

1. Method of *extirpation*: part of an animal's brain is destroyed, and the resulting losses of function are noted.

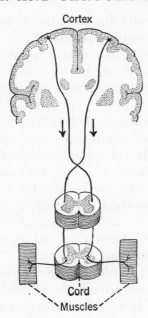

Cortex

Cord
Muscles

FIG. 57.—The principal motor path. Axons from the giant pyramids in the motor area pass down through the brain stem to some part of the spinal cord where they connect with the motor neurons and so with the muscles. Note the right-left crossing.

2. *Pathological* method: disturbed function is observed in a human patient, and autopsy sometimes reveals a more or less sharply localized brain injury.

3. *Stimulation*: weak electric currents are applied to an exposed region of the cortex to see what movements, if any, are elicited.

4. *Fiber tracing*: the connection of a certain part of the cortex with the eyes, of another with the ears, of another with the muscles, is established by tracing the fibers connecting the cortex with the lower centers.

The fiber-tracing method is especially convincing. When we find that the motor nerve fibers supplying the muscles of the arm come from nerve cells in the spinal cord at the level of the shoulder, we are convinced that this part of the spinal cord is the lower motor center for the arm. When we find that the giant pyramids in a certain region of the cerebral cortex send their axons down to this shoulder level of the cord, connecting with the lower motor center for the arm, we cannot doubt that this particular cortical region is a higher motor center for the arm (Fig. 57).

It must not be supposed that this fiber tracing is an easy matter. The fibers are not tough cords that can be teased out over long distances. Bundles of nerve fibers course in every direction through the white matter and only very special methods make it possible to trace any one bundle for any considerable distance. One special method is that of "degeneration." An axon severed from its nerve cell loses its vitality and degenerates. It then stains differently from a normal axon and can be traced in a series of cross sections.

By the concordant results of these various methods the following functional areas have been established.

**The motor area.**  If we ask which part of the immense surface of the hemispheres is most directly concerned with bodily movement, the fiber-tracing method points to a strip of cortex just in front of the central fissure, called the *precentral gyrus.* Here are the *giant cells* which send axons down to the lower motor centers in the cord and brain stem. Weak electrical stimulation of this strip of cortex produces movements of different parts of the body according to the part of the area stimulated. Stimulation at the top of the brain (just at the crown, where Gall located the center for veneration) gives movements of the feet and legs. A little further down stimulation gives movements of the trunk; still further down movements of the arms. Near the bottom of this precentral gyrus movements of the head, face and mouth are obtained. Injury to any part of this gyrus produces paralysis, temporary or permanent, in the corresponding part of the body. For all these reasons this narrow strip of cortex deserves the name of motor area.

The complete motor region however includes something more. It includes the cortex just in front of the motor area, which is often called the *premotor area*. This connects with the motor area and also has its own connections downward to the lower motor centers in the cord and brain stem. Stimulation of the premotor area gives movements which are more complex than those obtained from the motor area. The motor area seems to control single movements, the premotor area combinations of movements (6).

Even the motor and premotor centers taken together do not cover all the motor functions of the cortex. Eye and head movements can be obtained from the occipital lobe (as if in looking at a seen object), from the temporal lobe (as if in response to a sound) and from the frontal lobe (as if in spying out one's way).

Outgoing fibers lead from all parts of the cortex to the brain stem. A large share of them link the cerebrum through the brain stem with the *cerebellum*. This large organ has much to do with maintaining posture, equilibrium and muscular steadiness. The cerebrum and cerebellum work as a team, the cerebrum taking the initiative and providing the trained skill, as for example in kicking a football at the right time and in the right direction, while the cerebellum insures such an adjustment of posture as enables the player to kick and still maintain his balance.

**Sensory areas of the cortex.** The cortex is not connected directly with any of the sense organs, but it is connected with certain lower centers for these organs which all lie rather close together in the *interbrain*. The interbrain lies underneath the cerebrum. It may be called the upper end of the brain stem (Figs. 53, 54). Nerve fibers from the eye, the ear and the other sense organs lead to it, and relay fibers lead from it to different parts of the cortex. So the interbrain is an intermediate station or junction. It probably makes some essential contribution to sensory experience. Possibly it gives us the vaguer groundwork of sensation, leaving to the cortex the more definite perception of objects, shapes, colors, tones and noises. This is speculative; what we certainly know is that each sense organ

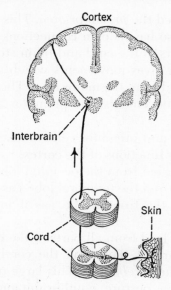

Fig. 58.—Sensory path from the skin of any part of the trunk or limbs. The path extends from the skin to the cord, from the cord to the interbrain, and thence to the somesthetic area of the cortex. See also Figures 45, 54.

communicates its messages to the cortex only by way of the interbrain. Each sense organ connects with a different part of the interbrain, the localization there being quite minute.

The somesthetic area.   The strip just behind the motor area, the *postcentral gyrus,* is the chief cortical center for the body senses, that is, for the skin and muscle senses. Injuries here cause losses of sensation in the skin or limbs. The limbs are represented in the same order as in the motor area, with the leg at the top and the face at the bottom.

The auditory area.   Sensory fibers from the ear run to the interbrain from which relay fibers run to a small portion of the *temporal lobe,* the auditory receiving center of the cortex. If this small region is destroyed in both hemispheres the individual is rendered deaf, but such injuries very seldom occur.

The visual area.   The sensory nerve fibers from the retina of the eye run back to a certain part of the interbrain, from which

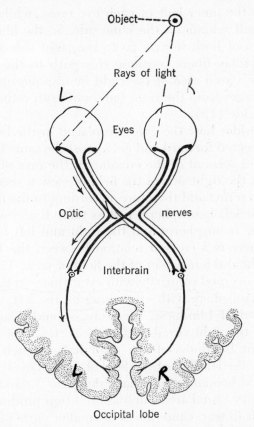

Object----

Rays of light

Eyes

Optic          nerves

Interbrain

Occipital lobe

FIG. 59.—Path of light and nerve impulses from a visible object to the visual area of the brain. The eyes are looking straight ahead. An object on the right affects the left half of each retina, the left side of the inter-brain, and the left occipital lobe.

relay fibers run to a limited region of the *occipital lobe*. This limited region is the visual receiving center, the primary visual center of the cortex.

This connection of the eyes with the brain is interesting enough to warrant a more detailed description (Fig. 59). From each eye the sensory fibers run back in the large optic nerve. The two optic nerves come together and appear to cross, but the fiber-tracing method shows that they do not all cross. The fibers from the inner half of each eye cross, while those from the outer half remain on the same side. So the fibers from the right halves of both retinas go to the right side of the inter-brain, and relay fibers continue this path to the right hemisphere. The visual area of the right hemisphere gets the combined messages from the right halves of both retinas; similarly on the left side (12).

Now consider how the eyes are placed in the head. In man they are directed forward and get almost the same field of view. (Try it!) On account of the crossing of the rays of light inside the eyeball, the right side of the field of view is seen by the left half of each retina and therefore, according to the fiber connections, by the left hemisphere. Just as there is a crossed relation between the hemispheres and the right and left halves of the body, so there is a crossed relation between the hemispheres and the right and left halves of the field of view. The left hemisphere is concerned primarily with everything on the right, and the right hemisphere with everything on the left.

What kind of blindness, therefore, should result from destruction of the right visual area of the cortex? Not blindness of one eye, but blindness of the right half of each retina, i.e., blindness to the left half of the field of view. This type of blindness is called *hemianopsia* ("half blindness"). Smaller injuries to the primary visual area, such as are often produced by gunshot wounds in war, cause losses of smaller parts of the field of view. The study of such injuries and the fiber-tracing method agree in showing that each part of the retina is connected with a different part of the visual area. The central part of the retina where vision is most distinct has a large share of the visual area devoted to it.

The primary visual area, then, consists of two parts, one part in each occipital lobe. It is rather curious that this division produces no discontinuity in the appearance of the field of view—no line or gap between the right and left halves of the field. The integration of the visual field must be accomplished by numerous fibers which connect the right and left visual areas.

There is still another method of studying the visual area which gives striking and convincing results. When the skull is opened up and the occipital lobe is exposed to view for the removal of a tumor, a weak electric current can safely be applied to points on the cortex and the patient (under local anesthetic) can report his experience. We might hastily assume that he would report pain, on the supposition that the brain must be very "sensitive." But no, stimulation of the visual area ought to give visual sensation. A leading student of these matters (3) reports the following results in one especially clear case: stimulation at the rear of the visual area caused the subject to see a bright light straight in front; at the upper part of the area it caused him to see a flickering something down below; at the lower part of the area it gave the same appearance in the upper part of the field of view. These localizations correspond to the results obtained by the other methods.

When the electric stimulus was applied outside the primary visual area but on neighboring parts of the occipital lobe, the subject reported more meaningful visual appearances; flames, stars, shiny balls, butterflies, various objects and even persons. Most of the occipital lobe is concerned in one way or another with vision. The primary visual area, receiving nerve impulses from the retina, passes the stimulation along by short association fibers to the neighboring regions and the latter contribute to the understanding of what is seen. Injuries to the occipital lobe not involving the primary visual area do not produce blindness but do impair the subject's ability to recognize objects, to read, to distinguish colors, or to find his way by the sense of sight.

## THE COMBINING OR ORGANIZING AREAS

The primary sensory areas are relatively small and the motor region also is not large in comparison with the whole extent of the human cortex. These primary areas provide for the intake of sensory data and the outgo of motor responses. But these sensory data and motor responses must be organized if the

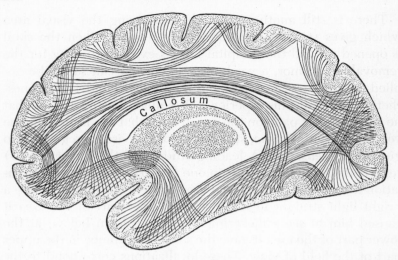

FIG. 60.—Sample axons connecting one part of the cortex with another. There are many millions of these "association fibers," connecting neighboring and distant parts of the same hemisphere or connecting one hemisphere with the other through the callosum.

individual is to deal effectively with the objective environment. Most of the cortex is concerned with this major job of organizing.

We might expect to find the "faculties" of memory, reason, feeling, and will, located in different parts of the cortex, but there is no evidence for any such localization. The distribution of functions over the cortex follows an entirely different principle, as we have just seen in the case of the occipital lobe. The cortex near the primary visual area is concerned with grasping the facts presented to the eye, and the cortex adjacent to the auditory area is concerned with the meaning of auditory data. In the neighborhood of the motor area the cortex seems to combine movements so as to reach certain goals and accomplish certain results. With the cortex adjacent to the primary areas thus accounted for, there still remain two large "association areas," one in the parietal, temporal and occipital lobes between the several sensory areas, and the other in the frontal lobe forward of the motor and premotor areas. Some evidence regarding the function of these areas has been obtained in cases of brain injury in man. The results of such injuries are classed under several heads (*11*).

**Aphasia** is a loss or impairment of speech and language usage, not due to either sensory loss or motor paralysis. Following brain injury there may be great difficulty in speaking sensible connected sentences, or in understanding spoken language. One speech center lies in the temporal and parietal lobes not far from the auditory area. This is not strange since speech is primarily an auditory affair. The child understands words before he can speak them, and the importance of hearing in the normal language process is shown by the fact that deaf children never learn to talk except with very special training. Because of injury in the neighborhood of the auditory area, an individual may be unable to understand spoken speech or to find the right words to express his own meaning even though he speaks fluently enough. One old gentleman mystified his friends by saying that he "must go and have his umbrella washed," until it was discovered that he wanted his hair cut!

Besides this sensory type of aphasia there is a motor type in which the great difficulty is to get the words out. Some patients can speak only one or two words of frequent usage (as "yes" and "no" and swear words), while others can pronounce separate words but cannot put them together into sentences. In this class of cases the injury is found in the lower part of the premotor area. Usually the brain injury is rather diffuse and the individual's intellectual processes are disturbed in many respects.

One striking fact about aphasia is its one-sided localization in the cortex. Although the basic sensory and motor functions are all represented in both hemispheres, language functions are controlled in one hemisphere only—the left one in right-handed persons. Aphasia thus results from injuries of the left hemisphere while corresponding injuries on the opposite side have no effect on language (*13*).

**Apraxia,** loss of ability to "do," is akin to aphasia. Give the individual a box of matches and a cigar, and he may be unable to make the right combination, though capable of executing all the necessary single movements. The brain injury varies in location but is usually not far from the motor area.

**Agnosia** is loss of ability to know or perceive. Visual agnosia consists in inability to recognize seen objects, to read, to recognize shapes and colors, etc. It is caused by injuries in the occipital lobe. In auditory agnosia sounds cannot be recognized or music cannot be followed and appreciated as before. The injury here is in the neighborhood of the auditory area. When the injury is close behind the somesthetic area the subject cannot recognize objects placed in his hands, or judge weights by lifting them, etc. In any form of agnosia the subject still sees, hears or feels but does not utilize the sensory data as signs of definite objective facts.

Language as we said a moment ago is primarily auditory and secondarily motor. Obviously language is not the mere production of certain sounds. It is a means of communication, and the sounds carry meaning. Language is symbolic and the trouble in brain injuries which give aphasia may be that the patient has lost his ability to use symbols. Agnosia similarly can be regarded as an inability to get the meaning of signs and symbols. Apraxia can be thought of as inability to connect one's meanings and intentions with the concrete acts which are necessary to carry out these intentions. Symbols and skilled movements are tools in intelligent behavior. These tools apparently depend on definite parts of the cortex but their use in intelligent behavior depends on the integrity of the cortex as a whole.

**The frontal lobes.** When Gall in his system of phrenology located the intellect in the forehead, he was following our everyday notions. We think of the high-browed individual as intellectual, and we point to the low-browed animals in confirmation of our view. The frontal lobes are in fact much larger in the human than in any animal brain. Let us ask ourselves, however, whether the human being is characterized exclusively by intellectual superiority. Is it not equally remarkable how he manages his activity, seeking distant goals and planning his actions? The frontal lobes might be concerned with management rather than with knowledge. The whole frontal lobe might be an adjunct to the motor area, a supermotor area organizing action into large units.

Frontal lobe injuries in man sometimes produce remarkably little change in behavior or intellectual processes. One sometimes wonders whether this part of the brain has any function at all beyond filling up the expansive forehead. The changes observed, however, do lie rather in the realm of management and character than in that of intellect and knowledge.

**Behavior after removal of the frontal lobes** (2).  A successful broker on the New York Stock Exchange when about 40 years of age began to suffer from severe headaches, absent-mindedness and failures of memory which culminated in a prolonged loss of consciousness. X-ray examination revealed a tumor involving both frontal lobes. An operation was performed which at first seems inconceivably daring but which has been successfully performed several times in the last few decades: the skull was opened and both frontal lobes were removed as far back as the premotor area (5). Care was taken not to disturb the motor and premotor areas including the motor speech center.

The patient made a good general recovery from the operation and was promptly relieved of his headaches and other intolerable symptoms. He showed no inclination to go back to work and in other respects was not his old self. He had no consideration for the feelings of his friends and was incapable of sustained and serious effort. In the hope of re-educating him he was kept under careful medical observation for over a year, in his home and elsewhere. His behavior showed some improvement but not enough to enable him to resume active business. Our interest in the case is to discover the losses, intellectual or behavioral, caused by removal of the prefrontal portion of the brain.

He had lost his zest for business. Yet he was far from somnolent or inactive. He was overactive in trifling ways, unwilling to sit still, preferring to walk or dance around the room and to sing, whistle or shout on all occasions.

He had lost his customary restraint and control of such natural impulses as those of sex and self-aggrandizement. He became very free in sex talk and playful sex behavior, but serious marital behavior disappeared nor did he make any serious advances to other women. He gratified his desire for self-aggrandizement by boasting of his prowess in athletics, in dancing, in business, and by claiming the ability to do anything that was mentioned. He made threats freely but did not carry them out.

In the psychologist's examining room he was overactive, facetious and distractible, and needed constant prodding to complete the tests. When allowance was made for these disturbing factors, his intelligence appeared to be normal. He was especially poor in sentence completion, picture completion, and similar tests which demand putting things together to make a meaningful whole. He seemed to have more intellectual ability than he was able to marshal for the purpose in hand.

What, essentially, had the patient lost? No faculty such as observation, attention, memory or reasoning was absent after the operation, though none of them, perhaps, was displayed to the full extent of the subject's previous ability. The investigator concluded that the deficiency lay in getting the various mental processes to work together. What was impaired was synthesizing or combining ability. The subject's free expression of emotion in the postoperative state was due not to an exaggeration of the emotions but to a lack of restraint, and the lack of restraint was a result of loss of synthesizing ability. Without this ability the individual cannot plan his actions or restrain impulses that are likely to lead to undesirable consequences. From lack of synthesizing ability he is impulsive and distractible, and does not steer his behavior consistently toward a distant goal. In other cases of frontal lobe injury the symptoms vary somewhat but can be brought under the formula stated, though different students of the matter formulate their interpretations in various ways.

Recently brain surgeons have found that the symptoms of certain mental illnesses can be helped by cutting or removing some of the brain tissue in the frontal lobes (5). In some patients whose mental processes have been distorted into severe anxiety, apathy, or depression, an operation on the frontal lobes may relieve the symptoms without greatly reducing the abilities needed to get along in ordinary situations.

**Two kinds of synthesis or combination.**   The brain must perform two kinds of synthesis or combination (see p. 213). One we may call incoming and the other outgoing. When you recognize a person, the stimulus is very complex, the picture on your retina has many parts. In seeing him as a person you combine the many into one, you make a unitary response to a plurality of stimuli. When you see a motion picture what you get on the retina is a rapid sequence of different stimuli, but what you "see" is a continuous unitary movement or action. When you hear a piece of music your ear receives a succession of tones but you hear a tune, having the character of a unit. All these are cases of incoming synthesis, with plurality in the stimulus and unity in the response.

Outgoing synthesis is illustrated in every coordinated movement, since several muscles are brought into play, either in response to a single stimulus as in reflex action, or in response to a unitary intention. The intention to catch a ball brings both your hands simultaneously into position. The intention to open a door puts you through a sequence of movements leading toward the desired result. In outgoing synthesis the unitary antecedent produces a multiple consequent; the one gives rise to the many.

Obviously the two kinds of synthesis call for different neural mechanisms. A collecting mechanism is required for the incoming synthesis, a distributing mechanism for the outgoing type. The rudiments of such mechanisms have already been described (pages 244–246). When several nerve fibers converge upon a single cell as they do in every nerve center, we have a collecting mechanism. When a single axon branches and stimulates several neurons, we have a distributing mechanism.

Of the two great association areas of the brain the posterior one, lying between the various sensory areas, may probably carry out synthesis of the collective type. It would thus be concerned in knowing and understanding. The frontal association area may be concerned with the distributive type of combination. It would thus be concerned with planning, organizing and managing action. This allocation of the two types of synthesis to the two great association areas is a fascinating idea but not demonstrated by any means.

## GENERAL FUNCTIONS OF THE WHOLE CORTEX

Seeing and hearing are known to be specific functions of small areas of the brain. The two types of synthesis are perhaps functions of certain large areas. There may also be general functions of the entire cortex. One general function is probably that of learning and remembering. Though there may be some of this in the lower centers the cerebral cortex is the part of the nervous system principally concerned in learning. The study of animal learning has been very active since about 1900 and has made important contributions to general psychology some of which will be noted in a later chapter. It has also made some important contributions to our knowledge of the cortex. The method of experimentation combines animal training and localized brain injury (4). An animal is trained to perform a certain act, then a part of the brain is removed and the animal tested to see if he can still perform the learned act.

The method seems a good one but its results are surprising. A performance such as following a path to a goal or as manipulating a door latch, learned by a monkey before removal of the frontal lobes, is *lost* as the result of that operation but can be *relearned* with further training. The only possible conclusion seems to be that different parts of the cerebrum can function in learning the same performance.

**Loss of learning ability dependent on amount of cortex removed.** A similar result is obtained when a white rat has learned to find his way quickly through a maze, a complicated set of paths and blind alleys. Injury to almost any part of the cortex impairs or obliterates this learned performance, which can however be relearned. Loss of almost any part of the cortex

impairs the rat's learning ability, and the larger the amount removed the greater is the impairment. The impairment is seen
in the following table from the increase in errors committed
before the maze is mastered.

MAZE LEARNING BY RATS AFTER OPERATION (8)

| Amount of Cortex Removed | Number of Errors Committed |
|---|---|
| none | 33 |
| 1–9% | 53 |
| 10–19 | 143 |
| 20–29 | 293 |
| 30–39 | 449 |
| 40–49 | 964 |
| 50–59 | 950 |

These results show that a learned act is not necessarily controlled by one particular cortical center. We cannot hope to
map the cortex into small, distinct centers, each presiding over
a specific mental or motor performance.

These results suggest that it is proper in a way to go back to
Flourens and say that the cerebrum functions "as a whole." But
the words must not be taken in a literal sense as if every cell
and fiber of the brain were simultaneously active all the time.
For then there could be only one brain activity, instead of the
thousands of varied brain activities which are vouched for by
the varieties of behavior. The best conclusion is that *the brain
acts in wide-spreading patterns,* patterns that involve many
cortical areas and their connecting association fibers. The pattern of brain activity must *shift* from moment to moment; a bit
of behavior that takes only a minute may bring most parts of
the cortex into action during the minute. Loss of any large
amount of cortex will disturb the interaction of parts and break
up the usual pattern.

**Situation set as a general function of the cortex.** Rats with
large losses of cortex lack energy in exploring a strange place
and in attacking a problem such as that of securing food from
a closed box (7). They lack persistence and variety of attack.
They wander about vaguely and appear only half alive to the

situation. It appears that the loss of any considerable portion of the cortex impairs the rat's ability to get up a good situation-and-goal set. Such an adjustment is probably an activity of the brain as a whole rather than of any single center. The frontal lobes may be concerned with directing activity toward a goal, while the posterior half of the cortex is concerned with grasping the situation. Since, however, situation-and-goal set is one adjustment and not two, the frontal and posterior parts must work together whenever the individual is dealing effectively with the environment.

### SUMMARY.

1. The nervous system is composed of nerves which connect with all the receptors and with all the effectors.

    a. The organism is enabled to act as a unit since all the nerves lead to or from a coordinating center consisting of the brain and spinal cord.

    b. The organism is enabled to carry out a variety of different actions since the nervous system consists of millions of nerve fibers, each connecting one point with another.

    c. A *neuron* is a single nerve cell with its *axon* and *dendrites*.

    d. The *synapse* is the point of contact between one neuron and another.

    e. The *nerve impulse* is an electrochemical wave transmitted in the nerve fiber. The energy of the nerve impulse does not depend on the intensity of the stimulus which aroused the impulse—this is the *all-or-none law*.

    f. The strength of response in nerve or muscle depends upon the number of impulses per second, this number depending partly on the number of impulses in each fiber and partly on the number of active fibers.

2. A *reflex arc* is the nerve path from a sense organ through the nerve center to a muscle. It consists of two or three or more neurons in sequence, with many neurons working abreast.

3. The brain is the chief coordinating and integrating center of the nervous system.

a. The *brain stem* is the continuation of the spinal cord in the head. Lower centers in the brain stem and cord carry out reflex actions and simple coordinations.

b. The *interbrain* lies between the brain stem and the cerebum and contains a center for each of the sensory pathways on the way to the cortex.

c. The *cerebellum,* connected by fibers to the brain stem, is a coordinating center for motor pathways.

d. The *cerebrum* is divided into two hemispheres which fill the skull. It is made up of fibers connecting all parts (white matter), and of intricately organized collections of nerve cells (gray matter).

e. The *cortex* is a thin layer of gray matter covering the entire convoluted surface of the cerebrum.

4. Different areas of the cortex are specialized for different functions.

a. The *motor area* contains neurons whose axons run to lower motor centers in the brain stem, the cerebellum, and the cord. Electrical stimulation produces movements of specific parts of the body, and injury to the motor area results in paralysis.

b. The *somesthetic area* is the cortical center for the skin and muscle senses. It is closely connected with the motor areas for the corresponding parts of the body.

c. The *auditory area* is in the temporal lobe and its destruction results in deafness.

d. The *visual area* of each hemisphere receives fibers from the same half of both eyes. Destruction of one visual area results in *hemianopsia* or blindness in the opposite half of the field of view.

5. The cortex surrounding and between the primary motor and sensory areas functions in combining and organizing sensory data and motor responses.

a. *Aphasia* is the loss of language functions not due to sensory impairment or motor paralysis. Cortical control of speech is localized in only one hemisphere of the cerebrum—the left side in right-handed persons.

    b. *Apraxia* is the loss of skilled coordinations resulting from brain injury near the motor area.

    c. *Agnosia* is the loss of the ability to recognize and perceive, although the basic sensory functions are not disturbed.

    d. Extensive injuries of the frontal lobes impair the synthesizing and combining abilities which are necessary for planning and effective management of behavior.

6. Learning and remembering are functions of the entire cortex.

    a. Injury of any area of the cortex interferes with learning.

    b. The loss of learning ability depends on the amount of cortex removed.

# CHAPTER NINE

# How the Individual Develops

O n reading the title of this chapter students will be of two minds as to the need of including the study of development in a general course in psychology. Some will say, "Let us get on at once to the behavior of the adult. Of course children are fascinating creatures and we understand that psychologists are investigating their behavior in much detail and writing whole books on the subject (6, 23). But for that very reason let there be a special course for those who are interested in children, and spare the rest of us." Others will point out that young adults are likely within a few years to have a very practical interest in certain children, so that it is well to be prepared. And even though a student is most interested in his contemporaries, still he will find it worth while to look at the adult from the developmental point of view. "How did he, or she, get that way?" is a question we often ask when a person's behavior strikes us as being queer. If we knew the person's past life, how he had been treated as a child, what problems he had encountered in growing up and how he had handled them, we should understand him better than we can by simply taking him as he is today. What is true regarding the peculiar individual is true of people in general: we can understand them better when we have learned something of their life history.

[In trying to deal with his environment the child adopts certain attitudes and ways that persist and become his personal traits. What attitude he adopts depends both on his own nature and on his particular environment.] To one child the environment appears hostile and overwhelming, and his reaction is to play safe and keep to himself as much as possible. Another child, more vigorous and aggressive by nature, adopts a belligerent, antisocial attitude. Still another child will readily adopt a friendly, participating attitude. These attitudes may become so ingrained in childhood that they are very difficult to change later on, and in many individuals they never are changed. [It would be going too far to say they never can be changed, for we have evidence to the contrary (pp. 143–147), but there can be no doubt that the attitudes formed in childhood often persist and are either helps or hindrances to the young adult as he starts to make his way in the world.]

If you take a critical look at a newborn baby you may ask yourself, "How in the world is that helpless creature ever going to become a competent adult? His head is too large for his body, his legs and feet are too small, he cannot stand or even hold his head up, his hands are no good for any kind of skill, he has no teeth, his voice may be loud enough but it is too monotonous for human speech, he has eyes and ears but makes no real use of them, he sleeps most of the time and his brain seems to be torpid in spite of his big head." That is true enough, the answer would be, but the baby is capable of development. He has the power of growth, the capacity to grow if given the proper environment. His legs will grow to the length appropriate for a human being and their muscles will grow to a size and strength sufficient for standing, walking and running. His hands will grow into excellent instruments for manipulating objects. His teeth, already present in rudimentary form, will grow and harden and break through his gums at the proper ages. His mouth and larynx will grow into flexible speech organs. His brain will grow not only in size but also in fineness of microscopic structure and so become capable of doing its share in human activities. This growth of any organism from an immature to a mature state is called *maturation*.

"Yes, but . . . ," you reply, "it seems to me this power of growth is not enough. For if I were able to speed up a child's growth and have it complete in a single week, would that week-old grownup be a true adult, a competent adult? In a week's time it would be impossible for him to know much about the world, or to master the language and the thousands of skillful acts which the adult normally has at his command." In other words, you are insisting that we must add to the power of growth another important capacity, the *power of learning*. The point is well taken. Development consists of both growing and learning. In human development, especially, learning is extremely important. While many animals reach maturity in a few weeks or months after being born, it takes the human being about 18 years, and during all these years he is learning. What he is as an adult depends on how well he has grown, and also on what he has learned.

## DEVELOPMENT BY MATURATION

Maturation and learning go on at the same time in the developing individual. Growth of the structures of the body makes it possible to begin a series of new activities, and these new activities make new learning possible. Most of the abilities of the adult, therefore, are dependent on both maturation and learning. But there are some which are primarily the result of maturation and which do not depend on learning.

**Instinct.** An instinct is an unlearned form of activity. It is an activity which enables an animal (or human being) to deal competently with something in the environment, without preliminary experience and practice. You might call it a natural technique as contrasted with an acquired or learned technique. Human techniques, in general, must be learned by each individual. Speech must be learned, good manners must be learned, the use of any tool must be learned. By contrast, the bird does not learn how to build its nest, nor the beaver how to build its dam. These are instinctive techniques. Animals do learn a great deal, as we shall see in a later chapter devoted to the process of learning, but a large share of their ability to deal with the environment—a larger share in some animals than in others—comes from instinct and not from learning. Some of the best examples of complex instincts are found in various kinds of insects. The female wasp does beautiful work in constructing a nest in which to lay an egg. The nest is always of the same type in the same species, and you might suspect, from your knowledge of human ways of passing along a technique, that each generation of wasps learned the art from the preceding genera-

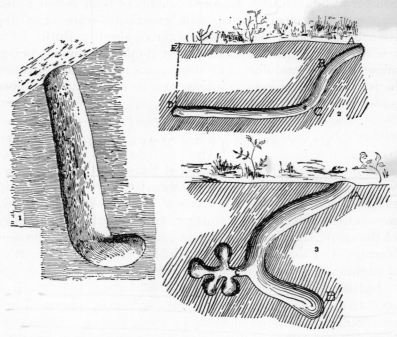

Fig. 61.—Nests characteristic of three different kinds of digging wasps. Other solitary wasps build their nests of mud above ground. The familiar large "paper" nests are built by social wasps. The tunnel in the first nest is about 8 inches long; in the second nest, ABCD is 22 inches; in the third nest, the distance from A around to B is less than 4 inches, and the cells at C are used for storage of food (Peckham).

tion. But that is impossible since the generations of wasps do not overlap. After laying her eggs the mother wasp goes away and dies before the young hatch out. There you have a complete demonstration of the reality of instincts.

In human beings the generations do overlap, the developmental period is prolonged, and the young learn a great deal from their elders. However, the child does possess certain techniques at birth. He breathes, coughs, sneezes, swallows. These might be called instincts, though they are much simpler than the wasp's nest building. They are more commonly called reflexes, being direct motor responses to sensory stimuli. There are many still simpler reflexes, such as the closing of the eyelids when the eye is touched or blown upon. It would seem safe to assume that the reflexes are unlearned since they are present in the newborn child.

Is it perfectly safe to assume that the child learns nothing before birth? Birth is undoubtedly an important turning point in the individual's career but it is not the start of life. It occurs earlier in some lives than in others; a premature baby is born at the six-month or seven-month stage instead of the usual nine-month stage of development. And some species of animals are born, or hatched, at a more immature stage than others. The newborn kitten is more immature and helpless than the newborn guinea pig; and the newly hatched robin than the newly hatched chick. All this goes to show that the moment of birth is not a sharp dividing line between two kinds of development. There may possibly be some learning before birth, and there certainly is some maturation after birth.

Prenatal development. If the contrast between the infant and the adult makes us wonder how the one can ever develop into the other, what shall we say of the contrast between the fertilized ovum and the newborn baby? How can this microscopic single cell ever become an eight-pound baby, with arms and legs, eyes and ears, heart and lungs and brain and all the other organs? As far as the mere matter of size is concerned, the one-celled individual has a supply of nourishment provided by the mother and he takes in nourishment and proceeds to grow and divide into two cells, four, eight and so on up to an enormous number of cells. But the remarkable thing is not so much the number as the variety of these cells. Some are muscle cells, some nerve cells, some skin cells, some bone cells. Yet they are all descended from the same fertilized ovum and they all have the same assortment of chromosomes and genes (p. 164). Since all these cells have the same heredity they must differ because of different stimulation received from their respective environments. Such was our previous reasoning when we were trying to explain the differences between individuals and it holds good now when we are considering the differences between cells in the same individual. They all have the same heredity and we must look to their environments for the factors that make them different. But the unborn child's environment in the mother's uterus or womb is certainly a very sheltered environment, free from the heat and cold, the pushes and pulls, the lights and odors and other forces of the outside world. It is

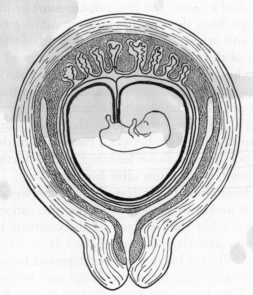

FIG. 62.—Diagram of the young embryo suspended in the mother's womb, protected from the external environment by the surrounding fluid and membranes, while having access to nourishment.

smooth and uniform and the same for all the cells of the growing organism. We cannot explain the differing cells by appealing to the individual's environment. We cannot say that some cells develop into muscle tissue and other cells into nerve tissue because of different influences reaching them from the external environment. We cannot say that the organism develops an arm at one place and a leg at another place because the external environment is different at these two places.

Differentiation is the name given to this developing of different kinds of cells out of the single original cell. Maturation consists very largely of differentiation. Since all the cells of the same organism carry the same genes and are subjected to the same prenatal environment, how can differentiation possibly be explained?

Probably you have already seen the answer. The environment of a cell within an organism is not the same thing as the environment of the organism as a whole. For the prenatal organism as a whole the effective environment is the uterus with its supply of the general requirements for growth such as food and warmth. For any cell within the organism, however, the effective environment consists of the other cells surrounding it. As soon as some differentiation has taken place, the cells in different parts of the organism have different surroundings and receive different stimulation from the surrounding cells. Certain genes respond to one kind of stimulation and other genes to another kind, and so the cells in different parts of the same organism develop differently. Differentiation starts in a small way in the fertilized ovum and builds up by degrees. At a very early stage there are three layers of cells; the skin develops from the outer layer, the internal organs from the inner layer, the muscles and bones from the middle layer. These three layers interact and stimulate each other and combine in various ways in producing the various parts of the body. The whole process is extremely intricate and the embryologists do not pretend to understand it thoroughly, but we can safely say that the decisive factor in differentiation is the *interaction of parts within the organism*.

Head end

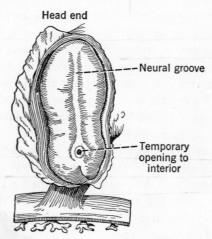

Neural groove

Temporary
opening to
interior

FIG. 63.—Dorsal view of a two-weeks human embryo,
magnified 20 diameters (Von Spee).

**Development of the brain and nervous system.**  One might suppose that the brain, like the bones, would develop from the middle layer of the embryonic organism. But no, it develops from the outer layer. In response to stimulation from the deeper layers, the outer layer bends in and forms a groove up and down the back of the very young embryo (Fig. 63), and this groove soon closes over into a tube. The neural tube develops rapidly at the head end so that by the early age of four weeks (counted from fertilization) the main parts of the brain are distinguishable (Fig. 64). The brain is very forward in its growth: at an early stage it makes up $\frac{1}{3}$ of the whole organism, at birth about $\frac{1}{10}$, but at maturity only about $\frac{1}{50}$.

In spite of its relatively enormous size, this embryonic brain is not functional, for the cells composing it are not nerve cells. They are rudimentary embryonic cells, but they soon divide and produce cells which take on the characteristics of neurons, with axons and dendrites, capable of conducting nerve impulses. Axons from some of these nerve cells reach out to the muscles and sense organs and begin to conduct impulses a long while before birth. The lower centers of the spinal cord and brain stem begin to function before birth, or are ready to function as

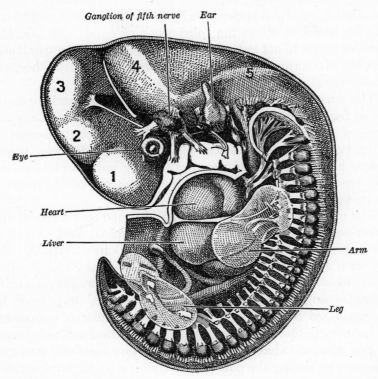

Fig. 64.—Human embryo of four weeks, magnified about 10 diameters. The numbered parts are the main divisions of the brain, 1 being the cerebrum, 2 the interbrain, etc. The spinal cord is continuous with 5, the rear portion of the brain stem. An arm and a leg appear as transparent buds (Streeter).

soon as the child is born. The cerebral cortex is very extensive by the time of birth, but its inner structure is not very far advanced and it may not be functional until several weeks after birth. The cortex probably has little to do with the behavior of the newborn child.

Prenatal activity. Up to the time of birth the individual's main job, we might say, is a construction job. He has to construct his heart and blood vessels, his arms and legs, his brain and nerves, and all his fundamental organs. His operational job, i.e., his behavior, can wait till later. Yet the unborn child is far from being wholly inactive. His heart begins to beat and circulate his blood at about the third week of embryonic life. His muscles begin to act in the third month, bending the trunk and moving the arms and legs, and these movements become stronger and more varied in the later months (5).

The sense organs and their nerves develop early and are capable of function some time before birth (as shown by the reactions of infants who are prematurely born), but the senses of sight, taste and smell can scarcely receive any effective stimuli before birth. Sounds can penetrate to the unborn child's ears. His sense of touch and his muscle sense are stimulated whenever he moves.

The movements of the unborn child prove that some of the lower nerve centers in the brain stem and spinal cord, as well as the nerves and muscles, get into action before birth. So the question arises whether the child is *learning* anything by this prenatal activity. The activity of the muscles may play a part in strengthening them, and the nerve centers, too, may be strengthened by their own activity. So much it is reasonable to believe. Before we start to trace the postnatal development of behavior, we shall do well to look more carefully into this question regarding the part played by exercise in development.

## DEVELOPMENT BY EXERCISE AND BY LEARNING

The first stage of development must consist wholly of maturation. It seems undeniable that an organ must have developed to a certain point before it can begin to function. The heart could not start pumping blood into the arteries until it had developed far enough to be a workable pump. The lungs afford a convincing example. No air can possibly enter the child's lungs before birth to distend and exercise them, and yet at birth they are well enough developed to play their part in breathing. After birth they get plenty of exercise and their further development probably results from this exercise as well as from continued maturation. A muscle, too, must mature to a certain degree before it can contract. Each muscle first makes its appearance, long before birth, as a little bud consisting of embryonic cells which have no contractile power. These cells multiply and combine into muscle fibers which can contract. Meanwhile a nerve is growing out from the nerve center to the muscle. When this development has gone far enough the muscle begins to receive nerve impulses and to respond by contracting. It continues to mature while probably gaining strength also from exercise.

**Exercise, or functional activity, as a factor in development.** Once maturation has provided an organ that can work or function, does the activity of this organ help to develop it more fully? Is there a law of growth through use, and of atrophy (the reverse of growth) through disuse? The growth of a muscle from exercise is a matter of "common knowledge," but in psychology we have to be on our guard against common knowledge and to insist on having definite facts to support our "laws." It is a fact that repeated exercise will build up the strength of a muscle, but the gain in strength is much greater than can be accounted for by the relatively slight increase in the size (thickness) of the muscle. The increase in muscular strength is partly due to better circulation and oxygen supply, partly to increase of reserve fuel stored in the muscle, and partly to greater effort, i.e., stronger stimulation from the brain. The shrinking of a muscle when immobilized for several weeks in a splint, and its gradual recovery after the splint is removed, certainly look like good evidence for atrophy from disuse and growth from use. But a well-controlled experiment would be much more conclusive.

There is one experiment, dating from 1897 and apparently so well done that the physiologists have not thought repetition necessary (22). A large, full-grown dog was first kept inactive for a month. Then one of the thigh muscles (the slender sartorius muscle which could easily be spared) was removed from one hind leg and preserved for later microscopic examination. After recovery from this operation the dog was trained in running a treadmill. He ran but little at first but after 20 days of training he was running the equivalent of 40–50 miles a day. He kept this up for 40 days and ran the equivalent of 2,000 miles in all in the treadmill. Now the sartorius muscle was removed from the other thigh, and the two muscles, one exercised and the other unexercised, were compared. The exercised muscle was 50 percent larger in cross section than the other, so that an actual growth of the muscle substance had resulted from the exercise.

Microscopic examination showed that the number of muscle fibers was the same in both muscles. Exercise had not increased the number of fibers; there had been no cell multiplication as there is in maturation. What exercise had accomplished was to thicken up the fibers, especially the numerous very slender fibers present in the little-used muscle. These slender fibers were a reserve stock available for development through exercise. A second dog was put through the same experiment with the same results.

Is the brain, too, as well as the muscles, developed in part by its own activity? Evidence on this question is hard to obtain, for we could not expect any large growth in mere size. The most we could expect would be to find a finer microscopic structure of the cortex in individuals who had used their brains. By comparison of the brains of children dying at different ages it is found that, while no new nerve cells are formed after birth, the cells grow in size, their axons and dendrites lengthen, and contact between the cells is increased. This development is rapid in early childhood and continues at a slower rate on into adult life. It is probably due in part to brain activity. The best evidence comes from comparing the primary visual area of the cortex (p. 259) in individuals who became blind early in life with the same area in those who have been using it all their lives in seeing. The nerve cells of the visual area are relatively underdeveloped in the blind (8, 9, 14). The conclusion is evidently that use of the visual cortex does develop its intricate internal structure.

**Learning as a process of development.**    Near the beginning of the chapter we said that development consisted of maturation and learning. Since then we have not used the word *learning* but have been talking of exercise as a factor in development.

Exercise strengthens the activity that is exercised but does not, by itself, add any new activity to the individual's repertory. How then does he develop all the new knowledge and skill that he certainly does acquire? The process of acquiring new knowledge and new responses is the process of learning.

Psychologists regard learning as one of the most fundamental and important topics in the whole science. Whatever other topic they take up, whether intelligence, personality, sense perception, thinking, or even emotion, they always find that learning plays an important part. Learning includes much more than school learning and study of any sort. A tune that you have heard several times with no intention of learning has been learned, nevertheless, if you can now hum it or even if it simply sounds familiar. All knowledge and skill, all habits good and bad, all acquaintance with people and things, all attitudes built up in your dealing with people and things, have been learned.

Sometimes the novelty of a learned act consists in the skillful combination of two acts which previously could only be performed separately, as when the young pianist learns to play with both hands at once; and sometimes it consists in doing separately what previously could only be done together, as when the same young pianist learns to strike notes with each separate finger instead of moving the last three fingers together. Most often, perhaps, the novelty consists in getting acquainted with a new situation, a new person, or a new object, and in finding some effective way of dealing with this situation, person, or object.

When a child gets a new toy he examines it attentively and proceeds to experiment with it and find out what it will do and what he can do with it. He brings into play the ways of acting that he already knows but he finds that this toy has its own little ways and that he must adjust himself to the toy. If it is a hoop it does not behave like a ball. He strikes the hoop in various ways with his stick, usually knocking it down or into the bushes, but when he hits it just right and keeps it rolling he is delighted. In time he comes to know his hoop intimately and to make just the right movements to keep it rolling.

**Reinforcement a factor in learning.** Exercise or activity is necessary for learning. It may be motor activity as in playing the piano, or sensory activity as in listening to a piece of music, but there must be activity in some form. "We learn by doing"— an old psychological proverb which is true enough but does not fully cover the ground. Another factor is involved which is suggested by a few words added to the proverb: "We learn by doing and getting results." When the young pianist succeeds in striking the proper notes with both hands, the good result encourages him to do the same thing again. When the listener finds he can follow through a sequence of notes and get a tune out of it, he is getting results and beginning to learn the tune.

Reinforcement is the individual's reaction to the results of his own activity. It is his check-up on results. Results are important to him in all his dealings with the environment, and he checks up on them more or less consciously, more or less carefully. Check-up is easy when there are just two clear alternatives— two doors to choose from in entering a certain office—and the right door is learned in a single trial, after a single check-up and reinforcement. In this case a single perfectly conscious "O.K. reaction" or "confirming reaction" establishes the correct response for future use (30). When the child strikes his hoop just right and sees the good result, he confirms and reinforces the successful stroke, but the reinforcement is not perfectly definite because the whole situation is less clear than in the case of the two doors. He has to keep on trying and checking up as well as he can, and gradually he establishes the successful ways of managing his hoop. There are many skillful performances which, like hoop rolling, have to be learned by much practice and many reinforcements.

Reinforcement does not necessarily mean satisfaction and pleasure. The sequence, lightning followed by thunder, is disagreeable to many persons but is evidently well learned. The reinforcement has come about in this way: when thunder has followed lightning several times, a child begins to expect a thunder peal after each new flash of lightning. He gets set to "take" the thunder, and this set is confirmed when the thunder comes.

In learning to deal with the environment the individual must learn what to expect as well as what to do. This matter of reinforcement and of learning in general will be much more fully considered in a later chapter.

## BEHAVIORAL DEVELOPMENT

We wish now to estimate the relative importance of our three developmental factors in the transformation of the infant's behavior into that of the adult. Up to the time of birth maturation must play the major role, with some strengthening of the muscles and lower nerve centers by exercise, but with very little chance, as far as we can see, for reinforcement or for learning the successful ways of dealing with the environment. After birth, exercise and learning come in strongly but there is no reason to assume that maturation stops short. Maturation certainly has much to do with the development of the teeth, of the bones, and also of the cerebral cortex which as we have seen is so immature at birth as perhaps to be nonfunctional. What we should especially like to know is whether the child's increasing strength and skill are wholly due to activity and learning or partly to continued maturation.

The pecking behavior of young chicks gives a clear picture of the relation between maturation and learning. Very soon after coming out of the shell a chick will peck at kernels of grain scattered on the ground. It pecks in the approximate direction of a kernel, but its aim is not very sure and it succeeds only 20 percent of the time in seizing and swallowing the grain. Its score improves rapidly from day to day, and experiments indicate that some of this improvement is due to continued maturation after hatching, while most of it is due to practice and learning. Evidently the pecking movement is instinctive and provided by maturation, but accurate pecking must be learned by trial and error, with reinforcement of the more accurate movements (4).

Maturation, then, does not do away with the necessity of exercise and reinforcement; but maturation prepares the way for learning Each forward step in maturation equips the young individual for commencing new activities in which learning is possible. When the baby's teeth come through (maturation) he starts to learn the arts of biting and chewing. When the adolescent boy's larynx matures and his voice changes he has a chance to learn how to sing tenor or bass.

**Activity of the newborn child.** Though the infant sleeps a large share of his first few days, he exhibits quite an assortment of movements if carefully watched and tested. His equipment includes especially what might be called the "service" acts of breathing, sneezing, coughing, yawning, sucking, swallowing, urinating and defecating. When hungry he cries, squirms and slashes his arms and legs around, so bringing someone to his assistance though at first he cannot possibly anticipate this beneficial result. He bends and extends his arms and legs, opens and closes his hands and even grasps a rod with such force as to suspend his weight. He wriggles his toes, opens and shuts his mouth and his eyes. In short, he uses all his muscles. Some of the service acts such as sneezing and swallowing are obviously well-coordinated performances, clever instinctive techniques. The arm and leg movements, while appearing random and diffuse to an adult observer, are really well-coordinated movements when taken singly, requiring good teamwork from the muscles that operate the different joints. The teamwork is controlled by the lower centers of the cord and brain stem.

But though these movements show admirable teamwork at a primitive, physiological level, they cannot be said to "deal with the environment" except in a very limited way. A month or two after birth the infant begins to have some dealings with the environment. He begins to take notice, especially of persons at first, and his movements begin to have some reference to persons and things. This important development in his behavior is probably due to maturation of the cortex to a point where it can begin to function. Interest in the environment and in doing things to the objects in the environment is surely a cortical function. As the cortex develops it begins to take charge of bodily movements. It makes use of the coordinated movements provided by the lower centers and directs them toward objects in the environment. It gets to know these objects by use of the senses. The sensory activity of observing things and the motor activity of acting on things go hand in hand. The infant observes things in a rudimentary way and recognizes them when he sees them again. He shows recognition of a person who has been good to him by smiling, cooing and waving his arms and legs whenever that person comes in sight. This sort of behavior makes its appearance, not in the first days or weeks after birth, but in the second or third month, when the cortex has matured sufficiently to play its part in simple forms of learning.

**Eye and hand.** In dealing with the environment, the eye and the hand serve as most important tools, the eye for obtaining information about objects, and the hand for acting upon objects. The two work together as a team but this teamwork or *eye-hand coordination* is not present in the newborn child. His eyes may fixate a bright object but he makes no move to reach for it. His hands may grip an object with much force but he does not look at this object. He gives no sign of being aware of objects or of attempting to do anything to objects. Within the first two months, however, his eyes begin to follow a moving thing or person and to focus for the distance of the object, so that he evidently is aware of certain objects. He keeps on looking at objects with increasing definiteness for some weeks before his hands show any sign of taking part. Then the hands begin to make excited waving movements on the appearance of an interesting object, as if they wished to do something with it but did not know how. A few weeks later they are clearly reaching for the object by a forward swing of both arms without much participation of the fingers or much success in actually reaching and grasping the object. By the age of seven months the child will have considerable success in securing the object, grasping it with all his fingers against the palm of the hand. His reaching movement becomes more direct, and in the last three months of the first year we shall find him taking the object between the thumb and the tips of the first two fingers, turning it about and examining it. All in all, we must credit the child

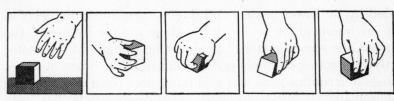

FIG. 65.—Stages in reaching and grasping. The ages vary but the sequence is fairly constant: first a reaching without grasping, then a raking-in, then a grasp with the whole hand, then opposition of thumb and fingers, finally limitation to thumb and first two fingers (Halverson, *11*).

with very marked progress during his first year in dealing with objects by the combined use of eyes and hands. This progress is partly due to maturation of the hands and of the brain, and partly to exercise and learning. When the child is trying to reach an object, any successful movement will be reinforced. So by trial and error and reinforcement the most efficient reaching and grasping movements are selected (*11, 18*).

**Learning (?) to walk.** In spite of common belief, it is not certain that the human child learns to walk. Certainly the parents do not *teach* him to walk, for very few people understand the act of walking well enough to teach it. The adult can stimulate and encourage the child and protect him from bad falls, but if the child learns to walk he does so through his own efforts. Many animals walk as soon as they are born; maturation does the spadework for them, and the mere fact that the human child's development is slower need not mean that maturation is any less helpful in his case. It is clear that the newborn child's legs and feet are not mature enough for any efficient walking movement, and with his relatively large head he would be a top-heavy little walker at the best. Besides, considerable maturation of the baby's brain is necessary before he can learn so complicated a performance as walking.

Granted all this, we still have no sure answer to our question. Two possibilities remain open. (1) Walking may be a natural movement controlled by a nerve center which develops by maturation and is ready to function a year or more after birth.

Fig. 66.—Stages in the development of locomotion. The numbers give approximate ages in months when the stages begin. The later creeping stages overlap the earlier stages in walking (McGraw, *18*).

(2) Walking may be a learned combination of movements built up by experimenting with various movements and adopting those which are most successful. To get any light on our problem we should follow the child through from birth till he starts to walk.

During his first year the child develops two lines of activity which come together in the act of walking. One line is *locomotion* and the other is *balancing*. For the first few months he makes no effort to move from place to place. At the age of 6–7 months he does try to move himself along the floor and by 8 months probably succeeds in crawling. A little later he can get up on his hands and knees and by the age of 9 months he usually develops a good creeping movement. Next he makes more use of his feet, getting one or both of them on the floor in creeping, and some children walk on all fours before passing over to erect walking. Though children differ in rate of development, nearly all of them go through the same main sequence of crawling-creeping-walking in much the same order (2).

Balancing, too, goes through a regular sequence, a head-trunk-leg sequence. The child holds his head up steadily at 3–4 months, sits up steadily at 7–8 months, stands with support at about 10 months and without support at about 12 months. He walks with some support from 10–11 months on and at 14 months usually walks alone. In walking he at first keeps his feet wide apart and his arms spread, but as his balance improves still further his feet keep to a narrower path and his arms are free for other uses (3, 10, 18, 27).

These regular sequences, especially the balancing sequence, are best explained by maturation. Why must the baby hold his head up before he can sit up? A good reason is seen in the fact that the nerve centers controlling neck movements mature earlier than those for the hip and leg region. The probability—though we cannot be certain as yet—is that the human erect posture and mode of locomotion are dependent on a complex nerve mechanism which develops by maturation and reaches a functional state about the time when the child starts to walk. Even so, learning may play a part. Exercise and reinforcement may be needed to insure efficient balancing and locomotion. Nothing is more characteristic of the growing child than the eager use of his powers as they develop. He gives them abundant exercise and so strengthens them. Reinforcement comes in when the child succeeds in crawling to an object that he wishes to get, and still more when he succeeds in the more rapid movement of creeping, and again when he succeeds in walking to the object of interest. Blind children tend to be very quiet in comparison with seeing children. They have much less stimulation and reinforcement for balancing and locomotion. They often are 9–10 months retarded in standing and walking alone. Since the nerve mechanism for walking probably matures as rapidly in the blind as in the seeing children, the difference must lie on the side of exercise and learning. We can conclude that both maturation and learning contribute to the development of walking (7, 17).

Learning to talk.   Here there is no question; the child certainly learns to talk. There is no natural language which all children begin to bring out when they reach a certain age. Each child picks up the language of his particular social environment. Nevertheless, maturation plays an essential part here, too. There are several ways in which the newborn child is not mature enough to start learning a language. He cannot make his speech organs perform the delicate movements of the spoken language. He is incapable of listening attentively to what people say or of distinguishing one word from another in what he hears. And his ability to associate words with their meanings is still undeveloped.

The child's progress toward motor speech can be followed by observing what sounds he makes at different ages. He uses his vocal organs from the start in crying. Grunts are made during the first few weeks and syllables like *goo* at about 2 months, followed by many other syllables and later by two-syllable units such as *da-da*. Baby talk which is conversational to the extent that it is directed to another person, with give and take, starts at about 6 months, and expressive tones and inflections are heard at about 9 months. The first recognizable word picked up from other people is spoken at about 14 months on the average. During the second year the number of words increases slowly and then rapidly, and phrases and short sentences make their appearance near the end of this year. Some children progress through these stages more quickly than others, but they all go through practically the same stages in the same order. The regular sequence here, as in the case of walking, suggests that a process of maturation underlies the learning of the language (27).

The child exercises his vocal powers as fast as they become available, and reinforcement comes in whenever he understands the words that are spoken to him (as he does considerably before he can say those words himself) and whenever he makes other people understand the words he is trying to speak.

**Social development.** As has been well said, the child's development consists largely in becoming a social being. You could not call the newborn baby a social being even though in a passive way he is very dependent on other people. By the end of his first year he is in active give-and-take relations with his social environment, and this interaction develops further with each succeeding year. He is taught by precept and example, by reward and punishment, how he must and must not act. The social environment, in short, takes an active part in socializing each new addition to the group. One might think that the child was simply forced to become a social being. But no, the child meets the social environment halfway. As soon as he is able to take notice at all, he notices people. The first object that he definitely looks at is some person's face. By the age of 2 months his own face will brighten into a smile at the sight of a person. At 10 months he delights in playing little games such as peeka-boo with an adult. By 12 months he is entering the imitative stage and doing as well as he can what he sees other people doing.

For the first year and more the social environment of most young children consists of persons who are his superiors in strength and ability. By this experience he cannot learn how to deal with his equals. When he is placed in a group of his contemporaries at the age of 18 months in a nursery school, he at first pays little attention to the other children and plays mostly by himself. In a few months he will pay more attention to them and make rudimentary social contacts by touching, pulling and pushing. By the age of 3 years children like to play side by side with the same materials, each busy on his own project, but by the age of 4 years they are undertaking larger projects such as playing house, with several children engaged in the same project. Year by year we see more cooperation and division of labor in the play group. This social development depends very largely on the growth of intelligence and knowledge (25, 29).

The beginnings of sympathetic behavior can be seen in the early years, though any real help to a fellow in need is impossible till the child's intellectual development has made some progress. He must comprehend the situation before he can do any good. For reasons that are not at all clear some children are much more sympathetic than others of the same age. The same child may be very helpful and very selfish, too, probably because he is very active and uninhibited (24).

**Personality development.** Both the biological and the social factors in personality change to some extent as the child advances in age, especially in adolescence (p. 143). On the social side we have to reckon with the individual's desire to be popular with his contemporaries, a desire which seems to be especially strong in adolescence. Behavior which wins popularity is reinforced. The adolescent group is eager to be grownup, eager to learn adult ways of behavior. The shift of interests that occurs early in adolescence, away from the aspirations and recreations of a child toward those of an adult, is sometimes supposed to be due to learning alone and so entirely to the social factor. But why does this shift of interests occur two years earlier in girls than in boys? Is it not tied up with the biological maturation which occurs two years earlier in girls than in boys? Just before puberty physical growth takes a spurt, as shown in Figure 67. Soon the girl begins to menstruate and her figure becomes that of a woman, and the boy in his turn develops a man's voice and the beginnings of a beard. These physical changes are largely due to the hormones of the gonads and pituitary and belong on the side of maturation.

The outstanding personality changes in adolescence are the increased interest in the opposite sex and the new spirit of independence, and both of these changes depend largely on biological maturation though they are fostered also by the influence of the adolescent group. Sex interest certainly depends

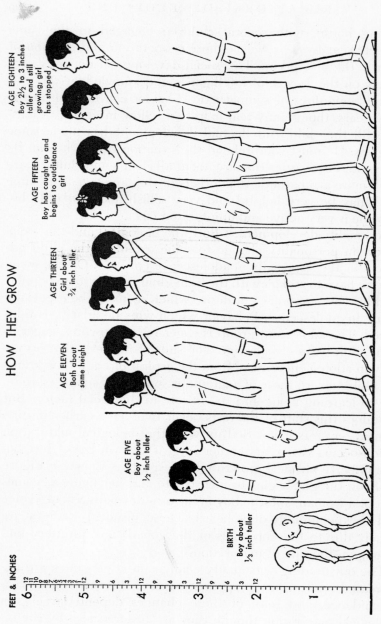

HOW THEY GROW

FEET & INCHES

BIRTH
Boy about ⅓ inch taller

AGE FIVE
Boy about ½ inch taller

AGE ELEVEN
Both about same height

AGE THIRTEEN
Girl about ¾ inch taller

AGE FIFTEEN
Boy has caught up and begins to outdistance girl

AGE EIGHTEEN
Boy 2½ to 3 inches taller and still growing; girl has stopped

FIG. 67.—The different course of maturation in boys and girls (Scheinfeld, 26).

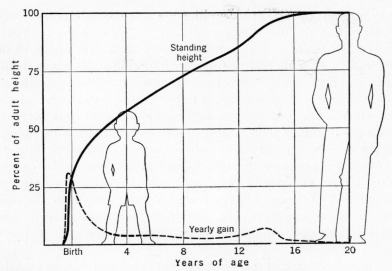

FIG. 68.—The growth of stature from before birth to maturity. Just before puberty each individual shows a second spurt of growth. The first spurt, as shown in the dotted curve of yearly gain, is at its peak before birth. The second spurt occurs at a variable age, from 10 to 15 years in girls, from 12 to 17 in boys. Because the prepubertal spurt occurs at different ages, it will not appear in an average of all boys or girls. This curve was obtained by averaging only boys who showed the greatest gain in height at the same age. Repeated measurements of the same individuals are necessary in order to obtain an accurate picture of growth (Data from Shuttleworth, 28).

in large part on the hormones, and the spirit of independence on the attainment of adult size and strength. A child may have rebelled in a rather futile way against adult authority, but as an adolescent he feels large and strong enough to assert his independence. He enters a new world because he is taller, stronger, and more interested in the other sex. However, he has to learn how to deal successfully with that other sex, and how to be independent without making himself ridiculous.

**Development of intellectual ability.** Binet, we remember, based his method of measuring intelligence on the fact that children become more capable mentally as they advance in age. We remember also that the upper limit of this advance seemed to occur in adolescence, but whether early or late in the teens was not certain (p. 51). Intelligence test scores increase only slowly, if at all, after the age of 15 or 16, though the best evidence at present would indicate a very slow gain up to 18 or even 20 (13). College students, given intelligence tests as freshmen and again as seniors, usually register considerable gain on the whole. The gain is greatest in the verbal tests, such as tests for vocabulary and for reading comprehension, and there is even a loss rather than a gain in the arithmetical tests, except in the case of students who have used their arithmetic in connection with courses in mathematics and science. The others have forgotten some of their arithmetic for lack of continued practice. And the gain in the verbal tests is more probably due to abundant practice in the use of the language than to any considerable maturation of the brain during the college years (12).

The exact shape of the mental growth curve cannot be exactly the same as that for the growth of stature shown in Figure 68. There cannot be much mental growth before birth. But there is a rapid rise in the first two years after birth. In our pride as adults, especially as young adults, we belittle the young child's intellectual attainments and assume that, of course, the greatest mental development occurs in adolescence. But consider the achievements of the two-year-old. He has established contact with the environment, both physical and social. He can manipulate objects with some skill and communicate with people. The gain from birth to the two-year level is certainly striking. Can we find as striking a gain in any two-year period during adolescence? In physical development there are striking changes at puberty, including a rapid gain in stature. A parallel spurt in mentality is possible but very difficult to prove or disprove. Some individuals show what looks like a spurt just before or after puberty, but others show no spurt. If there is an adolescent spurt in intellectual ability, it is much less striking than the physical spurt in adolescence, or than the child's gain in the first two years (1).

*Advance and decline during adult life.* The common opinion is no doubt that mental ability increases up to middle age and

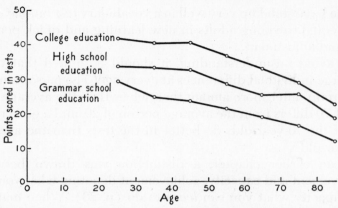

FIG. 69.—Age curves for intelligence test scores. At each age, 40–50 for example, individuals were tested who had gone through college, others who had gone only through high school, and others who had gone only through grammar school. At each age the better-educated group made the better average score, as would be expected. But the important point here is that in each educational group the older persons averaged lower than the younger ones (Miles & Miles, 19).

then declines. Intelligence test scores, however, show a decline starting as early as 25 or 30, though this decline is at first very slow. Such is the result obtained by several investigators who have tested large numbers at the different ages (13, 19, 20, 32). Great care has been taken to secure comparable samples of the different age groups, since it would not be fair to compare educated young persons with uneducated older persons, or the reverse. In a California study, samples of equal educational and social status were tested, with the results shown in Figure 69. In a New England study, practically the entire population of certain small towns and rural districts was tested, with results as shown at the bottom of Figure 70. Here the result is quite different with the tests that depend largely on knowledge and with those that depend mostly on alertness. The curve for general knowledge remains practically level from 20 to 60 years of age, while the alertness curve falls off quickly from its high point at 17 years. In another large-scale investigation, the ability to learn was found to decline at a moderate rate from its high point at about 20 years of age (31). In still other studies, old people have stood up very well in a vocabulary test but have not been equal to young adults in new learning and quick perception and adjustment.

To avoid misunderstanding, it should be added that there are large individual differences at every age⌊The persons in any age group differ more among themselves than the average person of 70 differs from the average person of 20, and a good number of the 70-year-olds do better in the tests than the average 20-year-old.⌉

In an earlier chapter, a distinction was drawn between achievement and capacity, achievement denoting what you *can* do, capacity what you can *learn* to do (p. 23). When maturation is completed, sometime in adolescence, the individual has reached his full capacity. But he has not necessarily reached his full achievement. He can go on learning for many years, mastering his chosen line of work, improving his ways of dealing with people, and building up a background of knowledge, poise and wisdom.

After maturation has done its work, learning has to continue for some years before the individual reaches the peak of his ability and achievement. Yet not for very many years. Some of the most original achievements in art, science and invention are the work of men in their twenties, though achievement is greater on the whole in the thirties, after which a decline sets in according to the facts summarized in Figure 70. If we ask why achievement should rise for 10–15 years after maturity is reached, the answer has already been given. "Art is long," and so is science. Much learning is needed in order to work up the background of one's subject and in order to discover one's own best leads and ideas. But if we ask why achievement should not remain at its highest level once that level has been attained, the answer is not altogether clear. There is such a thing as "resting on one's oars" from lack of motivation to keep up the strenuous effort required for creative work. There is such a thing as "running out of ideas," for we cannot expect any single individual to have an unlimited supply of original ideas that are also fruitful and important. And there is such a thing as "growing old."

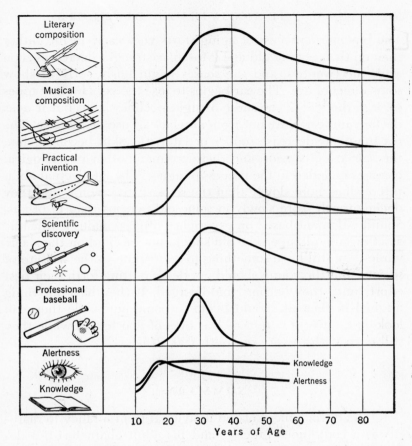

Fig. 70.—Intelligence and superior achievement as related to age (Data from Lehman, *15, 16*, and from Jones & Conrad, *13*).

The two curves at the bottom show the average scores of comparable age groups in the Army Alpha intelligence test (p. 43). The curve for Knowledge shows the run of the scores in the sub-tests that depend largely on knowledge, while the Alertness curve shows the scores in the sub-tests that depend mostly on close attention and mental flexibility. The Knowledge curve stays up while the Alertness curve begins to sag early.

The other curves picture the rise and fall of great achievements during the lives of leading creative workers. The uppermost curve shows the relative number of great works produced by the writers of modern times (now dead) at different ages; their output was high from 30 to 45 years of age, without any sharp peak. The curve for baseball has a rather sharp peak at 25–30. The peak for great scientific, inventive or musical achievement falls in the thirties, and a similar curve for the world's greatest paintings has its peak near age 35.

301

The biological process of aging starts very early in life rather than on the verge of old age. Muscular strength decreases soon after the twenties, and the senses begin fairly early to show some effect of age. The ear begins to lose the very highest tones even in the teens. The sense of sight declines later, but it does decline and certainly not from any lack of use or exercise. The sex functions decrease sooner or later; the skin becomes thin; the hair loses its color; and there are many other physiological changes included in the process of aging. The intellectual abilities decline more slowly than the sensory and motor, and they decline much more slowly in some old persons than in others. Sound judgment based on experience often remains a valuable asset even in old age. The old should not be "laid on the shelf" while they still have something to contribute to the welfare of society. But the young should not delay putting forth their best efforts until they become middle-aged. If they have anything original in them it should begin to come out while they still look on the world with the clear eyes of youth, and while they still burn with the fire of youth (20, 21).

## SUMMARY

1. The development of the individual from infancy to maturity is a continuous process, and his adult characteristics depend on his previous growth and experience.

2. *Maturation* is the growth and differentiation of the cells, tissues, and organs of the body.

   a. *Instinct* is an activity which enables an individual to deal competently with the environment without previous experience and practice. Instinctive activities are more common in animals than in human beings.

   b. In the *prenatal* period the fertilized ovum develops by increase in the number and variety of cells.

   c. The *differentiation* of cells, which necessarily carry the same genes, depends on the interaction of parts within the young organism, and results in the maturation of the various kinds of cells, tissues, and organs to a point where they can begin to function.

d. Most neurons develop to a functional stage before birth, but the cortex does not function to any great extent until after birth.

3. Development by *exercise* and by *learning* depends on interaction between the organism and its environment.

a. Once an organ has matured so that it can function, its *exercise* will further develop and strengthen it.

b. *Learning* is any relatively permanent change in an individual which results from experience.

c. *Reinforcement* is a response of the individual to the results of an activity, confirming and tending to select and establish the acts that produce desirable or meaningful consequences.

4. *Behavioral development* depends on maturation to provide a mechanism that will function, and on exercise and learning to strengthen and modify the mechanism.

a. The activity of the new-born infant consists of undirected movements of all parts of the body, as well as certain coordinated reflexes and instinctive acts.

b. Eye-hand coordination develops gradually and progressively during the first year after birth.

c. The regular sequence of stages in the development of *walking* and of *talking* indicates that maturation plays an important part.

d. *Social development* begins with the infant's responses to parents and adults; with his nursery school playmates the child shows progressively more social participation and cooperation from year to year.

e. *Personality development* is greatly influenced by the individual's learning in his social environment, but the personality changes of adolescence clearly show the maturational influences of puberty.

f. *Intellectual development* is rapid in childhood, leveling off between the ages of 15 and 20. Although knowledge and judgment may continue to improve, measures of intellectual alertness show a gradual decline on the average from that time on.

# CHAPTER TEN

# *Motives*

A person's achievement may fall far short of his ability. The college teacher will readily think of students with A-grade ability but C-grade achievement, and it is also true in athletics or dramatics that some persons who seem to have plenty of ability are very disappointing in actual performance. Sometimes their ability has been overrated, but quite often their mediocre performance is due to lack of effort or to a scattering of effort. They are not interested in an activity, or they have taken a personal dislike to the teacher or director or to their fellow-performers, or perhaps they simply have not the energy to carry all the activities they have undertaken. What they lack is not ability but motivation (*18*).

Even in the case of a machine a similar distinction can be made. A machine now standing idle in the shop is capable of doing a certain kind of work, but to make it work "motive power" must be applied. Just so, a person because of his structure has the ability to run instead of walking, but why should he run just now? If you see a person running you wonder whether he is in a hurry to get away from something behind or to get to something ahead. You assume he must have some motive.

In a recent chapter (p. 198) the What, How, and Why questions were mentioned as problems of psychology. We have now reached the Why problem and shall devote to it these next three chapters. After that we shall return to the How question which has been our major concern in the last two or three chapters. All these questions are so closely interrelated that they cannot be kept entirely separate.

When you ask why a person is acting in a certain way, the answer may be to point to a motive or simply to a stimulus. The two should not be confused. Consider a very simple example. If my hand touches a hot stove and I jerk it away, there is no excuse for saying that my motive is to escape the painful heat. The escape movement is a direct response to the hot stimulus and no motive *present in advance* prepared me to make this response. But suppose, while the pain in my hand continues, I see a pail of water and plunge my hand into it. This is not my usual response to a pail of water, but at this moment something unusual is going on in me, a seeking to escape from the pain in my hand. This seeking is the motive, while the immediate stimulus is the sight of the pail. A stimulus comes to the individual at a certain moment; a motive, if there is any motive acting, is already present in the individual before the stimulus appears.

Using the S—O—R formula as a guide, we inquired once before for the causes of a response (p. 208), and decided that, besides S, there are causal factors in O and that the O-factors belong under the three heads of structure (or permanent characteristics of the individual), temporary state, and activity in progress. When any motive is operating it belongs under the head of activity in progress. It is a readiness or preparation for certain kinds of behavior. A motive, then, is practically the same as a *set*.

An *incentive* is a goal toward which a motivated activity is directed. When hunger or food-seeking is the motive, food is the goal object or incentive. Food is an effective incentive, of course, only when O is hungry. Incentive and motive are aspects of the same process.

## ORIGIN AND DEVELOPMENT OF MOTIVES

Since the development of the individual depends on the factors of maturation, exercise, and learning, these same factors are undoubtedly concerned in the development of his motives. Some motives, resulting from maturation only, are his natural, instinctive, unlearned motives. Others, built up by his experiences, activities, and reinforcements, are his learned motives. Any motive of an adult human being is likely to be partly instinctive and partly learned; it probably includes both unlearned and learned components.

The hunger of a newborn puppy is certainly an unlearned motive. There is no reason to suppose that the puppy "knows" what it is seeking, and it is perfectly clear to an observer that the puppy does not know exactly where and how to secure nourishment. But a hungry puppy is exceptionally active and vigorous in its movements. Its successful movements are reinforced by finding food, and in this way the puppy learns how to act when motivated by hunger.

The human infant—if anything even more helpless than the puppy—at least need not *learn* to accept the nipple when hungry and reject it when satiated. His sucking movements are strengthened by exercise, and the bottle-fed baby learns a technique for handling his bottle efficiently. Moreover he becomes attached to his bottle because it brings satisfaction and reinforcement. His demand for the bottle is a learned motive built on the foundation of his unlearned hunger motive. When the time comes to wean him from the bottle, he objects because this learned motive is being frustrated. But the fundamental hunger motive persists and leads to some new desire for certain foods and certain ways of eating. By the time he becomes an adult his choice of foods and his table manners have undergone great changes, but the unlearned hunger motive still remains the basic factor in the whole business of eating.

**Unlearned motives necessary for life.** If the newborn organism is to survive and make its way in the world there are certain activities which are absolutely essential. Nourishment, water and oxygen must be supplied to every cell in the body, and waste products of metabolism must be removed. Serious injury and illness must be avoided or corrected. If the race as well as the individual is to survive, reproduction must take place and the young offspring must be cared for by the adults. Every kind of animal has some type of natural equipment to meet these requirements, though the equipment differs from one species to another. Sea-living animals do not need the thirst motive to assure taking in water. Protection from injury is not so essential for the housefly since survival of the species is assured by the enormous number of eggs that each female lays.

In the case of the human individual some of the vital requirements are met by instinctive motor responses and physiological mechanisms. A painful stimulus, typically a danger signal of injury, arouses an automatic response which tends to withdraw the individual from the danger. Oxygen is distributed from the lungs throughout the body by the blood stream, and a fresh supply of oxygen in the lungs is secured by the instinctive movements of breathing (3). But stereotyped responses of this sort will not meet all the requirements of life in a complex and changing environment. There is no conceivable specific act which would introduce water into the human body under all conditions. The human individual must vary his water-getting activity to suit his environment at the time. Thirst is the unlearned motive which impels the individual to meet this requirement for survival.

Each basic unlearned motive, then, is thrown into activity by some vital requirement such as a lack of water or nourishment in the body. No specific stereotyped response is adequate, but the whole natural equipment for dealing with such a situation includes the power of learning and three other features to insure learning:

1. A persistent stimulus which we feel as the sensation of hunger, thirst, pain, etc. These sensations have an impulsive or motivating quality.

2. An increase in the amount and vigor of general activity. The more active the individual, the more likely he is to discover

some way to satisfy the motive and terminate the unpleasant stimulus.

3. Reinforcement of any act which brings satisfaction of the motive. By this means the successful activity is confirmed and on future occasions will be aroused by the motivating stimulus.

**Likes and dislikes.** It is important to remember that there are likes as well as dislikes, desires as well as aversions, approaching as well as avoiding responses. Besides the unpleasant sensations that motivate the individual to escape, there are pleasant sensations that motivate him to hold them and get more of them; and some likes as well as some dislikes are natural and do not have to be learned. A sweet substance—but not too sweet—in the baby's mouth arouses the positive response of sucking, a bitter substance the negative response of spitting. One odor will arouse the positive response of breathing in deeply and so getting more of it, while another odor will arouse the negative response of checking the breath and turning away. A smooth, warm object touching the skin gets a positive response, while a very hot or cold object or one that is sharp and pricking gets a negative response. A smooth tone is naturally agreeable while a grating noise is disagreeable. With regard to the colors, perhaps there are none that are naturally disagreeable, but certainly bright colors attract the baby's eyes more than dull shades.

Besides having some importance in everyday practical life, these natural likes and dislikes furnish the foundation for the esthetic arts. Without pleasant tastes there could not be a culinary art, nor without pleasant odors a perfumer's art. The color art depends on human liking for colors and color harmonies, and music depends on pleasure in tones and rhythms and their manifold combinations. These natural likes and dislikes furnish only the foundation, and an immense amount of learning is necessary for appreciation of the complexities and refinements of artistic music or color decoration.

Reinforcement plays its part in the learning, or acquiring, of new likes and dislikes. On first drinking coffee a child, or perhaps anyone, is repelled by the bitter taste. Yet it has an agree-

able flavor and a stimulating temperature, and by savoring
these you reinforce the positive response of drinking coffee till
you come to enjoy it greatly. Imagine a simple experiment with
two bottles containing unknown liquids. You remove the stop-
per of the first bottle and inhale gently. The odor is agreeable
and your reaction is to inhale more deeply. This is a reinforcing
or confirming reaction. A gentle sniff from the second bottle
gives a disagreeable odor and your response is to recork the
bottle quickly. So you terminate the unpleasant sensation and
get *relief*. Is there any reinforcement in this case? Yes, the relief
obtained confirms your avoiding reaction. The next time you
see these two bottles, you smell from the first and avoid the
second, getting further reinforcement of the positive and negative reactions. Every time you take a whiff from the first bottle
your positive response is reinforced by the pleasant odor; and
every time the appearance of the second bottle suggests a disagreeable odor your avoiding response is reinforced by the
feeling of relief or escape. You might be making a mistake—
someone might have replaced the evil-smelling liquid by a de-
lightful perfume of the same color, and you would never discover the change because you would always avoid this bottle
and pat yourself on the back for having escaped the bad odor.
Many perfectly needless antipathies and fears are perpetuated
in this way, by continual avoidance of what are really only
imaginary dangers.

**Effects of learning.** In adjusting to his environment the individual modifies his unlearned motives. He does not usually
lose or outgrow them, but he does reshape them in several respects.

1. Goals and motives become more specific through learning, as already explained in the case of hunger. It should be
added that there is another kind of "specific hungers" dependent
not on learning but on the needs of the body for various foods
such as protein, fat, carbohydrate, salts and vitamins. An animal
that has had no salt to eat for a long time, or a man who has lost
much salt through rapid sweating, will manifest an intense salt
hunger when given access to salt; and the same seems to be true

with regard to the vitamin B complex and some other food substances. But the "food habits" of human beings depend mostly on learning and social customs and not on specific bodily needs (23). For example, we have learned to "get hungry" three times a day, but in some other societies the people get hungry once a day, or five times a day.

2. Motives are combined into more complex motives. This happens when the same object is the goal of two or more desires. Dinner in congenial company satisfies both hunger and the desire for companionship, and when you look forward to such a dinner it would be difficult to disentangle the two motives out of your total anticipation of a good time. In the same way, longing for home is not just desire for shelter, or for food, or for companionship, but all of these desires are combined and blended into the homing motive.

3. Intermediate goals, means to an end, come to be desired as a result of learning. You are at A and wish to find your way to Z; and you have learned from previous experiences that if you reach M you are on the right road and halfway to your goal. In the first half of your journey, M is your first goal and when you reach M you have a sense of getting somewhere. The effort to reach the intermediate goal may become so absorbing that the ultimate goal is temporarily forgotten. So the means to an end becomes an end in itself. Money is only a means to some further end, but the desire for money itself is very strong in many people.

4. New stimuli become associated with a motive and capable of arousing it to activity. The fear motive or desire to escape is aroused not only by visibly present danger but also by any danger signal, like the wailing of an air-raid signal in wartime. The siren would not have this effect except for previous learning. The natural stimulus for the hunger motive is an internal lack of nourishment, but you are unconscious of this internal condition while engaged in some interesting activity, until you hear the dinner bell when all at once you feel your hunger and start for the dining room. The meaning of any such signal has to be learned.

## CLASSIFICATION OF MOTIVES

Human behavior is animated by a great variety of motives: hunger and thirst, fear and anger, love and hate, desire to know and master the environment, self-interest and loyalty to family, friends, cause, country. Which motives are learned and which unlearned, or how far is any one of them learned or unlearned? Such a question is sure to be difficult. Perhaps the best way to approach it is to alter its form slightly and ask, "What are the goals of human activity?" Where does a given activity start and where does it terminate? If we know the start and finish of an activity, we can see its direction or aim, and sometimes we can detect a natural aim underlying all the learned behavior that is likely to develop on the foundation of any unlearned motive. In spite of all we have learned of what to eat, and when and how, we still wish to start a meal when hungry and to finish when relatively satiated, so that the direction and aim of our refined eating behavior still reveals the unlearned hunger motive. So it may be with many other forms of human activity, though not necessarily of all.

In the following list of outstanding human motives, the attempt is made to discover the fundamental aims and to show how each one is modified through learning. The motives are divided into three main classes. There are (1) motives which depend on internal bodily states; these are the *organic needs*. Other motives depend on the individual's relations to the environment, and are subdivided into two classes. There are (2) the *emergency motives*, aroused when the environmental situation requires quick and vigorous action. And there are (3) the *objective motives*, directed toward effective dealing with the objects and persons in the environment.

1. **Organic needs.**  *Hunger* and *thirst*, the typical examples of organic needs, have already been sufficiently considered. The *respiratory needs* for oxygen and for removal of excess carbon dioxide are scarcely felt under ordinary conditions but become absolutely imperative in drowning and other cases of suffoca-

tion. The *elimination needs,* too, become urgent when not promptly met, and create serious problems for the young child who is learning to harmonize his instinctive motives with the requirements of the social environment.

The *sex motive* is complex. Without the sex hormones, already mentioned as factors in personality (p. 132), it would not develop to any great strength and thus it belongs fundamentally with the organic needs. The hormone control of the sex motive is not only shown by the effects of puberty and of castration, but also clearly demonstrated by the cyclical changes in female mammals. The cycle varies in length from a few days to a month in different animals. Each cycle in the female includes a comparatively brief period of readiness for sex activity and a longer period of sex inactivity. In the active period an egg (unfertilized ovum) is discharged from the ovary toward the womb, ready for fertilization. The animal's external behavior during the active period is peculiar in two respects: she shows much more motor activity in general than at other times, and she shows specific sex activity. Her response to the male animal is very different in the two periods. During the inactive period she fights off any male that makes advances to her, but during the active period she is receptive. Physiological study reveals that the female sex hormone is secreted only during this active period. The male sex hormone does not follow any such cycle.

Though there are these excellent reasons for believing the sex motive to be fundamentally unlearned, there is also plenty of proof that it is modified by learning in all the four ways previously outlined. It becomes a specific interest in some particular person rather than an impartial interest in all members of the opposite sex. It is combined with other motives, since this particular person has other attractive qualities besides sex appeal, and since both parties have other interests in common. It generates interest in intermediate goals, in ways and means for winning the desired person, in customary or original forms of courtship. And it becomes responsive not only to the actual person but also to messages and gifts and tokens of affection. Without such learned modifications of the sex motive the novelists could never have found material for their thousands of fascinating stories.

*The needs for activity and for rest.* The need for rest after activity and the need for sleep at intervals are organic needs imposed by bodily conditions. Muscular fatigue is due partly to the using up of fuel stored in the muscle, and partly to the accumulation of the waste products of muscular activity, especially lactic acid. The activity may become painful from soreness of the muscles and joints, and there is a strong inclination to stop and rest even while the muscles still have plenty of strength left. In prolonged mental work there may not be much actual loss of power but there is an increasing boredom and distaste for the work, with an inclination either to take a complete rest or to turn to some different activity. In the drowsy state the tendency to go to sleep is certainly a powerful motive, even though, like fatigue, it can be overcome by strong motives to activity (*19*).

But is there an organic need for activity after rest, a true activity motive? At least the well-rested organism is very responsive to stimulation. More than that, there is a positive zest for activity at such times and a great deal of playful or unnecessary activity appears. The amount of such spontaneous activity depends on the hormones and vitamins and on the rested state of the muscles, sense organs and brain. The activity motive seems to be genuine and to have an organic basis. It is especially characteristic of early life and is an important factor in getting acquainted with the world, while the inclination to avoid excessive effort is a factor in the selection of activities that are worth while (*2*).

**2. Emergency motives.** In contrast to the organic needs which arise from internal conditions, the emergency motives depend on the environment. From time to time the individual gets into a situation calling for prompt action to avoid injury or to take advantage of a momentary opportunity. In such a situation the organism is likely to be thrown into an emotional state which will be more fully considered in the following chapter.

## THE EMERGENCY MOTIVES

| Situation or Start | Goal or Finish | Motive or Direction | Emotional State |
|---|---|---|---|
| 1. Danger | Safety | Escape | Fear |
| 2. Restraint | Freedom | Combat | Anger |
| 3. Obstacle | Mastery | Effort | Determination |
| 4. Prey | Capture | Pursuit | Eagerness |

So far as these motives are unlearned, they are aroused by emergencies of a very primitive sort and give rise to behavior that is equally primitive.

*a. The escape motive.* Danger is the typical emergency, and at the primitive level danger is the threat of immediate bodily injury. If injury is not merely threatened but actually taking place, a reflex withdrawal movement is the organism's response. The flexion reflex of the hand, which pulls it away from a burn, prick or pinch, is one of a host of simple avoiding responses—winking, scratching, coughing, sneezing, wincing, limping, squirming—most or all of them being unlearned responses. In speaking of the withdrawal of the hand from a burning stimulus we argued at the beginning of the chapter that no motive was involved but only a stimulus and a response. If the pain continues there will be a seeking to find some way of escape, and this seeking is the escape motive. Not only so; if the injury has not yet occurred but is merely threatened, there may be a seeking to avoid it, and here too we have the escape motive, often associated with fear of the threatened injury.

A situation that threatens injury presents some danger signal, and the meaning of the signal has to be learned. There may be some exceptions to this statement; the mother hen, for example, gives a terrifying squawk at the approach of a hawk and the young chicks immediately flee in all directions. They do not have to learn the meaning of this danger call. Possibly a similar shriek from a human mother would terrify the infant, though without doing the infant any good. But most danger signals are not terrifying in themselves but only after their meaning has been learned. Consequently the little baby is the most fearless of human beings. He makes the natural avoiding responses to stimuli that are painful but disregards danger signals. For example he is not afraid of a snake. If the snake test (a large but actually harmless snake, carried by the experimenter who invites everyone to feel the snake's nice, smooth, hard skin) is tried on people of various ages, no child under two years shows any fear or concern, children of three or four years begin to be somewhat wary, older boys and girls, many of them, shrink back from the snake, and college students show decided fear (9).

How are danger signals learned? By association or "conditioning" in some cases. Little Albert, a healthy child nearly a year old, was accustomed to play fearlessly with dogs, rabbits and white rats; but he was made the subject of an experiment on learned fears. A white rat was held out to the child, who reached for it; but before he got hold of it the experimenter, standing behind the child, produced a startling noise by striking a long steel bar with a hammer. The child shrank back in momentary fright. When this procedure had been repeated a few times, the child shrank back whenever the rat was presented and would no longer play with it. He was then tested by showing him a rabbit or a dog and he showed fear of them, too. The sight of one of these animals had become a danger signal to the child, a sign that unpleasantness was about to follow (22). This experiment does not succeed with all children. Some of them turn and scowl at the harsh noise and then resume their play with the pet animal. They seem to understand that the noise has really nothing to do with the animal, and their intelligence protects them from acquiring a needless fear.

Many danger signals are learned by the child from the warnings he gets from older people or from the fear the older people show under certain conditions. Children who are originally not a bit afraid of thunder and lightning may pick up a fear of them from adults who show fear during a storm. However, not all of the increasing number of a child's fears are due to associations of this sort. Part of the increase is due to maturation and better acquaintance with the world. The infant cannot be frightened by visual stimuli, but as he comes to see better, he is startled by sudden movements such as the jump of a frog, and the sight of a frog becomes a danger signal. At first he understands little of what is going on around him, but as he understands more he finds more need for caution.

Once a learned fear, even a wholly needless one, has been established, it is reinforced every time the child makes the avoiding reaction and has the feeling of escaping from danger (p. 310). It is not easy to rid a child of such a fear. Different methods have been tried without much success, but the following experiment was successful. Peter, nearly three years old, was for some unknown cause extremely afraid of rabbits. The experimenter undertook to remove this fear by introducing pleasant associations. The procedure was the reverse of that used with Albert but more difficult to carry through successfully. The plan was to have the rabbit present while Peter was enjoying his lunch. Without skill on the experimenter's part the procedure could have taken the wrong direction and the rabbit would have spoiled the lunch instead of the lunch making the rabbit endurable (as cod liver oil in orange juice may make a child hate orange juice rather than like cod liver oil). At first, the experimenter placed the rabbit in a cage quite far away where Peter could tolerate his presence during lunch. Day by day the rabbit was brought nearer and the child continued to tolerate the situation. Finally the rabbit could be placed right on the lunch table and released from his cage. Peter was soon playing with the rabbit even without the help of lunch. What happened here was that the child saw the rabbit in a favorable light because of the agreeable nature of the whole situation (10).

b. *The combat motive.* Angry behavior as seen in a child of one or two years is a surprising phenomenon. Prevented from doing what he wishes, or commanded to do what he does not wish, the child is likely to burst out into undirected motor activity, jumping up and down and screaming; or he may struggle against the interfering person or object; or he may attack that person or object. This outburst may last for a longer or shorter time but typically for 1–5 minutes. Such behavior is disapproved by adults who try not to reinforce it, and it becomes less frequent as the child grows up under normal conditions (5). In anger, as in fear, there is an internal, organic, emotional disturbance, and this internal activity is likely to remain even when the individual has learned to control his external pugnacious behavior, or when he has substituted angry talk for the primitive struggling, kicking and screaming.

Combative behavior is aroused by some restraint, restriction, or interference with the individual's course of action, and it reaches its goal when the interfering object or (more often) person is thoroughly beaten so that the angry individual is free to do as he wishes. The goal is reached by struggling and fighting, and this seems without doubt to be a natural direction of behavior, and an unlearned motive. But the behavior is modified in many ways by learning. Kinds of interference that would not disturb a young child will arouse antagonism in an older person, and the technique of fighting changes. An adult may not dare to scratch his opponent's skin but he would like to damage his reputation and lower his social prestige (17).

*c. Effort directed toward overcoming an obstacle.* Let the individual be engaged in any activity whatever and moving toward any goal, and let him encounter an obstacle. What will be his reaction? Several reactions are possible. He may give up and yield to the obstacle. He may find a way around the obstacle. He may become angry and make a pugnacious attack on the obstacle, as we have already said. Simpler and more common than this angry reaction is the reaction of effort, which consists in pressing toward the goal with increased energy. The direction of activity is from being blocked toward overcoming the obstruction.

This motive to overcome resistance is certainly unlearned. Obstruct a movement that the little baby is making and you can feel him putting increased muscular force into his movement. A more complicated reflex of the same sort is the movement of straining: a full breath is taken, the glottis is closed preventing the escape of air from the lungs, and then a strong movement of expiration is made. The most obvious result of this peculiar action is to produce pressure in the abdomen and so overcome any difficulty in evacuating the bladder or rectum; and that is the way the baby first uses the movement of straining. But it also stiffens the trunk for lifting a heavy weight or for any powerful muscular act, and it is a regular component of any such act. It is likely to occur whenever you make a strong effort of any kind, physical or mental.

There are many other expressions of effort: gritting the teeth, clenching the fist, stiffening the neck, frowning in the effort to see better, leaning forward tensely for the same purpose even when, as at a football game or in the gallery of a theater, getting a foot or two nearer the show cannot make the view appreciably better. Ask a child just learning to write why he grasps the pencil so tightly, why he bends so closely over the desk, why he purses his lips, knits his brow and twists his foot around the leg of the chair, and he might answer, very truly, that it is because he is *trying hard*. All this muscular effort may not make the writing any better but it does reveal the natural tendency to put in more effort whenever difficulty of any kind is encountered.

A good example at the level of mental work is seen in the distraction experiment (p. 229). When a person occupied in mental work is exposed to loud noises and other distracting stimuli, he is apt to throw in extra energy and overcome the distraction. Effort, just by itself, is not pleasant; it is unpleasant unless it is felt to be overcoming a difficulty. This motive might well be called the *mastery motive*. Why do people like to solve puzzles, or to master difficult "stunts"? Why are games and sports so devised as to create difficulties that can be overcome by strength and skill? Without difficulty overcome there would be no joy of achievement. The mastery motive, or zest for achievement, while based on the primitive motive to overcome an obstacle, is modified in various ways by experience and learning.

As a general proposition, and one of the most general propositions in the science of motivation, we can state that difficulty encountered in carrying through any activity stimulates the individual to throw more energy into the activity and makes the activity more worth while.

d. *The pursuit motive—seizing the momentary opportunity.* Thinking again of primitive conditions of life we see that the presence of prey creates an emergency, since the prey will escape unless quickly pursued and caught. More than a trace of this sort of behavior is seen in the young child; if you place an attractive toy before him, especially a new one, he makes a grab for it. Modified situations of this general kind are common in games; the ball must be caught at just such a time or the chance is missed; and the player who makes no "errors" is the one who makes good use of all his chances.

There are two reasons why the presence of prey is an emergency: the prey may get away, or some competitor may get to it first. The germ of *competition* is present whenever there are two individuals making a grab for the same thing, as often happens in animal life and child life. The competitive spirit is strongly fostered in some societies though not in all; no doubt it has its origin in primitive emergency behavior but it is developed and modified by learning from the group.

**3. Objective motives and interests.** The "will to live," often said to be the great inclusive motive of all living creatures, is in human beings not simply the will to stay alive but rather the will to live in active relations with the environment. Being equipped with sense organs and motor organs and a well-developed brain, the human individual has a fundamental inclination to deal with the environment. This motive is not primarily directed toward serving the organic needs and meeting the emergencies of life, but toward knowing objects and persons, doing things to them, and participating in what is going on in the environment. Just because this objective tendency of human activity is so all-pervasive, it is often overlooked and omitted from a list of fundamental motives, where it certainly belongs. It shows itself in the general tendencies to explore and manipulate the environment, and in a great variety of more specific interests.

*a. Exploration.* The exploring motive is obviously present in animals as well as in man. It appears in the baby before he is able to move around. He explores with his eyes, ears, hands and mouth. Looking at an object is a simple form of exploration. An object off to one side catches the baby's attention; he turns his eyes and focuses them on that object. The clear view he thus obtains of that object is the goal of this little act of exploration. He examines the object for a while and his active brain gets some knowledge of the object. Reinforcement occurs, first when he sees the object clearly, and then when he gets some knowledge of it. When the child is a little older he explores by moving around while using his senses. He also asks many questions, and when he gets an answer that satisfies his momentary curiosity he has reached the goal of one bit of exploration. He sometimes makes practical use of the information obtained, but often the only immediate goal is that of getting acquainted with the environment.

*b. Manipulation.* Playful manipulation is seen in the behavior of a kitten with a ball or of a puppy with a stick but it is still more characteristic of the human child because of his clever hands and because his brain is better equipped for understanding and managing objects. The child is not satisfied with simply looking at an object. He wants to get hold of it, turn it about, drop or throw it, meanwhile watching to see what happens. The immediate goal of this activity is the result accomplished. By exploration and manipulation combined the child builds up his acquaintance with the world. So he is preparing himself for the serious activities of later life, but his own motive is not to prepare for the future, but to deal actively with the present environment. We can judge of his motivation by noticing what kinds of objects are the child's favorite playthings. A large share of them fall into the following classes:

Movable objects: a book, a door, a drawer to open and shut, a water tap to turn on and off (especially on), a bag or box to pack and unpack. Almost anything that the child can move serves him as a plaything.

Plastic materials: damp sand, mud, snow, and other materials that can be worked in some way, like paper to tear or fold, blocks to pile or build, water to pour.

Noise-makers: rattle, drum, bell, horn, firecracker.

Vehicles: cart, bicycle, sled, skates, skipping-rope.

Space-annihilators enabling the child to act on a wider environment: balls to throw, bow and arrow, sling, mirror to flash light into the eyes of a distant person.

Things that defy gravity by floating, balancing or rising instead of falling: balloon, kite, top, rolling hoop, swing, seesaw, boat.

Adult-imitating toys: little tools, dishes, furniture, dolls, toy animals, toy trains and automobiles.

Play with such toys consists in manipulating them so as to produce some interesting results. The hoop is made to roll, the kite to fly, the arrow to hit something; the blocks are built into a tower and knocked down with a crash, the mud is made into a "pie," the horn is sounded. The child's motive is not simply that of engaging in motor activity; rather, he aims to produce interesting results. It is an objective motive. The child's vocal activity, too, produces objective results, audible sounds in the first place which seem to be the original goal of this activity. Besides, these sounds get response from other persons and enable the child to do something in the way of manipulating other people. The child finds animals and human beings to be extremely interesting objects to explore and manipulate. In group play a variety of other motives come into operation, especially the emergency motives, for an active game provides one emergency after another calling for effort to overcome an obstacle or for quick action to take advantage of an opportunity. Many games stimulate competition and team work and thus involve the mastery motive.

*c. Interests.* Exploration, including exploratory manipulation, is a necessary step in dealing with the environment, but it is only the first step. Some things, after the child has explored them, are of no further interest to him while other things become his favorite playthings. If the individual finds an object interesting, this interest of his is a motive leading to active dealing with the object. What is the difference between objects that are interesting and those that awaken no interest? Some will tell you that an object is interesting if it is found to be good to eat or if it is somehow associated with an organic need or with escape from danger. They will tell you, for example, that Peter's interest in the rabbit was derived from his interest in his lunch by a process of association or conditioning. But let us look into Peter's case a little more closely. Peter started the experiment with a fear of rabbits which had to be overcome before he could discover for himself how interesting rabbits really are. Rabbits have characteristics that make them interesting to many children without any association with lunch. Peter could not explore the rabbit and discover these interesting characteristics so long as he continued to avoid the rabbit. The association with lunch enabled him to overcome his fear but did not create the interesting characteristics of a rabbit.

Oftentimes an object has certain characteristics that are uninteresting or even repellent as well as other characteristics that are very interesting. A person's face may be scarred or homely and not at all "easy to look at"; but if you can overcome your first unfavorable reaction you may find a grand personality hidden behind the face. Your first impressions of a book or of a course of study may be unfavorable and it may take some determination to explore far enough to discover its interesting characteristics.

What then makes the difference between the interesting and the uninteresting object? The answer, in general terms, would run something like this: The individual has a fundamental tendency to deal with the environment, and is capable of dealing with it in certain ways. When he finds an object that he can deal with, he takes an interest in that object. Unless he can deal with it somehow, there is nothing in it for him. "Dealing," however, must be taken in a very broad sense so as to include appreciation and understanding as well as handling and managing the object. Smooth tones are interesting because you can listen to them with pleasure. Music is still more interesting if you are able to follow its rhythm and harmony, and making music yourself is better yet. Bright colors are interesting because you can gaze at them with pleasure, color designs are still more interesting if you can make out the pattern, and constructing your own designs is better yet. Places are interesting if you can see the lay of the land and find your way around, and by extending your explorations you build up quite an interest in local geography and perhaps in maps and the wider science of geography. Objects can be counted, and the child may take quite an interest in counting and go on to an interest in the characteristics of numbers.

Persons are interesting, partly because you can watch them and follow what they are doing and understand them to some extent, and partly because you can induce them to do things for you and with you. The fact that they differ in so many ways gives you still more opportunity to exercise and develop your powers of understanding and managing people.

Groups of people are interesting because they do so many things together—conversation, games, work—and as the child grows up he finds he can understand what they are doing and take part in their activities. Participation in group activities is one of the major goals of the individual's existence. It is fun for its own sake and not merely a means to some ulterior end such as greater individual prosperity and security.

Each individual comes to have an interest in himself. At first the child can scarcely be aware of himself as a person, and he explores things and other persons before he gives much attention to himself. Older people call his attention to himself by applauding him for some of his actions, blaming him for some, comparing him with other children, and urging him to improve and to show what he can do. To some extent he comes to see himself as others see him, i.e., as an object having certain characteristics. He boasts of his successes and is ashamed of his failures, and all this interest in himself may distract him too much from his interests in things and in social participation and teamwork. A man may be so eager to shine and win applause for himself that he "plays to the grandstand" and not for the success of the team. This motive of *self-assertion*, however, is often a powerful drive toward achievement. Sometimes it does good and sometimes harm. One thing that saves it is the individual's power to *identify* himself with his team, so that he takes pride in the achievements of the team.

**Purposes.** Though the word "purpose" is sometimes used so broadly as to cover any action directed toward a goal, it is better reserved for cases where the individual has some *foresight* of the end to be accomplished and where he has definitely *committed* himself to the action. If he were just strolling along, following vague inclinations but with no definite idea of where he was going, his behavior would scarcely be purposive. If he were thinking of something desirable and wishing he had it, he still might have no definite purpose. If he says, "I'd like to do this, or to have that," his wish is not yet a purpose, but if he goes on to say, "I'll do it, I'll get it," he has adopted the wish as his purpose. Having committed himself he will take steps to reach his goal; he will devise ways and means to attain his end. The planning and execution of a long-time purposive action demands imagination and intelligence as well as energy and persistence.

A purpose can be the most definite of motives and the most powerful. The more definite the goal, the more determined you are to overcome obstacles and put in the necessary effort.

Though a purpose has this definiteness it is often based on more than a single motive, and the individual may not understand why he is aiming so persistently at this particular goal. Any act accomplishes more than a single result. You start from A and go to Z. Is your motive to get to Z, or to get away from A, or perhaps to pass through M where there may be something attractive? And Z itself may appeal to more than one motive, as in the case of the good dinner in good company. It is sometimes very difficult for the individual to analyze his own motives, or for anyone else to analyze them for him. In being helpful to a friend he is also dominating over him to a certain extent. He himself may say, "I am simply trying to help you," while his friend may say, "But you insist on bossing me and showing how superior you are." The individual tends to see himself in a good light and to put a favorable interpretation on his motives, while others may be biased in the opposite direction. Neither bias gives a true picture, the fact being that the individual's motives are mixed. They spring from various sources, some being unlearned and some learned, some dating from forgotten experiences and associations of childhood and some from recently awakened interests in people and things. The old motives and the unanalyzed motives are sometimes called "unconscious," but this word is mystifying rather than explanatory.

## STRENGTH OF MOTIVES

If we were provided with a complete list of human motives, the next question we should want to ask would be as to which motives were the stronger and which the weaker. A motive might be so strong as to overpower all others and take complete charge of the individual's behavior, at least for a time; or it might be so weak as to have little effect on behavior. We often make some attempt to estimate the strength of a motive, as in asking a person how much he is willing to pay for a certain satisfaction, or how long he is willing to work for it, or what other satisfactions he is willing to give up in order to secure this particular one. Of course the answer to such a question would depend on the individual and still more on the circumstances. When Patrick Henry exclaimed, "Give me liberty or give me death," he was proclaiming, in effect, that the combat motive of fighting against restraint and bondage could be the strongest of all motives; and his assertion would seem to be borne out by the fact that a nation threatened with subjugation by a foreign tyrant will devote as nearly as possible all its energies to a defensive war. But the individual soldier's fighting spirit, no matter how keen and courageous, may finally yield to the imperative demands of fatigue. Under more normal conditions, some idea of the relative strength of different motives in the population at large can be obtained from statistics of their use of money. When the people of the United States in 1929 spent over twice as much for entertainment of all kinds as for education, the inference would seem to be that the entertainment motives were much stronger on the average than the education motives. Many students, to be sure, are putting much more money as well as much more time and effort into education than into entertainment. The entertainment motives are largely social motives, since in most forms of entertainment the individual participates in the enjoyments and activities of a group (*16*).

**The measurement of animal motives.**   Basic information on the relative strength of the most primitive motives can be obtained best from animal experiments, because conditions are much better controlled in the animal laboratory than they can be in the complex social life of mankind, and because of the animal's simplicity and freedom from self-consciousness. The basic motives revealed in animal behavior are usually called *drives*.

In one type of experiment, the animal's output of muscular energy is measured by an *activity cage* which is like a squirrel

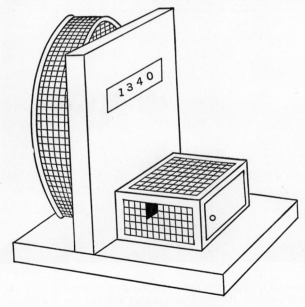

Fig. 71.—An activity cage.

cage in being provided with an upright wheel for the animal to run in as much as he will. A mechanical counter shows the number of times the animal's running has turned the wheel around. A healthy rat may spend a good share of the time running in preference to sitting still, and the counter often records the equivalent of 5, 10 or even 20 miles run during 24 hours (*14*). While hungry the animal runs a good deal but after a meal very little, as we should expect. An animal deprived of certain endocrine glands—pituitary, thyroid, gonads, or adrenal cortex—is very inactive.

The *obstruction method* offers the animal a reward or incentive but places an obstruction in the way to the goal. A convenient obstruction consists of an electrified grill in the floor of a tunnel through which the animal must pass in order to reach the incentive. The shocks are strong enough to make the animal avoid the tunnel unless there is some incentive present

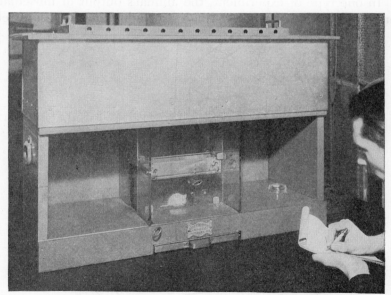

*Courtesy, C. J. Warden*

Fig. 72.—An obstruction box. The starting compartment is at the left. The rat is shown on the grid, advancing toward the food compartment at the right.

on the far side. After each crossing the animal is allowed only a little nibble of food, or a small portion of whatever reward is offered, and then is placed back at the entrance. He is given a total of 20 minutes, and the question is how many times he will cross the grill to the incentive.

With white rats as subjects, there are about 3 or 4 crossings in 20 minutes with no particular incentive. When the rats are hungry and food is the incentive, the number of crossings is about 18 on the average after a fast of 2–4 days, but after still longer periods of fasting the number of crossings declines. We may accept 18 crossings in the twenty-minute test period, then, as the maximum effect of the hunger drive (for the average white rat of a certain age). In the same way the maximum is determined for thirst and for other drives. The strength of the maternal drive is tested by taking a mother rat from her litter and making it necessary for her to cross the grid in order to reach the young. She makes a higher score within a few hours after childbirth than a week later; in this species, then, the maternal drive declines rather rapidly. The sex drive is tested by placing a mate beyond the grill. During the active period of the sexual cycle (p. 313) the female rat will cross the grid repeatedly to reach the male, but during the inactive period she will scarcely cross at all. (During the active phase she also makes an extremely high score in the activity cage.) The male rat, similarly tested, shows no cycle but crosses the grid much less after a period of free sex activity than after 24 hours or more of sex deprivation.

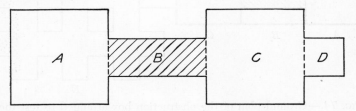

FIG. 73.—Ground plan of an obstruction box. The animal is in compartment A and the incentive in C or D. To reach the incentive the animal must cross through the narrow, low passage B and take electric shocks from the wires in the floor (Warden, 20).

In estimating the comparative strength of these various drives, we should take each one at its maximum. The results, expressed in numbers of crossings of the grill within the twenty-minute test period, are as follows (20).

| Drive Tested | Average No. Crossings |
|---|---|
| Maternal | 22.4 |
| Thirst | 20.4 |
| Hunger | 18.2 |
| Sex | 13.8 |
| Exploratory | 6.0 |
| No incentive | 3.5 |

Small differences in these averages are not well established, but there seems no doubt that the maternal, thirst and hunger drives, at their respective maxima, are more insistent than the sex drive at its maximum, and that the sex drive in turn is stronger than the exploratory. With regard to the last point, however, the animal psychologists report that the rat foregoes either food or sex activity in any strange locality until he has first explored the place. There seems no possible doubt of the

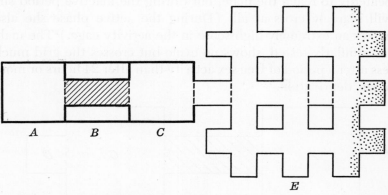

Fig. 74.—Ground plan of the obstruction box arranged to test the exploratory drive. The animal, placed in A, must traverse the passage B and step on the electrified grid in order to reach C and the enclosure E which contains sawdust and other objects such as rats are wont to investigate (Nissen, in Warden, 20).

genuineness of the exploratory tendency, at least in the white rat.

*Goal gradient.* Another interesting result from the animal laboratory is that an animal speeds up as it approaches the goal. When the goal is right close at hand an animal, or a child, finds it very difficult to take a necessary detour instead of plunging straight for the goal. The closer the goal, the greater its pulling power. This principle is probably applicable to men as well; the results are at least suggestive (*6, 8*).

## MOTIVATION OF WORK

It would be more satisfactory, in approaching the practical side of the subject, if we could entitle this section, "Motivation of work and play"—if we could promise information on the important problems of securing and retaining affection, winning friends and increasing the enjoyment of social life, by use of suitable incentives. A young wife wishes to keep her husband as much in love with her as he is during the honeymoon. She has a problem of motivation on her hands, and there are many such problems on which common-sense advice, "words of wisdom," could be offered. It is safe to recommend an outgoing, optimistic attitude rather than recourse to such negative suggestions as, "You don't love me any more" or, to a child, "You are a bad boy and will be a disgrace to the family." Such suggestions may be accepted as the truth! At any rate they create a barrier which interferes with confidential, friendly relations.

A genuine play situation fosters spontaneity and usually secures excellent motivation. Children who hang back from a piece of work will do the same thing eagerly if it is somehow made into a game. Not being commanded, they are not stimulated to resist and are left free to immerse themselves in the activity and find something interesting in the materials, operation and social give-and-take involved in the game. There is a suggestion here for anyone concerned with the motivation of serious work.

**Suggestions from the laboratory.** From numerous experiments on motivation a few are selected which demonstrate the effectiveness of certain incentives.

*Competition.* Pass a dynamometer around a group of men asking each to try squeezing it as hard as he can. You tell the first man his squeeze in pounds and hand it to the second man who perhaps does better than the first. At once the first man wants to try again and visibly exerts himself more than before.

*Pacemaking.* This is an outdoor rather than a laboratory experiment. A runner can make better speed against a competitor than when running "against time." He does better when paced by a bicycle rider who keeps just a little ahead of him than when running alone. The pacemaker is not a genuine competitor, and the runner does not really desire to overtake him. What, then, is the use of the pacemaker? The best answer is that the pacemaker provides an immediate goal, always close ahead of the runner, calling for the runner's best effort moment by moment. <u>A distant goal is less stimulating</u>.

*Self-competition.* A similar result can be obtained without a trace of competition between individuals. You give the subject a series of trials at the same performance and before each trial you show him his record on the preceding trial. He will usually try to beat his previous record. Practice with knowledge of results so far accomplished gives the subject at every stage something very definite as an immediate goal.

The output of muscular work can be considerably increased by these incentives. In one experiment the subject lifted a weight time after time with one hand (by pulling on a cord which passed up over a pulley and was attached to the weight at the other end). The apparatus made a visible record of each pull, and the question was how many times the subject could and would lift the heavy weight, one lift every two seconds, before giving up. In one condition the subject did not see the record being made but simply did "as much as he could." In another condition he saw the record as he made it and also saw ahead of him on the record a mark placed there by the experimenter as a goal. If he could reach this goal he would surpass his previous achievement. Under this latter condition he got

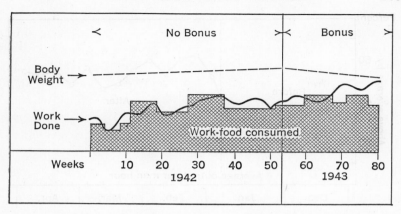

FIG. 75.—Output of heavy muscular work as affected by the food ration and by bonus incentives. A group of German laborers whose food ration was strictly controlled during World War II, and whose output was measured in tons per hour per man, were found to produce in proportion to the calories of food provided. This relation held good during the first year, during which the men gained some weight; they were not using quite all the available energy. From the beginning of the second year they were offered a bonus for additional speed of work, the bonus consisting of cigarettes, almost unobtainable otherwise. Their output in tons per hour increased considerably in the next half-year, at the cost of some loss of weight (Kraut & Muller, *11*).

20–40 percent more work out of his muscles, at the cost of some extra fatigue. In this experiment motivation came from the visible goal and the immediate knowledge of results (*4*).

Very different from muscular effort is accuracy of observation, but this too is improved by prompt reward for good work. In one experiment the "reward" was simply a bell ringing whenever the subject had done a very accurate job in his effort to divide a line into halves by the unaided eye. With this stimulation his accuracy improved far beyond the point reached by trying to do his best, time after time, without knowledge of results (*7*).

The pacemaker and similar experiments show the great value of visible, immediately attainable goals and the value of prompt check-up by the individual on the results he has accomplished. These incentives can be used in many practical situations. An-

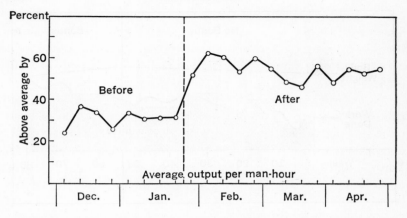

Fig. 76.—Teamwork in setting a goal and then reaching it. A group of industrial workers, paid by the piece, decided unanimously to try for a higher rate of output, and after experimenting to discover what maximum rate was feasible, set and maintained a goal which was well above their previous rate and far above the average rate for the entire plant (Bavelas, *1*).

other incentive that has proved to be very stimulating is praise for good work. Adverse criticism should at least be friendly and constructive and free from sarcasm and public ridicule and all needless wounding of the individual's ego. (*12*).

In teamwork the individual's output is merged into that of the team, and the problem is to motivate the individual to work for the team. Experiments such as those reported in Figures 75 and 76 show the motivating value of a goal adopted by the group and capable of attainment by cooperative effort.

How to secure action from yourself, or from others if you are responsible for their action, is a big practical problem. A few hints on the matter are suggested by what precedes.

**Getting action from yourself.** You wish to liberate your latent energies and accomplish what you are capable of accomplishing. A definite purpose is the first requirement; without that one merely drifts. The goal should be something that appeals vitally to you, and something which you can attain; not too distant a goal; or, if the ultimate goal is distant, there must be landmarks along the way to strive for as immediate goals; for a goal that can be reached by immediate action enlists more present effort. The student puts more energy into his study when the examination is close at hand; and, although this fact is regrettable, it reveals a side of human nature that can be utilized in the management of yourself or others.

The more clearly you can see your approach toward the goal, the more action. You cannot do so well when you simply "do your best" as when you set out to reach a certain level, high enough to tax your powers without being quite out of reach. You cannot jump so high in the empty air as you can to clear a bar; and, to secure your very best endeavor, the bar must not be so low that you can clear it easily, nor so high that you cannot clear it at all.

**Getting action from other people** is the business of parents, teachers, leaders, managers, officers, and of everyone who wishes to influence another (15). In war, the problem of morale is as important as the problem of equipment, and was so recognized by all the armies engaged in the two World Wars. Each side sought to keep the morale of its own soldiers at a high pitch, and to depress the morale of the enemy. Good morale means more than mere willingness for duty; it means a positive zest for action—"pep for the job in hand." It depends on several factors: on good physical condition, on competence for the job, on group solidarity, on confidence in the officers, and on intervals of relaxation from the strain of duty.

1. Morale is impaired by lack of "physical pep"—by sickness, unappetizing food, insufficient vitamins, excessive fatigue, lack of sleep. The Army and Navy take great care to provide for the organic needs. Yet the men have to learn by experiencing hardships that they can carry on even under unfavorable physical conditions. Ability to do so is part of their military competence.

2. Morale is impaired by any feeling of incompetence and futility. The men need to have assurance that their particular jobs contribute something to the winning of the war, and that they are being well trained for their jobs and are becoming experts in their particular lines. One motive that comes strongly into play is interest in the operations themselves—in guns,

tanks, airplanes and the techniques of handling them successfully. The bomber crew is motivated not so much by anger
against the crew of the warship down below as by the desire
to make a clean hit.

3. The raw recruit just entering camp may have good preparatory morale but he does not have the true military morale
until he has become an active member of a team, proud of his
unit, interested in its operations, competent to make his contribution to the teamwork of the unit, and animated by a feeling
of comradeship and solidarity.

4. Being accustomed to resist domination and to assert that
one man is just as good as another (or a little better) the recruit is apt to resent the authority of the officers. His morale is
not too good until he has come to recognize the importance
and difficulty of the officer's job and to respect and admire his
own officers for their competence, justice, and concern for the
welfare of their men.

5. Most of the soldier's life is a life of work, of strenuous
effort, of obedience and discipline, sometimes of hardship. To
maintain his morale he needs periods of relaxation. He needs
freedom some of the time, he needs ease and comfort some of
the time, he needs amusement some of the time. But his fur-
lough must not be too long, for he is likely to lose his military
set and to find it a long, hard task to get back into the swing of
active service (2).

Civilian morale was important in the total wars and was high,
as a matter of fact, in nations on both sides of the conflict. Nations that were attacked had the clear goal of defending their
liberty, while aggressor nations apparently believed their des-
tiny was to rule the world and saw this before them as their
goal. A clear national goal is the first requirement for high national morale, and the second is such an organization of the
energies of the people as will enable everyone to make some
contribution to the war effort. A third is confidence in the
leaders. In peacetime national morale tends to sag because the
first two requirements are not fully met. The national goal is not
so tangible, and the individual citizen does not see how he can

make any significant contribution. The postwar situation is a challenge to those who would be worthy leaders in national and community life (21).

## SUMMARY

1. A *motive* is a set which predisposes the individual for certain activities and for seeking certain goals.
   a. *Incentive* is a goal toward which a motivated activity is directed.
   b. A basic or primary motive is the unlearned instinctive component of a motive (often called a *drive*).
   c. *Likes and dislikes* are the conscious aspect of the approaching and avoiding motives. They are based on the naturally agreeable or disagreeable character of certain sensory experiences.

2. Motives develop in the individual through maturation, exercise, and learning.
   a. Unlearned motives become shaped and modified by learning.
      1. Goals become more specific.
      2. Motives are combined into complex motives.
      3. Means to an end become goals in themselves.
      4. New stimuli become capable of arousing a motive.
   b. The organism is so equipped as to guarantee the learning and carrying out of certain activities essential for survival of the individual and the race. The equipment includes a persistent stimulus, increased general activity, and reinforcement of successful acts.
      1. *Organic needs* (hunger, thirst , respiration, sex, activity and rest) are definite bodily states or conditions. The associated drives tend to assure the learning of activities which bring fulfillment of the organic needs.
      2. *Emergency motives* (escape, combat, effort, and pursuit) arise from external environmental stimuli. The

motives, themselves originally unlearned, come readily by learning to be aroused by new stimuli.

3. *Objective motives* (exploration, manipulation, interests) arise from drives to deal with the environment and lead to knowing objects (and persons), doing things to them, and participating in what is going on.

c. *Purpose* is goal-directed activity in which the individual has foresight of the end to be accomplished and has definitely committed himself to the action.

3. *Strength of motives* can be expressed in terms of the relative effectiveness of one motive which is pitted against another, or in terms of a third motive, such as money.

a. *Animal drives* can be measured in clearest fashion because of the absence of complicating social factors.

(1) An *activity cage* measures the gross amount of general activity induced by a drive condition.

(2) The *obstruction method* compares different drives by measuring the strength of electric shock which is just sufficient to block the drive.

b. Goal gradient is a statement of the principle that the nearer the individual comes to the goal, the stronger is his motivation.

4. Specific suggestions for improving motivation in practical situations of work and play are:

a. Avoid negative and disparaging suggestions.

b. Arrange competitive situations.

c. Establish intermediate goals in tasks that have only distant goals.

d. Encourage self competition by making available the results of each trial.

e. Get the individual or the group to discuss and set their own level of aspiration.

# CHAPTER ELEVEN

# Feeling and Emotion

As sometimes understood, the emotions are the same as the desires already considered in the chapter on Motivation. A desire is a motive, a set directed toward some goal. But that is not all there is to a desire. When you desire something strongly you certainly have a set directed to obtaining that thing, but you also feel strongly about it and as an organism you are not in your usual calm and placid state. When you desire to escape from some danger you are likely to feel afraid, and when you desire to fight and injure a person you are likely to have an angry feeling. In the scientific study of desire there are two main problems: (1) the problem of motive—"What is the individual trying to do?"—and (2) the problem of feeling and emotion—"What is his internal state?" His state can be discovered partly from his own introspective testimony as to how he feels, and partly by an objective study of his bodily condition. Motive, being directed toward a goal, belongs under the general head of "activity in progress," while feeling and emotion belong under the head of "temporary state of the individual." Desire includes both, and the two are closely related, both being parts of an integrated activity of the organism as a whole.

## FEELING

It is remarkable how many words there are in common use for various feelings and shades of feeling. It would be no great task to find a hundred words, some of them no doubt synonymous, to complete the sentence, "I feel . . ." Here are a few names of feelings and emotions, roughly grouped into classes.

Pleasure, happiness, joy, delight, elation, rapture
Displeasure, discontent, grief, sadness, sorrow, dejection
Mirth, amusement, hilarity
Excitement, agitation
Calm, contentment, numbness, apathy, weariness, ennui
Expectancy, eagerness, hope, assurance, courage
Doubt, shyness, embarrassment, anxiety, worry, dread, fear, fright, terror, horror
Surprise, amazement, wonder, relief, disappointment
Desire, appetite, longing, yearning, love
Aversion, disgust, loathing, hate
Anger, resentment, indignation, sullenness, rage, fury

The first word in each class is intended to give the keynote of the class. Other classifications could be made, and the classes could be made broader or narrower. Two broad classes, pleasant and unpleasant, would include most of the feelings. Still, you cannot say that the names simply designate different degrees of pleasantness or unpleasantness. Rapture and hilarity are both intensely pleasant, but scarcely the same; nor are fear and disgust the same, though both unpleasant. The fact is that there are many kinds of pleasant feeling, and of unpleasant. Some of the words do not indicate whether the feeling is pleasant or unpleasant; excitement may be happy excitement or unhappy excitement, and the same is true of expectancy and of surprise.

**Wundt's three dimensions of feeling.** This great leader in experimental psychology (who established the first active psychological laboratory in Leipzig in 1879) hoped to introduce some order into the motley variety of feelings by a system of three dimensions. Just as the position of an airplane can be designated by giving its latitude, longitude and altitude, so, Wundt suggested, the state of a person's feeling at any moment may be described by telling how pleasant (or unpleasant) it is, how excited, and how tense or expectant. States of feeling can be arranged in a series from the most pleasant down through lower degrees of pleasantness and through a neutral zone over into the minor and then the major degrees of unpleasantness. This pleasantness-unpleasantness dimension was universally recognized and commonly assumed to be the only scale of feelings. But states of feeling can be arranged in another series, from the most excited to the most calm, subdued or inert. Wundt proposed, then, to take inert feeling as the reverse of excited feeling, and thus he had his second dimension, excitement-inertness. For his third dimension, he selected tenseness-release, which might also be called expectancy-release. In expectancy you are waiting for something to happen, in relief or release something has happened and abolished the expectancy (27).

Wundt's scheme has some value, even though it is almost too neat to fit all the facts of feeling. There may be other dimensions worthy to be placed alongside of these three, such as the feeling of familiarity in a place that is well known, as against the feeling of strangeness and curiosity when you are in a novel situation. There is no reason why there should necessarily be just three dimensions of feeling, no more and no less; and in fact Wundt's pleasantness-unpleasantness and excitement-inertness are better established than his third dimension of expectancy-release.

**Feeling distinguished from motor activity.** Any muscular act produces external results and in most cases is aimed at some external result; it is dealing with the environment. Feeling is internal and by itself produces no external results. Yet feeling is often associated with a *motor tendency*. Unpleasant feeling accompanies action directed toward getting rid of the unpleasant object or state of affairs, of a disagreeable odor, for example. Pleasant feeling is just the opposite; it accompanies action keeping things as they are. But the feeling can be there

without any definite motor activity directed toward changing
the situation or toward keeping it as it is. You may do nothing
to get rid of the disagreeable odor; and you may enjoy a warm
bath while relaxing as completely as possible. Then, too, you
may be dealing actively with the environment while having no
strong feeling of either pleasure or displeasure; i.e., motor activity can occur with a minimum of feeling. Excited feeling
certainly *tends* toward much motor activity, and inert feeling
toward a minimum of motor activity; and yet you may keep
perfectly quiet externally while all excited internally, and you
may force yourself to act though feeling much inclined to do
nothing.

**Feeling distinguished from sensory activity.** Feeling is different from knowing. It does not consist in knowing anything
about the environment or in knowing anything about yourself.
You get to know the environment by use of the senses, since the
sensations they furnish can serve as indicators of external facts.
Some sensations can serve as indicators of internal facts, facts
concerning your own bodily condition. But of all the various
sensations received at any moment, only a few can be utilized
at that moment as indicators of facts. You cannot attend to so
many facts at once. Most of the sensations remain in the background as a mass of feeling. A pain from the region of the
stomach may be noticed carefully with the object of deciding
whether it is the pain of indigestion or a hunger pang, or it may
be left in the background and simply give an unpleasant tinge
to the momentary feeling. When you feel dull and heavy, if you
attend to different parts of your body you notice dull pains in
the eyes, neck, elbows and knees and dull pressure in the chest
and abdomen; these sensations, not attended to separately but
left as an unanalyzed mass, make up the general feeling of dullness. This dull, heavy feeling, often present in prolonged sed-
entary work, can be relieved by a little exercise or by lying down
for a few minutes, because the numerous dull pains from various
parts of the body are removed.

The active life of dealing with the environment by observing,
thinking and doing calls for more brain activity than the more

passive life of feeling. The mass of bodily feeling is almost lost in the background when you are absorbed in active work or play. At such times the "brainy activity" dominates; at other times it takes a rest and the mass of feeling comes more to the front.⌋

**Sources of pleasure and displeasure.** Some things are pleasant even when they are not desired in advance; other things are pleasant only after a desire for them has first been awakened. Unpleasant things fall into two similar classes. A sweet taste or odor is pleasant even when you get it without having sought for it, and an unexpected bitter taste is unpleasant. A beautiful chord of music suddenly reaching your ears gives you a thrill of unexpected pleasure, and a grating noise gives you an unpleasant surprise. These are pleasures and displeasures of the first class.

In the other class belongs the pleasure of a cold drink when you are thirsty, for you must first be thirsty in order to have this pleasure. What is true of thirst is true of hunger or of any motive. The motive must first be there; then pleasure or displeasure will come according as the motive is gratified or thwarted. At a football game, when a player kicks the ball and it sails between the goal posts, half of the spectators yell with joy, while the other half groan in agony. Strange that the mere sight of a ball sailing between two posts should be so pleasant to some persons and so unpleasant to others! First arouse any motive, and then you can give pleasure by gratifying it, or displeasure by thwarting it. The pleasure of achievement belongs in this second class. To have the joy of achievement you must first achieve, and to achieve you must strive, not for the joy but for the achievement, because your energies must be concentrated on the task in hand. Absorbed in your task you plow through to success; then, almost as a pleasant surprise, comes the joy of achievement.

No one has attempted to make a complete list of the common pleasures of life, but such a list has been gathered from many persons for the common annoyances, and the length of the list is surprising (8). A small sample of the most commonly reported annoyances is given here.

*Annoyances*

A person continually arguing
"     "     continually criticizing
"     "     monopolizing the conversation
"     "     bragging
"     "     bullying a child
"     "     always talking about his illnesses
"     "     assuming superiority
"     "     continually giving me unsolicited advice
"     "     interrupting when I am talking
"     "     paying no attention to what I say
"     "     prying into my affairs
"     "     nagging at me
"     "     trying to sell me something I don't want
"     "     crowding ahead of me in line
"     "     late for an engagement
"     "     swearing
"     "     spitting, belching, stuffing his mouth, picking his
               nose, etc.
Untidy room, clothes, hands, etc.
A mosquito buzzing when I want to sleep
Cats howling at night
A window rattling
False teeth

Hundreds of other annoyances have been reported. Some of them which seem quite innocuous may have originated by association with something that was genuinely unpleasant. Many varieties of annoying behavior suggest that the person so behaving feels himself superior or lacks consideration for others. Even when he is merely breaking an unnecessary social taboo his behavior suggests that he does not care what other people think. When a person behaves in any such way he offends your own desire for superiority or at least equality, and so causes a feeling of annoyance. Apparently this is one great source of unpleasantness in social life. When asked to think of people they most like and dislike and to say why in each case, college students mention a large number of traits, but the most frequently mentioned on the undesirable side are conceitedness

and deceitfulness. On the desirable side, most often mentioned
are intelligence and cheerfulness (28).

**Sympathy and empathy.**  [When other people are manifesting
feeling, it seems natural to have the same feeling yourself] Gay,
happy companions infect you with a happy feeling, sad companions with a gloomy feeling. In a stir of excitement you tend
to become excited yourself though you have no personal reason
for excitement, and when everyone around you is tense you
tend to become tense yourself. When you see a group of people
looking intently at the sky, you have a feeling of curiosity and
can scarcely refrain from looking up yourself. This "feeling
with" another person is sympathy. Whether it is an instinctive
imitative response, or a learned response, has not been proved
one way or the other. Often there is something more to it than
mere imitation. Often there is a positive motive involved, a
desire to feel the same as your friend is feeling, to like the same
things and dislike the same. This motive is strong in a couple of
young lovers. If they find they have the same likes and dislikes,
they feel closer; if in some matters they cannot deny that they
disagree, they feel that a slight barrier has come between them.
They have to learn to love without always having the same
feelings.

To sympathize fully with another person you need some
imagination, for you have to put yourself in his place and see
things from his point of view. To be helpfully sympathetic you
need more than fellow-feeling, for you must know how to deal
with the situation affecting your friend. You need experience
in helpful behavior.

*Empathy* means "feeling into" a person or thing, rather than
feeling with him or it. A person who is not manifesting any
feeling may be in a situation that would arouse feeling in you,
and by placing yourself in that situation, imaginatively, you get
the feeling appropriate to the situation. You identify yourself
with the person. Empathy is often visible in behavior. Observe
the spectators at an athletic contest or game and you will see
some of them "help" a player who is on the point of kicking
the ball, or a pole vaulter who is just clearing the bar. Such

Courtesy, Dartmouth Alumni Magazine. From Allport's Personality

FIG. 77.—Empathy in well-wishing spectators of an athletic feat.

behavior of the spectator is sometimes carelessly called imitative, which it cannot be since it tends to *precede* the player's movement. It is not doing what the player is observed to have done, but what the spectator imagines the player is about to do. The spectator is participating imaginatively.

In reading a novel you are likely to identify yourself with the hero (or heroine), feeling anxious when he is in difficulties, and elated when everything comes out right. This can be called empathy since you are placing yourself in the hero's situation rather than imitating any expressions of joy and sorrow which the author has put into print.

To watch a bird flying high in the air, especially if he is soaring without flapping his wings, gives you a thrill as if you were soaring yourself. This is empathy, and you may have the same thrill in watching an airplane or even a kite. In the enjoyment of fine architecture, too, empathy may play an important part; so at least it is held in certain theories of this kind of esthetic pleasure.

Look at a pillar (Fig. 78), for example. If the pillar is too massive for the load supported, it gives you the unsatisfactory impression of doing something absurdly small. If it is too slender for the load that seems to rest upon it, you get the feeling of strain and insecurity; but if it is rightly proportioned, you get the feeling of a worthy task successfully accomplished. The pillar, according to the empathy theory, pleases you by arousing and gratifying your mastery impulse; and many other architectural effects can be interpreted in the same way.

**Esthetic enjoyment.** One important source of pleasure is beauty in nature and art, but the explanation of this pleasure makes a difficult psychological problem. Some things are beautiful to us because of their pleasant associations. The baby is delighted at the sight of his bottle, and that shape may well be beautiful to him. But the theory that all pleasure in the beautiful stems from such associations is difficult to accept.

Beauty and ugliness can be seen in the very simplest objects. You would scarcely suppose that a mere rectangle could produce any esthetic effect; yet it is found that some rectangles are preferred to others, and that the popular choice falls along near the proportion known to art theorists as the "golden section," the width being about 62 percent of the length. Again, however much you may like symmetry, you can scarcely suppose it makes much difference exactly where a horizontal line is cut by a short cross line; yet nearly everyone on being put to the test selects the middle as the best point. Though the causes of these preferences are not surely known, we may hazard the conjecture that they are radically different in the two cases.

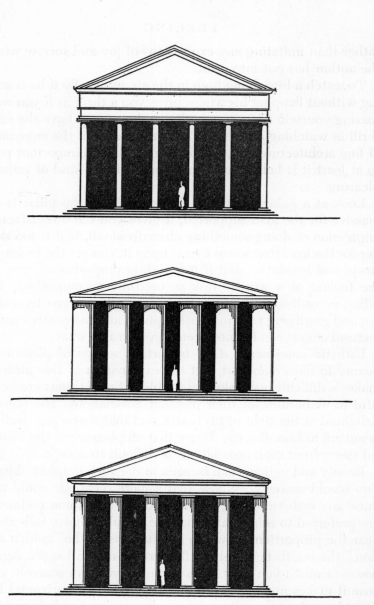

FIG. 78.—Empathy may explain the esthetic effect of suitable and unsuitable proportions in architecture.

Symmetry probably appeals to us, directly or indirectly, because we ourselves are symmetrical. We are symmetrical from side to side and we like a cathedral to be so, not insisting that it be symmetrical from front to back. On the other hand we are much slimmer than the golden section, and our preference here must have a less personal, more objective basis. Probably the golden-section rectangle appears typical for a rectangle, slim enough to be a successful rectangle without being extreme. There is a suggestion here of two ways of perceiving objects: either in relation to ourselves, or in relation to other objects— either egocentrically or objectively. There is no reason to assume that all esthetic interest springs from the internal needs of the organism. It may spring as well from the individual's interest in the objective world.

## EMOTION

Emotion is a "moved" or stirred-up state of the individual. It is a stirred-up state of feeling—that is the way it appears to the person himself. It is a disturbed muscular and glandular activity—that is the way it appears to an external observer, who sees the clenched fists and flushed face of anger and the tears of grief, or who hears the loud laugh of merriment and the pleading tones of love.

Each emotion can be located in the tridimensional scheme of feeling, but such an analysis does not do full justice to the emotion. Fear is a state of excited, unpleasant expectancy, and mirth is excited, pleasant relief, but each is something more.

Each emotion is a feeling, and each is at the same time a motor set. Fear is a set for escape, and anger for attack. Mirth is a readiness to laugh, and grief a readiness to cry. These sets are more specific than the accepting and rejecting motor tendencies of mere pleasantness and unpleasantness. Emotion is also an organic state. The heart and stomach and other internal organs of the body are disturbed in emotion. The organic state is reflected in such changes as sweating and pallor.

Though we all know the emotions as matters of personal experience, no one seems to be able to describe them adequately either as subjective feelings or as muscular and glandular activities. How, then, can we tell the emotions apart? How does it come about that we have that large vocabulary of names of different emotions? The several emotions are distinguished, in practice, by stating the *external situation* in which each occurs and the type of *overt response* demanded. Any particular emotion is the stirred-up state appropriate to a certain situation and overt response.

It is true that the situation and overt response may occur without emotion. You may fight off an attack without anger, or dodge an automobile without fear. If the overt response is prompt and successful, emotion may not be aroused. If the brainy life of dealing with the environment dominates the organism at the moment, the emotion is minimized. But if the situation gets out of hand, the emotion appropriate to the situation surges up. From the situation and overt response, then, you cannot safely assert that the individual is undergoing an emotion; but you are reasonably sure that, if he is undergoing an emotion, it is the one that usually goes with that situation and that response.

**The great variety of emotions.** Though fear or anger is usually mentioned as the standard example of an emotion, there are other stirred-up states which are very different, as for example the state of a person who is laughing heartily or of one who is radiantly happy at a piece of good news. What makes a person feel happy, hilarious, angry, or afraid? To answer this question in general terms, so as to identify the stimulus for each kind of emotion, is very difficult, but it is a question that the student will naturally have in mind as he thinks through a list of common emotions.

*Fear.* Along with anger, determination, and eagerness, fear was mentioned in the last chapter as an emergency emotion. A dangerous situation tends to arouse the internal state of fear as well as the external movements of escape. At the present time we have among us very many young men who have had personal experience of extremely dangerous situations, and these veterans are not ashamed to testify that they felt afraid in battle and especially just before a battle. They say that this stirred-up state, if kept under control, was of some value in the extreme exertions called for in battle. Fear is better than indifference, though not so good as anger directed against the enemy. Fear is troublesome when you have to wait in suspense without doing anything, but gives way during actual combat to the state of total activity which is much less painful and may be even exhilarating. Fear can be kept under control when you are well prepared, when you know your weapons, the terrain where you have to fight, and something of the plan of battle, and when you have confidence in your comrades and your officers (2, 11).

Strange as it may seem, many favorite forms of play and recreation depend on fear. The chutes, roller coasters, etc., of the amusement parks would have no attraction if they had no thrill; and the thrill is a form of fear. You experience some of the thrill of danger while knowing that the danger is not very real. Probably the sense of danger would not be worth much by itself, but danger quickly followed by the joy of escape is highly satisfactory. The same can be said of any adventurous sport; and the fascination (for many people) of gambling and taking risks probably stems from fear and the joy of escape.

*Surprise.* When you are set for a certain situation and for carrying on a certain activity, and something happens for which you are not set, there is a momentary emotional disturbance. It is like a brief gust of fear, even though after the momentary disturbance you recover your equilbrium and perhaps have a pleasant rather than an unpleasant surprise (15). While sitting on your chair you are set for continued stability, and if the chair suddenly gives way you are surprised to say the least. A startling stimulus such as a pistol shot will make anybody jump. Sometimes the "jump" consists of nothing more than a quick blinking of the eyelids, while sometimes it is a sort of protective shrinking reflex of the whole body, as shown in Figure 79.

*Anger.* The emergency here is not danger so much as interference or frustration, when the individual is thwarted in his

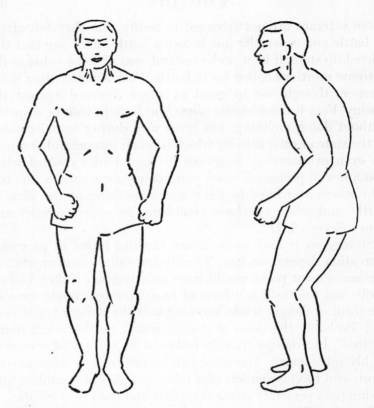

Fig. 79.—The startle pattern. When a revolver is discharged near a person, he always blinks his eyes and usually shows a more or less complete shrinking response of several parts of the body. The whole response is over in less than half a second but can be analyzed in motion pictures obtained with an ultra-rapid camera exposing 64 or even as many as 1500 frames per second. The film is later projected at a much slower rate so that what was a very rapid movement appears as a slow movement and can be studied in detail. The startle pattern or some elements of it are found to be present in all normal children and adults, even in experienced marksmen who are used to hearing pistol shots. A similar shrinking response is found in many subhuman animals. Other sudden stimuli such as a flash of light or a jet of cold water against the skin often elicit the startle pattern, though not so dependably as the loud noise of the pistol (Landis & Hunt, 20).

desires, especially when he can put the blame on some person or thing. "A bad workman quarrels with his tools," placing the blame for his failures on his tools rather than on his own awkwardness. But sometimes he gets angry with himself. As compared with fear anger is a more vigorous and outgoing emotion, and less unpleasant. Some persons seem even to enjoy being angry and go out of their way to pick a quarrel.

*Mirth* or *amusement*. The emotional state that goes with smiling and laughing must not be overlooked. No reaction is more clear-cut than that of hearty laughter, and the emotion is certainly very different from fear and anger. But what, in general terms, is the stimulus that gives rise to amusement and laughter? What is there common to all the various amusing situations? Many theorists have attempted to answer this difficult question. The baby laughs when tickled, or when he drops his rattle over the side of his crib and hears it bang on the floor. The boy is intensely amused by practical jokes which land someone on the floor instead of in a chair, etc. Adults laugh at puns (sometimes), at absurdities, and at stories with very unexpected endings. There is usually an element of surprise in a joke (12).

*Joy,* while pleasurable like mirth, is not the same emotional state. Victory is not amusing. The typically joyful situation is the winning of success after a hard struggle; the achieving of the goal after intense effort.

*Grief,* with its crying or weeping, is the emotion of one who is helpless in the face of loss or difficulty.

*Sex excitement* is not the same as other forms of excitement, for the situation is distinctive, the behavior likewise, and the strong accompanying emotion has its own particular characteristics.

Many other shadings of emotion could be listed. There are shame and jealousy on the unpleasant side, enthusiasm and warm affection on the pleasant side. There are combinations and refinements of the more elemental emotions, and combinations of emotion with agreeable or disagreeable sensations and ideas.

## EMOTIONAL EXPRESSION

A person who wishes to give expression to his feelings can of course attempt to describe them in language, or he may use expressive gestures. Apart from such intentional expression, there are involuntary forms of behavior which reveal the emotional state more or less clearly and truthfully.

**How emotions are revealed—expressive movements.**   Smiling, laughing, scowling, pouting, sneering, sobbing, screaming, shouting and dancing up and down accomplish no important external result, except for their effects on other people. What is the sense of these movements? At first thought, the question itself is senseless, the movements are so much a matter of course, while on second thought they certainly do seem queer. What sense is there in protruding the lips when sulky, or in drawing up the corners of the mouth and showing the canine teeth in contempt? Darwin, after studying these movements in men and animals, suggested that they were survivals of acts that were once of practical utility in the life of the individual or of the race (*10*).

Shaking the head from side to side, in negation or unwillingness, dates back to the nursing period of the individual, when this movement was made in rejecting undesired food. The nasal expression in disgust was originally a defensive movement against bad odors; and the set lips of determination went primarily with the set glottis and rigid chest that are useful in muscular effort (p. 318). Such movements, directly useful in certain simple situations, become linked up with similar but more complex situations in the course of the individual's experience.

Showing the teeth in scorn dates back, according to Darwin, to a prehuman stage of development, and is a useful act in animals like the dog or gorilla that have large canine teeth. Baring the teeth by these animals is a preparation for using the teeth; and often it frightens the enemy away and makes actual attack unnecessary. This movement, Darwin urges, has survived in the race even after fighting with the teeth has mostly gone out. Many other expressive movements can be traced back in a similar way, though it must be admitted that the racial survivals are usually less convincing than those from the infancy of the individual.

**Learning to control emotional expression.** [Some expressive movements, like smiling, laughing, crying, sobbing and screaming, are certainly unlearned; others are picked up by imitation.] As the child grows up, he learns to *moderate* his expressions of anger and of glee, and he even learns to *conceal his emotions.* He is ridiculed for crying or showing fear; he gives offense by showing anger, or by crowing and strutting in pride. Politeness requires him to smile many times when he feels like scowling, and to exclaim in surprise at information that is perfectly trite. Thus social pressure trains him to keep his feelings to himself. At the same time, other people are always trying to discover how he does feel, and he himself scans the faces of other people in the attempt to *read their emotions.* There is a race between concealment of the emotions on one side and detection of the emotions on the other, like the naval race between defensive armor and penetrating projectiles.

On the whole, expressive movements tend to become reduced as the individual grows older. [But in make-believe play and on the stage there is a development in the opposite direction, in the direction of *depicting the emotions.*] There is a language of the emotions, composed of gestures and postures, of exclamations and inflections and tones of the voice, and of facial expressions. This language is no doubt based upon the unlearned expressive movements, but it has become standardized through long ages, and now is largely a matter of social custom and convention. The child finds this language in use, and appropriates it to some extent. Actors appropriate it to a large extent, and introduce their own individual improvements. The result is that this language of the emotions is much more expressive than the average adult's facial and vocal behavior during emotion. When the actor poses for an emotion, he makes full use of his face; but when the ordinary citizen is in an emotional state, his face is little more than a mask.

FIG. 80.—Two poses, A being intended for surprise and B for hate. When shown to 100 persons they got a variety of judgments as shown by the following counts, and still most of the judgments of the same pose are rather similar (Feleky, *14*).

| *Pose A* | | *Pose B* | | *Pose B—Continued* | |
|---|---|---|---|---|---|
| surprise | 52 | ugliness | 13 | disregard | 1 |
| wonder | 12 | disgust | 11 | bore | 1 |
| astonishment | 11 | hate | 8 | fury | 1 |
| amazement | 9 | disdain | 8 | sulkiness | 1 |
| admiration | 3 | scorn | 7 | pouting | 1 |
| awe | 2 | defiance | 6 | pettiness | 1 |
| dismay | 2 | aversion | 5 | disagreeable | 1 |
| playful interest | 1 | repugnance | 5 | suspicion | 1 |
| earnestness | 1 | bitterness | 3 | self-assertion | 1 |
| enthusiasm | 1 | contempt | 3 | self-sufficiency | 1 |
| rapture | 1 | loathing | 3 | displeasure | 1 |
| hope | 1 | irritation | 2 | perturbance | 1 |
| romantic love | 1 | hardness | 2 | weeping | 1 |
| friendliness | 1 | sneering | 2 | timidity | 1 |
| altruistic pride | 1 | dislike | 2 | pain | 1 |
| repugnance | 1 | antipathy | 1 | mental pain | 1 |
|  |  | sullen anger | 1 | disgusted dread | 1 |
|  |  |  |  | sorrowful pity | 1 |

How expressive is the facial language of the emotions? To obtain evidence on this question—obviously an important question for social psychology—the experimenter presents photographed facial poses and asks you to judge what emotion is portrayed by each pose. The words used by different observers to characterize a given pose vary somewhat but do not usually indicate radical disagreement. Some poses are very clear and convey the same impression to almost all observers, while other poses are more ambiguous. A good pose for love will often be called "happiness"—not a large discrepancy—but will never be called "anger" or "disgust." It is possible to arrange a series of emotions (or of facial expressions) extending from love and happiness at one end to contempt at the other, with fear and anger about in the middle (Fig. 81). Many poses can be located very exactly in this series. Some of the ambiguous poses yield this curious result: half of the observers say the pose shows contempt, while the other half say it belongs with love, happiness and mirth (Fig. 82). Now love and contempt are far apart as emotions, and it would be too bad if your friend could not distinguish them in your face. But happiness and mirth are not always far removed from contempt—do we not know the "superior smile" of the disdainful person? There are different kinds of happiness, admiring happiness and contemptuous happiness. The arrangement of all emotions in a single series is somewhat forced but does serve to bring out the important fact that facial expressions are often understood very well (23).

**Emotional expression by gesture and by voice.** Emotions can be expressed by the hands, and a few gestures have been conventionalized and are readily understood. Everyone knows how to express by his hands an inclination to fight, to accept, to reject or to plead for mercy. Experiment shows that photographs of an actor portraying a large number of emotions by the hands alone can be judged by college students with fair agreement on a number of them. The agreement is somewhat better when motion pictures of the actor's manual poses are used instead of still views. The observers in this experiment testify, as they do also in experiments in the interpretation of facial expressions, that they use two devices to assist them. They imitate the pose to see how it feels; or they imagine a situation in which the given expression would be appropriate (7).

The voice is perhaps even more expressive than the face, and the speaking voice is more expressive than the singing voice because free to take on a harsh quality and to slide up and down in pitch as required by the emotion to be expressed. The rising inflection in questioning, the falling inflection in certainty, and the circumflex inflection in sarcasm are easily under-

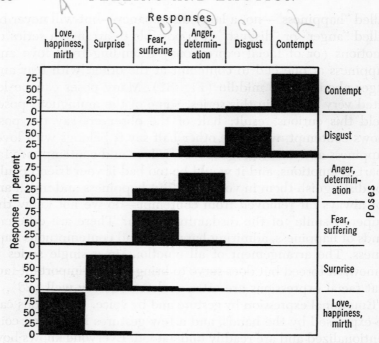

FIG. 81.—Judgments of posed facial expressions, showing general agreement with the actress's intentions. There were 100 judges, and 6 emotions (or classes of emotions) depicted by the actress. Reading along the bottom line we see that the poses for love, happiness and mirth were judged to represent this class of emotions by about 90 percent of the judges, the remainder judging "surprise." Reading across the line for the fear-suffering poses, we see more scatter but a strong preponderance of fear-suffering judgments. The oblique slant of the whole diagram indicates a fairly high positive correlation between the actress's intention and the observer's judgment (Data from Feleky, *14*).

stood by the listener. The little word, "No," can be made to carry several different meanings according to the way it is spoken. The following passage can be spoken in very different ways.

There is no other answer. You've asked me that question a thousand times, and my reply has always been the same. It always will be the same.

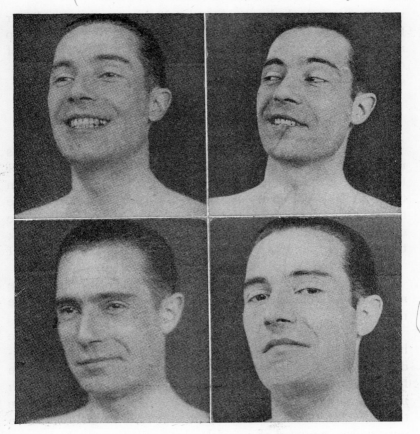

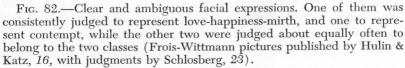

Fig. 82.—Clear and ambiguous facial expressions. One of them was consistently judged to represent love-happiness-mirth, and one to represent contempt, while the other two were judged about equally often to belong to the two classes (Frois-Wittmann pictures published by Hulin & Katz, *16*, with judgments by Schlosberg, *23*).

A competent actor read this passage five times before an audience, intending to express in the several readings: contempt, anger, fear, grief, indifference. The auditors judged what emotion was being expressed in each case and 78–94 percent of their judgments coincided with the actor's intention. Other actors, while not doing quite so well, still conveyed the intended emotion to a large majority of the audience. The actor's voice was pitched about an octave higher in anger and fear than in the other emotions (*13*). It is probably instinctive to raise the voice in both pitch and intensity during any state of excitement, but the inflections and other details of vocal expression may be social customs differing from group to group.

## ORGANIC STATES IN EMOTION

Traditionally, the heart is the seat of the emotions, and this means, no doubt, that they are felt in the general region of the heart; and other ancient "seats," in the diaphragm or in the bowels, agree in pointing vaguely to the interior of the trunk as the general location where emotions are felt. There may be something in this primitive location of the emotions; there may be some internal disturbance in strong emotion that makes itself felt by obscure sensations.

To understand what goes on in the interior of the trunk, we need to add to our previous information some knowledge of the nerve supply of this region.

The autonomic nerves.   These are the nerves that run to the heart, blood vessels, lungs, stomach, intestines and other viscera, and also to the sweat glands, the little muscles of the hairs, and the iris of the eye. They run, that is, to the *smooth muscle,* a slower-acting, but more automatic type of muscle than that of the limbs, and they run also to glands. These nerves are composed of extra-slender nerve fibers, which grow out from cells in the brain stem and cord, and so are part of the general nervous system. There are three divisions of the autonomic, the upper, middle and lower. The *upper division* comes out from the brain stem, and, among other effects, slows the heart beat, but stimulates the glands of the stomach to pour out the gastric juice, and the muscular wall of the stomach to make its churning movement. Thus the upper autonomic is active in digestion. The *middle division* of the autonomic consists of the *sympathetic* nerves, which come out from the spinal cord at the level of the chest, and which have the opposite effects on the heart and stomach to those of the upper division.

The sympathetic hastens the heart, raises the blood pressure, checks stomach activity, and has other effects described as "signs of emotion." The sympathetic in its wide distribution also overlaps the *lower division* of the autonomic (which comes from the lower part of the spinal cord), and it antagonizes the latter's stimulating effects on the genital and excretory organs.

In speaking of the sympathetic as opposing or antagonizing the other two divisions of the autonomic, we should not think of two independent teams struggling against each other with no higher control. The two teams are coordinated and balanced, the balance shifting to one side or the other according to the changing demands of the situation.

There is a brain center for the autonomic system in the hypothalamus, a part of the interbrain (pp. 250–251). This fact becomes the more interesting when we learn that many students of the brain are convinced that the interbrain plays an important part in feeling and emotion. Indirectly, the autonomic is influenced by the cerebral cortex, as we see from the fact that something you merely *think* of may hasten or slow the heart, make you blush or turn pale, and promote or disturb your digestion (22).

**Breathing and heart beat in emotion.** Excitement, attended as it is apt to be with muscular activity, calls for increased breathing and heart action.

The chest movements in breathing can easily be recorded by suitable apparatus, and various peculiarities of the movement pattern are found in emotional states. Laughing and sobbing give very peculiar breathing curves. Psychologists, after becoming expert in the analysis of breathing curves, have attempted to detect a subject's emotional state from his breathing record. They have been especially interested to see whether they could detect the suppressed excitement incident to giving false testimony before a court or inquisitor. In an experimental setup, the subject is instructed to give true or false testimony before a group of persons, and this "jury" attempts to decide whether the witness is lying or telling the truth. Meanwhile his breathing record is taken, and from this alone the experimenter at

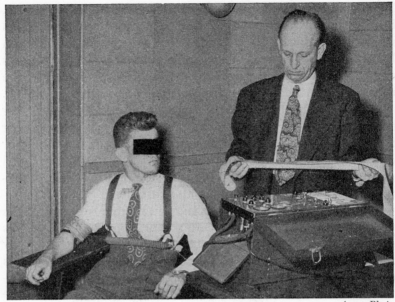

FIG. 83.—The *"lie detector"* apparatus. The suspect's breathing is recorded by use of the air-filled belt around his chest. Changes in his pulse and blood pressure are obtained from the inflated cuff around his arm. Changes in the electrical conductance of his skin are obtained from electrodes attached to the palm and back of one hand. The apparatus on the table makes the records. The test indicated (correctly) that this particular suspect was innocent.

tempts to reach a decision on the same question. With a fairly competent liar in the stand, the jury has only a 50–50 chance of guessing right, but some experimenters have scored almost 100 percent by analysis of the breathing record. On the whole, however, the method is not as successful as the one described just below.

The *blood pressure,* or pressure in the arteries, depends on complex physiological factors, the chief of which are the output of blood from the heart, and the resistance offered by the small arteries to the passage of blood. In the lying experiment, the blood pressure rises in about 80 percent of the cases. This indicator of deception is now often used in the police examination

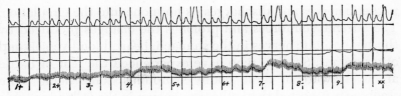

FIG. 84.—Lie-detector records obtained in a Chicago case. The upper line records breathing, the middle line skin conductance, the lower line pulse and blood pressure changes. Questions (to be answered "Yes" or "No") were asked at the points indicated by numbers. The rise in blood pressure at questions 4, 7 and 9, where the suspect denied his guilt, was strongly indicative of an intention to deceive (Inbau, *18*).

of suspects (*18*). There is no mysterious connection of lying with blood pressure or breathing. The blood pressure is apt to rise in excitement, whether the excitement is brought on by the exigencies of making up a plausible story, by taking an intelligence test, by watching a "sexy" motion picture, or by receiving strong electric shocks.

**Stomach changes in anger.** Suppose we have a cat that knows us well, and after feeding her a good meal containing some substance that is opaque to the X-rays, suppose we place her on a table and pass X-rays through her body, so as to get a visible shadow of the stomach upon the plate of the X-ray machine. While the cat is contentedly digesting her meal, the X-ray picture shows her stomach to be making rhythmical churning movements. In comes a fox terrier and barks fiercely at the cat; she shows the usual feline signs of anger but is held in position and her stomach kept under observation—when, to our surprise, the stomach movements abruptly cease, not to begin again till the dog has been gone for about fifteen minutes. The churning movements of the intestine cease along with those of the stomach, and, as other experiments show, the gastric juice stops flowing into the stomach. The whole business of digestion halts during the state of anger. In man also it is an excellent rule not to get angry or worried on a full stomach (*3, 26*).

Stomach inhibition is not the only internal response during fear and anger. The heart beats more forcibly than usual. The medulla of the adrenal glands (p. 130) is aroused by the sympathetic nerves and discharges its hormone into the circulation. The adrenin reinforces and prolongs the changes produced by the sympathetic nerves in the stomach, heart, blood vessels and other organs. Soldiers who have experienced the fear of battle are well aware of these bodily symptoms, some being more frequently reported than others, as shown in the following table obtained from combat troops in the American Army (2, p. 384):

### AUTONOMIC SYMPTOMS OF FEAR

| | | |
|---|---|---|
| Violent pounding of the heart, reported by | 86 | percent |
| Sinking feeling in the stomach | 75 | " |
| Feeling sick in the stomach | 59 | " |
| Trembling and shaking | 56 | " |
| Cold sweat | 55 | " |
| Tense feeling in stomach | 53 | " |
| Feeling of weakness and faintness | 51 | " |
| Vomiting | 24 | " |
| Involuntary defecation | 10 | " |
| Involuntary urination | 10 | " |

**Other signs of emotion.** The cat's hair rises in fear or anger, and goose flesh in the human being is the same response, produced by tiny muscles under the control of the sympathetic nerves. The pupil of the eye dilates in the same conditions, from the action of another sympathetic nerve. The sweat glands are similarly aroused, and in strong emotion the perspiration may stand in beads upon the skin. Even in momentary thrills of fear, surprise, embarrassment or expectancy—i.e., in small "emergencies"—the sweat glands are stimulated to a slight degree by their nerves, and the result is a momentary change in the electrical condition of the skin, which can be registered by a galvanometer and is called the *psychogalvanic reflex*. This electrical change is a delicate indicator of activity in the sympathetic nerves.

**The autonomic organic state as a useful preparatory reaction.** Apparently there are two types of fear: one, full of energy and showing itself in vigorous movements of escape; the other, inactive, shrinking and timid. Though we know too little about the autonomic balance in these two types of fear, it would seem that the organic state is about the same in the energetic type as in anger, and rather different in the timid type. The organic state in anger and energetic fear, though useless and perhaps a handicap in most of the activities of civilized man, does make a first-class preparation for intense muscular activity, such as is demanded in fighting or running away. Rapid circulation and abundant fuel are needed in the emergency, while digestion can bide its time.

Essentially the same organic state can be detected, physiologically, in strenuous muscular activity such as running a race. It has been found in football players before a game, and in students just before an examination. Probably the organic state was useful to the football players, and far from useful to the students. In both cases the emotion was scarcely fear or anger; the subjects said they felt "all on edge" or "all keyed up." It was, in a word, a state of *excitement*.

Excitement, as already suggested, is a readiness for great activity—not for any special kind of activity but for whatever activity is on foot. There are two kinds of excited feeling: the tense, fidgety, shivery kind, when one is eager to get started and is only waiting for the time to arrive; and the hot, hyperkinetic kind, when one is in the thick of action. Athletes awaiting a contest are well aware of the tense, expectant kind, which may make itself felt a day or more before the contest and increase till the event actually starts, giving way then to the state of intense overt activity. The latter state does not appear emotional to the subject because he is thoroughly absorbed in the game, i.e., in the objective situation and the results accomplished or attempted. The two states are seen also in the public speaker while waiting his turn, and while successfully making his speech. Possibly there are two somewhat different organic states of excitement, the shivery state being a one-sided sympathetic-adrenal affair, and the hot state being produced by a more equally balanced activity of the autonomic nerves (*17, 25*).

Pure excitement is neither angry nor afraid. Angry feeling

is excited feeling, to be sure, but it has its own special impulsive quality which is different from the impulse of fear. These impulses are directed toward overt activity: toward attack in anger, toward escape in fear. In anger and fear, then, we find (a) a set of the organism toward certain types of overt activity, and (b) an organic state which is a physiological preparation for those types of activity. The set for the special overt activity, occurring alone, would be felt simply as an impulse to attack or escape. The organic state, occurring alone, would be felt as excitement. The combination of set and organic state is experienced as an emotion of anger or of fear.

**Organic states in other emotions.** The foregoing analysis of anger and fear raises the question whether a similar pattern can be found in the various other emotions. Is each emotion a set for a certain kind of external behavior, combined with an appropriate internal state? The studies already cited of *sex appetite* do show a similar pattern, since there is a set for sex behavior, with an organic state due to the sex hormones. This is quite a different state from that of fear or anger though it does involve excitement. No specific organic state has been identified for other emotions.

## THEORY OF THE EMOTIONS

Our final task in this chapter is to put together the main facts that have emerged from our study of feeling and emotion, with the object of discovering (a) the difference between emotional behavior and unemotional, and (b) the difference between one emotion and another.

The main facts we have to work with are:

1. The situation in which the individual is placed, and his intellectual perception of the situation.

2. His set for a certain overt activity or for a certain result, such as escape from danger.

3. The organic state, present in some emotions, though perhaps not in all, this state not being the same for all emotions, nor yet different for every different emotion. It appears to be

the same in anger, fear and other excited states, but something else in sex appetite or in grief or joy. The organic state depends largely on the autonomic nerves and their center in the inter-brain.

4. The sensations produced by the internal organic activity, by expressive movements, and by the overt activity, these sensations being felt as a mass.

5. The greater or less dominance of the organism by the practical or intellectual activity as against the more diffuse and undirected type of activity which occurs in strong feeling and emotion.

**The James-Lange theory of the emotions.** The American psychologist, James, and the Danish physiologist, Lange, inde-pendently of each other, put forward this theory about 1880, and it has ever since remained a great topic for discussion. It has mystified students more than it would have done if they had noticed exactly what the authors were trying to explain. They were thinking of the conscious state of excited feeling and wanted to know how that feeling originated. When you find yourself in a dangerous situation, why should you not simply take measures to escape, without having any upsurge of fear? The older common-sense theory was rather vague but seemed to assume that the knowledge of danger gave rise di-rectly to the feeling of fear and that the feeling then stirred up the body internally and also produced the escape behavior. The James-Lange theory held, on the contrary, that the feeling of fear was not the cause but the effect of the stirred-up bodily state. It was simply a mass of sensations from all over the body, especially from the internal organs. The emotion, according to the theory, is the *way the body feels* when in a disturbed or-ganic state and when making the various movements charac-teristic of the emotion.

As a test of the theory, James suggested a sort of experiment. Think away from the emotion of fear all the sensations of rapid heartbeat, shallow breathing, trembling lips and weakened limbs, goose flesh and visceral disturbance—and what have you got left? Only the knowledge of danger and the cool intention to escape. "Without the bodily states," James urged, we might "see the bear, and judge it best to run, receive the insult, and deem it right to strike, but we should not actually *feel* afraid or angry" (*19*).

The James-Lange theory is a "peripheral" rather than a "central" theory, i.e., it holds that the emotional state results from sensations arising in the periphery (the body in general) rather than from any activity occurring primarily in the brain. So it can be tested by physiological experiments.

**Evidence against the James-Lange theory.** Sherrington attempted a physiological examination of this question (*24*). Having a dog in the laboratory that showed a markedly emotional temperament, affectionate toward some individuals and hostile to others, he performed certain nerve-cutting operations which deprived the animal of nearly all sensation from the interior of the trunk. This loss of sensation produced no obvious change in the dog's emotional behavior. "Her anger, her joy, her disgust, and when provocation arose, her fear, remained as evident as ever." A visitor who had previously awakened her anger was again received with signs of rage—wide-open eyes, dilated pupils, vicious growls—while the attendant who fed her was received with all signs of joy.

This experiment certainly proves that the overt behavior and expressive movements of emotion do not depend upon sensations from the interior of the trunk. Of course, it is impossible to say, absolutely, what the dog *felt*. It might be argued that the dog went through the external movements with no emotional feeling. But so strained an interpretation of the dog's behavior could only be justified by very strong evidence from some other source of the truth of the James-Lange theory.

Another physiological experiment, by Cannon, carries us a step further. The sympathetic nerves of a cat were severed, and the organic state of anger, so far as dependent on those nerves, was made impossible, and still the cat continued to show the overt behavior and expressive movements of anger—growling, hissing, showing the teeth, drawing back the ears, lifting the front leg to strike. So far as we can judge from an animal's behavior, the organic state is not an essential part or factor in the emotion of anger (4).

For sure evidence on the subjective feeling in emotion, we need testimony from human subjects. One important case bearing on the problem is that of an intelligent woman of forty whose neck was broken by a fall from her horse. The breaking of the spinal cord in the neck interrupted all the sensory and motor nerve pathways between the brain and the trunk and limbs, except for the connections by way of the upper division of the autonomic with some of the internal organs. The sympathetic or middle division was entirely disconnected from the brain, and all sensations from the trunk and limbs were abolished. According to the James-Lange theory, practically all emotional experience should have been abolished; yet, during the year that the patient survived the accident, the expert neurologist who attended her reported that he "saw her showing emotions of grief, joy, displeasure and affection. There was no change in her personality or character." We should have more cases, but this one certainly indicates that emotional experience can arise in the brain without the help of sensations from the body and limbs. If the emotional experience is not a mass of sensations, what can it be? Probably it is simply the experience of behaving in a certain way, i.e., of letting oneself go in the direction of a certain impulse or attitude (9).

What would happen if the organic state characteristic of fear and anger could be artificially produced, without any external cause for fear or anger? This experiment has been tried, by giving adrenin to human subjects—under medical advice, as an overdose has bad effects. Definite physical symptoms are produced, such as rapid pulse, cold hands and feet, trembling of the arms, legs and voice. The subjects commonly report that they feel nervous, uneasy, tense, excited, or "on edge," as before a game or race in which they are to take an active part. Many of the subjects go a little further and say they feel "as if anticipating an emergency of some sort," or "as if they were awaiting a great joy," or "as if they were going to weep without knowing why." These subjects admit having an "as if" emotion, but not a true emotion. They say they have some of the feeling of fear, but no real fear because there is no cause for fear. In a few instances a "vague, nameless fear" is reported, and very rarely a gust of genuine though still causeless fear. In most cases, it appears, the subject in this experiment keeps his head and is not really frightened, knowing he has nothing to fear. But while under the influence of the adrenin he is more easily frightened than in the normal state (5, 6).

The experimental evidence is certainly against the peripheral theory of emotion and therefore in favor of a central theory. The organic state, normally present in emotion, is directly under the control of the autonomic nerves and of their center in the interbrain. This center has two-way connections with the cortex; it can influence the cortex and be influenced by it. Something like this may be true: When the cortex dominates, behavior is relatively calm, practical and goal-directed; but when the interbrain dominates, behavior is disturbed, diffuse and emotional. When the individual "loses his head," the interbrain takes control; but as long as he keeps his head, the cortex is master (1, 21).

Under what conditions is the individual likely to lose his head? When the situation is so confused and difficult that he loses his grip on it. When the goal cannot be reached, or not quickly enough. When the goal has been reached, and there is nothing more to do except to burst forth in jubilation. When the organic state is strong and lively, like a horse that is all warmed up and hard to control. During intoxication or anoxia, when the cerebral cortex is partially thrown out of action, it ceases to dominate the lower parts of the brain, and the interbrain, left to itself, carries out the blinder and more impulsive life of emotion.

We have been speaking too much in antithetical terms, as if the individual at any moment must be either in a storm of emotion or else in a state of perfect calm. Actually there are all degrees of emotion, and a moderate degree does not prevent the individual from using his head. A perfectly cold intellectual activity, free from any tinge of emotion, may never occur. If you are engaged in an activity that bores you, that boredom has an emotional quality; and if the activity interests you, the interest, too, partakes of emotion. If an activity neither bores nor interests you it is probably going on automatically, leaving you free to think of something that does have interest. Usually the intellectual and the emotional are harmoniously combined in the total activity. The cortex and the lower brain centers usually work together in harmony, with the cortex dominating but not suppressing the activity of the lower centers.

## SUMMARY

1. *Feeling and emotion* are temporary states of the individual, associated with motives, and together with motives comprising what are called *desires*.

2. *Feelings* are conscious states of various kinds and intensities.

   a. Wundt proposed a classification of feeling in three dimensions: pleasantness—unpleasantness, excitement—inertness, and expectancy—release.

   b. Feeling is differentiated from motor activity, although feeling often accompanies activity.

   c. Feeling is differentiated from sensory activity in that it provides no knowledge of environmental or internal events and objects.

   d. Pleasure and displeasure may be derived from sensory activity itself, and from the satisfaction or thwarting of a motive.

   e. *Sympathy* is the tendency to feel the same as another person is feeling. *Empathy* is the tendency to feel what you would feel if you were in another person's situation. Both tendencies are often expressed in overt behavior.

   f. *Esthetic enjoyment* of beauty in nature and art is sometimes based on associations; but esthetic preferences for symmetry, proportion, and balance seem to be more general and more basic.

**3.** *Emotions* are stirred-up states of the individual. Each emotion can be described in terms of the feeling, the motor set for response, the organic state, and the kind of external situation arousing the emotion.

    a. *Fear* is aroused by danger situations, i.e., by stimuli which the individual has learned are signs of impending unpleasantness. Sudden, strange or unexpected stimuli likewise arouse fear (surprise) because they are so frequently signals of danger.

    b. *Anger* is aroused by situations in which an activity in progress, or a set, is thwarted by some obstacle.

    c. *Mirth* is evoked by a variety of situations which do not have any clear-cut single feature in common. One theory of humor emphasizes the sudden release from tension.

    d. *Joy* occurs when an anticipated goal or pleasure is achieved.

    e. *Grief* results from the unalterable deprivation of an accustomed or expected source of gratification.

**4.** *Emotional expressions* are derived from responses which were serviceable to our remote ancestors, or are learned in the course of individual development.

    a. The child gradually learns to control his emotional expressions in line with the social pressures of his environment. He conceals the expression of many emotions and he acquires the standardized expressions of social custom.

    b. The emotional state of an individual can be judged with fair accuracy from his facial expression, and to a certain degree from his gestures and his vocal inflection.

**5.** An *organic state* with characteristic physiological changes is associated with the excited emotion of fear or anger.

    a. The bodily changes result largely from activity of the sympathetic nerves—the middle division of the autonomic nerves.

    b. Changes in breathing and blood pressure during emotion can be recorded to provide indicators of deception.

    c. During anger the stomach ceases its normal digestive functions.

d. Other signs of sympathetic nerve activity during emotion can be seen in goose flesh, pupil dilation, and sweating.

e. The organic state in emotion is a useful preparation for energetic vigorous activity.

6. *Theory of emotions* tries to relate the stimulus situation, the set, the organic state, and the bodily sensations.

a. The James-Lange theory proposed that the emotional feeling is the mass of sensations coming from the body, especially the internal organs.

b. Experimental results show that emotion is not abolished when the sensory nerves from the body are cut, nor does clear-cut emotion result from giving adrenin which produces the characteristic organic state.

c. Emotion probably results from the activity of the interbrain when the dominance of the cortex is removed.

# CHAPTER TWELVE

# Choice, Conflict, Frustration

L ife would be simple if each stimulus infallibly gave one sure response—if heredity and past environment provided the individual with only one possible way of acting in a given situation—if it were perfectly clear to him at each successive moment that there was only one thing he could do, or only one thing he wanted to do, so that he "had no choice in the matter." Daily routine is often like that, with everything running along in a familiar groove and no alternatives suggesting themselves. Yet even in the course of an ordinary day you will find, if you notice your behavior closely, quite a number of choices made, quite a number of decisions on minor matters arrived at after some consideration of possible alternatives. And in the course of a lifetime there are sure to be several, or many, important moments of choice and decision. Is it a privilege or a hardship to have alternative courses open before you with freedom to choose but obligation to decide? Consulting their own feelings some persons would answer this question one way and some the other.

The will. [This noun like many others used in psychology is best regarded as a verb.] "To will" is to choose, or to intend, or to overcome obstruction. You *choose* one goal as preferable to another, and having selected your goal you choose one route to the goal, one means to the end, as better than another.

You do not *intend* to wink when some object suddenly approaches close to your eyes, that wink being an involuntary, unlearned reflex. Some learned movements become so automatic as to be made involuntarily. Especially the part movements that compose a larger act are apt to be involuntary. You voluntarily sign your name, but you do not make each separate letter as a voluntary act, because once you start to sign your name the series of movements runs off automatically. Intentional acts were considered before under the name of "purposes" (p. 325). Will, as exemplified by purposive behavior, includes two elements, motive and foresight. In acting purposefully you desire certain results and foresee that you will obtain those results, probably at least, if you act in a certain way. You may also foresee certain incidental results which you do not especially desire and which you may even dislike, but they are part of the price you are prepared to pay for the desired results. You foresee hard work and much drudgery on the way to your goal, and perhaps other inconveniences to yourself and other people, but you determine to "take these things in your stride" because you are fully committed to that goal. To reach such a decision and stick to it may be very difficult.

*Overcoming obstacles* by increased effort—this form of will, too, was discussed before (p. 318). Obstacles are of many sorts and the effort that overcomes them is not always muscular. When we say of a child that he has "a will of his own," we mean that he persists in what he undertakes, in spite of hindrances, and that he insists on having his own way in spite of the commands and coaxings of other people. He is free with his "I will too" and "I won't either." Of course his will is not absolutely unconquerable. He may yield to persuasion or to fear of punishment or to fatigue. Or he may give in to laziness, inertia, the attraction of the easy life as compared with the strenuous life. There are always alternatives, and when a person says that he has no choice he really means that only one alternative has any appeal. In the face of difficulty there is always the alternative of giving up, which is sometimes the most rational choice that can be made under the circumstances.

Ideally choice should be based on rational considerations. We are creatures with motives, foresight and a "will of our own," to be sure, but also with excitable emotions. Often our actions emerge from a stirred-up inner state rather than from a dispassionate view of the desirable and undesirable consequences of different lines of action. Our cautious attitude passes over into blind fear of the unknown, our effort to overcome obstruction into wild rage, our normal distaste for useless work into the pessimism of "What's the use?" In considering conflicting motives and frustrated efforts we must bear in mind the emotional as well as the rational factors in human behavior.

## CONFLICTING MOTIVES

When a conflict of motives occurs there are alternative goals and courses of action. To keep matters simple let us say there are two alternatives, and let us speak of two "objects" between which you are supposed to choose. An object may be either attractive or repellent; it is one which you desire to approach so as to have it, use it, enjoy it; or it is one which you wish to avoid and get away from because of its undesirable qualities. Let us mark the attractive object with a + sign, the repellent one with a − sign, and diagram the different situations that may arise.

**Choice, compromise and vacillation responses.** Choice is selective; in a clean-cut choice one alternative is taken and the other altogether rejected, response being made to only one of the two objects. In a compromise, the response tends to approach both desirable objects, or to avoid both undesirable ones, or to approach a desirable one while keeping away from one that is undesirable. The tendencies to move toward or away from the objects can be represented by arrows, as in Figure 85.

When the alternatives are a plus object and a minus one, a clean-cut choice would be either to approach the plus object or to move away from the minus object, disregarding the other object in either case. One of these choices usually does occur, but if the minus object is greatly feared while the plus object is much desired, there may be a compromise response, a movement along the diagonal between the two arrows, bringing O (the subject) around behind the plus object where, the minus object being now too far away to be very fearsome, he may change his course and go straight for the plus object (compare the case of Peter and the terrible rabbit, p. 317).

If both objects are repellent there will be no conflict, no choice necessary and no true compromise, though O may follow the diagonal by running away from both at once. If both objects are attractive and equally so, the compromise would follow the diagonal and not reach either one, but so futile a response would certainly not persist very long; a choice is easily made• since the conflict is so slight. If you were a small boy offered a choice between two equal pieces of cake, you might scrutinize

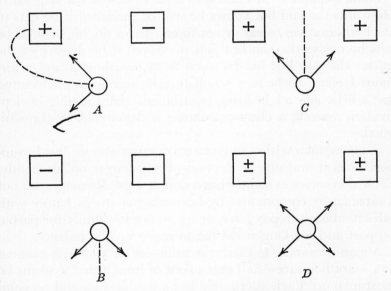

FIG. 85.—Choice, compromise, vacillation. The plus sign denotes an attractive object or alternative, the minus sign a repellent one. The arrows indicate tendencies to move toward or away from the objects. The dotted diagonal lines indicate the possible compromise responses.

them carefully to see if one were not a little larger than the other, but you would not vacillate long.

In spite of diagrams B and C vacillation does often occur when a choice must be made between two good things or between two evils. You swing this way and that like a pendulum, almost deciding for one good thing but taking a last glance at the other and finding it too good to relinquish—or almost selecting one of the two evils but then wondering whether the other might not after all be more endurable. When such vacillation occurs it is because each alternative has a double sign; it has its advantages and its disadvantages in comparison with the other alternative (diagram D). Though perhaps equally good or bad, they differ in kind, and you have to decide which kind of good you prefer, or which kind of evil you can better endure. Difficult choices probably always involve such double-sign alternatives (6, 9, 13).

Some examples.   A child sees a jar of jam in the cupboard. He wants the jam but knows he will be punished if he eats it. Each alternative, to eat or not to eat, has a double sign. If he eats he enjoys the jam but gets punished; if he doesn't eat he misses the jam but has freedom from punishment and a virtuous feeling. So he may vacillate. The compromise of eating just a little jam might bring punishment and a feeling of deprivation as well; a clean-cut choice is demanded by the situation.

A young man wishes to go to college but also desires to support himself and not be dependent any longer on his family. Each alternative evidently has a double sign. He may work out a satisfactory compromise by borrowing from his family with full intention to repay later, or by asking his family for partial support and working part-time to make up the balance.

A man is running to catch the train—or an athlete is running in a Marathon race—and gets so out of breath that it seems he must give up. Each alternative has a double sign and no compromise is possible. If he keeps doggedly on (and is in good condition) he may get his second wind and find his task easier than seems possible at present. Something like second wind occurs in other, non-athletic tasks calling for prolonged effort. You feel you cannot work any longer; but you must work longer, or else . . . ; so you decide to stick to it a little longer and are surprised to find the tired feeling passing away.

**Decision.** The state of indecision is likely to be very unpleasant and sometimes full of confused emotions, though at other times the decision is reached by a process of calmly examining the advantages and disadvantages of the alternatives, perhaps writing out a list of all the arguments for and against each side. Sometimes the decision comes gradually as the weight of the arguments makes itself felt. At other times the vacillation is so prolonged, irritating and almost humiliating that you say, "Any decision is better than none; here goes, then, *this* is what I will do," so breaking the deadlock by what seems just like tossing a penny. When, after long deliberation, you still find yourself hopelessly vacillating between two alternatives, you may well let the matter rest for a while. On taking it up afresh after a rest and perhaps after a night's sleep you may find that one alternative is clearly superior to the other.

By one means or another a decision is finally reached and then it usually sticks. A student vacillates for a long time between the almost equal attractions of two colleges, but when he has finally chosen one, the other promptly loses its appeal. Now he is all for one and not at all for the other. Some people, indeed, being abnormally prone to vacillation or compromise, never accept their own decisions as final, but normally a decision, once reached, is reinforced by the satisfaction of now having a definite goal. It is reinforced also by the self-assertive tendency, for when the student has chosen a college he has made it *his* college. He identifies himself with his college; when anyone praises it he feels proud as if he himself were being praised, but if anyone disparages it he feels personally insulted.

**Is choice determined by the strongest motive?** The old debate on "free will versus determinism" has many non-psychological ramifications which do not concern us here. Psychologically, a person who is free from external compulsion feels himself free to do what he wants as against what he does not want, and to do what he wants more as against what he wants less. From his point of view it is logical to say that choice follows a motive and that when motives conflict choice follows the strongest motive. By "strongest" he means strongest at a given moment when decision is reached. Such a statement may create the false impression that the individual is passive and driven this way and that by conflicting forces which, though internal rather than external, are not under his control. Actually, being a single unitary organism or system of forces, he does have some control, as any whole system controls its parts. No motive has any force unless it appeals to him, and if a motive appeals to him against his total interest and best judgment, he can mobilize other motives and organize a team of motives that shall be stronger than the single motive. This so-called "will power" is really the whole individual mobilizing all his powers so as to accomplish what he most wants to accomplish. Take a very commonplace example: I am absorbed in reading a story when the dinner bell awakens my hunger motive. I start to lay my book aside but take a last glance and become absorbed again in the story. Then I remember that promptness at meals is much appreciated at my eating place and that I have a reputation for promptness. The desire to maintain my good reputation awakens and I drop the book and hasten to dinner. Here hunger alone was not strong enough to overcome my interest in the story, but I mobilized stronger motives and overcame the story interest. Something of the same sort occurs when you resist a more serious temptation. A desire that would be overpowering if you were driven by separate impulses loses out when you pause to consider the consequences, because it cannot compete with your self-respect and loyalty to your ideals and to your friends.

Sex interest is naturally strong in young adults and often has to be controlled by the individual. If he joins with people of both sexes in social activities he thus combines his sex motive with other interests and keeps above the primitive level. Or he may work off his steam in athletic activities which do not gratify the sex impulse in the least but do provide other satisfactions

—and it is the individual that must be satisfied, rather than any particular one of his motives. If he becomes attached to an unworthy mate, his sex motive conflicts with self-respect and with a distaste for the inferior personality. But if he finds a worthy mate he can combine the sex motive with self-respect, admiration and other interests into the powerful team of motives which we call love.

## FRUSTRATION

Minor difficulties and obstacles are encountered every hour of the day, most of them being easily surmounted, and more serious difficulties are not at all uncommon. Anything that obstructs your progress to a chosen goal, anything that interferes with the satisfaction of a motive, is an obstacle. The most natural response to an obstacle, as has been said before, is to put in greater effort toward the goal. If this does not remove or surmount the obstacle, the next natural response is to vary your attack, to explore the situation in the hope of finding a way around the obstacle. This problem-solving behavior may consist in moving around and looking around or in thinking how best to handle the difficulty. Problem solving will be the theme of later chapters on learning and thinking. But if the effort, the exploration, the thinking result only in *failure*, what happens then? What is the reaction to failure? That is our present problem.

The word *frustration* is used in two ways which however will probably not cause much confusion. Sometimes it refers to a stimulus and sometimes to a response. Sometimes it means the unsurmounted obstacle, or the failure to surmount it, and sometimes it means the subject's reaction to failure, especially when that reaction is very emotional. A person who is "frustrated" may be one who is simply blocked in all his attempts to solve a problem, or he may be one who has responded to his failure by anger, worry and anxiety. Some individuals continue their problem-solving attempts longer than others before becoming emotionally frustrated. They are said to have more "frustration tolerance." Happy, self-confident, secure individuals are less likely to be upset (frustrated) by failure (frustration) than those who are insecure and always on the defensive.

Considered in a perfectly matter-of-fact way, failure means simply that an obstacle is stronger than the force directed against it. If you try to break a stick but fail, you may say either that the stick is too stiff or that you are too weak, and as long as you maintain the matter-of-fact attitude the two statements amount to the same thing. But if you become emotional over your failure, you will either feel angry at the stick for being so stiff, or else feel humiliated and upset because you are so weak. If angry at the stick you can call it names and throw it away, but if personally humiliated you have to do something to restore your self-esteem. The emotional response to failure takes many forms, some of which we will examine after first considering different kinds of failure.

**Sources of emotional frustration.**   Sometimes an emotional upset is brought about by failure in what seem like very unimportant matters. A young child may be quite upset in situations which seem trivial to an adult though they doubtless are important to the child with his limited perspective. Usually, we can say, serious and prolonged emotional frustration occurs only when a strong, persistent motive cannot be gratified in spite of a person's best efforts. The most common frustrating situations fall into four main classes:

1. *Motivated individual blocked by impersonal obstacle.* A man is driving to catch an important train or to keep an important engagement, when his car stalls. Minute after minute passes and he still fails to locate the trouble. He is likely to become agitated and angry. Monotonous work and drudgery are frustrating to some people who feel the urge within them to attempt something creative. Prolonged unemployment during a recent depression was very frustrating to some people though not to all. Many prisoners of war had a deep sense of frustration.

2. *Motivated individual blocked by another person.* This situation is more disturbing than the first because a person is

supposed to be more reasonable and sympathetic than an in-
animate object.)But persons can be very stubborn; they have
their own motives and purposes which may conflict with yours.
A young married couple get into an angry quarrel because each
of them wants his own way in some unimportant matter. "If
you loved me you wouldn't insist on my doing what I don't
want to do." "If you loved me you wouldn't refuse to do what
I ask." Once in this mood they are apt to air many other com-
plaints, till their love and happy companionship, so precious to
both of them, are as if lost forever and they are left desolate
and hopeless. They have to learn that neither one can dominate
the other. The tendency to dominate and the resistance to being dominated cause periodical disturbance in any group of
friends. A knowledge of the psychology of motives should enable each member of the group to recognize the masterful
tendency in himself and to tolerate some self-assertion in his
friends. (But the happiest solution for this type of conflict is
found in teamwork, where the members of the group are unit-
ing their efforts toward a common goal. They can accept leadership and management aimed at the common goal and not at
petty domination and self-assertion.

(3.) *Conflict of positive motives in the same person.* This sort
of conflict, already analyzed in this chapter, may give rise to
emotional frustration. The young girl who desires to accept an
invitation to a dance and at the same time desires to please
her mother who disapproves of "dates" is bound to be disturbed
if both motives are strong and equally balanced. To choose one
course of action inevitably means that the other motive is
thwarted. The mother, too, may be torn as mothers often are
between the desire to have her child happy and the feeling of
responsibility for the child's upbringing.

(4.) *Conflict of a positive motive and a negative one.* This
sort also was illustrated before. A desirable goal beckons you
forward but something within you keeps holding you back.

a. The negative motive may be inertia, laziness or weariness.
A lazy person may be quite cheerful about it, or he may become upset because he has no energy or ambition. In some

other people it is not laziness but a sense of weakness or lack of ability, an "I can't" feeling of some sort, that hampers free approach to the desired goal. A young person desires to join in social activities, but from lack of experience feels awkward in the group and remains on the outskirts while still upset and rebellious at his own failure to participate.

b. Often the negative motive is fear of something or other, fear of punishment, for example. The trusted bank teller, caught by unfortunate gambling debts, spends his working days looking at money which he might "borrow" to tide him over the emergency. Yet he may experience no severe conflict since the fear of punishment is strong enough to settle the issue. Or, if he were already a hardened criminal, the fear of punishment would be too weak to cause conflict. But if the positive and negative motives are equally strong he suffers the persistent agony of indecision. The negative motive in other cases may be not fear of punishment exactly but fear of social disapproval or of being ridiculed for failure. Failure sometimes results from fear of failure, as in the case of stage fright.

c. Instead of fear of other people's criticism it may be one's own code or conscience that stands in the way of gratifying some desire. If conscience is strong enough it will rule out the desire without much conflict. If the two are equally balanced there will be a period of painful vacillation. "I want to do it— I mustn't do it—But I want so much to do it—But I mustn't, mustn't do it." If the desire wins, there will be remorse afterward, a state of hopeless frustration because what has been done cannot be undone.

Although frustration may arise in any of life's situations it is inevitable in the discipline of the home and in the social group with its code and taboos. Such motives as hunger, thirst and the need for sleep are seldom thwarted for long in our society, but when they are thwarted by the unusual conditions of war or desert travel very serious states of frustration do occur. In civilized conditions of life, however, there is continual and persistent frustration of the egoistic impulses of children, of the sex drive in adolescents, and of the desire for social status in adults.

**Behavior in emotional frustration.** When a person fails in all his attempts to solve his problem, but still cannot give up because his desire is too strong and persistent, he is indeed in an unhappy state. His behavior no longer seems intelligent; instead of being directed toward the problem it is directed toward escaping somehow from the agitated, emotional state of frustration. The reaction in frustration takes many forms which can be classified under three heads according to the amount of intelligence brought into play.

1. *Unthinking emotional reactions.* The primitive reactions of anger and fear, sometimes more the one and sometimes more the other, are aroused by frustration.

a. Angry "aggression." A child's temper tantrum is an example. He is "mad all over," scarcely dealing with the environment at all but simply venting his emotion. He shows a little more sense when he attacks the person or thing that is thwarting him, but when he attacks a person, that person is likely to fight back and so prolong and increase the frustration. An angry response of some kind is very common in older children and adults when they are subjected to frustrating situations (3, 17).

b. Helpless anxiety. Instead of temper the child may have a fit of heartbroken crying and sobbing. So far, again, he is not dealing with the environment. He seems to feel helpless, insecure, in need of comfort and support. In older people, too, the emotional state in frustration is often a state of anxiety and hopelessness, giving up and withdrawing from the situation.

c. Regression. Literally this word means going back in time, doing six-year stuff when a child has failed to do what is appropriate to his age level of nine years. Thumb-sucking, baby-talk, and even bed-wetting are sometimes observed in eight or ten year old children who have been seriously frustrated. An experimental study has shown that children restricted to playing with their ordinary toys while much more attractive toys were in full view behind a wire screen, regressed to relatively infantile kinds of play (2).

d. Fixation. Faced with failure in his repeated efforts, a person may sometimes lapse into repetitive stereotyped behavior, which does not contribute toward solution of the problem. Such reactions have been demonstrated in animal experiments (*11*), and are seen in the compulsive actions of maladjusted persons.

These primitive responses in frustration are not learned through experience but are natural reactions of the individual to his frustrated state. Of course learning may modify frustration behavior if it is followed by some form of reinforcement. If the child who has a temper tantrum when his parents repeatedly block his efforts to play with the vacuum cleaner is finally allowed to play with it, he will be more likely to have another tantrum when he is thwarted again. He learns to use the tantrum as a means to an end, as another child may learn to put on a show of desolate weeping as a way of bringing pressure to bear on his parents.

e. Repression. The state of helpless anxiety is almost intolerable; yet it may last a long time, until the child has had his cry out and gone to sleep. The angry emotion is not so bad from the subject's point of view, but it may be complicated by punishment received from anyone who is attacked by the angry subject. All in all this frustrated emotional state is something to be avoided and if the person feels it coming on again he recoils as much as possible. If the desire that led to failure and frustration awakens again he feels the danger and checks that impulse. So he represses the desire and the memory of the frustration. By doing this repeatedly, every time the desire awakens, he may practically forget the whole experience and deaden that specific desire, though he cannot of course eliminate any basic motive from his system. The psychoanalysts believe that repressed desires and experiences live on in "the unconscious," breaking into normal waking activities to some extent as well as expressing themselves in dreams (*4*). This is an interesting theory but there are other ways of explaining the facts.

2. *Placing the blame.* If a little thinking creeps into the emotional state, so that the person asks why he has failed, he is most likely to put the blame on the environment. He says that the task was too hard, or that it was unfair. If this explanation

does not satisfy, he may try to place the blame on someone other than himself. This may lead to argument and hostility and the person feels angry or guilty. Usually, however, he saves himself and "defends his ego" by some explanation or *rationalization* which is satisfactory to him and perhaps even justified. For example:

a. The task is too hard, at least for one of my youth and inexperience.

b. The task may be all right but it is not in my line and of no importance to me. I can laugh over my failure.

c. "Sour grapes," as the fox said of the fruit he failed to reach.

d. I am not bad and hateful; I am not angry at these people, but they hate me. This reaction is called *projection*, the idea being that the individual projects into other people the undesirable attitudes which he is unwilling to recognize in himself. In international affairs projection is illustrated by a nation accusing its neighbors of a plot to "encircle" it, when the real fact is that it plans to encircle them. But the individual's projection is said to be "unconscious" in the sense that it is impulsive and not a deliberate and planful deception either of other people or of himself.

3. *Finding a substitute goal.* More rational, and certainly more enterprising, than the reactions to frustration so far mentioned is the effort to escape from failure by finding some activity offering a better chance for success. The subject may renew his efforts to attain the original goal by finding some new approach, or he may try for another similar goal, or he may shift to some altogether different goal which appeals not to the original motive but to some other interest. Sometimes failure occurs because you have aimed too high, and you may lower your sights, lower your "level of aspiration," temporarily at least, and so keep up your self-confidence. Some people, however, are so afraid of any failure that they will never aim high (*10*).

a. Sublimation. A young man strongly in love with a certain girl but unable to win her approval may start writing sonnets in her honor and perhaps write some eloquent lines. The earlier psychoanalysts believed that art and science were sublimated outlets for a frustrated sex drive, but it has become clear that the artists and scientists have the same sex cravings as other people and that the organic sex need is not drained off into these higher activities. Less emphasis than formerly is now placed on sublimation. Besides, the young man writing sonnets is certainly animated by an interest in his poetry as well as desire for his ladylove. Art and science, even if they sometimes serve as an outlet for frustrated love, also have a strong human appeal on their own account. The frustrated lover who throws himself into athletics or any worthwhile activity is finding a new goal rather than a new approach to the old one.

b. Compensation. In a broad sense any substituted successful activity compensates for failure in the original activity, at least if it satisfies the individual in question. More particularly, however, compensation refers to individuals suffering from a feeling of inferiority because of some physical or other handicap, who regain their self-esteem and prestige by developing outstanding ability in some line, often in a line related to the one where they are handicapped. Theodore Roosevelt, dissatisfied with being a sickly boy, developed his physical stamina and became a rough rider, an explorer, and an exponent of the strenuous life. Some compensatory activities are not so admirable. A schoolboy who is failing in his lessons may compensate by any attention-getting devices that occur to him, such as noisy clownishness.

c. Fantasy or daydreaming. Failing in a real activity which has to deal with a stubborn environment the individual can find some satisfaction in imagining himself as engaged in highly successful activity of the same or a different sort. He "remolds the world to his heart's desire." Or, instead of doing his own inventive imagining, he reads a story and identifies himself with the hero who meets with many difficulties but struggles through to triumphant success.

These "mechanisms" or stratagems for defending the ego against frustration appear in exaggerated forms in neurotic and psychotic individuals (14) but in moderation also in the daily life of children and adults (*3, 11, 17, 18, 19, 21*). And they can be demonstrated experimentally (*12, 19, 22*).

## ADJUSTMENT AND MALADJUSTMENT

Aside from the important matter of general health, most personal problems are concerned with the individual's relations to his fellows, who are his parents, brothers and sisters, playmates, teachers, friends and associates, wife or husband and children. "How to get along with one's fellows" is the basic problem—how to live the life of a socialized human being, and enjoy it. The infant soon encounters this problem; if he finds a good solution he has made a start toward a good life. He needs some help in getting away from the purely selfish attitude of always having his own way and using other people only as tools for ministering to his own pleasure. Unless he gets away from this attitude he becomes a social problem rather than a social being. It would be too much to expect the child or anyone else to adopt the entirely unselfish, altruistic attitude of seeking only to be of service to other people. Nor is such an attitude socially desirable. It is undesirable in the child's mother because it spoils the child. Give-and-take, participation and teamwork represent the true principle of social living.

The child encounters obstacles and has to learn how to overcome them or by-pass them. At times his desires conflict with each other and he must learn how to manage such conflicts. He must learn how to avoid or tolerate frustrating situations. He has problems on his hands when the adults insist on weaning him and on training him to control his bladder and bowel movements, and when other children compete with him for playthings and for the attention of his parents. These problems are but the forerunners of many others encountered by the growing child, the adolescent and the adult. An adjustment is a way of dealing with a problem situation, a way of accomplishing the desired results. A good adjustment secures the desired results without also producing undesirable results. It solves the problem without creating worse problems to be handled. Adjustments are learned and used again and again so that they become habitual and easy. Maladjustments also are learned and may become habitual and automatic. In solving their immediate problems they create new and difficult problems; in securing certain desired results they incidentally produce an excess of unfortunate consequences. So daydreaming enables a person to escape from his present difficulties, but if too much indulged in it leaves him helpless and futile in dealing with the real environment. Putting the blame for your failures on other people relieves your present humiliation but makes you a very unsatisfactory companion and so tends to isolate you from your fellows.

**Severe maladjustments.** So-called normal people differ from the so-called abnormal not in complete freedom from maladjustments but in the minor severity and persistence of their maladjustments. The social lives of normal people are not thrown out of gear by their maladjustments. The nature of a maladjustment can often be seen more clearly in the severe cases, and for that reason the study of abnormal psychology throws much light on normal psychology as well as helping in the treatment of the abnormal.

A special course in abnormal psychology, rather than a few pages here, would be required for opening up the large subject of the neuroses and psychoses with their manifold manifestations. Some persons are beset with fears and anxieties which they themselves admit are foolish but which they cannot overcome. Some persons are haunted by strange ideas which they cannot shake off. Some have an unaccountable lack of energy and self-confidence. Some have physical symptoms like loss of appetite and apparent loss of muscular power or of sensation. So far we have *neurotic* symptoms. Still more serious are the *psychoses* or insanities, showing as extreme excitement or depression, or as withdrawal from the environment to such an extent as to be incapable of effective contacts with other people, or as terrible suspicion coupled with an overweening assertion of superiority (8).

The causes of these abnormal conditions are by no means

clear. Quite possibly, the body chemistry is involved. The belief of many psychiatrists, with regard to the neuroses at least, is that they are forms of maladjustment different in degree rather than in kind from the minor maladjustments of which everyone has some small share, maladjustments due largely to frustration and conflict of motives.

Psychiatrists have devoted a great deal of thought to the problem of how these neuroses originate, and have formulated a number of theories contradicting one another except on the point that the neuroses are due to conflict of motives or to frustration of desires. To evaluate these theories would obviously be too great a task for us here. Just a little may be said regarding these theories. Freud held that maladjustments originate in the child's demand for love and pleasure and in his hostility toward anyone who thwarts this demand. This desire to be rid of the interfering persons being also blocked, the child has a difficult problem on his hands. If his solution of this problem is inadequate he is left with a basic maladjustment which may show itself later in the neuroses of adult life (4).

Adler set up a different theory. The child's fundamental desire is conceived to be a demand for superiority and for overcoming the inferiority inherent in his status as a little child. His demand for superiority is subject to continual frustration and makes it difficult for him to adopt the give-and-take of a socialized human being. Unless the socializing process is tactfully managed by the parents, the child devises for himself a peculiar "style of life" which gives him some sense of superiority though it is unsuited for real achievement. According to Adler, then, maladjustment arises from frustration of the individual's demand for achievement (1).

Others of the general psychoanalytic group lay most stress on the demand for security. There are many ways of making the little child feel insecure. He is weak and helpless if left to himself. He is perhaps warned too much against the common dangers of life. If his mother takes a brief vacation from home duties, he is apt to feel deserted. If he is scolded, he feels deprived of affection and, momentarily at least, cast adrift in a hostile world. The child does not always outgrow this feeling of insecurity, and it may be accentuated in the adult struggle for existence and social recognition (5).

Without undertaking the almost hopeless task of deciding between these theories as explanations of the neuroses, we may at least admit that every one of them has pointed out certain difficulties in the way of an easy adjustment to life's conditions. As we advance from infancy toward maturity, pleasures of the more childish sort must be relinquished, increased responsibility and decreased protection must be accepted as a matter of course, and higher and higher standards of achievement must be met. Every such change costs effort, calls for readjustment and opens the door to maladjustment.

**Ways of helping maladjusted individuals.**   A child's maladjustments are handled quite directly, though not always successfully. A counselor from outside the home (or schoolroom) secures the child's confidence, and enlists his cooperation in an effort to see what the trouble is, what the conflicting demands are that have not been properly adjusted. If the problem arises in the home, or leads back into the home, as most problems of young children do, the cooperation of the parents must be secured, and often their behavior toward the child needs to be changed. The general plan is to lead the parties to see the situation clearly and to work out a solution in the light of the facts. "Facing the facts" is the main principle (p. 146).

The maladjustments of an adult cannot be handled so directly, because their sources may lie far back in the individual's experience and may have been forgotten. An irrational fear often dates back to childhood. If old memories can be revived, so that the original facts can now be faced squarely, the individual may throw off the childish fear and regain his self-confidence. But there is no sure cure for all cases. Strange as it may seem, the individual may cling to his fear or other maladjustment, in spite of its inconvenience, because it has come to mean something for his personality. He feels lost without it.

Anyone who is poorly adjusted to a life situation may find a useful suggestion in the proverb that "two heads are better than one." What he needs is not advice altogether. He needs the chance to use his own head in explaining the problem to an understanding friend, and if the friend does not understand the whole difficulty instantly, so much the better. The person who is in difficulty will understand it better himself after making it plain to his friend. Silent brooding over a troublesome personal matter is almost sure to give a distorted view. Minor maladjustments usually clear up in a confidential talk with a friend, without calling on the professional counselor. More difficult problems, however, do require the assistance of the expert. "Giving advice" is not exactly what the counselor does, for he is careful to give the individual a large share in solving his own problem and planning his own further course of action. The counselor, from his experience with similar problems, can see the ins and outs of the present problem better than anyone who is new to this type of difficulty. The counselor sees the situation objectively while the individual personally concerned is likely to be biased and emotional. When the emotional disturbance cuts deeply into the personality and upsets the individual's life with nameless fears and fixed ideas, the expert with experience in this type of cases is the psychiatrist.

The various methods of treating the neuroses may be examined with quite a modest purpose. We cannot attempt to decide which of the various rival methods is the best or only true method, but we may obtain a little information on ways in which maladjustment can be overcome.

There are two main steps in psychotherapy, as the treatment of maladjustments is called. The first step is to find the source of the trouble and to get the individual to face the facts. The second step is to induce him to advance hopefully toward full health and well-adjusted living. There are several methods of psychotherapy.

*Suggestion and hypnosis.* A "suggestion," in the sense here intended, is an idea or plan of action adopted by the individual without calling it in question.

One person is more suggestible than another, and the same person is more suggestible at certain times, or in certain states, than otherwise. The most suggestible state is hypnosis, a passive and sleeplike state that is nevertheless attentive and concentrated. The hypnotized subject, it appears, is awake simply to what the hypnotizer suggests, and inaccessible to other stimuli. His field of activity is narrowed down almost to a point (7).

Hypnosis may be deep or shallow. Comparatively few persons can be deeply hypnotized, but many can be put into a mild state of suggestibility. Where the waking person is alert, suspicious and assertive, the hypnotized subject is passive and submissive. The subject's cooperation is necessary, as a rule, for inducing any hypnotic state.

The means of inducing hypnosis are many and varied, but they all consist in gently wafting aside all extraneous thoughts and interests, and getting the subject into a quiet, receptive state with all his attention focused on the operator.

With the subject in this state, the operator's suggestions are accepted with less resistance than in the waking state. In deep hypnosis, gross illusions and hallucinations can be produced. The operator hands the subject a bottle of ammonia, assuring him it is the perfume of roses, and the subject takes a deep whiff with every sign of enjoyment.

In mild hypnosis, these very striking phenomena are not obtained, but suggestions of curative value may be accepted with useful results. Hypnosis is employed in both the main steps of psychotherapy: to revive a forgotten memory which reveals the origin of the trouble, and to fill the subject with the idea that the old trouble is of no consequence and that he is going to be well. Hypnosis should be reserved for serious therapeutic uses.

A young woman who was subject to serious hysterical attacks was able under hypnosis to remember how they had originated. While watching a fire she had been terrified to see children jumping out of the windows. She was induced to remember also that these children had been caught in the fireman's net and saved from harm. So the memory was relieved of most of its terror, and the suggestion was then given that this experience would not trouble her any more. This treatment was successful in putting a stop to the hysterical attacks( While removing a distressing symptom, however, suggestion may fail to reach an underlying maladjustment, and for that reason many psychotherapists regard hypnotism as of little value. They believe that the subject must do more than accept suggestions and that he must take an active part in working out a good adjustment to his life problems.)

*Psychoanalysis.* (In the strict sense, psychoanalysis is Freud's theory and practice and does not include any of the similar theories and methods that have been developed by his successors. In Freud's view the only way to treat a neurotic individual is to get back to the origin of the trouble in childhood) Instead of hypnotizing the patient, Freud had him recline and relax and become as uncritical as possible while letting thoughts and memories come by "free association." The association or recall process was controlled to this extent, that the patient must not let his mind wander to trivialities but should be looking for memories of personal significance. Freud usually asked the patient first to relate a dream of the previous night, and then the dream was "analyzed" by free association. Taking each item in the dream as a starting point, the patient let his mind play freely about that item so as to find what it suggested in the way of personally significant material. In this way, often after many visits, memories of childhood came up, revealing such attitudes as desire for the mother and opposition to the father, in a male patient. By dwelling long on these memory fragments, the patient came to revive some of the emotional attitudes of childhood. The child's attitude toward the father— an attitude partly of love and dependence, partly of resentment and rebellion against authority—on being revived, attached itself to the psychoanalyst as the most available present substitute for the father. When this "transference" had been secured, the next stage of the treatment consisted in re-education of the patient. Under the guidance of the psychoanalyst he practiced for many weeks in handling the difficulties of his present life, being gradually weaned from his dependence on the psychoanalyst and becoming more and more capable of managing his own affairs ( *4* ).

Freudian psychoanalysis takes a long time and should not be begun unless the patient is prepared to see it through to the finish, for if dropped in mid-course it leaves the patient worse off than before. It is not usually undertaken except by one whose difficulties in life are quite serious. It is not regarded, even by the psychoanalysts, as providing a "cure" in the usual medical sense, but it does enable many much-disturbed persons to "carry on" better than they could before the treatment.

What interests us here, in regard to psychoanalysis, is the benefit obtained from getting back to the source of a difficulty. An attitude that disturbs a person's life may have arisen in some situation of childhood which has little importance from the adult's point of view. Once he sees and "feels in his bones" that this attitude is a mere carry-over from childhood, he can treat it lightly. An adult's terrible fear of running water disappeared when it was traced back to a childhood experience of terror combined with guilt. Even without being able to trace back all of our irrational fears and antipathies to specific events, we can rest assured that they arose by some kind of "conditioning" and that they have no real importance for our adult lives.

Freud has many partial followers who owe much to his psychological approach to the problems of neurosis, and to his emphasis on conflict of motives and on the "unconscious" or unanalyzed character of many motives, but who do not accept the whole of his complicated theory nor follow his methods in detail. Adler had considerable success, at least with young persons suffering from minor maladjustments, by use of much simpler and quicker methods. In a few interviews he could discern the subject's "style of life," adopted in early childhood and adhered to throughout life. He led the subject to see his "style" and to adopt useful ways of reaching his goal instead of the inefficient and troublesome ways carried along from childhood ( *1* ).

Other independent psychoanalysts believe that less depends on going back to childhood and finding the infantile origin of the maladjustment than on tracing out its consequences in the adult's present ways of handling his problems. The neurotic person not only suffers from his maladjustment but he uses it; it is his way of getting something he cherishes. To take a simple example: the person who has a headache whenever a desirable group activity is in prospect puts other people out as well as himself and thus achieves a measure of dominance—or he may have a sense of social insecurity that makes him dread a large party. The ramifications of these motives are often very surprising (1a, 5, 20).

*Nondirective counseling* sounds like a contradiction in terms, for what can a counselor do except counsel and direct the maladjusted client who comes to him for help? What can a therapist do except to diagnose the patient's trouble and help him to eliminate the bad motive that is causing the trouble? What, indeed, except to help the client bring to light the good motive, the constructive forces within him, the *vis medicatrix naturae* or "healing power of nature" on which any physician really must rely in combatting a disease? (The nondirective or client-centered counselors trust the client's will and power to find his own way out of his trouble, if only they supply a psychological atmosphere of warmth and understanding, a "permissive" atmosphere in which he is free to express his thoughts and feelings.) The client talks about himself, at first at a relatively superficial level. The counselor, avoiding both praise and blame, reflects back to the client what he has revealed of his motives and thus stimulates the client to go further and deeper in exploring himself. Constructive motives gradually come into view and assert their power so that the client freely chooses a better course than the one he has been blindly following. The task of the counselor in such a series of interviews is by no means easy, for he has to lay aside the superior attitude of the professional expert and meet the client on the client's own ground. The client may at times feel that the counselor is not taking hold as he should, yet he comes back for further interviews because he finds the oppressive load of frustration growing lighter from week to week (15, 16).

## SUMMARY

1. *Choice* occurs in those numerous situations in which no reflex or automatic involuntary response is present and there are alternative courses of action open to the individual. *To will* is to choose a course of action, to foresee the probable results, and to exert effort to overcome obstacles.

2. A *conflict situation* is one in which the motives for the alternatives are nearly equally balanced. The response may be a clean-cut choice, a compromise, or a state of vacillation and indecision.

    a. *Indecision* is unpleasant; a decision may sometimes be achieved by further examination of the alternatives, by coming back to the choice after a rest, or by making an arbitrary choice.

    b. *Freedom of choice* is an expression of the individual's ability to mobilize additional motives to support one course of action.

3. When the satisfaction of a motive is blocked by conflict or other obstacles, problem-solving responses may be made. If this results in failure the individual may react emotionally. *Frustration* refers to the failure situation and the reactions it evokes.

    a. Frustration may be seen in situations in which a motivated individual is blocked by (1) an impersonal obstacle, (2) another person, (3) another positive motive in himself, or (4) a negative motive such as laziness, fear of punishment, or guilty conscience.

    b. Behavior in frustration is characteristically emotional, unintelligent and unadaptive.

        (1) Least thoughtful are reactions of *angry aggression, helpless anxiety, regression, fixation,* and *repression.*

        (2) *Rationalization* and *projection* are reactions which defend the individual against the admission of failure by placing the blame elsewhere.

        (3) More rational reactions sometimes are directed at

finding a substitute goal for the thwarted one. Examples are *sublimation, compensation,* and *fantasy.*

4. The process of growing up in a social environment involves numerous and recurrent frustrations. *Adjustment* is a way of dealing with a problem situation which does not create worse problems.

a. *Maladjustments* occur in all individuals, but in some persons they are so severe and persistent as to disrupt effective living. *Abnormal psychology* is the study of such extreme persons.

(1) *Neurotic* symptoms are severe manifestions of maladjustment. Different theories emphasize the importance of frustration of the child's demand for love and pleasure (Freud), or of the demand for superiority and achievement (Adler), or the need for security (Horney).

(2) *Psychoses,* or insanities, are more severe disorders involving most of the individual's activities, and usually requiring institutional care.

b. *Psychotherapy* depends on diagnosing the real source of trouble, which may date back to forgotten childhood, helping the person to face the facts clearly and with insight, and arranging environmental changes or reeducational opportunities which promote healthy adjustment.

(1) *Hypnosis* is a state of exaggerated suggestibility in which repressed memories may be revived and helpful positive ideas will be accepted by the individual.

(2) *Psychoanalysis* is a lengthy process of discovering childhood sources of conflict by recall, free association, and dream analysis, with subsequent interpretation and re-education.

(3) *Nondirective counseling* creates a permissive warm atmosphere in which the individual feels free to express his thoughts and feelings and in which he gains insight into his own problem and works out his own solution to it.

# CHAPTER THIRTEEN

# *Observing*

We have reached another turning point in our study. We are returning to the How question after devoting the last three chapters to the Why, the motivation of behavior. In the first part of the book, it will be remembered, we considered individual differences in ability and personality, and sought for their causes in heredity and environment. We concluded that individuals were bound to differ but that they could probably be much improved. From a practical standpoint what we have been considering in the subsequent chapters is the scientific basis for improving human behavior. We have seen how the individual develops through maturation, exercise and learning, and we have examined the motives that spur him on to activity.

Since the individual deals with the environment, it is important for him to know the environment and to master it sufficiently for his needs and purposes. He gets to know it by using his senses, and he acts on it and masters it to some extent by using his muscles. So much was said in the chapter on Interaction with the Environment, and something more was added in the chapter on Development. But we have left to this latter third of the book any full consideration of the question, how he knows and masters the environment. It is a difficult question but one on which psychologists have done a large amount of investigation. It branches out into many special questions on the senses, learning, memory and thinking.

The word *observation* in its everyday meaning points to the first of the main questions to be considered, the question how the use of the senses enables a person to get acquainted with the environment. The answer to this question will come partly from the study of the different senses in the following two chapters, but the present chapter will bring out some of the more general facts regarding this process of observation.

The question of how to get to know the environment is really a very practical question, though it is likely to lead into technical details which seem much less interesting, at first, than the study of motives, emotions and personality. When we analyze an unsatisfactory personality, we often find that the trouble is due to poor observation. Such a person does not notice what other people desire nor how they feel about things. He does not observe people sympathetically and so fails to understand them, and without understanding them he can scarcely hope to do the right thing by them. Again, many people complain of having a poor memory when the trouble is that they are unobservant. What they do not observe they cannot hope to remember. Observation is a topic of central importance in the whole field of psychology.

There are two steps in the process of observation. *Attention* is the preparatory step, the getting ready to observe. *Perception* is the final step, the actual observing of some fact. When some one says to you, "Observe this," or, more probably, "Notice this," he wants to have you *attend* to something in the hope that you will then *perceive* some interesting or important fact. A "poor observer"—and some people come to the psychologist complaining of poor powers of observation—may be one who is inattentive or one who is careless in perceiving facts. He may not notice the right things because of other interests, or he may not be clear and accurate in his observations because of difficulties to be indicated later.

## ATTENTION

*Attention* is another of those nouns that are properly verbs (p. 19). When a teacher says, "Please give me your attention," she really means, "Please *attend* to what I am going to say." When a person is said to have "strong powers of attention," the real meaning is that he can attend strongly to his work or to an object he is trying to observe. To attend is to concentrate your activity. The fact that everyone does attend, more or less, is a fundamental characteristic of the behavior of organisms. Instead of responding equally to the numerous stimuli received at a given moment, the organism responds selectively, focusing on one stimulus or one group of stimuli and practically neglecting the rest. The next moment the focus may shift to another stimulus. We can say the same thing in terms of attention. You attend to many objects, one after another, but at any one moment you are attending to a particular object out of the many that are present to your senses. You sometimes wish you could attend to two or more important objects at the same time or keep two or more interesting activities running simultaneously, but your powers are limited and compel you to focus on a single object or activity at a time. The word *attention* points to this limitation of an organism's powers.

In the chapter on Interaction with the Environment several elementary facts were brought forward that belong under the head of attention. Mention was made (p. 211) of "two main factors in dealing efficiently with the environment," factors which go by the names of *selectivity* and *set*. "Selectivity refers to the fact that the activity of any moment is *focused* on certain stimuli and certain responses instead of being spread over all the stimuli present and all the possible responses. Set refers to the fact that the organism is usually *prepared* at any moment for the stimuli it is going to receive and for the response it is going to make." To attend is, in short, to get set and ready to perceive a certain object or to perform a certain act. The runner on the mark is selectively set to catch the sound

of the pistol and to dash forward without delay. This is a case
of momentary attention, but mention was also made of a "set
to continue an activity" which is the same thing as "sustained
attention." The experiments on distraction and on "doing two
things at once," reported in that earlier chapter, belong here as
well. Along with the principle of selectivity two other principles were found to be important, the principles of "shifting"
and of "combination," and we shall see that all of these principles are important in attention and perception.

**Attention and consciousness.** You can attend to an object
such as an approaching automobile, to an act such as printing
your name very legibly, or to the thought of some absent
person or scene. Whatever you may be attending to, of that you
are fully conscious. You are more fully conscious of it than of
anything else at the moment, and yet you are somewhat conscious (or aware) of objects, acts and thoughts to which you
are not attending. If you are looking out of the window while
absorbed in some problem, you are most conscious of your
problem but you are somewhat conscious of the scene before
your eyes, and you are not wholly unconscious of sensations
from various parts of your body. Some physiological activities
of the internal organs lie entirely outside of your consciousness.
The total activity of an organism at any moment can be thought
of as divided into three concentric fields: the central field of
attention and full consciousness, the intermediate field of dim
consciousness, and the outer field of completely unconscious
processes. The boundaries between these fields are not perfectly sharp or perfectly fixed. The central field is sometimes
very narrow, as when for some reason you are trying to observe a minute object with great care; while at other times it is
broad enough to include a whole landscape, your interest being
to drink in the general impression. The intermediate field of
vague consciousness must usually be quite wide, including
everything visible except the object you are attending to, including the sounds you hear while attending to a seen object,
including a mass of bodily sensation, and including an undercurrent of feeling which may be more or less pleasant or un-

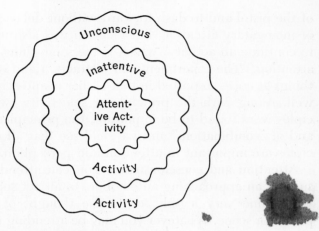

Fig. 86.—Some activity is clearly conscious, some only vaguely conscious, and some purely physiological and unconscious.

pleasant, more or less excited, more or less tense. Besides all this, often you are partially rather than fully conscious of where you are and what you are doing. If you are figuring out your accounts, that fact is in the background throughout the operation, while at any one moment you are focused on obtaining the correct sum of a certain column of numbers. Or again, if you are doing a routine job that is perfectly familiar, you can safely think of something else and be only partially conscious of this semiautomatic performance.

**Catching and holding attention.**    What do people attend to? At one time or another they attend to everything, large or small, new or old, abstract or concrete, pleasant or unpleasant. But they are more likely to attend to some things than to others, and the psychological problem is to find out what kinds of things are more likely to catch and hold attention. Many stimuli are competing for $O$'s attention, and we wish to know what factors give the advantage to one stimulus rather than another in this competition. The S—O—R formula will serve as a guide in seeking the answer. If $R$ is the response of attending, what factors in $S$ or in $O$ give the advantage to one object over others in attracting and holding attention?

[Certain kinds of *stimulus* have the advantage in attracting attention.]

The *intensity* of the stimulus is a factor. A strong stimulus is more likely to be noticed than a weak one. A loud noise has the advantage over a low murmur, a bright flash of light over a faint twinkle. With visible objects *size* has the same effect as intensity; the large objects, rather than the small details, are likely to catch the attention.

*Repetition*, or the summation of stimuli, is a factor. "Help, help, help!" will arrest attention when a single "Help!" would pass unnoticed. But if a stimulus is repeated many times, it ceases to hold attention because of its monotony. It yields to some other stimulus that has the advantage of change and novelty.

*Change* is a powerful factor. A steady noise ceases after a while to be noticed, but let it change in any respect and it catches attention. You become so accustomed to the steady ticking of a clock as scarcely to hear it, but if it stops you wonder what has happened. An object that starts to move is almost sure to catch the eye. Any change must have some degree of suddenness to be effective; a very gradual change may go to considerable lengths before being noticed.

*Difference* or contrast is very much like change in its effects. Anything that is very different from its surroundings is likely to stand out and catch the eye; it may be a dark spot in a bright landscape, or a red spot in a green field, or even a motionless spot in the midst of general movement. It may be a smudge on the smooth wall, or a tear in a garment. It may be an *x* in a mass of *o*'s, or an *o* in a mass of *x*'s.

| | |
|---|---|
| ooooooooo | xxxxxxxx |
| ooooooooo | xxxxxxxx |
| ooxooooo | xxxxxxox |
| ooooooooo | xxxxxxxx |
| ooooooooo | xxxxxxxx |

So much for the stimulus factors. [The *internal factors*, present in *O* at a given time, may be classified under two main heads: (1) the permanent or "structural" characteristics of the individual, and (2) the temporary factors of state and activity in progress (p. 209).

Among the permanent factors are the individual's habits of attention and inattention. He has learned to attend to certain things and to disregard other things. The automobile driver has the habit of listening to his motor, since the sound tells him whether the motor is laboring or running freely. The botanist has become attentive to such very inconspicuous specimens as the lichens on the rocks and trees. Habits of attention and inattention are established by the child through the influence of older people who point out to him what they regard as worth noticing. So he becomes acquainted with the things that other people know and his knowledge follows the traditional lines.

Among the temporary internal factors the most important is interest. You notice what is in line with your interest at the moment. In a show window the article you wish to buy catches your eye, even though other articles are more prominently displayed. The interest of the moment often takes shape in a question. The question of price comes to mind and immediately an inconspicuous price card catches your attention.

To catch attention is one thing, to hold it is another. The stimulus factors such as novelty and intensity attract attention, but some genuine interest must be tapped in order to hold attention for long. The principle of reinforcement comes into play (p. 286). An object of striking appearance catches your attention, and if it appeals to some interest of yours, the interest reinforces your momentary inclination to observe that object and holds attention there, while another article of equally striking appearance wins only a passing glance because it awakens no personal interest and so gets no reinforcement.

An advertisement must first of all catch attention by use of the stimulus-factors that have been mentioned. Illuminated street signs make much use of intensity and striking color; the flashing signs depend on change and repetition; and the big signs outbid the little ones. Newspaper and magazine advertisers competing for the reader's attention use similar devices. A picture, especially one with people in it, is often effective in catching the reader's attention for a moment. But to hold his attention the advertisement must appeal to some genuine interest. If the newspaper reader happens to be seeking a job, even a little "want ad," with all the factors against it except the factor of interest, will catch and hold his attention (2).

**Sustained attention.**   Attention tends to *shift* quickly from one object to another, as you can tell from watching a person's eyes while he is surveying a scene. Every second or two they shift from one point to another. And attention is even more mobile than the eyes, for often while the eyes remain fixed on an object attention will shift away from that object to some interesting thought. Even while one is lying in bed with the eyes closed attention shifts rapidly from one thought to another.

In spite of this continual shifting there is such a thing as sustained attention. An exciting game holds the spectator's attention. Not for an instant does his mind wander from the game. For all that, his attention is as nimble as ever. His eyes follow the movements of the players. He keeps pace with the game which is certainly mobile and changing. Sustained attention, then, is not rigid and motionless but consists rather in movement within a certain field of interest. It does not wander outside that field nor yield to distractions. The livelier it is within its proper field, the more surely it resists allurements to wander outside (p. 229).

Teachers sometimes complain of inattentive pupils, and students are known to complain of their own poor powers of attention. The trouble with the children is not inattentiveness in an absolute sense, but *attention to something else;* and this is usually the source of the students' difficulty, too. Not many of them get into the trance-like state in which there is no concentrated activity of any sort. With live young adults the main problem is to sustain attention in spite of competing interests. We can learn something here from the story reader. He is in little danger of dawdling and mind wandering; he leaves his other interests aside and presses forward eagerly to discover how the story is coming out. The efficient reader of serious matter has a similar eagerness. He sees the question at issue and presses forward to find the answer. Such a reader is both quick and retentive.

For the student the ideal sustainer of attention is of course a genuine interest in the subject. Any branch of science, literature or art will probably interest him if he can once advance far enough into it to discover how interesting it really is, but he may have to force himself into it by arousing such personal motives as fear of failure and determination to master the task he has undertaken.

There is a problem here for the speaker or writer who wishes to hold the attention of his audience. How shall he present his subject so as to secure sustained attention? He needs first of all to awaken in his audience an interest in the question which he is going to answer, and then he must lead the way to the answer without too many detours. Side issues which may seem worth while to him will lead the audience astray. Even illustrative examples, however necessary for clarifying his meaning, may be so interesting in themselves as to distract the audience from the main line of thought. The audience will often remember the example but forget the point it was meant to illustrate.

## PERCEPTION

The word *perception,* as we are using it, denotes the process of getting to know the environment by use of the senses. The definition should be enlarged a little, however, to do justice to the fact that the individual can discover facts about himself by use of his senses. He can observe that his skin is tanned or that a certain muscle is sore. Although these are not strictly environmental facts, they are objective facts and the process of observing them is the same as when attention is directed to external objects. The most correct statement, then, is that perception is the process of getting to know objects and objective facts by use of the senses.

The practical importance of perceiving and knowing objective facts is very clear when we consider the individual's relations with the environment. They are "active give-and-take relations," as was said before (p. 199). The individual is constantly dealing with the environment. He is acting on objects in the environment, and to act effectively he must know those objects, not completely of course but to some extent. He knows them through the senses, i.e., by means of the stimuli that reach his receptors. The stimuli come from objects in the environment, but the stimuli are not the objects. The stimuli and the objects are entirely different. When you see a lake down there in the valley, what happens is obviously not that the lake comes shooting up to your eyes, but merely that light reflected from the surface of the lake strikes your eyes. The light shimmers and you perceive that the surface of the lake is being ruffled by a breeze. You hear a low hum growing louder and louder, and you perceive that an airplane is approaching. Now an airplane is not a hum any more than a breeze is a shimmer or a lake a bright spot of light. The objective facts are somehow indicated to the observer by the stimuli he receives, but they are very different from the stimuli. How is it possible for the organism, confined as it is within its own skin, to know anything "out there" and deal with it effectively?

The problem of explaining how the individual can perceive objective facts is a fascinating but difficult one for the psychologist. Some help toward an explanation is provided by our old formula:

$$W—S—O_w—R—W$$

The environment is sending out stimuli which reach $O$'s receptors, and $O$ is responding by muscular movements which produce effects in the environment. The small $w$ attached to $O$ stands for the important fact that $O$ is *set* for the environment. At any given moment he is set for the present situation, so far as he has already perceived it, and he is set to reach some goal. He is trying to deal with certain objects and he is trying to perceive them sufficiently for his purpose. It does not follow that he can perceive them, but trying helps. He might be listening to a low hum just as a smooth tone, without caring about the source of the sound; but if he is trying to make out what that sound can be, he is more likely to perceive it as the hum of an airplane.

More than that—if he has already perceived the situation in general and built up a situation set, each new fact that he perceives must fit into the situation. If he is attending a football game, a sudden outburst of yelling does not suggest to him that a revolution has broken out, but only that one side has made a spectacular gain. He perceives the single fact in the light of the total situation. One fact perceived helps in perceiving further facts. This process of fitting facts together and so building up a knowledge of the environment begins as soon as the child starts to "take notice," and that is, probably, as soon as his cerebral cortex starts to function. With his cortex functioning the child already has this objective attitude of trying to perceive objects and do something with objects. He is not satisfied merely to receive stimuli; he is always trying to discover the meaning of the stimuli.

**Observing objects and observing stimuli.** In the main it is true that objects rather than stimuli are observed. But the stimuli are there and can be observed if the individual trains himself to hold his attention on the stimuli themselves and not, for the time being, to follow his natural tendency to pass at once from the stimuli to their objective meanings. With your eyes closed, lift a chair and report what you observe. You probably report that the chair is fairly heavy, an objective fact. But now ask yourself what actual stimuli you receive from the chair, and you will notice a pressure on the skin of the hand that lifts the chair, a pull at the elbow joint increasing till the chair comes up, etc. Normally, instead of noticing this pressure and pull, you notice the weight of the chair, i.e., you pass at once from the stimuli received to the objective fact indicated

by the stimuli. Similar examples will be cited under the senses
of sight and hearing.

Signs and meanings.   Perception is a process of utilizing signs
so as to get their meanings. Stimuli from the environment are
the signs; objective facts are the meanings. Several important
characteristics of perception emerge from a study of signs and
their meanings.

1. As has already been brought out, the observer is ordinarily
so intent on knowing the objective facts that he does not dwell
on the signs but passes as quickly as possible to their meanings.
In reading, which is one kind of perception, you seldom dwell
on the appearance of a printed word more than just enough to
catch its meaning. In many cases you perceive the facts without being able to point to the signs that reveal the facts. You
see clearly enough that a certain object is close by and another
object far away; but what are the signs by which you perceive
their distances? You perceive that a sound is coming from a
certain direction; but what are your signs of the direction of
the sound? Such problems call for keen psychological investigation, and one of the main tasks of the psychologist in his study
of perception is to discover the signs that are constantly being
used by everyone in perceiving objective facts. The psychologist often speaks of "cues" instead of signs. He asks, "What
are the cues of distance or of direction or of weight or of the
passage of time?" He experiments by excluding one cue after
another until the observer can no longer perceive the objective
fact. Thus he obtains some idea of the relative value of different
signs or cues.

2. The meaning of a sign must usually be learned from experience. There may be some signs of distance and direction
that are instinctive rather than learned, as would seem to be
true from the behavior of some young animals, but certainly the
multitude of signs that human beings use have been learned.
To follow up the question, how the connections of signs and
their meanings are learned, would take us too far afield, but
one fact should be noted. Signs are of two types, which may be
called *symbols* and *signals*. Symbols are stimuli which "stand

for" an object, as a name stands for a person and a word stands for a concept. The choice of any particular symbol is purely arbitrary in the first instance, but through constant use we learn the connection with its meaning so thoroughly that they seem to belong together naturally. A child who is learning names may ask how anyone could possibly have found out the names of the stars which are so far away.

Signals, on the other hand, have a more realistic and inevitable connection with their meanings. The signal of an object is typically some stimulus received from the object. Smoke is a signal of fire; the word "fire" is a symbol standing for fire. So the hum is characteristic of an airplane in motion, and shimmering light is a characteristic effect of a breeze blowing on a lake. By observing objects with their various characteristics the child learns to use certain characteristics as signals of the objects. He learns to take a smile as a sign of good humor and a scowl as a sign of crossness. A good share of the child's early self-education consists in observing how people behave under different circumstances, and in learning to perceive their attitudes and purposes from characteristic behavior signs. So he is making a start in what we may call social perception.

3. *Reduced cues.* In first getting acquainted with an object we like to observe it from all sides and put it through its paces so as to know all (or many) of its characteristics. Later, when it has become familiar, a single characteristic may be enough to reveal the presence of the object. The signal may be very sketchy in comparison with the whole object. Just a brief glimpse, a whiff of odor, or a snatch of sound will be enough. Such reduced cues save time and trouble though they sometimes lead to mistakes in perception.

4. *Ambiguous signs.* With its free use of reduced cues, perception is certainly a rapid-fire process, but it is not the sure-fire process it would be if every sign had only a single meaning. Stimuli are like words in that many of them have two or more meanings. A word such as "case" taken by itself is ambiguous, though its meaning will be clarified by the context, and so it

is with other signs. A stimulus may come from different objects according to circumstances, and which object will be perceived depends on the observer's situation set. If you are out in the fields at night, a large mass looming before you may be a distant mountain or a haycock a few feet away; both would deliver the same stimulus to your eyes. Any size of stimulus might come from any size of object according to the distance of the object. When looking at familiar objects in a good light you have no doubts and make few mistakes. But when the object is unfamiliar and not clearly presented, you may be confused and go through a series of *trial-and-error perceptions* before being satisfied. In night driving what seems at first to be a piece of road may soon reveal itself as the roof of a barn. Noises are often ambiguous. In one instance what sounded at first like distant thunder was perceived the next moment as somebody walking on the floor above. When touching an object in the dark you may perceive it as several different things before reaching a meaning that fits the situation and is accepted as satisfactory (reinforced).

Not only is it true that the same sign may have different meanings, but it is also true that different signs may have the same meaning. You view an object from different angles; it sends you different stimuli but is still perceived as the same object. You approach it and it looms large in your field of view, you go further away and it shrinks, and yet it appears to be of the same size. You see it in a strong light when it reflects much light into your eyes, and again in a dim light when it can reflect but little light, and yet it still appears white if it is a white object, or black if it is black. This important line of facts goes by the name of "perceptual constancy," which means that the same object will be perceived as the same and as having the same characteristics (within limits) in spite of the different stimuli which it sends to you under different conditions. There will be more to say about "constancy" in the next chapter.

"Ambiguous figures" are specially drawn so as to represent two or more objects equally well. The observer can readily perceive the different objects, but only one at a time. The

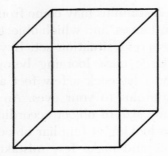

FIG. 87.—The ambiguous cube.

transparent cube drawing, showing near and far edges alike, is a famous example. Looked at steadily, this figure is seen in three different ways. It is seen simply as a flat drawing. But it is more likely to be seen as a cube, and the near and far sides of the cube change places from time to time if the drawing is examined steadily.

Another celebrated figure is the reversible staircase, which can possibly be seen as a flat drawing but is much more likely to appear either as the upper side or as the under side of a flight of stairs. If you look steadily at it for a long time, it will shift repeatedly from one appearance to the other. Since the drawing itself does not change, the shifting must be due to factors in the observer. He may fixate different parts of the drawing, and certain fixation points favor one appearance or the other, but with steady fixation the appearance will still shift in time while with change of fixation point the appearance may remain unchanged (10).

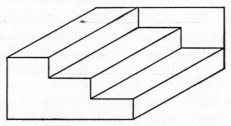

FIG. 88.—The reversible staircase.

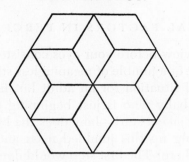

Fig. 89—An exceedingly ambiguous figure. Stared at for a long time, it may take on at least eight different appearances, some flat, others three-dimensional. The three-dimensional appearances are more interesting and have a definite advantage which points to a preference of the individual for seeing objects in the three dimensions. If there were no such preference or predisposition, the sketchy line drawing of persons, animals, houses and whole landscapes that do good service in children's books could scarcely have the realistic effect which they do have for the child.

The best theory of these shifting perceptions starts with the fact that any perception is a response of $O$ to stimuli received. When the stimuli are ambiguous, two or more responses are available, and after $O$ has made one response for a while he has had enough of it and shifts to another response. Perhaps a slight fatigue effect is involved. It is much the same sort of thing as was seen in shifting of attention, and there are many similar instances in reflex action and other simple forms of behavior.

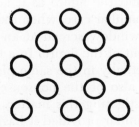

Fig. 90.—An example of shifting perception. This dot figure, if looked at steadily, may appear in several different forms and groupings (Sanford, 9).

## FIGURAL FACTORS IN PERCEPTION

If the field of view before your eyes consisted not of familiar objects at all, but of a jumble of meaningless stimuli, you would be in an unusual situation for an adult but in very much the situation of the baby who is just beginning to "take notice." How could you make a start—how does the baby make a start —toward breaking up this jumbled mass and perceiving the objects that are there? The first step would doubtless follow the principle of selectivity: some bright spot or moving spot would stand out, attract the eyes, and be seen more distinctly for a time than the rest of the field. The next step would probably be the appearance of some shape or figure standing out from its surroundings. This shape might be a space between objects rather than any one object. The baby sometimes looks intently at a corner of the room where there is a sharp contour that seems to fascinate him. He sees figures before he finds real objects, and the ability to see shapes must be a great help in perceiving objects, since most objects present quite definite shapes to the eye. Figure-seeing is an essential step toward object-seeing.

Figure and ground. When a figure "stands out," it stands out from a ground. A contour, more or less sharp, separates the two. To the adult observer, at least, the contour appears to belong to the figure and not to the ground. In the familiar case of an object standing out from its background, the ground seems to extend behind the figure as it actually does in that case. But in another familiar case, when the observer is looking through a lattice or window screen at an object beyond, the ground extends in front of the figure. In a third case the figure and its ground are actually in the same plane; this is true not only of pictures but also of the nonsense drawings used by psychologists in investigating this matter. They find that the figure need not be familiar provided it has some visible shape. If it is compact, it stands out strongly, but it may be comparatively large provided it has a definite total shape that holds its parts together. The ground itself may have some figure in it,

Fig. 91.—Reversible figure and ground (Rubin, 8).

especially a repeated figure like that of wall paper, but this is entirely subordinate to the main figure. In some drawings it is easy to make figure and ground change places—another example of shifting. When such a shift occurs, the appearance of the drawing changes greatly.

Figure and ground are not confined to the field of view but appear also in the world of sound. Often there will be a background of dull noises and a person's voice standing out as the figure. In music the tune (air or melody) stands out from the background of chords and accompaniment. The accompaniment may have a subordinate rhythmical and melodic figure of its own which enhances the total effect but is not allowed to submerge the main figure. From all these observations it seems certain that figure-finding is a natural process which plays an important part in perception.

**Building up a figure by combining parts.** When the field of view consists of a "jumble of meaningless stimuli," i.e., of a large number of spots of various colors and brightnesses, but without any familiar objects, these spots could conceivably be combined in many ways into various shapes. Some groupings, however, are natural and easy while others can be seen only with great difficulty. The psychological problem, then, is to discover the factors that make for ease of grouping. It is a companion problem to the one we met before under the head of attention, and we can once more take the S—O—R formula as a guide and look for S-factors or stimulus factors, and O-factors or internal factors which favor the response of combining certain spots into a figure. Psychologists make much use of dot assemblies in experimenting on this question.

The following *stimulus* factors are found (*6, 11*):

1. *Proximity*. Dots that lie near together are easily combined into a group, dots that lie far apart not so easily. Dots that lie far apart tend to fall into different groups.

2. *Similarity*. Dots that are alike are easily combined into a group. A collection of dots naturally breaks up into two combinations when the dots are of two shapes or colors.

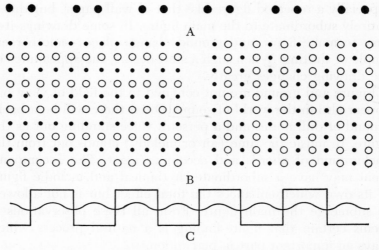

FIG. 92.—Dot assemblies showing the influence of proximity, similarity and continuity. In looking at each assembly, notice which is the easy and natural grouping. In A it is possible to group dots 2 and 3, 4 and 5, 6 and 7, etc., but it certainly is easier to yield to the force of proximity and group 1 and 2, 3 and 4, 5 and 6, etc. In B you can probably see columns or rows composed of dissimilar dots, but lines of similars are more easily seen. In C it would require much effort to resist the continuities and actually *see* a design made up of alternate parts of the wavy and angular lines (Wertheimer, *11*).

3. *Continuity*. Dots that lie along a straight line or regular curve are easily seen as so combined.

These factors operate in the auditory field as well as in the visual. Three drum beats close together in time are heard as a group, but three coming at long intervals are heard as separate beats. In listening to an orchestra, you readily combine a series of high notes, or a series of low notes, or a series of notes played by the same instrument, or any such series of similar notes. If the series also has continuity, as in running up or down the scale or following any regular tune, you are still more likely to hear such a series of notes as a unit.

The *internal factors,* or *O*-factors, are practically the same here as in catching attention. *Habit* based on past experience makes it easy to see familiar figures such as the letters of the alphabet or the shapes of familiar objects. *Set* is a selective factor enabling you to find figures if you are looking for them and to overlook them when you are looking for something else. These two factors are covered by the statement that you tend to see figures that are *meaningful* either because of your past experience or because of your present interest. There is an *esthetic* factor, too, shown by the fact that a symmetrical or pleasing figure will be seen while an irregular one is overlooked, and by the further fact that asymmetries and other defects are apt to be disregarded if they are not too glaring. A piece of music played on a piano that is slightly out of tune will sound all right to anyone who is not especially critical. One who is habitually critical or just now in a critical mood will notice the defects rather than the approaches to beauty. The principle of *reinforcement* operates in various ways in perception. What is meaningful is reinforced and emphasized and brought out clearly; what is pleasing is reinforced and made more pleasing; but what is defective may be emphasized and made still more unsatisfactory. One who is overcritical will actually take great satisfaction in the unsatisfactory.

**Hidden figures—camouflage.**   The factors which make it easy to see a figure must be borne in mind when for any reason it is desired to conceal an object which must nevertheless be left in

FIG. 93.—A hexagon more or less concealed by added
lines (Hanawalt, 4).

full view. A simple figure can be quite effectively concealed by embedding it in a larger figure which has characteristics of its own conflicting with those of the smaller figure. The slant of the smaller figure may be lost when certain additions are made, and its clean contour may be destroyed by simply prolonging some of its sides beyond the corners.

The contour of an object can be destroyed in another way, by avoiding contrast between the object and its surroundings. A soldier's helmet is painted or draped to match the terrain. A large object such as a ship can be so painted as to produce striking contours that are altogether different from those of the object itself. The proximity factor is responsible for the current rule that a body of soldiers must advance spread out instead of in close formation. It is still better if they can manage to get themselves grouped with rocks and bushes, utilizing proximity combined with some similarity of appearance. Good camouflage is shown by the protective coloration of animals (1, 3).

## ACCURACY AND INACCURACY OF OBSERVATION

Perception is sometimes sure and easy, sometimes difficult and uncertain. You cannot expect it to be perfectly correct all the time. Sometimes the stimuli received by the senses are ambiguous and do not enable you to identify the object, and sometimes two objects are so much alike that you cannot tell them apart with any certainty. If you are asked to tell which of two persons is the taller, it is easy when the two differ by several inches, but difficult when the difference is only half an inch. Telling two things apart, or observing a difference, is called *discrimination,* and evidently discrimination is easy

*U. S. Army Signal Corps Picture*

FIG. 94.—Camouflage.

when the difference is large, but difficult when the difference is small. In a discrimination test, the observer is shown two objects and asked to tell which is the larger, for instance, or which is the darker in color; or he lifts them and tries to tell which is the heavier. The purpose is to discover how small a difference in size or color or weight can be perceived—or how accurately such differences can be observed. This is one form of test for accuracy of observation.

In another form of test the observer is given a single object and asked to identify it, classify it, or estimate its size, weight, etc. He might be shown a specimen of wood and asked whether it is pine, maple, oak, walnut, redwood or mahogany. Here he depends on his memory as well as his senses, and the same is true when he is asked to estimate the length of a line in inches, or the weight of an object in pounds, or the temperature of the room in degrees.

Whether the observer's task is to *estimate* the size of a single object or to *discriminate* one object from another, he is bound to make some errors if the task is at all difficult, and these errors are especially interesting to the psychologist, who uses them as indicators of the observer's accuracy or inaccuracy. In order to determine the errors, the psychologist needs a good thermometer to tell him the accurate temperature, or a good balance to tell the accurate weight, or a good measuring instrument of some kind. Human ingenuity has provided these instruments to aid the senses in accurate observation; the psychologist uses them to ascertain the facts and then asks how accurately the facts can be observed without any such aids. The psychologist has to be interested in errors. For suppose that an observer gets through a test with no errors. That test is obviously too easy for that observer. How much better he could do we cannot tell until we have tried him with more difficult tests on which he begins to make errors. It is the same as with the high jump in athletics. We set the bar fairly low and the athlete clears it every time. We have to raise the bar until he begins to fail in order to get his measure. Both successes and failures must be taken into account in the measurement of any ability.

**The perception of number—the span of apprehension.** The height of the bar that the jumper can just barely clear might be called his "high jump span." It is his limit. There is a limit also to the amount of material that an observer can grasp or "apprehend" in a single act of perception, and this limit is his *span of apprehension*. Let the material to be grasped consist simply of objects of the same kind, such as oranges lying on a table. You look at them and say there are "a great many," or "several," or "just a few." Human ingenuity long ago provided a measuring device for obtaining the exact number by counting. But we wish to find out how well you can do, without

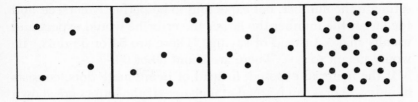

Fig. 95.—The number of dots in each collection is to be perceived or estimated from a single glance.

counting, by taking a single glance with attention directed to the number of objects. This is one of the oldest experiments in psychology, made at first with very rough apparatus. We place a few marbles in a small tray, you take a single glance and tell, if you can, how many there are. The span is about 5 or 6 if no errors are allowed.

In the laboratory we have exposure apparatus for displaying a card a fifth of a second or less, just time enough for a single view and not enough to look the card over or do any counting. The experimenter has cards containing different numbers of dots, and exposes the cards one at a time. The subject attempts to perceive or at least estimate the number of dots. With only 2, 3 or 4 on a card, he probably reports the number correctly every time; with 5 he may make an occasional error, and the errors increase till at about 12 exact perception of the number is entirely gone and the observer can only give an estimate. The span is not an absolutely fixed quantity, but varies somewhat from one individual to another and from moment to moment in the same individual. Sometimes the observer will be perfectly clear that the number of dots is 8, neither more nor less; while at other times he is not sure whether the number is 6, 7, or 8. But how can the observer ever grasp a number as large as 8 without the aid of counting? Mostly, it seems, by the aid of *grouping.* When there are only 3 or 4 dots they form a single group; when there are 7 or 8 they may fall into two groups. Unless they do fall instantly into small groups the observer cannot grasp a number greater than 5 in a single glance (7). That is, he cannot grasp it clearly and exactly. He can estimate the number, not expecting to be perfectly correct; and the larger the number the larger the error he would expect and usually make. Instead of saying, "There are 54 or 55 dots," he would be apt to say, "There are about 50 or 60."

If the material exposed, instead of being mere dots, consists of letters, 3 or 4 can be read at a glance. If the letters are shown combined into familiar words, 2 or 3 words can be read at a glance; and if the words are shown combined into a familiar phrase, the whole phrase containing as many as 20 letters can often be read at a single glance. In this experiment, as in ordinary reading, groups of letters rather than separate letters are being perceived.

**Constant and variable errors.** If collections of 12 dots are shown (interspersed with larger and smaller collections) the observer's estimates of the 12-dot collections will vary, perhaps all the way from 9 to 13. In technical language, he shows a *variable error*. And he is more likely to underestimate the number than to overestimate it; that is, he shows a *constant error*. His errors of observation can be broken down into these two, just as a marksman's errors in shooting at a target can be broken down into the variable error, shown by the scatter of his shots, and the constant error, shown by the preponderance of shots to the right or left, or above or below the bull's-eye. Constant error can be pretty well eliminated by practice with knowledge of results (p. 286), but the variable error of perception, or of any kind of activity, can never be wholly eradicated, for it is inherent in the organism. It can be diminished, however, by long practice.

Constant errors are sometimes quite large, and they themselves vary with the conditions. A minute, when you are impatiently waiting for it to come to an end (as in taking your temperature), seems incredibly long; but when you are working against time, a minute seems very short. The professor is shocked when the closing bell rings, and thinks that certainly the hour cannot be up, but some of the students have been consulting their watches for quite a while. In a court of law, when a witness is required to testify regarding the length of time occupied by a certain event, he is likely to give a very erroneous estimate. Whether he will overestimate or underestimate the time in question depends on his attitude and desire when he witnessed the event. Under conditions of tense waiting for something to happen, an actual time of one minute might seem to be fully five minutes.

**Weber's law.** In estimating the number of dots or marbles or oranges in a collection, your constant error may change from overestimation to underestimation as the number increases, or in some other way, for constant errors are rather unpredictable and dependent on special circumstances. But the variable error is predictable to this extent at least, that it will increase with the number of objects. In the same way, in estimating the weight of an object by lifting it, you will make a larger error when the object weighs several pounds than when it weighs only a few ounces. In estimating the length of a line you will not be off more than a fraction of an inch when the line is only an inch or two long, but you may err by a couple of inches when the line is about a foot long, and by several feet when the line is around 20 feet long. Your variable error in estimating a foot is about 12 times as great as in estimating an inch, and it is about 20 times as great in estimating 20 feet as in estimating one foot. *According to Weber's law, the variable error of estimate is strictly proportional to the quantity estimated.* This famous law, however, is approximately rather than precisely true. It does not hold for very small quantities (such as $\frac{1}{32}$ of an inch), where the error of estimate is relatively (not absolutely) large. Except for these very small quantities, the law is nearly enough correct to serve as a practical guide. Even a good observer would not undertake to estimate a length of about 20 feet to the nearest inch, and it would be absurd to demand any such accuracy from him, though he could easily estimate to the nearest inch a length of 10–15 inches.

Weber's law can be stated in several different ways. The statement just given applies to the task of estimating a single quantity. When the task is to discriminate two quantities, the law takes this general form: In any particular kind of percep-

tion, *equal relative differences* (*not equal absolute differences*)
*are equally perceptible.* A less general statement of the law is
that, in any particular kind of perception, *the least perceptible
difference is*—not a certain absolute amount, but—a *certain
constant fraction of the total quantity.* So, the least perceptible
difference in length is, not one inch or one foot or any such
absolute amount, but (under the most favorable conditions of
observation) about ⅟₅₀ of the length of the lines compared.
According to Weber's law, the least perceptible difference increases in direct proportion to the magnitudes compared.

According to the law, the difference between two weights of
10 and 11 ounces is just as easy to perceive as the difference
between 10 and 11 pounds. The difference is 1 part in 10 in
both cases. In illumination, the difference between 20 and 21
candlepower is just as perceptible as the difference between
400 and 420 candlepower, the difference being ½₀ in each
case. A difference of 1 part in 10 is much more easily perceived
in illumination than in weight; but that fact is not contrary to
the law, which states, for each separate kind of magnitude only,
that the stimuli must be in a constant ratio in order to make the
difference equally perceptible.

Different *kinds* of magnitude are, as a matter of fact, perceived with quite unequal accuracy. Perception of brightness is
probably the most accurate, as under favorable conditions a
difference of 1 part in 100 can here be perceived with very few
errors. Visual perception of length of line is good for about 1
part in 50, perception of lifted weights for about 1 part in 10,
and perception of intensity of sound for about 1 part in 4.

As an example of the data used to check Weber's law, we
cite an experiment in discrimination of brightness. The subject
sees before him a disk of white light; its upper and lower halves
are illuminated from two separate sources; the brightness of the
lower half is kept constant while the brightness of the upper
half is varied by the experimenter and compared by the subject
with the lower half. The experimenter starts with both halves
the same and increases the brightness of the upper half, step
by step, till the subject perceives the difference. The experi-

Fig. 96.—What the subject sees in an experiment on discrimination
of brightness: two semicircles of different brightness.

menter then starts with the upper half much brighter and di-
minishes its brightness, step by step, till the subject no longer
perceives any difference. The test is repeated till the average
difference is determined that the subject can barely perceive.
Suppose this difference to be 2 physical units when the lower
half of the disk has a brightness of 100 units; then the just perceptible difference is .02 of the basic brightness. The experiment is extended to other values of the basic brightness to see
whether this fraction is the same for all values, as it should be
according to Weber's law. The results obtained from one subject are given in the following table.

| Basic Brightness in Millilamberts | Just Perceptible Difference as a Fraction of the Basic Brightness |
|---|---|
| .01 | .35 |
| .1 | .13 |
| 1 | .05 |
| 10 | .03 |
| 100 | .02 |
| 1,000 | .02 |
| 10,000 | .02 |
| 100,000 | .03 |

One millilambert is the brightness of matt white paper lying on a table and illuminated by a 10 candlepower lamp (without reflector) one meter above the table. This is quite moderate brightness. (Reference to this classical experiment can be found in 5.)

Is Weber's law verified or not? Confining our attention to moderate and high intensities, we find the fraction nearly constant, but at low intensities it is much larger. Weber's law, then, is approximately a true statement for moderate and high intensities of light, but breaks down at low intensities (perhaps because the rods, not the cones, do most of the work at low intensities, p. 444) In the other senses, Weber's law has about the same degree of validity. It always breaks down at low intensities but stands up fairly well at moderate and high intensities. The basis of the law is probably physiological.

The practical importance of Weber's law is very great, especially in the use of the eyes to perceive objective facts such as size, shape and color. You see two men approaching from a distance, one slightly larger than the other. While they are still far away, they are very small figures in your eyes, but as they come nearer their figures become larger and the absolute difference between them increases while the relative difference remains the same. In agreement with Weber's law they appear the same to you, one slightly larger than the other, whether they are near or far; and this appearance agrees with the objective fact. Or you see two objects side by side in fairly dim light (but not too dim), both being gray objects but one slightly darker than the other. As the light increases both grays reflect more light to your eyes and the absolute difference between the two stimuli increases while the relative difference remains the same. In agreement with Weber's law you continue to see one as just slightly darker than the other—which is objectively correct since the two gray objects remain the same in spite of changes in the illumination. Weber's law is thus a help and not a hindrance to the perception of many objective facts. On the other side of the ledger, Weber's law points to the limits of our powers of estimation and discrimination. Why are the stars invisible by day? The stars are there and still sending their light through to us, but the background of the daytime sky is so bright that the stars are only imperceptibly brighter points of light. They are perfectly camouflaged by the brightness of the sky.

**Illusions.** When any process, physical or mental, goes wrong its inner workings may be more clearly revealed than when it is running smoothly. For that reason we can learn something regarding the process of perception from a study of illusions. An illusion is an error of perception. Any of the errors already studied might be called illusions but the term is usually reserved for errors that are large and surprising. An illusion consists in getting a false impression of the objective facts that are presented to the senses. The stimulus is ambiguous or misleading, and the observer falls into the trap and gets a false meaning from the sign received. Some illusions are due to external, physical causes and some to causes within the organism.

1. *Illusions due to physical causes.* The mirror illusion and the echo illusion are good examples. They are similar in that one is due to the reflection of light and the other to the reflection of sound. The mirrored object seems to be behind the mirror because that is the direction from which the light actually reaches your eyes; and the echo seems to come from somebody across the lake because the sound actually reaches you from that direction. These physical illusions have some psychological interest simply because *we learn to overcome them* and to perceive the objective facts in spite of the misleading stimuli. We even learn to make good use of mirrors in dressing and

driving an automobile. However, concealed mirrors can still fool us.

2. *Illusions due to habit and familiarity*. You are accustomed to use a certain stimulus (or combination of stimuli) as the sign of a certain objective fact. Usually your perception is correct but it may go wrong when a stimulus resembling the usual one is received, for the objective fact may be different. One illusion of this type dates from Aristotle (B.C. 330), the first man to write books on pyschology. Cross two fingers, and touch a marble with the crossed part of both fingers, and you seem to feel two marbles. A pencil can be used in place of the marble. In the usual position of the fingers, the stimuli thus received would be rceived from two objects, not from one.

Another good instance of this type of illusion is called the "proofreader's illusion," though the professional proofreader is less subjcet to it than anyone else. It is almost impossible to find every mispelled word and other typographical error in reading proof. Almost every book comes out with a few errors, in spite of having been scanned repeatedly by several people. Several misprints have purposely been left in the last few lines for the reader's benefit. If the word as printed has enough resemblance to the right word, it arouses the same response and enables the reader to get the sense and pass on satisfied.

3. *Illusions due to set and expectancy*. When you are all ready to perceive a certain fact you are liable to accept very inadequate stimuli as the signs of that fact. To take an extreme

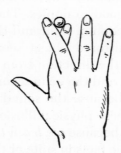

FIG. 97.—Aristotle's illusion.

case: an insane person hears the creaking of a rocking-chair as a voice calling him bad names. He expects to be reviled because he is preoccupied with his suspicions. In a milder form, similar illusions are often momentarily present in a perfectly normal person. While looking for a lost object you may mistakenly perceive it whenever you get a glimpse of any similar object. A mother, with the baby upstairs very much on her mind, hears him cry—so it seems to her—when it is only a cat yowling out of doors. The ghost-seeing and burglar-hearing illusions belong here.

4. *Illusions due to unanalyzed total impressions.* The stimuli received are often so complex as to conceal the objective fact that you wish to perceive. The real fact can only be got at by analysis and close attention to detail—a laborious process which anyone tends to avoid. Under this head belong a whole army of special illusions designed by psychologists. A figure is so drawn as to make it difficult for the observer to single out the fact he wishes to perceive. A famous example is the Müller-Lyer figure: two objectively equal lines or distances are so embedded in the total figure as to lead the observer astray. While wishing to compare the two particular lines he is much more likely to take the whole figure in the rough and compare the

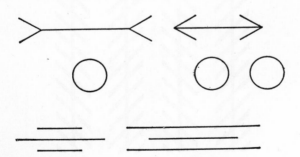

FIG. 98.—The Müller-Lyer illusion in three of its many forms. In the upper figure the two horizontal lines are to be compared in length. In the second figure the open space between the first and second circles is to be compared with the space including the second and third circles. In the third figure the lengths of the two middle lines are to be compared. All the six lengths in question are drawn to be objectively equal.

large masses instead of the particular lines. Illusions of this
type are of practical importance to the architect and dress
designer. An oblique line or complication of any sort is sure to
alter the apparent proportions of an object. A broad effect, a
long effect, a lopsided effect, may be produced by extra lines
in a dress or in the front of a building.

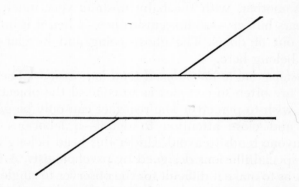

FIG. 99.—The Poggendorf illusion. Are the two oblique lines
parts of the same straight line?

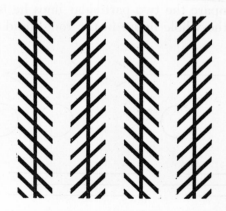

FIG. 100.—The Zoellner illusion. The long lines are really parallel. The
illusion is increased by holding the page in an oblique position. It is more
difficult to "deceive the eye" regarding horizontal and vertical lines than
regarding oblique lines.

If you hold the page flat and sight along the oblique lines you get a
three-dimensional appearance.

## IMPROVEMENT OF OBSERVING

On the important question of how to become a better observer the first thing to notice is the principle of selectivity. No one observes everything; no one could possibly do so, there is so much that might be observed even at a single moment. To be a good observer means first of all to observe what is most worth while, and this differs from person to person and from time to time. Since observation requires attention and attention depends on interest, it is clear that the good observer must be interested in what is worth while. It is well, then, to build up an interest in what is most worth observing and to give some thought to this matter. When two people are living or working together, for example, it is surely worth while for each one to observe the other's signs of pleasure and displeasure instead of forming a "habit of inattention" to the other person as so often happens between two close associates.

Having decided what you need to observe, you can improve by practice in observing this thing. Practice with "knowledge of results" is especially valuable. That is, you should have a check on the correctness of your observations, so as to reinforce the successful methods and discard the rest. Just for an example, not a very important one, you can practice estimating the temperature every morning and check by consulting the thermometer; so you can build up considerable ability in this specific kind of observation. Whether any such specific training is going to make you a good observer in general, a good all-round observer, is doubtful. It seems, rather, that each kind of observation, depending on specific interests and specific methods, has to be trained for itself. Still, there are some principles of good observation to be learned from the study of illusions and from the experience of scientific observers.

**Inferences from the study of illusions.** To judge from the different classes of illusions, poor observation results (1) from misleading stimuli, (2) from the force of habit and blindness to new impressions, (3) from preoccupation and bias, and (4) from being satisfied with total or general impressions. A good observer must be on his guard against these sources of error. In observing his friend, for example, the good observer must know whether his friend does not sometimes mislead him bv pretending to be pleased when really displeased. The gooa observer must be alert to slight changes in his friend's customary behavior. The good observer must guard against his own bias which may be in the direction of doubt and suspicion or in the direction of complacency. And the good observer must sometimes be specific and analytical and not satisfied to say merely, "Everything seems to be all right," or, "Something seems to be wrong." But we should notice that these sources of error are also factors in efficient observation. Once you know of the misleading stimuli, like those from a mirror, you can allow for them and make good use of them. Once you are well acquainted with a certain class of objects you can use reduced cues in perceiving them quickly and easily, while without past experience you would be lost and not know what to observe. Bias is certainly to be avoided, but a set for making a certain observation is necessary; without preparatory set you would be looking for nothing in particular and would probably observe nothing of importance. And without the ability to take in total impressions you would be lost in isolated details. What the good observer needs is some flexibility so that he can swing to the total impression or to the analysis of detail, to the regular routine or to the novel and unexpected, as the occasion may demand.

**Scientific observation.**   We should be able to learn something from the scientists on the essentials of good observation. The first thing we notice is their strong reliance upon observation. They submit their theories to the test of observation and abide by the result. All of us would probably become better observers if we imitated the scientists in this respect. The second thing to notice is that the scientist approaches nature with *questions to be answered by observation.* Of course he has his eyes open for unexpected phenomena, and his background of knowledge enables him to seize the significance of an unexpected phenomenon, as happens from time to time when striking discoveries are made "by accident." But in most instances he observes the answer to a definite question that he has in mind. A good question is a great sharpener of observation. Where possible, the best plan is to decide beforehand exactly what needs to be observed and then to focus attention on this precise point.

The scientist takes great pains to make his decisive observations as sure as possible. Instead of straining his eyes to see a small specimen, he uses a microscope. He invents instruments of precision and makes them as foolproof as possible. He repeats each observation and has it checked by another observer. He records his observations on the spot to avoid error of memory.

How does the scientist escape the error of bias in making his observations? Often he has a personal interest in a theory and cannot but hope, however devoted he is to the truth, that the facts will support his theory—or, perhaps, disprove someone else's theory. But he cannot afford to let bias creep in, because so much depends on his data. He may propose to make practical application of his findings, and certainly they are to be built into the larger edifice of his science, and if they are not right something is sure to go wrong. His fellow-scientists will discover the error. Science, even pure science, is a social enterprise, and the scientific group provides the best corrective for the bias of the individual.

In all these respects, the would-be good observer can learn from the experience of the scientists.

## SUMMARY

1. *Observing* is the process of knowing the environment by means of the senses. Two steps in observation are attention and perception.

2. *Attending* is selective observation—the process of getting set to perceive a particular object. Attention can be focused maximally on only one thing at a time.

a. Whatever is attended to is most fully *conscious*, but you are dimly aware of other things and activities at the same time.

b. Stimulus factors and internal factors determine what will catch and hold attention.

   (1) *Stimulus factors* include intensity and size, repetition, change, and contrast.

   (2) *Internal factors* include permanent characteristics of the individual such as his habits of attention, and more temporary characteristics such as interests and set.

c. Attention tends to shift quickly from one object to another. *Sustained attention* consists of shifts which are restricted to a certain field of interest.

3. *Perception* is the process of knowing objects and objective facts on the basis of stimuli from the objects which affect the senses.

a. Stimuli can be observed if the individual trains himself to attend to the stimuli themselves rather than the objects.

b. Psychology studies the *signs* (stimuli) by which we perceive the *meanings* (objective facts).

   (1) We often are not aware of the signs which furnish the basis for perception.

   (2) Signs are of two types: *symbols,* which are arbitrary names standing for objects, and *signals,* which are stimuli coming directly from the object.

   (3) Signals are *reduced cues*—often sketchy characteristics of an object.

   (4) Signs are sometimes ambiguous, and if a sign can represent two objects equally well, perception will shift from one meaning to another.

4. In perception, a *figure* stands out naturally from a *ground.*

a. If the field of view contains many meaningless items, they will tend to combine into a figure depending on their proximity, similarity, and continuity, and on internal factors such as familiarity, set, and pleasingness.

b. *Camouflage* is the concealment of an object by reducing its figural characteristics.

5. The accuracy of perception is measured by tests of *discrimination* and *estimation*.

    a. The *span of apprehension* is the number of items which can be correctly estimated in a single glance without counting. The span depends on the observer's grouping of the items.

    b. Errors of perception can be divided into *variable errors,* which scatter on both sides of the true value, and *constant errors,* which lie on one side. Variable error can be reduced but not eliminated by practice; constant error can be eliminated by proper training of the observer.

    c. *Weber's law* states that the variable error of estimate is proportional to the quantity estimated. It is true at moderate and high stimulus quantities, but the errors are disproportionately greater in estimating very minute stimulus quantities.

6. *Illusions* are striking examples of errors in perception. They illustrate fundamental principles of perception.

    a. The false localization of a mirror image or an echo is due to physical causes.

    b. False perception may result from habit and familiarity.

    c. Set may lead an individual to perceive (falsely) what he is expecting to perceive.

    d. The total impression may influence the perception of a part which the observer is unable to single out for independent perception.

7. Although the basic sensory abilities are unchanged, observation can be improved by developing interests which regulate the direction of attention, and by practice with knowledge of results.

    a. From the study of illusions it is clear that a good observer must be on his guard against misleading signs, against the blindness of habit or bias, and against being satisfied with total or general impressions.

    b. *Scientific observation* takes advantage of every means to secure accurate unbiased observation.

# CHAPTER FOURTEEN

# *The Sense of Sight*

O bservation, besides being considered in general as was done in the last chapter, can be investigated in much greater detail. An enormous amount of information is available on the senses, which have been studied by physiologists as well as by psychologists. Most of this material lies outside the scope of this book, but a few especially significant points will be brought to the reader's attention.

**What do we see?** The common-sense answer is that we see the objects that are before our eyes. But when we ask *how* we see the house over there, we learn that what we actually see is sunlight reflected from the house into our eyes. Do we see objects or do we see light? Do we see the colors of objects or the colors of light? This last question is a very practical one to the painter. Suppose his subject to be a white cow lying on the green grass in the shade of a tree. He sees the cow to be white and the grass to be light green, but if he lays on pure white for his cow and light green for his grass, he has altogether lost the shade of the tree. To reproduce the picture that he has before his eyes, he has to darken the cow and the grass, he has to paint the white cow gray and the light green grass dark green. The painter has to learn to see lights and shades and the color of the light, instead of the colors of objects. It is a difficult task for the novice in painting to see light and the colors of light— which might be called picture colors—and to get away from the customary seeing of objects and their colors. For ordinary purposes it is more useful to see the colors of the objects them- selves than to see the picture colors which those objects deliver to the eye at any moment. There is no doubt that ordinarily we go as far as we can away from seeing light and toward seeing objects.

**Sensation and perception.** Evidently there are two mean- ings of the verb "see," and it would be desirable to have two psychological terms to mark the distinction. Let us call the see- ing of light by the term "visual sensation," and for seeing objects or environmental facts let us use the term "visual per- ception." Similarly in the case of smell, olfactory sensation is the sensing of the odor stimuli that enter the nose, while olfac- tory perception is the noticing of odorous objects present in the neighborhood. In general, when we speak of sensation we are thinking of stimuli and investigating the relationship of the in- dividual's experiences to the various stimuli which reach his receptors; and when we speak of perception we are thinking of objects and are investigating how well the individual's experi- ences correspond with the objective facts. In his practical life of relation with the environment, the individual is bent on percep- tion; but his receptive apparatus seems built for sensation. He certainly knows the environment only by utilizing the stimuli received.

## MECHANISM OF THE EYE

Before following up any further the process of seeing objects, we need to know something of the eye and of visual sensation. The eye, of course, is only part of the visual apparatus. The eyes are connected by their sensory nerves, the optic nerves, with the interbrain, and this in turn with the occipital lobes of both cerebral hemispheres. The eyes receive the stimuli, which produce nerve currents passing back to the interbrain and cor-

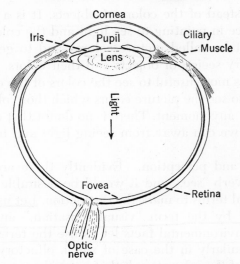

FIG. 101.—Horizontal section of the eyeball.

tex, and in the cortex occur the processes which make possible the grouping, patterning and recognizing of objects (p. 262).

The human eye is a registering optical instrument, like the camera. In fact, it is a camera, the sensitive plate being the *retina,* which differs from the photographic plate in recovering after each exposure so as to be ready for the next. Near the front of the eye, where light is admitted, is the colored *iris,* with the hole in the center that we call the pupil of the eye. The iris has little muscle fibers in it, which regulate the size of the pupil; it corresponds to the adjustable diaphragm of the camera. At the front of the eye is the curved, transparent *cornea,* which is a powerful lens. Just behind the pupil is another *lens,* adjustable in curvature by the action of the little ciliary muscle. This muscle corresponds to the focusing mechanism of the camera; by it the eye is focused on near or far objects. Transparent fluid allows light to pass through to the retina. The retina is a thin membrane, lining the rear of the eyeball, and containing the sensitive cells, from which neurons make connection to the brain.

**The visual receptors.** The retina contains sense cells of two

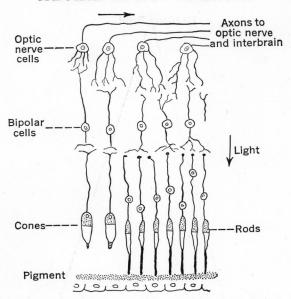

FIG. 102.—Sense cells and nerve cells of the retina. The light, reaching the retina as shown in Figure 101, passes through the nearly transparent retina till stopped and absorbed by the pigment layer, and there produces chemical changes which stimulate the tips of the rods and cones. The rods and cones pass the impulse along to the bipolar cells and these in turn to the optic nerve cells. The axons of these latter cells extend by way of the optic nerve to the interbrain. See page 259.

forms, the *rods* and the *cones.* The incoming light produces chemical and electrical changes in the rods and cones.

The cones are more highly developed cells than the rods. At the *fovea,* a little depression in the retina, straight back from the pupil, only cones are present, and this is the "center of clear vision." In looking straight at a small object so as to see it distinctly, we turn the eyes so that the light from that object falls on the fovea. Outside of this little central region, rods and cones are intermingled, with fewer and fewer cones the further out in the retina you go. The further out you go, also, the less distinctly both form and color are seen, from which fact it is inferred that form and color vision depend mostly on the cones.

**Eye movements.** The eyeball is turned in its socket by six

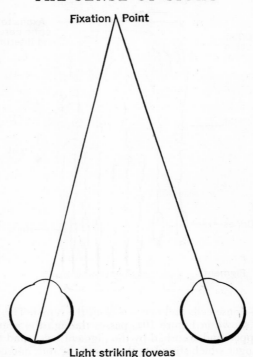

Fic. 103.—Convergence of eyes on near fixation point. When looking at a distant object convergence is unnecessary and the eyes assume their parallel position.

muscles, and the two eyes are so harnessed together in their motor nerve centers that they show almost perfect team-work in their movements. They execute two types of coordinated movement. In looking here and there about the landscape, the two eyes turn like a pair of horses in parallel, and this is the *conjugate* movement of the eyes. But in turning from a far to a near object, the eyes *converge*, so that the foveas of both eyes receive the light from the particular object looked at.

The conjugate movement, on being recorded photographically (2), is found to have two varieties, called the jump or *saccadic* movement and the *pursuit* movement. The saccadic movement carries the eyes from one object to another, while the pursuit movement follows a moving object.

Watch the eyes of someone who is looking at a scene and you will see them jumping from one part of the scene to another. The eyes fixate one point for a short time, jump to another point and remain there for a moment, and so on about the field of view. In reading, as the result of practice, the eyes follow a more regular procedure, fixating a series of points in a line of print, with short jumps from each fixation point to the next, and a longer reverse jump to the beginning of the next line (p. 226). As each jump occupies but a thirtieth to a fiftieth of a second, while the fixation-pauses between jumps last much longer, the result is that over 90 percent of the time spent on a line of print is fixation time, less than 10 percent being consumed in making the jumps. It has been found that nothing of any consequence is seen during the jumps, and that the real seeing takes place only during the fixations. The saccadic movement is simply a means of passing from one fixation to another with the least waste of time.

The eye sees an object distinctly only when stationary with respect to the object. If the object is still, the eye must be still. But if an object is moving with moderate speed, the eyes can keep pace by a pursuit movement, so remaining fixed upon the moving object, and getting a clear picture of that object, while the stationary background is reduced to a blur.

**Adaptation of the retina to dim and strong light.** The first reaction of the eye to change of illumination is a widening or narrowing of the pupil. A slower but more effective change occurs in the retina itself, and sensitizes the retina to the degree of illumination. Go into a dark room, and at first all seems black, but by degrees, provided there is a little light filtering into the room, you begin to see, for your retina is becoming dark-adapted. Come out of the dark into a bright place, and at first you are "blinded," but you quickly get used to the bright light and see distinctly, your retina having become light-adapted.

Complete dark adaptation requires a stay in the dark of half an hour, and leaves the eye a full million times as sensitive to faint light as on first entering the dark from bright sunlight.

While in the dark, after becoming dark-adapted, you will notice that you see only light and shade and no colors. Another significant fact is that the fovea, which has only cones and no rods, does not become well dark-adapted and is almost blind in very dim light. These facts mean that vision in dim light, or *twilight vision* as it is called, is rod vision and not cone vision. The rods become sensitized to very faint light, far outstripping the cones in this respect. On the other hand, not the rods, but only the cones, have color vision.

Individuals differ considerably in their powers of dark adaptation. Lack of vitamin A in the diet prevents the formation of "visual purple," a chemical pigment in the rods. Individuals whose diet is deficient in vitamin A show some degree of night blindness, due to imperfect dark adaptation. In an experiment to test the importance of vitamin A, "all dairy products, colored vegetables, liver, kidney and other selected foods" were excluded from the diet of a healthy young man for a period of 34 days (all other requirements except vitamin A being supplied). His power of dark adaptation declined gradually till the sensitivity of the cones was reduced to $\frac{1}{3}$ of normal, and that of the rods to $\frac{1}{9}$ of normal. At the end of the period ample amounts of vitamin A were administered and the subject's dark adaptation promptly returned to normal (16). The small differences in sensitivity of twilight vision among normal persons, however, are not usually due to vitamin A deficiency, and cannot be corrected by eating carrots.

## VISUAL SENSATION

**The stimulus for vision.** Without going into the physics of light to any extent, we can say that light is electromagnetic energy of wavelike character, so that we can speak of its *wave length*. In the rainbow, or spectrum, light of the different wave lengths is separated and spread out in order before us. At the red end of the spectrum, the wave length of the light is 760 millionths of a millimeter, and at the violet end it is 390 millionths. In between are waves of every intermediate length, appearing to the eye as orange, yellow, green and blue, with all their transitional hues. A wave length of 580 gives yellow, one of 520 gives green, one of 480 gives blue, etc. Outside the limits of the visible spectrum, there are longer and shorter waves, incapable of arousing any sensation of light, though the long waves, the infrared, excite the warmth sense of the skin, and the very short waves, the ultraviolet, while arousing none of the senses, do tan the skin and produce other physiological effects.

Seldom does the light reaching the eye from any point consist of waves that are all of the same wave length. Sunlight contains waves from all parts of the spectrum and appears as white. The light from an electric bulb appears pale yellow because while containing waves from all parts of the spectrum it is relatively strong in the middle wave lengths. Light that has passed through a sheet of good red glass comes out pure red because all but the red waves are strained out by the pigment in the glass. Thus light varies in amount of *mixture* of different wave lengths. Light varies also in *intensity* or energy.

The stimulus entering the eye from any point can vary, then, in three ways: in wave length, in energy, and in amount of mixture; and we now ask what difference in sensation corresponds to each of these differences in the stimulus.

**Dimensions of visual sensation.** To the energy or intensity of the stimulus corresponds the *brilliance* of the visual sensation. The brilliance dimension of visual sensation extends from dark to light—from absolute darkness to glare.

To the wave length of the stimulus corresponds the *hue* of the visual sensation. The hue series extends from red through yellow and the other colors of the spectrum to violet and then by way of the purples back to red again. It is a circular series, as indicated in Figure 104.

To the mixture of wave lengths in the stimulus corresponds the *saturation* of the color sensation; the more mixture the less saturation. A full, pure color is saturated, a pale or a dull color is unsaturated. A saturated color need not be very bright, and a bright color need not be saturated at all. Pink and reddish

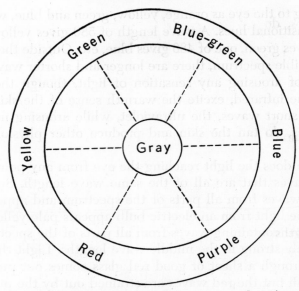

FIG. 104.—The color circle. Complementary colors (see later) are placed diametrically opposite each other.

brown are both unsaturated red; pale blue and bluish gray are alike in being unsaturated blue. See Color Figure A, facing page 446.

These are the general correspondences between the physical light and the visual sensation, but the whole relationship is much more complex. Brilliance depends, not only on the energy of the stimulus, but also on its wave length. The retina is most sensitive to waves of medium length, corresponding to the yellow of the spectrum. A given amount of physical energy arouses a much stronger light sensation if its wave length is medium than if it is near the red or the blue end of the spectrum.

Color mixing. Hue, as has been said, depends on the wave length of the light stimulus, each hue being a response to one particular wave length. But this is not the whole truth. Any hue can be got without its particular wave length being present at all, by mixing wave lengths lying on both sides of this particular one. For example, the orange color given by wave length

# A

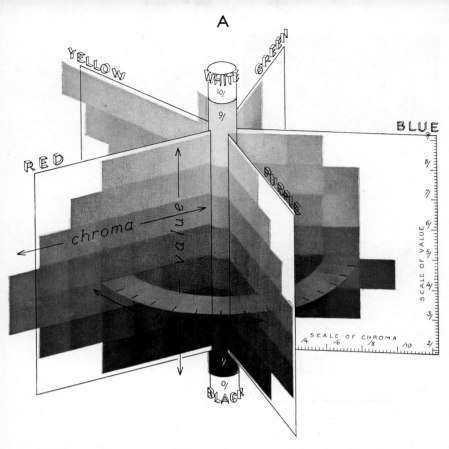

**A** MUNSELL COLOR SYSTEM. This is a diagram of the Munsell system for relating and describing pigments and other physical standards. The three variables of color sensation are assigned to three dimensions of space: *value,* or brightness, is vertical; *chroma,* or saturation, extends outward from the neutral axis; and the *hues* are arranged around the axis.

The actual Munsell papers are highly accurate laboratory standards produced (from pigments tested for permanency) under controlled conditions to specified tolerances. The colors displayed in the diagram are produced from printing inks and are only approximations of the Munsell standards. The number of colors shown is limited by the need for simplicity and by the lack of printing inks of stronger chromas. The Munsell space plan provides for the exact designation of an unlimited range of pigments.

Using this diagram, make an estimate of the hue, value and chroma of colors around you, such as a book cover or necktie.

*(The color plates on this and the following three pages were prepared by Dean Farnsworth, Lt. Comdr., H(S) USNR, especially for this book.)*

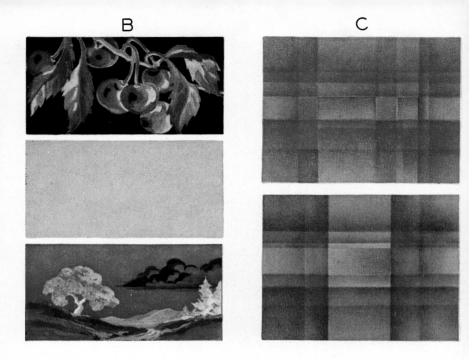

**B** INDUCED AFTER-IMAGES. Place book under a strong light, such as a desk lamp, stare at the cherries for 10 or 15 seconds, and then look at the gray square. Repeat with the landscape. How much detail is retained? Are all the after-images exactly complementary to the original color? What relation has this demonstration to color negatives in color photography?

**C** SIMULTANEOUS CONTRAST. Punch or cut a hole in a card and, holding it near the eye so as to exclude the rest of the page, look through it at one of the plaids. Try to describe each color accurately and note the effect of juxtaposition. In order to see the independent colors of the pigments, place the card right against the page. Note that when isolated the center rectangles of the two plaids do not match and are not actually gray. The esthetic quality of color depends heavily upon induced color contrast. Note its use in decoration and dress design.

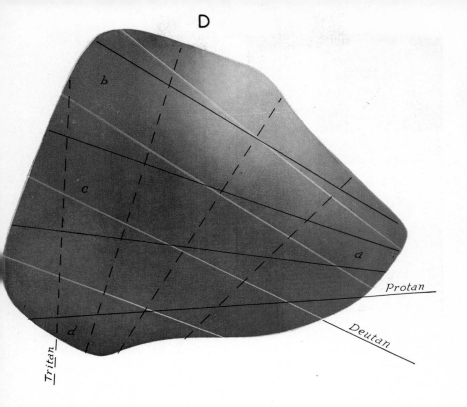

**D** ZONES OF COLOR-BLIND CONFUSIONS. The question "How do color-blind persons see?" is well answered by this chart. Protanopes confuse the colors which lie within the zones indicated by black lines; deuteranopes confuse the colors within the zone indicated by the white lines; and tritanopes (a rare type) confuse the colors within the dashed lines. For example, the spot at *a* and the spot at *b* will look alike, or nearly alike, to a deuteranope; but the spot at *a* will appear about the same as the spot at *c* for a protanope; but *b, c* and *d* would appear about alike to a tritanope. It is upon these systems of color confusion that most tests for color deficiency are based.

Protanopes are commonly called "red blind," deuteranopes called "green blind." Is it apparent from the chart why the latter names are oversimplifications and misleading?

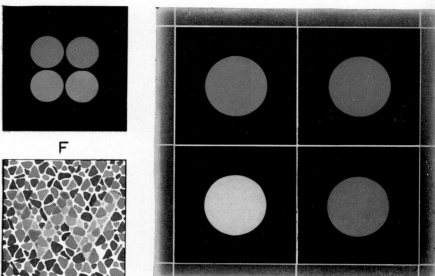

**E** FOVEAL COLOR VISION. The colors of lights and pigments depend upon the area of the retina upon which the image falls. When viewed at reading distance the image of the colors in *E* is large enough to extend beyond the fovea. Notice how distinct they are. Set the book at a distance of 8 or 10 feet and observe the change in color when the light falls only on the fovea; then fixate a little to one side of the spots and see what the colors are when viewed just outside the fovea. At reading distance again, notice which colors can be recognized out of the corner of the eye.

**F** A "POLYCHROMATIC" PLATE. This is a simple test for color deficiency. A color normal will see a colored "W" against a gray background. Deuteranopes will see one "V" more clearly; protanopes will see the other "V" more clearly. Can you pick which "V" will be seen by each type?

**G** BINOCULAR FUSION AND RIVALRY. Hold the page a few inches from the eyes, so that the green circle is before the left eye, the red one before the right eye, and let the eyes relax. Can you by superimposing the red and green figures secure a yellowish color? By overlapping the yellow and blue-purple, can you secure a neutral? What colors would you expect to result from a mixture of red and yellow, green and blue, red and blue? You can make these mixtures by turning the book sidewise and at a 45° angle. The fusion experiments must be performed under a strong light. The effect of "rivalry," an alternation of the two color impressions, must be suppressed in order to achieve fusion.

650 is given also by mixing wave lengths 700 and 600; a mixture of red and yellow lights gives orange.

A point of experimental technique: in mixing colored lights for the purpose of studying the resulting sensations, we do not depend on mixing paints, but we throw both lights together into the eye or on a white screen. We can also, by virtue of a certain lag or hang-over in the responses of the retina, mix lights by use of the "color wheel," which throws them in rapid alternation into the eye.

By mixing black and white in different proportions we obtain the whole series of dead grays. By mixing white or gray with any saturated color we make it less saturated. By mixing black with any color we lower the brilliance of that color.

By mixing red and yellow, in different proportions, we get all the hues intervening between red and yellow—all the oranges. By mixing yellow and green we get all the yellowish greens, and by mixing green and blue, all the greenish blues. Finally, by mixing blue and red, we get violet and the purples. Purple has no place in the spectrum, since it is a sensation which cannot be aroused by the action of any single wave length, but only by the mixture of long and short waves.

Now what happens if we add yellow to blue? Those who know about mixing paints will say that blue and yellow will give green; but mixture of paints is decidedly not adding lights, for each paint *absorbs* or subtracts part of the light, and the effect of the double subtraction is very different from *adding* blue and yellow. If we add blue and yellow, we get white or gray. Two wave lengths which, when acting together on the retina, give a white or gray sensation, are called *complementary*. Yellow and blue, then, are complementary. The complementary of red is bluish green, and that of green is purple.

Red and green are not complementary but, like blue and yellow, may be called a *disappearing color pair*. When we mix blue and yellow, both disappear, and we get the sensation of white, in which there is no resemblance to either yellow or blue. When we mix red and green, too, both disappear, and the sensation of yellow emerges.

**Elementary, primary and salient hues.**   There are hundreds of distinguishable colors and every one is simple or elementary in that we cannot actually *see* any other colors in it. We can see the resemblance of orange to both red and yellow, but as we look at the orange color we do not actually see a good red and a good yellow. The red and yellow are so perfectly blended in the orange as to lose their own specific qualities, and the orange has a specific quality all its own. In this respect all colors are equally elementary.

But some colors are more salient or outstanding than others. White and black are the clearest examples. They are the extremes in the white-black series of grays, and there is no gray in the series that stands out above the rest. If the hues are arranged in a circle, red, yellow, green and blue stand out and might well be made the corners of a square diagram to be substituted for the circle.

It would seem reasonable to conjecture that the salient colors are also primary and that all the other colors are derived from them by combination. At least, it is reasonable to suppose that the retina has just a few primary activities which go on together in varying proportions and give numerous resultant effects.

The facts of color mixture suggest a very small number of primaries, since all the hues, and also white and gray, can be obtained by mixing four wave lengths corresponding to red, yellow, green and blue. Moreover, yellow is not needed since it is obtained by mixing red and green. All the colors, including white, can be obtained by mixing red, green and blue in the proper proportions. This striking fact is the basis of the well-known Young-Helmholtz (6) theory of color vision, which assumes just three primary responses of the retina to light, giving the sensations of red, green and blue.

**Color-blindness.**   There are two main kinds of color-blindness, total and partial. *Total color-blindness* amounts to rod vision, which gives light and dark, but none of the spectral colors. The outermost zone or ring of the normal retina, where cones are very scarce, is almost totally color-blind. Some individuals, very few, are totally color-blind over the whole retina, having apparently no cones but only rods; their daylight vision is poor, as would be expected.

[*Partial color-blindness,* though uncommon among women, is present in 6 or 8 per cent of men.] It is not a disease, and is not associated with any other defect of eye or brain. Nor can it be cured or corrected by training. It is simply a hereditary peculiarity of the color sense, a reduced or simplified form. The partial-color-blind individual is unable to distinguish all the hues, and he therefore confuses certain colors seen by the normal individual. His range of colors can be duplicated by mixtures of only two wave lengths instead of the three which are necessary to produce the full scale of colors. There are three kinds of partial color-blindness in which different sets of hues are confused (see Figure D). The most frequent kinds are those in which reds and greens are confused, and individuals of this sort are often referred to as red-green blind. They are not blind of course—they see something when looking at reds and greens—but they do not see as many different colors as normal individuals. We have learned from a few persons who are red-green blind in one eye and have normal color vision in the other eye that the red-green blind has the sensations of yellow and blue, along with white, black and the grays—but no red or green. What appears to the fully equipped eye as red or green appears to him as dull yellow, and what appears to the normal eye as greenish blue, violet or purple appears to him as dull blue. He has difficulty in picking strawberries, in obeying the traffic lights, and in selecting his neckties, because red and green are not differentiated.

Now everyone is red-green blind in the intermediate zone of the retina, between the central region which has full color sense and the outermost zone which is almost totally color-blind. This statement can be checked by taking bits of various colors and moving them slowly from the very margin of the field of view towards the center, all the while keeping the eyes directed straight ahead. When the bits first become visible, at the margin of the field of view, they have no color other than gray, then they take on a blue or yellow tinge, and finally, near the center of vision, they acquire their red or green components and show in their true colors. See Figure E.

These "zones" are not sharply separated. An intense, saturated color can be recognized farther out from the fovea than a weak color. At high intensities red, yellow and blue are perceived even out to the periphery of the field of vision.

**After-images.**   A better name would be after-sensations. Any response outlasts its stimulus. This is true of a muscle, and it is true of a sense organ. The ear is very quick in recovery, and gives almost no after-sensations, but touch after-sensations can easily be felt after a momentary touch on the skin. Visual after-sensations are the most interesting. If you look toward a lamp, but with a book in front of your eyes to serve as a screen, remove the screen for an instant and then replace it, you continue for a short time to see the light after the stimulus is cut off. This *after-lag* is like the main sensation, only weaker. The *after-image* can be obtained by looking steadily at a black-and-white or colored figure for fifteen seconds, and then looking at a gray background. See Figure B. An after-sensation develops in which black takes the place of white, and white of black, while for each color in the original the complementary color now appears. When so appearing, the after-image is "negative," but it can be transformed into a positive by closing the eyes or turning them upon a black background. After strong stimulation the after-image may last for a long time and be switched back and forth repeatedly between the positive and the negative. The colors, however, are rather undependable. The after-image of a bright white light may go through a long sequence of different colors before it disappears.

**Visual contrast.**   Contrast is another effect that occurs in other senses, but most strikingly in vision. After looking at a bright surface, one of medium brightness appears dark, while this same medium brightness would seem bright after looking at a dark surface. After looking steadily at one color, and then turning the eyes upon the complementary color, the latter appears more saturated than usual; in fact, this is the way to secure the most saturated color sensations—it is worth trying.

These successive contrast effects are essentially negative after-images.

Simultaneous contrast is peculiar to the sense of sight. If you take two pieces of the same gray paper, and place one on a black background and the other on white, the one on black looks much brighter than the other. Spots of gray on a colored background are tinged with the complementary color. Any two adjacent colors produce contrast effects in each other, though we do not usually notice them any more than we notice the after-images which surely occur many times in the course of a day. We disregard sensations that do not indicate objective facts. See Figure C.

A word should be added about *black*. Black is sometimes said to be simply the absence of light. But black is as positive a sensation as any. We even speak of an "intense black." Black is a response made to the absence of light, but it occurs in its full intensity, as absolute black, only just after light is withdrawn from the eye, or else in an unlighted area surrounded by light. An object may reflect considerable light to the eye and yet be seen as black if the surrounding field is very much brighter, for example, a piece of coal in direct sunlight.

## VISUAL PERCEPTION

When you look out of the window on even the most ordinary scene, what you see is simply astounding. It is so to a psychologist. You see objects of various shapes, sizes and colors, lying at different distances, some of them in sunlight and some in shadow. What is there strange about all that? The strange thing is the great divergence between this objective situation which you perceive, and the medley of juxtaposed color patches which is all your retinas get from the environment. Move about a little while watching the scene; you see constant motion in the visual field—in the picture, we may call it—yet the objects do not seem to move. Look at a near-by object like a table or chair from different positions, and the picture is very different; yet the object looks the same. The stimuli change but the appearance remains the same. Things appear to the observer as they are objectively, not as they are pictured on the retina.

That there is a problem here will be brought home to anyone who, without previous experience in drawing or painting from nature, attempts to reproduce the picture his eyes give him. Like the child or the primitive artist he will doubtless try to put on the canvas what he sees to be out there in space. The realistically inclined painters struggled for centuries to discover what was in the visual picture, as distinguished from what was out there in space. Their job was to put on canvas, as far as possible, the same aggregate of color patches as the scene presents to the retina. Instead of interpreting the stimuli from an object, as we do in practical life, the painter has to disregard the object and reproduce the stimuli.

**Seeing distance or the third dimension.**   The stimuli received from the environment are spread out in two dimensions on the retina like a picture projected upon a screen. The picture has the left-right and up-down dimensions, but no front-back dimension. How then does it come about that we see the distance of objects from us, and the solidity and relief of objects? This problem in visual perception has received much attention and been carried to a satisfactory solution.

A *single, motionless eye* receives a picture similar to one painted on canvas, and the available indications of distance are the same in the two cases. The painter uses *perspective*, or foreshortening, and makes a man smaller in the picture when he wants him to appear farther away; and in the same way, when any familiar object casts a small picture on the retina, we perceive the object, not as diminished in size, but as far away. The painter colors his near hills green, his distant ones blue, and washes out all detail in the latter—*aerial perspective,* he calls this. His distant hill peeks from behind his nearer one, being partially *covered* by it. His *shadows* fall in a way to indicate the relief of the landscape. These signs of distance also affect the single eye and are responded to by appropriate spatial perceptions.

Ewing Galloway

Fig. 105.—Signs of distance.

If the head is moved from side to side, while the eye continues to look forward, distant objects seem to move with the
head, and nearer objects to slide in the opposite direction. Try
this in the woods some time, and see how clearly the nearer
and farther branches are distinguished. If you look to the side
from a rapidly moving train or car, the effect is still more pronounced.

**Binocular perception of depth.** An observer looking at a near
object sees the third dimension more clearly with two eyes than
with one. The signs described above are unchanged but there
are two important additional signs.

1. *Stereoscopic effect.* The two eyes get slightly different

views of the same object. If you hold your finger up near your face and look at it first with the right, then the left eye, you will notice that you can see more of the fingernail in one case. The right eye sees a little more around to the right, and the left eye a little more around to the left. The brain responds to these slightly different simultaneous views of the same object by seeing the solidity of it, its third dimension.

Judgment of distance is correspondingly more accurate with two eyes. Take a pencil in each hand, close one eye and bring the pencil points horizontally from the two sides till they seem to be almost touching; then open the other eye, and see if you can improve the setting.

2. Another binocular sign of distance is afforded by *double images*. When the eyes are converged on a near point, more distant objects are seen double; and when the eyes are directed to a distant point, nearer objects are seen double. Hold a pencil about a foot in front of the nose, directly in line with some more distant object. When you look at the pencil you see the farther object double, and when you look at the farther object the pencil is seen double. These double images usually remain unnoticed but help greatly in perceiving the relative distances of objects in the field of view.

The *stereoscope* is a convenient instrument for experimenting upon binocular vision. It presents separate views to the two eyes. If the views show the same object or scene, photographed from two positions close together, the third dimension comes out very realistically. If the two pictures are taken by cameras whose lenses are separated by the distance between our two eyes, the stereoscopic view will have normal depth. If the cameras are separated by a greater distance, the depth effect is exaggerated. This result, amusing in the parlor stereoscope, is utilized in taking aerial reconnaissance pictures so as to bring out the height of a building—height being the third dimension of a scene as viewed from above.

All these signs of distance are utilized together in the visual perception of three-dimensional space, sometimes one sign and sometimes another being more useful. In learning the spatial meaning of these signs, the child is undoubtedly helped by watching objects as they approach or recede from him, or as he approaches them. The chick reacts correctly to distance as soon as hatched, and it is quite possible that some sign of distance, probably the binocular sign, does not have to be learned (8).

**Erect vision in spite of the inverted retinal picture.** The picture thrown upon the retina by the lens of the eye is inverted It is upside down and reversed right and left. How then can we see the field of view right side up? Stratton (*13, 14*) prepared a system of lenses that reinverted the field of view, and wore this device constantly for a week, except at night when he was blindfolded. The retinal picture was now right side up, but the relation of visual field to hand, foot and body movements was reversed, with great resulting disturbance of movement and orientation. At first, movements in response to seen objects were entirely false; the subject reached in the wrong direction for any seen object, and ran into anything that he tried to avoid. Movements guided by the eye were laborious and nerve-racking, and had to be performed either by patient calculation or else by mere trial and error. By the end of the week, the subject was able to walk freely about the house, and to perform all sorts of manual operations, and his behavior in familiar surroundings became almost normal, though the field of view still did not appear right side up. When he removed the lenses at the end of the week, the first effect was one of pleased surprise at finding himself back in his old, familiar visual space; but there was considerable bewilderment and movements were false again, since they continued to follow the new system of eye-hand coordination. After a few hours, however, the old system was fully re-established. Erect vision, according to the results, must be largely a matter of integration between vision and movement (3).

**Visual perception of object size and shape.** A novice in drawing or painting from nature has difficulty in representing the shapes and relative sizes of objects. He *sees* two men to be of the same height when one of them is standing ten feet from him and the other twenty feet; but if he makes them of the same

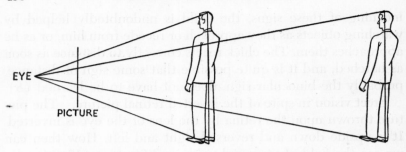

EYE

PICTURE

FIG. 106.—Picture size in relation to distance.

size in his drawing, something is wrong. His teacher shows him how to measure the picture size of objects by extending his arm, holding a pencil upright and marking off the intercepted height of the object with his thumb; and he then finds that the man who stands farther away has much less height in the field of view and should be correspondingly diminished in the picture. Picture size (or stimulus size) depends on both the real size of the object and on its distance from the observer.

It is the same with the shape of objects. A novice seeing a circle draws it as a circle, while according to the stimulus received it is an ellipse unless it chances to be seen square on.

In looking at a real scene the observer uses the signs of distance which have been mentioned and perceives the spatial relations in the objective situation and the relative distances of the various objects. His adjustment to these spatial relations is part of his situation set. Each particular object fits into this general framework. As he looks at an object he see its distance and he has given its stimulus size or size in the "picture." Since he is set for the distance of the object, its picture size immediately *means* its real size.

However, the observer is not likely to be perfectly accurate in his perception of the real sizes of objects at various distances. He may not allow adequately for their distances. In an experimental test of this matter, the subject looked down a long table and saw two circular gray disks, one 5 feet away, the other 10 feet. The nearer one was 4 inches in diameter, the farther one might be larger or smaller. The subject was asked which disk looked larger, and the farther disk was changed till the size was found that looked the same as the nearer one. Exact equality of real size would of course require the farther disk to have a diameter of 4 inches, while exact equality of stimulus size would demand a farther disk of 8 inches diameter. The 25 women college students who took this test varied somewhat but their average choice for the far disk was 4½ inches, very close to objective equality though with a slight compromise effect (*12*).

**Perception of object colors.** We return now to the problem in color perception that was raised at the beginning of the chapter. How can the observer see objects in their real colors in spite of the various illuminations in which they may stand? If a white cow goes out of the sun into the shade of a tree, she does not seem to our eyes to change color. A black cow in the sun still looks black, though more light is reaching our eyes from her black surface than from the white cow standing in the shade. To a remarkable degree we are able to identify the color of an object in spite of changes in the illumination. This fact is known by the name of "color constancy," meaning the constancy of object color as perceived (*9, 11*).

If you take two sheets of the same paper and place one near the light and the other far from the light, the latter is more dimly illuminated and consequently reflects less light to the eye, as you can easily verify by holding the near sheet so that it partly overlaps the farther one in your field of view. Nevertheless you have no difficulty in seeing that both sheets are of the same color as pieces of paper. This experiment has been tried out systematically on children and adults, who were asked to match various shades of gray, always matching a well lighted with a dimly lighted specimen. As the gray papers were alike in all other respects, they could be matched only by their shade. The matching was accomplished readily and with little error even by four-year-olds (*1*). In accurate tests, individuals are found to differ somewhat and color constancy is seldom perfect, the usual match being a compromise between the stimulus color and the object color (*7, 12*).

The psychological problem is fundamentally the same here

as in regard to perceiving object size. We wish to discover how the observer is able to read off the approximate color of an object instantly, whether it stands in good light or shadow. We must first ask what it is that he perceives.

*What object colors are, physically.* [A white object or substance is one that reflects all the light it receives, absorbing none, and a black substance is one that absorbs all and reflects none. (These are the "ideal" white and black; a good white paper does absorb some of the light, about 20 percent, reflecting 80 percent, and a good black paper reflects about 5 percent of the light.) A dead gray object absorbs some fraction of the light, and absorbs it unselectively, all wave lengths alike. A colored object is one that absorbs the light selectively, and therefore reflects selectively; a red object reflects the red rays predominantly, and a blue object the blue. The surface of any object is a light filter; a white surface does not change the light, a black surface kills the light, and a gray partially deadens it; a red surface reddens the reflected light; and so on. When we perceive object color, it is this physical property of the object which we perceive.

*Taking account of the illumination.* It is easy to prove that object color cannot be perceived unless the observer is enabled to allow for illumination.

The simplest way of concealing the illumination conditions is to look at a plain surface through a tube or "hole screen." Roll a paper tube small enough so that on looking through it you can see only a single uniform surface. Or cut a hole in a sheet of paper and hold it a few inches in front of the eye. It is not always possible to find perfectly plain surfaces to examine, but if such a surface is examined through the tube it loses its object character and the visible spot is seen simply according to its stimulus color.

From what has been said of the physical fact of object color, we see that the observer could arrive at that fact by deduction from two given facts, the illumination received by an object and the stimulus reflected by that object to the eye. If the observer saw the light reflected from the object to be the same in color and brightness as the illumination, he could infer that the object was white. If he saw the light reflected to be redder than the illumination, he could infer that the object was red. The observer does not actually go through any such process of reasoning and calculation, but he sees object colors instantly—actually *sees* them—provided the illumination is sufficiently revealed.

*The set for illumination.* There are several good indications of illumination: the general brightness and color of the field, the shadows and high lights, and the minute shadows and high lights on a rough surface. These are all seen in relation to the space characters of the visible field of objects. Under normal conditions the observer promptly becomes set or adjusted for the illumination, and consequently does not need to reason out the color of an object. He receives the light from the object while set for the total situation, illumination included. The principle is the same as in perceiving object size. There, one is set for the distance of the object and reads off the object size from the stimulus size. Here, one is set for the illumination and reads off the object color from the stimulus color.

**Seeing movement.**    Motion in the field of view is easily seen, and fully as easily in indirect as in foveal vision. Part of the utility of the external zones of the retina is their ready picking up of any movement and arousing a saccadic eye movement which brings the fovea to bear on the moving object.

Motion pictures set an interesting problem in the perception of movement. What is projected on the screen is a series of still pictures, a series of instantaneous snapshots, no single one of which shows any motion. Whence comes the motion that you see in looking at this series of motionless views? Evidently the seen motion is your response. The film has enough in common with an actually present moving object to arouse the same perception.

The after-lag of visual sensation quite obviously plays a part here, for without it the picture would be seen to be intermittent, as it is physically. But a more important factor is that the brain is tuned to see motion, and grasps at any chance to see it. It sees motion much more readily than it can pick out the successive positions through which a moving body passes. Everyone who has examined snapshots has been surprised at the queer positions into which a man, or a horse, gets in the course of his movements. We can scarcely believe that he actually takes these positions. We perceive the movement as a continuous pattern, and do not perceive the consecutive positions (p. 213).

*Apparent movement* can be seen with much simpler stimuli than those of the moving pictures. All you need is two lines, a short distance apart, presented one after the other to the eyes with a little blank interval between them. You can try the experiment by simply holding the forefinger upright three or four inches in front of the nose, and looking at it while winking first one eye and then the other. To the right eye it appears more to one side and to the left eye more to the other side; and when one eye is closed and the other simultaneously opened, the finger seems actually to move from one position to the other. This result is confirmed by careful laboratory experiments. If the time interval between the exposures of the two lines is very short, the lines are seen as present together, each in its own position; and if the interval is rather long, one line is seen in its position and then the other in its position, without apparent motion. But if the interval is just right, apparent movement occurs (*4, 5*).

Motion pictures are based on the proneness of the organism to see movement patterns rather than successions of discrete stimuli. They afford a striking example of the tendency to see objects and their behavior and not simply to see the light by which the objects are revealed.

## SUMMARY

1. The *eye* admits light through the *pupil*, the size of which is regulated by contraction of the *iris*. The light passes through the *cornea* and the *lens*, which is adjustable in curvature to focus the light on the *retina*, where it produces a photochemical

reaction in the *rods* and *cones,* from which nerve impulses proceed to the brain.

   a. The cones are specialized for response to detailed form
     and to color in ordinary illumination.

   b. The rods are specialized for response in very dim light,
     and do not differentiate color or fine detail.

   c. The *fovea* is a small region in the center of the retina con-
     taining only cones and serving clearest vision.

   d. Eye movements are of two types. *Conjugate movements,*
     both *saccadic* and *pursuit,* turn the eyes in parallel so that
     light from the object seen falls on the foveas of both eyes.
     *Convergence movements* turn the eyes toward each other
     so as to see a near object.

   e. Adaptation of the retina to dim light is due to increased
     sensitivity of the rods and cones, especially the rods. Night
     blindness, or inadequate rod function, may be due to
     deficiency of vitamin A.

2. *Visual sensation* is the process of seeing in which the individual's experiences are related to the *stimuli* falling on the
receptors.

   a. The stimuli for vision are light waves, differing in *wave
     length,* in *mixture,* and in *intensity.*

   b. Visual sensations differ correspondingly in *hue,* in *satura-
     tion,* and in *brilliance.*

   c. Mixture of light of all wave lengths arouses a colorless
     (white or gray) sensation. Mixture of two wave lengths
     gives a hue corresponding to an intermediate wave length.
     Mixture of two *complementary* colors gives a colorless
     (gray) sensation.

   d. Any hue can be secured by the mixture in proper propor-
     tions of three colors such as red, green and blue. The
     Young-Helmholtz theory goes on from this fact to postu-
     late that there are three types of cones.

   e. *Color-blindness* is a hereditary peculiarity of the retina,
     present in 6 to 8 percent of men.

     (1) In red-green blindness, reds are not distinguished
        from greens, both being seen as yellow.

(2) In total color blindness, which is very rare, none of the hues are distinguished, and everything is seen as shades of gray.

f. The center of the retina has full color vision; the surrounding zone is relatively red-green blind; the outermost zone is totally color blind (except to very bright colors).

g. *After-images* may be positive (similar to the sensation) or negative (complementary colors).

h. *Visual contrast* is the heightening of visual sensation when a complementary color precedes or adjoins the stimulus.

3. *Visual perception* is the process of seeing in which the individual's experiences are related to the objects he is looking at.

a. *Seeing distance* or the third dimension of space is achieved in spite of the fact that the stimuli on the retina are only two-dimensional.

(1) The single eye can react to certain signs of distance such as size perspective, aerial perspective, covering of objects, and shadows.

(2) When the head and eyes are moved back and forth, we see distant objects moving with the head and near objects moving in the opposite direction.

(3) In *binocular vision* there are two additional signs of distance. Each eye gets a slightly different view of the object, and the difference becomes a sign of distance. Also when the eyes are converged on a near point, the more distant objects are seen double; and when the eyes are directed to a distant point, the nearer objects are seen double.

b. *Erect vision* in spite of the inverted retinal image is a matter of integration between vision and the bodily movements by which we locate objects.

c. In judging size, an observer comes closer to *object size* than stimulus size. Using the signs of distance, he is set for the distance of the object and perceives its real size.

d. *Object color* is perceived much the same in spite of differences in illumination and consequently of the light stimulating the eye.

SUMMARY                                 **463**

(1) Object color is the reflecting property of the surface.
(2) If the observer cannot allow for the illumination, as in looking through a tube, he does not perceive the object color.

e. *Apparent movement* is seen when two stimuli are presented successively with the proper interval between them.

# CHAPTER FIFTEEN

# *The Other Senses*

Though sight may well be regarded as the most important of the senses, all the others make significant contributions to the individual's welfare. He uses nearly all of them in exploring the environment, though the internal sensations such as hunger, thirst and fatigue inform him rather of his own organic state than of external facts. He uses the skin of the hands and of various other parts of the body in exploring objects by feeling them, so discovering their roughness or smoothness, hardness or softness, moistness or dryness, warmth or coldness (*11*). By lifting and manipulating objects he discovers their weight, elasticity and other mechanical properties. By smell and taste he discovers important facts relating to foods and other substances. By the sense of hearing he obviously learns a great deal about the environment. Several of the senses contribute also to the enjoyment of life by the agreeable sensations they provide. Hearing, smell and taste deserve emphasis in this respect, but the skin should not be forgotten since it provides agreeable warmth and coolness, agreeable sensations of smooth contact, and erotic sensations. There are also, to be sure, disagreeable noises, tastes and odors, disagreeable heat and cold, pain from the skin and ache from the interior, all of these being indicators, however, of external or internal conditions that demand correction.

As already illustrated in the treatment of vision, the study of any sense includes two main problems. (1) There is the problem of sensation, concerned with the stimuli received by each sense organ, with the operation of the sense organ, and with the individual's sensory impressions as related to the stimuli and receptors. (2) There is the problem of perception, concerned with the individual's use of each sense in discovering objective facts in the environment or in the individual's own body. Sensations correspond to stimuli, while perceptions correspond more or less to objective facts.

**The sense organs in general.**   The most primitive animals, the protozoa, though sensitive to various stimuli, are sensitive all over, rather than in certain spots. They respond to mechanical stimuli (contact or jarring), to certain chemical stimuli, to thermal stimuli (heat or cold), to electrical stimuli and to light. They have no special light-sensitive spot, but respond to light no matter where it strikes them.

In the development of the metazoa, or multicellular animals, specialization has occurred, some parts of the body becoming muscles, some parts digestive organs, some parts conductors (the nerves), and some parts specialized receptors or sense organs. A sense organ is a portion of the body that has very high sensitivity to some particular kind of stimulus. The eye responds to very minute amounts of energy in the form of light, but not in other forms; the ear responds to very minute amounts of energy in the form of sound vibrations, the nose to very minute quantities of chemical energy.

A useful classification of the senses divides them into the exteroceptors, the interoceptors, and the proprioceptors. The exteroceptors receive stimuli from outside the organism, and the interoceptors from the interior of the mouth, throat, gullet, stomach, intestines and lungs, while the proprioceptors are located in the proper substance of the body, i.e., in the muscles, tendons, joints, and are stimulated by movements of these parts. Of the exteroceptors, the eye, ear and nose are singled out as *distance receptors,* because they receive stimuli from sources that are not in contact with the organism. The distance receptors enable the organism to adjust itself to a wide environment.

**Mechanism of a sense organ.** Each sense organ is a receiving instrument or indicator, as the thermometer is an indicator of temperature. The sensitive part of a sense organ is not visible from outside, but lies in the depth of the organ—that for smell being well back inside the nose and that for hearing, the inner ear, being embedded in the bone beneath the external ear. Each sense organ has its *sensory nerve* which connects it with the nerve centers and through them, indirectly, with all parts of the body. Without this nerve connection the sense organ could have no influence on the activities of the organism. The fibers of the sensory nerve divide into fine branches within the sense organ, and the high sensitivity of the organ is partly due to these fine nerve endings. In addition, there are special *sense cells* in the eye, ear, nose and mouth. Besides these sensitive structures most of the sense organs contain *accessory apparatus* which conveys the stimulus effectively to the nerve endings and sense cells. The lens, the iris and the muscles of the eye belong in the category of accessory apparatus.

The efficiency of a receptor depends (a) on its being *selective,* tuned to one kind of stimulus, and not indifferently responsive to every stimulus, (b) on its being very *sensitive* to its particular kind of stimulus, (c) on its responding differently to different *intensities* of the stimulus, and (d) on its responding differently to different qualities or *varieties* of the stimulus. For example, the sense of smell is selective in that it responds to odors and not also to sounds entering the nose—which would be confusing; it is sensitive in that it indicates the presence of incredibly small quantities of an odorous substance in the air; it responds differently to faint and strong odors by smell sensations of different intensities; and it gives different smells for different substances. Few man-made instruments can vie with the nose in these respects—or with the eye and ear.

## THE SKIN SENSES

Moist and dry, hot and cold, itching, tickling, pricking and stinging are skin sensations; but some of them are certainly complex. Relatively simple sensations are obtained by exploring the skin, point by point, with weak stimuli. As a cool stimulus, a pencil point at room temperature will serve for a hasty exploration. Passing it lightly along the skin, one gets at most points merely a sensation of contact, but at certain points there is a clear cold sensation. Within any half-inch square on the back of the hand, several of these *cold spots* can be found, and painstaking work, with adequate apparatus and procedure, shows them to be relatively stable. Similarly, *warmth spots* are located by using a stimulus a few degrees warmer than the skin. If a sharp point is pressed moderately against the skin, it gives at many places a small, sharp pain. These are the *pain spots*. Finally, if the skin is explored with a hair of just the right flexibility—too flexible to stimulate the pain spots—nothing at all is felt in most places, but at some points there is a definite sensation of touch or contact; and these are the *touch spots*. The pain spots and touch spots are much more numerous than the temperature spots, and the cold spots are more numerous than the warmth spots.

As no further varieties of sensory spots are found, touch, warmth, cold and pain are believed to be the only primary cutaneous sensations. Itch, stinging and aching seem to be variations of pain. Tickle seems to be a variety of touch.

Hard and soft combine touch from the skin with resistance encountered by the muscles and detected by the muscle sense. They are qualities of objects rather than of stimuli and are perceived rather than sensed. Somewhat the same is true of rough and smooth, which are felt by moving the skin over a surface and so obtaining a vibratory stimulus (*12*).

**The elementary stimuli of the skin senses.**   Exactly how is the skin acted on to give each primary sensation? In the case of *touch,* the exact stimulus is a bending of the skin, either in or out, at any touch spot, or at many touch spots at once. The stimulus that gives *pain* may be mechanical (as a needle prick), or thermal (heat or cold), or chemical (as a drop of acid), or electrical; but in any case it must be strong enough to injure or almost injure the skin. The pain receptors, then, are not highly sensitive, but require a fairly strong stimulus; their use is to detect the presence of stimuli that threaten injury.

Temperature stimuli require more discussion. The internal body temperature is steady, in health, at about 98° Fahrenheit, but the surface of the skin is likely to be about 85–90°, which feels neither warm nor cool, because neither the warmth nor the cold spots are aroused. They are "adapted" to the skin temperature. Let a metal object, or other good conductor of heat, be laid upon the skin. If the metal object is warmer than the skin, it will raise the surface temperature. If the stimulus is a single degree above the skin temperature, it will feel warm —or cool, if a single degree below. Regarding the organism as a thermometer, we may say that its zero lies at skin temperature, and that its sensitiveness is very good for temperatures just above or below its zero.

This psychological zero shifts up and down according to the temperature of the skin. Immerse the hand for five minutes in water at some temperature between about 60° and 100° F., and you change the skin temperature and the zero point. Stimuli a degree or two warmer or cooler than the new zero will give the warm or cool sensation. Beyond the limits mentioned the temperature sense cannot fully adapt itself, so that a very cold object continues to feel cold, and a very warm object to feel warm or hot (3).

An easy and striking demonstration of temperature sense adaptation proceeds as follows. Take three bowls of water, one at skin temperature and feeling neither warm nor cold to the hand, one definitely hot and one definitely cold. Hold one hand in the hot water and the other in the cold water for half a minute, and then place both hands in the medium water which doubtless will feel warm to the cold-adapted hand and simultaneously cold to the warm-adapted one.

As a thermometer the skin tells us whether an object is above or below skin temperature, and it also gives some indication as to how warm or cold an object is. With colder and colder objects applied to the skin the cold sensation increases in intensity, and finally the pain sense also is aroused. With objects farther and farther above the psychological zero, the warmth sensation becomes more and more intense and finally the pain sense is aroused and the sensation is one of burning heat.

The touch sense, as well as the temperature sense, shows a striking adaptation effect. A perfectly steady pressure on the skin soon ceases to be felt. Pull on a tight glove and hold the hand perfectly quiet (so as to avoid changing the pressures), and you soon cease to feel the glove (15).

The skin receptors.  Innumerable sensory nerve fibers grow out to the skin, where each one divides into many fine branches. Not in the outermost, horny layer of the skin, but just a little way in, is a perfect thicket of fine nerve branches. On hairy

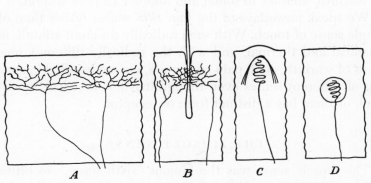

*A*            *B*            *C*            *D*

Fig. 107.—Diagrams of skin receptors. The surface of the skin is at the top, and nerve fibers are seen entering from below, i.e., from inside the skin.

A, the most common skin receptor, certainly serving the pain sense and probably other senses as well.

B, the hair as a touch organ.

C, a touch corpuscle.

D, an end-bulb, probably responsive to cold. Several other varieties of end-bulbs are found in the mucous membrane, the surface of the eyeball, the depths of the skin and elsewhere. They are certainly receptors but their exact stimuli have not been discovered.

parts, the hairs extend down into this thicket and, when touched on the outside, act as little levers in stimulating the nerve ends. They are accessory apparatus to the sense of touch.

On hairless surfaces, especially the palms, some of the sensory nerve fibers terminate in little cones of skin tissue, and these "touch corpuscles" are believed to be touch receptors. Spherical end-bulbs, which are minute round or oval bodies, with a sensory nerve fiber terminating in each of them, are probably cold receptors (19).

Sensory nerve endings are present not only in the skin but also in the subcutaneous tissue, and deep pressure and dull pain can be felt even when the skin is anesthetized. Cutaneous sensation extends into the mouth and nose, and the tip of the tongue is a keen touch organ, but on the whole these extensions of the skin senses are less keen than the skin itself. As everybody knows, the skin is much keener in some parts than in others, and one region is especially sensitive to cold, another to warmth, another to touch and another to pain stimuli.

We speak nowadays of the *four skin senses* rather than of a single sense of touch. With such radically different stimuli, mechanical and thermal, and with the radically different sensations of warmth, cold, pain and touch, we are justified in speaking of different senses even though it is not yet clear whether each of them has a distinct form of receptor.

## THE MUSCLE SENSE

The muscle sense was the famous "sixth sense," so bitterly objected to in the middle of the nineteenth century by those who maintained that the five senses that were good enough for our fathers ought to be good enough for us, too. The question was whether the sense of touch did not account for all sensations of bodily movement. It was shown that there must be something besides the skin sense, because weights were better distinguished when "hefted" in the hand than when simply laid in the motionless palm, and because the coordinated movements of a limb were much more disturbed by loss of *all* its

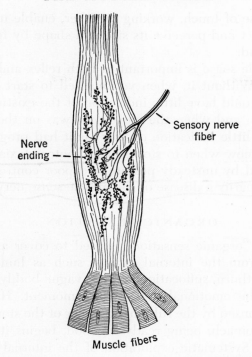

Sensory nerve
fiber

Nerve
ending - -

Muscle fibers

FIG. 108.—A tendon spindle, similar to the muscle spindle mentioned in the text, but found in the tendon instead of in the muscle substance. When the tendon is made taut by the contraction of its muscle, the nerve endings are squeezed and stimulated (Ramon y Cajal).

sensory nerves than by loss of its cutaneous nerves alone. Later, the crucial fact was established that sense organs (the "muscle spindles") existed in the muscles, and similar sense organs in the tendons and about the joints. This sense is the muscle, tendon and joint sense rather than simply the muscle sense. It is sometimes called the *kinesthetic* sense, from the Greek words meaning "sense of movement."

This sense is stimulated by muscular contractions, by postures, by passive movements and by external resistance encountered by a movement. It furnishes important information regarding the weight of objects, their firmness or looseness, hardness or softness, stiffness or flexibility. The muscle sense and the sense of touch, working together, enable us to recognize an object and perceive its size and shape by feeling of it with the hand.

The muscle sense is important in both reflex and voluntary movement. Without it, when you wanted to start any movement, you would have little indication of the existing position of the limbs; and when the movement was on the way, you would have little indication of how far it had progressed and would not know when to stop it. Locomotor ataxia, a disease characterized by unsteady posture and poor control of movement, is primarily a disease of the muscle sense nerves.

## ORGANIC SENSATION

The term "organic sensation" is used to cover a variety of sensations from the internal organs, such as hunger, thirst, nausea, heartburn, suffocation and the vague bodily sensations that color the emotional tone of any moment. Hunger is a sensation aroused by the rubbing together of the stomach walls when the stomach, being ready for food, begins its churning movements. Systematic exploration of the internal organs reveals astonishingly few sensations arising there, but there can be little doubt that those just listed really arise where they seem to arise, in the interior of the trunk.

## THE SENSE OF TASTE

A simple experiment shows that the numerous so-called tastes of foods and drinks are only partly tastes proper. The subject holds his nose, so as to prevent any odor from reaching the olfactory receptors, and then is unable to distinguish coffee from a weak solution of quinine, or apple juice from onion juice. Coffee and quinine have the bitter taste in common, and that is all the taste they have; onion and apple have the sweet taste in common. The primary tastes are limited to *bitter*, *sweet*, *sour* and *salty* (10).

The interior of the mouth is supplied with the skin senses as well as with taste. A biting "taste" is partly pain, and a smooth "taste" partly touch sensation. The temperature of a food or drink also contributes to what we inaccurately call its taste. In addition to all these sensations from the mouth, food in the mouth stimulates the sense of smell by way of the throat and the rear passage to the nose; and the *flavor* of food consists largely of odor.

Analysis of tastes, like that of skin sensations, is greatly assisted by the fact that the different sensations are aroused by stimulation of different spots. Some of the papillae or little protuberances on the surface of the tongue contain taste receptors, and correspond roughly to the sensory spots of the skin. A few of the papillae give a single taste sensation, and many give only two or three of the four primary tastes. The bitter taste is got principally from the rear of the tongue, sweet from the tip, sour from the sides, and salty from the tip and the adjacent part of the sides. A sweetened bitter solution tastes sweet when applied with a little brush to the tip of the tongue, and bitter when applied to the rear of the tongue.

The actual taste receptors, called taste buds, are located not on the surface of the tongue, but in little pits which extend down from the surface. The taste buds are bunches of sense cells, each cell having a slender tip that projects into the pit,

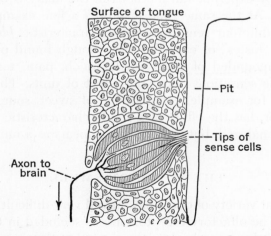

FIG. 109.—A taste bud, showing its location and nerve supply.

where it is exposed to the sugar or salt or other tasting substance present in the mouth. The sense cell, being thus aroused to activity, arouses in turn the sensory nerve fiber which twines around the base of the cell. Thus nerve impulses are started along the sensory nerve to the brain.

The stimulus to the sense of taste is of a chemical nature. The tastable substance must be in solution in order to penetrate the pits and reach the sensitive tips of the taste cells. If the upper surface of the tongue is first dried, a dry lump of sugar or salt laid on it gives no sensation of taste until a little saliva has accumulated and dissolved some of the substance.

Exactly what the chemical agent is that produces a given taste sensation is a problem of some difficulty. Many different substances give the sensation of bitter, and the question is what there is common to all these substances. The sweet taste is aroused not only by sugar, but also by glycerine, saccharine, and even "sugar of lead" (lead acetate). The sour taste is not aroused by all acids, and is aroused by some substances that are not chemically acids. The chemistry of taste stimuli is not yet fully understood.

Though there is this uncertainty regarding the stimulus, on the whole the sense of taste affords a fine example of success achieved by experimental methods in the analysis of complex sensations. At the same time it affords a fine example of the fusion of different sensations into characteristic *blends*. The numerous "tastes" of everyday life, though found on analysis to be compounded of taste, smell, touch, pain, temperature and muscle sensations, have the effect of units. The taste of lemonade, for example, compounded of sweet, sour, cold and lemon odor, has the effect of a single characteristic sensation. It can be analyzed, but ordinarily it appears as a unit.

## THE SENSE OF SMELL

The great variety of odors has proved very difficult to reduce to order. The olfactory receptors are so secluded in their position, in a little alcove back in the nose, that they cannot be ex-

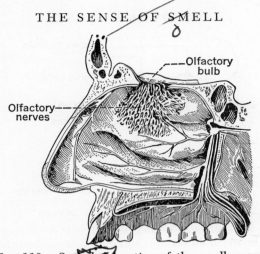

Fig. 110.—Secluded location of the smell organ.

plored as the skin and tongue have been. The receptor cells
are embedded in the mucous membrane lining the nasal cavity
and have fine tips which are exposed to the air in the cavity
and so to chemical stimulation by odorous substances inhaled
in the air.

Since we cannot apply stimuli to the separate receptors,
about all that can be done in the way of analysis is to assemble
a complete assortment of odors, and become thoroughly acquainted with their similarities and differences. Series can be
arranged, grading off from one salient odor through intermedi-
ates to another salient odor. Recent work indicates about six
salient odors, but whether these are true primaries or not is
still uncertain. The following is Henning's classification, or list
of the salient odors (9):

1. Spicy, found in cloves, cinnamon, etc.
2. Fragrant, found in heliotrope, vanilla, etc.
3. Ethereal, found in orange oil, ether, etc.
4. Resinous, found in turpentine, pine needles, etc.
5. Putrid, found in hydrogen sulphide, etc.
6. Burned, found in tarry substances.

These being the outstanding odors, there are many inter-
mediates. The odor of roasted coffee is intermediate between

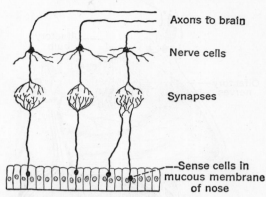

Axons to brain

Nerve cells

Synapses

--Sense cells in
mucous membrane
of nose

Fig. 111.—Four olfactory sense cells and their nerve connections. The nasal cavity, in which an odorous vapor may be present, lies below the mucous membrane in the figure.

resinous and burned, that of peppermint between ethereal and spicy.

The lower portion of the interior of the nose is supplied with the cutaneous senses, which are stimulated by many inhaled substances and contribute to what we call the "odor" of those substances. The "smell" of camphor or of menthol is partly cold sensation, and the "pungent odor" of ammonia, acetic acid, chlorine or iodin is partly pain.

The stimulus of the sense of smell is undoubtedly chemical, but the chemical correlations are not yet well worked out. It is an extremely sensitive sense, responding to very small quantities of certain substances diffused in the air. Other substances arouse no olfactory response at all. Many animals, such as the dog, make much more use than we do of this sense in exploring the world; but we probably use it more than we suspect.

## THE SENSE OF HEARING

Sound is physically a wave motion or vibration in the air or other conducting medium. In the air, it consists in a slight back and forth motion of the air, a motion usually too slight to be felt by the sense of touch. The ear is much more sensitive, by virtue of its sense cells and accessory apparatus.

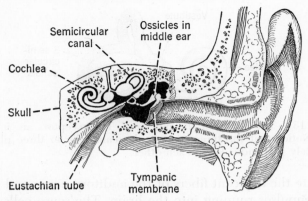

FIG. 112.—The ear, outer, middle, and inner. Sound waves entering the outer ear strike the tympanic membrane (ear drum) and throw it into vibration. The vibration is transmitted by the ossicles to the liquid filling the inner ear and so reaches the cochlea. The middle ear is filled with air which comes in by way of the throat and the Eustachian tube. (The *ch* in "cochlea" and "Eustachian" is pronounced like *k*.)

**The sound-receiving apparatus of the ear.** We speak of the outer, middle, and inner ear. The outer ear is a collector, the middle ear a transformer, and the inner ear the sensitive receptor. In man, the outer ear has little of the ear-trumpet action so beautifully shown by the donkey, and can be cut off with no noticeable effect upon hearing. Sound waves, entering the ear hole, strike the *tympanic membrane* within and set it into vibration. The membrane communicates its motion to the *ossicles,* an assembly of three little bones in the middle ear, and these concentrate the vibration upon a small opening from the middle to the inner ear. Thus the middle ear mechanism achieves the important result of setting into vibration the fluid that fills the inner ear.

The inner ear is first of all a cavity in one of the skull bones— a very small cavity, but complicated, with a *vestibule* in the middle, and a spiral passage and three *semicircular canals* opening out of the vestibule. The spiral passage, called the *cochlea* ("snail"), contains the auditory receptors. These are cells with delicate hair branches for picking up the sound vibrations. When the cells are thus thrown into activity they

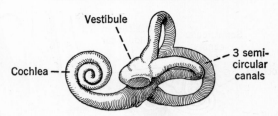

Fig. 113.—The cavity of the inner ear. The receptors are inside this cavity. Notice that the three semicircular canals lie in three planes approximately perpendicular to each other.

stimulate the adjacent fibers of the auditory nerve and so start nerve impulses running into the brain. The sense cells rest on the *basilar membrane,* which is a fibrous ribbon stretched sideways between two shelves of bone and extending the length of the cochlea, widening from one end to the other, and as it widens becoming slacker and more heavily loaded by the overlying cells. These details agree in suggesting that one end of the basilar membrane is tuned to rapid sound vibrations and the remainder to slower and slower vibrations, like the strings of a harp or piano.

**How the inner ear operates.**   Helmholtz's "piano theory" or *resonance theory of hearing* accepts this suggestion and assumes that each region of the basilar membrane, being tuned to a certain vibration rate, is thrown into sympathetic vibration whenever the liquid filling the cochlea is vibrating at that rate. (Sympathetic vibration is illustrated by pressing the piano pedal that lifts the dampers from the strings and singing a note into the piano. On ceasing to sing you hear the piano answering with the same note, because the strings tuned to that note have been thrown into vibration by the air waves produced by your singing.) When a tone of a certain vibration rate is transmitted by the middle ear mechanism to the liquid of the inner ear, the corresponding region of the basilar membrane is supposed to be thrown into vibration. When, as usual, more than a single vibration rate is present in the incoming sound, two or more regions of the basilar membrane are thrown into vibration. Whatever part of the basilar membrane is made to vibrate, the

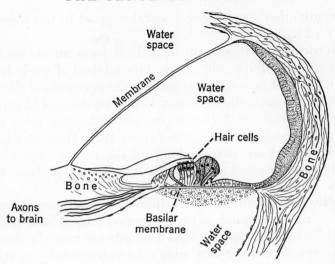

FIG. 114.—Cross-section of the cochlea, showing a single row of the sense cells. There are about 5000 such rows standing on the basilar membrane. Each of the three "water spaces" is a long slender tube. The sound waves come in from the middle ear and vestibule by the uppermost of the three tubes, pass through the membranes, and are carried back by the lowest tube to a vent leading to the middle ear. They do their work while passing through the basilar membrane.

hair cells located on that part are shaken and stimulated; they in turn stimulate the connected nerve ends and start nerve impulses toward the brain. Differential tuning of different parts of the basilar membrane would explain the individual's ability to distinguish sounds of different vibration rate, to hear high, low and intermediate tones, and to "hear out" single tones from a chord or single noises from a medley of sound (1, 8, 17).

If this theory is correct, an injury to a limited portion of the cochlea should impair hearing, not for all tones alike, but for tones of a certain approximate vibration rate. In human subjects loss of hearing for the very high tones is fairly common. Post-mortem examination of many individuals whose loss of the high notes had been accurately determined shows that the narrow end of the basilar membrane, which according to the theory is tuned to the high notes, is the part affected. These and many other results give general support to the resonance theory (2).

Electrical oscillations can be led off from an active nerve and recorded after amplification. This method of study has revealed much of importance regarding the operation of the inner ear (20). In general the resonance theory seems to hold good for the reception of the higher tones, with vibration rates above 1000 per second, while the lower tones affect the entire basilar membrane and are passed along up the nerves somewhat as vibrations are passed along to the wire by a telephone transmitter.

**Auditory sensations and their stimuli.** An auditory sensation, the hearing of a sound, is a response of the ear and brain to vibrations striking the ear. Heard sounds are roughly classified into tones and noises, tones being relatively smooth and steady, and noises mixed and irregular. Noise is produced by an unsteady medley of vibrations, tone by a sequence of uniform vibrations.

Heard sounds differ in loudness, in pitch and in timbre. By *pitch* is meant the highness or lowness of a tone. The soprano voice has a high pitch, the bass a low pitch. By *timbre* is meant the characteristic sound of different instruments and other sources of sound. A violin, a cornet and a human voice may all give the same note or pitch with the same loudness, but they can easily be distinguished by their timbre.

Now we must find three ways in which the vibratory stimulus can differ, to account for these three differences in the sounds heard. Air vibrations, if simple, differ in only two independent ways, in amplitude or extent of the back-and-forth swing, and in the frequency or rate of the swing, the number of vibrations per second. Compound vibrations differ also in composition, i.e., in the number and relations of the simple vibrations of which they are composed.

Loudness depends on the amplitude of the vibrations; the greater the amplitude the louder the sound. Pitch depends on the frequency of vibration; the greater the frequency, the higher the pitch. Timbre depends on the combination of dif-

ferent frequencies in a complex vibration. These general statements require some explanation and qualification.

The deepest audible tones have a vibration rate of about 20
per second, and the highest a rate of about 20,000. Outside of
these limits there are plenty of physical sounds, but they arouse
no auditory sensation. A giant organ pipe may emit vibrations
at the rate of only 16 per second, and shake the whole audi-
torium, but these vibrations cannot be heard. A tiny whistle
gives out 30,000, 50,000 or more vibrations per second, and
these can be heard by some animals but not by the human
ear. Individuals differ in their upper and lower pitch limits,
and the upper limit declines gradually after the age of twenty
years.

Though the ear is tuned to respond to this wide range of
vibration rates, it is most sensitive to the middle part of the
range, from 500 to 5,000 vibrations per second. Weaker vibrations can be heard at these middle rates than toward the extremes of the audible range. In this way, loudness depends on
vibration rate as well as on amplitude.

Middle C of the piano, a note within the compass of all
voices, though rather low for the soprano and rather high for
the bass, has a vibration rate of about 260 per second. Go up
an octave and you double the vibration rate; go down an octave
and you halve the rate. It takes a deep bass voice to go down
two octaves below middle C (i.e., to a note of 65 vibrations),
and a high soprano to go up two octaves (i.e., to a note of 1040
vibrations). The whole range of audible tones from 20 to 20,000
vibrations per second amounts to approximately 10 octaves, of
which music employs about 8 octaves, finding little esthetic
value in the highest and lowest audible tones. The smallest step
on the piano, called the semitone, is $\frac{1}{12}$ of an octave; but this
is by no means the smallest pitch difference that can be perceived. Most people can distinguish tones that are 4 vibrations
apart, and keen ears can detect a difference of less than one
vibration; whereas the semitone, at middle C, is a step of about
16 vibrations. The semitone is simply the smallest step utilized
by the European scale, which came down from the Egyptians

and Greeks. Oriental music uses different scales and some steps
smaller than the semitone of our music.

**Tone combinations, overtones and timbre.** When two or
more notes sound together, a chord or discord is heard.
Whether it shall seem pleasant or unpleasant depends primarily
on the relative vibration rates of the combined notes, but
partly also on the hearer's being accustomed or not to the
particular combination—it requires some practice with close
harmonies to enjoy them—and partly on the sequence of chords
in a piece of music.

A chord is a blend, a unit, but after practice you can hear out
the notes which make up the chord. The ear is an *analyzer,*
making it possible to isolate the separate sounds out of a combination. For a familiar example, you can hear what one person
is saying in spite of the din of other voices or of street noises.
One sound does mask another to some extent, especially when
both are of about the same pitch, but you can hear out the
separate sounds to a remarkable degree. These sounds are not
separate in the air; as they enter the ear they are not separate
but combined into a complex vibration. According to the piano
theory, different parts of the basilar membrane, being tuned
to different vibration rates, pick up the component notes of a
chord or medley of sounds.

Even a single note of an instrument gives a combination of
different vibration rates. Every sounding body produces overtones along with the fundamental tone. Any note sounded on
the piano is a combination of fundamental and overtones, and
the sensation aroused by the complex stimulus is a blend. With
practice you may be able to hear out some of the overtones, but
ordinarily you take the blend as a unit (just as you take the
taste of lemonade as a unit), and simply get the characteristic
quality of piano notes. Another instrument will give a different
combination of overtones, and so a different blend, a different
total quality. The timbre of an instrument depends on the particular combination of overtones which it gives out.

**Speech sounds.** These are perhaps the most important of all
sounds for human beings to hear. The great handicap of the

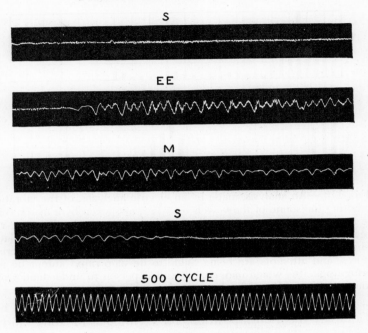

FIG. 115.—An oscillograph record of the sound waves produced in speaking the word, "seems." The unvoiced s gives only small, rapid mouth waves, but as the vowel ee begins, the vocal cord tone and overtones appear. The bottom line shows the simple waves produced by a tuning fork vibrating 500 times per second (Fletcher, 4).

deaf child, which shows in his IQ, is probably his inability to hear what other people say. If we had time for a thorough study here, we should begin with the production of speech sounds by the vocal cords and by the mouth. One important fact is that the vocal cords supply the voice element in speech sounds— an element that is absent in whispering and in the "unvoiced" consonants such as k, p, t, f, and s. The vocal cords emit overtones along with the fundamental tone that is being spoken or sung. But the vocal cords by themselves produce no vowels or consonants. These are due to the various positions of the mouth, tongue and lips. Any one of these positions forms a resonance chamber that strengthens certain of the vocal cord overtones, and by so doing gives the vowel or consonantal quality.

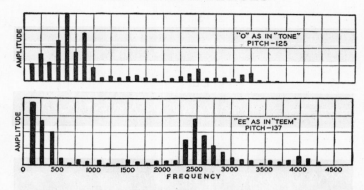

FIG. 116.—An analysis, made by an electric analyzer, of the vibrations composing the sound of the vowels *o* and *ee*, as spoken by a man's voice. The location of the bars along the base line indicates the vibration rate of each overtone, while the height of the bars indicates the relative strength of the several overtones. The speech sounds have characteristic pictures, and attempts are being made to develop rapid automatic registering apparatus which may enable a deaf person to understand words through the eye (*16*) (Fletcher, *4*).

Compare the mouth positions for saying *o* as in "tone" and *ee* as in "teem." The *o* position reinforces the vocal cord overtones in the region of 500 per second, the *ee* position reinforces those in the region of 2,500 per second. Notice also the position for saying *s*: the tongue is brought up to the base of the upper teeth, leaving a narrow passage for the air, which whistles through giving a very rapid vibration (about 7,500 per second), which can readily be heard in whispering the sound *s*. If you sound *z*, the corresponding voiced consonant, you can hear both the vocal cord tone and the hissing at the front of the mouth. You can feel them both, as well, in pronouncing this letter. Each speech sound is a different combination of tones. The development of telephone, phonograph and radio engineering has made it possible to obtain beautiful records and analyses of speech sounds.

In hearing speech, we do not hear out the component tones to any great extent, but recognize the total complex as a familiar blend. Even a whole syllable, composed of several successive speech sounds, is heard as a unit.

From the high pitch of many of the overtones that enable us to distinguish one vowel or consonant from another, we see how useful it is to have ears very sensitive to what might otherwise seem absurdly high vibration rates, from 2,000 to 10,000 per second, away above the range of the human voice, i.e., of its fundamental tones. These high overtones are weak in comparison with the vocal cord fundamental, and, as the sensitiveness of the ear to high tones decreases with age, one finds it more difficult to hear what people are saying, though one can still hear the rumble of their voices.

**The elementary auditory sensations.** Simple tones, free from overtones and noises, can be arranged in a continuous pitch series, from the lowest to the highest audible tones, with no "salient sensations" such as we have found in the other senses. The notion of a few primary sensations, which was useful in understanding the cutaneous senses, sight, taste and possibly smell, has no value in the case of hearing. Every tone, provided it is a single tone, is as primary as any other. This continuous scale of auditory responses makes the ear a much better registering instrument for pitch than the eye is for color. The ear registers the component vibrations of a chord much more adequately than the eye can do for a mixture of light rays. In compensation, the eye is far superior to the ear in registering space relations.

**Auditory perception of objects.** In the chapter on vision the question was discussed whether we see light or see objects. A similar question could be raised with regard to hearing. The obvious answer is that we certainly hear sounds, but there is something more to be said. Noises are usually heard as the *sounds of objects*. We ordinarily speak of hearing the wind or the waves, an airplane or a bee, a man sawing or a horse trotting. When we hear a noise that we cannot identify we are uneasy and dissatisfied, for our strong tendency in hearing as well as in seeing is to get at the objective fact indicated by the stimulus.

In listening to music we may care only for the esthetic effect and be perfectly contented to close our eyes and take in the sequence of tones and chords without asking whether they are coming from the violins or from the brass instruments. Sunset colors, in the same way, are viewed for their beauty and not as signs of objects, though there is as yet no elaborate art of pure colors comparable to the tonal art of music.

In listening to a person talk, what do we really hear? We hear the stimuli, the sounds that reach our ears. We hear the speaker, the source of the sound, as in another case we hear an airplane or a man sawing wood. We hear the words and sentences as patterns of sound. But what we are really listening for is the speaker's meaning. To penetrate behind the patterns of sound to the meaning is our whole intention, just as in numerous other cases we get as much meaning as possible from the stimuli received by the senses.

At times this strong tendency to jump instantly from the stimulus to its meaning leads us astray. Sometimes the sign is ambiguous and the part of prudence is to avoid plunging to any definite meaning. On shipboard we see a vague something along the horizon and exclaim, "I see land!" only to be assured by a sailor that it is only a cloud. In the middle of the night we "hear a burglar" when it is only some creaking thing about the house. It is well to be able to strip off the meaning and get down to the bare stimuli. But the natural tendency, useful for the most part, is just the reverse.

**Locating the source of a sound.**    Auditory space perception is not nearly so good as visual, but still there is some ability to hear where a sound is coming from, i.e., to perceive the distance and direction of the source of sound. If the sound is familiar, its loudness indicates how far off, roughly, the source must be. But how can its direction possibly be perceived? This question has given rise to many fine experiments and the results are surprising, though well established. The experiments are best conducted in an open field or padded room, free from reflected sound that would confuse the listener. The first result is that he can tell very well whether the sound is coming from the right or left; even if it deviates only a few degrees from straight forward or back he can detect the deviation. He can face very accurately toward an unseen source of sound. That is about all; up from down, front from back, he cannot surely distinguish so long as he holds his head motionless and straight forward, though by twisting his head he can convert these other dimensions of space into a temporary right-left dimension and so utilize his excellent ability to distinguish sounds from right and left.

This ability is due to his having two ears. A sound reaches the nearer ear a little sooner and with a little greater intensity, so providing two possible cues of right or left. But if we examine the physics of the matter we find that the time difference and intensity difference, as between the nearer and farther ear, are very small. Since sound travels 1100 feet a second in the air, the time difference between the two ears can never be as much as $\frac{1}{1000}$ of a second. You would think that so small a time could have no appreciable effect on the organism. You can test the matter by providing your subject with two earphones on separate circuits, and sending separate clicks to the two ears. He will hear the two clicks as a single click coming from a certain direction. When the two are exactly simultaneous the sound seems to come from straight in front (or straight behind), but when the right ear gets its click $\frac{1}{10,000}$ sec. sooner than the left, the sound seems to come from about 10° to the right. To test the intensity cue, give both clicks simultaneously but make one stronger than the other: the sound seems to come from the right when the right ear gets the stronger stimulus. By such experiments the time and intensity cues are shown to be effective, time being more effective in certain conditions and intensity in other conditions (22).

Recalling the famous experiment with inverted vision (p. 455), we wonder what would be the effect of reversing the cues of sound direction by interchanging the stimuli that affect the two ears. The experiment has been tried (21, 23), as illustrated in Figure 117. Each ear got the stimulus that would normally enter the other ear. The effect was a complete right-left reversal in the apparent direction of sounds, with a good deal of front-back reversal as well. A door would creak, ap-

Fig. 117.—Diagram of Young's pseudophone (23). Each ear trumpet is continued by a tube that runs over the head and is plugged into the opposite ear. Padding is required to minimize leakage of sound directly into the nearer ears.

parently behind and to the left, but the visitor would be seen to enter at the front and right. Finding a ticking clock, with the eyes closed, was an almost impossible task, for the more one went "toward" it the more it receded. With the eyes open the effect was a little different, for if the subject saw the person or thing making the noise, the visual location would often suppress the auditory, so that the sound was accepted as coming from the visible source. Subjects who wore the reversing apparatus all the waking time for a week became accustomed to disregarding the misleading auditory cues (in traffic, for example), but they did not overcome the reversal effect. The time and intensity cues are too deep-seated physiologically to be easily unlearned and given a new meaning.

*Perceiving the intensity of distant sounds.* We can see the true size of an object at various distances (p. 456) and just so we can compare the proper loudness of sounds coming from different distances; i.e., we can take account of the distance and perceive the loudness as at the source. This "loudness constancy" is demonstrated as follows. Two loudspeakers are placed at different distances from the subject, say at 3 feet and 30 feet. Phonograph records are played into the loudspeakers through controlled amplification, first a bit into one loudspeaker and then, after a few seconds, a bit into the other

loudspeaker, and so on. The subject adjusts the amplification
of the nearer loudspeaker till it appears to be emitting sound of
the same intensity as the farther loudspeaker. He tries to equate
intensities *at the source,* and he does so with great accuracy.
Though less important than the ability to perceive the size and
shape of seen objects, this ability to perceive objective loudness fits in well with the general tendency to perceive the objective environment (*14*).

*Perceiving objects by echoes.* We see objects for the most
part by the light they reflect, but so far what we have said of
hearing objects refers to hearing the sources of the sound, such
as the person speaking or the automobile blowing its horn. If,
however, we hear an echo from a certain direction, we know
there must be some object over there reflecting the sound. A
river boat in a fog blows its horn so that echoes will reveal the
proximity of the shore. The blind make much use of reflected
sound for indicating the presence of walls, houses or any obstacles in their path (*13*). They perceive not only the direction
of an object but also its distance or at least whether it is very
near or not. Usually they cannot explain what cues they use
or how they perceive obstacles. Some of them have subscribed
to the theory of "facial vision" which supposed that the touch
and temperature senses of the face were affected by air currents or waves coming from the obstacles. But an auditory
theory was evidently possible. To test these theories a screen
was set up as an obstacle in a variable position in a large room,
and the blind (or blindfolded normal) subject was started toward the screen and told to signal as soon as he detected the
presence of the screen, and then to approach as near to it as he
could without touching it. Several important facts were established. The blind subjects detected the presence of the screen
from a considerable distance, often as great as 10–15 feet. The
normal-sighted but blindfolded subjects could not do very well
at first but improved with practice. The subjects' ability to perceive the screen from a distance was reduced by diminishing
the noise of their footsteps (stocking feet on a strip of heavy
carpet), and was entirely destroyed by plugging their ears,

whereas this power was only slightly reduced by shielding the face with a heavy veil (which also cut down the sounds to some extent). These and other experiments showed clearly that the blind person uses his ears and not the skin of his face in perceiving the presence of walls and other objects (*18*). A blind person is accustomed to make some noise as he walks, perhaps by thumping his cane on the sidewalk. He thus produces noises of high pitch which echo back more clearly than low-pitched tones. It has been discovered that bats flying in the dark and cleverly avoiding obstacles do so by the aid of echoes. They emit rapid series of "supersonic" cries, tones of vibration rates over 50,000 per second, far above the range of the human ear. If their ears are stopped, or if their mouths are gagged, they lose the power of avoiding obstacles. The principle of locating objects by reflected waves is employed in several modern devices, as in radar, only in this last it is radio waves and not sound waves which are sent out and reflected back to the perceiver (*5, 6, 7*).

## THE SENSE OF HEAD POSITION AND MOVEMENT

It is a surprising fact that some parts of the inner ear are not connected with hearing at all. In fact, if we trace the ear back in the animal series, we find that its first use was to respond not to vibrations, but to movements and positions of the head. The cochlea is a recent addition to the ear, and so also are the middle and outer ear. The vestibule and the semicircular canals are the old parts, and they are fundamentally more important than hearing, because, being stimulated by positions and movements of the head, they provide the sensory data for the maintenance of posture, orientation with respect to gravity, equilibrium, and steadiness of movement. They enable the fish to keep right side up in the water, the bird in the air, the frog to right himself instantly if placed on his back, and the cat to land on her feet when falling from a tree.

There are receptors in the vestibule and semicircular canals, consisting of hair cells, somewhat similar to those in the

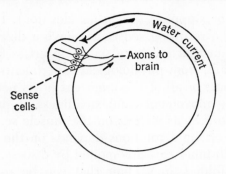

Fig. 118.—How the sense cells in a semicircular canal are stimulated by a fluid current. This current is an inertia back flow produced by a turning of the head in the reverse direction.

cochlea. In the vestibule, the hair-tips of the sense cells are matted together, and in the mat are embedded little particles of stone, the *otoliths*. When the head is inclined in any direction, these heavy particles sag and bend the hairs, so stimulating them; and the same result occurs, by inertia of the heavy particles, in any sudden starting or stopping of the body's motion. Around the base of the hair cells twine the fine terminations of sensory nerve fibers, which are excited by the activity of the sense cells, and pass the activity on to the brain.

Each semicircular canal has a bunch of sense cells, with long hairs sticking up into the fluid like reeds growing in a stream. Now, though the canals are called "semicircular," each is considerably more than a semicircle and, opening at each end into the vestibule, amounts to a complete circle. Rotating the head produces, by inertia of the fluid, a back flow in one or more of the canals, which bends the hairs and stimulates them. As the semicircular canals lie in three planes at right angles to each other, they provide a complete analyzer for head rotations in any direction. Meanwhile, the otolith receptors, which are also arranged in different planes, analyze the positions and rectilinear movements of the head. Thus the inner ear as a whole— quite apart from the cochlea—provides a complete analyzer for head positions and movements.

This sense is strongly stimulated by whirling, swinging, sud-

den starting or stopping (as in an elevator), turning somer-
saults, etc. The resulting sensations have a dizzy quality, but
it is not certain that all dizzy sensation arises from the inner
ear. It is certain, from physiological experiments involving destruction of part or all of the inner ear or its nerves, that postures, righting movements and steadiness of progression depend on this organ, as well as on the muscle sense.

Perception of slight rotations depends on the canals, and is
lost when both inner ears are spoiled by disease. If a person is
placed, blindfolded, in a chair that can be rotated without
sound or jar, he can easily tell when you start to turn him, and
in which direction. If you keep on turning him at a constant
speed, he soon ceases to sense the movement, and if you then
stop him, he believes you are starting to turn him in the opposite direction. He perceives the beginning of the rotation because this causes a back flow in the canals; he soon ceases to
sense the uniform rotation because friction in the slender canals
stops the back flow; and he mistakes the arrest of rotation for
the start of an opposite rotation because the fluid in the canals
continues flowing by inertia for a short time after the rotation
ceases.

Aside from the dizzy sensations resulting from strong stimulation of the semicircular canals, the impressions we get from
this source are perceptions rather than sensations. We perceive
the fact of being rotated without being aware of any particular
sensation from the ears or head. Reflex movements of the head
and eyes are another effect of stimulation of the canals.

## SUMMARY

1. The study of each sensory function includes two main
problems: the relation of *sensation* to stimuli, and the relation of
*perception* to objective facts.

    a. *Sense organs* are specialized tissues that have very high
      sensitivity to a particular kind of stimulus.

      (1) *Exteroceptors* receive stimuli from outside the or-

ganism. The *distance receptors* are the eye, ear, and nose.

(2) *Interoceptors* receive stimuli from the interior of the organism.

(3) *Proprioceptors* are located in the tissues of the body itself (muscles, tendons, joints), and are stimulated by movement of these parts.

b. Sense organs contain special *sense cells* from which the *sensory nerve fibers* run to the nerve centers. Many of the sense organs have *accessory apparatus* to convey the stimulus effectively to the sense cells.

2. Primary sensations from the skin are warmth, cold, pain and touch. Complex experiences such as burn, itch, tickle, or ache are variations or combinations of the primary sensations.

a. Stimuli for the skin senses may be mechanical, thermal or chemical. Thermal stimuli are sensed when they are above or below the temperature to which the skin receptors are *adapted* at the time.

b. Sensitivity is not uniform over the skin surface but is found in small discrete *spots*, each of which responds with only one type of sensation. Different kinds of nerve endings and accessory apparatus underlie the different kinds of spots.

3. *Muscle sense*, or kinesthetic sense, gives information about movements, postures and strains of parts of the body.

a. Receptors for the muscle sense are located in the muscles, tendons, and joints.

b. Normal coordination of movement depends on muscle sense.

4. *Organic sensations*, arising from sense cells in the internal organs, are important in motivation and emotion.

5. *Taste* sensations are limited to bitter, sweet, sour, and salty. The so-called tastes of foods and drinks are usually blends of several taste sensations combined with smell and sometimes temperature and touch sensations.

a. Sense cells are located in taste buds on the surface of the tongue. Different regions of the tongue are more sensitive to one taste than the others.

b. Stimuli for taste are chemical substances in solution.

6. *Smell sensations* may be roughly classified into six basic types which combine in various blends. Sense cells, embedded in the mucous membrane lining the nasal cavity, respond to minute quantities of chemical substances in the air.

7. *Hearing* is a sensation induced by slight wave vibrations in the air.

a. Sound waves set the *tympanic membrane* into vibration, from which the vibration is transmitted to the fluid in the *cochlea*.

b. Sense cells, located on the *basilar membrane* of the cochlea, respond selectively to certain frequencies of vibration.

c. Heard sounds differ basically in *loudness, pitch,* and *timbre,* corresponding to differences in the sound waves in *amplitude, frequency,* and *composition.*

d. Combinations of tones can be analyzed and heard separately but are ordinarily heard as a blend (chord or discord). A musical tone contains overtones which result in its particular quality.

e. Speech sounds are produced by vibration of the vocal cords with certain frequencies and amplitudes, modified by the positions of the mouth, tongue and lips.

f. In hearing there is less tendency than in seeing, to perceive the object rather than the stimuli, but in listening to speech we do tend to hear the meaning rather than the sounds themselves.

g. *Localization* of the source of sound is less accurate than visual localization. It depends on the time and intensity differences between the stimuli reaching the two ears, and so is effective in right-left localization but not in up-down or front-back.

h. The *intensity of a sound source* can be judged even when the distance, and the resulting stimulus intensity, are varied.

i. *Echoes* provide clues for the perception of the direction and distance of an object. Bats and blind persons utilize such clues to avoid obstacles in their paths.

8. Head position and movement are perceived on the basis of stimulation of the *vestibule* and *semicircular canals*.

# CHAPTER SIXTEEN

# *Learning*

O ne large and important question remains to be considered in this last part of the book. It is a question of achievement. How does the individual master the environment? And, we may add, how does he master himself? What psychology has to offer toward an answer to this question belongs largely under the headings of Learning, Remembering, and Thinking. Our task from now on is to discover how the individual attacks and masters new situations and problems, retains what he has achieved and puts it to use when he meets the same situation again or a similar situation. Thinking is a distinctively human way of attacking a problem. Learning and remembering are common to men and animals. Whenever the individual learns anything he is evidently dealing with a novel situation, for if the situation were perfectly familiar he could depend on memory and would not need to learn anything.

Although the intensive study of the processes of learning has been left until now, earlier chapters were compelled to take some account of learning in order to do justice to their own special topics. It was impossible to trace the individual's development without indicating how largely his abilities and personal traits depend on experience and learning. It was impossible to study unlearned motives alone without noticing the modifications due to experience and the new interests derived from acquaintance with the environment. And it was impossible to discuss observation without saying that through learning stimuli acquire meaning and become signs of objective facts. But while repeatedly emphasizing the importance of learning we have not yet made any serious study of the process of learning. This is one of the principal fields of psychological research and one in which the experimental method, from about 1880 to the present time, has been employed with great success.

**Definition.** A broad definition of learning was given in the chapter on Development. The individual, we said, is not passively molded by environmental forces. Instead he responds actively to stimuli, and it is in activity that he learns. Activity or exercise strengthens the muscle fibers and probably the neurons of the brain. But learning means something more than simple strengthening. A learned act is something new added to the individual's repertory. Typically at least learning consists in doing something new, provided this something new is retained by the individual and reappears in his later activities. The "something new" may be a combination of movements, as when the beginner in automobile driving learns to depress the clutch along with the brake; or it may be the noticing of a new object, as when you observe a stranger's face and can recognize him later. Learning is not any one special kind of activity, except that it must be new, either wholly or partially new.

But not every "something new" is learned. In attempting to master a novel situation you are likely to do a variety of things which get you nowhere and which are left behind and not retained, but a successful act is reinforced and learned. A proper combination of foot movements on brake and clutch pedals brings the car to a stop without stalling the engine, and so this particular movement gets reinforcement. Looking out at a "sea of faces" you see hundreds that make no particular impression and will never be remembered. They are not learned, but some one face may arrest your attention and awaken your interest, and this reinforcement will make that face rememberable. From such instances we came before to the idea that "reinforcement" was an essential factor in learning. In the present chapter we shall see how this idea works out.

**The importance of including animal learning in our study.** Many people are surprised when informed that much of the productive experimental work on learning has been done with animals as the subjects (8, 12, 14, 19, 29, 33). Why should psychologists be especially interested in animal learning? Of course they would like to know whether animals are capable of learning, but a few experiments were sufficient to prove that the higher animals learn a great deal and that some power of learning is present far down the animal scale. Why, then, not leave the animals aside and study learning where it is best developed, i.e., in human beings? The answer is that the fundamental processes of learning can be seen more clearly where they are relatively simple and not complicated by the higher intellectual processes of human beings. The power to learn, seen in both men and animals, is one of the most remarkable facts of nature, in a class with the power of reproduction and heredity. Such phenomena are a challenge to the scientist. He wants to know what goes on in the process of learning, whether in men or animals. He believes, too, that the more fundamental his knowledge, the more useful it will prove to be in the life of mankind. The rat learning the psychologist's mazes may help mankind to solve the international problems of the atomic age. Why not? Mankind has certainly got into a maze and must learn the way out. Men must learn the secret of peaceful international behavior. They must learn by exploring this maze, by discovering and eliminating the blind alleys, and by "reinforcing" the true paths when found.

In order to derive much benefit from animal experiments we must observe our animal subjects as objectively as possible, without reading human characteristics into their simpler behavior. If we carelessly assume that an animal is thinking and feeling as we do in a similar situation, we miss our chance of getting a glimpse of the more primitive subhuman way of at-

tacking a problem. We must be on our guard against anthropo-
morphism. This principle was laid down by one of the founders
of animal psychology and is named, in his honor, *Lloyd
Morgan's canon*. As he put it: "In no case may we interpret an
action as the outcome of a higher psychical faculty, if it can be
interpreted as the outcome of the exercise of one which stands
lower in the psychological scale" (*21*).

If we see a dog open a gate by lifting the latch with his
muzzle, we should not assume that he has reasoned out the
solution of this problem. We should take a dog that has not
learned the trick and watch him through the process of learning it, as was done by Lloyd Morgan with his fox terrier. When
the dog was first placed in a small front yard enclosed by a
picket fence, his behavior showed an eagerness (or a goal set)
to get out of the yard into the street. He pushed his nose between the pickets in one space after another. The gate latch
was in one of these spaces and in pushing his nose there he happened to raise the latch. The gate swung open and the dog
went out into the street. Next day and on several subsequent
days the dog still tried one space after another but more and
more in the neighborhood of the gate, till finally he always went
directly to the right place and raised the latch with a definite
lift of his head.

Nothing in this dog's behavior looks like reasoning, which
would be a more deliberate, less impulsive attack on the problem. His attack consisted in varying his activity while trying
all the time to get out. This line of attack is often called *trial
and error*, because it consists in trying many leads, most of
which turn out to be false leads or errors. The essentials of trial
and error are:

1. A "set" to reach a certain goal.
2. No obvious way to reach the goal.
3. Exploring the situation, finding possible leads and trying
them, backing off when blocked in one lead and shifting to
another.
4. Finally finding a good lead and reaching the goal.

All this could go on without any learning, but learning did

take place, as shown by the improvement from day to day. If we ask what the dog learned, his behavior shows that he learned *where* to work. First he learned *approximately* where to work, i.e., in the region of the gate, and later he learned *exactly* where to work, i.e., in one particular space between the pickets. This we may call *place learning*. Finally he learned how to manipulate the latch, and this we may call *thing learning* or *tool learning*.

In saying that the animal learns places and things, or learns to deal with places and things, we do not mean to prejudge the question of the psychological level of his learning. Lloyd Morgan's canon requires us to credit the animal with no higher mental processes than are necessary to account for the facts of his behavior. At the lowest possible level the animal would merely learn to respond to certain sensory stimuli by making certain muscular movements. At a somewhat higher level the animal by exploring a place would get to know the place, and by manipulating an object would get to know the object, so that his motor behavior would be governed by this knowledge rather than directly by the stimuli received. A great number and variety of experiments on place and tool learning have been carried on by psychologists in the hope of discovering exactly *what* the animal does learn, and *how* he learns.

## PLACE LEARNING

All animals, except perhaps some of the invertebrates, explore places and so learn to get around in them without much lost motion. The favorite animal of the psychologists for the investigation of place learning is the rat, especially the white or albino rat. The white rat is bred in laboratories so that his heredity, age and past experience are known. These important variables are thus much better controlled than they can be in most experiments on human subjects.

**Negative adaptation.** When a rat is placed in a new place—a box, pen or other small enclosure—he shows signs of fear or caution. He may struggle frantically to escape or he may cower timidly in one corner. His emotional disturbance subsides after a while, and he begins to explore the place. If he is taken out then but replaced next day in the same enclosure, his behavior shows that he has learned something, since his emotional upset is less marked and he wanders freely from one part of the enclosure to another, sniffing at the walls and at any object he may find. If the place is pretty bare, with no food present nor anything of importance to a rat, this exploratory activity ceases after a time, and next day in the same enclosure there will be less of it. Again, the rat's modified behavior shows that he has learned something.

The learning so far goes by the name of "negative adaptation." The rat became adapted to the place and the adaptation consisted in the elimination of certain responses. First the fear responses dropped out and later the exploratory responses. The fear responses were not reinforced by finding anything dangerous in the enclosure, and the exploratory responses ceased when the place had been thoroughly explored.

Negative adaptation, a fundamental kind of learning, is important in many ways. The horse gets used to the harness, and the dog to the presence of a cat in the house. Taming an animal consists largely in getting him accustomed to handling which at first arouses a violent reaction of escape or attack. Man also becomes negatively adapted to situations which at first make him feel frightened or insecure. His fear responses "adapt out," and the same is true of his exploratory responses as illustrated by the fact that a noise which at first arouses sharp attention ceases to be noticed at all after it has been repeated many times. Negative adaptation eliminates responses that are not worth the trouble. It leaves the individual free to deal with the important things in the situation. It is a part of his situation set (p. 222).

The rat in the maze.    In a maze consisting of narrow passages between walls, with some blind alleys and a crooked through route leading to a food box, the rat cannot see far ahead (as the human subject can in working his way through a pencil maze like the one on p. 42), and at first the rat has no definite goal.

Fig. 119.—The white rat exploring a maze. This is the old Hampton Court type of maze, mostly replaced for animal experiments by more standardized forms. The wire-mesh cover has been removed for photographic purposes. The rat is seen in a blind alley. The experimenter is taking the time with a stopwatch.

But he soon begins to explore, wandering through the various passages and sniffing everywhere. In the course of these wanderings he reaches the food box and eats. Taken out and replaced at the starting point, he shows that he has already learned something, for his behavior is less leisurely, more hurried, and with less dallying in the blind alleys. He now has a definite goal. If given one or more trials a day in the same maze, he goes less and less deeply into the blind alleys, later merely hesitates at the entrance to a blind alley before going on, and finally passes by without so much as turning his head. Eventually he passes all the blind alleys and runs swiftly from the starting point to the food box. Now exactly what has this rat learned?

According to the *chain reflex theory* he has learned a fixed series of movements. At first he made a lot of miscellaneous movements and most of them, as in exploring the blind alleys, were superfluous. These useless ones being gradually eliminated, what remains is a regular chain of movements, made in response to the regular series of stimuli from the successive parts of the maze. This theory has the merit of simplicity but has been disproved by a variety of experiments which show that the rat's movements in running a well-learned maze are by no means so stereotyped as the theory demands. The following

Courtesy, C. J. Warden

FIG. 120.—A modern type of maze. The rat is being placed at the starting point by one experimenter, while another experimenter stands near the food box ready to time the run.

experiment is especially convincing. A maze was so constructed that it could be flooded with water, either shallow water permitting the animal to wade or deep water forcing him to swim. Rats that learned to follow the correct path to the food while wading continued to follow the same path when the water was deep and forced them to swim; and *vice versa*. Now a chain of wading movements cannot be carried over into deep water, nor a chain of swimming movements into shallow water. Therefore what the rats learned and carried over from one condition to the other was something quite different from a chain of movements; they had learned the correct *path* to the food box —just as a dog that has hurt one foot and is hobbling along on the other three is not lost by any means but still knows the way home (*18*).

The *fixed path theory*, however, is not adequate. One fixed path through the maze is not all the animal learns. Place a rat several times in a simple square enclosure with the food box always in a certain corner, and after he has learned to go promptly from the entrance to the food box introduce partial barriers into the middle of the enclosure. The rat still heads for the food box and negotiates the necessary detours without much trouble (*10*). Or place a rat in a strange maze with no food present in the food box; after he has thoroughly explored the maze, start giving the food; he now learns the correct path

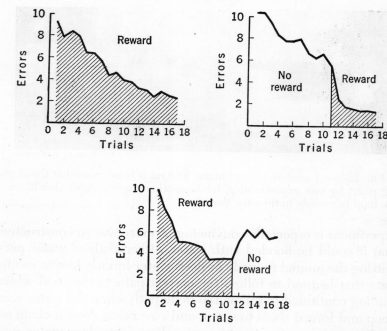

FIG. 121.—Learning curves of three groups of rats, the first group being rewarded at every trial, the second group not until trial No. 11., and the third group having no reward from trial No. 11 on. The errors, consisting of entrance into blind alleys, become fewer as the rat masters the maze (Tolman & Honzik, *30*).

very quickly, showing that his preliminary exploration taught him a good deal though it gave him no fixed path to the food box. The results of one experiment of this sort are shown in Figure 121. There were three "groups" of about 35–40 rats, the rats being run singly, however, not in groups. Each rat had one trial per day. The rats of the first group found food in the food box on every trial; their learning curve shows the usual gradual improvement. The second group explored for 10 trials without any reward except that of being taken out when they reached the empty food box, but beginning with the eleventh trial they found food there; they then mastered the correct path so quickly as to prove that they had already accomplished most of the necessary learning. The third group found food for 10

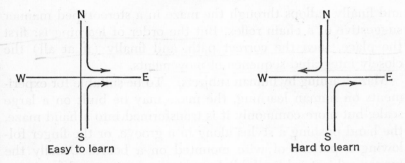

Easy to learn                              Hard to learn

FIG. 122.—In an experiment specially designed to test the place-learn-
ing theory, one group of rats always found food at the same place, E,
whether they were put in at N or at S. They had to turn left at the
junction when approaching from N, but to turn right when approaching
from S. Another group had always to make a right turn at the junction,
finding food at W when approaching from N, but at E when approaching
from S. It proved to be very much easier for the rat to learn to go to a
fixed place than to learn to make the same motor response at the junction.
Suitable variations in the experiment excluded any other interpretation
(31).

trials and no more; they soon began again to explore, so
proving that mastery of the maze is not the same as an inner
compulsion to follow a fixed path. Notice also Figure 122.

From all the evidence the best answer to the question as to
what the rat learns in a maze seems to be just this, that he
learns the maze itself. He discovers walls, corners, dead ends,
clear paths, and locates them more or less definitely in the maze
as a whole. He discovers the food box and locates this more or
less definitely. He perceives these facts and retains some of the
facts perceived so that the maze gradually becomes a familiar
place. He gets acquainted with this particular environment,
"set" for this objective situation, and his movements, while still
varying more or less, are governed by this set.

There are probably several stages in the full mastery of a
maze. There is first the emotional adjustment, followed by exploring the maze and becoming familiar with it. Blind alleys are
gradually left aside and the economical through route adopted.
The problem, we may say, has now been solved "in principle."
If many additional trials are given, the rat increases his speed

and finally gallops through the maze in a stereotyped manner suggestive of a chain reflex. But the order of learning is: first the place, then the correct path, and finally (if at all) the closely integrated sequence of movements.

**Maze learning by human subjects.**   To be suitable for experiments on human learning, the maze may be built on a large scale, but more commonly it is transformed into a hand maze, the hand pushing a stylus along in a groove, or the finger following a pattern of wire mounted on a board. Usually the human subject is blindfolded or somehow prevented from getting a comprehensive view of the entire maze. Comparison of rats and men in their learning of the same maze pattern tends to increase our respect for the rat. Often the rat learns it as quickly as the man. The rat makes more numerous errors at first and may re-enter the same blind alley time and again in the same trial. The human adult is more deliberate and tries to check off the blind alleys as he discovers them so as not to repeat the same error. He is apt to be self-conscious and to feel ashamed when he finds himself in a blind alley. We do not credit the rat with any self-consciousness or with any feelings of shame.

Nor do we credit the rat with anything corresponding to the *verbal aids* which the human subject uses to good advantage in some mazes. A formula like "once to the right, then twice to the left, then twice to the right," and so on, is useful for fixing the details rather than for grasping the general spatial pattern of a maze; it does not take the place of genuine place learning (32).

The human subject, after learning a maze, can make a rough drawing of the correct path; he can remember the path when he is not actually in the maze. He "recalls" the maze and the path (p. 569). We need not credit the rat with any recall memory, for there is no way to demonstrate that the rat remembers anything about the maze when he is not in the maze. We probably can credit the rat with recognition memory, since he shows familiarity with the maze by doing the right thing at the right place. In fact "place learning" implies that after a rat has sufficiently explored a maze he recognizes its parts as he comes to them.

The introspections of a human subject yield some valuable indications of what he learns in a maze. *General orientation* and *specific landmarks* are learned, according to his testimony. After one or two trials he is somewhat "oriented," i.e., he knows the general direction of the goal. And after a few more trials he reports that he has noticed certain outstanding parts of the correct path, and that he recognizes these landmarks when he comes to them again and so knows he is on the right path. They serve as intermediate goals which he strives to reach. Such landmarks, along with the start and finish of the maze, are learned quickly and provide a framework into which the remaining details are fitted as they become known (5). There are indications in the rat's behavior that he, too, soon becomes oriented toward the goal and that he recognizes landmarks along the way.

The maze is simply a small sample of the problem of finding your way in the environment. Many animals—many kinds of mammals, birds and fishes—show such remarkable ability in finding their way over long distances as to raise the question whether they do not possess some special "sense of direction" not present in man. Without going into the evidence on this question we may simply say that it is against the theory of a special sense of direction. The carrier pigeon, for example, depends on landmarks which he can see with his keen eyes (33).

Man certainly possesses no mysterious sense of direction, though we sometimes speak as if he did because he has considerable ability to maintain his orientation, or "keep his bearings," as well as superior ability to observe landmarks and recognize them later. When two persons are motoring together along the back country roads, or hiking together in the woods where the trails are not marked with signs, it often happens that one of the two relies more on keeping his bearings, the other more on finding landmarks which he can recognize. Either person may go wrong, since the one may become "turned around" more or less completely, while the other may

forget or confuse his landmarks. It is a case where two heads
are better than one. Man performs surprising feats of finding
his way, assisting himself however by various devices which
he has invented—the road sign, the map, the lighthouse, the
mariner's compass, the radio beam—and man has the intellectual ability to plan his route in advance as well as to recall
it afterwards.

## THING LEARNING, TOOL LEARNING

If place learning is learning by exploration, what we are
now to consider is learning by manipulation. To get acquainted
with a place, you move around while using the senses; you combine locomotion with observation. To get acquainted with a
thing you often have to handle it and put it through its paces
—especially if the thing is a tool. A tool, we may say, is a thing
to be manipulated so as to produce certain results. You get
acquainted with a tool by manipulating it and observing the
results. Though the use of tools and the manipulation of things
are seen most extensively in human beings, from childhood up,
such behavior is not lacking by any means in animals. Instead
of hands (as demanded by the strict meaning of the word
*manipulate*) the animal may use fore feet or hind feet, teeth,
tusks, snout, beak, or any part of the body in moving objects
and getting acquainted with them.

Our main question here, as in the case of maze learning,
is what the animal learns. Does he learn certain movements or
does he learn certain characteristics of the things he employs
as tools?

The cat in the Thorndike puzzle-box.   Place a hungry young
cat in a small cage, with a bit of fish lying just outside, and you
usually get plenty of action. The cat extends her paw between
the bars of the cage but cannot reach the fish; she pushes her
nose between the bars but cannot get through; she bites the
bars, claws at anything small, shakes anything that is loose,
and is likely to try every part of the cage, though mostly the
parts near the fish. Sooner or later she attacks the button which

is holding the door shut and in manipulating it she happens to turn the button; the door swings open and the cat goes out to her reward. The experimenter, having recorded the time consumed in this first trial, replaces the still hungry cat in the cage with another bit of fish outside. Trial-and-error behavior again, though probably less of it than before. In further trials the useless movements are gradually eliminated, till finally, on being placed in the cage, the cat promptly turns the button and gets out within a couple of seconds. Perhaps 10–20 trials, distributed over several days, have been required to master the trick.

Older cats, or placid cats, or cats that for some reason are not so eager, go through less of this motor activity and yet may learn the trick in fewer trials than the excited ones—a fact which suggests that the use of the senses rather than vigorous motor activity is an important factor in learning. Another relevant fact is that the cats, after getting out once, concentrate their activity in the region of the door; they have already achieved some *place learning*. In one type of puzzle-box a loop of string or wire, hanging in the cage, will release the door if given a pull. The cats soon concentrate their activity upon this loop. If the experimenter moves the loop to another part of the cage, the behavior of the cats is interesting in two ways. They go first to the place where the loop has been and claw in the air there as if expecting to find the loop—thus showing that they have learned the *place*—and later when they find the loop in its new position they pull it as they have learned to do in its former position, showing that they have learned the *thing*. They are dealing with things rather than going through a gymnastic exercise. But, one may ask, have they not learned simply to make certain movements at sight of certain things? If that were a fair statement, they should always, after learning a trick, execute it with the same movement. As a matter of fact, the cat that has learned to pull a loop sometimes uses her claws and sometimes her teeth to secure the same result. Sometimes the movement becomes stereotyped but usually not (*1, 9, 28*).

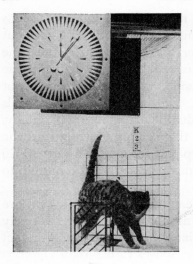

Fig. 123.—Cat opening the door of a puzzle-box by pushing a pole with her side. The cat entered the box or cage by the small door at the back and advanced toward the wire door in front, meanwhile pushing the upright pole with her left side. Any push on this pole opened the front door. The two views show the same cat in two trials, and the clock gives the time up to the moment of pushing the pole; it reads 6 seconds for trial 23, and 5 seconds for trial 38. This particular animal always pushed the pole with her left side. Other animals used a paw or the head, many of them in this situation adopting a stereotyped procedure. In other puzzle-boxes each animal's procedure is apt to vary from trial to trial. Even here, close inspection of the pictures shows that the cat is improving her technique. In the second picture she has not turned so far away from the door and is more ready to approach it as soon as it opens.

It appears, then, that what the cat learns is not a certain movement or series of movements, but the useful character of certain objects and the useless character of others. She finds the spaces between the bars useless, too narrow to let her through; she finds the door button movable and useful for opening the door. These characteristics of objects are gradually borne in on her and finally well learned. On the motor side there is very little new learning required, for the movements needed to pull a string or turn a door button are old, familiar movements. In the mastery of simple tools, as in the mastery of a maze, old and familiar movements will do the trick once the objective situation is perceived. Once the rat has discovered what path to follow through the maze, his customary walking and running movements enable him to follow that path; and once the cat has discovered the turnable button or the pullable string in the puzzle-box, her customary clawing and biting movements enable her to use this tool successfully. In both cases, to be sure, continued practice may develop a higher degree of motor skill.

**Tool learning by monkeys and chimpanzees.** As compared with cats and dogs, monkeys have better hands for manipulating, better eyes for observing, and larger brains for learning. They learn more quickly and master more complicated tools. The anthropoid apes, especially the chimpanzee, surpass the monkeys in brain size and probably approach more nearly to the human tool-using ability.

Some psychologists are not pleased with the maze and puzzle-box experiments which place the animal in a blind situation. Such a situation has to be explored bit by bit, and this long-drawn-out trial-and-error behavior may conceal rather than reveal the essential process of mastering and learning the problem. Relatively free from such complications is the *reaching-stick problem* for monkeys and chimpanzees. The monkey is in a cage with a banana or other bait lying on the floor outside, too far away to be reached by the hand and arm; but a stick is lying conveniently near. The monkey soon learns to pull the banana in by use of the stick. He is then given the two-stick problem: a short stick lying close at hand will not reach the banana but will reach a longer stick which has to be pulled in first and then used on the banana. The monkey learns this trick and others requiring the use of three or more sticks.

A chimpanzee, having already learned to use a stick to pull in a banana, was given two sticks of bamboo, neither of them being long enough to reach the banana, but one being small enough in diameter to fit into the open end of the other. Would the animal have intelligence enough to construct and use a *jointed stick?* After an hour of fruitless efforts with the single sticks, the chimpanzee had thoroughly learned that these were

FIG. 124.—Monkey working at a multiple stick problem. To reach the incentive the longest stick is needed, and a series of shorter sticks must be pulled in, one after the other, in order to secure the longest stick.

512

too short. He gave up and went to the rear of his cage. While there he began playing with the two sticks and in his play got them end to end and pushed the smaller one a short distance into the larger. Up he jumped, ran to the front of the cage, and started to pull in the banana with his jointed stick. The loosely joined pieces fell apart, but he promptly put them together again and secured the banana. Without stopping to eat, he pulled in everything else within reach of his new tool. The next day, on being retested, he began with a few useless movements but in just a few seconds reconstructed his jointed stick and used it as before (16). This experiment has been repeated with similar results on young children (2).

**Insight.** The dramatic moment when this chimpanzee passed from a state of helplessness to one of assured mastery of the problem may be called a moment of *insight,* though this word is really too strong since it usually implies a penetration below the surface of things, while all we mean here is that the animal saw he now had a good long stick in place of the useless short ones. He perceived or observed something helpful in solving his problem. Even the word *observation* is too strong if it suggests any deliberate effort to perceive. All we mean is that the animal, by using his senses, gets acquainted with objects and especially with those he can use in reaching his goal.

Insight is sometimes *foresight* and sometimes *hindsight.* When the chimpanzee ran with his jointed stick to the front of the cage and reached for the banana, he showed foresight —he foresaw success. He saw the way clear to his goal. The cat in the puzzle-box, the rat in the maze, the dog behind the picket fence, could not see any sure way to reach the goal. They could see leads, possible ways to the goal. When they tried a lead and were blocked they may have had some hindsight, i.e., they may have observed that this was a false lead; and when they tried something that worked they may have observed the goodness of that lead. Foresight is seeing the way to the goal before taking it—or perceiving the uselessness of a certain lead without trying it—and hindsight is observing that a lead is good or bad after trying it. When the whole situation is clear and aboveboard, there is a good chance for foresight, but when important characteristics of the situation have to be discovered by exploration and manipulation, hindsight is the best we can expect.

**Tool learning by human subjects.**    Instead of the simple puzzle-boxes used with animals, a mechanical puzzle is difficult enough for the human adult. The puzzle is to be taken seriously, and practice continued until the subject can manipulate the puzzle quickly and uniformly with no errors or hitches in the performance. The experimenter notes the time required by the subject to take the pieces apart and observes his mode of attack, while the subject reports after each trial what he can remember of his efforts and difficulties.

The human subject's first attack on a puzzle consists largely of trial and error. Impulsively he tries one possible opening after another, sometimes following the same false lead repeatedly, till, more or less by chance, the pieces come apart to his surprise and gratification. Some few individuals make a more deliberate attack and attempt to study out the puzzle by looking at it; but this apparently rational procedure seldom succeeds because the three-dimensional movements of the pieces cannot be discovered without actual manipulation.

In the second trial the subject may still be at a loss and proceed in the same haphazard manner as at first; but usually he has observed one or two helpful facts. He is most likely to have noticed what part of the puzzle he was working at when he succeeded; for *locations* are about the easiest facts to observe —easiest for men as well as animals. In the course of a few trials the subject eliminates many of the false leads and perhaps "sees into" the puzzle more or less clearly, though he may learn to manipulate the thing correctly without really knowing what happens.

The insight that occurs in solving a three-dimensional puzzle is mostly of the hindsight variety. It need not be at all profound to be useful in solving the immediate problem. The more profound it is the wider is its sphere of possible application. One interesting question is whether *skill in manipulating* an object

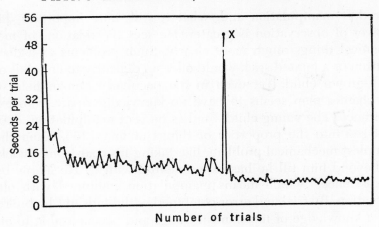

FIG. 125.—Learning curve of a human subject in mastering a mechanical puzzle. The trials are arranged in their order from left to right, the time taken in each trial being indicated by the height of the point above the base line. Improvement is shown by the gradual descent of the curve. At the point X the subject observed something about the puzzle that he had not noticed before and studied it out carefully, so increasing his time for this one trial but permanently bettering his performance (Data from Ruger, 25).

is acquired by observation. When the subject first succeeds in solving one of these mechanical puzzles his manipulation is awkward, but he acquires skill by repeated trials. Sometimes he reports noticing some characteristic of the puzzle and being helped by this observation in his efforts to handle the puzzle smoothly and quickly. An instance is recorded in Figure 125. To assert that all skill is gained by observation and that all learning is accomplished by observation is going pretty far— much beyond the evidence now available. But it is clear that in handling any sort of tool, whether hammer or golf stick, you attend more to the tool and other objects concerned, like the nail or the golf ball, than you do to your own movements; and this fact suggests that observation of the objects and of the results accomplished plays an important part in mastering the operation.

In understanding and handling mechanical things man's superiority to animals is very great. His hands are more suited for deft manipulation and, what is still more important, his power of observation is greater. He sees the relations of mechanical things much more clearly. Such problems as a door button or a jointed stick would offer no difficulty to an adult or half-grown child. Yet even in the peculiarly human field of mechanics man seems to have no knowledge apart from experience. The young child, fond as he is of manipulation, does not see into the properties of things at first (15). Even the simplest mechanical problem, like taking his coat from a hook, is beyond him till he has experimented with it. He learns by "experience," which means manipulation combined with observation. By trial and error combined with hindsight he builds up a knowledge of mechanical things and becomes able to attack new mechanical problems with some degree of foresight.

Not only mechanical things but even social requirements are learned by the child through trial and error combined with observation, as we saw in the case of the group code of ethics (p. 138). After acquiring a fund of knowledge of these matters he is able to proceed with some foresight.

**Differences between human and animal learning.**   The main points of human superiority, so far revealed in our study, seem to be the following.

1.  Man is a better observer; he observes many characteristics of things, people and situations that lie beyond the animal's scope.

2.  Man uses more deliberation, management and control in attacking a problem.

3.  Man makes much use of names, numbers and in general of language in learning.

4.  Partly by aid of language, man is able to think about problems even when the materials are not before him. After struggling vainly with a puzzle, a subject has been known to reach a solution while lying in bed the next morning. Ideation, the thinking of things that are not present to the senses at the moment, is doubtless much more highly developed in man than in any other animal.

**"Higher units" in skillful activity.**   Among the tools which a human being learns to operate with great skill are such instruments as the typewriter, the violin, the airplane. These call for complex combinations and sequences of muscular movements nicely adjusted to the instrument. Another "tool" consists of the subject's own mouth, tongue and larynx—his vocal and speech apparatus—which he certainly operates with great skill in talking and singing. How does the individual learn these skills and exactly what does he have to learn in order to become expert? Take typewriting for example, since it has been studied experimentally.

In learning to typewrite you must first do some place learning. You learn the arrangement of the letters on the keyboard, and to do the job right you learn which finger to use in striking each letter. If you are going to adopt the "touch system" you learn to locate the letters without seeing the actual keyboard. After some practice you can hit the right letter almost every time and without much feeling around. In writing a word you spell it out and respond to each separate letter by the appropriate finger movement. Having accomplished so much you naturally assume that you have mastered the problem "in principle" and have only to build up your speed of striking the letters.

But there is much more to it than that. So far you have learned the correct responses to single letters, you have acquired the necessary *letter habits*. As you continue your practice you will find after a while that you are beginning to use some *word habits*. You are now responding to a short familiar word as a whole, without spelling it out, and you are combining the necessary finger movements into an integrated act of writing the whole word. Take the word *and,* for example, the first and last letters being written with the left hand, the middle one with the right hand. Instead of writing three separate letters—*a*, pause; *n*, pause; *d*, pause—as you did at first, you now, after striking *a* with the left hand, hold that hand ready to strike *d*, meanwhile inserting the *n* with the right hand. So it is with many other common words and with common prefixes, suffixes and other letter sequences. Your two hands and your

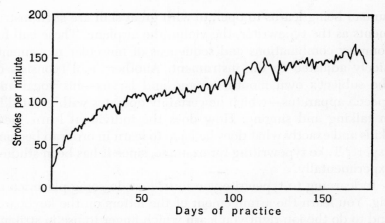

FIG. 126.—Learning curve of a young man in typewriting. Each point on the curve shows a day's record in number of strokes per minute (Book, *4*).

ten fingers are now making team plays instead of individual plays. Such integrated responses are true units, and they are "higher units" in relation to the letter habits. It is a smoother and quicker process to write a word as a whole than to write a series of separate letters. By developing these higher units, then, the learner advances toward expert work.

What happens, however, goes beyond the mere acquisition of a certain stock of higher units. If we notice how the word unit "and" is executed, we see that the typist, while writing the first letter, is already getting ready for the subsequent letters of the word. He is free to do this because he has his letter-striking movements under good control and does not need to give them close attention, one by one. Not only in the familiar words but also in all his writing, the expert typist is preparing in advance for the letters he is about to write. *Preparation* for what has to be done next is an important key to skill (*4*).

Higher units, and preparation for the later phase of an act while the earlier phase is being executed, are present in many kinds of skilled performance, as in talking, in singing or playing any musical instrument, in the running high jump or the pole vault. A word consists of a sequence of sounds, produced by a sequence of speech movements, but it is certainly a unit to the speaker and to the listener as well. A familiar phrase is spoken and heard as a unit. In connected speech the speaker is always preparing in advance for what he is about to say, and the listener, too, is getting ready for what the speaker is about to say. Often he knows what is coming before the speaker can get the words out.

**The progress of skill learning.**   To reach perfection in quality and quantity of work, in accuracy and speed, a typist would certainly need much practice. But would practice, no matter how much of it, guarantee perfection? Because of individual differences in capacity for this kind of work, we must in fairness regard a typist as perfect if he has reached the maximum of which he is individually capable. The maximum of which an individual is capable is his *physiological limit,* a limit imposed by the characteristics of his sense organs, muscles, nerves, etc. The eyes have their limits of keenness, the muscles their limits of possible strength, the nerves their limits of conducting speed. A clear example of the physiological limit is found in the hundred-yard dash, since apparently no one can lower the record below 9 or 10 seconds, and relatively few individuals reach that speed, no matter how long and hard they train. But has a much-practiced individual necessarily reached his physiological limit?

If we look closely at the typist's learning curve in Figure 126, we can notice some facts that bear on our problem. We see that the gain in speed was rapid at first and became less rapid as the practice continued. This gradual flattening of a learning curve is very common though not universal. Beginning after about 42 days and continuing for about 30 days, this learner scarcely gained at all, and he may have thought he had reached his limit. It was not his physiological limit, however, for with further practice he began to improve again, and he gained a good deal more before the end of the record, with no clear indication even then that his limit had been reached.

A long flat stretch in the learning curve, a long period of almost no improvement, is picturesquely called a *plateau,* provided it is followed by more improvement or is somehow

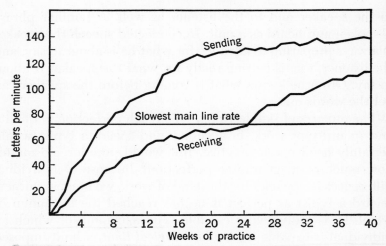

Fɪɢ. 127.—Learning curves of a student of telegraphy. The height of a curve above the base line shows the number of letters sent or received per minute. A rise of the curve denotes improvement. There is a plateau in the receiving curve. This old figure is a classic in the psychology of learning (Bryan & Harter, 6).

known to be below the physiological limit.] Many learning curves, though not all by any means, show more or less of a plateau (6).

There are two main causes of these plateaus: poor motivation, and poor method of work. By "poor" is meant that the motivation is not strong enough, nor the method efficient enough, to push the learner on toward his true limit. Motivation is poor when the learner becomes discouraged and feels that he does not have the ability or energy to reach an expert level. (He may be right, too, for many young people aspire to be professional musicians, for example, who can never "make the grade" though they could advance somewhat beyond the point where they give up.)

Motivation is poor in another way when the learner is well satisfied with moderate achievement and perhaps is really doing good enough work to hold a job. He may jog along for years without making any further improvement, so that in his case a large amount of practice does not make perfect. After these years on a plateau some special incentive may stimulate the routine worker to greater effort with the surprising result of marked improvement—as has been demonstrated in certain industrial experiments. See pages 333, 334.

In spite of excellent motivation a learner may continue on a long plateau because his method of work is not well adapted to the instruments and materials he is using. A clear case is shown in Figure 125. As this curve is plotted in time per unit of work instead of work per unit of time, improvement makes the curve go down instead of up as in Figure 126. This curve starts down rapidly and then flattens out. It reaches a plateau and stays there until the learner discovers a better way of handling the material, when it descends to a lower level which was probably close to the physiological limit.

In most cases when we think we are doing about as well as we possibly can, the chances are that we are on a plateau and not at our physiological limit. Of course there is no point in attempting to be perfect experts in everything we do. A person with such an aspiration must certainly be over-motivated. But if what we lack is good methods of work, there can be no undue strain in substituting them for inferior methods, if we can discover what are the best methods. The good teacher or coach can be of great assistance both on the side of motivation and on that of expert method of work.

## CONDITIONING OR
## THE LEARNING OF SEQUENCES

To be well acquainted with the environment and well equipped to deal with it, an individual has to do a great deal of place learning and thing learning, as we have already seen, and now we must notice that something more is necessary. The world is something more than a world of places and things; it is also a world of happenings, of events, of changes. Many of the changes are regular and dependable so that when the event A occurs the event B is pretty sure to follow. If the individual is capable of learning the sequence, A-B, he can take

A as a signal that B is coming and be ready for B when it arrives. To be prepared in advance for what is about to happen would be a great help in dealing with the environment.

Now it is certain that the human individual does become acquainted with many regular sequences and does know what to expect in many familiar situations. From early childhood he has been learning sequences. He has learned the lightning-thunder sequence so that when he sees the lightning he expects to hear the thunder very soon. He has learned to expect a bounce when a ball falls to the ground, a crash when a dinner plate falls, a wail when a baby falls. He has learned the sequence of words in a familiar proverb, and the sequence of notes in a familiar song. He has learned the normal sequence of parts in any sentence so that on hearing the subject he expects a predicate to follow. Even a single heard word is a sequence of speech sounds, and he certainly is well acquainted with many words. In short there are numberless regular sequences of stimuli which he observes, learns and remembers.

In his own movements, too, there are many regular sequences which become familiar and almost automatic in his behavior. When he speaks a familiar word he is making a learned sequence of speech movements. A song which he sings from memory is another example. The "higher units" in typewriting and other skilled performances are excellent examples.

Besides these sequences of stimuli and sequences of movements, there are many well-learned sequences consisting of both sensory stimuli and motor responses. Such a sequence will have the form,

$$S_1—R_1—S_2—R_2,$$

and may run on to quite a number of stimuli and responses. In many cases $S_1$ is a signal or warning that $S_2$ is coming, and $R_1$ is a preparation for $R_2$. The two stimuli may be "Ready!—Go!" and the first response, $R_1$, is a posture of readiness for the quick getaway which is $R_2$. This ready posture of the runner was used once before as the classic example of a preparatory set (p. 215). The reaction time experiment, mentioned in the same connection, furnishes another good example of an $S_1$—$R_1$—$S_2$—$R_2$ sequence. To the ready signal ● responds by placing his finger on the reaction key and looking at the place where the flash of light is going to appear, and when the flash comes he responds by lifting his finger in the quick time of ⅕ of a second. His reaction time would be much longer if he were not prepared.

In this experiment the preparatory response of placing the finger on the key is definitely voluntary and purposeful. O knows what he is doing and why. But he is not definitely conscious of the muscular tension in his arm which is an *involuntary* part of his preparation for a quick reaction. If electrodes are placed over the finger muscles in the forearm and the muscle currents tapped, amplified and recorded, it is found that the muscles are already beginning to act before the reaction stimulus ($S_2$) arrives, though their action is usually not strong enough to lift the finger prematurely. The preparatory set, $R_1$, includes this involuntary muscular tension as well as the voluntary act of placing the finger on the key (7).

In the same way the runner voluntarily assumes some standard ready posture which the trainer has taught him, but even if he had received no training he would involuntarily take some sort of a ready posture and his muscles would be tense because of his eagerness to get started. There are many similar cases. During roll call you follow along the series of names and just before your own name is reached you make the preparatory (and probably involuntary) response of drawing in air which you then exhale in the final response of saying "Here!"

We see from these examples that the preparatory response may be either voluntary or involuntary, or partly one and partly the other. We see, too, that the preparatory response may be either similar to the final response or quite dissimilar. The slight activity in the finger muscles is similar to the strong action of the same muscles in lifting the finger from the key, but the inhalation of air in preparation for vocalization is an altogether different movement from the exhalation of air in actual vocalization.

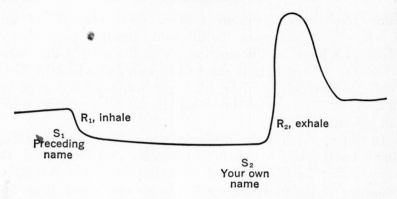

FIG. 128.—The sequence of events in answering the roll call. Here S₁ is the calling of the name preceding your own name, and S₂ is the calling of your own name. Your R₁ is the inhalation preparatory to speaking, and R₂ is the exhalation involved in saying "Here!"

The typical "conditioned response" is an involuntary preparatory response, called out by a signal which regularly precedes an important stimulus—such a stimulus as calls out an important final response. The conditioned response may resemble the final response more or less, or it may be altogether different, so long as it is preparatory. Though the conditioned response is typically involuntary, it is sometimes more or less voluntary. But a definitely planned preparatory response, or one that is taught by a trainer, would scarcely be called a conditioned response. Essentially, conditioning is the process of learning a new $S_1$—$R_1$—$S_2$—$R_2$ sequence. This form of learning has been studied with very instructive results.

Pavlov's classical experiments on conditioning. About the year 1900 this eminent Russian physiologist, while engaged in the study of digestion, using dogs as subjects, devised a method for measuring the flow of saliva. The duct of one of the salivary glands was made to discharge on the outside of the dog's cheek so that the saliva could be drained off into a measuring instrument. While using this apparatus Pavlov incidentally observed saliva flowing not only when food was in the mouth but also when the dog saw food in his dish before starting to eat, or saw the attendant bringing the food dish, or even heard the attendant's footsteps approaching from the next room. The flow of saliva when food is actually in the mouth is a natural reflex (p. 243), but when it was aroused by such stimuli as the sight of a dish or the sound of footsteps it was obviously a learned response and dependent on the conditions in which the animal had previously been fed in the laboratory. Pavlov accordingly called it a "conditioned reflex." Not being a reflex in the strict sense it is better called a conditioned response (23).

The sight of the dish or the sound of the footsteps was a signal that food was coming, and the advance flow of saliva before food was actually in the mouth was a preparatory response. The dog had evidently learned an $S_1$—$R_1$—$S_2$—$R_2$ sequence. Here:

$S_1$, also labeled CS (the conditioned stimulus) is the sight of the dish or the sound of the footsteps;

$R_1$, also labeled CR (the conditioned response) is the advance flow of saliva;

$S_2$, also labeled US (the unconditioned stimulus) is food in the mouth; and

$R_2$, also labeled UR (the unconditioned response) is the reflex flow of saliva aroused by food in the mouth.

**Pavlov's laws of conditioning.** Believing he had struck a good lead toward the study of brain functions, Pavlov devoted his energies and those of his students to experimenting on the conditioned response. They performed a great variety of experiments and discovered laws which have since been confirmed by investigators in other laboratories. For the student of learning the most important of Pavlov's laws are the following.

*1. Establishment of the CR by repetition with reinforcement.* In the hope of discovering how such responses were acquired, Pavlov attempted to "condition" the salivary response to a perfectly arbitrary stimulus like the sound of a bell, a touch on the skin, or any stimulus which would attract attention without greatly disturbing the animal. He succeeded by using a certain regular procedure. A hungry dog—a well-treated animal, fully at home in the laboratory—was placed on a table, standing but with slings under his body that prevented his walking away. When the animal had become quiet and adjusted to this situation, an electric bell was started, and food was placed in his mouth after the bell had been ringing for a certain time, such as 15 seconds. A few minutes later the same sequence of stimuli was repeated; the same after another pause, and so on. After several repetitions of the stimulus sequence, bell—food, saliva began to flow while the bell was ringing and *before* the food was given. The quantity of this conditioned saliva increased trial by trial up to a certain maximum which, it is important to note, was much smaller than the flow produced by food in the mouth. Thus the salivary CR was established for that day.

Next day there was no flow of saliva the first time the bell sounded, but it appeared after a few repetitions, and a few days of this regular procedure established the CR so thoroughly that it held over from day to day. Once well established, a conditioned response may be retained for many months.

Though Pavlov's interest was focused on the measurable flow of saliva, he also observed a conditioned motor response accompanying the glandular response. While the bell was sounding and before the food was given, the dog would turn his head toward the food. The total CR, glandular and motor, was

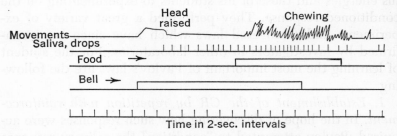

FIG. 129.—Graphic record of a dog's well-established conditioned response. At the sound of the bell the dog raised his head toward the food pan and his saliva began to flow slowly. On obtaining the food he began to chew vigorously and his saliva came more rapidly. Recording apparatus registered the flow of saliva in drops and the movements of the head and jaws (Zener & McCurdy, 35).

a preparation for receiving the food. On the whole this preparatory response was quite different from the final response of
eating the food, for while the glandular part of it was the same
except in amount, the preparatory movement of approaching
the food was entirely different from the final act of chewing.

*Reinforcement* here refers to the fact that food was always
given after the bell had sounded for its regular time.

2. *Extinction of the CR by repetition without reinforcement.*
One of Pavlov's main discoveries is that a conditioned response
can be *extinguished* by repeatedly giving the conditioned
stimulus and not following it with the unconditioned stimulus.
Sound the bell but give no food; give $S_1$ but not $S_2$.

In one of Pavlov's experiments, with the sound of a beating metronome as the conditioned stimulus, the salivary CR
was well established in a series of days, and then, on a certain
day, the metronome was sounded as usual, bringing a good
flow of saliva, but no food was given (no reinforcement). On
the next trial, three minutes later, the flow was less abundant.
Still no food was given, and the same procedure was repeated
till the metronome failed to excite any salivary response. The
gradual extinction of the CR can be seen in the following table
of Pavlov's results.

| Stimulation by the Metronome Began | Quantity of Saliva Produced, in Drops |
| --- | --- |
| 12.07 P.M. | 13 |
| 12.10 " | 7 |
| 12.13 " | 5 |
| 12.16 " | 6 |
| 12.19 " | 3 |
| 12.22 " | 2.5 |
| 12.25 " | 0 |
| 12.28 " | 0 |

The word "extinction" is rather too strong, for the "extinguished" CR can be easily restored in either of two ways.
(1) Give one or two reinforcements, and the CR comes back
at once. (2) Give no reinforcements after extinction but simply
give the animal a rest, and next day *spontaneous recovery* of
the CR will be seen, for saliva will again flow at the sound of

the metronome. But if the food is withheld this day also, extinction is more rapid than before; and repetition of this procedure, day after day, with never any reinforcement, finally leads to permanent loss of the CR.

Extinction may be fundamentally the same thing as negative adaptation (p. 501). In both we see the gradual elimination of a useless response to a repeated stimulus.

3. *Delayed CR when reinforcement is delayed.* Let the bell or metronome always sound for a full minute before the food is given. Early in the process of conditioning, when the CR

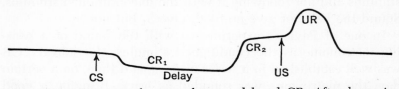

Fig. 130.—Diagram of a two-phase or delayed CR. After becoming habituated to the sequence, Signal—Long Wait—Food, the dog makes a double CR: slump during the delay, followed by attention and salivation as the time for food draws near.

first appears, it comes almost as soon as the sound begins; the flow of saliva starts then and continues for the whole minute of delay. Day by day, however, as the conditioning proceeds, the CR is more and more delayed till near the end of the minute. During the first half minute or more the dog slumps drowsily in his harness and no saliva flows, but toward the end of the minute he perks up and saliva begins to flow. He has become adjusted to the timing of the stimuli. He has learned a two-phase CR: first slump in preparation for a long wait, then wake up and salivate in preparation for food.

4. *Selective conditioning accomplished by selective reinforcement.* The conditioned response is likely to be rather unselective in the sense that it can be aroused by any sudden stimulus that resembles the regular stimulus employed as the signal in the conditioning. If the regular CS so far used has been an electric bell, and a buzzer is substituted, the regular CR will be made though it may be rather weak. If the regular CS has been a certain musical tone, a higher or lower tone will

produce the CR; if the regular CS has been a touch on the shoulder, a touch on the flank can be substituted. How can the CR be made more selective? The procedure is simple though many trials may be necessary before the animal can discriminate consistently between the two stimuli. Intersperse the two stimuli, A and B, in irregular order, with food always following A and never following B. Always reinforce A and never reinforce B. The response to B is gradually extinguished through non-reinforcement, while the response to A is maintained by reinforcement. In effect, two conditioned responses are thus established: the positive response to A consists of perking up and salivating, and the negative response to B consists of slumping down and not salivating. A has become a signal of "food coming," B a signal of "no food this time."

The standard terms used to cover these facts are rather difficult. *Stimulus generalization* refers to the fact that a CR established to a specific CS will be made also to other stimuli which more or less resemble that specific CS. *Generalization gradient* refers to the fact that these substituted stimuli are less effective the less they resemble the specific CS. *Differentiation* is the overcoming of the initial generalization by use of selective reinforcement. The word "differentiation" here means just what it says, since the animal learns to make different responses to different stimuli. When the little child calls any attractive man "Papa," he is showing "stimulus generalization" which will soon be corrected by selective reinforcement from his social environment.

*Adjustment to the situation is necessary for successful demonstration of conditioning.* These experiments do not succeed unless the dog (or the sheep in some other instructive experiments, *17*) is familiar with the experimenter and well adjusted to the laboratory conditions. Any distracting stimulus that occurs may momentarily break up the animal's adjustment and interfere with conditioning, with extinction, or with differentiation. Pavlov found it so important to avoid distracting the animal that he had a special laboratory built for conditioned reflex experiments, with elaborate provision for excluding all extraneous lights and sounds and even for keeping the experimenter out of the dog's sight during an experiment.

**The conditioned response in human beings.** Would experiments like Pavlov's succeed with human subjects? Babies have been tried with a buzzer-bottle sequence; just before the bottle is given a buzzer starts to sound. After this procedure has been employed regularly for a few days the babies show signs of being conditioned, since they stop crying at the sound of the buzzer, open their mouths or make sucking movements (*20*). Conditioning becomes easier and quicker as the child advances in age up to about four years, but beyond that age the human being *seems*, at least, to become less and less easily conditioned. The salivary CR can be experimentally established in some human adults but it is not so dependable as in dogs. Non-experimentally, i.e., in ordinary life, the mouth waters at the sight of food, at the sound of the dinner bell, or on hearing a person describe the delights of a juicy steak. But in the laboratory the human adult is likely to feel that he is being made a fool of when the experimenter causes his mouth to water at the sound of the buzzer or in any way makes him do something he had no intention of doing. Some individuals object more seriously than others and the same individual's attitude may change from time to time. Consequently the laboratory CR is undependable (*24*).

It would be a mistake to leave the impression that conditioning experiments on human adults usually result in failure. They usually result in establishment, extinction, or differentiation of conditioned responses, provided the experimenter uses good technique. Success has been achieved in building up conditioned responses preparatory to the knee jerk (*26, 34*), to the pupillary reflex (*13*), to the psychogalvanic response, and to other reflexes including the two which will now be mentioned.

*The eyelid reflex.* The quick, sharp closing of the eyes in response to such a stimulus as a puff of air against the front of the eye is a true reflex. As a conditioned stimulus give a weak flash of light just $2/5$ of a second before every puff. In the course of an hour's work nearly every subject will give a few conditioned responses at least, consisting of partial closure of the eye

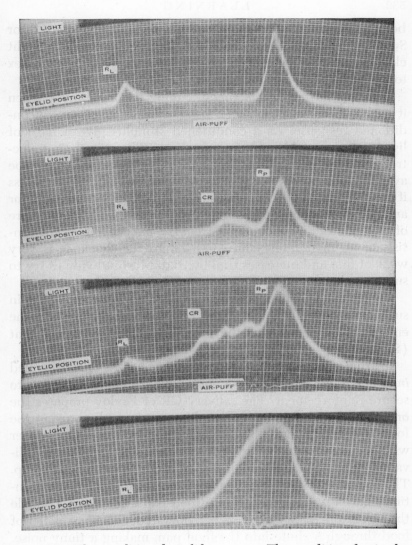

Fig. 131.—The conditioned eyelid response. The conditioned stimulus was a weak light which in this subject gave a weak lid reflex, marked $R_L$ on the tracings, while $R_P$ is the strong reflex to the puff of air used as the unconditioned stimulus. The first record shows these two reflexes before any conditioning, and the other records show different forms of the CR. In the bottom record the CR merges smoothly into the UR. The heavier vertical lines record time in units of $\frac{1}{20}$ second (Hilgard and Marquis, *12*).

531

before the puff. Conditioning builds up a neat little pattern or $S_1$—$R_1$—$S_2$—$R_2$ sequence, consisting of a relatively slow, slight closure at the preliminary signal followed by the quick reflex to the puff (12).

*Hand withdrawal from shock.* Pulling the hand away when it gets a strong electric shock is a natural reaction, an unconditioned response. As a conditioned stimulus give a flash of light half a second before every shock. The stimulating electrode may be attached to the hand so that the shock cannot be avoided by any advance withdrawing movement. Nevertheless if the flash-shock sequence is repeated about twice a minute for an hour you will get conditioned responses from a good share of college students though not from the majority. This CR consists of an involuntary shrinking before the shock. It is very weak at first and increases trial by trial. Most individuals try to suppress the shrinking movement (11).

Conditioned responses probably play an important part in such activities as control of the bladder and rectum and the emotional expressions of the face, breathing and heart beat (22).

**Instrumental conditioned responses.** A CR can be called *instrumental* if it acts on the environment in such a way as to secure reinforcement. The salivary CR of Pavlov prepares the organism for food but it has nothing to do with securing the food which is given at the regular time by the experimenter whether the animal has started to salivate or not. So the salivary CR is not instrumental. But consider this different setup. The animal, usually a rat, is placed in a small box which is entirely bare except for a little tin food pan at one end. Outside the box is a machine which, when operated, delivers a pellet of food through a chute into the food pan, making a tinny noise. When the rat has become adjusted to the empty box, the experimenter works the machine and delivers a pellet. The rat investigates, finds the pellet and eats. A few minutes later the experimenter delivers another pellet and the rat approaches the food pan more promptly than before; and with a few more repetitions the approaching response is well established. The rat has learned an $S_1$—$R_1$—$S_2$—$R_2$ sequence, $S_1$ being the tinny noise, $R_1$ the approach to the food pan, $S_2$ the food, and $R_2$ the act of eating. Here $R_1$ is obviously a preparatory response and it can be called an instrumental conditioned response since it acts on the environment so as to secure the food.

Complicate the setup a little. Near the food pan introduce a horizontal bar along one wall, so connected with the machine that pressing down the bar delivers a pellet into the food pan. In exploring the box the rat encounters the bar, gets his paws on it and accidentally delivers a pellet which he promptly secures since he has already learned to respond to the tinny noise. Whenever he presses the bar he gets a pellet, and this response is quickly established. It is clearly an instrumental CR. It can be extinguished by stopping the reinforcement, i.e., the delivery of pellets. Extinction requires a greater number of unreinforced trials here than in Pavlov's experiment.

This particular form of conditioning experiment was developed by Skinner (27). Compared with the Thorndike puzzle box the Skinner box offers little for the animal to explore. There are few if any false leads to eliminate, and consequently the learning proceeds very rapidly. But the positive process of establishing the successful response must be essentially the same in the two kinds of problems. The cat in the puzzle box also learns an $S_1$—$R_1$—$S_2$—$R_2$ sequence, $S_1$ being the sight of the door button, $R_1$ the act of turning it, $S_2$ the food, and $R_2$ the act of eating. So Skinner's experiment bridges the gap between Pavlov's conditioning and Thorndike's trial and error, two forms of learning which have often been regarded as totally different. All three involve the learning of a sequence. In all three the meaning of a stimulus is learned, since a stimulus becomes a signal or cue, indicating what is going to happen next or what can be had by making a certain reaction.

## IMPORTANT FACTORS IN LEARNING

A comprehensive theory of learning would have to take account of other experiments besides those described in this chapter. Some of them are included in the following chapter on Memory. No general theory of learning commands the universal approval of psychologists at the present time. Approaching the problem from different sides and by the aid of different experiments they are inclined to emphasize different factors. What we shall attempt here is to bring out the factors that are certainly important.

**Observation.** This factor has just been strongly emphasized in the discussion of conditioning, and it was emphasized in the earlier discussions of place learning and thing learning. In learning to deal with the environment, what has to be learned is primarily the characteristics of the environment. Once these are learned, little motor learning is required, at least in simple cases, since the necessary movements of approach or avoidance are already well learned or even instinctive. When a rat has learned that a tinny noise from the food pan means food, he does not have to learn in addition how to approach the pan.

Observation of results deserves a word or two more. You aim a missile at a target, let go and watch the result. If the result shows that you have aimed too high you "lower your sights" and try again. So you learn to take a better aim. If you were somehow prevented from observing results you would have no guide toward better performance, and practice would be uninteresting and unprofitable. The motivating value of *knowledge of results* was mentioned once before (p. 332).

Another practical suggestion: The more clearly you perceive the situation and understand the problem, the better off you are for learning what is essential. Any of the factors which favor attention and observation (intensity, interest, etc., see p. 405) will also favor quick and appropriate learning.

**Stimulus patterns.** The short sequences learned in conditioning experiments are patterns of a simple sort, and depend on "temporal contiguity," the quick following of one stimulus after another. The sequence of stimuli in a maze is a stimulus pattern, and when a rat has thoroughly learned a maze he runs through it with a speed and smoothness which indicate that he is ready for each turn before actually reaching it. Though

his smooth performance looks like a pure motor automatism
he is still using his senses to pick up the necessary cues. Besides
these sequential performances which depend on regular sequences of contiguous stimuli there are simultaneous combinations of movements, movements of both hands for example,
which become almost automatic with practice. They depend on
detailed observation to get them organized but become so
closely integrated by practice that only a minimum of observation is still required.

**Exercise and repetition.**    Simple acts are sometimes learned
in a single trial, but more complex acts usually require repeated
trials, and even simple acts are remembered longer if the trials
have been repeated. In being introduced to a stranger, if you
find him interesting and attend closely to his name, you will
probably remember the name from this single intense activity.
But if you are halfhearted about it, you may need several re-
minders before you are sure of the name.

**Timing of repetitions.**    If the particular learning situation
does not occur again for a long time the effect of the first learning will be lost or forgotten. It is important to follow up right
away if the progress of learning is to be rapid. On the other
hand it is possible to crowd the repetitions so close together
that learning is actually impaired. There is an optimal spacing
of repetitions for any task that is being learned. The effect of
this factor on memorizing will be discussed in the next chapter
(pp. 552–554).

**Reinforcement.**    While exercise is necessary for learning,
even repeated and well-timed exercise is not sufficient. Have
we not seen that long-continued routine repetition, in the absence of good motivation, may leave a person on a plateau, and
that knowledge of results is an important factor in improvement? And have we not seen that the conditioned response,
established by repetition with reinforcement, is extinguished by
repetition without reinforcement? The differentiation experiment shows that reinforced responses are maintained while the
non-reinforced ones are discarded. In the maze or puzzle box,
too, the learner eliminates responses which are not reinforced

by reaching the goal, and keeps those which are reinforced by success. Exercise alone may tend to strengthen all the responses, but reinforcement is a selective factor.

To grasp the full meaning and scope of reinforcement we need to remember that it is a factor in learned perceptions as well as in learned movements. In the chapter on Observing we spoke of "trial and error perception." You hear a rumbling noise which suggests thunder, but reject this suggestion because the weather is clear; then the noise suggests somebody walking on the floor above, and you accept this suggestion because it fits the situation. *Fitting the situation* is a kind of reinforcement. While on a visit in the country you are warned "not to touch those leaves; they are poison ivy," and if you are wise you observe those particular leaves closely and their appearance strikes home or is reinforced by your feeling of the importance of the matter. You cannot tell the color of your friend's eyes because you have never asked yourself what color they are, but now that the question is raised, you notice and remember, because you get an answer to your question. In all these cases reinforcement consists in an emphasis placed on certain observed facts. Many other facts, perceived casually and without emphasis, are soon forgotten while the emphasized facts stand a good chance of being remembered. So reinforcement is a strong factor in perceptual learning.

Instead of using the word "reinforcement" some psychologists prefer to speak of *reward and punishment*. The rat is rewarded for taking the correct path through the maze by finding food in the food box. He is punished for entering a blind alley by finding no food there and he may be more drastically punished by getting a shock. If he afterward keeps out of that alley he is "rewarded" by avoiding the shock.

Punishment has two important effects. When the child gets a burn from a hot radiator he learns to *avoid* the radiator. When anyone in following a certain lead to his goal meets with punishment, more or less drastic, he tends to *shift to another lead*.

The idea of reward has to be stretched a good deal in order to cover all cases of reinforcement. The food in Pavlov's experiment can be regarded as a reward, but how about the puff of air in the eyelid experiment? In the lightning-thunder sequence, is the thunder a reward? Perhaps we could say that the *preparation* for what is going to happen is rewarded. And how about perceptual reinforcement? When you have any question in mind an answer is rewarding, and whenever you are exploring the environment you are rewarded by discovering what is there. So by stretching the idea of reward we can make it fairly equivalent to reinforcement.

**Motivation.** Motives might well have been emphasized more than they have been in this chapter, though their importance for learning has been implied many times. Usually the motive involved in learning is not the motive to learn. Animals certainly are not motivated to learn for future use, and in human learners, too, the motive is commonly aimed at dealing with the present situation and accomplishing immediate results. The motive may be to obtain food, to escape from danger, to win social approval, to play an interesting game, or any of the motives that were listed in an earlier chapter (p. 312). Whatever the motive, mastery of the present situation may require learning and so actually prepare for the future.

If perceptual learning is so important as we have been urging, the exploring and manipulating motives must play a great part in learning. Other, more insistent motives may indeed be too strong; a very hungry animal is so excited at the prospect of food that he plunges straight for the goal without pausing to examine the situation, and he may go into a temper tantrum when blocked in his plunging, instead of exploring around for some less direct approach to his goal (3).

Evidently reinforcement depends on motivation. If an animal is hungry, food is a reward and finding food in the food box reinforces his choice of the correct path through the maze. If he is not hungry he does not get this reinforcement, though he may observe the food and utilize this observation later when hungry.

Extinction and negative adaptation are examples of an important kind of learning—the learning *not* to do something.

What is the motive for this sort of learning? It might be called the economy motive, the natural inclination to avoid useless effort. Since this motive is stronger in some individuals than in others, and stronger at some times than at others, extinction is rather undependable. A useless act, i.e., one that gets no reinforcement, ought to be eliminated rather quickly, but sometimes it is continued for many repetitions. It may be getting some internal reinforcement, or *assumed reinforcement*. The individual may assume he has accomplished something when objectively he has accomplished nothing.

An example of assumed reinforcement is a needless fear (p. 317). When a child who has a fear of dogs runs away from a harmless dog, the child assumes that he has avoided a bite and congratulates himself on his narrow escape. So he gives that fear plenty of reinforcement and keeps it alive in spite of getting no external reinforcement. Superfluous antipathies are kept alive in much the same way. A different kind of example can be seen in the plateau of the learning curve, when this is due to poor motivation or low "level of aspiration"; here the individual does accomplish something and assumes he is doing well enough. So he continually reinforces his inefficient methods of work.

Assumed reinforcement is all to the good when good work is being done without an objective check. If you do much arithmetical work you know the multiplication table so well that you need no objective check when you say that 7 times 9 are 63. Every time you say this you know you are right; so you keep this response alive by continued reinforcement. It is not extinguished as it probably would be without any reinforcement whatever. Many well-learned acts are kept alive in this way.

## SUMMARY

1. *Learning* consists in doing something new, provided the new activity is reinforced and reappears in later activities.

a. In research on the fundamental processes of learning, animals are often used as subjects in order to avoid the com-plications of the higher intellectual processes.

b. Animal learning is observed as objectively as possible and is not interpreted as the outcome of a higher mental proc-ess if it can be interpreted in terms of one which stands lower in the psychological scale (Lloyd Morgan's canon).

2. *Place learning* is basic in most situations. It is learning by exploration where to work, where the goal is, and what the landmarks are in the goal-direction.

a. *Negative adaptation* is the reduction and elimination of unnecessary (non-reinforced) activities such as fear or exploratory behavior.

b. In *learning a maze,* a rat adapts to the new situation, ex-plores, gradually eliminates entrances to blind alleys until he can run swiftly through the correct path without errors.

(1) According to the *chain reflex theory,* the rat learns a fixed series of movements. This is disproved by the demonstration that an animal which has learned to run a maze will still follow the correct path when the maze is flooded so that he has to swim.

(2) According to the *fixed path theory,* the rat learns the single correct pathway. This is disproved by the fact that after the introduction of partial barriers in the pathway, the rat still heads for the food box, taking the necessary detours.

(3) From the evidence it appears that what the rat learns is the direction of the goal in a situation with which he has become familiar.

c. Human subjects learn a maze in the same way but in ad-dition are able to use verbal and number aids in identify-ing the details (blind alleys) and other landmarks.

3. *Tool learning,* a second basic type of learning, depends on manipulation of things and observation of the results.

a. A *cat in a puzzle box* scratches, pushes, claws and bites at various parts of the box until she turns the button that re-leases her. On later trials her attack is directed more exclusively toward the button and escape is more rapid. The cat has learned, not a stereotyped movement, but the useful character of certain objects.

b. *Monkeys and chimpanzees* learn more complicated problems by the same processes of manipulation and observation.

c. *Insight* refers to the moment of sudden solution of a problem. *Foresight* is seeing the way to the goal before taking it; *hindsight* is observing that a lead is good or bad after trying it (reinforcement).

d. Human tool learning is superior to that of animals with respect to observation, managed manipulation, language usage, and ideational activity.

e. In learning skillful activities, the individual progresses from mastery of single part units to higher units involving sequences and combinations of the single units. Execution of a sequence as a unit involves preparation for the next movement while one movement is being made.

4. *Sequences* of stimuli, of responses, and of stimulus-response units are learned by the process of conditioning. A *conditioned response* is an involuntary preparatory response called out by a signal which regularly precedes an important stimulus.

a. Pavlov first studied in dogs the conditioned response of salivating to a signal for food. The sequence of events is indicated as follows:

$S_1$ conditioned stimulus (bell, light, sight of food, etc.)
$R_1$ conditioned response (preparatory salivation)
$S_2$ unconditioned stimulus (dry food in mouth)
$R_2$ unconditioned response (reflex salivation)

The chief laws of conditioning formulated by Pavlov are:

(1) The CR is *established by repetition* of the sequence CS followed by US-UR (reinforcement).

(2) The CR is *extinguished* by repetition of the CS without subsequent reinforcement. The extinguished CR can be restored by a few reinforcements or by *spontaneous recovery* during a rest period.

(3) A *delayed CR* will be established when the US follows the CS by an appreciable interval of time.

(4) *Selective conditioning* (discrimination) is established by reinforcement of one CS and non-reinforcement of another similar stimulus which, by *generalization,* elicits the CR.

b. Conditioned responses in human adults are usually complicated by the sophisticated attitudes and the voluntary control of the subjects. Conditioning can best be demonstrated with involuntary reactions or with young children.

c. *Instrumental conditioned responses* are learned reactions to a signal which are instrumental in producing the second stimulus or reinforcement.

**5.** A *theory of learning* identifies the important factors which determine the occurrence and degree of learning.

a. *Observation* of stimulus features and of the results of any activity is essential for learning. Any of the factors favoring attention and observation will likewise favor learning.

b. *Stimulus patterns* must be present to provide the opportunity for learning. Patterns may consist of two or more stimuli which occur in temporal relation (contiguity), or spatial relation (nearness), or which are similar to each other.

c. *Exercise and repetition* of an activity with reinforcement strengthens the learning.

d. The *spacing of the repetitions* should not be too long or too short for most rapid learning.

e. *Reinforcement* is a selective factor determining which of the individual's activities will be learned. Non-reinforcement of a learned act produces extinction or elimination of the act.

f. *Motivation* is essential for learning in two respects:

(1) Exploring, manipulating and related motives drive the animal to perform some kind of act in a learning situation.

(2) Reinforcement depends upon motivation.

# CHAPTER SEVENTEEN

# *Memory*

W HEN the poet sings of the joys of memory—or sometimes of its terrors—he is depicting for us a human
ability which is truly remarkable. In some degree,
though never perfectly, we are able to revive our own past
experiences, live them over again and enjoy them—or shudder
at them—for the second or the hundredth time. The friends of
earlier years are not wholly lost, for they "come back" in memory; and when old friends come together in reality their conversation is sure to "bring back" the old days.

In the practical affairs of life, as well as in leisure moments,
memory has much to contribute. So much depends on a good
memory in all kinds of work, and especially in brain work,
that many people become worried about their poor memories
and take up some form of memory training in the hope of improvement. But just here scientific study has proved to be of
great practical value, and the best way to go about improving
memory is to know the facts and laws of memory. To discover
these laws and organize them into a comprehensive theory of
memory—such is one of the great problems of psychology, a
problem only partially worked out at the present time.

Memory consists in remembering what has previously been

542

learned. It would be better, however, to say that memory consists in *learning, retaining and remembering* what has previously been learned. For when you actually remember a person's name, for example, you demonstrate both that you learned the name at some previous time, and that you have retained it during the intervening time when you may never have once thought of it. Retention is inactive, remembering is active, and both are included under the general head of memory. And there are several different ways of remembering, the two principal ones being *recalling* and *recognizing.* When you recall a person's name you say it either aloud or to yourself. But you may be unable to recall the name and still feel you have not entirely forgotten it. Some one suggests, "Was it Harris?" No. "Was it Marshall?" No. Was it "Randall?" Yes, that was it. So you recognize a name that you could not recall. We have thus three main topics under the general head of memory: Learning, Retention, Remembering.

Though the topic of learning has been considered rather extensively in the preceding chapter, there are yet other experiments on human learning and "memorizing" that will add to our knowledge, and there are many instructive experiments on retention, recall and recognition. The general plan of any memory experiment has this form,

$$L—I—R,$$

where L stands for the act of learning, R for the act of remembering, and I for the interval of time between the learning and the remembering, i.e., the interval during which what has been learned is retained. Exactly how the experiment will be arranged depends on the particular question to be answered. If we are seeking for conditions favorable to rapid learning, we vary the conditions under L while keeping the I interval short and holding R constant as a test of the learning. But if we are trying to discover the laws of retention, we vary the length of the interval I or we vary O's occupation during this interval, while still holding R constant as a test of retention. If we are interested in recall or recognition, we vary the conditions of the

R test while holding L and I constant. All sorts of combinations are possible, so that the variety of memory experiments is amazing. We shall make no attempt to survey them all.

## MEMORIZING

In a typical memorizing experiment O's task is to master a certain "lesson" so as to pass a memory test on it later. The lesson must be at least partially new and unfamiliar, so that he will have something to learn. Wholly unfamiliar material can scarcely be found, but much use is made of relatively meaningless material such as nonsense syllables, nonsense drawings, and arbitrary lists of words or numbers. Meaningful material can be used if the lesson is long enough to require some study. The lesson must be difficult enough so that O will make some errors in the memory test—otherwise there is no way of telling the degree of success in his task of memorizing the lesson (p. 422). The subject's purpose, then, is to learn and remember; the experimenter's purpose is to discover what is learned, how it is learned, and what conditions are favorable for learning and remembering.

**The immediate memory span.** How much material can a person grasp in one trial well enough to recall it perfectly (compare the "span of apprehension," p. 422)? He need not retain it for long, but only for a few seconds; the interval I is reduced to a minimum. One of the simplest memory experiments consists in presenting lists of numbers (digits) so as to discover how long a list O can reproduce perfectly after a single presentation. Lists of increasing length are presented:

70461
927358
4016372
24971306
176028395
6381470259
85079153624

Several lists of each length should be given, since O will vary somewhat. A given individual may have no trouble with the short sequences of three, four or five numbers and may succeed every time with six and seven, and usually with eight, but only seldom with the longer lists. His "immediate memory span for digits" would then be approximately eight, about the average for a college student. Children of four to six years have a span of about four digits, and the average increases gradually up to the age of eighteen. It increases also with practice. Individual differences in immediate memory span are related to individual differences in general intelligence, and a test of digit span is included in most intelligence tests. Repeating the digits in backward order is a more difficult test.

**Memorizing of longer lessons.** If the list of numbers to be memorized exceeds the memory span, several readings are necessary before it can be recited. Of course!—but it is really rather strange. Suppose your memory span is eight digits; why should you not be able to hold eight digits while reading another eight, and then recite the whole sixteen, after a single reading? There is some sort of interference or confusion between the parts of the list. Grasping the second handful, or span of digits, loosens your hold on the first handful. We have here an important elementary fact of memorizing.

Another elementary fact comes to light if you go over the long list time after time. Though for a while it seems beyond your power, with *repetition* it becomes more and more familiar till finally it can be recited without error. The number of repetitions required for memorizing a list increases greatly as the length of the list is increased.

2 6 0 1 3 6 4 2 8 1 9 4 7 6 8 9 0 1 2 7

Mere repetition, however, does not describe the process of intelligent memorizing. The learner is very much on the alert. Suppose he has a list of twenty digits to memorize. As he wades into the long list and finds himself getting out of his depth, he grasps at anything to help. He does not simply take the numbers as they come but looks for *groups* that will hang together.

Any familiar group, such as the sequence 1492, he hails with joy. Even if he finds no especially easy spots, he at least notes the *locations* of certain numbers and groups in the list, and he notes similarities and other *relationships* that tie the different parts of the list together.

This process of memorizing conforms very well to the formula suggested by maze learning—fitting parts into a framework (p. 507). In memorizing a list, the learner starts with a general impression of its length and make-up, and he proceeds to find parts and to locate them in this framework. The beginning and end of the list, where locating is easy, are usually learned first, but landmarks are soon found in the middle also. The mastered portions grow and finally unite. Lists of nonsense syllables, such as

wok pam zut bip seg ron taz vis lub mer koj yad

are usually learned by grouping, by observing similarities and contrasts, and by reading meaning into the single syllables or their combinations. Often the subject divides the list into pairs, accents the first syllable of each pair, and finds that the *rhythm* thus introduced aids in memorizing. Many are the devices hit upon, and some of them work better than others, but they all reveal the learner as actively searching for combinations that shall be familiar, meaningful, or somehow characteristic, and thus useful in tying the items together, and in transforming the list from an amorphous mass into a well-articulated pattern

## ECONOMY IN MEMORIZING

Memorizing—of substance at least—is a time-consuming job for students and others, but fortunately it is a job that can be laid out and arranged in such a way as to economize time and effort. Conditions can be *managed* so as to favor efficient learning. An obvious rule is to shut out distractions. Other rules, or guides at least, have been worked out in the laboratory.

**Identifying the task in memorizing.** The learner's line of attack differs according to the particular test that is later to be made of his memory. Suppose an experiment is conducted by the method of "paired associates." The subject is handed a list of paired words, such as

| | |
|---|---|
| soprano | emblem |
| grassy | concise |
| nothing | ginger |
| faraway | kettle |
| cedar | captain |
| mercy | scrub |
| hilltop | internal |
| recite | shoestring |
| narrative | thunder |
| seldom | harbor |
| jury | eagle |
| windy | occupy |
| squirm | hobby |
| balloon | multiply |
| necktie | unlikely |
| supple | westbound |
| obey | inch |
| broken | relish |
| spellbound | ferment |
| desert | expect |

He must learn to answer with the second word of each pair when the first word of that pair is given. The way he learns this lesson is to take each pair as a unit and look for something in it to bind it together—the mere swing or rhythm of the two words, or some connection of meaning. A few readings fix most of the pairs.

But suppose the experimenter now springs a surprise, by asking the subject to recite the pairs in order. The subject fails almost completely, and protests that the test is not fair, since he has paid no attention to the order of pairs, but only to each pair by itself. Had he expected to recite the whole list, he would have taken note of the sequence of words right through the list, instead of noticing only the combination of words in

Fig. 132.—A memory drum. The upper cut shows the apparatus as it appears to the subject; the lower cut shows some of the hidden mechanism. The cylinder carrying the words to be memorized is turned in a series of little jumps, so allowing the subject a certain time (as 2 seconds) in which to anticipate the word that is coming next. When he succeeds in anticipating all the words in the list he has learned the list.

each separate pair. <u>Mere repetition, without taking notice (a kind of reinforcement), is not enough to establish associations.</u>

Much more difficult than a list of word-pairs is a memory task which was undertaken by many thousands of young soldiers and sailors during the War, the task of learning the signals of the telegraphic code for use in communication by radio or blinker. (See Fig. 133.) Here we have 26 pairs to be learned, besides the signals for the 10 digits. Half an hour would be enough for mastering 36 word-pairs, but eight hours and more, on the average, were needed by highly motivated college students to reach a moderate degree of mastery of the 36 telegraphic signals, and many more hours were needed before they could receive code messages at any satisfactory speed. The difficulty is not in associating the signals with the letters, so much as in getting the signals themselves clear and distinct so as to identify each signal and distinguish it from all the rest. <u>That is, the learner's great problem is one of "differentiation"</u> (p. 529). On paper the signals for C and Y, for example, look quite

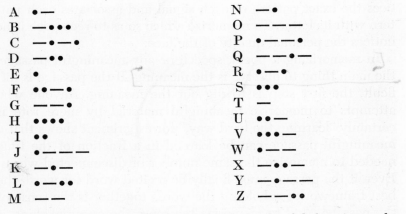

| | | | | |
|---|---|---|---|---|
| A | •— | | N | —• |
| B | —••• | | O | ——— |
| C | —•—• | | P | •——• |
| D | —•• | | Q | ——•— |
| E | • | | R | •—• |
| F | ••—• | | S | ••• |
| G | ——• | | T | — |
| H | •••• | | U | ••— |
| I | •• | | V | •••— |
| J | •——— | | W | •—— |
| K | —•— | | X | —••— |
| L | •—•• | | Y | —•—— |
| M | —— | | Z | ——•• |

Fig. 133.—The International Morse Code for the alphabet. As sent by radio the dots and dashes are short tones, all of the same pitch. Each dash lasts about ⅕ second, and each dot about a third as long as a dash. A beginner is allowed a pause of 3 seconds after each letter for identifying and "copying" the signal before the instructor announces its name. Later the pause is cut down (and the announcement is omitted) as the learner becomes able to take 50, 75, 100 and more letters per minute.

different, but when sounded rapidly they are often confused. The same is true of the signals for K and R, for those for H and S, and for many others to some degree. After making a few such mistakes the learner sets to work seriously to clarify his perception of each signal. On receiving a signal he tries to "echo" it or imitate its pattern in some way, before giving it a name, i.e., a letter. This emphasizing of the pattern is a kind of reinforcement (15).

**Learning by observing.** In memorizing any sort of lesson, the learner has the "will to learn." He is making an effort to learn. How shall he direct his effort? At first he is apt to depend on mere repetition of the lesson over and over again, but he finds this rote learning very slow and inefficient. So he is driven to adopt some kind of reinforcement which amounts to learning by observation. He tries to find and emphasize rememberable characteristics of the lesson. To memorize a list of numbers he observes the positions and sequences of the numbers. To memorize pairs of words he notices something characteristic of each pair taken as a unit. To memorize the telegraphic code he notices the exact pattern of each signal and associates each pattern with its letter. To memorize a face so as to recognize it he notices the personal quality of the face.

In memorizing a poem, speech or any meaningful passage, the main thing to observe is the meaning. If the passage is difficult, the first step is to dig out the meaning. Anyone who attempts to memorize meaningful material by mere rote is certainly "learning the hard way," for experiment shows that a meaningful passage can be learned in a fraction of the time needed to memorize the same number of disconnected words. Even if the passage must finally be recited word for word, the best framework for holding the words together is the sense of the passage. And to memorize the sense the essential thing is to get the sense. If the main idea is grasped in the first reading, that main idea is already learned, though further readings may be necessary in order to fit all the subordinate thoughts into the framework.

**The value of recitation in memorizing.** Recitation here means reciting to oneself. After the learner has read his lesson once or twice, let him attempt to recite it, prompting himself when he is stuck. The question is whether this active method of study economizes time, and whether it fixes the lesson durably in memory. The matter has been thoroughly tested and the answer is unequivocally in favor of recitation. The results of one experiment are summarized in the following table.

THE VALUE OF RECITATION IN MEMORIZING

| Material studied | 16 nonsense syllables | | 5 short biographies, totaling about 170 words | |
|---|---|---|---|---|
| Distribution of Learning Time | Percent Immediately | Remembered After 4 Hours | Percent Immediately | Remembered After 4 Hours |
| All time devoted to reading | 35 | 15 | 35 | 16 |
| ⅕ of time devoted to recitation | 50 | 26 | 37 | 19 |
| ⅖ of time devoted to recitation | 54 | 28 | 41 | 25 |
| ⅗ of time devoted to recitation | 57 | 37 | 42 | 26 |
| ⅘ of time devoted to recitation | 74 | 48 | 42 | 26 |

The time devoted to study was in all cases 9 minutes, and this time was divided between reading and recitation in different proportions as stated at the left. Reading down the first column of numbers, we find that when nonsense syllables were studied and the test was conducted immediately after the close of the study period, 35 percent were remembered when all the study time had been devoted to reading, 50 percent when the last ⅕ of the study time had been devoted to recitation; and so on. The next column shows the percents remembered four hours after the study period. Each subject in this experiment had before him a sheet of paper containing the lesson to be studied, and simply read till he got the signal to recite, when he started reciting to himself, consulting the paper as often as necessary, and proceeded thus till the end of the study period. The subjects in this particular experiment were eighth grade children; adult subjects gave the same general results (9).

Two facts stand out from the table: (a) Reading down the columns, we see that recitation was always an advantage. (b) The advantage was present in the test conducted four hours after study as well as in the test immediately following the study. Recitation favors permanent memory.

What is the advantage of recitation? For one thing, it is more stimulating than the continued re-reading of the same lesson. The latter procedure easily degenerates into a meaningless reading of the words which contributes very little toward learning the sense of a passage. Each recitation shows you what you already know and what still demands close attention. It makes you more observant.

Continued re-reading does not at once give you the reinforcement of success or failure. Recitation applies reward and punishment earlier in the game.

If attempted too soon, recitation of course wastes time. The material should first be explored to see what it contains. Then take a chance at recitation. So you find out more about the material, just as you learn about a mechanical puzzle by observantly manipulating it.

One form of recitation, especially valuable when the substance rather than the exact wording of a passage is to be learned, consists in outlining the thought after the first reading, and fitting in the details after a second reading.

**Problems of timing.** A rule which is useful in memory work, if not carried too far, is the old rule to "make haste slowly." If you wished to memorize a telephone number, such as "Academy 2–7223," which you can easily recite after a single reading, you might say it over and over several times without any pause. But you would probably remember it longer if you paused a few seconds after each repetition. "Spaced repetitions" would probably give you better results than "massed repetitions." In a laboratory experiment a list of 12 nonsense syllables was exposed, one syllable at a time, at the rate of 2 seconds per syllable, and with a pause of only 6 seconds at the end of the list before starting over again. As soon as O was able to anticipate

any syllable he did so, and the learning continued till he anticipated every syllable and so recited the whole list correctly.
This was massed learning. In a parallel experiment on spaced
learning, everything was the same except that the pause at the
end of the list was lengthened by two minutes. To prevent the
subject from rehearsing the syllables during this long pause he
was kept fully occupied with a color-naming test. It took the
subjects (32 college students) 15 trials on the average to master
the list by massed learning, and only 11 trials by spaced learning. The total time was of course greater with spaced learning
because of the long pauses. But another variation of the experiment proved to be the most economical of all: the syllables
were presented at a slower rate, 4 seconds per syllable, and
with only the short pause of 6 seconds at the end of the list. In
this case the subjects learned in 7 trials and saved time, too, as
compared with the other methods (13).

In endeavoring to interpret these results, we can readily see
how the learner could make good use of the 4-second interval
between syllables, for the purpose of grasping the separate syllables and noting their sequences—in short for getting in some
reinforcement—and no doubt the suggestion from this experiment could be carried over to the learning of meaningful material. Instead of hurrying through the material time after time
you will probably find it more economical in the end to read
slowly enough to understand and appreciate the meaning.

But when we ask what can be the value of the pause of a
minute or two between readings, the answer is not easy. One
thing is certain: after a pause you can attack the lesson with
renewed vigor and freshness. A good practical rule for any lesson is to attack it at intervals and to have the intervals long
enough to make a fresh attack possible. If you read an interesting paragraph over and over without any pause, you soon lose
the meaning and merely keep on grinding out the words. After
an interval the paragraph becomes meaningful once more, and
then a new reading will add to your memory of the meaning.

The interval between repetitions can be as short as one minute or as long as 24 hours and still give good results. With a long and meaningful lesson the interval should be fairly long, long enough to make a fresh attack possible.

When we say that spaced repetitions give the best results in memorizing, we do not mean that study should be in short periods with intervals of rest. The probability, since most students consume some time in getting "warmed up" to study, is that fairly long periods of consecutive study will yield larger returns than the same amount of time divided into many short periods. What we have been saying here is simply that repetition of the *same material* fixes it better in memory, when an interval elapses between the repetitions.

**Whole versus part learning.** In memorizing a long lesson, is it more economical to divide it into parts, and study each part by itself till mastered, or to keep the lesson entire and always go through the whole thing? Most of us would probably guess that study part by part would be better, but experimental results have usually been in favor of study of the whole.

If you had to memorize 240 lines of a poem, you would certainly be inclined to learn a part at a time; but notice the following experiment. A young man took two passages of this length, both from the same poem, and studied one by the whole method, the other by the part method, in sittings of about thirty-five minutes each day (22). His results appear in the table.

LEARNING PASSAGES OF 240 LINES, BY WHOLE AND PART METHODS

| Method of Study | Number of Days Required | Total Number of Minutes Required |
|---|---|---|
| 30 lines memorized per day; then whole reviewed till it could be recited | 12 | 431 |
| 3 readings of whole per day till it could be recited | 10 | 348 |

In this experiment, the whole method gave an economy of 83 minutes, or about 20 percent, over the part method. Other similar experiments have given smaller differences, and sometimes the advantage has been with the part method.

These contradictions in the experimental results warn us against accepting whole learning as necessarily advantageous under all circumstances. Instead of slavishly following mechanical rules, you need in practical work to apply general principles and adapt them to your circumstances and individual peculiarities. If you have a great deal of memorizing to do— whether verbatim or for substance only—spaced whole study is a good general principle. But you should feel perfectly free to interrupt this regular procedure and concentrate for a time on some detail that can be mastered by a little intensive work. Some poise and skill are needed to handle the whole method efficiently. Anyone who finds the part method so much more comfortable that he prefers it at all odds should at least divide the material into fairly large parts, much larger than his memory span. If you can recite two lines of a poem after a single reading, it will do you little good to keep on reciting this bit time after time. It would be much better to make four lines the unit. Even if you prefer the part method, it is best to begin with one or two careful readings of the whole and to review the whole occasionally, so as to have a framework into which the parts will fit as they are mastered.

## RETENTION

After considering thus far the process of learning or "committing to memory," we come now to the second of the three main divisions of our subject and ask how what has been learned can possibly be retained. Some have said that it is retained "in the unconscious." But what can this mysterious statement mean? It might mean unconscious activity or unconscious inactivity. Unconscious activity would mean that a boy who has learned the multiplication table must be continually reciting it to himself, though unconsciously, and that the same boy, since he has also learned to skate, swim, and climb a tree, must be continually going through all these activities, and singing all the songs he knows, remembering all the people he knows, etc., etc. Any theory of retention that demands continued activity of all learned responses breaks down from its own weight. But if retention is unconscious inactivity, the word "unconscious" is superfluous and misleading; for the meaning must be that learning modifies the structure of the organism, and that the structural changes persist though remaining inactive until aroused by some effective stimulus. Exercise and reinforcement produce changes in the brain structure, changes which are sub-microscopic in size but sufficient to enable a person to do again what he has learned to do and to see things again as he has learned to see them (pp. 209, 284).

The modified structure which retains a given memory is called a *memory trace.* We do not know the exact nature of this trace but we have a right to assume that every learning process leaves some trace in the brain. These traces, persisting for some time at least, make it possible to remember what has been learned. We need not assume that an inactive memory trace will necessarily last to the end of a person's life. It may die out gradually with the result that what was once learned is finally forgotten.

But is anything once learned ever completely forgotten and lost? Some say no, being strongly impressed by the occasional recovery of memories that were thought to be gone forever. Experiences of early childhood have sometimes been recovered after a long and devious search. Persons in a fever have been known to speak the language of their childhood which in their normal state they could not remember at all. Such facts have been generalized into the extravagant statement that "nothing once known is ever forgotten." For it is an extravagant statement. It would mean that all the lessons you ever learned, all the stories you ever read, all the faces, scenes and happenings that ever attracted your attention are still retained and could be recalled if only the right means were taken to revive them. There is no evidence for any such extreme view. Probably a great deal is forgotten, as we shall see.

**How to observe and measure retention.** Since we cannot see the memory trace, our only evidence of retention is the fact that what has been learned can be remembered after an interval.]You can prove that you retain a lesson in three ways. You can *recall* the content of the lesson, as in the essay type of examination. You can *recognize* statements taken from the lesson, and distinguish them from statements not contained in the lesson, as in the true-false examination. These two methods are often used in testing retention. There is a third, less obvious method, called the *relearning method*. If some time ago you memorized certain stanzas of a poem, it may be you cannot now recall any of the lines; it may be you cannot even recognize or identify the stanzas you once learned; but you may find you can now learn certain stanzas quite easily, because you are *relearning* what you learned before. If it takes you 10 minutes to learn a new stanza but only 8 minutes to relearn a comparable stanza which was previously learned, the retention produces a *saving* of 2 minutes, or 20 percent, in the time of learning. Here the traces retained from the previous learning reduce the labor of relearning by 20 percent; or, we may say, retention amounts to 20 percent, forgetting to 80 percent.

Measured by this relearning or saving method the retention often turns out to be much better than would be indicated by the recall score. You may recall almost nothing of a previously learned lesson and still find it very easy to relearn. And you may recognize more than you recall. Referring to our general plan of a memory experiment,

$$L—I—R,$$

we see that the R test for retention may be a recall, a recognition, or a relearning test, and that the three measures will not necessarily give the same result. Still, all three are useful in one problem or another.

The psychological problems of retention are concerned especially with the I interval. During this interval the lesson which has been learned is not studied any more but remains totally inactive (as far as possible). The I interval may vary (1) in duration or (2) in filling. (1) As the time since learning increases, retention decreases, but we should like to know more about this loss of memory with time. (2) Since the interval is

558 MEMORY

not empty but is filled with activities, the question arises whether certain activities disturb the memory trace and so impair retention.

**The curve of forgetting.** The curve picturing the decline of retention with lapse of time was first worked out by the relearning method and later verified by the recall and recognition methods. There is a gradual loss of retention, but the loss is much more rapid in the first hours after learning than it is later.

Though this flattening of the curve is well established by numerous and varied experiments, the absolute speed of forgetting varies enormously. (a) One individual forgets more rapidly than another. (b) Material that has been "overlearned," i.e., studied beyond the point where it can barely be recited without error, is forgotten more slowly. (c) Most important of all, meaningful material, besides being much more

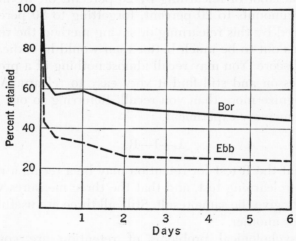

FIG. 134.—The curve of forgetting, or curve of retention. Lists of nonsense syllables were memorized, laid aside, and relearned after the stated intervals. The percent retained was measured by the saving in relearning. The Ebbinghaus curve (Ebb) is from one practiced subject who learned many lists; the Boreas curve (Bor) is the average from 20 students, each learning and relearning one list for each interval. While the Boreas curve shows much slower forgetting than that of Ebbinghaus, both curves have the same general course (Ebbinghaus, 7, and Boreas, 3).

quickly learned than nonsense material, is much more slowly forgotten. A list of nonsense syllables, just barely learned, shows no retention by any test at the end of four months, but barely learned poetry has shown a little retention even after twenty years. When meaningful material has been greatly "overlearned," it may be retained almost indefinitely. A popular song of long ago that you have not sung or heard for many years will come back to you, slowly perhaps, if you now try to remember it. A student who had practiced on the typewriter for 200 hours, and then dropped it entirely for a year, recovered all the lost ground in less than an hour of fresh practice, so showing a retention of over 99 percent. The cases sometimes regarded as proving that "nothing once learned is ever forgotten" were cases of greatly overlearned material, such as the everyday speech and the vivid experiences of childhood.

**The causes of forgetting.** The mere lapse of time cannot conceivably destroy the memory traces. It is not time, but what goes on in time, that produces effects. If there could be a perfectly blank interval of time, with nothing happening to the organism or in the organism—all life simply suspended as in the "Sleeping Beauty" story—then, when life started up again, everything would resume just as if there had been no blank interval, and no memories would be lost in such a lapse of time. The causes of forgetting must be sought in the processes which go on in time, i.e., in the "filling" of the I interval. Two quite different processes go on, suggested by the words *behavior* and *metabolism,* and accordingly there are two theories of forgetting, the interference theory and the atrophy theory.

*Interference.* My boyhood chum was "Clarence," let us say, and for years that name meant that boy and no one else. But as time went on he dropped out of my life and other "Clarences" came in with the result that I have almost (not quite) forgotten what the name originally meant to me. The original meaning has been extinguished by nonreinforcement, and displaced by new meanings for the same name. The original S—$R_1$ connection has been broken up by the later S—$R_2$ connection. This is interference in its clearest form. Rather vaguely, we can see how various daily activities, being partially alike and partially unlike, may interfere with each other to some extent and disturb each other's memory traces.

*Atrophy from disuse.* If the brain were made of copper with nice clean contacts which, once made, would stay put till the switches were thrown another way, the interference theory would be good enough. A connection once established would be permanent until displaced by the establishment of an alternative connection. But a living organ or tissue needs to be maintained in prime condition by the chemical processes of bodily metabolism. A muscle that is active or has just been active takes in nourishment from the blood, while a muscle that is kept inactive, as when a broken arm is bound in a splint, loses some of its substance to the blood and gradually atrophies. The muscles compete with each other in their demands for nourishment, and an inactive muscle loses out in the competition. The same thing is probably true, on a microscopic scale, of the brain structures which provide the memory traces (p. 284). Traces that have been unused and inactive for a long time will scarcely be in prime metabolic condition even if no interference has occurred at the behavioral level. Like muscle fibers which have long been inactive the traces will at best be weak and unable to function effectively.

Forgetting is not wholly a disadvantage, and the tendency to forget should not be regarded as wholly a weakness of the biological organism. To some extent forgetting is a restorative process, a getting back to normal. The healing of a wound is a sort of biological forgetting. Many things that you learn have only temporary value for you. If everything you ever learned were perfectly retained, it would be continually bobbing up and interfering with your adjustment to new situations. For interference works both ways. Learning the new interferes with the retention of the old, and recall of the old interferes with the learning of the new. When you learn $S$—$R_2$ you impair the retention of $S$—$R_1$, and when you revive $S$—$R_1$ you hinder the learning of $S$—$R_2$. So the (probable) metabolic decline of unused memory traces is sometimes an advantage. Metabolic decline works against interference in the learning of the new, though it works with interference in impairing the retention of the old.

**Slow forgetting during sleep.**   Behavior is at a low level during sleep, and interference with memory traces is reduced. Forgetting should therefore be less rapid during sleep than during waking hours. This expectation is borne out by experimental results. Fig. 135 gives the results of a human experiment and Fig. 136 those of a still more adequate animal experiment —more adequate because the state of sleep or inactivity began more promptly after the learning and was probably more complete and less disturbed. The curves show that forgetting during sleep is slower than during activity. Yet some forgetting did occur during the first few hours of sleep. The rapid initial drop typical of curves of forgetting is present even in the well-controlled animal experiment but it is slight in sleep compared with the big drop in the first hours of activity after learning.

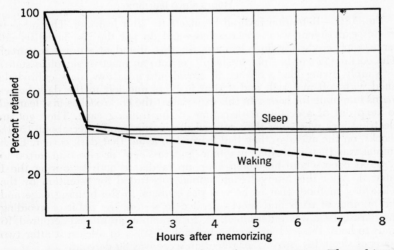

Fig. 135.—Retention favored by sleep after memorizing. The subjects, after memorizing lists of nonsense syllables, either went about their daily activities or else went to sleep as soon as possible and were awakened after a certain interval to relearn the lists. Forgetting was more rapid during waking hours than during sleep, except during the first hour of partial wakefulness (van Ormer, 25).

The conclusion that forgetting is slow during sleep—or rapid during daytime activity—can be accepted with certain reservations. First, it is *barely learned* material that shows this effect;

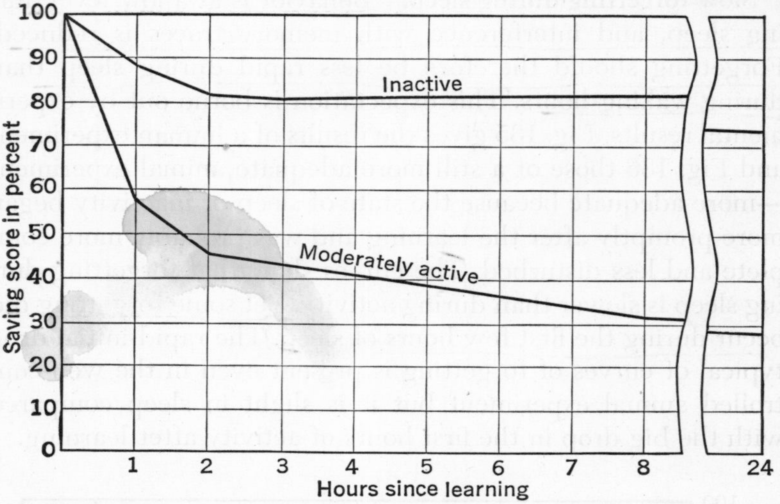


FIG. 136.—Retention favored by inactivity after learning. The subjects in this experiment were cockroaches—and do not the psychologists deserve some credit for finding a use for this abundant natural resource? The cockroach can be "put to sleep" (or into an inactive sleeplike state) by simply giving him a chance to crowd into a narrow, dark cubbyhole lined with soft material; and if shut in there and left in the dark he remains immobile for hours. In this experiment the cockroaches first learned to keep out of a certain dark corner of the training cage. They got an electric shock whenever they entered that corner, and after about 15–18 shocks, on the average, they had learned to avoid that dark corner. Each animal was then immediately either "put to sleep" or else transferred to a round cage where he would keep up moderate activity during the I interval. After this interval each animal was tested for retention by the relearning method; that is, he was placed back in the training cage and the number of trials and shocks needed to restore the habit of avoiding the dark corner was determined. If, for example, an animal required 15 trials to learn the trick originally, but only 3 trials to relearn it after two hours of sleep, his "saving" or retention score was 80 percent.

Check experiments showed that learning ability itself was not much affected one way or the other by a preceding period of sleep—or, we might say, learning ability was not affected by a preceding period of moderate activity. A period of extreme activity (treadmill) just before learning greatly impaired the learning ability, and just after learning it greatly impaired retention (H. Minami & K. M. Dallenbach, *19*).

better learned material is remembered about as well after eight hours of ordinary activity as after eight hours of sleep; a strong trace holds out better than a weak one against the forces of atrophy and interference. Second, it is the *brand-new traces* that are disturbed by activity and favored by sleep. If you could be perfectly wideawake while learning a lesson and then pass instantly into a perfect sleep, you would have the best possible chance of remembering that lesson next day. For practical purposes each individual has to consider his own learning ability at different hours of the day. If he learns poorly in the evening, it would be no advantage to him to put off the important lessons till then. If his learning ability is about equal, morning and evening, he might try out a scheme for combining the advantages of whole learning, spaced learning, and sleep right after learning: Give the lesson one good reading just before bedtime; sleep on it; and go over it again in the morning.

**Experiments on direct interference.** You are serving as *O* in a memory experiment, and *E*, the experimenter, asks you to memorize the paired associates given on p. 547, the list beginning:

| Stimulus words | Response words |
| --- | --- |
| soprano | emblem |
| grassy | concise |
| nothing | ginger |
| faraway | kettle |
| etc. | etc. |

*E* shows you a stimulus word for 2 seconds and then the response word for 2 seconds, and so on through the list. When he goes through the list the second time you are able to anticipate a few response words. The third time you get more of them, the fourth time still more, and on the fifth round, let us say, you get 16 of the 20 response words correct. *E* says, "Very good. Now you may rest, and please look at these pictures to occupy your mind while resting a few minutes." At the end of a 15-minute rest period he says, "Now we will go through that list once more." By this time you have forgotten

some of the words but you still get 12 correct, so that your retention is $12/16$ or 75 percent of what you knew at the end of
the original learning.

But suppose $E$, instead of giving you a rest period immediately after the original learning, had said, "Now I am going to
ask you to learn new responses to those same stimulus words,"
and had proceeded to show you the following pairs:

| Stimulus words | Response words |
|----------------|----------------|
| soprano | index |
| grassy | foreign |
| nothing | leather |
| faraway | yellow |
| etc. | etc. |

The previously learned response words would be apt to come
up and interfere with the learning of the new ones, but these
old responses, not being reinforced, would be extinguished
after a few rounds, and you would make a good score of the
new responses. Then $E$ gives you the pictures to amuse you
during a short rest period and at the end of it he says, "Now
we will return to the original list. I will show you the stimulus
words and ask you to give the original responses." In trying
to recall the original response words you experience some interference from the substitute responses that you have since
learned. These substitute responses are apt to intrude and delay
the recall of the original responses even if not actually spoken.
However, this interference with retention and recall is not
complete; you find that the original responses are not totally
lost, and you may make a score of 8 correct, to be compared
with the 12 correct after a rest interval free from any such
direct interference. Of the 16 you knew at the end of the
original learning, you lose 4 in a rest interval without obvious
interference, and 4 more through interference. The exact numbers will vary but some such result has been obtained in many
similar experiments (16, 18, 24).

If the second list of responses has been pretty well learned,
it will interfere more than if it has been only slightly learned.

This result is easily understood, but suppose the second list has been so well learned that the word pairs in it are perfectly familiar—what would you expect then? Of course these new responses are very ready to use, but they are instantly recognized as belonging to the second list, and since you are now set for recalling the first list you can reject these second responses instantly, and their interference is not so troublesome as when the second list is not so familiar. Or, if the first list is the one that has been thoroughly learned, any intruding responses from the second list are instantly recognized as not belonging. If both lists have been thoroughly learned, you can shift from one list to the other with very little difficulty. For example, if you are thoroughly familiar with both English and French, you can give either the French or the English names for the numerals 3, 5, 8, 1, 9, 2, etc., with no hesitation. When you are set for French you get the French names, and when you are set for English you get the English names; the factor of "set" does away with the interference in such cases (p. 221).

**Indirect interference.**  In the interference experiment just described the two alternative responses to the same stimulus were in direct competition with each other. But suppose the second list to be learned does not contain the same stimulus words as the first list. Let the two lists be composed of entirely different words. You learn the first list of pairs (not too well), and the second list, and after a rest period you try to recall the responses of the first list. You do not do as well in this recall test as when you have no second list to learn but rest during the entire interval between original learning and recall. This indirect interference is not easily explained but has to be accepted as a fact. It is slight unless the second lesson is similar to the first. If the first list consists of word pairs but the second list of number pairs, the interference is very slight.

Anyone who attempts to explain *all* forgetting as due to interference has to rely mostly on indirect interference. To explain the forgetting that occurs even during a period of comparative rest he must assume that any activity whatever exerts some interference on anything previously learned, and that the accumulation of slight interferences gradually reduces retention toward zero. When pressed to the limit the interference theory becomes too vague to have much scientific appeal or practical value.

**What happens directly after learning—recency effects.** One fact not easily explained by interference is the shape of the curve of forgetting with its sharp drop in the first minutes and hours after learning. Why should interference be worse in the first hour than in the second or fiftieth hour after learning? The explanations offered are all very speculative. But it is worth while to give special attention to the period directly after learning, or to what may be called the *recency effects,* since they are of considerable practical importance to the learner.

By recency effects we mean short-time effects, effects that last for a short time and soon disappear. Take that first rapid drop in the curve of forgetting: instead of asking how so much can be forgotten after a short time, ask how so much can be remembered for a short time. Someone sounds a note for you to sing: a second or two later you can strike the exact note but if you wait half a minute you get it only approximately. At first the note seemed to "ring in your ears"—really in your brain— and you did not seem to recall it but only to hold on to it. In many such cases you have the feeling that the just-past sensation or experience is still "echoing" or continuing in weaker intensity. This feeling may not prove anything but it suggests the hypothesis that a brain activity started by a stimulus does not cease abruptly when the stimulus ceases, but rather continues for a short time. Such continuing activity would explain many recency effects.

*The warming-up effect.* The pitcher "warms up" before going into the box, and other athletes do practically the same thing. They find that some preliminary exercise increases both strength and skill. After a moderate amount of vigorous activity the muscles are in a different physiological state, more ready for work and more responsive to stimulation; and the same seems to be true of the brain. During rest the warmed-up state gradually dies away, so that short rest periods are more beneficial than long ones in the course of the day's work. One short-time effect of activity, then, is this warmed-up state of special readiness to continue the same activity.

*Short-lived interference.* In experiments on interference, the most interference is obtained when the second list is learned immediately after the first or else immediately before the recall test (*21*). Of course whenever the second list requires you to unlearn the first and substitute new responses to the same stimulus words, the substitutes are likely to persist, but when the interference is "indirect" a sufficient lapse of time between the lists enables you to learn both without much interference. Exactly how long a time interval is sufficient has not been worked out experimentally and probably varies a good deal, but it is safe to say that a few minutes of relaxation after mastery of one proposition in geometry will tend to prevent the next proposition from interfering with retention of the first.

*Speed of recall.* Recent experiences and ideas are recalled quickly, while older ones are apt to come up with some delay. If you know the names of the capitals of France, Italy, Sweden, Denmark, Spain and Greece, but have not thought of them recently, you may need several minutes to get them all; but when you have once recalled them, you can recall them very quickly a few minutes later, because they are now "fresh in mind," i.e., recent. Because old traces are apt to act slowly while recent responses are repeated easily and quickly, the recent ones often get in the way and prevent recall of the old.

*Recency effects and the curve of forgetting.* The first rapid drop in the curve of retention may be due to the disappearance of the recency effects, rather than to any rapid weakening of the memory traces. If the intense activity of learning leaves behind a less intense activity or at least a warmed-up state of the learned responses, good memory for a short time is possible even if no strong traces have been established. Next day the recency effects have gone and memory depends on the traces.

*Recency effects and the establishment of traces.* Any continuing activity of a learning process would strengthen the memory traces just being formed, especially of course if the continuing activity broke through into spontaneous recall which would amount to partial review of the lesson. So we may assume that the establishment of a trace is not completed with the cessation of the learning period but continues for a short time. Any interfering activity during this short time would disturb this process of establishing the traces and leave them weaker than they would otherwise have been. Later on, when the traces are simply inactive brain structures, they may be immune to "indirect interference" though disturbed when a definite substitution of new responses is attempted.

*Shock effects on the establishment of traces.* If the biological process of establishing a memory trace in the brain takes a short time to complete itself, we should expect that a blow to the head throwing the brain out of commission temporarily (producing unconsciousness) would halt the process, so that the traces of experiences occurring just *before* the shock would not be well formed and these experiences would not be remembered afterwards. Many cases of just this sort have been reported. Recently, with the introduction of "shock therapy" in the treatment of certain mental diseases, it has become possible to obtain more clear-cut evidence on the question. The shock effect can be produced by passing a strong electric current momentarily through the patient's head. The patient loses consciousness for a time but afterward his mental condition is improved in many cases. Ten patients were tested in the following manner. Shortly before receiving the current they learned a list of paired associates, and later in the day after recovery from the shock they were tested for retention. Their retention was very poor on these days compared with control days when the procedure was the same except for the omission of the shock. Yet their learning ability was not impaired by the shock. They could form new traces but had lost the traces formed just before the shock. Probably they had not fully established these traces because the process of forming them was interrupted by the shock. Experiments on animals have given similar results, though many angles of the problem have not yet been explored (6, 27).

**Reviewing.**   One very practical fact about retention has not been brought out so far. When a lesson has been learned, partly forgotten, and then relearned, it sticks better the second time; and if it is partly forgotten again and relearned again, it sticks still better the third time; and so on. In a review it is best to depend on recitation as much as possible. Let the old traces do the work and so build themselves up.

## RECALL

Earlier in the chapter recall and recognition were said to be the two principal ways of remembering, and the difference between them was illustrated by an example. For a working definition we may say that "Recognition is remembering something that is present," while "Recall is remembering something that is not present." By "present" is meant "presented to the senses."

A person stands before you: you recognize his face and recall his name. A person's name is mentioned: you recognize the name and recall the person's face.

Recall memory is also known as reproductive memory, and sometimes the word *reproduce* is more suitable than *recall*. If you ask me whether I can recall Hamlet's soliloquy, my saying "Yes" may mean only that I remember the first words and the general nature of that speech; but if you ask me to reproduce it from memory, my task is much more serious. If you ask whether I recall the Sistine Madonna, my saying "Yes" means that I have a general impression of the picture, but if you ask me to reproduce it I must make a sketch from memory—or perhaps you would be satisfied with a good verbal description. However, the word *recall* can be used in a sense broad enough to cover all degrees and varieties of remembering what is not present.

**Memory images.**   If a recalled fact or experience comes back with a decided sensory character—if it is realistic and like actual seeing or hearing or smelling, it is called a memory image. Can you recall the blue of the sky, or the tone of the violin or of a friend's voice, or the odor of camphor, or the feel of a lump of ice in the hand, or the way it feels to jump, or kick, or yawn, or clench your fist? Almost everyone will answer "Yes" to some of these questions. One person will report getting a vivid picture of a scene, and another a realistic mental rehearsal of a piece of music. What they recall seems to them essentially the same as an actual sensory experience.

Individuals seem to differ greatly in the vividness or realism of their memory images (8). Most memory images are inferior in realism and completeness to actual sensory experience. From the practical standpoint they are inferior in that facts cannot be found in the image of a thing unless they were observed in the actual presence of the thing.

At one of the universities, there is a beautiful library building with a row of fine pillars across the front, and the students pass this building every day and enjoy looking at it. A favorite experiment in the psychology classes at that university consists in first asking the students to call up an image of the front of the library, and then asking them to count the pillars from their image. But at this point the students begin to object. "We have never counted those pillars, and cannot be expected to know the number now." In fact, few of them give the correct number, and those whose images are vivid and realistic are little better off in this respect than those whose images are dim and vague.

Ordinarily, in looking at a beautiful building, we simply take in the general effect; and when we later get an image, it is just this general effect which we recall. If we pick out details, we can later recall them. If we study the color scheme, or the balance of masses, while looking at the building, we can recall what we have observed and no more.

*The primary memory image—eidetic images.* What has been said of images, so far, refers to those recalled some time after the original experience. The primary memory image is different in that the experience is simply persisting for a few moments after the original stimulus has ceased. For a few seconds after somebody has stopped talking, you can still hear his voice, as if in an echo—a *recency effect.* You may be able to recover what he has said, though you were not closely attending to it at the instant when he was speaking. In the same way, immediately after you have looked over the landscape out of your window, you can still see it better than you can recall it later. This primary memory image is not the same as the "after-image" mentioned previously (pp. 16, 450).

Now it appears that many children under fourteen years of age, perhaps half of them, if they examine any complex object or picture in an absorbed way for half a minute, and then shut their eyes, or, still better, turn them upon a plain gray background, can *see* the object as if it were still before them, and can answer questions about it which they did not have in mind during the actual presence of the object. This image is not strictly photographic, but rather plastic, and likely to be modified by the subject's interest. The object may grow larger, or may become more regular, or may appear to move. The color may become more brilliant, or may change to a different color. Such changes may be either voluntary or involuntary. This type of image, then, is quite subjective, though on the whole it conforms rather closely to the scene from which it was taken.

These peculiarly vivid and detailed primary memory images have been called *eidetic images*, and the individuals who have them *eidetic individuals*. Eidetic imagery seems to be most common in later childhood, and to fade out, usually, during adolescence, though a few adults can still obtain images of this sort. Such images, though usually appearing, if at all, immediately after being immersed in the actual contemplation of an object, may reappear later (1, 14, 17, 20).

**Hallucinations.** Since a vivid memory image may be "in all respects the same as an actual perception," according to the testimony of some persons, the question arises how such an image is distinguished from a perception. Well, the image does not usually fit into the objective situation present to the senses. But if it does fit, or if the objective situation is lost track of, then, as a matter of fact, the image may be taken for an actual perception.

You are half asleep, almost lost to the world, and some scene comes so vividly before you as to seem real till you awaken to the reality of your surroundings. Or you are fully asleep, and then the images that come in your dreams seem entirely real, since contact with the objective situation has been lost.

Images taken for real things are common in some forms of mental disorder. Here the subject's hold on objective reality is loosened by his absorption in his own fears and desires, and he hears reviling voices, smells suspicious odors, or sees visions that are in line with his fears and desires.

Such false perceptions are *hallucinations*. A hallucination is a memory image taken for a perception; it is something recalled or built up out of past experience and taken for a present objective fact.

**Limitations of memory.**   While the ability to remember at all is a remarkable property of the organism, it is a limited ability even in human beings. It is subject to incompleteness, inaccuracy and even falsification. These deficiencies come to light in recall and recognition, but they are due to inadequate learning and inadequate retention as well as to difficulties arising in the process of recalling. If we confine our attention to verbal memory, or especially to verbatim memory, we are sure to overlook some of the limitations. A poem can be memorized completely and exactly, as far as the words go, and it can be retained well enough to give a complete and exact recitation later. But the substance of a lecture, the course of events in a story, the content of a picture, or even the appearance of a single thing or person, is never completely and exactly observed. The memory traces needed for complete and exact recall are not formed in the first place, and some of those that are formed fade out quickly. The result is that when you try to remember a story or picture or any concrete thing, the traces are not sufficient to do a complete job. They furnish some material but not enough. You have to depend on your general stock of knowledge to supplement the traces, so as to "reconstruct" the story or rather to construct one that shall be reasonably complete in itself, probable enough, and perhaps conforming to your own preferences and prejudices. You cannot really reproduce the original but you do produce a story that resembles the original more or less, though it is partly a work of imagination rather than of memory (2).

*Memory for nonsense figures.* These causes of incomplete and inaccurate recall are brought out clearly by experiments with relatively simple shapes which are exposed briefly for the subject to examine and later draw from memory. If the figure were a square or circle or any familiar geometrical figure, he would have no trouble in "nailing it down." If it were an outline drawing of a cat, a bottle or any familiar object, he would name it and later draw something representing the object. But since it is a nonsense figure, his task is not so simple. He either tries to analyze it geometrically or, more commonly, asks him-

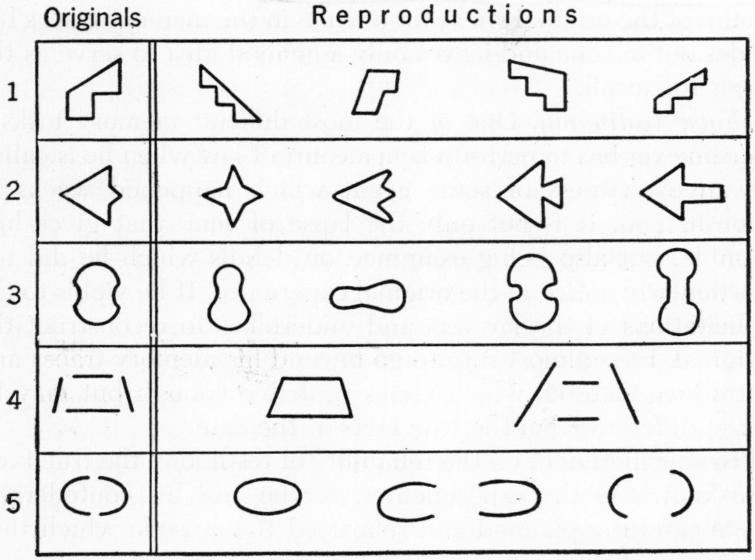

Fig. 137.—Attempted reproduction of nonsense figures from memory. The subjects were working under pressure, having a series of 14 nonsense figures to memorize. The first figure usually suggested stairs, but reminded one subject of a ship's ventilator. The second figure was seen by different subjects as a star, a bird, an arrowhead, and an arrow. The third was seen as a woman's torso, a footprint, a violin, a dumbbell. In reproducing the broken figures the subjects tended either to close the gaps or else to exaggerate them (Gibson, *10*).

self what sort of object it roughly resembles. But when he comes to reproduce it, he finds that his observation was not exact and detailed enough to specify the exact shape (*4, 11, 12*).

For example try to reproduce original No. 2 in Fig. 137 from memory. Geometrically, it is an equilateral triangle with an extra point projecting from one side; but when you try to reproduce it you are not sure how large and how sharp to make that projecting point. Or, if you take it for an arrowhead without noting the exact size and shape of the projection, you have to improvise that part of your drawing, and probably draw a more typical arrowhead than the original. In observing the original you formed some idea of it, and what you remember is this idea rather than the original itself. Some of the concrete detail of the original sticks for a while in the memory traces but fades out in time and leaves only a general idea to serve as the basis for recall.

*False testimony.* One of the most difficult memory tasks a person ever has to perform is in a court of law when he is called as an eyewitness of some event which happened weeks or months ago. It is not only the lapse of time that gives him trouble, but also being examined on details which he did not particularly notice in the original experience. If he yields to the solicitations of the lawyers and undertakes to reconstruct the original, he is almost sure to go beyond his memory traces and introduce material which seems probable enough but may be quite different from the true facts of the case.

In an experiment on the reliability of testimony the true facts are known to the experimenter, for he and his confederates have carefully planned and rehearsed the episode which they then enact before a group of unsuspecting witnesses—students, very likely, in a psychology class. Either directly afterward or some days later these eyewitnesses write out reports of the episode and answer a list of questions. They give a surprising amount of hazy and even false testimony. If the episode has been so designed as to create a false impression of what is going on and of the actors' motives, all the witnesses may agree in giving a perfectly false interpretation of the incident. Though recognition is on the whole more reliable than recall, mistakes may be made in the attempt to identify the individuals concerned. Court cases are on record in which a suspect was convicted and sentenced to a long term in prison, only to have it proved later that this suspect was not on the ground and had no possible connection with the crime. Such instances of mistaken identity warn us to be critical of our own memories in respect to recognition as well as recall. When called upon to give testimony either in court or elsewhere, we ought in all fairness to maintain a critical attitude, because our original observations were certainly incomplete and possibly biased, because our memory traces have become less definite, and because in attempting to reproduce the original experience we are very apt to introduce extraneous material.

**Interference in recall.** Learning does not guarantee later remembering, for forgetting may take place during the interval. Even good retention does not absolutely guarantee recall. We retain a person's name, as we prove by recalling it later, but at the moment we cannot get it. We know the answer to an examination question, but in the hurry and worry of the examination we give the wrong answer, and only later does the right answer come to mind. Some sort of interference is operating here.

One type of interference is emotional. Fear can paralyze recall. Anxious self-consciousness, or stage fright, is a terrible distraction. If the victim could only forget about himself, his memory of the well-learned speech or act would serve him perfectly. Repression (p. 386) is an extreme example of emotional forgetting.

Another type of interference occurs when two responses are aroused at the same time and get in each other's way. A speaker may hesitate and stumble, not because he has forgotten what he wants to say, but because two ways of expressing his thought occur to him at the same instant and one recall blocks the other. Something of the same sort often happens when you start to recall a person's name. You get some other name more or less similar to the desired name, such as "Underwood" instead of "Overstreet," and try in vain to get away from the false lead and on the trail of the right name. Drop the matter, and a little later the desired name is easily recalled, because the interfering suggestion has lost its temporary advantage, its recency effect. This way of escaping from temporary interferences by dropping the matter after one good effort, and taking it up afresh a little later, works well in many other cases besides the search for a name. You may find it almost impossible to make up your mind as between two alternative courses of action. Each has advantages and also disadvantages, and you vacillate between them interminably. This turmoil may be merely a recency effect, and next morning you find no difficulty in reaching a decision. Another important example can be found in the following chapter (p. 610).

## RECOGNITION

Recognition was defined, in distinction from recall, as "the remembering of something that is present, *i.e.*, presented to the senses." You recognize your friend by his visible appearance or the sound of his voice. His dog may recognize him by the sense of smell. The other senses, too, sometimes furnish the cues by which an object is recognized. [Cues or signs are used in recognition as they are in perception, and in fact recognition is a kind of perception] (p. 411). You see a small black object approaching and say, "It's a dog," and then, "It's a Scotty," and finally, "Why, it's Mac, the Parkers' dog!" To recognize the individual object you need more definite cues than simply to perceive the kind of object, for you must be able to distinguish the particular object from others of the same class. Often you are not aware of the exact cues which enable you to recognize an individual. You could not describe your friend accurately enough to enable a stranger to distinguish him from others who are more or less like him, unless he has a peculiar scar or some such identification mark. In general you use cues in recognition as in other forms of perception, without being distinctly aware of them, your interest being in the object and not in the cues.

When you see a casual acquaintance outside of his usual surroundings he may arouse a curious feeling of partial recognition. "I know him," you say, "Who is he?" Or you say, "I recognize him but cannot place him." It is an intriguing experience and stimulates you to search your memory, i.e., to try to *recall* the time, place and circumstances of your previous contact with this person. Recall, if successful, enables you to make your recognition complete. Here we have the processes of recall and recognition cooperating; first comes partial recognition, then recall leading to full recognition.

In another important kind of remembering the process starts with recall and is completed by recognition. When you are trying to remember a name, you are not satisfied with any name you happen to recall. Some names that come up you reject, but finally you recall a name that rings true. You recognize it and so complete the job of remembering. In the same way, when you are attempting to answer a question from memory, you are not satisfied with any answer that suggests itself; you wish to recognize the recalled material as belonging to the appropriate context.

**Errors of recognition.** On the whole, recognition seems to be a simpler and more dependable process than recall. A name, a face, a picture, a piece of music that you cannot recall may be recognized without any trouble. However, recognition is not infallible by any means. If an object now presented *resembles* one seen before, false recognition may occur, as can be easily demonstrated by a simple experiment. A dozen pictures are first shown, one at a time, to be "learned" by the subject. After an interval which need not be long these same pictures are shown again one at a time, but interspersed with a dozen new ones, some of the new ones being similar to some of the old but others quite dissimilar. O's task in the recognition test is to distinguish the old and the new, and to say "Yes" if he recognizes a picture and "No" if it seems new. Even though responding correctly most of the time he is likely to make errors of two sorts, by failing to recognize some of the old ones and by mistakenly saying "Yes" to some of the new but similar ones.

If the reaction time is measured in this experiment, the correct responses are found to be quicker on the whole than the incorrect—quicker and more confident. The response to a new but similar picture is not a decisive "Yes!" but a hesitant "Ye-es," perhaps with a question mark after it. The response to a new and dissimilar picture is a quick, decisive "No!" Non-recognition, or the knowing of a thing to be new, is not a mere absence of recognition, but is a positive and emphatic act (23). The feeling of novelty is just as definite as the feeling of familiarity.

**Behavior in recognition.** A person can show whether he recognizes an object by other forms of behavior than the verbal responses of "Yes" and "No." If his present behavior toward a certain object has evidently been learned in previous dealing with that particular object, it shows recognition; if his behavior is of the exploring type, it indicates novelty and non-recognition. When a baby smiles, not at everybody alike, but at a particular person who has pleased him before, he recognizes that person. On some previous occasion this person appeared before him and proceeded to amuse him. Now he smiles as soon as he sees that person without waiting for anything amusing to happen. This smile is a *conditioned response*, and when Pavlov's dog began to salivate at the sound of a bell, he recognized the bell. The conditioned response is behavioral evidence of the recognition of the conditioned stimulus. The bell was perceived as the food signal. So we saw once before (p. 521). The dog showed *stimulus generalization* by salivating somewhat in response to similar stimuli substituted for the regular CS; and just so the human subjects in the last paragraph showed stimulus generalization by hesitantly responding "Ye-es" to pictures similar to those seen before.

As the child grows up and moderates his emotional expressions (p. 355), he recognizes his friend without making that broad grin but still with a feeling of expectant pleasure which

is a sort of shorthand internal behavior or at least an adjustment to the friend's presence, a readiness or preparatory set for
a pleasant visit. In many other cases, perhaps in all cases of
recognition, there is a readiness to deal with the object in the
accustomed way. The complete recognition of your own room
is a readiness to behave there as you usually do. The partial
recognition of someone seen out of his usual surroundings is
more specific than a mere general feeling of familiarity. This
person, it seems to you, belongs behind a window, selling
something; later you identify him as the ticket agent in a railroad station. This other person seems like a man of some authority; later you identify him as the manager of the bank
where you have your account. A third arouses in you an attitude of vague hostility, and a fourth arouses the feeling that
you once saw him at the seashore or some resort. These feelings
suggest that recognition is the revival of an attitude of readiness
to deal with an object as we learned before to deal with it. Or
we may say that recognition is a perception of the object as
having characteristics which it was formerly found to possess.
These two seemingly opposed theories of recognition—one regarding it as a kind of perception, the other as a set or readiness for behavior—really come down to the same thing; for in
perceiving an object you are getting ready to deal with it according to its perceived characteristics, and in recognizing it,
*i.e.*, in perceiving it again as the same object, you are getting
ready to deal with it again as you dealt with it before.

## MEMORY TRAINING

When a person complains of his "weak memory" or "poor
powers of retention," his diagnosis of the trouble may be correct—for individuals differ in memory as they do in other
abilities and capacities—but quite possibly what he needs is
not to increase his "power" so much as to adopt better management and better methods in his memory work. By management
we mean the over-all planning and layout of the work, and by
methods the more detailed technique and ways of learning and

remembering. A person with just ordinary memory power can do a good job in memory work if he plans intelligently and practises good methods.

A large share of this chapter has been concerned with conditions favorable to efficiency in learning and remembering. Under the head of "economy in memorizing" we noticed the advantages of reciting and outlining a lesson as against merely reading it over and over, the advantages of studying the lesson as a whole rather than piecemeal, and the advantages of spaced as against massed repetitions so as to have some freshness in each new attack on the lesson. We also noticed, however, that individuals differ in respect to these alternatives, so that good management requires each individual to do some experimenting on his own account. Under the head of retention we saw the advantage of relaxing after learning important material, and perhaps even studying the most important lesson just before bed time—though here again individuals differ and good management requires that each should experiment and discover his own best hours for intensive study. There seemed to be no doubt of the advantage and even necessity of reviewing at suitable intervals any material that must be retained permanently. Under the head of recall we noticed that temporary interferences may disturb the process and that it is often good management to have one good try at recalling a name, for example, and then let the matter rest for a while. Recognition, we noticed, depends on previous observation and even on very close observation if one object is later to be safely identified in distinction from similar objects. In both recall and recognition we saw the desirability of maintaining a critical attitude toward our own memory, though this attitude should be balanced by another excellent habit, that of depending on our memory when the material in question has been well learned.

**Improvement of memory through practice.** The important question whether memory can be improved by training can be divided into the four questions: whether memorizing, or retention, or recall, or recognition can be improved. Regarding recall and recognition there is not much to be said, apart from the matter of good management, already discussed. Regarding retention, which people are most apt to be worried about, what can be said is mostly negative, apart again from questions of management. You can make sure of thorough learning, you can review, you can avoid interferences, but it is hard to see how otherwise you could go about to improve the memory traces or the sheer retentiveness of the brain. About all that can be suggested is to keep the organism, and with it the brain, in good physical condition. Retentiveness can be protected by hygienic measures, but not improved, so far as we know, by any sort of training.

The process of learning or memorizing, however, being a straightforward and controllable activity, is exceedingly susceptible to training. The beginner in learning lists of nonsense syllables is emotionally wrought up and insecure, goes to work in an uncertain way, perhaps tries to learn by mere rote or else attempts to use devices that are ill-adapted to the material, and has a slow and tedious job. With practice in learning this sort of material, he learns some appropriate technique, becomes sure of himself and free from emotional disturbance, and may even enjoy the work. Certainly he improves greatly in speed of memorizing nonsense syllables. If, instead, he practices on Spenser's "Faerie Queene," he improves in that, and may cut down his time for memorizing a stanza of that poem from fifteen minutes to five. This improvement is due to the subject's finding out how to organize this particular sort of material. He gets used to Spenser's style and range of ideas. And so it is with any kind of material; practice brings great improvement in memorizing that particular material.

**Transfer of training.** Whether practice in memorizing one sort of material brings skill that can be "transferred," or carried over to a second kind of material, is quite another question. Usually the amount of transfer is small compared with the improvement gained in handling the first material, or compared with the improvement that will result from specific practice with the second kind. What skill is transferred consists partly in the habit of looking for groupings and relationships, and partly in the confidence in one's own ability as a memorizer. It is really worth while taking part in a few memory experiments, just to know what you can accomplish after a little practice. Most persons who complain of poor memory will be convinced by such an experiment that their memory is fundamentally sound. But these laboratory exercises do not pretend to develop any general "power of memory," and the much advertised systems of memory training are not justified in any such claim. What is developed, in both cases, is skill in memorizing certain kinds of material so as to pass certain forms of memory test.

What has just been said of the transfer of memorizing skill holds good of other skills as well. In using any given tools and materials, the learner adjusts himself to the specific character of his particular job and is very likely not to discern any general principles that can be carried over to other jobs. Fortunately, however, it has been found that suitable instruction in good methods of work, with a moderate amount of practice devoted to using the methods, does build up a body of transferable ability (5). And the same has been found true of memory training. A moderate amount of practice in memorizing nonsense syllables and poetry, with instruction on the best methods of memorizing, enabled a class of college students to attack other kinds of memory material with unusual success. In the training, emphasis was placed on the value of a confident attitude, alertness and concentration, attention to meaning and grouping, recitation, and learning by wholes rather than in small parts (26).

Numerous experiments on transfer prove that it is not safe to trust to any automatic spread of ability from one activity to another. What is successfully transferred is usually something you can put your finger on—a principle, a good emotional attitude, a technique.

When anyone complains of a "poor memory" for any special material—names, errands, engagements—the trouble can usually be found in his heedless way of committing the facts to memory, not in his power of retention. President Seelye of Am-

herst College, back in the 1880's, never failed to call a student
or alumnus by name, after he had interviewed the man in the
freshman year. In this interview, besides fatherly advice, he
asked the man personal questions and studied him intently. He
was interested in the man, he formed a clear impression of his
personality, and to that personality he carefully attached the
name. Undoubtedly this able scholar was possessed of an un-
usually retentive memory; but his remarkable memory for
names—a definite social asset—depended largely on his technique.

Contrast with this the casual procedure of many of us on
being introduced to a person. Perhaps we scarcely notice the
name, and make no effort to attach the name to the personality.
To have a good memory for names, one needs to give attention
and practice to this specific matter. It is the same with memory
for errands; it can be specifically trained. Perhaps the best general hint here is to associate the errand beforehand in your
mind with the place where you should remember to do the
errand.

Often some little *mnemonic system* will help in remembering disconnected facts, but such devices have only a limited
field of application and do not in the least improve the general
power of memory. Some speakers, in planning out a speech,
locate each successive topic in a corner of the hall, or in a
room of their own house; and when they have finished one
topic, look into the next corner, or think of the next room, and
find the following topic there. It would seem that a well-con-
structed speech should supply its own logical cues so that arti-
ficial aids would be superfluous. In training the memory for
the significant facts of one's business, the best rule is to inter-
relate the facts into a system.

## SUMMARY

1. The process of memory consists in learning, retaining, and
remembering.

2. Experiments on *memorizing* (learning) make use of unfamiliar or lengthy material so that the degree of success in memorizing can be measured.

    a. *Immediate memory span* is the number of items (such as digits) that can be remembered after a single presentation of the material. The span increases with age and with practice.

    b. Material which is longer than the memory span can be memorized in repeated trials. The difficulty of memorizing increases greatly as the number of items of material is increased. Difficulty will be reduced if the material can be grouped into a smaller number of units according to meaning, location, similarity, or any other characteristics.

3. Economy in memorizing can be secured by proper management of the conditions of efficient learning.

    a. The subject must determine the particular task and direct his effort toward it.

    b. Memorizing is more efficient if the subject observes the distinguishing characteristics of the material—the meanings.

    c. *Recitation* is superior to passive re-reading in economy of memorizing and in retention. The advantages of recitation depend on better opportunities for observation and for reinforcement.

    d. Memorizing by *spaced repetitions* requires fewer trials than by *massed repetitions.*

    e. Memorizing is usually faster if the material is studied by the *whole method* rather than by the *part method,* but the evidence is not completely consistent.

4. *Retention* does not imply continuous activity but rather a modification of the structure of the brain, called a *memory trace.*

    a. Retention can be demonstrated only by the fact of remembering. *Relearning* tests are more sensitive than *recognition* tests which in turn are more sensitive than *recall* tests.

b. Retention decreases with the passage of time between learning and remembering. The loss is much more rapid at first than it is later in the retention interval.

c. *Forgetting* cannot be caused by the mere lapse of time; it must be due to the processes which go on during the time.

   (1) *Interference* from new learning may disrupt memory traces.

   (2) *Atrophy,* or metabolic changes resulting from disuse, may also disrupt memory traces.

d. Retention is better during sleep than during waking hours, presumably because interference is reduced.

e. *Direct interference* from learning new responses to the original stimuli produces marked loss of retention. If the original and the second list are both thoroughly learned, the interference effect can be overcome.

f. *Indirect interference* from learning a second list composed of different words is less than direct interference. The interference effect is slight unless the second material is similar to the first.

g. *Recency effects* are the phenomena of retention which immediately follow a perception. The process appears to be different from long-time retention and to depend on continuing activity in the brain.

   (1) *Warm-up* is a temporary state of readiness induced by activity.

   (2) Interference between two lists is greater if no time elapses between them.

   (3) Recall time is shorter for very recent than for older experiences and responses.

   (4) The initial rapid drop in the curve of forgetting may be due to the rapid disappearance of the recency effects.

   (5) The establishment of a memory trace continues during the period of the recency effect.

   (6) A blow to the head, or a strong electric shock through the head, produces forgetting of material learned just prior to the shock.

h. *Reviewing,* by recitation and relearning, improves the memory traces and reduces forgetting.

5. *Recall* is remembering something that is not present. Full recall requires the *reproduction* of the material.

　　a. *Memory images* are usually inferior to the actual sensory experiences in that facts cannot be found in the image unless they were observed at the time of the original perception.

　　b. *Primary mental images* are recency effects. Many children have *eidetic images*—vivid and detailed primary mental images.

　　c. *Hallucinations* are vivid images which are not distinguished from actual perceptions. Hallucinations are typical in dreams, and occur in some forms of mental disorder.

　　d. Recall may give a distorted, incomplete, and sometimes false reproduction of the original. The limitations are due both to inadequate learning and to difficulties in the process of recall.

　　　(1) In the recall of nonsense figures, persons tend to remember a word standing for a single general idea, and forget the details of the actual figure. The reproduction is often distorted to conform to the person's general idea.

　　　(2) Legal testimony of witnesses is subject to the same limitations. When the details of the original event were not specifically observed, the recall may be hazy, incomplete, or false.

　　e. *Interference with recall* may occur even when retention is adequate. Such interference results from emotion, or from a strong tendency to recall some other (incorrect) response.

6. *Recognition* is the remembering of something present, identifying it as something you have previously perceived. Full recognition involves recall of the circumstances of the previous perception.

　　a. Although recognition is simpler than recall, errors may result from failure to distinguish between two similar experiences.

   b. Recognition may be demonstrated by non-verbal behavior —a revival of a set toward an object which was established in prior experience.

7. Individuals differ in memory ability, but any person can improve his remembering by better management and better methods of memory.

   a. *Practice* is effective in improving memorizing, but is ineffective on the processes of retention, recall, and recognition.

   b. Practice in memorizing one sort of material does not *transfer* completely to other material. The amount of transfer is proportional to the identities and similarities between the two tasks. Transfer is therefore increased if the learner observes and concentrates on those features of the task which will be common to other tasks: principles, attitudes, and techniques.

# CHAPTER EIGHTEEN

# *Thinking*

While the superiority of the human race to the rest of the animal kingdom is marked in many respects—in diversity of motives and interests, in powers of observation, learning and memory—it is nowhere more marked than in a kind of intellectual activity which has been mentioned only incidentally in the preceding chapters. Man is distinctively a thinker. Hunched over his desk with only a pencil and a scrap of paper to work with, or even lost in thought with his feet on the desk, he may be all alive with inner activity and perhaps taking the crucial steps toward some great achievement. Man is notably a doer as well as a thinker. He loves to manipulate and change his environment. He engages in large enterprises and accomplishes far-reaching results. But these large enterprises depend on previous thinking. They are planned activities, and planning is a form of thinking. Man is distinctively a talker as well as a thinker, and his talking and his thinking are closely related in many ways. Language helps him to crystallize his thoughts and also to communicate them to his fellows. Language enables a group of people to pool their thinking, and the large enterprises of men are usually social enterprises which depend on teamwork in planning as well as in execution.

## IDEATION

All through the preceding chapters the individual has been represented as "dealing with the environment" or being in "active give-and-take relations with the environment." He receives stimuli which he uses as signs of objects present in the environment and of events going on there; and he responds by moving around in the environment, manipulating objects and taking part in what is going on. He learns to know and manage the environment.

In human beings, however, and to some extent in the higher animals, there is such a thing as *ideational activity* which does not deal with the *present* environment. Ideation, or "having ideas," is a distinctly "mental" activity in that it is not distinctly sensory or motor. It does not make use of sensory stimuli as signs of present objects, nor does it make use of muscular movements for producing any change in the present situation. In reading an absorbing story you take the stimuli from the

*By Burton Holmes, from Ewing Galloway*

FIG. 138.—The Thinker (Rodin).

printed page as signs of imaginary events and not of anything going on in your actual surroundings. In planning for tomorrow you may use your muscles, pacing the floor and even shaking your fist at your future adversary, but you are not trying to change your present environment. At other times you think of your absent friend, recall a pleasant or perhaps a painful experience, wonder what is happening at some distant place or what is going to happen at a future time. Shall we regard this "inner life" of thought and feeling as altogether separate from the practical life of dealing with the environment?

**Dreams and daydreams.** In a moment of relaxation and reverie, your thoughts may wander hither and yon, one thing reminding you of another, one memory recalling another, till you find yourself surprisingly far from your starting point; but if you carefully review the sequence of thoughts you can usually discover the associations that led from one to another. Sometimes long-forgotten memories are revived in such a process of *free association*. It is "free" because not controlled by any purpose nor directed toward any goal (see p. 220).

In a daydream there is apt to be more continuity. You are building a "castle in the air," imagining things as you would like to have them rather than as they are in reality. Or you are concocting a story with yourself as the hero. Usually you are a "conquering hero" in the daydream, winning your ladylove, outdoing your competitors, or displaying remarkable ability in some line. But you may make yourself a "suffering hero," jilted by your best girl or misunderstood by your best friends. It is easy to see into the motivation of the conquering hero dream, but why should anyone imagine himself worse off than he is in reality? Why should anyone "make a mountain out of a molehill" if he has been slighted or criticized in some unimportant way? Well, a person who has received just a little injury is left in a rather ridiculous position, and unless he can laugh it off his recourse is to magnify the injury and so restore his sense of self-importance. So both types of "hero" daydream bolster the dreamer's self-esteem. The motives of the daydream are the motives of daily life, and the materials of which the

dream castle is built are derived from the experiences of daily
life. The daydream is thus not entirely an escape from the
active give-and-take of life in the environment.

As a kind of play activity, a "play of the imagination," daydreaming has some of the value of other kinds of play. As an
escape from the difficulties and responsibilities of real life, it
obviously has its dangers. Carried to an extreme, as it is by
some insane individuals, it incapacitates one for real life. Some
of these unfortunate people are so immersed in fantasy as to
lose all contact with the environment, at least with the social
environment. Others, while maintaining some contact with the
world about them, transform it into an imaginary world in
which they are conquering heroes or suffering heroes or both
at once; that is, they have delusions of greatness and of perse-
cution.

Let us turn from daydreams to dreams of the night. In sleep
the brain activity sinks to a low level. Contact with the environment is mostly lost, though some stimuli are perceived in a
crude and bizarre way, as when the alarm clock is taken for
an orchestra, or cold air on the feet for a wet sidewalk. More
often, a dream resembles a daydream in being a train of
thoughts and images which make a story, though usually without much plot or continuity. The events of the dream seem real
at the time because not checked by any set for the objective
situation. Some dreams are obviously wish-fulfilling, as for example the boy's dream of finding a whole barrel of jackknives,
or the sex dreams of a sexually abstinent person, the feasting
dream of a starving person, or the polar explorer's often-repeated dream of warm, green fields. Many dreams seem too
fantastic to have any personal meaning or to fulfill any wish,
though Freud, the psychoanalyst, believed that all of them
were disguised gratifications of some wish or other, often of
repressed wishes dating from childhood (6). Even if a dream
runs along without any apparent goal or motive, the materials
of the dream are obviously derived from the experiences of
waking life.

**Purposive thinking.**   Even daydreaming serves a legitimate purpose in providing temporary relaxation from strenuous work and temporary escape from serious responsibilities. Story reading does the same. But ideation has its uses also in the practical life of dealing with the environment. It plays an important part in the great human enterprises of *discovery* and *invention*. Discovery is the goal of scientists, investigators and explorers of all types, from the least to the greatest; and invention is the goal of engineers and artists and creative designers of all types. Even the young child discovers and invents in a small way, for in exploring the environment he finds much that is new to him, and in manipulating the environment he devises little stunts and games that show at least a trace of originality. The essential role of ideational thinking in the process of discovery or invention can be seen in very ordinary, humble examples.

Suppose you need the hammer and go to the place where it is kept, only to find it gone. Now if you impulsively begin to ransack the house without any guiding idea, that would be motor exploration pure and simple. But if after a little of this you sit down and say, "Let me think. Where could that hammer be? Perhaps where I used it last!" you may remember using it in a certain place, go and find it there. You have substituted mental exploration for mere motor exploration and saved time and effort. Two ideational factors have played a part: (1) a guiding idea, "Look where you had it last"; and (2) a specific fact supplied by memory.

For an example belonging under the head of invention rather than discovery, suppose you are dissatisfied with the arrangement of the furniture in your room, and instead of shifting the pieces about with much labor suppose you sit down and say, "Let me think. What exactly is the matter with the present arrangement and what effect do I want to secure by rearrangement?" This question and the answer you give will steer your thinking in a certain direction and remind you of other rooms you have liked or disliked. When you think of a possible rearrangement of your furniture you may be able to imagine the effect without actually moving the pieces about.

There are then three ways in which ideation is useful in discovery and invention. (1) Most obvious is the recall of facts
previously observed and pertinent to the present problem. (2)
Equally valuable is the recall of guiding ideas. A rule or principle painfully worked out in the effort to solve one problem
can sometimes be profitably *transferred* to a new problem (p.
581). (3) Once you have a lead toward the solution of your
problem, you may decide whether it is a good lead by following it through ideationally. You invent a fine joke to play on
your friend, but then you ask yourself how he is likely to take
it. You imagine the joke tried out and the victim's reaction, and
perhaps see that the prospects are not very good. You "see"
this ideationally, not by actual use of the eyes but as you "see"
the point of a joke. To *see* means here, in dictionary language,
to "discern, to perceive by mental insight." Since we use "perceive" to refer to sense perception, the word "discern" will
serve us better when we refer to this ideational seeing. The important point is that by merely thinking we sometimes discover
whether a statement is true or false, whether a plan of action
will succeed or fail. At other times we cannot be sure of our
solution till we have actually tried it out and seen the result
with our eyes; but even so, ideational discernment prepares the
way for the experiment and without discernment the experiment would not prove anything. Purposive thinking is a process of seeking and finding. Guiding ideas direct the seeking but
discernment is the finding.

## TOOLS OF THOUGHT

Thinking is not always a difficult or strenuous form of activity, for nothing could be easier than the free flow of ideas
in reverie and daydreaming. Thinking out a problem, however,
is more difficult because of the tendency of the thoughts to
wander, and because of distracting stimuli from the present surroundings. These difficulties are overcome to some extent by
the use of *symbols,* which are present objects used to stand for
absent objects. If you are trying to explain how your car hap-

pened to collide with another car at an intersection, you will say something like this: "Here is one road and here is the other; this book is my car and this other book is the other car"—and so on. You are using symbols for the absent roads and cars, and really you are using symbols of two kinds, diagrams and words. The books and the spaces designated as the two roads make up a diagram of the situation, and your words, "my car" and "the other car," are verbal symbols distinguishing one absent object from another. Both words and diagrams serve as tools of thought.

Memory might be called a tool of thought, or better a tool chest since from it you draw previously acquired knowledge that may be useful in solving your present problem. In your stock of knowledge there are many concepts and principles which can be used as tools of thought.

**Thought and language.** If you ask a little child "what he thinks with" he is most apt to point to his mouth. Some behavioristic psychologists have pointed to the larynx; the ancient Greeks pointed to the diaphragm. All these authorities agree in connecting thought closely with speech, and they are supported by the introspection of many of us who will testify to the presence of "silent speech" when we are thinking.

Language is undoubtedly a great aid in thinking. First and foremost, thinking develops largely out of social situations. The child is stimulated to think by being questioned and by trying to describe what he has seen and to explain what he wants. Discussion and argument stimulate thought in older people, and even when an individual is alone and "thinking to himself" he is apt to speak and gesture as if defending his ideas before an audience.

Language helps in assembling materials for thought to work on, because it facilitates recall. Verbalized facts and principles are especially easy to remember. If you have put into suitable words a principle discovered while solving one problem, you recall that principle the more readily when you encounter a similar problem. This is partly because well-phrased sentences are easy to learn and remember, and partly because a principle has to be seen clearly in the first place, if it is to be clearly expressed.

But language can be a treacherous tool. A well-turned phrase may mislead you into assuming you understand something you have not really grasped at all. Then there are the ambiguous words, the weasel words, the question-begging words, which say one thing while meaning something else. And there are the boastful words, the mournful words, the hand-clapping words, the mud-slinging words, which awaken emotion and prejudice and close the door to clear thinking (8).

Mere talk, mere verbalism, is not thinking. A boy memorizes a speech, goes on the platform and rattles it off without the slightest sense of what he is talking about. That "silent speech" that goes with thought is meaningful speech, and thought is concerned with the meaning and not with the words, even though the words can be of great value to the careful thinker.

There is often some actual muscular activity during silent speech, as we might expect from the fact that the little child is apt to think aloud. Urged to make less noise he learns to whisper or simply move his lips and finally to think without any visible speech movement. In learning to read he passes through a similar sequence from reading aloud to silent reading. From this course of events we should expect some residual muscular activity during the silent reading or thinking of the adult. The muscles can be slightly active without producing any visible (or audible) movements, as is proved by tapping and amplifying the electrical changes or "muscle currents" that occur during slight activity of the muscles. If an electrode is inserted into the tongue, feeble muscle currents are detected during some silent speech, as when the subject recites a poem to himself (10). The speech muscles of a deaf person who talks largely with his fingers are more accessible, situated as they are in the forearm. With electrodes applied to the forearms of such a subject no muscle currents will be detected during easy reading or easy arithmetical work, but as the thinking becomes more difficult muscle currents appear (14). In the same way any one of us who usually reads silently will sometimes move

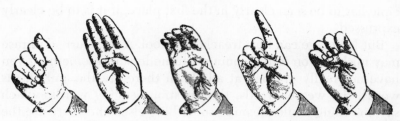

Fig. 139.—Talking with the fingers—the first few letters of a standard alphabet used by the deaf. Many other standard signs and gestures are used. If anyone talks with his hands, should he not also think with his hands?

his lips or speak aloud when he encounters difficult reading matter. Slight gesturing as well as speaking movements often occur during hard thinking.

**Diagrams.** A verbal description of a complex situation or plan of action would be very unwieldy and hard to piece together. Imagine an architect trying to explain to the carpenters and plumbers how he wishes a house built, without any blueprints to make his ideas plain! Or imagine a conductor trying to get his orchestra to play a new piece by describing it in words without any use of musical notation! A blueprint, a musical score, a map, or an organization chart is an elaborate symbol possessing certain advantages over a verbal description. It affords a comprehensive view of the whole plan or situation; and it is constructed so as to embody certain important characteristics of the real thing. By studying a blue print or organization chart you may detect flaws in the plan and discover how to correct them. By studying a road map you work out a satisfactory route for your trip. Much less elaborate diagrams are often useful in thinking out a problem.

**Concepts.** If a word is to be a tool of thought it must mean something. The meaning of a word is a concept. The definition of a word as given in the dictionary is an attempt to give expression to the concept, and examples help to make the meaning clear. Often you know the meaning of a word that you cannot define very exactly. That is, you have concepts that you cannot formulate, and you doubtless have concepts for which you have no convenient names.

A person who is having his first experience of mazes enters a
certain passage, explores it, finds a dead end and comes out
where he went in. If he takes note of the peculiar character of
that passage before proceeding further, the next time he
reaches the entrance to a passage he will ask himself if this is
"another of those things," so that he explores this second passage with a definite question to be answered. By recalling his
previous observation he is freed from the necessity of beginning from scratch in each new problem. If he picks up some
more definite name for "those things," the name will be a convenient symbol for his conceptual tool. The concept of "blind
alley" will be a useful tool in exploring mazes and in a figura-
tive sense it may be transferred and used in thinking out other
kinds of problems.

An example at a higher level is that of a group of people discussing the problem of inflation. One says, "If prices go up,
wages have got to go up." Another replies, "But when wages go
up, prices rise to meet the increased cost of production." "All

*Press Association, Inc.*

Fig. 140.—Group thinking; planning for world-wide democracy. But
does this word carry the same concept to all members of the United
Nations Council of Foreign Ministers?

right," says a third person, "So the only way to escape from this vicious circle, or spiral, is to increase production." Here we have quite a number of words which may be spoken glibly, in parrot fashion, or which may stand for definite concepts and serve as tools of clear thinking.

Your own concept of a thing may not agree in all respects with the standard definition, for your concept consists of what you know or believe about the thing; it includes also your own attitude toward the thing. Your concept of a church may be quite different from mine. In discussing churches you of course use your concept and I mine and we may fail to understand each other.

There are concepts not only of things and persons but also of their qualities, actions and interrelations. So there are concepts of the height of mountains, of the fluttering and falling of leaves, and of the distance between two places; and concepts of the optimism of some people, of the walking, talking and breathing of people, and of the friendship or hostility between people.

The child undoubtedly forms some concepts for himself before he can talk. He observes and remembers how certain people and things behave. From the way he likes to drop things out of his crib and hear them bang on the floor he must have a concept of dropping and of droppable things. From his different behavior toward his mother and father he must have different concepts of these two persons. When he begins to pick up the language he has the task of finding out what the words mean, and in proportion as he uses words correctly we can infer that he has acquired the corresponding concepts. On this basis we infer that he easily acquires concepts of objects such as he can manipulate or deal with in any active way, and concepts of operations that he performs or that are performed upon him (such as "carry," "tickle"). Color names and number words he learns easily enough but uses at first with little discrimination. He needs to *use* colors and numbers in some way in order to grasp the precise meanings of these words. His concepts of natural phenomena are very naive at first (*17*).

*Generalization and differentiation* play an important role in concept formation as they do in conditioning (p. 529). The child's concepts often show a crude generality which has to be overcome by taking note of differences. A little girl on seeing a squirrel for the first time called it a "funny kitty." She was generalizing by assimilating the new to the old, but as she noticed that the new kitty was "funny" she was ready to learn a new name and differentiate a fresh concept. To advance from vague general concepts to more precise concepts, observation and suitable reinforcement are necessary.

Besides the crude, primitive type of generalization there is a more advanced type which consists in finding common characteristics in things that at first seem quite different. To discover what is common to rats, rabbits and squirrels and so to arrive at the concept of the rodents, while distinguishing them from the cat family and the dog family, is an example of generalization of the advanced type.

*Abstraction.* In order to generalize at the higher level, it is necessary to notice the common characteristics of different individual objects. It is possible, for human beings at least, to single out a certain characteristic of an object while for the moment disregarding all its other characteristics. You "abstract" this characteristic and so form an abstract concept of the characteristic itself. When you say of a person that he "is tall," the adjective "tall" designates a characteristic observed in this person but also in many other persons. For the moment you are disregarding all other characteristics of this particular person and mentioning only a single characteristic which is common to him and others. Whenever you try to describe a person you have to use words that designate some of his qualities or characteristics; and the same is true when you describe a thing or tell what happened on a certain occasion. You use words that mean qualities and relations, and make yourself understood because the one listening knows the meanings of these words, i.e., knows the abstract concepts designated by these words.

*The process of forming a concept* is illustrated by experiments such as the following. A series of nonsense drawings is

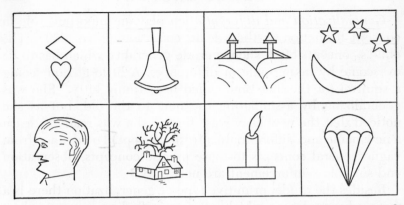

Fig. 141.—Establishing a concept. Let the figures in the upper row be called "Uppos" and those in the lower row "Downos." The reader is to find the answers to the questions, "What is an Uppo?" and "What is a Downo?" The next figure gives further examples of the two concepts.

shown, all of them having a certain characteristic in common while differing in other respects. A nonsense word is given as the name of this class of figures, and there are one or more other classes of figures, each with its name. The subject's task is to observe the figures as they are shown, one at a time, and to discover the common characteristic of each class of figures, so as to give a definition of each of the nonsense names. Being very much on the alert in such an experiment, the subject takes note of some striking characteristic of the first figure, looks for it in the second figure and, if he finds it there, looks for it in the third figure, and so on. As long as he finds it he accepts it with growing confidence as the common characteristic of the class. But if he cannot find it in one or more of the figures, he drops it and looks for some other characteristic. He is testing tentative concepts suggested by his observation of the figures. His tentative concepts are reinforced as long as they work and enable him to name the figures correctly, but become extinguished when they fail to work (5, 20, 21).

Some common characteristics of figures are much more easily found than others. Thinglike features (resemblance to a concrete thing) are more easily spotted than less tangible characteristics such as shape or number of parts. Very likely the

Fig. 142.—Continuation of Fig. 141.

ability to abstract, i.e., to deal with an object as the possessor of one particular characteristic while disregarding all its other characteristics, develops first in very practical situations. When you need "something to pound with" and use a shoe, disregarding for the moment the ordinary use of shoes, you are building up an abstract concept. To perceive an object is to be ready to deal with it, and to discern a common characteristic of many objects is to be prepared to deal with any object possessing this common characteristic. Abstract concepts serve practical purposes besides the purpose of communicating knowledge from one person to another, and they are of great value to the scientist or inventor (9).

Combinations of concepts—principles, rules, laws, systems. Thinking is guided and aided not only by single concepts but also by concepts combined in various ways. In considering how to remedy an undesirable state of affairs you recall the proverb, "The cure was worse than the disease," and are led to think carefully of all the possible effects of a suggested remedy. The proverb brings the concepts of cure and disease into a relation which needs to be considered. When you have learned a proposition in geometry, such as, "The sum of the angles of a triangle equals two right angles"—a statement which brings certain concepts into relation with each other—you have a tool useful in the solution of many geometrical problems. The rules of arithmetic, the rules of the road, the rules of a game, are combinations of concepts which guide thought as well as action. The same is true of the laws of a state and also of the laws of nature which are used in scientific thinking. Any of these laws, rules and propositions may be called *principles* or we may reserve that word for the higher and more important ones. On analysis a principle will be found to combine two or more concepts in certain relations.

*A conceptual system* contains several or many concepts which are interrelated in definite ways. Arithmetic is such a system, including concepts of numbers, of the four fundamental operations and of fractions, decimals, percents, averages, etc. When you see that a certain problem is one in arithmetic, your thinking is guided into the appropriate channels. If the problem is one of esthetic effect you will think in terms of symmetry, balance, contrast and this system of concepts. If it is a problem in personal relations, you will think in terms of motivation and frustration, likes and dislikes, rivalry and sympathy, family background, education and other psychological concepts which are, to be sure, not so well integrated into a system as the concepts are in arithmetic, but still are of some use in guiding your study of a human problem.

Just because your concepts and principles—and your beliefs, we should add—guide and facilitate your thinking, it does not follow that they always guide you aright. You may try to use the wrong set of concepts or the concepts themselves may be too self-centered or too traditional for clear, objective thinking. Your personal feelings and the prejudices of your group may falsify your ideas and lead you to erroneous conclusions. There is no way of protecting yourself completely from such errors, but it is possible to accomplish a good deal by resolute practice in objective observation and straight thinking (22).

## PROBLEM SOLVING

A problem exists when the way to a desired goal is not plain, when the means for accomplishing a desired result is not perfectly obvious. The problem is solved when ways and means are found. The process of solution, then, is a process of seeking and finding, and often some of the work can be done by thinking instead of by motor exploration and manipulation. The "tools of thought" are put to use. Concepts learned in previous experience are applied to the new problem, usually being recalled by aid of their verbal symbols; and new concepts may be invented for handling the novel problem. Principles are remembered and given a trial. Language enables the thinker to talk to himself about his problem and also to talk it over with his fellows and enlist their assistance.

Most of the situations which confront us in daily living are readily met by the transfer of knowledge and skill from our past experience. A quick look at the situation suggests that such and such concepts are relevant, the known principles embodying these concepts are recalled, and an appropriate solution is immediately achieved. Such instances are not really problems. When a real problem arises, which does not readily yield a solution by our habitual methods, we usually manage somehow to push it aside. But intellectual curiosity or practical necessity may cause us to continue our efforts. The process of reaching a solution may be long and troublesome even though the solution, when it is finally reached, proves to be surprisingly simple. So we are informed by scientists, engineers, musical composers and creative thinkers of all varieties.

**Obstacles to clear thinking.** In a problematic situation there is a starting point and there is a goal. Something is given and something is required. What is given are certain "data" already available to the thinker, certain facts that he knows, certain materials that he can use. What is required is typically an explanation of the known facts or a satisfactory way of using the given materials so as to accomplish the desired result. The difficulty may be (1) that the available data are insufficient so that more data must first of all be obtained; (2) that some of the given facts and materials are superfluous and confuse the thinker; (3) that the data do not fall readily into a unified pattern or over-all view of the entire problem.

These difficulties stand out clearly in the task of a detective attempting to solve the mystery of a crime (or in the task of the reader of a detective story who attempts to solve the mystery for himself). (1) Certain facts are known from the start but these are not enough and the first job is to gather more data. (2) Inevitably some of the circumstances of the crime are irrelevant and create a false impression of what has happened and raise suspicions against some innocent party. (3) Even when all necessary data have been secured and irrelevant data weeded out, the facts may not make sense or fall into any consistent pattern. The detective may say (at least in the stories) that he is not yet ready to offer a possible solution, because "something is wrong with the picture." The parts do not fit together. He tries to maintain an open-minded view of the mass of data until he can discern some pattern that holds everything together.

**The value of guiding ideas.** The thinker's task varies of course with the nature of his problem. In a mathematical problem such as an "original" in geometry or one of the concrete problems in algebra or arithmetic, what is "given" is usually sufficient and there is no need to obtain any more data. Some of the data may be irrelevant. "How many square yards of green carpet will be needed to cover one end of a pine box that is 3 feet high, 3 feet wide, and 8 feet long?" In the schoolroom such "trick questions" would be condemned though they are not unlike the arithmetical problems of everyday life. To solve this problem you have to disregard the irrelevant data regarding material and length of the box, and concentrate on the mere size of the end of the box. Under the guidance of this abstract concept the problem is easily solved.

Let us take a slightly more difficult example. My friend has driven up the highway, making an average of 40 miles per hour. One hour later I start out to overtake him, making an average of 50 miles per hour. How long will it take me to overtake my friend?

I examine the data: one hour start and 40 miles an hour for him, 50 miles an hour for me. These elements of the problem do not instantly fall into a usable pattern. Some unifying, guiding idea is needed. I shall be *gaining* on him, and this abstract concept of gain furnishes a guiding idea. How much distance am I gaining per hour? He makes 40, I make 50; so I gain 10 miles per hour. How much total distance have I got to gain? He has been out an hour and is now 40 miles ahead. I have to gain 40 miles, I gain 10 miles per hour, and therefore it will take me 4 hours to overtake him.

If I am doubtful about this answer and wish to check it somehow, I must approach the problem from another angle and use another guiding idea. I think of algebra and say, "Let $x =$ the number of hours I have to go." Then I must make an equation, I must find two quantities that are equal. Well, yes— when I overtake him we shall both have gone the same distance from the starting point. Since I shall go $x$ hours at 50 miles per hour, the distance for me will be $50x$ miles. Having an hour the start of me he will have driven $x + 1$ hours, and, making 40 miles per hour, he will have gone $40(x + 1)$ miles. As these two distances will be the same, I have the equation, $50x = 40(x + 1)$. Working this out I get $x = 4$ hours, the same answer as before.

Since both my guiding ideas have led to the same conclusion, I am greatly surprised when I overtake my friend after only two hours, and my first impression is that my mathematics must have been at fault. But he tells me that after the first hour he slowed down to 30 miles per hour so as to let me catch up. Checking back I see that my reasoning was correct but my data partially incorrect.

One more problem of a different sort. The five little "blocks" in Fig. 143 are to be fitted together so as to make a perfect square (with no gaps). Different individuals attack this problem in quite different ways.

1. *Hit-or-miss motor manipulation.* One subject may say, "I must cut those shapes out of stiff paper and just experiment with them, putting them together in various ways until I get a square." This subject seems to have no over-all view of the problem nor any guiding idea, though as he goes along he will

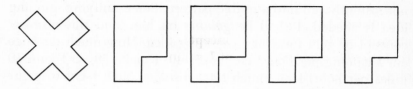

FIG. 143.—A construction puzzle. The five shapes represent blocks which are to be fitted together into a square (Durkin, 4).

probably observe certain characteristics of the pieces that have to be considered. He is making a slow job of it.

2. *Guidance by outstanding characteristics of the pieces.* Another subject notices at once that the projecting parts of the 4 similar pieces will fit into the 4 inner angles of the little cross, and proceeds to experiment in this way. He may be able to do this ideationally, without actual manipulation. He builds a good rectangle and a nice cross but not the required square. But he will probably see a way to modify this procedure slightly and so reach a solution.

3. *Guidance by size of the required square.* Another subject may ask himself how large the square is going to be. In this particular puzzle he can answer this question rather easily; for the cross is divisible into 5 little squares, and each of the other pieces also into 5 of the same little squares. Since the whole area of the square, then, is going to be 25 of these little squares, the side of the big square will equal 5 times the side of the little squares. He then asks how to put together the pieces so as to obtain straight edges of the required length and soon sees how this can be done. His procedure is more planful and we may say more rational than those of the other two subjects. More than the other subjects he keeps the goal before him while exploring the given material (4).

A guiding idea may be obtained by examination of the present situation without much attention to the goal; or one may be obtained from thought of the goal without much attention to the present situation or data; but it is most likely to lead to a solution if it manages to take account of both what is given and what is required (3, 13).

**Hypotheses.**   A hypothesis is a question that leads to thought and observation. It is a definite question, suggesting a tentative answer that is worth investigating. In a perfectly familiar situation there is no question as to the facts or as to the proper line of action. In a novel and problematic situation the first questions to suggest themselves are very general and indefinite. They are questions like these: "What's the matter? Why has the car stopped running? What shall we do now?" These questions are not definite enough to be called hypotheses. But more pointed questions may quickly arise. "Have we run out of gas?" If so, the gauge will register zero—but it says half full. "How about the spark?" And so on. These more definite questions stimulate thought and observation, thought indicating the way to find an answer, and observation then finding the answer.

Much more original hypotheses and more elaborate thinking and observing are demanded by the problems confronting the scientific investigator, but in outline his procedure is the same as illustrated in the simple case of the stalled car. An example from the history of science is afforded by Harvey's discovery (about 1628) of the circulation of the blood. From examination of the beating heart Harvey was led to the hypothesis that the heart acts as a pump forcing blood into the arteries and that the blood circulates through the body and returns to the heart by way of the great veins. If this is so, Harvey saw (discerned by thinking), the flow of blood in any artery must be away from the heart, and in any vein it must move toward the heart. He found by observation that this was the fact. Further, there should be little tubes leading from the smallest arteries over into the smallest veins, and this consequence of the hypothesis was verified later when invention of the microscope made observation of the capillaries possible. Other consequences of the hypothesis were thought out and verified from time to time, and the circulation of the blood became an accepted law.

Many hypotheses are not so fortunate as this one, because some of their logical consequences are not verified by observed facts. They have to be abandoned or at least modified. Even when destined to die, hypotheses are temporarily useful to the scientist as stimuli to thought and observation. The psychological process of scientific discovery is about as follows. You start with certain facts that demand explanation and try to fit them into the existing body of knowledge. If you can find no accepted scientific principle that explains these facts you try to invent a hypothesis that fits the new facts while being consistent with existing knowledge. If you succeed in devising such a hypothesis you are naturally proud of it as "your baby," but if you have the true scientific spirit you put a question mark after your beautiful hypothesis and use it simply as a guiding idea. You combine it with existing knowledge and figure out its logical consequences; that is, you see (discern) that *if* the hypothesis is correct certain results will follow and be observable. Then you go into the laboratory or into the field and arrange matters so as to observe whether the predicted results are obtained. If they are found, your hypothesis is verified to that extent, though it may be upset later. If contradictory facts are found, the hypothesis is disproved and you must modify it or begin all over again (p. 11).

The would-be investigator, even when he knows his subject well, may slip up at several points. He may not get hold of any fruitful hypothesis. Or he may not be able to discern any consequences of his hypothesis that can be put to the test of observation. Or he may not have the enterprise and industry to gather the necessary data by experiment or field work.

"How shall I proceed so as to think of fruitful hypotheses?" This is a difficult question for the psychologist, because the thinking process is hidden and variable. You first take in your problem as clearly and fully as you can. You draw on your stock of knowledge. You try intensely to find a good clue. If you find no clue that has any promise you shift for a while to a more passive, receptive attitude, just letting the problem soak in. It is well at this point, if not earlier, to *question your assumptions*, for you may be blinding yourself to some possible leads by taking something for granted that is not necessarily so in the present situation. You may need to examine the problem from a fresh angle in order to see any fresh leads. Sometimes, on the contrary, you reject a lead that is actually good without following it up sufficiently. So the successful investigator has to preserve a proper balance (1) between active seeking and watchful waiting, and (2) between thoroughness and flexible openmindedness.

*Hypotheses compared with "guiding ideas."* A hypothesis is itself a guiding idea of the most definite sort but it is usually based upon knowledge which provides a more general guiding idea. A good hypothesis is not often a wild guess or "shot in the dark." The better the problem is understood, the more likely the thinker is to be guided toward a reasonable hypothesis. When a car is stalled on the road, the problem is so clearly one of engine mechanics—and not one of arithmetic, for example— that the driver searches in that field and finds his definite hypotheses there. When the problem has to do with overtaking another car that has an hour's start, it is so clearly one of arithmetic that he tries to think arithmetically. In this second case he does not need any definite hypothesis, for if he can formulate the problem exactly he need not guess at the answer but can work it out in a straightforward manner. If he were not much of an arithmetician he might set up a hypothesis, as by saying, "I guess it will take about two hours," and test this hypothesis arithmetically by figuring as follows: "In two hours I'll be 100 miles from here, and the other driver will be 80 miles from where he is now, that is 120 miles from here. So he will still be ahead. Perhaps it will take me three hours to overtake him." This way of attacking the problem looks like the standard scientific procedure of setting up a hypothesis and then testing it; but it would be rather absurd since he can reach the answer without guessing once he has the right guiding idea. In mathematics it is often possible to do without hypotheses because a clear view of the problem suggests a procedure which will certainly lead to the solution. In most sciences, as well as in practical affairs, it is usually necessary to let the guiding idea suggest more definite hypotheses which can be tested by experiment or some form of factual observation. Even the mathematical thinker does not usually advance in a straight course from the problem to the solution. If he does not need hypotheses, at least he needs a guiding idea and he may have to search in different directions before finding a good one. But the more clearly and fully he grasps the problem the surer he is to find a good guide.

"Incubation" of a difficult problem.  In working on a problem you may find yourself "going round and round in a circle" and unable to reach a solution. At such times it is a good rule to lay the matter aside for a time. Many creative thinkers, whether in science or invention, in art or literature, have found this rule to work well. On the basis of their testimony it seems possible to divide the whole process of original thinking on a difficult problem into *four stages of creative thought*:

1.  Preparation, "loading up."
2.  Incubation, while the problem is laid aside.
3.  Illumination, the "happy thought" or guiding idea that suggests a hypothesis leading to the solution.
4.  Verification and elaboration.

In the stage of preparation, the problem is analyzed, and all available information is assembled and studied intensively. Preliminary attempts are made to reach a solution, but if these fail the matter is laid aside. In the stage of incubation no serious work is done on the problem though it may come to mind at odd moments. In one of these odd moments—on awaking in the morning, or while daydreaming, or during conversation, while out for a walk, or even while taking a bath (remember Archimedes!)—illumination comes in the form of an idea that looks so promising that it immediately engrosses the thinker's attention and leads to the most intense concentration. If the idea is good, it must then be worked over in detail so as to produce a complete machine or scientific discovery, or a complete poem or picture, according to the nature of the creative thinker's problem (*16, 18*).

The word "incubation" implies a theory, the theory that unconscious work is being done on the problem while it is laid aside and "out of mind," just as important hidden processes are going on inside an egg that is being incubated. There is no positive evidence for this theory, and a different theory is at least possible. Why does a thinker who has all necessary data well in hand not reach a solution immediately? He may be confused by irrelevant data, he may be making a false assumption or following a poor lead, he may be lost in details and unable to discern the whole pattern of the problem. All these interferences have a strong hold on him as long as he continues thinking on the problem without any respite, but their recency effect will fade out during a rest period, as it does in the much simpler but parallel case of the forgotten name (pp. 566, 576). What he needs is a fresh view of the problem, such as he is more likely to get when physically well rested and when not anxiously continuing to pursue old and fruitless lines of inquiry. But to secure the advantages of incubation he must first have made thorough preparation.

**Rational thinking compared with trial and error.** A thinker engaged in solving a problem is in somewhat the same predicament as a rat in the maze or a cat in the puzzle box. He has his data to start from and he has his goal to steer for, but he sees no straightforward way to advance to the goal. If he could see the way to the goal the problem would be no problem for him. He has to proceed by exploring the possibilities, by finding leads and trying them out, by backing off when blocked in one approach and trying another. So the thinker's procedure has something of the character of trial-and-error behavior (p. 499). It differs from trial and error in two respects. First, the thinker tries out his leads, or some of them, ideationally instead of by motor exploration and manipulation. Second, by first grasping the problem as fully as he can, he gets hold of guiding ideas that conform to the nature of the problem. He rejects foolish suggestions that do not conform to the structure of the entire problem. He makes a planned attack on the problem. Even so, he cannot be sure of selecting the best lead at first, and since he must often give very close attention to details he cannot always keep the entire situation in mind. So thought tends to take a zigzag course, and this is true even of the best thinkers when they are working on really difficult problems (23).

## LOGICAL AND ILLOGICAL THINKING

When a thinker, from the examination of his data, reaches a conclusion which he accepts as certain or at least probable, he has been *reasoning*. When he reaches a conclusion that follows from his data, he has reasoned logically. When, as is sometimes the case, he reaches a conclusion that does not follow from his data, his thinking has been loose and his conclusion is illogical.

A conclusion "follows" from the data when it can be discerned in the pattern of the data. If George is William's son and John's father, it follows that William is John's grandfather. The pattern of these particular data can be diagramed by a vertical line with George in the middle, William at the top, and John at the bottom. Here the pattern is simple and the logical conclusion easily seen. In the old riddle,

> Sisters and brothers have I none,
> But this man's father is my father's son,

the pattern is not so obvious, but once it is constructed a conclusion can easily be discerned.

**The use of a "middle term" in reasoning.** George, in the example given, is a middle term standing in certain relations to both William and John and so making it possible to discern a relation between these two. Reasoning very often depends on the use of some middle term. You wish to compare the girths of two trees, and find you can reach all the way around the one but only part-way around the other. Using your own reach as a middle term you discern which tree is larger. Any kind of measurement provides middle terms for comparing things that cannot be brought into direct relation with each other, like the weights of two persons or the temperature on two days.

The middle term may be a mere number. "Have we set the

table for all the people?" "Wait till they all come to the table
and we can tell." "Oh! but we can tell beforehand by counting
How many people are coming? One, two, three . . . fifteen in
all. Now count the places at the table—only fourteen. We must
make room for one more." Here the middle term consists of
the two numbers, 14 and 15, and the relation between these
two abstract numbers is seen to hold good for the concrete
objects that have been counted, the people and the chairs.

If two things are equal to the same thing they are equal to
each other. Here the third thing is the middle term. But can
we say that two things which *resemble* a third thing must resemble each other? If Mary and Jane both resemble Winifred,
can we conclude that they resemble each other? Hardly, for
Mary may resemble Winifred in one respect, while Jane resembles her in another respect, and there may be no particular
resemblance between Mary and Jane. Winifred is not a good
middle term unless we define her more exactly. The middle
term must not be ambiguous.

We wish to reach a conclusion of the form, "S is P," or "S is
related in a certain way to P," where S is the "subject" or what
we are talking about, and P the "predicate" or what we can say
about the subject. The middle term, M, must be so related to
S on the one hand and to P on the other, that it forms a bridge
between them. If our data are that the country S lies north of
the equator, but the country P south of the equator, the equator
is a true middle term and we can draw the conclusion that S
lies farther north than P. But if we are told that S lies north
of the equator and that P also lies north of the equator, we
see of course that S and P are alike in that respect but we cannot tell which of them lies farther north, because the equator
is not a genuine middle term in this case. If we are told that S
is 40° north of the equator and P only 30°, we see that S is the
farther north, but our middle term now is not simply the equator. The middle term need not always lie literally between S
and P, but its relations to S and P must be such as can combine
into a single relation between S and P.

There are still other requirements which must be met by a

satisfactory middle term. In complicated arguments the conclusions reached are often illogical and deceptive because of inadequate middle terms.

**Psychology and logic.** Psychology is not the only subject interested in reasoning. Logic was well developed before psychology began to examine the actual processes of thinking, the conditions that make reasoning easy or difficult, the growth of reasoning ability in the child, the effect of training, individual differences, and other problems that are clearly psychological. Logic is concerned especially with the question whether the conclusion follows from the data and with ways of insuring logical procedures throughout the reasoning process. What we have been saying about the middle term belongs rather to logic than to psychology, and we will dip into logic a little more, for the purpose still of bringing out pitfalls that beset the thinker.

**The syllogism.** In order to check the logic of an argument, all the data on which the conclusion is supposed to rest must be made perfectly explicit. The reasons for a conclusion are often only partially expressed in ordinary talk and writing. We say, "this flying creature cannot be a bird, for it has six legs." If made perfectly explicit, the argument takes this shape:

> This creature has six legs.
> No birds have six legs.
> Therefore, this creature is not a bird.

In many cases, if not in this one, the explicit formal statements make it easier to see whether the conclusion does or does not follow from the data. The formal statements show what is the middle term and what are its relations to the S and P terms. The statements giving the relations of the middle term to the other two terms are the *premises* from which the conclusion is supposed to follow. The two premises and the conclusion, taken together, make up a *syllogism*. (In long arguments and complicated reasoning processes there may be many more than two premises, but they are often combined in pairs to yield intermediate conclusions which then serve as the premises yielding the final conclusion.)

By using our symbols, S, M and P, we can express the syllogism just given in generalized form, thus:

S is M.
P is not M.
Therefore, S is not P

We see that the conclusion is logical whenever an argument can be thrown into this precise form—provided, also, that M is a good, unambiguous middle term standing in suitable relations with S and P. The relation intended by the little word "is" ought to be made more explicit. Here it means "is included in," while "is not" means "is excluded from." These are the relations to be understood when nothing more is said. Put in this form the syllogism about the flying creature is as follows:

This creature is included in the six-legged creatures.
No birds are included in (or all birds are excluded from) the six-legged creatures.
Therefore, this creature is not included in the class of birds.

Another standard syllogism, leading however to a positive instead of a negative conclusion, has this form:

All S is M.
All M is P.
Therefore, all S is P.

The conclusion is clearly logical, and this is about the easiest form of syllogism to see into clearly. The two following forms look simple, but they are illogical:

All S is M.                    No S is M.
All P is M.                    No P is M.
Therefore, all S is P.(?)      Therefore, all S is P.(?)

No conclusion can be drawn from either of these two, except of course that S and P are alike in one respect, i.e., in being M or not being M.

**A logical conclusion not necessarily true in fact.**   The distinction between logical correctness and factual truth is important in reasoning. A logical conclusion is one which follows from the

premises; but it is not necessarily true in fact. A logical conclusion is true *if* the premises are true. Reasoning has two uses.
If the premises are known to be true, correct reasoning yields
additional knowledge; the truth of the conclusion can be inferred from the true premises. If we are sure that bears are
mammals and that all mammals are warm-blooded animals,
then we see that bears must be warm-blooded animals (in spite
of the fact that they hibernate). But if we are not sure of the
truth of one of our premises, what can we do? We can accept
it as a hypothesis and draw the logical conclusion; and if the
conclusion then proves to be *false* as a matter of fact, we see
that our premise or hypothesis must be false. This testing of
hypotheses by deducing their consequences, and then observing whether the consequences hold good in fact, is a very important use of reasoning, as we have already seen (p. 607). If
the predicted consequences are found to be true in fact, the
hypothesis is not thus proved to be certainly true, for a conclusion that is both logical and true sometimes follows from partially or wholly false premises. For example, "All whales are
mammals; man is a species of whale; therefore man is a mammal." Or even, "All lizards are mammals; man is a species of
lizard; therefore man is a mammal."

Though the truth of a conclusion is something quite different
from its logical correctness, it is easy to get the two confused
and to overlook the poor logic of a conclusion that is known or
believed to be true. Notice the following argument:

All Mongolians have slant eyes.
The Chinese have slant eyes.
Therefore, the Chinese are Mongolians.

Over 50 percent of a group of college students marked this conclusion as correct. They would doubtless have responded very
differently to the same syllogism with changed terms, as for
example:

All birds have wings.
Bees have wings.
Therefore, bees are birds.

To escape from such confusion and pin ourselves down to the pattern of the data, letter symbols can be substituted for the meaningful terms of a syllogism. In place of either of these last two we should have:

All P is M.
S is M.
    Therefore, S is P.

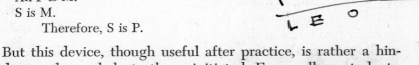

But this device, though useful after practice, is rather a hindrance than a help to the uninitiated. Even college students, with all their training in algebra, commit more errors in such symbolic syllogisms than in those stated in ordinary language. In order to reason easily, it seems from the experiments, we need something concrete to hold on to, though with something concrete given we are prone to be swayed unduly by our knowledge, belief or prejudices regarding the conclusions reached (*11, 12, 15, 24*).

But what harm does it do to reason illogically, provided the conclusions are true? Well, the human being prefers to be clearheaded rather than muddled, and there is often practical harm from basing a true conclusion on false premises or loose reasoning. When a child is told to "be good or the goblins will get you," and later finds out that there are no goblins, he is apt to think there is no reason for being good. And when a political orator offers unsound arguments for his party, those who see through his flimsy reasoning are apt to conclude that the party is no good.

**Verbal difficulties in reasoning.**  As has already been said (p. 594), language is both a great aid in thinking and a source of error and confusion. Data are sometimes expressed in a form that obscures their interrelations. An instance is afforded by the efforts of 8-year-old children to solve the following problem:

Edith is fairer than Olive; but she is darker than Lily.
    Who is darker, Olive or Lily?

Only 46 percent of the children got this right; but the percent rose to 72 when a simple verbal change was made, giving the same problem this form:

Lily is fairer than Edith; Edith is fairer than Olive.
   Who is the fairer, Lily or Olive?

In the first form the mix-up of the two opposite relationship words, "fairer" and "darker," was the source of confusion. This type of syllogism, as already suggested, can be made clear by a straight-line diagram with the middle term in the middle and the other two terms at the ends (1, 2).

Syllogisms of the other type, based on inclusion and exclusion, are usually expressed in language which does not show the exact relations of the data. This source of difficulty is present even in the simple problem of deciding whether the "converse" of a proposition is logical. Consider which of the following converse statements follow logically from their respective original statements.

| *Original* | *Converse* |
|---|---|
| (1)  All X's are Y's | All Y's are X's  *NO* |
| (2)  Some X's are Y's | Some Y's are X's  *yes* |
| (3)  No X's are Y's | No Y's are X's  *yes* |
| (4)  Some X's are not Y's | Some Y's are not X's  *no* |

Most people find it easy to accept all of the converse statements, though careful examination will show that only (2) and (3) are logical. From "All X's are Y's" it surely follows that "Some Y's are X's," but not that "All Y's are X's." The difficulty here is one of language. "All X's are Y's" has an *atmosphere* of strong positive assertion which makes the strong converse seem all right; and "Some X's are not Y's" has an atmosphere of weak negation which seems to justify the similar converse statement (*19*).

That the difficulty in these cases is largely one of words is seen from the fact that a diagram may make everything clear. Represent the class X by a circle and the class Y by another circle. Then the statement that "All X's are Y's" is diagrammed by placing the X circle inside the Y circle, and from the diagram it is perfectly clear that some, but not all Y's are in the X class. The diagram for (2) consists of two intersecting circles,

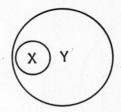

Fig. 144.—Diagram of the statement, "all X is Y."

and that for (3) of two entirely separate circles; and these diagrams reveal the correctness of the converse statements. The diagram for (4) can be two intersecting circles, but it can also be composed of a Y circle inside the X circle, so that no sure converse can be obtained.

Three circles are needed to diagram a syllogism. The argument that bears are warm-blooded, because they are mammals which are all warm-blooded, is readily seen to be sound reasoning. If S is included in M, and M in P, then S must be included in P.

But the syllogism about Chinese being Mongolians because both are slant-eyed is seen to be unsound. The premises tell us that S and P are both included in M, but within the M circle the two smaller circles have perfect freedom. They might coincide, overlap, be entirely separate, or be so placed that either one was entirely included in the other. It is the same way with the other incorrect syllogism (p. 615) where both S and P are excluded from M; the appropriate diagram shows that no logical conclusion can be drawn from such premises.

**Reasoning from probabilities.** The syllogisms we have been considering are mostly of the all-or-none variety, with premises such as, "All bears are mammals," or, "No birds have six legs." We did mention the "Some" premises from which, however, not much can be inferred. Consider these premises:

Some members of the Spanish class flunked the examination.
Ten members of the Gamma fraternity were in the Spanish class.
    Therefore what?

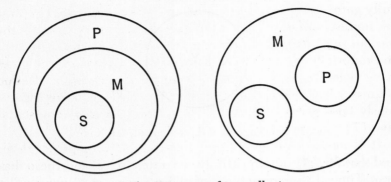

FIG. 145.—Diagrams of two syllogisms:
1. "All S is M; all M is P: therefore all S is P"—logical.
2. "All S is M; all P is M; therefore all S is P"—illogical.

We cannot assert that any of the Gammas flunked, though there is that possibility. If the first premise is made more definite so as to read that 20 percent of the Spanish class flunked, we can infer that probably about 2 of the 10 Gammas flunked —more than that if the Gammas are usually low in scholarship, fewer if they are usually high. Such a conclusion has to contain the qualifying words, "probably" and "about." In everyday life we often have to act on probabilities instead of certainties, and in reasoning about human affairs, too, absolute certainty is not often attainable. We have to allow for varying conditions and for the variability of human reactions. "If prices shoot up excessively, people will refuse to buy"—a good probable prediction, but subject to exceptions, since some people will buy for fear of still higher prices to come, and some people will even boast of the high prices they have paid.

The scientific approach to probabilities is to quantify them so as to replace the indefinite words, "probably" and "possibly," by numerical statements of the odds for or against a given prediction. Many large predictions can be based on results obtained from relatively small samples, as we see from straw ballots and opinion polls. A few thousand persons state their opinions on a certain issue and these data furnish the basis for predicting how the population at large will vote or think on this issue. To have any predictive value the data must be very carefully gathered. The sample must not be too small, and it must be representative, i.e., it must include representatives of the various sections of the country, of the various occupations, etc., in proportion to their size in the whole population. Straw votes have yielded some surprisingly accurate predictions of election returns when the sampling was well done, and some ridiculously false predictions when the sampling was unrepresentative (7).

It is more difficult to think clearly regarding probabilities and variable phenomena than to reason from all-or-none premises. There are several common errors. (1) A conclusion is based on altogether too small a sample. You will hear a person assert that he has "invariably" found such-and-such to be the

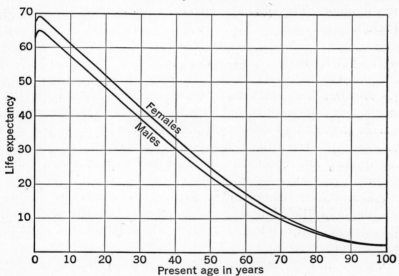

Fig. 146.—Reasoning from probability—here from life expectancy at different ages. At age 20, for example, the average young man may reasonably expect to live approximately 48 years longer, and the average young woman about 52 years. These expectations are reasonable because they correspond with the current mortality rates for the white population of the United States. How long a given young man will live depends of course on many individual factors and cannot be exactly predicted from the averages, but the averages are of great value to those who think in terms of averages and probabilities in providing life insurance, annuities and pensions.

case, but on questioning him you may find that he has observed one or two striking instances and no more. (2) "Negative instances" are often waved aside as mere exceptions to the general rule, instead of being kept in the record until the odds for and against the rule can be counted up. (3) The sample on which a generalization is based may be unrepresentative. You think you know the general opinion on a certain matter because you have discussed it with your friends and found them in substantial agreement. But do your friends fairly represent the general population in all respects? (4) A conclusion that is only probable is often taken for a certainty. The doubts regarding it may be forgotten and it may stand for a long time as the accepted doctrine, until someone takes the trouble to obtain more evidence. This has happened time and again in the history of science.

## SUMMARY

1. *Ideation* is mental activity which does not depend directly upon sensory and motor contact with the present environment.

   a. In *dreams and daydreams,* ideational activity is not deliberately controlled in specific directions, but the sequence and continuity of ideas and images result from their past association together in the person's experience. Dreams are related to the motives and desires of the individual; the content of the dream may be a distorted and symbolic expression of motives which he does not admit even to himself.

   b. *Purposive thinking* is ideational activity which is controlled and directed toward the goals of discovery and invention.

2. The tools of ideational activity are *concepts. Symbols* are objects or expressions or activities which stand for concepts in the absence of the actual items.

   a. *Language symbols* are vocal and written expressions used in the first place for communication between persons and in the second place for ideational activity. Young children often clearly demonstrate the role of language symbols in thinking by talking aloud as they work on a problem. As they grow up they learn to talk subvocally and eventually without any motor expression.

b. *Diagrams, maps, musical scores*, etc., are useful symbols to represent complex situations with multiple relationships among the items.

c. *Concepts* are ideas which refer to objects, events, qualities, etc. Concepts are formed by noticing the similarities and differences among items, and learning a word or other symbol for each concept. The concept thus becomes the meaning of the word.

   (1) *Generalization* is the mental process of forming a concept of a class of items on the basis of experience with a certain number of instances.

   (2) *Differentiation* is the opposing process of making distinctions among the items of a class; of forming two or more concepts out of one.

   (3) *Abstraction* is the related process in which some attribute or characteristic is considered independently of other characteristics or of the object as a whole.

d. *Principles* are relations between concepts, usually expressed in the form of sentence statements or mathematical equations.

3. *Problem solving* behavior occurs in novel or difficult situations in which a solution is not obtainable by the habitual methods of applying concepts and principles derived from past experience in very similar situations.

a. Certain problems contain *obstacles to clear thinking*, as when the situation presents insufficient data, irrelevant data, or inconsistent data.

b. *Guiding ideas* determine what kind of attempts at solution will be made. If all the attempts arising from a certain guiding idea are fruitless, it is wise to discover a different guiding idea.

c. A *hypothesis* is a principle which is invented and applied in a problem situation in the form of a question. It is tested by figuring out its logical consequence in the situation, trying it out, and observing whether the predicted results are obtained.

d. An *incubation* period is an interval of time during which the problem is laid aside after preliminary attempts at solution have failed.

e. Rational thinking has something of the character of trial-and-error behavior, but it differs in being ideational rather than motor, and in being a planned attack on the problem.

**4.** *Logical thinking* proceeds from the data to a correct conclusion by a proper process of *reasoning*.

a. Reasoning often depends on the use of a *middle term,* and will be correct only if the middle term is not ambiguous and if it is related in a single way to both the subject and the predicate.

b. *Logic* is a system of rules for correct reasoning.

c. A *syllogism* is a formal statement of a process of reasoning, consisting of two explicit *premises* and a *conclusion*.

d. A conclusion is *logical* if it follows from the premises; it is not necessarily *true* in fact unless the premises are true.

e. The *verbal form* of stating a syllogism affects the likelihood of correct reasoning. For many persons symbols are harder to handle logically than words, and diagrams may make clear the logic that is confused by verbal expression.

f. *Reasoning from probabilities* is usually necessary in dealing with human reactions. Such reasoning can be made more accurate by quantitative statements of the probabilities and by careful attention to the size and representativeness of the sample on which a statement is based.

# Questions and Exercises

## Chapter One. The Aim and Method of Psychology

1. How is psychology related to other sciences—and is it related more closely to some than to others?

2. Show that language is a human activity about which psychological, physiological and sociological questions can be asked.

3. Formulate a psychological question concerned with education, one concerned with government, and one concerned with automobile driving.

4. Why are ordinary reports of human activities often unsatisfactory as scientific data?

5. Why does the psychologist ever use any other method besides the experimental?

6. A student from school A has a poor opinion of the students from school B because he remembers an incident in which two boys in school B's rooting section at a basketball game were very unsportsmanlike in their actions. How would you criticise the conclusion drawn by the school A student? What errors of method has he made in arriving at this conclusion?

7. A student wished to find out whether he studied more efficiently in the morning or in the evening. So he studied his mathematics every morning and his English every evening, and found that he got much better marks in English. He concluded that he studied more efficiently in the evening. What was wrong with his experiment?

8. When you consult a physician, you probably give him both introspective and objective data regarding your condition. Give examples of each kind, and show what is meant by calling one kind "private" and the other "public."

9. From the Table of Contents select the chapters which deal with differences between people, and those which deal with mental activities in general.

10. From the Index select 10 psychological nouns that have the meaning of verbs.

625

## Chapter Two. Individual Differences in Ability

1. Using singing as an example, bring out clearly the distinction between capacity, achievement, and aptitude.

2. Explain what is meant by the statement, "A raw score tells very little without certain background information."

3. How is a psychological test like a scientific experiment?

4. Explain the steps a psychologist would take in preparing a standardized test for mathematical ability.

5. Plot the distribution and locate the 10-centile, 25-centile, 50-centile, 75-centile and 90-centile points from the following marks obtained by 20 students in an examination: 68, 72, 74, 76, 78, 80, 82, 82, 84, 84, 86, 86, 86, 86, 86, 88, 88, 90, 92, 96.

6. By test results two men are both morons, yet one is legally feebleminded and the other not. How can this be explained?

7. What is the approximate IQ of a 35-year-old man with an MA of 17 years? If his IQ has remained constant since he was 10 years old, what was his MA at that age?

8. How can you explain the fact that a person's IQ may change by 5 or 6 points when he is retested within a week?

9. To be a productive genius, what does one need besides an IQ of perhaps 160?

10. If you were giving a talk on the subject of intelligence, what use would you make of the distribution curve?

## Chapter Three. The Correlation of Abilities

1. What do the cases of idiot savants and arithmetical prodigies show with regard to specialization of abilities?

2. Define the term *correlation*. What is indicated if the correlation between the scores in two tests is +.95? −.75? +.03?

3. If we should find a low positive correlation between athletic and scholastic achievement, what could we infer?

4. What evidence indicates that there must be many very specific abilities, and also some abilities of wider scope?

5. Which of the known "group factors" would be needed by a lawyer, a mathematics teacher, a dress designer?

6. Explain this statement: A test may have high reliability without much validity, but it cannot have high validity unless it has high reliability.

7. Why is it that a battery of tests often proves to be valid for the selection of employees, although any single test in the battery has only low validity by itself?

8. How might the fact that different abilities correlate more highly in children than in adults be reasonably explained?

9. In one test there were 20 items and the scores ranged from 8 to 18. In a second test there were 50 items and the scores ranged from 35 to 45. There were 11 subjects who took both tests, and these were their scores, each parenthesis containing the two scores of the same individual: (18, 45), (8, 37), (15, 44), (10, 36), (13, 39), (11, 38), (16, 42), (9, 35), (14, 41), (10, 40), (12, 43). Plot these data in a scatter diagram.

10. Compute the correlation (rho) between the two tests.

## Chapter Four. Personality

1. Without looking back at the definition given in this chapter, define "personality" as you would use the term in ordinary conversation. Then compare your definition with that given in the book.

2. What difficulties would you encounter if you attempted to classify people on the basis of opposite extremes in personal traits?

3. What traits and attitudes are desirable in one who would be an interviewer?

4. Explain the common errors that a supervisor may commit in rating the personality of his subordinates.

5. Rate a large number of your acquaintances in some one trait. Use a separate line (graphic rating scale) for each individual, and finally assemble all the individual ratings on a single line so as to show their distribution. What kind of a distribution do you get, and does it suggest any criticism of your ratings?

6. What considerations would influence you in deciding whether a number of raters who are to judge the same individual should fill out their rating blanks separately and then average the ratings, or should secure a consensus after discussing the individual?

7. Why is it that personality questionnaires are not widely used in selecting people for jobs in which personality is important?

8. Design a situation test for cooperativeness.

9. What does the experimental evidence reveal in respect to the generality of honesty as a trait of school children? How would the

conclusions of this study apply to the old saying that there is "honor among thieves"?

10. Does a personality profile give a satisfactory picture of a person's total personality? Reasons?

## Chapter Five. Physiological and Social Factors in Personality

1. What is meant by a "factor in personality," and what is the distinction between physiological and social factors?

2. Make a list of personality traits you might expect a very beautiful girl to have, and the same for a homely girl. What traits might be the same in both?

3. Considering the effects of undernourishment on the individual, would you expect the most underprivileged section of the population to be the most aggressively radical in their demands for reform? Explain.

4. Construct a table of the endocrine glands, indicating the hormone provided by each, its physiological effects, and the possible effects on personality of overactivity and of underactivity of the gland.

5. Explain what is meant by "endocrine balance."

6. Why are personality difficulties resulting from encephalitis very difficult to correct?

7. How does the group code affect the personalities of the members of the group?

8. Analyze some one you know quite well in respect to the roles he plays in different social situations.

9. A child of very high IQ was conceited and arrogant up to the age of adolescence when he gradually shifted over to quite a modest type of behavior. How can this be explained?

10. Analyze Mark Twain's career in terms of the social code and the individual's role in the social group.

## Chapter Six. Heredity and Environment as Causes of Individual Differences

1. Discuss this statement: Though a child inherits all his genes from his parents, he does not inherit his own particular combination of genes.

2. What conclusions can be drawn from hybridizing experiments

as to the importance of heredity in producing individual differences?

3. What is meant by the "effective environment," and how does it depend, partly, on the individual's own tendencies, so that children who grow up in the same home do not necessarily have the same effective environments?

4. Since genetic studies show that acquired characteristics are not passed on by way of heredity, what factors would explain the fact that a boy whose father was a great tennis player becomes an excellent tennis player himself?

5. In a certain college a great deal of attention is paid to instruction and practice in public speaking. How will the graduates of this college compare (a) with each other and (b) with other college graduates in their skill in public speaking? What general principles are illustrated in this case?

6. Explain this situation: Extremely intelligent individuals are usually more intelligent than their parents, and also more intelligent than their children.

7. What can a nation do to improve the heredity of its population?

8. What evidence has been contributed by psychologists on the question of racial differences in intelligence?

9. Do you think that sex differences in mechanical ability are due mostly to heredity or to environment? Your reasons?

10. Which of the following facts are evidence for heredity, and which for environment, as a factor in producing individual differences?

a. It has not been found possible to make any randomly selected child into a genius.

b. Identical twins who were separated and reared in very different environments have been found to differ considerably in IQ.

c. Even separated identical twins differ on the average much less than children from different homes.

d. Children reared in a relatively common environment, such as an orphanage, differ in IQ almost as much as the children of an average community.

e. Fraternal twins are slightly more alike than other siblings in respect to intelligence.

f. Children reared in superior foster homes seem to surpass their own parents by 5 or 10 points in IQ.

g. The own children of professional men exceed the adopted children of professional men by 10 points of IQ on the average.

## Chapter Seven. Interaction with the Environment

1. How does the approach of general psychology differ from that of differential psychology in the study of human behavior?

2. Show that the emphasis on environment in the present chapter is not inconsistent with the balanced view of heredity and environment advocated in the preceding chapter.

3. How are your daily activities related to environmental conditions? In what different ways do you deal with the environment?

4. In the adjustment process represented by the W-O-W formula, what part is played by the receptors? By the effectors?

5. What is meant by "inhibition"? With reference to the S-O-R formula show that inhibition is sometimes due to an S-factor, but sometimes to an O-factor.

6. Explain in terms of selectivity and set why the associative reaction is slower than the simple reaction.

7. Illustrate the principle of combination by the muscular action in throwing a ball.

8. Show that the runner's set for a quick getaway is a situation set as well as a goal set.

9. What is the situation set when you are reading an interesting story, and how does it make for rapid and enjoyable reading?

10. An experimenter found that classical music was less distracting to most students than popular music. How might this be explained?

## Chapter Eight. The Nervous System

1. How does the structure of the nervous system make it possible for the organism to act as a whole?

2. What neural arrangements make it possible for two or more stimuli to combine in arousing a response, and what neural arrangements make it possible for two or more muscles to act together in a coordinated movement?

3. Describe the "reflex arc." How does reflex action differ from most motor behavior?

4. What parts of the cerebrum are known to perform different functions?

5. What is the all-or-none law? Does it imply that a muscle contracts as a whole or not at all?

6. What is the difference, structurally and functionally, between the white and the gray matter?

7. What lines of evidence indicate that the visual area lies in the occipital lobe?

8. What sensory and motor centers of the cortex are active in speaking?

9. Summarize the evidence supporting the hypothesis that the entire cortex functions as a whole in learning a complex act.

10. Considering the speed of transmission along a nerve and the distances to be covered, estimate how much of the simple reaction time to sound is required for the necessary transmission of nerve impulses to and from the brain.

## Chapter Nine. How the Individual Develops

1. What is the relationship between maturation and (a) instinct, (b) learning?

2. If maturation, like other activities of the organism, is a process of responding to stimulation, where does the stimulation come from?

3. What is the reason for thinking that the cerebral cortex probably has little to do with the behavior of the newborn child?

4. Discuss the question whether the unborn child can be aware of his environment.

5. Do you think that the average child could be taught to walk at nine months of age (CA) if enough practice were given him at that age and earlier? Defend your view.

6. Show how reinforcement plays its part in the child's mastery of the reaching trick.

7. What changes in adolescence are probably due to maturation?

8. What sampling difficulty is encountered in determining the curve of mental advance and decline during adult years, and how has this difficulty been overcome by the investigators?

9. In what respects are men and women of 40 mentally superior to those of 18–20?

10. On the whole it is probably true that people become more conservative as they advance from early adult life to middle age. Why might this be so?

## Chapter Ten. Motives

1. Distinguish accurately between these terms: *motive, incentive, stimulus*.

2. Give an example of your own for each one of the four kinds of modification that an unlearned motive undergoes through the individual's experience.

3. Analyze the development of interest in money.

4. Why does a needless fear or antipathy often persist in spite of receiving no reinforcement from the environment?

5. Careful observation will show that small emergencies of the various sorts distinguished in the text occur very frequently in ordinary life. Give examples.

6. How is the human individual equipped by nature for advancing from primitive to more socialized ways of eating?

7. What is the unlearned basis for:
   a. Desire to master difficulties?
   b. Attraction to new objects?
   c. Playful running and jumping?
   d. Competition?

8. How can the strength of animal drives be measured?

9. How is the principle of goal gradient often demonstrated by students in their studies?

10. How can the Army's experience in maintaining the morale of soldiers be applied in a college fraternity or social group?

## Chapter Eleven. Feeling and Emotion

1. What do people mean when they say, "I feel that you are right," and why don't they say, "I think you are right?"

2. Give two examples of pleasures that do, and two of pleasures that do not, depend on an active desire.

3. List 10 kinds of behavior in other persons that give you pleasure? How do these "pleasures" contrast with the common "annoyances"?

4. Explain, with examples, the differences between these three: sympathy, empathy, imitation.

5. Trace the cause-and-effect relation between worry and indigestion.

6. List several reasons why the normal person gains more and more control over his emotions from birth to maturity.

7. What pitfalls have to be avoided in the practical use of a lie detector?

8. What is lacking in an "as if" emotion that is present in a true emotion?

9. Ask several persons to judge the facial expression shown in each picture in Figure 82, using the categories given in Figure 81. How do your results compare with those cited in the text?

10. Preferred proportions of a rectangle. Take a sheet of blotting paper, or some similarly shaped strip of colored paper, and lay it vertically on a white sheet of paper, covering its upper part with a second white sheet. Adjust the height of the visible colored rectangle till its proportions are most agreeable; measure them and compute the ratio of height to width. Repeat with other individuals as subjects. How near do the preferred shapes come to the golden section, and how much do they scatter?

## Chapter Twelve. Choice, Conflict, Frustration

1. Analyze according to Figure 85 some situation in which you have had to make a difficult choice.

2. Suggest a rational procedure for reducing the amount of vacillation in a situation demanding a difficult choice.

3. What is meant by "compromise responses"?

4. Why does a decision usually stick, even when reached after much doubt and vacillation?

5. Compare two ways of dodging frustration, a strong way and a weak way.

6. How can "will power" be understood on the basis of motivation?

7. How is a frustrating situation apt to arouse excessive emotion?

8. Illustrate by an example not given in the text each of the following:

a. Sublimation      e. Projection
b. Rationalization      f. Compensation
c. Regression      g. Fantasy
d. Repression

9. Of what value is hypnosis in psychotherapy? Why do many psychoanalysts consider it of little value?

10. How does a non-directive counselor help a maladjusted person solve his problems.

## Chapter Thirteen. Observing

1. What is learned about attention from experiments on doing two things at once. (See Chapter Seven also.)

2. Compare the requirements of camouflage with the advertiser's devices for catching attention.

3. Show that certain habits of inattention may interfere with cordial relations between husband and wife.

4. Bring out the difference between stimuli and objects in the experience of exploring a room in the dark.

5. Give two examples of signs and their meanings in social perception (as in perceiving anyone's intentions and emotions).

6. What is meant by "reduced cues" and by "ambiguous signs"? Give an original example of each.

7. Making the radio play softly does not wash out the difference between the loud and soft passages in the music. Show how this fact agrees with Weber's law.

8. Show some analogy between Weber's law and this fact: The loss of a dollar means more to a poor man than to a rich man.

9. Give one example from everyday life of an illusion due to physical causes in the stimulus, and two examples of illusions due to causes within the organism.

10. In what ways are the observations of scientists likely to be superior to those of ordinary life?

## Chapter Fourteen. The Sense of Sight

1. List all the motor responses of the eyes and indicate the utility of each of them.

2. When it seems that our eyes are sweeping smoothly across the page in reading, what is actually happening as far as eye movements are concerned? (See also Chapter Seven.)

3. What are the differences between the rods and the cones?

4. Why is the concept of color saturation so hard to make clear?

5. If you sent a red-green blind person after a brown tie, what mistakes might he make and what mistakes would he surely not make?

6. In many games it is important for a player to be able to keep track of his teammates out of the corner of his eye. Considering this fact and the facts of retinal zones, what colors of uniforms would

you recommend for an athletic team, and what colors would you avoid?

7. What advantage in depth perception does a person with two good eyes have over a person blind in one eye? What cues are available to the one-eyed person in perceiving the distance of objects?

8. What principles explain the motion that we see in a motion picture?

9. Elaborate this statement: The picture size of an object is an ambiguous sign analogous to an ambiguous word, but both get definite meaning from their contexts.

10. Which eye do you use in sighting? With both eyes open sight along your pencil toward a more distant object. Then, by closing one eye, find out whether you were sighting with it or with the other one. Repeat several times to make sure.

## Chapter Fifteen. The Other Senses

1. Construct a table of all the senses, showing the stimulus for each, the dimensions of the stimulus and the corresponding sensation dimensions.

2. Show that the skin serves to a limited extent as a distance receptor.

3. In what ways would the loss of the kinesthetic sense be a handicap to a person?

4. What sensations other than taste actually contribute to what we commonly call the "taste" of foods? Does vision ever have any influence?

5. Arrange the six classes of odors in the order of their agreeableness.

6. How can you explain the fact that the water in a swimming pool feels very cold when you first go in, though after a while it no longer seems cold?

7. What characteristics of the stimuli enable you to recognize the sounds of different musical instruments? Of different vowels?

8. Describe the sequence of events from the source of a sound to the conscious experience of hearing the sound.

9. Compare the spatial information derived from binocular vision with that derived from binaural hearing.

10. What cues are used in locating the source of a sound? How could a person deaf in one ear do this?

## Chapter Sixteen. Learning

1. Compare negative adaptation and sensory adaptation.

2. Summarize the evidence for place learning.

3. Show that the manipulation of an unfamiliar object is a kind of exploration.

4. How are place learning and tool learning illustrated in the process of learning to operate an automobile or to play a violin?

5. Give an example of a human learning problem where insight is possible.

6. What is meant by a "plateau" in the learner's progress? How might it be eliminated?

7. Show that the elements of skill found in typewriting are present also in fluent speaking.

8. How is the extinction of a conditioned response accomplished? Why does it not work sometimes in getting rid of a needless fear?

9. Show that reinforcement acts as a selective factor in conditioning and other forms of learning.

10. Show that the following examples of learning can be represented by the CR formula or by the formula, $S_1$–$R_1$–$S_2$–$R_2$.

    a. Response to the dinner bell.

    b. Response to the closing bell in a lecture room.

    c. The meaning of a foreign word.

    d. A reduced cue.

## Chapter Seventeen. Memory

1. Explain in detail how the rules for efficient learning could be applied to the task of learning a lesson in psychology.

2. Why are nonsense syllables and nonsense figures often used as material to be learned in memory experiments?

3. Explain the fact that we often master a subject more thoroughly if, in addition to merely reading up on the subject, we discuss it with other people.

4. What is meant by a memory trace? Why is it placed under the head of "structure"? What evidence do we have for the existence of such traces?

5. Discuss the different methods of demonstrating retention. Which are the best for demonstrating the existence of very weak traces?

6. Assemble the various instances of interference in learning and remembering.

7. How does the loss of memory due to an electric shock passed through the head support the theory that the establishment of a memory trace continues for a time after active learning ceases?

8. Study of one's own memory images. Try to call up the images mentioned below, and rate each image on the following scale:

3. . . . *image clear, bright, realistic*
2. . . . *image only moderately clear and realistic*
1. . . . *image almost devoid of realistic sensory quality*
0. . . . *no sensory image even though the object is remembered*

a. Call up the visual appearance of: a sunflower, a large dog, automobile headlights, your own signature.

b. Call up the sound of: a church bell, a dog barking, a siren whistle, paper tearing.

c. Call up the feel of: velvet, a lump of ice, lifting a heavy weight, turning over in bed.

d. Call up the odor of: coffee, apple, onion, camphor.

Having made these ratings, compare the average rating for each of the four classes.

9. A simple experiment: Make up a short story, write it down, then tell it to a friend. Have him tell it from memory to a third person, this person repeat it to a fourth person, and so on. Have the sixth person in this sequence write down the story as he remembers it, and compare his story with the original. What kind of changes have occurred? What bearing have such experiments on the psychology of rumor?

10. From this and previous chapters (by aid of the Index) make a list of all the different varieties and uses of reinforcement.

## Chapter Eighteen. Thinking

1. Show how language is often an aid but sometimes an obstacle to clear thinking.

2. What different motives may be gratified by daydreams?

3. Does muscular activity in silent thought always occur only in the speech organs? Think of some active game, of a spiral staircase, of the location of two books in your bookcase, etc.

4. What is the difference between a guiding idea and a hypothesis?

5. Give an example of an abstract concept usefully applied to a concrete problem. (See the discussion of the nature of intelligence in Chapter Two.)

6. Illustrate the ways in which past experience is useful in solving a problem in mathematics—or in millinery.

7. What is meant by the "atmosphere effect" in reasoning? How is this principle often utilized in propaganda?

8. Can any logical conclusion be drawn from these two premises?

Some X is Y;

No X is Z.

Try to think this out verbally and then by use of diagrams. How did you reach an answer, and how sure of it are you?

9. Several instances of incubation have turned up in the course of the book (see the Index). Taking them all into account, what do you regard as the best theory of incubation?

10. Again by aid of the Index, assemble the various cases in which "set" has been mentioned, and indicate how it is useful (but sometimes harmful) in problem solving.

# References

## Chapter One. The Aim and Method of Psychology

1. Cattell,J.McK. The conception and method of psychology. *Pop.Sci. Mon.*, 1904, *46*, 176–186.
2. Crafts,L.W., Schneirla,T.C., Robinson,E.E., Gilbert,R.M. *Recent experiments in psychology.* N.Y., McGraw-Hill, 1938.
3. Davis,A.M., Dollard,J. *Children of bondage.* Washington, American Youth Commission, 1940.
4. Garrett,H.E. *Great experiments in psychology.* N.Y., Appleton-Century, 1941.
5. Haldane,J.S., Priestley,J.G. *Respiration.* 2d ed. New Haven, Yale University Press, 1935.
6. Hulin,W.S. *A short history of psychology.* N.Y., Holt, 1934.
7. Keller,F.S. *The definition of psychology.* N.Y., Appleton-Century, 1937.
8. McFarland,R.A. Psychophysical studies of high altitude in the Andes. *J.comp.Psychol.*, 1937, *23*, 191–225.
9. Munn,N.L. *Psychological development.* Boston, Houghton Mifflin, 1938.
10. Pratt,C.C. *The logic of modern psychology.* N.Y., Macmillan, 1939.
11. War work of psychologists. See many reports in *Psychol.Bull.*, 1945, and in *Amer.Psychologist*, 1946, 1947.

## Chapter Two. Individual Differences in Ability

1. Abel,T.M., Kinder,E.F. *The subnormal adolescent girl.* N.Y., Columbia University Press, 1942.
2. Anastasi,A. *Differential psychology.* N.Y., Macmillan, 1937.
3. Binet,A., Simon,T. Sur la nécessité d'établir un diagnostic scientifique des états inférieurs de l'intelligence. *Année psychol.*, 1905, *11*, 163–190; *The Development of intelligence in children.* Baltimore, Williams & Wilkins, 1916.
4. Bingham,W.V. Inequalities in adult capacity—from military data. *Science*, 1946, *104*, 147–152.
5. Freeman,F.N., Flory,C.D. Growth in intellectual ability as measured by repeated tests. *Soc.Res.Child Develpm.Monogr.*, 1937, *2*, No. 9.
6. Garrett,H.E. *Statistics in psychology and education.* 3d ed. N.Y., Longmans, Green, 1947.
7. Goodenough,F.L. *Measurement of intelligence by drawings.* Yonkers, World Book Co., 1926.

8. Greene,E.B. *Measurements of human behavior.* N.Y., Odyssey Press, 1941.

9. Guilford,J.P. *Fundamental statistics in psychology and education.* N.Y., McGraw-Hill, 1942.

10. Hollingworth,L.S. *Children above 180 IQ, Stanford-Binet.* Yonkers, World Book Co., 1942.

11. Lindquist,E.F. *A first course in statistics.* Rev. ed. Boston, Houghton Mifflin, 1942.

12. Selz,O. Versuche zur Hebung des Intelligenzniveaus. *Z.Psychol.,* 1935, *134,* 236–301.

13. Smith,G.M. *A simplified guide to statistics.* N.Y., Rinehart, 1946.

14. Terman,L.M., and others. *Genetic studies of genius.* Stanford University Press. 3 vols., 1925–1930.

15. Terman,L.M., Merrill,M.A. *Measuring intelligence.* Boston, Houghton Mifflin, 1937.

16. Thorndike,E.L., and others. *Adult learning.* N.Y., Macmillan, 1927.

17. Thurstone,L.L. *Primary mental abilities.* University of Chicago Press, 1938. (Supplement.)

18. Tredgold,A.F. *Mental deficiency.* 6th ed. Baltimore, Wood, 1937.

19. Wechsler,D. *The measurement of adult intelligence.* 3d ed. Baltimore, Williams & Wilkins, 1944.

20. Yerkes,R.M. *Psychological examining in the United States Army.* Washington, National Academy of Sciences, Memoirs, Vol. 15, 1921.

## Chapter Three. The Correlation of Abilities

1. Bingham,W.V. *Aptitudes and aptitude testing.* N.Y., Harper, 1937.

2. Brown,W., Stephenson,W. A test of the theory of two factors. *Brit.J. Psychol.,* 1933, *23,* 352–370.

3. Crawford,A.B., Burnham,P.S. *Forecasting college achievement; a survey of aptitude tests for higher education.* New Haven, Yale University Press, 1946.

4. Garrett,H.E. *Statistics in psychology and education.* 3d ed. N.Y., Longmans, Green, 1947.

5. Garrett,H.E. A developmental theory of intelligence. *Amer.Psychologist,* 1946, *1,* 372–378.

6. Guilford,J.P. *Psychometric methods.* N.Y., McGraw-Hill, 1936.

7. Lindquist,E.F. *A first course in statistics.* Rev. ed. Boston, Houghton Mifflin, 1942.

8. McCullough,C.M., Strang,R.M., Traxler,A.E. *Problems in the improvement of reading.* N.Y., McGraw-Hill, 1946.

9. Schiller,B. Verbal, numerical and spatial abilities of young children. *Arch.Psychol.,* 1934, No. 161.

10. Shartle,C.L. *Occupational information, its development and application.* N.Y., Prentice-Hall, 1946.

11. Smith,G.M. *A simplified guide to statistics.* N.Y., Rinehart, 1946.

12. Sommerville,R.C. Physical, motor and sensory traits. *Arch.Psychol.*, 1924, No. 75.
13. Spearman,C.E. *The abilities of man.* N.Y., Macmillan, 1927.
14. Staff. Psychological activities in the training command, Army Air Forces. *Psychol.Bull.*, 1945, *42*, 37–54.
15. Staff. Research program on psychomotor tests in the Army Air Forces. *Psychol.Bull.*, 1944, *41*, 307–321.
16. Super,D.E. *The dynamics of vocational adjustment.* N.Y., Harper, 1942.
17. Thomson,G.H. *The factorial analysis of human ability.* London University Press, 1939.
18. Thorndike,E.L., and others. *The measurement of intelligence.* N.Y., Teachers College, Columbia University, 1926.
19. Thurstone,L.L. *Primary mental abilities.* University of Chicago Press, 1938.
20. Tiffin,J. *Industrial psychology.* N.Y., Prentice-Hall, 1942.
21. Traxler,A.E. *Techniques of guidance.* N.Y., Harper, 1945.
22. Tredgold,A.F. *Mental deficiency.* 6th ed. Baltimore, Wood, 1937.

## Chapter Four. Personality

1. Allport,G.W. *Personality.* N.Y., Holt, 1937.
2. Anon. A good man is hard to find. *Fortune*, 1946, *33*, 92–95, 217–223.
3. Asch,S.E. Forming impressions of personality. *J.abnorm.soc.Psychol.*, 1946, *41*, 258–290.
4. Beck,S.J. *Rorschach's test*: Vol. I, *Basic processes;* Vol. II, *A variety of personality pictures.* N.Y., Grune & Stratton, 1944, 1945.
5. Bingham,W.V., Moore,B.V. *How to interview.* Rev. ed. N.Y., Harper, 1934.
6. Cattell,R.B. *Description and measurement of personality.* Yonkers, World Book Co., 1946.
7. Cantril,H., Allport,G.W. *The psychology of radio.* N.Y., Harper, 1935.
8. Dashiell,J.F. Experimental studies of the influence of social situations on the behavior of individual human adults. *Handbk.soc. Psychol.*, edited by C.Murchison. 1935, 1097–1158.
9. Estes,S.G. Judging personality from expressive behavior. *J.abnorm. soc.Psychol.*, 1938, *33*, 217–236.
10. Franz,S.I. *Persons one and three.* N.Y., McGraw-Hill, 1933.
11. Guilford,J.P. *Fundamental statistics in psychology and education.* N.Y., McGraw-Hill, 1942. (Esp. pp. 118–122.)
12. Guilford,J.P., Guilford,R.S. Personality factors $S$, $E$, and $M$ and their measurement. *J. Psychol.*, 1936, *2*, 109–127; Guilford,J.P., Martin,H. Age differences and sex differences in some introvertive and emotional traits. *J.gen.Psychol.*, 1944, *31*, 219–221.
13. Harriman,P.L. A follow-up study of the Woodworth-House mental hygiene inventory. *Amer.J.Orthopsychiat.*, 1938, *8*, 255–259.
14. Hartshorne,H., May,M.A. *Studies in deceit.* 1928; *Studies in service*

*and self-control.* 1929; *Studies in the organization of character.* 1930. N.Y., Macmillan.

15. Heidbreder,E. Measuring introversion and extroversion. *J.abnorm. soc.Psychol.*, 1926, *21,* 120–134.

16. Hollingworth,H.L. *Vocational psychology and character analysis.* N.Y., Appleton, 1929.

17. Jung,C.G. *Psychological types.* N.Y., Harcourt Brace, 1923.

18. Klopfer,B., Kelley,D.McG. *The Rorschach technique.* Yonkers, World Book Co., 1946 Supplement.

19. Kuder,G.F. *Manual for the Kuder Preference Record.* Chicago, Science Research Associates, 1946.

20. Landis,C., Katz,S.E. The validity of certain questions which purport to measure neurotic tendencies. *J.appl.Psychol.*, 1934, *18,* 343–356.

21. Lecky,P. *Self-consistency, a theory of personality.* N.Y., Island Press, 1945.

22. McDougall,W. *Outlines of abnormal psychology.* N.Y., Scribners, 1926. (Esp. pp. 482–506.)

23. Murphy,G., Murphy,L.B., Newcomb,T.M. *Experimental social psychology.* N.Y., Harper, 1937. (Esp. pp. 769–888.)

24. Murray,H.A., and others. *Explorations in personality.* N.Y., Oxford University Press, 1938.

25. Newcomb,T.M. *The consistency of certain extrovert-introvert behavior patterns in 51 problem boys.* N.Y., Teachers College, Columbia University, 1929.

26. Paterson,D.G. *Physique and intellect.* N.Y., Century, 1930.

27. Preston,M.G. Note on the reliability and the validity of the group judgment. *J.exp.Psychol.*, 1938, *22,* 462–471.

28. Prince,M. *Clinical and experimental studies in personality.* Cambridge, Mass., Sci-Art, 1929.

29. Prince,W.F. *The Doris case of multiple personality.* York, Pa., York Printing Co., 3 vols., 1915–1917.

30. Ryans,D.G. An experimental attempt to analyze persistent behavior. *J.gen.Psychol.*, 1938, *19,* 333–371.

31. Schmidt,H.O. Test profiles as a diagnostic aid: the Minnesota Multiphasic Inventory. *J.appl.Psychol.*, 1945, *29,* 115–131.

32. Sears,R.R. Experimental studies of projection. 1. Attribution of traits. *J.soc.Psychol.*, 1936, 7, 151–163.

33. Stagner,R. *Psychology of personality.* N.Y., McGraw-Hill, 1937.

34. Strong,E.K. *Vocational interests of men and women.* Stanford University Press, 1943.

35. Terman,L.M., and others. *Psychological factors in marital happiness.* N.Y., McGraw-Hill, 1938.

36. Thorndike,R.L. The effect of discussion upon the correctness of group decisions, when the factor of majority influence is allowed for. *J.soc.Psychol.*, 1938, 9, 343–362.

37. Thurstone,L.L., Thurstone,T.G. A neurotic inventory. *J.soc.Psychol.*, 1930, *1,* 3–30.

# Chapter Five. Physiological and Social Factors in Personality

1. Adler,A. *Problems of neurosis.* N.Y., Cosmopolitan Book Corp., 1930. (Esp. pp. 151–178.)
2. Beach,F.S. Effects of cortical lesions upon the maternal behavior pattern in the rat. *J.comp.Psychol.*, 1937, *24*, 393–440.
3. Bender,L. The Goodenough test (drawing a man) in chronic encephalitis in children. *J.nerv.ment.Dis.*, 1940, *91*, 277–286.
4. Brown,A.W., Jenkins,R.L., Cisler,L.E. Influence of lethargic encephalitis on intelligence of children. *Amer.J.Dis.Child.*, 1938, *55*, 304–321.
5. Burt,C.L. *The young delinquent.* 4th ed. London University Press, 1945.
6. Cannon,W.B. *Bodily changes in pain, hunger, fear and rage.* 2d ed. N.Y., Appleton, 1929.
7. Carpenter,J., Eisenberg,P. Some relations between family background and personality. *J.Psychol.*, 1938, *6*, 115–136.
8. Emerson,H., editor. *Alcohol and man: the effects of alcohol on man in health and disease.* N.Y., Macmillan, 1932.
9. Freud,S. *A general introduction to psycho-analysis,* N.Y., Liveright, 1935.
10. Furfey,P.H. Pubescence and play behavior. *Amer.J.Psychol.*, 1929, *41*, 109–111.
11. Guetzkow,H.S., Bowman,P.H. *Men and hunger.* Elgin, Ill., Brethren Publishing House, 1946.
12. Healy,W., and others. *Reconstructing behavior in youth.* N.Y., Knopf, 1929.
13. Horney,K. *New ways in psychoanalysis,* N.Y., Norton, 1939. (Esp. pp. 88–100.)
14. Hoskins,R.G. *Endocrinology.* N.Y., Norton, 1941.
15. Ingle,D.J. Endocrine function and personality. *Psychol.Rev.*, 1935, *42*, 466–479.
16. Jack,L.M. An experimental study of ascendant behavior in preschool children. *Univ.Iowa Stud.Child Welfare*, 1934, *9*, No. 3, Pt. 1, 1–65.
17. Jones,H.E. Order of birth. *Handbk.Child Psychol.*, edited by C. Murchison. 2d ed., 1933, 551–589.
18. Keister,M.E. The behavior of young children in failure. *Univ.Iowa Stud.Child Welfare*, 1938, *14*, 29–82.
19. Lashley,K.S. Experimental analysis of instinctive behavior. *Psychol. Rev.*, 1938, *45*, 445–471.
20. Leacock,S.B. *Mark Twain.* N.Y., Appleton, 1933.
21. Lehman,H.C., Witty,P.A. A study of vocational attitudes in relation to pubescence. *Amer.J.Psychol.*, 1931, *43*, 93–101.
22. Levy,D.M. *Maternal overprotection.* N.Y., Columbia University Press, 1943.
23. Lurie,L.A. Endocrinology and the understanding and treatment of the exceptional child. *J.Amer.Med.Ass.*, 1938, *110*, 1531–1536.

24. Mead,M. *Coming of age in Samoa*. N.Y., Morrow, 1928.
25. Moore,J.E. A comparative study of the intelligence of delinquent and dependent boys. *J.educ.Psychol.*, 1937, *28*, 355–366.
26. Page,M.L. The modification of ascendant behavior in preschool children. *Univ.Iowa Stud.Child Welfare*, 1936, *12*, No. 3, 1–69.
27. Paine,A.B. *A short life of Mark Twain*. Abridged ed. N.Y., Doubleday, Doran, 1928.
28. Piaget,J. *The moral judgment of the child*. London, K.Paul, 1932.
29. Regensburg,J. Studies of educational success and failure in supernormal children. *Arch.Psychol.*, 1931, No. 129.
30. Shaw,C.R. *Delinquency areas*. University of Chicago Press, 1929.
31. Sherman,M., Henry,T.R. *Hollow folk*. N.Y., Crowell, 1933.
32. Shock,N.W. Some psychophysiological relations. *Psychol.Bull.*, 1939, *36*, 447–476.
33. Slawson,J. *The delinquent boy*. Boston, Badger, 1926.
34. Thrasher,F.M. *The gang*. 2d ed. University of Chicago Press, 1936. (Esp. pp. 328–363.)
35. Tryon,C.M. Evaluations of adolescent personality by adolescents. *Soc.Res. Child Develpm.Monogr.*, 1939, *4*, No. 23.
36. Willson,G.M. A case of post-encephalitic conduct disorder. *Training Sch.Bull.*, 1925, *22*, 25–27.
37. Witty,P.A., Shacter,H.S. Hypothyroidism as a factor in maladjustment. *J.Psychol.*, 1936, *2*, 377–392.

## Chapter Six. Heredity and Environment as Causes of Individual Differences

1. Bennett,G.K., Cruikshank,R.M. Sex differences in the understanding of mechanical problems. *J.appl.Psychol.*, 1942, *26*, 121–127.
2. Bingham,W.V. Inequalities in adult capacity—from military data. *Science*, 1946, *104*, 147–152.
3. Burgess,E.W., Wallin,P. Homogamy in personality characteristics. *J.abnorm.soc.Psychol.*, 1944, *39*, 475–481.
4. Burks,B.S. The relative influence of nature and nurture upon mental development. *27th Yearb.Nat.Soc.Stud.Educ.*, 1928, Part I, 219–316.
5. Burks,B.S. On the relative contributions of nature and nurture to average group differences in intelligence. *Proc.Nat.Acad.Sci.*, 1938, *24*, 276–282.
6. Burks,B.S. A study of identical twins reared apart under differing types of family relationships. *Studies in personality contributed in honor of Lewis M. Terman*. N.Y., McGraw-Hill, 1942, pp. 35–69.
7. Byrnes,R., Henmon,V.A.C. Parental occupation and mental ability. *J.educ.Psychol.*, 1936, *27*, 284–291.
8. Chein,I. The problems of heredity and environment. *J.Psychol.*, 1936, *2*, 229–244.

9. Cook,R., Burks,B.S. *How heredity builds our lives.* Washington, American Genetic Association, 1946.

10. Dennis,W. The performance of Hopi children on the Goodenough draw-a-man test. *J.comp.Psychol.*, 1942, *34*, 341–348.

11. Evans,H.M., Swezy,O. *The chromosomes in man, sex and somatic.* University of California Press, 1929.

12. Freeman,F.N., Holzinger,K.J., and others. The influence of environment on the intelligence, school achievement, and conduct of foster children. *27th Yearb.Nat.Soc.Stud.Educ.*, 1928, Part I, 103–217.

13. Glass,B. *Genes and the man.* N.Y., Teachers College, Columbia Univ., 1943.

14. Harrell,T.W., Harrell,M.S. Army general classification test scores for civilian occupations. *Educ.psychol.Meas.*, 1945, 5, 229–239.

15. Havighurst,R.J., Hilkevitch,R.R. The intelligence of Indian children as measured by a performance scale. *J.abnorm.soc.Psychol.*, 1944, *39*, 419–433.

16. Jones,H.E., Conrad,H.S., Blanchard,M.B. Environmental handicap in mental test performance. *Univ.Calif.Publ.Psychol.*, 1932, *5*, 63–99.

17. Klineberg,O., editor. *Characteristics of the American Negro.* N.Y., Harper, 1944. (Esp. pp. 23–138.)

18. Leahy,A.M. Nature-nurture and intelligence. *Genet.Psychol.Monogr.*, 1935, *17*, 234–308.

19. Macmeeken,A.M. *The intelligence of a representative group of Scottish children.* London University Press, 1939.

20. McNemar,Q. *The revision of the Stanford-Binet scale.* Boston, Houghton Mifflin, 1942 (Esp. pp. 42–54.)

21. Newman,H.H. *Multiple human births.* N.Y., Doubleday, Doran, 1940.

22. Newman,H.H., Freeman,F.N., Holzinger,K.J. *Twins: a study of heredity and environment.* University of Chicago Press, 1937.

23. Outhit,M.C. A study of the resemblance of parents and children in general intelligence. *Arch.Psychol.*, 1933, No. 149.

24. Roe,A., Burks,B.S., Mittelmann,B. Adult adjustment of foster children of alcoholic and psychotic parentage. *Mem.Alcohol Stud.Yale Univ.*, 1945, No. 3.

25. Rohrer,J.H. The test intelligence of Osage Indians. *J.soc.Psychol.*, 1942, *16*, 99–105.

26. Scheinfeld,A. *You and heredity.* N.Y., Stokes, 1939.

27. Schneidler,G.G., Paterson,D.G. Sex differences in clerical aptitude. *J.educ.Psychol.*, 1942, *33*, 303–309.

28. Shaw,C.R., and others. *Delinquency areas.* University of Chicago Press, 1929.

29. Skodak,M. Children in foster homes. *Univ.Iowa Stud.Child Welfare*, 1939, *16*, No. 1.

30. Skodak,M., Skeels,H.M. A follow-up study of children in adoptive homes. *J.genet.Psychol.*, 1945, *66*, 21–58.

31. Smith,S. Language and non-verbal test performance of racial groups in Honolulu before and after a fourteen-year interval. *J.gen. Psychol.*, 1942, *26*, 51–93.
32. Stockard,C.R. *The physical basis of personality*. N.Y., Norton, 1931.
33. Sturtevant,H., Beadle,G.W. *An introduction to genetics*. Philadelphia, Saunders, 1939.
34. Terman,L.M., and others. *Genetic studies of genius*. 3 vols. Stanford University Press, 1925–1930.
35. Terman,L.M., Merrill,M.A. *Measuring intelligence*. Boston, Houghton Mifflin, 1937.
36. Visher,S.S. Where our notables come from. *Scient.Mon.*, 1937, *45*, 172–177.
37. Wheeler,L.R. A comparative study of the intelligence of East Tennessee mountain children. *J.educ.Psychol.*, 1942, *33*, 321–334.
38. Wilson,P.T. A study of twins with special reference to heredity as a factor in determining differences in environment. *Hum.Biol.*, 1934, *6*, 324–354.
39. Wingfield,A.H. *Twins and orphans*. London, Dent, 1928.
40. Witty,P.A., Jenkins,M.D. The educational achievement of a group of gifted Negro children. *J.educ.Psychol.*, 1934, *25*, 585–597.
41. Witty,P.A., Theman,V. A follow-up study of educational attainment of gifted Negroes. *J.educ.Psychol.*, 1943, *34*, 35–47.
42. Woodworth,R.S. *Heredity and environment*. N.Y., Social Science Research Council, 1941.
43. Yerkes,R.M. *Psychological examining in the United States Army*. Washington, National Academy of Sciences, Memoirs, Vol. 15, 1921.

## Chapter Seven. Interaction with the Environment

1. Baker,K.H. Pre-experimental set in distraction experiments. *J.gen. Psychol.*, 1937, *16*, 471–488.
2. Buswell,G.T. Remedial reading. *Suppl.educ.Monogr.*, 1939, No. 50.
3. Gates,A.I. *The improvement of reading*. N.Y., Macmillan, 1935.
4. Hovey,H.B. Effects of general distraction on the higher thought processes. *Amer.J.Psychol.*, 1928, *40*, 585–591.
5. Luchins,A.S. Mechanization in problem solving, the effect of *Einstellung*. *Psychol.Monogr.*, 1942, No. 248.
6. Mowrer,O.H. Preparatory set (expectancy)—some methods of measurement. *Psychol.Monogr.*, 1940, No. 233.
7. Poffenberger,A.T. *Principles of applied psychology*. N.Y., Appleton-Century, 1942. (Esp. pp. 141–143.)
8. Rees,H.J., Israel,H.E. An investigation of the establishment and operation of mental sets. *Psychol.Monogr.*, 1935, No. 210, 1–26.
9. Triggs,F.O. *Remedial reading: the diagnosis and correction of reading difficulties at the college level*. University of Minnesota Press, 1943.
10. Woodworth,R.S. *Experimental psychology*. N.Y., Holt, 1938.

## Chapter Eight. The Nervous System

1. Adrian,E.D. *The basis of sensation.* London, Christophers, 1928.
2. Brickner,R.M. *The intellectual functions of the frontal lobes.* N.Y., Macmillan, 1936.
3. Foerster,O. Beiträge zur Pathophysiologie der Sehbahn und der Sehsphäre. *J.Psychol.Neurol.*, 1929, *39*, 463–485.
4. Franz,S.I. On the functions of the cerebrum: the frontal lobes. *Arch. Psychol.*, 1907, No. 2.
5. Freeman,W., Watts,J.W. *Psychosurgery.* Springfield, Ill., Thomas, 1942.
6. Fulton,J.F. *Physiology of the nervous system.* 2d ed. N.Y., Oxford University Press, 1943.
7. Lashley,K.S. Studies of cerebral function in learning. *Comp.Psychol. Monogr.*, 1935, *11*, No. 52.
8. Lashley,K.S., Wiley,L.E. Mass action in relation to the number of elements in the problem to be learned. *J.comp.Neur.*, 1933, *57*, 1–55.
9. Martin,H.N. *The human body.* Revised by E.G.Martin. N.Y., Holt, 1934.
10. Morgan,C.T. *Physiological psychology.* N.Y., McGraw-Hill, 1943.
11. Piéron,H. *Thought and the brain.* Trans. by C.K.Ogden. N.Y., Harcourt, Brace, 1927.
12. Poljak,S. A contribution to the cerebral representation of the retina. *J.comp.Neur.*, 1933, *57*, 541–617.
13. Weisenburg,T.H., McBride,K.E. *Aphasia.* N.Y., Commonwealth Fund, 1935.

## Chapter Nine. How the Individual Develops

1. Abernethy,E.M. Relationships between mental and physical growth. *Soc.Res.ChildDevelpm.Monogr.*, 1936, *1*, No. 7.
2. Ames,L.B. The sequential patterning of prone progression in the human infant. *Genet.Psychol.Monogr.*, 1937, *19*, 409–460.
3. Bayley,N. The development of motor abilities during the first three years. *Soc.Res.ChildDevelpm.Monogr.*, 1935, *1*, No. 1.
4. Bird,C. Maturation and practice: their effects upon the feeding re-actions of chicks. *J.comp.Psychol.*, 1933, *16*, 343–366.
5. Carmichael,L. The onset and early development of behavior. Pp. 43–166 of the following.
6. Carmichael,L., editor. *Manual of child psychology.* N.Y., Wiley, 1946.
7. Dennis,W. On the possibility of advancing and retarding the motor development of infants. *Psychol.Rev.*, 1943, *50*, 203–218.
8. Donaldson,H.H. Anatomical observations on the brain and several sense-organs of the blind deaf-mute, Laura Dewey Bridgman. *Amer.J.Psychol.*, 1890, *3*, 293–342; 1891, *4*, 248–294.
9. Filimonoff,I.N. Zur embryonalen und postembryonalen Entwicklung

der Grosshirnrinde des Menschen. *J.Psychol.Neurol.*, 1929, *39*, 323–389.

10. Gesell,A., Thompson,H. *The psychology of early growth*. N.Y., Macmillan, 1938.

11. Halverson,H.M. The development of prehension in infants. In *Child development and behavior*. Edited by Barker and others. N.Y., McGraw-Hill, 1943, 49–65.

12. Hartson,L.D. Does college training influence test intelligence? *J.educ. Psychol.*, 1936, *27*, 481–491.

13. Jones,H.E., Conrad,H.S. The growth and decline of intelligence. *Genet.Psychol.Monogr.*, 1933, *13*, 223–298; Mental development in adolescence. 43d *Yearb. Nat.Soc.Stud.Educ.*, 1944, *I*, 146–163.

14. Kappers,C.U.A. *The evolution of the nervous system in vertebrates*. Haarlem, Bohn, 1929. (Esp. p. 144.)

15. Lehman,H.C. The creative years. *Sci.Mon.*, 1937, *45*, 65–75; The creative years in science and literature. *Sci.Mon.*, 1936, *43*, 151–162; The most proficient years at sports and games. *Res.Q.Amer. Ass.Hlth.Phys.Educ.*, 1938, *9*, 3–19; The creative years: oil paintings, etchings, and architectural works. *Psychol.Rev.*, 1942, *49*, 19–42.

16. Lehman,H.C., Ingerham,D.W. Man's creative years in music. *Sci. Mon.*, 1939, *48*, 431–443.

17. Maxfield,K.E., Fjeld,H.A. The social maturity of the visually handicapped preschool child. *ChildDevelpm.*, 1942, *13*, 1–27.

18. McGraw,M.B. *The neuromuscular maturation of the human infant*. N.Y., Columbia University Press, 1943.

19. Miles,C.C., Miles,W.R. The correlation of intelligence scores and chronological age from early to late maturity. *Amer.J.Psychol.*, 1932, *44*, 44–78.

20. Miles,W.R. Age and human society. *Handbk.soc.psychol*. Edited by C.Murchison, 1935, 596–682.

21. Miles,W.R. Psychological aspects of ageing. *Problems of ageing*. Edited by E.V.Cowdry. 2d ed. Baltimore, Williams & Wilkins, 1942, 756–784.

22. Morpurgo, B. Ueber Activitäts-Hypertrophie der willkürlichen Muskeln. *Arch.path.Anat.*, 1897, *150*, 522–554.

23. Munn,N.L. *Psychological development, an introduction to genetic psychology*. Boston, Houghton Mifflin, 1938.

24. Murphy,L.B. *Social behavior and child personality*. N.Y., Columbia University Press, 1937.

25. Parten,M.B. Social participation among pre-school children. *J.abnorm. soc.Psychol.*, 1932, 27, 243–269.

26. Scheinfeld,A. *Women and men*. N.Y., Harcourt, Brace, 1944.

27. Shirley,M.M. *The first two years*. 2 vols. University of Minnesota Press, 1931, 1933.

28. Shuttleworth,F.K. Sexual maturation and the physical growth of girls age six to nineteen. *Soc.Res.ChildDevelpm.Monogr.*, 1937, *2*, No. 12.

29. Slater,E., and others. Types, levels, and irregularities of response to a nursery school situation. *Soc.Res.ChildDevelpm.Monogr.*, 1939, *4*, No. 21.
30. Thorndike,E.L. *Man and his works*. Cambridge, Mass., Harvard University Press, 1943.
31. Thorndike,E.L., and others. *Adult learning*. N.Y., Macmillan, 1927.
32. Wechsler,D. *The measurement of adult intelligence*. 3d ed. Baltimore, Williams & Wilkins, 1944.

## Chapter Ten. Motives

1. Bavelas,A. See Maier, Ref. 12, p. 265.
2. Boring,E.G. *Psychology for the armed services*. Washington, The Infantry Journal, 1945.
3. Cannon,W.B. *The wisdom of the body*. N.Y., Norton, 1939.
4. Crawley,S.L. An experimental investigation of recovery from work. *Arch.Psychol.*, 1926, No. 85.
5. Goodenough,F.L. *Anger in young children*. University of Minnesota Press, 1931.
6. Gottschaldt,K. Der Aufbau des kindlichen Handelns. *Z.angew.Psychol.*, 1933. Beiheft 68.
7. Hamilton,H.C. The effect of incentives on accuracy of discrimination. *Arch.Psychol.*, 1929, No. 103.
8. Hull,C.L. The rat's speed-of-locomotion gradient in the approach to food. *J.comp.Psychol.*, 1934, *17*, 393–422.
9. Jones,H.E., Jones,M.C. A study of fear in young children. *Childhood Educ.*, 1928, *5*, 136–243.
10. Jones,M.C. A laboratory study of fear: the case of Peter. *Ped.Sem.*, 1924, *31*, 308–315.
11. Kraut,H.A., Muller,E.A. Calorie intake and industrial output. *Science*, 1946, *104*, 495–497.
12. Maier,N.R.F. *Psychology in industry*. Boston, Houghton Mifflin, 1946.
13. Morgan,C.T. *Physiological psychology*. N.Y., McGraw-Hill, 1943.
14. Richter,C.P. Animal behavior and internal drives. *Q.Rev.Biol.*, 1927, *2*, 307–343.
15. Roethlisberger,F.J. *Management and morale*. Cambridge, Mass., Harvard University Press, 1941.
16. Thorndike,E.L. *Human nature and the social order*. N.Y., Macmillan, 1940.
17. Tolman,E.C. *Drives toward war*. N.Y., Appleton-Century, 1942.
18. Troland,L.T. *The fundamentals of human motivation*. N.Y., Van Nostrand, 1928.
19. Viteles,M.S. *Industrial psychology*. N.Y., Norton, 1932.
20. Warden,C.J., and others. *Animal motivation*. N.Y., Columbia University Press, 1931.
21. Watson,G., editor. *Civilian morale*. Boston, Houghton Mifflin, 1942.
22. Watson,J.B., Raynor,R. Conditioned emotional reactions. *J.exp.Psychol.*, 1920, *3*, 1–14.

23. Young,P.T. The experimental analysis of appetite. *Psychol.Bull.*, 1941, *38*, 129–164; Studies of food preference, appetite and dietary habit. *J.comp.Psychol.*, 1946, *39*, 139–176.

## Chapter Eleven. Feeling and Emotion

1. Bard,P. The neuro-humoral basis of emotional reactions. *Handb.gen. exp.Psychol.* Edited by C.Murchison, 1934, 264–311.
2. Boring,E.G., editor. *Psychology for the armed forces.* Washington, The Infantry Journal, 1945.
3. Cannon,W.B. *Bodily changes in pain, hunger, fear and rage.* 2d ed. N.Y., Appleton, 1929.
4. Cannon,W.B. The James-Lange theory of emotions. *Amer.J.Psychol.*, 1927, *39*, 106–124.
5. Cantril,H. The roles of the situation and adrenalin in the induction of emotion. *Amer.J.Psychol.*, 1934, *46*, 568–579.
6. Cantril,H., Hunt,W.A. Emotional effects produced by the injection of adrenalin. *Amer.J.Psychol.*, 1932, *44*, 300–307.
7. Carmichael,L., and others. A study of the judgment of manual expression as presented in still and motion pictures. *J.soc.Psychol.*, 1937, *8*, 115–142.
8. Cason,H. Common annoyances. *Psychol. Monogr.*, 1930, *40*, No. 182.
9. Dana,C.L. The anatomic seat of the emotions: a discussion of the James-Lange theory. *Arch.Neurol.Psychiat.*, 1921, *6*, 634–639.
10. Darwin,C. *The expression of the emotions in man and animals.* London, John Murray, 1872.
11. Dollard,J. *Fear in battle.* New Haven, Yale University Institute of Human Relations, 1943.
12. Eastman,M. *Enjoyment of laughter.* N.Y., Simon & Schuster, 1936.
13. Fairbanks,G., Pronovost,W. Vocal pitch during simulated emotion. *Science*, 1938, *88*, 382–383.
14. Feleky,A. *Feelings and emotions.* N.Y., Pioneer Publishing Co., 1924.
15. Hebb,D.O. On the nature of fear. *Psychol.Rev.*, 1946, *53*, 259–276.
16. Hulin,W.S., Katz,D. The Frois-Wittmann pictures of facial expression. *J.exp.Psychol.*, 1935, *18*, 482–498.
17. Husband,R.W. A study of the emotion of excitement. *J.genet.Psychol.*, 1935, *46*, 465–470.
18. Inbau,F.E. *Lie detection and criminal interrogation.* Baltimore, Williams & Wilkins, 1942.
19. James,W. *Principles of psychology.* 2 vols. N.Y., Holt, 1890.
20. Landis,C., Hunt,W.A. *The startle pattern.* N.Y., Farrar & Rinehart, 1939.
21. Lashley,K.S. The thalamus and emotion. *Psychol.Rev.*, 1938, *45*, 42–61.
22. Morgan,C.T. *Physiological psychology.* N.Y., McGraw-Hill, 1943.
23. Schlosberg,H. A scale for the judgment of facial expressions. *J.exp. Psychol.*, 1941, *29*, 497–510.

24. Sherrington,C.S. *The integrative action of the nervous system.* New Haven, Yale University Press, 1906. (Esp. p. 259.)
25. Stratton,G.M. Excitement as an undifferentiated emotion. *Wittenberg Symposium.* Edited by M.L.Reymert, 1928, 215–221.
26. Wolf,S., Wolff,H.G. *Human gastric function, an experimental study of a man and his stomach.* N.Y., Oxford University Press, 1943.
27. Wundt,W. *Grundriss der Psychologie.* 1896. Translated by C.H.Judd. *Outlines of psychology.* Leipzig, Engelmann, 1897.
28. Young,P.T. *Emotion in man and animal.* N.Y., Wiley, 1943.

## Chapter Twelve. Choice, Conflict, Frustration

1. Adler,A. *Problems of neurosis.* N.Y., Cosmopolitan Book Corp., 1930.
1a. Alexander,F., French,T.M. *Psychoanalytic therapy.* N.Y., Ronald Press, 1946.
2. Barker,R.G., Dembo,T., Lewin,K. Frustration and regression: an experiment with young children. *Univ.IowaStud.ChildWelfare,* 1941, *18,* No. 1.
3. Dollard,J., and others. *Frustration and aggression.* New Haven, Yale University Press, 1939.
4. Freud,S. *A general introduction to psycho-analysis.* N.Y., Liveright, 1935.
5. Horney,K. *New ways in psychoanalysis.* N.Y., Norton, 1939.
6. Hovland,C.I., Sears,R.R. Experiments on motor conflict. *J.exp. Psychol.,* 1938, *23,* 477–493.
7. Hull,C.L. *Hypnosis and suggestibility.* N.Y., Appleton-Century, 1933.
8. Landis,C., Bolles,M.M. *Textbook of abnormal psychology.* N.Y. Macmillan, 1946.
9. Lewin,K. *A dynamic theory of personality.* N.Y., McGraw-Hill, 1935.
10. Lewin,K., Dembo,T., and others. Level of aspiration, in Hunt,J.McV., *Personality and the behavior disorders.* N.Y., Ronald Press, 1944, *1,* 333–378.
11. Maier,N.R.F. The role of frustration in social movements. *Psychol. Rev.,* 1942, *49,* 586–599. *Psychology in industry.* Boston, Houghton Mifflin, 1946. Esp. pp. 65–68.
12. McClelland,D.C., Apicella,F.S. A functional classification of verbal reactions to experimentally induced failure. *J.abnorm.soc.Psychol.,* 1945, *40,* 376–390.
13. Miller,N.E. Experimental studies of conflict, in Hunt,J.McV., *Personality and the behavior disorders.* N.Y., Ronald Press, 1944, *I,* 431–465.
14. Richards,T.W. *Modern clinical psychology.* N.Y., McGraw-Hill, 1946.
15. Rogers,C.R. *Counseling and psychotherapy.* Boston, Houghton Mifflin, 1942; Significant aspects of client-centered therapy. *Amer Psychologist,* 1946, *1,* 415–422.
16. Rogers,C.R., Wallen,J.L. *Counseling with returned servicemen.* N.Y., McGraw-Hill, 1946.

17. Rosenzweig,S. An outline of frustration theory, in Hunt,J.McV., *Personality and the behavior disorders*. N.Y., Ronald Press, 1944, *I*, 379–388.
18. Shaffer,L.F. *The psychology of human adjustment*. Boston, Houghton Mifflin, 1936.
19. Sears,R.R. Experimental analysis of psychoanalytic phenomena, in Hunt,J.McV., *Personality and the behavior disorders*. N.Y., Ronald Press, 1944, *I*, 306–332.
20. Sherman,M. *Mental conflicts and personality*. N.Y., Longmans, Green, 1938.
21. Symonds,P. *The dynamics of human adjustment*. N.Y., Appleton-Century, 1946.
22. Zander,A.F. A study of experimental frustration. *Psychol.Monogr.*, 1944, No. 256.

## Chapter Thirteen. Observing

1. Boring,E.G., editor. *Psychology for the armed services*. Washington. The Infantry Journal, 1945.
2. Burtt,H.E. *The psychology of advertising*. Boston, Houghton Mifflin, 1938.
3. Friedmann,H. The natural-history background of camouflage. *Smithsonian Institution War Background Studies*, 1942, No. 5.
4. Hanawalt,N.G. The effect of practice upon the perception of simple designs masked by more complex designs. *J.exp.Psychol.*, 1942, *31*, 134–148.
5. Holway,A.H., Pratt,C.C. The Weber-ratio for intensitive discrimination. *Psychol. Rev.*, 1936, *43*, 322–340.
6. Köhler,W. *Gestalt psychology*. N.Y., Liveright, 1929.
7. Oberly,H.S. The range for visual attention, cognition and apprehension. *Amer.J.Psychol.*, 1924, *35*, 332–352.
8. Rubin,E. *Visuell wahrgenommene figuren*. København, Gyldendal, 1921.
9. Sanford,E.C. *Experimental psychology*. Boston, Heath, 1898.
10. Sisson,E.D. Eye-movements and the Schröder stair-figure. *Amer.J. Psychol.*, 1935, *47*, 309–311.
11. Wertheimer, M. Untersuchungen zur Lehre von der Gestalt. *Psychol. Forsch.*, 1923, *4*, 301–350.

## Chapter Fourteen. The Sense of Sight

1. Burzlaff,W. Methodologische Beiträge zum Problem der Farbenkonstanz. *Z. Psychol.*, 1931, *119*, 177–235.
2. Dodge,R. Five types of eye movement in the horizontal meridian plane of the field of regard. *Amer.J.Physiol.*, 1903, *8*, 307–329.
3. Ewert,P.H. A study of the effect of inverted retinal stimulation upon spatially coordinated behavior. *Genet.Psychol.Monogr.*, 1930, *7*, 177–363.

4. Fernberger,S.W. New phenomena of apparent visual movement. *Amer.J.Psychol.*, 1934, *46*, 309–314.

5. Gilbert,G.M. Dynamic psychophysics and the phi phenomenon. *Arch. Psychol.*, 1939, No. 237.

6. Helmholtz,H.L.F.von. *Helmholtz's treatise on physiological optics.* Translated from the 3d German ed. Edited by J.P.C.Southall. Rochester, N.Y., Optical Soc. Amer., 1924–1925. 3 vols. (Esp. vol. 2, p. 426.)

7. Henneman,R.H. A photometric study of the perception of object color. *Arch.Psychol.*, 1935, No. 179.

8. Johnson,B., Beck,L.F. The development of space perception: stereoscopic vision in preschool children. *J.genet.Psychol.*, 1941, *58*, 247–254.

9. Katz,D. *The world of colour.* Translated from the German by R.B. MacLeod and C.W.Fox. London, Paul, 1935.

10. Ladd-Franklin,C. *Colour and colour theories.* N.Y., Harcourt, Brace, 1929.

11. MacLeod,R.B. An experimental investigation of brightness constancy. *Arch.Psychol.*, 1932, No. 135.

12. Sheehan,M.R. A study of individual consistency in phenomenal constancy. *Arch.Psychol.*, 1938, No. 222.

13. Stratton,G.M. Some preliminary experiments on vision without inversion of the retinal image. *Psychol.Rev.*, 1896, *3*, 611–617.

14. Stratton,G.M. Vision without inversion of the retinal image. *Psychol. Rev.*, 1897, *4*, 341–360; 463–481.

15. Troland,L.T. *Principles of psychophysiology.* Vol. 2. N.Y., Van Nostrand, 1930.

16. Wald,G., Steven,D. An experiment in human vitamin A deficiency. *Proc.Nat.Acad.Sci.*, 1939, *25*, 344–349.

## Chapter Fifteen. The Other Senses

1. Banister,H. Auditory phenomena and their stimulus correlations. *Handbk.gen.exp.Psychol.* Edited by C.Murchison. 1934, 880–923.

2. Crowe,S.J., Guild,S.R., Polvogt,L.M. Observations on the pathology of high-tone deafness. *Johns Hopkins Hosp.Bull.*, 1934, *54*, 315–379.

3. Culler,E.A. Thermal discrimination and Weber's law. *Arch.Psychol.*, 1926, No. 81.

4. Fletcher,H. *Speech and hearing.* N.Y., Van Nostrand, 1929.

5. Galambos,R. Cochlear potentials from the bat. *Science*, 1941, *93*, 215.

6. Griffin,D.R. Echolocation by blind men, bats and radar. *Science*, 1944, *100*, 589–590.

7. Griffin,D.R., Galambos,R. The sensory basis of obstacle avoidance by flying bats. *J.exp.Zool.*, 1941, *86*, 481–506.

8. Hartridge,H. Theories of hearing. *Handbk.gen.exp.Psychol.* Edited by C.Murchison, 1934, 924–961.

9. Henning,H. *Der Geruch.* Leipzig, Barth, 1924.

10. Henning,H. Psychologische Studien am Geschmackssinn. *Handbh. biol.Arbeitsmeth.*, 1927, *6*, A, 627–740.
11. Katz,D. *Der Aufbau der Tastwelt.* Leipzig, Barth, 1925.
12. Katz,D. *The vibratory sense and other lectures.* Orono, Maine, University Press, 1930.
13. Mansfeld,F. Die Verdunklung und die Blinden. *Arch.ges.Psychol.*, 1940, *107*, 411–436.
14. Mohrmann,K. Lautheitskonstanz im Entfernungswechsel. *Z.Psychol.*, 1939, *145*, 145–199.
15. Nafe,J.P., Wagoner,K.S. The nature of sensory adaptation; The nature of pressure adaptation. *J.gen.Psychol.*, 1941, *25*, 295–321, 323–351.
16. Potter,R.K. Visible patterns of sound. *Science*, 1945, *102*, 463–470.
17. Stevens,S.S., Davis,H. *Hearing, its psychology and physiology.* N.Y., Wiley, 1938.
18. Supa,M., Cotzin,M., Dallenbach,K.M. "Facial vision": the perception of obstacles by the blind. *Amer.J.Psychol.* 1944, *57*, 133–183.
19. Walshe,F.M.R. The anatomy and physiology of cutaneous sensibility: a critical review. *Brain*, 1942, *65*, 48–112.
20. Wever,E.G., Bray,C.W. The nature of acoustic response. *J.exp. Psychol.*, 1930, *13*, 373–387.
21. Willey,C.F., Inglis,E., Pearce,C.H. Reversal of auditory localization. *J.exp.Psychol.*, 1937, *20*, 114–130.
22. Woodworth,R.S. *Experimental psychology.* N.Y., Holt, 1938. (Esp. pp. 518–534.)
23. Young,P.T. Auditory localization with acoustical transposition of the ears. *J.exp.Psychol.*, 1928, *11*, 399–429.

## Chapter Sixteen. Learning

1. Adams,D.K. Experimental studies of adaptive behavior in cats. *Comp. Psychol.Monogr.*, 1929, *6*. No. 27.
2. Alpert,A. The solving of problem-situations by pre-school children. *Teachers College, Columbia University, Contrib.Educ.*, 1928, No. 323.
3. Birch,H.G. The role of motivational factors in insightful problem-solving. *J.comp.Psychol.*, 1945, *38*, 295–317.
4. Book,W.F. *The psychology of skill.* N.Y., Gregg, 1925.
5. Brown,W. Spatial integrations in a human maze. *Univ.Calif.Publ. Psychol.*, 1932, *5*, 123–134.
6. Bryan,W.L., Harter,N. Studies in the physiology and psychology of the telegraphic language. *Psychol.Rev.*, 1897, *4*, 27–53.
7. Davis,R.C. Set and muscular tension. *Indiana Univ.Publ.Science Series*, 1940, No. 10.
8. Guthrie,E.R. *The psychology of learning.* N.Y., Harper, 1935.
9. Guthrie,E.R., Horton,G.P. *Cats in a puzzle box.* N.Y., Rinehart, 1946.
10. Hebb,D.O., Williams,K. A method of rating animal intelligence. *J.gen. Psychol.*, 1946, *34*, 59–65.

# REFERENCES 655

11. Hilden,A.H. An action current study of the conditioned hand withdrawal. *Psychol.Monogr.*, 1937, *49*, No. 217, 173–204.
12. Hilgard,E.R., Marquis,D.G. *Conditioning and learning.* N.Y., Appleton-Century, 1940.
13. Hudgins,C.V. Conditioning and the voluntary control of the pupillary light reflex. *J.gen.Psychol.*, 1933, *8*, 3–51.
14. Hull,C.L. *Principles of behavior.* N.Y., Appleton-Century, 1943.
15. Kellogg,W.N., Kellogg,L.A. *The ape and the child.* N.Y., McGraw-Hill, 1933.
16. Köhler,W. *The mentality of apes.* N.Y., Harcourt, Brace, 1925. (Esp. p. 132.)
17. Liddell,H.S., James,W.T., Anderson,O.D. The comparative physiology of the conditioned motor reflex. *Comp.Psychol.Monogr.*, 1934, *11*, No. 51.
18. Macfarlane,D.A. The role of kinesthesis in maze learning. *Univ.Calif. Publ.Psychol.*, 1930, *4*, 277–305.
19. Maier,N.R.F., Schneirla,T.C. *Principles of animal psychology.* N.Y., McGraw-Hill, 1935.
20. Marquis,D.P. Can conditioned responses be established in the newborn infant? *J.genet.Psychol.*, 1931, *39*, 479–492.
21. Morgan,C.L. *An introduction to comparative psychology.* London, W.Scott, 1894. (Esp. p. 53.)
22. Mowrer,O.H., Mowrer,W.M. Enuresis—a method for its study and treatment. *Amer.J.Orthopsychiat.*, 1938, *8*, 436–459.
23. Pavlov,I.P. *Conditioned reflexes.* N.Y., Oxford University Press, 1927.
24. Razran,G.H.S. Attitudinal control of human conditioning. *J.Psychol.*, 1936, *2*, 327–337.
25. Ruger,H.A. The psychology of efficiency. *Arch.Psychol.*, 1910, No. 15.
26. Schlosberg,H. A study of the conditioned patellar reflex. *J.exp. Psychol.*, 1928, *11*, 468–494.
27. Skinner,B.F. *The behavior of organisms.* N.Y., Appleton-Century, 1938.
28. Thorndike,E.L. Animal intelligence. *Psychol.Monogr.*, 1898, *2*, No. 8; *Animal intelligence.* N.Y., Macmillan, 1911.
29. Tolman,E.C. *Purposive behavior in animals and men.* N.Y., Century, 1932.
30. Tolman,E.C., Honzik,C.H. Maze learning in rats; Maze performance in rats. *Univ.Calif.Publ.Psychol.*, 1930, *4*, 241–275.
31. Tolman,E.C., Ritchie,B.F., Kalish,D. Studies in spatial learning. II. Place learning versus response learning. *J.exp.Psychol.*, 1946, *36*, 221–229.
32. Warden,C.J. The relative economy of various modes of attack in the mastery of a stylus maze. *J.exp.Psychol.*, 1924, *7*, 243–275.
33. Warden,C.J., Jenkins,T.N., Warner,L.H. *Comparative psychology.* 3 vols. N.Y., Ronald Press, 1935–1940.
34. Wendt,G.R. An analytical study of the conditioned knee-jerk. *Arch. Psychol.*, 1930, No. 123.

35. Zener,K., McCurdy, H.G. Analysis of motivational factors in conditioned behavior. *J.Psychol.*, 1939, *8*, 321–350.

## Chapter Seventeen. Memory

1. Allport,G.W. Eidetic imagery. *Brit.J.Psychol.*, 1924, *15*, 99–120.
2. Bartlett,F.C. *Remembering*. N.Y., Macmillan, 1932.
3. Boreas,T. Experimental studies of memory. (Greek.) *Praktika Acad. Athènes*, 1930, *5*, 382–396.
4. Carmichael,L., Hogan,H.P., Walter,A.A. An experimental study of the effect of language on the reproduction of visually perceived forms. *J.exp.Psychol.*, 1932, *15*, 73–86.
5. Cox,J.W. Some experiments on formal training in the acquisition of skill. *Brit.J.Psychol.*, 1933, *24*, 67–87.
6. Duncan,C.F. The effect of electroshock convulsions on the maze habit in the white rat. *J.exp.Psychol.*, 1945, *35*, 267–278.
7. Ebbinghaus,H. *Über das Gedächtnis*. 1885. Translated by H.A.Ruger and C.E.Bussenius. *Memory*. N.Y., Teachers College, Columbia University, 1913.
8. Galton,F. *Inquiries into human faculty and its development*. London, Macmillan, 1883.
9. Gates,A.I. Recitation as a factor in memorizing. *Arch.Psychol.*, 1917, No. 40.
10. Gibson,J.J. The reproduction of visually perceived forms. *J.exp. Psychol.*, 1929, *12*, 1–39.
11. Hanawalt,N.G. Memory trace for figures in recall and recognition. *Arch.Psychol.*, 1937, No. 216.
12. Hanawalt,N.G., Demarest,I.H. The effect of verbal suggestion in the recall period upon the reproduction of visually perceived forms. *J.exp.Psychol.*, 1939, *25*, 159–174.
13. Hovland,C.I. Experimental studies in rote-learning theory. *J.exp. Psychol.*, 1938, *23*, 172–190.
14. Jaensch,E.R. *Eidetic imagery*. N.Y., Harcourt, Brace, 1930.
15. Keller,F.S., and others. Studies in International Morse Code. *J.appl. Psychol.*, 1944, *28*, 254–266; 1946, *30*, 265–270.
16. McGeoch,J.A. *The psychology of human learning*. N.Y., Longmans, Green, 1942. (Esp. pp. 453–512.)
17. Meenes,M., Morton,M.A. Characteristics of the eidetic phenomenon. *J.gen.Psychol.*, 1936, *14*, 370–391.
18. Melton,A.W., vonLackum,W.J. Retroactive and proactive inhibition in retention: evidence for a two-factor theory of retroactive inhibition. *Amer.J.Psychol.*, 1941, *54*, 157–173.
19. Minami,H., Dallenbach,K.M. The effect of activity upon learning and retention in the cockroach. *Amer.J.Psychol.*, 1946, *59*, 1–58.
20. Murphy,G. *An historical introduction to modern psychology*. N.Y., Harcourt, Brace, 1932. (Esp. supplement by H.Klüver, pp. 437–442.)

21. Pillsbury,W.B., Sylvester,A. Retroactive and proactive inhibition in immediate memory. *J.exp.Psychol.*, 1940, *27*, 532–545.
22. Pyle,W.H., Snyder,J.C. The most economical unit for committing to memory. *J.educ.Psychol.*, 1911, *2*, 133–142.
23. Seward,G.H. Recognition time as a measure of confidence. *Arch. Psychol.*, 1928, No. 99.
24. Underwood,B.J. The effect of successive interpolations on retroactive and proactive inhibition. *Psychol.Monogr.*, 1945, *59*, No. 273.
25. vanOrmer,E.B. Retention after intervals of sleep and of waking. *Arch.Psychol.*, 1932, No. 137.
26. Woodrow,H. The effect of type of training upon transference. *J.educ. Psychol.*, 1927, *18*, 159–172.
27. Zubin,J., Barrera,S.E. Effect of electric convulsive therapy on memory. *Proc.Soc.exp.Biol.Med.*, 1941, *48*, 596–597.

# Chapter Eighteen. Thinking

1. Burt,C. The development of reasoning in school children. *J.exp.Ped.*, 1919, *5*, 68–77; 121–127.
2. Burt,C. *Mental and scholastic tests.* London County Council, 1921.
3. Duncker,K. On problem solving. Tr. by Lynne S. Lees. *Psychol. Monogr.*, 1945, *58*, No. 270.
4. Durkin,H.E. Trial-and-error, gradual analysis, and sudden reorganization. *Arch.Psychol.*, 1937, No. 210.
5. Fisher,S.C. The process of generalizing abstraction. *Psychol.Monogr.*, 1916, *21*, No. 90.
6. Freud,S. *The interpretation of dreams.* Tr. by A.A.Brill from 8th German ed. London, Allen & Unwin, 1937.
7. Gallup,G. *A guide to public opinion polls.* Princeton University Press, 1944.
8. Hayakawa,S.I. *Language in action.* N.Y., Harcourt, Brace, 1941.
9. Heidbreder,E. The attainment of concepts: I. Terminology and methodology; II. The problem. *J.gen.Psychol.*, 1946, *35*, 173–189, 191–223.
10. Jacobson,E. Electrophysiology of mental activities. *Amer.J.Psychol.*, 1932, *44*, 677–694.
11. Janis,I.L., Frick,F. The relationship between attitudes toward conclusions and errors in judging logical validity of syllogisms. *J.exp. Psychol.*, 1943, *33*, 73–77.
12. Lefford,A. The influence of emotional subject matter on logical reasoning. *J.gen.Psychol.*, 1946, *34*, 127–151.
13. Maier,N.R.F. Reasoning in rats and human beings. *Psychol.Rev.*, 1937, *44*, 365–378.
14. Max,L.W. Action-current responses in the deaf during awakening, kinesthetic imagery and abstract thinking. *J.comp.Psychol.*, 1937, *24*, 301–344.
15. Morgan,J.J.B., Morton,J.T. The distortion of syllogistic reasoning produced by personal convictions. *J.soc.Psychol.*, 1944, *20*, 39–59.

16. Patrick,C. Creative thought in poets. *Arch.Psychol.*, 1935, No. 178; Creative thought in artists. *J.Psychol.*, 1937, *4*, 35–73; Scientific thought. *J.Psychol.*, 1938, *5*, 55–83.
17. Piaget,J. *The child's conception of the world.* London, K.Paul, 1929.
18. Rossman,J. *The psychology of the inventor.* Washington, Inventors Publishing Co., 1931.
19. Sells,S.B. The atmosphere effect. *Arch.Psychol.*, 1936, No. 200.
20. Smoke,K.L. An objective study of concept formation. *Psychol. Monogr.*, 1932, *42*, No. 191.
21. Stevanović,B.P. An experimental study of the mental processes involved in judgment. *Brit.J.Psychol.Monogr.*, 1927, No. 12.
22. Thouless,R.H. *How to think straight.* N.Y., Simon & Schuster, 1939.
23. Wertheimer,M. *Productive thinking.* N.Y., Harper, 1945.
24. Wilkins,M.C. The effect of changed material on ability to do formal syllogistic reasoning. *Arch.Psychol.*, 1928, No. 102.

# Index of Authors

# Index of Subjects